READINGS IN FISCAL POLICY

THE SERIES OF REPUBLISHED ARTICLES ON ECONOMICS

Volume VII

Selection Committee for This Volume

ARTHUR SMITHIES

J. KEITH BUTTERS

The participation of the American Economic Association in the presentation of this series consists in the appointment of a committee to determine the subjects of the volumes and of special committees to select the articles for each volume

READINGS IN FISCAL POLICY

Selected by a Committee of

THE AMERICAN ECONOMIC ASSOCIATION

1955

Published for the Association by

RICHARD D. IRWIN, INC.

HOMEWOOD, ILLINOIS

First Printing, June, 1955

Library of Congress Catalogue Card No. 55-8513

PRINTED IN THE UNITED STATES OF AMERICA

Introduction

Fiscal policy as the term has been used over the past twenty years is a branch of economics that partially overlaps the fields of public finance, money and banking, and business cycles. Its central concern is with the aggregative effects of government expenditures and taxation on income production and employment. The present compilation adheres in the main to this delimitation of fiscal policy but attempts also to show the relation that should be recognized between fiscal policy so conceived and other closely related policies.

The American Economic Association has already sponsored readings on monetary theory and business cycles. Those volumes will help the student to cross the arbitrary boundaries of the present volume in two important directions. But there is still room for an additional volume that deals with the traditional subject of public finance.

As with other volumes in the series, the editors have been mainly concerned with the need to make periodical and pamphlet literature available to students. Consequently, some pioneering articles, such as R. F. Kahn's classic article on the multiplier, which are readily available in other collections of readings have been omitted from the current volume. On the other hand, a volume on fiscal policy could hardly be considered complete without representation of the works of Keynes, Schumpeter, and Hansen. But to achieve adequate representation, it was necessary in each case to depart from the usual practice and include extracts from books rather than articles.

The volume attempts not only to cover the field of fiscal policy but to show how doctrine on the subject has evolved over the past generation. To facilitate the attainment of this dual objective, several authors have kindly consented to the republication of articles written some time ago, even though their views may have been refined and modified in the meantime.

The editors are indebted to experts in the field for their suggestions and particularly to Wilbur A. Steger of the Harvard Department of Economics for invaluable spadework in the selection process.

ARTHUR SMITHIES
J. KEITH BUTTERS

June 1955

Contents

I. INTRODUCTION

II. FISCAL POLICY IN RECOVERY

III. FISCAL POLICY AND INFLATION

IV. FISCAL POLICY AND THE NATIONAL DEBT (MONETARY POLICY)

V. FISCAL POLICY AND STABILITY

VI. BURDENS OF THE BUDGET AND DEBT

I. INTRODUCTION

1

The Balanced Budget[*]

By JESSE BURKHEAD[†]

. . . the practical nature of the problem is invading the sanctuary and is troubling the priests. (Thurman Arnold, *The Folklore of Capitalism*, p. 330.)

In a world in which Keynesianism abounds, one might reasonably expect that balancing the government's budget would be regarded as an outmoded policy goal. A great many other pre-Keynesian fiscal notions have pretty well gone by the boards. One seldom hears these days that a dollar of government expenditures causes a corresponding reduction of a dollar of private outlay, or that government expenditures cannot raise the level of national income, or that we can never achieve full employment by government spending. But amidst the wide acceptance of the goals and tools of Keynesianism, even in those circles where the name is still anathema, there is remarkable persistence in the notion that government budgets ought to be balanced, even balanced annually.[1]

This article proposes to examine our intellectual heritage in this matter of budget balancing. The first section will be devoted to the views of the classical economists on national debt and deficits. Here it will be pointed out that while there is a common body of doctrine which may be characterized as the classical view of debts and deficits, this doctrine changed substantially, in accordance with the changing

* *Quarterly Journal of Economics*, May 1954. Reprinted by courtesy of the *Quarterly Journal of Economics* and the author.

The author is grateful for criticisms and suggestions from his colleagues Sidney Sufrin and Melvin Eggers and from Richard Goode of the International Monetary Fund.

† Syracuse University.

[1] Documentation is everywhere evident. For example, "The first order of business is the elimination of the annual deficit. . . . A balanced budget is an essential first measure in checking further depreciation in the buying power of the dollar. . . . As the budget is balanced and inflation checked, the tax burden that today stifles initiative can and must be eased. . . ." (President Eisenhower in the "State of the Union Message," Feb. 1953.) And, although somewhat more guarded, "We should make it the first principle of economic and fiscal policy in these times to maintain a balanced budget, and to finance the cost of national defense on a 'pay-as-we-go' basis." (President Truman in the *Economic Report of the President*, Jan. 1951.)

nature of the problems, from the time of Adam Smith to that of Alfred Marshall. The second section will review briefly the major characteristics of Keynesian thinking about national debt and deficits and attempt to analyze the reasons for the relative positions of the classicists and Keynesians. The third section will attempt to explain the failure of Keynesianism to influence the "practical nature of the problem" and will assess the degree to which the classical heritage is "real" and the extent to which it is "folklore."

"Practical men, who believe themselves to be quite exempt from any intellectual influences, are usually the slaves of some defunct economist," said Keynes. This article is devoted to an examination of the degree of enslavement.

It should be noted at the outset that this subject is not marked by conceptual clarity either in the writings of economists or in public policy. Considerations relating to balanced budgets are tied to considerations relating to increases in national debt. Annual increases in debt, in turn, are tied to problems of the size of the debt and the annual payment of interest thereon. And all these are linked, in the literature and in past and current public policy, with notions about the role of the state vis-à-vis the private sector.

In the review of classical doctrine, only the writings of the major classical economists will be examined and the work of others, including important and influential writers on government finance, will be neglected. This neglect, however, may be justified on the ground that the main stream of classical economics has defined the character of our intellectual and technical heritage in governmental financial practice. Also, the term "classical" will be used here as it was used by Keynes, to include both the classical and neoclassical school.

I

It is commonly held that the classicists assumed that the economic role of the state must necessarily be limited and they then adduced certain rationalizations regarding the nature of governmental fiscal operations to support this assumption. It seems more likely that such economists as Adam Smith looked first at the objective requirements of the economic order and then proceeded to theorize about the proper role of the state therein.[2]

Adam Smith's views on balanced budgets were conditioned very

[2] See Harvey S. Perloff, "Budgetary Symbolism and Fiscal Planning," *Public Policy*, Vol. II (Cambridge, Mass., Graduate School of Public Administration, Harvard University), pp. 40–44.

largely by his views on national debt.[3] And his views on the latter are a clear and direct product of his antimercantilism. It is difficult to dissociate Smith, the antimercantile-polemicist, from Smith the economist. His often quoted passages defining, in restrictive terms, the proper and legitimate functions of the state should probably be viewed not so much as an evidence of his pro-laissez-faire position as an evidence of his antimercantilism. Smith was an antimercantilist because he saw that the state apparatus as it then existed was an inefficient organization from the standpoint of wealth and income creation. It was the bulwark of a pattern of special trading privileges, grants of monopoly and tariffs. More importantly, the state was wasteful; it took funds from merchants and industrialists and spent these funds in riotous living. This deprived industry and commerce of capital which was badly needed for the furtherance of production and trade by diverting the national product toward consumer goods and away from capital goods.

This was the major reason for Smith's opposition to unbalanced budgets: governments would borrow from industry and commerce and thus deprive a capital-poor society of revenue which could be productively reinvested.[4] From this major ground for opposition to public borrowing stemmed other arguments. Once the sovereign started to borrow, his political power was increased, because he was no longer dependent on tax exactions from his subjects. Therefore, borrowing encouraged the sovereign to wage needless wars. On the other hand, if taxes were raised to meet current costs, "Wars would in general be more speedily concluded, and less wantonly undertaken."[5] In short, the ability to engage in loan finance makes for irresponsibility in the sovereign.

England's experience with national debt after the beginning of the eighteenth century adequately justified Smith's concern. In the years from 1713 to 1739 the South Sea Bubble and the war with Spain had added to the national debt. The war of 1739–48 raised England's debt from £47,000,000 to £78,000,000. At the end of the Seven Years' War in 1763, the debt stood at about £136,000,000. Furthermore, the intervening peacetime years did not bring important debt reductions.[6]

---

[3] For a discussion of pre-Smithian practices and views on these matters see C. F. Bastable, *Public Finance* (London, Macmillan & Co., Ltd., 1922), pp. 611–57; Gustav Cohn, *The Science of Finance,* T. B. Veblen, trans. (Chicago, University of Chicago Press, 1895), pp. 691–703.

[4] Adam Smith, *The Wealth of Nations,* Vol. II (Cannan ed.) (London, Methuen & Co., Ltd., 1930), pp. 409–11.

[5] *Ibid.,* p. 411.

[6] Bastable, *op. cit.,* pp. 630–32.

For Smith these increases in debt were most serious when they were *created;* the burden of an *existing* debt, although important, was much less significant. The most important loss came when industry and trade lent their funds to the state. Contemporaries of Smith had pointed out that an internally-held debt occasioned no loss through the annual interest transfer from taxpayers to bondholders. Smith replied that, "This apology is founded altogether in the sophistry of the mercantile system, . . ."[7] In confounding the sophistry Smith contended that the public creditor was not a good manager. Unlike the private creditor, he ". . . has no interest . . . in the good management of any particular portion of capital stock."[8] Further, the annual tax burdens occasioned by the interest payment may drive capital from the country. "The industry of the country will necessarily fall with the removal of the capital which supported it, and the ruin of trade and manufactures will necessarily follow the declension of agriculture."[9]

And, finally, there is a long-run danger in the debt. Once "accumulated to a certain degree" it leads inevitably to national bankruptcy. Since the days of Rome, sovereigns had resorted to all manner of juggling and trickery to "liberate the revenue." Bankruptcy had been disguised by "pretended payments" in debased currency; sovereigns adulterated the coin.[10]

Jean-Baptiste Say, conditioned no doubt by a French debt experience which was even more irresponsible than the English, was as vehement as Smith in opposition to debts and deficits. He was very much impressed with the wastefulness of government outlay, and cited example after example to the point.[11] The sovereign is engaged in pomp and circumstance; the preservation of etiquette and custom is a very expensive affair. The wealth which passes from the hands of the taxpayer to the taxgatherer is consumed and destroyed.

Say based these views on the argument that public consumption is not, in principle, different from the consumption of individuals or families. In either case there is a destruction of values and a loss of wealth.[12] The limitation of public consumption, like the limitation of private consumption, is necessary to provide capital for industry and trade. Public borrowing is not only unproductive because the capital is consumed and lost, but, in addition, the nation is burdened by the

---

[7] *Ibid.,* p. 412. [8] *Ibid.,* p. 413. [9] *Loc. cit.* [10] *Ibid.,* pp. 415–18.

[11] "It would be curious to calculate the time wasted in the toilet, or to estimate, if possible, the many dearly-paid hours lost, in the course of the last century, on the road between Paris and Versailles." J. B. Say, *A Treatise on Political Economy,* translated from the 4th edition by C. R. Prinsep (Philadelphia, Lippincott, Grambo & Co., 1853), p. 428.

[12] *Ibid.,* p. 412.

annual interest payment. It cannot be argued that the annual circulation of interest payments is a net addition to capital. "The tax-payer would have spent what is now spent by the public creditor; that is all."[13]

A national debt of moderate amount which had been judiciously expended in useful public works might be attended by the advantage of providing an investment outlet for the minute forms of capital which might otherwise be squandered by individuals.

> This is perhaps the sole benefit of a national debt; and even this is attended with some danger, inasmuch as it enables a government to squander the national savings. For, unless the principal be spent upon objects of permanent public benefit, as on roads, canals or the like, it were better for the public, that the capital should remain inactive, or concealed; since, if the public lost the use of it, at least it would not have to pay the interest.[14]

It is irresponsible government which is to be feared. When the government credit is strong, Say said (apparently quoting with approval from contemporary political scientists):

> they are too apt to intermeddle in every political arrangement, and to conceive gigantic projects, that lead sometimes to disgrace, sometimes to glory, but always to a state of financial exhaustion; to make war themselves, and stir up others to do the like; to subsidize every mercenary agent, and deal in the blood and the consciences of mankind; making capital, which should be the fruit of industry and virtue, the prize of ambition, pride, and wickedness.[15]

It is not surprising that David Ricardo, writing at the end of the Napoleonic Wars, should have generally shared the antipathy of his classical predecessors to national debt. By 1816 England's debt stood at about £500,000,000, approximately double what it had been at the turn of the century.[16] It was appropriate, in these circumstances, for Ricardo to refer to the debt as ". . . one of the most terrible scourges which was ever invented to afflict a nation . . ."[17] However, by this time the industrialization of England was much further advanced than it had been in 1776. Irresponsible sovereigns, in league with merchant-princes, were no longer the threat to economic progress that they had been in Smith's time. The national debt was a significant problem, but in his *Principles,* Ricardo did not devote the attention to this subject that Smith had. When he did discuss it, Ricardo made important modifications in the arguments of Smith and Say.[18]

---

[13] *Ibid.,* p. 480. [14] *Ibid.,* p. 481.

[15] *Ibid.,* p. 483. [16] Bastable, *op. cit.,* pp. 634–35.

[17] David Ricardo, "Funding System," *The Works and Correspondence of David Ricardo,* Vol. IV, Piero Sraffa and M. H. Dobb, ed. (Cambridge, Eng., 1951), p. 197.

[18] David Ricardo, *Principles of Political Economy and Taxation, The Works and Correspondence of David Ricardo,* I, 243–49.

Ricardo pointed out that the important burden of the national debt was not in the annual interest transfer, but in the loss of original capital:

> When, for the expenses of a year's war, twenty millions are raised by means of a loan, it is the twenty millions which are withdrawn from the productive capital of the nation. The million per annum which is raised by taxes to pay the interest of this loan, is merely transferred from those who pay it to those who receive it, from the contributor to the tax, to the national creditor. The real expense is the twenty millions, and not the interest which must be paid for it.[19]

The effects of the annual interest transfer, Ricardo argued, would depend on what A and B, taxpayer and creditor, did with the revenue. Either A or B might squander the revenue; either might employ it productively. The annual transfer was in no sense lost to the economy.

Once a nation has incurred a debt, no great *economic* advantage accrues from retiring it. The presence of the debt does not affect the nation's ability to pay taxes. There is the same taxable capital with or without the debt:

> It is not, then, by the payment of the interest on the national debt, that a country is distressed, nor is it by the exoneration from payment that it can be relieved. It is only by saving from income, and retrenching in expenditure, that the national capital can be increased; and neither the income would be increased, nor the expenditure diminished by the annihilation of the national debt.[20]

Neither does the presence of the debt place the nation at any particular disadvantage with respect to foreign countries. Taxes will be higher, it is true, and the price of labor will be increased, but the real capital of the nation is unchanged; the only problem is a transfer problem.

Why, then, should the national debt be retired? Why does it justify the appellation of "scourge"? Here Ricardo shifts ground and abandons aggregative analysis to contend that, even though there is no loss of capital in the aggregate, the particular taxes which may be levied to pay the interest will encourage every individual contributor to "withdraw his shoulder from the burthen," and,

> . . . the temptation to remove himself and his capital to another country, where he will be exempted from such burthens, becomes at last irresistible, and overcomes the natural reluctance which every man feels to quit the place of his birth, and the scene of his early associations. . . . That which is wise in an individual, is wise also in a nation.[21]

Ricardo's most important writing on the national debt was the essay on the funding system, contributed to the *Encyclopaedia Britannica.* His contemporary, Dr. Robert Hamilton, had authored *An Inquiry*

[19] *Ibid.*, p. 244. [20] *Ibid.*, p. 246. [21] *Ibid.*, pp. 247–48.

Concerning the Rise and Progress, the Redemption, and Present State of the National Debt of Great Britain, which included a critical attack on the debt retirement schemes which had been in force since 1716. The sinking fund schemes had not proved efficacious in eliminating the debt; ministers always abused the arrangements. Ricardo was apparently in essential agreement with Hamilton in his criticism of these schemes and in this essay he elaborated Hamilton's arguments and discussed at some length the distinctions between annual revenue, paid as interest on the debt, or as contribution to the sinking fund, and the capital of taxpayers which was available for productive investment.[22] Although in his *Principles,* Ricardo had pointed out the limitations in the arguments of those who advocated retirement of the debt, in the *Britannica* article he simply assumed that debt retirement was desirable.

Ricardo proposed that in future (war) emergencies the government adopt a pay-as-you-go financial plan. Thus, "When the pressure of war is felt at once, without mitigation, we shall be less disposed wantonly to engage in an expensive contest, and if engaged in it, we shall be sooner disposed to get out of it, unless it be a contest for some great national interest."[23] A pay-as-you-go plan might encourage a higher level of current saving, in order to meet the temporarily heavier taxes. At the termination of hostilities there would be no continued interest (and taxation) burden. Further, to extinguish the outstanding debt, Ricardo proposed a once-over special levy of two or three years' duration on property. Thus, "by one great effort" we should get rid of this "terrible scourge."[24]

The dissenter, whose views on public debt ought to be examined before continuing the main stream of classical development, is Thomas Robert Malthus. The national debt is not the evil which it is generally supposed to be, said Malthus. Those who live on the interest from the national debt, like statesmen, soldiers and sailors, ". . . contribute powerfully to distribution and demand . . . they ensure that effective consumption which is necessary to give the proper stimulus to production. . . ."[25] Therefore, the debt, once created, is not a great evil:

It is, I know, generally thought that all would be well, if we could but be relieved from the very heavy burden of our debt. And yet I feel perfectly convinced that, if a spunge could be applied to it tomorrow, and we could put out of our consideration the poverty and misery of the public creditors, by supposing them to be supported comfortably in some other country, the rest of the society, as a nation, instead of being enriched, would be impoverished. It is the greatest mistake

[22] "Funding System," *op. cit.,* pp. 149–200.

[23] *Ibid.,* p. 186. [24] *Ibid.,* p. 197.

[25] Thomas R. Malthus, *Principles of Political Economy* (2nd ed.; London, William Pickering, 1836), p. 409.

to suppose that the landlords and capitalists would either at once, or in a short time, be prepared for so great an additional consumption as such a change would require; . . . and I feel very little doubt that, in five years from the date of such an event, not only would the exchangeable value of the whole produce, estimated in domestic and foreign labour, be decidedly diminished, but a smaller absolute quantity of corn would be grown, and fewer manufactured and foreign commodities would be brought to market than before.[26]

Since the greatest powers of production are comparatively useless without effective consumption, Malthus argued, ". . . it would be the height of rashness to determine, under all circumstances, that the sudden diminution of the national debt and the removal of taxation must necessarily tend to increase the national wealth, and provide employment for the labouring classes."[27] But having made his case as forcibly as possible, Malthus almost immediately modified his position to bring it closer to that of his classical colleagues. There are, after all, evils in the debt. The taxation which is required to meet the interest payments may be harmful; people think the debt should be paid off, so the interest on it is always to some degree "insecure"; the presence of the debt aggravates the evils arising from changes in the value of money.[28] These disadvantages must be weighed carefully against the advantage of maintaining a body of "unproductive consumers" who encourage wealth by maintaining a balance between production and consumption. The need for the unproductive consumers, in turn, varies with time and place, and the skill and tastes of a people.

In 1848 John Stuart Mill could appropriately suggest some further modifications in the body of classical thinking on national debt and deficits. Apparently, by this time industry's need for capital was not as pressing as it had been earlier. In some circumstances, Mill said, government loans are not charged with pernicious consequences.

. . . first, when what is borrowed is foreign capital, the overflowings of the general accumulation of the world; or, secondly, when it is capital which either would not have been saved at all, unless this mode of investment had been open to it, or, after being saved, would have been wasted in unproductive enterprises, or sent to seek employment in foreign countries.[29]

Further, Mill suggested an "index" for determining whether there are pernicious consequences stemming from government loans. If the loan

[26] "Notes on Malthus's Principles of Political Economy," *The Works and Correspondence of David Ricardo,* II, 434–35. To this Ricardo replied, "I should think that Mr. Malthus must be the only man in England who would expect such effects from such a cause." (*Ibid.*)

[27] Malthus, *op. cit.*, p. 411.

[28] *Ibid.*, pp. 411–12.

[29] John Stuart Mill, *Principles of Political Economy* (Ashley ed., London, Longmans, Green & Co., 1929), p. 874.

raises the rate of interest it could be concluded that capital is taken which could have been productively employed, and ". . . those loans are chargeable with all the evils which have been described."[30] But if interest rates are unchanged, the pernicious consequences are not evident.

Mill continued to stress that government borrowing is harmful if it destroys capital which could otherwise be used for productive employment.[31] However, he finds it somewhat paradoxical that in these years of capital destruction—mainly war years—there is apparent prosperity. He concluded that this occurs because loan finance is an effective subtraction from the portion employed in paying laborers, and the laborers suffer accordingly. But if production is the same, the country is no poorer. "The breach made in the capital of the country is thus instantly repaired, but repaired by the privations and often the real misery of the labouring class."[32]

Regardless of whether a country has wisely or unwisely incurred a national debt, it is expedient to pay it off as rapidly as possible.[33] Mill discussed the two methods available—immediate payment by a general contribution and gradual payment with surplus revenue, and concluded that the former was preferable but that the latter was more practicable.

After J. S. Mill, the major classical economists devoted less and less attention to problems of the national debt. This is evidently a direct reflection of the fact that from this time until 1914 the outstanding British debt remained almost constant. The increase at the time of the Boer War was wiped out by debt reduction in the immediately subsequent years. At the same time, the level of national income increased tremendously; Britain grew out of her debt.[34] The writings of the classicists of this period reflected the lesser significance of the debt. Cairnes, in 1874, has no organized discussion of national debt or government fiancial problems. Sidgwick, writing in 1883, briefly discusses the effects of government borrowing, but adds little to the views of J. S. Mill.[35]

---

[30] *Ibid.*, p. 874. Mill obviously assumed that there is a "free" market in funds and that supply is relatively inelastic.

[31] *Ibid.*, pp. 76–78. [32] *Ibid.*, p. 76.

[33] It seems to be characteristic of Ricardo, Malthus, and Mill that after partially destroying the "scourge concept" of the national debt they embrace it in their policy conclusions. It is almost as if they are arguing, "The debt is not so bad as is supposed, but nevertheless we ought to pay it off."

[34] The ratio of debt service to national income was about the same in 1923 as it had been in 1818. (See *Report of the Committee on National Debt and Taxation,* Cmd. 2800, pp. 235–36.)

[35] Sidgwick incorporates in his discussion the distinction between productive and unproductive government debt, a distinction observed but not fully developed by his predecessors, and also suggests that borrowing tends to increase inequality in the distribution of

The culmination of the classical tradition—Marshall's *Principles*—devotes no attention whatever to the subject. And, significantly enough, the passing references to national debt in Marshall's *Money, Credit and Commerce* exhibit almost no concern for the problem, even though this book appeared immediately after World War I. Marshall's attitude toward the possibly wasteful spending practices of the sovereign is strikingly different from Smith's:

> The work of credit in the modern age differs from that of earlier times. . . . Formerly a great part of it was given by professional money-lenders to spendthrift heirs; now it is chiefly given by people who are living within their incomes to States which do not spend recklessly; and to strong businesses. . . . Monarchs used to be large borrowers: chiefly for the purposes of war; largely to support extravagance on the part of themselves and their favorites; and occasionally for financing expenditure on good roads, and other requisites of national well-being. . . .[36]

At about the turn of the century public finance dropped out of the main stream of classical economics and developed as a partially independent "science of finance." The views of Bastable are representative of this approach.[37]

It seems likely that Bastable, writing the first edition of *Public Finance* in 1892, was influenced by the German and French writings and experience in government finance, and possibly by the financial practices of private industry.[38] Whatever the reason, Bastable now presses the

---

national wealth. (Henry Sidgwick, *The Principles of Political Economy* [3rd ed.; London, Macmillan & Co., Ltd., 1901], pp. 549–53.)

The main body of American writing on governmental financial policy did not differ in general outlook from that of the British classicists in the last half of the nineteenth century. Henry C. Adams, for example, was as strong, but no stronger in his condemnation of public debts and deficit financing than his British contemporaries. (Henry C. Adams, *Public Debts,* p. 78). The prevalence of these views in the United States indicates not only the strength of the classical outlook but also the triumph of Gallatin's position over Hamilton's. The latter had contended forcibly that any evils inherent in the debt were more than offset by the advantages derived from a high level of federal expenditures and from the resulting stability of private credit. Gallatin, however, had apparently been more influenced by *The Wealth of Nations* and was in general agreement with Jefferson's pungent phrase that the national debt was "swindling futurity on a large scale." (For a summary of this controversy see Paul Studenski and Herman E. Kroos, *Financial History of the United States,* pp. 69–71; also, George Rogers Taylor (ed.), *Hamilton and the National Debt;* and Henry Adams (ed.), *The Writings of Albert Gallatin,* III, 143–52.)

[36] Alfred Marshall, *Money, Credit and Commerce,* pp. 69–70.

[37] The style of writing on this subject altered drastically from the time of Smith and Say to the time of Bastable. For the former, the history of governmental financial practice was cited for purposes of drawing a moral, or citing a horrible example of malpractice. With Bastable, history is history—this happened, and that was said. The issues are no longer burning. One can afford to be dispassionate.

[38] A wholly different view of the role and function of public credit was developed by the German economists in the last half of the nineteenth century. This approach stressed the "productive" character of much public expenditure and the role that public credit had

". . . fundamental difference between two classes of debt, the one contracted for non-economic ends, the other for purposes of reproductive employment."[39] This distinction should not be stretched, however, to embrace nonrevenue producing assets.[40] "National culture, education, the promotion of social progress are all most desirable; but their promotion is not so urgently required as to need the use of borrowing by the public powers."[41] It is appropriate to finance the purchase of the Prussian railways or the English telegraphs by borrowing, but not the construction of school buildings. The latter may be generally and indirectly productive, but the results of such expenditure are ". . . hard to trace or measure, and any statement respecting them must rest in a great degree on conjecture."[42]

Unless there is an equivalent revenue obtained from the application of the proceeds of borrowing, Bastable argued, there will inevitably be a curtailment of the future power of spending. Heavy borrowing cripples the ordinary revenue and compels retrenchment in the future. However, there are conditions under which loan finance is to be preferred to heavy taxation. Nonrecurrent and large expenditures may be financed by loans with less disturbance than if heavy taxation were used. Where the expenditure extends over a period of years, there may be limits to the productiveness of specific taxes and of the tax system as a whole, so that borrowing is necessary. And, in some circumstances, it may not be politically expedient to press heavily on the taxpayers.[43] In developing an adequate financial policy for a government it is of greatest importance to have a budget system, and a strong minister of finance who will undertake "prudent reduction of outlay" and "skilful adjustment of resources."[44] ". . . the creation of the budget is therefore a work of administrative art, in which the use of proper methods will very materially improve the financial position, and contribute to the public advantage."[45]

---

played in the development of private credit instruments. It further argued that governments could appropriately borrow for permanent improvements that would benefit future generations. For an excellent discussion of this literature, and German national and state financial policy which accompanied it, see Gustav Cohn, *op. cit.*, pp. 718–26.

This approach seems to have had very little impact on the literature or practice of fiscal policy in Great Britain and the United States, unless it can be contended that the distinction between productive and unproductive debt came from this source. However, in the Keynesian attack on classical fiscal principles, some inspiration was apparently derived from the most prominent of the German writers of the nineteenth century. See Walter F. Stettner, "Carl Dietzel, Public Expenditures, and the Public Debt," in Lloyd A. Metzler (ed.), *Income, Employment and Public Policy*, pp. 276–99.

[39] Bastable, *op. cit.*, p. 627.

[40] *Ibid.*, p. 670.

[41] *Loc. cit.*

[42] *Ibid.*, p. 671.

[43] *Ibid.*, pp. 678–79.

[44] *Ibid.*, pp. 734–36.

[45] *Ibid.*, p. 736.

A final and important addition to this body of doctrine developed from the application of the principles of marginalism to public finance. Marginalism in public finance seems to have been first elaborated as a conceptual framework for analyzing the distribution of tax burdens, then applied to the distribution of government expenditures, and finally utilized to bring together the revenue and expenditure activities of government.[46] Dalton's is one of the first complete elaborations of this approach:

> Public expenditure in every direction should be carried just so far, that the advantage to the community of a further small increase in any direction is just counterbalanced by the disadvantage of a corresponding small increase in taxation or in receipts from any other source of public income. This gives the ideal total both of public expenditure and of public income.[47]

It may be assumed that public income from borrowing involves no disutilities to the lender. Therefore, utilities and disutilities are balanced when the budget is balanced.[48]

From this summary account of the classical approach to budget balancing and national debt it is evident that attitudes and analyses changed substantially from the time of Smith to the time of Bastable and Dalton. Perhaps the greatest change is that the degree of antipathy to debts and deficits was modified sharply downward.

In spite of the changes it is possible to summarize the classical doctrine in a set of propositions, intermingled though the propositions are. In some cases these are clearly set forth in the writings of the classicists. In other cases they must be inferred. Parts of the doctrine were accepted by some but rejected by other writers. These propositions on debts and deficits, together with an assessment of their current validity, are as follows:

1. Government loan finance withdraws funds from productive private employment.

Where this point is interpreted to mean that an economy has an aggregate funds shortage it is a generalization which has no applica-

[46] Emil Sax is credited with being the first to apply marginalism to public finance. For an excellent discussion of the development of this approach see Mabel L. Walker, *Municipal Expenditures,* pp. 28–51.

[47] Hugh Dalton, *Principles of Public Finance,* pp. 18–19.

[48] Smithies has pointed out that the application of marginalism to the division of resources between public and private use does not require a balanced budget where there is a defined fiscal policy goal of raising the money level of national income and where tax reduction is one of the means available for reaching this goal. However, this possibility was not considered by the marginalists; for them, budget balancing was the end product of the application of their principles. (See Arthur Smithies, "Federal Budgeting and Fiscal Policy," *A Survey of Contemporary Economics,* I, 192–95.)

bility whatsoever in an advanced industrial economy possessed of a fractional reserve banking system and central banking techniques. Government bonds sold to commercial banks and to the central bank do not absorb funds which would otherwise be invested in the private sector. Indeed, J. S. Mill, as noted, did not attempt to support this generalization so long ago as 1848. Where the argument is advanced, as it was by Say, to mean that funds should be expended on capital goods by industry rather than on consumer goods by the state, what is really implied is that government expenditures do not add to productive capacity and that there are unfulfilled investment opportunities in industry and trade. This makes the point much more complex and eliminates any general validity which it may possess.

2. Deficits are less painful than current taxes. Unbalanced budgets therefore expand governmental activity and invite irresponsible governmental action.

There is no doubt that deficits are relatively painless, as compared with increased taxes, but it is much less certain that deficit spending necessarily leads to irresponsibility, unless it has been defined in advance as equivalent to irresponsibility. In a modern budgetary system it would be most difficult to demonstrate that the legislature scrutinizes less closely the outlays financed by loans than the outlays financed by taxes, or that wartime deficits or deficits incurred to combat a depression represent a fiscal policy which is more irresponsible than peacetime surpluses.

The point at issue here is the general one of securing a responsible and democratic government. The emergence of such government over the last several hundred years is not at all equivalent to the avoidance of governmental deficits. Modern budgetary systems have been most important in the development of responsible government but their contribution is not to be judged solely in terms of the elimination of deficits.

There is another point which remains in this argument, the point which Adam Smith was most concerned about. Deficit finance expands the relative power of government, vis-à-vis the taxpayers. Where governments can control resources without immediately diverting them from private incomes, there is, beyond doubt, an augmentation in the political and economic power of the sovereign. If the sovereign is irresponsible, he will resort to loan finance under conditions where it is not justified; loan finance, in turn, will increase his power. Strict adherence to the limitations of a balanced budget will operate to restrict the growth of the public sector.

3. Government borrowing makes future financing more difficult by

increasing the proportion of the budget which must go for fixed charges and by increasing the amount of taxes which must be paid to finance the transfer of interest on the debt.

This proposition is applicable and important to the extent that governmental revenues are restricted by constitutional, statutory or economic factors. Therefore, it is more applicable to state and local governments than to a national government. Moreover, for a strong national government, the increase in fixed charges and accompanying taxes may be offset by lowered interest rates, unless these are institutional barriers which require orthodox financial practices. Additions to government debt need not bring higher tax rates, even with the level of national income unchanged, if interest rates are continuously brought down by central monetary authority.

Where interest payments do increase, together with taxes, to support these payments, the possibly deleterious consequences depend, as Ricardo pointed out, on the pattern of taxpaying and the pattern of bondholding. A domestically-held debt is burdensome in so far as the transfer is burdensome. Economic burdens will obtain only where the additional taxes levied to finance the interest payments discourage economic activity more than the receipts of interest encourage it.[49]

4. Loan finance is costly; public outlays financed in this way must be paid for twice—once in meeting interest charges and once in amortizing the debt.

Viewed as a matter of arithmetic, this proposition cannot be doubted. Where debts are amortized, the finance of capital outlay by means of borrowing entails an increasing volume of annual charges which soon mount to the point where less outlay is possible than if all financing had been undertaken out of current revenue.[50] However, as in the case of budgetary inflexibility, the importance of "costliness" must be judged in relation to the nature of the governmental receipts and expenditures.

The "costliness" of governmental borrowing, again, is most serious for governmental units with limited tax and credit resources. It is not

[49] This subject received much attention in the years immediately after World War II when public and professional concern over the national debt was at its height. In one careful analysis of the problem it was concluded that interest on the federal debt, and the corresponding pattern of tax payments to support that interest, operated moderately in the direction of reducing concentration in the disribution of total income, a consequence which is desirable if the economy is tending toward underconsumption. See Henry C. Wallich, "The Changing Significance of the Interest Rate," *Am. Econ. Rev.*, Dec. 1946, pp. 770–75. Also, Jacob Cohen, "Distributional Effects of the Federal Debt," *Jour. Finance*, Sept. 1951, pp. 267–75; Jesse V. Burkhead, "Full Employment and Interest-Free Borrowing," *So. Econ. Jour.*, July 1947, pp. 1–13.

[50] For a demonstration of this point, see James A. Maxwell, "The Capital Budget," *Quart. Jour. Econ.*, May 1943, pp. 454–56.

hard to convince city officials that a pay-as-you-go plan for municipal improvements is to be preferred to loan finance; the latter is too expensive. The interest payments may be a serious drain on a city's financial resources, and the interest payments are likely to be made "abroad," that is, to bondholders outside the city's jurisdiction.

But "costliness" in these terms does not apply to the federal government of the United States. Here the interest payments are not made "abroad"; instead, they are transfer payments within the economy.

Of these propositions the first and fourth appear to possess little validity. The second—that deficits expand the scope of governmental power—is significant, particularly where government officials and legislators are irresponsible and require the fiscal discipline of rigid rule-making. The third—that debt finance raises the level of future tax payments—is important in those cases where governments choose to make it so, that is, where policy decisions are limited by fiscal orthodoxy.

The two remaining propositions in the classical doctrine can be evaluated only after an examination of the Keynesian contribution to the theory and practice of government debts and deficits. These are:

5. Unbalanced budgets lead to currency deterioration.
6. Balanced budgets provide a guide for the transfer of resources from the private to the public sector.

II

The Keynesian attack on the classical principles of budgeting and public finance was a logical extension of the Keynesian attack on the view that the economy tends to equilibrium at full employment. If there were unemployed resources which the private sector would not or could not employ, these resources might be put to work by the state by means of additional public outlay, which need not be matched by additional government revenue. Orthodox financial rules must be abandoned, even as orthodox economics must be abandoned.[51]

Keynes himself did not elaborate the role of fiscal policy in the maintenance of full employment. This remained for Alvin Hansen and the Keynesians. Writing at the end of a decade of depression, Hansen, in *Fiscal Policy and Business Cycles,* made a number of significant

---

[51] "The local corollary of orthodox economics is orthodox finance. If it is believed that all factors of production are normally and inevitably utilized by private business, it follows that the State can obtain the use of such factors only by preventing private business from using them. . . . From this it follows that the first principle of 'sound' Public Finance is that the budget should be balanced." (E. F. Schumacher, "Public Finance—Its Relation to Full Employment," *The Economics of Full Employment,* Oxford University Institute of Statistics (Oxford, Basil Blackwell, 1946), p. 86.)

contributions.[52] He attempted to restore public finance, as fiscal policy, to its place in the main stream of economics. He reinterpreted the nineteenth century experience of national governments in their debt-creating capacity. And he attempted to establish a new set of guide lines for government borrowing and deficit financing.

The general outlines of Hansen's contribution are well-known and need be summarized only briefly. Hansen argued that fiscal policy had been forced to serve as a compensatory device more by accident than by design. Public finance had been broadened by the political necessity of coping with unemployment. Most of the "principles" intended to cover public debt policy had been borrowed from private finance, but the analogies were misleading. "If one adopts wholeheartedly the principle that governmental financial operations should be regarded exclusively as instruments of economic and public policy, the concept of a balanced budget, however defined, can play no role in the determination of that policy."[53]

Hansen contended that success or failure of public debt policy can be determined only in relation to the aggregates of national income and its distribution. Whether or not the public debt should be reduced depends on the general economic situation and not on principles applicable to private commercial accounting. Economic activity in the government sector is not "sustained out of" private economic activity; it is an independent sector in the production of goods and services. Government outlay financed by debt creation will increase the level of national income, regardless of the productivity of the assets which may be acquired. Moreover, the importance of the public debt in the establishment of the credit system in western European countries and in the United States had not been fully appreciated.

Hansen pointed out that the limits to the public debt must be determined in relation to a nation's taxable capacity, the danger of price inflation, and the distribution of income; the limits are flexible and not fixed. The implementation of compensatory fiscal policy required a recasting of traditional budgetary policy, in order to view the expenditure and receipts side of government budgets in relation to the total level of economic activity.

The attack by the American Keynesians on the classical principle of budgetary equilibrium was accompanied by numerous suggestions to improve budgetary techniques with a view to making the federal budget in the United States more flexible and of greater usefulness in a compensatory fiscal policy. Many of these contributions were evi-

[52] Esp. pp. 135–222. [53] *Ibid.*, p. 188.

dently inspired by Hansen and appeared in the 1941 volume of *Public Policy.*[54]

Experience with capital budgets in the Scandinavian countries had impressed Hansen with their usefulness as tools of fiscal policy. By varying the rate of expenditure for capital outlay, the Swedish government had apparently made a major contribution to economic stabilization. Although he did not recommend that the United States adopt this technique, he did suggest that the experience be carefully examined. The capital budget might offer means for the expansion of governmental expenditures, loan financed, but in accordance with a set of rules and procedures which could be readily understood.[55]

The Hansenian contribution is not, however, the whole of the development of Keynesian fiscal theory. The culmination is A. P. Lerner's functional finance.[56] This approach to fiscal policy views government revenue and expenditure and government debt solely as instruments for the control of aggregate community expenditure. These are the tools, and the goal is the maintenance of stable employment at constant prices. Taxes and expenditures should be increased or reduced solely to affect the community's rate of spending; debt instruments should be sold to the public to absorb their idle balances and reduce liquidity in times of inflation, and redeemed to increase liquidity in times of depression. Perhaps to gain currency for his views Lerner formulated his propositions in terms of "laws."

Unfortunately, the enactment of the "laws" of functional finance would provide no workable guides for the formulation of budget policy. The policy-making official would have three instruments of stabilization available for use—taxation, expenditures, and the purchase and sale of debt instruments. But he would have no criteria available for choosing among them. Beyond this, functional finance provides no guides for the selection of alternative government expenditures. Lerner gives no assistance to the budget-maker who must determine both the aggregates of receipts and expenditures and their components. Government responsibility for stable full employment is substituted for government irresponsibility in the determination of the kinds of programs which are undertaken.

[54] Yearbook of the Graduate School of Public Administration, Harvard University (Cambridge, Mass., 1941).

[55] Spencer Thompson, "The Investment Budget," *ibid.*, pp. 63–77. For a critical examination of capital budgeting see Richard A. Musgrave, "The Nature of Budgetary Balance and the Case for the Capital Budget," *Am. Econ. Rev.*, June 1939, pp. 260–71, and James A. Maxwell, *op. cit.*, pp. 450–65.

[56] A. P. Lerner, *The Economics of Control,* pp. 302–22; "Functional Finance and the Federal Debt," *Soc. Research,* Feb. 1943, pp. 38–51.

From this brief examination of the Keynesian impact on budgetary theory certain conclusions may be drawn.

It is evident that the major difference between the outlook of the classicists and the Keynesians turns on their analyses of the nature of economic society and the role of the state therein. The classicists, particularly Adam Smith, were completely explicit on this point: economic society is characterized by a fundamental harmony of interest. The invisible hand, operating in a competitive society, will reconcile all conflicts. The role of the state must and should be narrow. With fundamental harmony prevailing there is no need for extensive intervention.

The Keynesians have not been so explicit—modern economists appear to shun political theory. But running through almost all of the Keynesian literature there appears to be an unstated assumption that the economic order is harmonious *except for* its inability to achieve stability. This defect can be overcome by governmental fiscal action.[57] The enlarged role of the state is necessitated by the requirement for erecting a balance wheel for economic activity. Stable full employment is identical with the general welfare and this general welfare is greater, *Gestaltische,* than the aggregate of specific interest groups and economic class welfares.[58]

The Keynesians conceive the state to be primarily ameliorative but with a program of its own and an internal dynamic of its own making. The state operates with a high degree of independence above and beyond the interest groups which comprise it. The government is not a pawn in the hands of these groups, nor does it merely serve as a device for reconciling conflicting pressures. Rather, governmental organizations contribute to policy-making as an independent force.[59]

III

Two questions remain for consideration. First, why has there been so little Keynesian impact on prevalent attitudes toward government debts and deficits in this country? Second, what are the reasons, whether

[57] Keynes' attack on wage cutting as an antidepression remedy does not reflect any feeling on his part that the economic order is characterized by deep-seated struggles over the relative shares of national income. In fact, he points out that the willingness of trade unions to work for unchanged money wages even when real wages are falling makes for harmony and stability. (*General Theory,* pp. 4–22.)

[58] For a critical dissent see Paul A. Baran, "National Economic Planning," *A Survey of Contemporary Economics,* Vol. II (Homewood, Illinois, Irwin, 1952), pp. 355–77.

[59] For an excellent statement of this position in terms of the administrator's role in policy formulation see Emmette S. Redford, *Administration of National Economic Control* (New York, Macmillan Co., 1952), pp. 220–36.

"practical" or "folklore," which explain the widespread acceptance of the doctrine of balanced budgets for the federal government?

The answer to the first question is undoubtedly to be found, in good part, in the behavior of the American economy since World War II. Full employment has been maintained almost consistently, and the federal budget has been generally in balance. It may be that the high level of federal expenditures has been a major factor in maintaining prosperity, but the fact is that these high expenditures have been matched by high receipts. From 1947 to 1952 the economy did not require deficit spending for the maintenance of prosperity; only in 1953 did a substantial deficit appear.

Since full employment has been maintained without compensatory spending, it is not surprising that American Keynesians have devoted little attention to the development of workable concepts and techniques for flexible budgeting. The importance of the federal budget in economic stabilization is widely recognized, but this recognition has not been accompanied by implementation.

An implementation would require two things. First, there must be a more or less "official" adoption of flexible concepts of budgeting with a view to the use of the budget for stabilization purposes. Second, there must be a classification of governmental receipts and expenditures which will provide at least an approximation to the measurement of the economic efforts of government activity. This classification must be used and useful in budgetary planning.

Sweden is an outstanding example of a country where the national government has abandoned the budget-balancing philosophy. This abandonment has evolved gradually. The capital budget which was used in that country in the 1930's required a balance in the current account, but capital expenditures could be varied for purposes of stabilization. By 1937 there was official abandonment of annual budget balancing for either the current or capital account and balancing over the cycle was substituted therefor. Since 1944 cyclical budget balancing is no longer regarded as important; the total impact of state finances on the level of national economic activity is now the major determinant of budgetary policy.[60]

The second requirement involves a thoroughgoing reclassification of governmental activity—an economic character classification. This classification should, at minimum, provide estimates of the net effect of current and proposed government activities on private income ac-

[60] United Nations, Department of Economic Affairs, *Budgetary Structure and Classification of Government Accounts* (New York, 1951), pp. 68–81.

counts. Such a classification was proposed for Great Britain by J. R. Hicks,[61] and one has been set forth in generalized terms by the Department of Economic Affairs of the United Nations.[62] To be used and useful an economic character classification should be developed in the process of budgetary formulation at a time and place in the governmental hierarchy where it enters into budgetary decision-making.

In this country neither of these developments has occurred. Rigid and inflexible concepts of budget balancing have the greatest influence on public policy and there has been no governmental effort to introduce alternative and more flexible concepts.[63] Further, there has been no development of an economic character classification to accompany the U.S. budget, although there have been important developments in other areas of budgeting technique in the federal government in recent years.[64] The Budget Message continues to be a review of agency and departmental programs, rather than a document reflecting an analysis of the economic character of governmental operations.

The practical influence of Keynesian economics on budgeting concepts and procedures in the United States has been almost nil. We continue to be dominated by adherence to the goal of a balanced budget buttressed by the phrases and arguments of the classical economists.

The answer to the second question—the explanation for the adherence to balanced budgets—would appear to be provided by a combination of considerations, some of which relate to the economics of debts and deficits, and others which are the product of popular attitudes.

---

61 *Budgetary Reform* (Oxford, 1948).

62 *Budgetary Structure and Classification of Government Accounts,* pp. 1–50.

63 For one important set of suggestions for more flexible budget concepts see Morris A. Copeland, "The Capital Budget and the War Effort," *Am. Econ. Rev.,* Mar. 1943, pp. 38–49. The Committee for Economic Development has proposed a budgetary policy which would set tax rates at a point to provide a surplus for debt retirement at an agreed high level of income and employment. These rates would be unchanged except in a severe depression or critical inflation. (*The Stabilizing Budget Policy,* New York, 1950.) This proposal, if adopted, would serve to reduce, not increase, flexibility in the use of the budget as a stabilization measure, since variations in expenditures for stabilization purposes would be almost precluded. For a critical examination of the CED and similar proposals see Paul A. Samuelson, "Principles and Rules in Modern Fiscal Policy: A Neo-Classical Reformulation," in *Money, Trade, and Economic Growth* (in honor of John Henry Williams), pp. 157–76.

64 The development of performance budgeting at the agency level is probably the most significant of these, together with some major improvements in the form and structure of agency and departmental accounting. There are two budgetary statements which have some significance for the analysis of the economic character of governmental activities—the statement of "Receipts from and Payments to the Public" and the statement of "Investment, Operating, and Other Budget Expenditures." These, however, fall considerably short of what is needed. (See *Budget of the United States Government for the Fiscal Year Ending June 30, 1954,* pp. 1076–77, 1098–1106.)

These may be labeled "real" and "attitudinal." The "real" considerations are those previously summarized in the review of classical doctrine. These are:

1. Unbalanced budgets contribute to currency deterioration.

There is no doubt that, from the time of Adam Smith to the present day, unbalanced budgets have evoked great concern on this ground. History, even recent history, is replete with cases of corrupt or inefficient governments which went to their ruin in a shower of paper currency.

Unbalanced budgets could conceivably lead to inflation in one of two ways. Either the deficit itself could be inflationary, as governments made net contributions to levels of demand, or the accumulated deficits, by their additions to money supply, could contribute to inflationary pressure. These influences are not always separated in popular discussion.[65]

It is almost a truism that government deficits add to levels of effective demand and that, unless the supply of resources is elastic at current price levels, prices will rise. However, from this relationship it should not be concluded that an increase in the federal deficit will inevitably lead to an increase in prices. Examination of the behavior of the wholesale price index and federal deficits since 1930 shows that it has not worked out this way. In only eight of the twenty-three fiscal years from July 1, 1930 to June 30, 1953 was there a positive association between an increase in the federal deficit and an increase in the price level. In fifteen of these years changes in the deficit and changes in wholesale prices moved in opposite directions. In some recent years the inverse association has been striking. In fiscal 1951 the budget moved from a deficit of $3.1 billion to a surplus of $3.5 billion, that is, a *decrease* in the deficit of $6.6 billion. In the same fiscal year there was an *increase* in the wholesale price level by 15 per cent. In fiscal 1953 the budget deficit increased from $4.0 billion to $9.3 billion, but the level of wholesale prices dropped slightly.

It is evident that in any one year currency stability cannot be assured by balancing the budget.[66] It can be assured only by "balancing" the

[65] For Adam Smith it was the debt itself which produced the currency deterioration, as sovereigns attempted to reduce its crushing burden by clipping coins and printing paper money. This view, surely, was the product of an age of irresponsible sovereigns, and of a time when, at least in part, the debts of the state were the personal debts of the crown, to be retired in depreciated currency when the crown could temporarily gain an advantage over the merchant-bondholders with whom it was engaged in a more or less continual struggle. Smith did not argue that there was a causal relation between current deficits and currency depreciation.

[66] It should also be noted that balancing the federal budget balances only a set of accounts, which are not the whole of federal financial operations. Trust accounts are ex-

combined operations of the government and the private sectors. If the outlook is inflation, then, clearly, a balanced or overbalanced budget is not out of order. But there can be no assurance that the surplus will not be offset by activities in the private sector.

It is very frequently contended that accumulated deficits (debt) are an inflationary force. The additions to money supply occasioned by the debt may add to bank reserves, which, in the absence of countervailing action, may encourage banks to extend loans to business firms and households. Debt holdings by persons, by adding to the stock of liquid assets, may conceivably lead to a higher consumption ratio out of current income. Business firms may liquidate their debt holdings to bid up the price of inventory or producers' durables. Debt holdings by the public are thus an inflationary potential, which, if not offset by other controls, may be a destabilizing influence. But again, the point to be stressed is that accumulated deficits and the concomitant increased liquidity do not, in themselves, generate an inflationary movement. They may feed it but they do not start it. Liquidity is significant only in relation to its distribution among those who are motivated to make their demands effective. It is not significant in the aggregate. Liquid asset holdings did not prevent the 1949 recession.

2. A balanced budget provides an easily-understood rule to guide the transfer of resources from the private to the public sector.

Here the advocates of budget balancing appear to be on firm ground. Whether or not this proposition is grounded in the economics of marginal utilities and disutilities, there is no doubt that budget balancing, particularly annual budget balancing, has a definite and precise character which is lacking in any other available guide to fiscal policy.[67] The concept of "balancing over the business cycle," for example, always generates uncertainty as to the precise point in the cycle where one finds oneself. Moreover, budget balancing is a practicable guide for policy-making officials, who can roughly gauge the amount of taxation which the community can "stand" and then trim expenditures to fit the revenue.

Unfortunately, however, this guideline is valueless when there are unemployed resources which may be put to work producing goods and services. The employment of such resources is virtually costless

---

cluded from the budget and their surpluses or deficits are excluded from the definition of budget surplus or deficit.

[67] For the limitations which attach to a strict application of marginalism in this area see A. C. Pigou, *A Study in Public Finance* (3rd rev. ed., London, Macmillan & Co. Ltd., 1951), pp. 31–34.

to the economy as a whole. In the vocabulary of the marginalists, there are only utilities—no disutilities.

The remaining possibility is that it is not economic factors, but "attitudinal" factors which account for the prevalence of the balanced budget doctrine.

1. It may be that popular thinking about government budgets is based on popular thinking about household budgets.

It matters not, that, as Hansen pointed out, the analogies are all faulty. Household budget balancing is in accord with the kind of Poor Richard economics which has made up the code of conduct of the American economy for many generations. Thrift and frugality in personal affairs; economy and efficiency in government. Saving is a virtue; for governments as for individuals, the rule is "waste not, want not."

2. It may be that there is a fear of the economic and political consequences of government spending rather than direct concern over the debt itself.

This is a variant of the argument that deficits expand governmental authority. Those who are most vocal in opposition to an increase in the debt may, in reality, be opposing only the increase in expenditures. Certainly, conflict over whether activities shall be conducted collectively by government or by firms in the private sector is one of the most persistent in the history of economic systems. Those who are in a position to feel government competition directly, as in electric power or housing, will diligently oppose the extension of governmental expenditures in these areas. It is understandable that in seeking to combat such competition, those who are most affected thereby will both oppose the expenditure directly and utilize the concern over the national debt and deficits to bolster their case. The extent to which this type of attitude is significant is, of course, impossible to determine.

3. The opposition to an increase in debt may be explained by opposition to compensatory fiscal policy.

If the adherence to balanced budgets is based on opposition to what its opponents call "a managed economy," the practical nature of the problem is likely to force this kind of folklore out of the sanctuary.

Undoubtedly, there are difficulties in applying government compensatory action. Forecasting techniques are not well developed; governmental programs cannot be administered with sufficient rapidity to prevent either rapidly-moving inflation or rapidly-moving deflation; the increase in governmental authority which is required for compensatory action may be difficult to control—policies may be irresponsibly conceived.

Nevertheless, and in spite of the difficulties, it can hardly be doubted that any modern and responsive government will use the weapons at its disposal, including budgetary policy, for purposes of economic stabilization. The government may act less promptly than some would like; expenditures may be increased when some would prefer that taxes be reduced; pyramids may be built when some would prefer that resources be developed. But, surely, compensatory fiscal policy will continue to be used by the federal government for purposes of stabilizing levels of economic activity, even as it has been used since the 1930's.

To summarize. The classical case for budget balancing rests on a series of interrelated propositions, some of an "economic" nature and some of a "political" nature reflecting attitudes toward the role of the state and the responsibilities of sovereign authority. Two of these propositions possess at least a limited validity for budget-making in strong national governments: (1) deficits may encourage irresponsibility and contribute to the growth of the public sector, and (2) deficits may require a higher level of future tax rates. In addition, one of the propositions—that current deficits contribute to inflation—has validity, although recent U.S. experience would indicate that a federal government deficit is by no means a sufficient condition for inflation. Accumulated deficits may contribute to inflation through effects on the money supply, if the inflationary movement is already under way and unless offset by the actions of monetary authority. Finally, the classical proposition that balanced budgets provide an automatic rule-making authority for government budgeting is significant and important and at the basis of the "practical nature of the problem." The prevalence of the balanced budget philosophy is, however, not fully explainable by the propositions of the classical case. Beyond doubt, the "attitudinal" factors are at least as important as the "real" factors.

The Keynesian contribution to budgetary theory and practice is reducible to the proposition that government activities should be used to stabilize the level of total economic activity. The classicists stressed the control of the budget; the Keynesians the effects of the budget. Unfortunately, the Keynesian attention to budgetary effects has been accompanied by inattention to the problem of control.

This would seem to be the remaining and challenging task for the critics of conservative fiscal policy: to provide a guide to governmental budgeting which will serve two purposes simultaneously. The first purpose is to guide the transfer of resources from the private to the public sector; the second is to guide the selection of the aggregate level of receipts and expenditures with a view to stabilization. The guidelines must be widely understood and capable of political implementation. Until this is done we can confidently anticipate a continuation of discussion over national debts and deficits, a discussion which will abound in semantic confusion.

Since this article was initiated with the suggestion of Thurman Arnold that our theorizing in these matters partakes of folklore, it may appropriately be closed on a practical point:

> Mr. Micawber solemnly conjured me . . . to observe that if a man had twenty pounds a year for his income, and spent nineteen pounds nineteen shillings and sixpence, he would be happy, but that if he spent twenty pounds one he would be miserable. After which he borrowed a shilling of me for porter . . . and cheered up.[68]

[68] Charles Dickens, *David Copperfield* (Philadelphia, John C. Winston Co., 1948), p. 73.

II. FISCAL POLICY IN RECOVERY

2

An Open Letter

By JOHN MAYNARD KEYNES

London, Dec. 30.

Dear Mr. President:

You have made yourself the trustee for those in every country who seek to mend the evils of our condition by reasoned experiment within the framework of the existing social system.

If you fail, rational change will be gravely prejudiced throughout the world, leaving orthodoxy and revolution to fight it out.

But if you succeed, new and bolder methods will be tried everywhere, and we may date the first chapter of a new economic era from your accession to office.

This is a sufficient reason why I should venture to lay my reflections before you, though under the disadvantages of distance and partial knowledge.

OPINION IN ENGLAND

At the moment your sympathizers in England are nervous and sometimes despondent. We wonder whether the order of different urgencies is rightly understood, whether there is a confusion of aims, and whether some of the advice you get is not crack-brained and queer.

If we are disconcerted when we defend you, this is partly due to the influence of our environment in London. For almost every one here has a wildly distorted view of what is happening in the United States.

The average City man believes you are engaged on a hare-brained expedition in face of competent advice, that the best hope lies in your ridding yourself of your present advisers to return to the old ways, and that otherwise the United States is heading for some ghastly breakdown. That is what they say they smell.

There is a recrudescence of wise head-wagging by those who believe the nose is a nobler organ than the brain. London is convinced that we

---

* *New York Times,* December 31, 1933. Reprinted by the courtesy of the North American Newspaper Alliance, Inc.

only have to sit back and wait to see what we shall see. May I crave your attention, while I put my own view?

THE PRESENT TASK

You are engaged on a double task, recovery and reform—recovery from the slump, and the passage of those business and social reforms which are long overdue. For the first, speed and quick results are essential. The second may be urgent, too; but haste will be injurious, and wisdom of long-range purpose is more necessary than immediate achievement. It will be through raising high the prestige of your administration by success in short-range recovery that you will have the driving force to accomplish long-range reform.

On the other hand, even wise and necessary reform may, in some respects, impede and complicate recovery. For it will upset the confidence of the business world and weaken its existing motives to action before you have had time to put other motives in their place. It may overtask your bureaucratic machine, which the traditional individualism of the United States and the old "spoils system" have left none too strong. And it will confuse the thought and aim of yourself and your administration by giving you too much to think about all at once.

NRA AIMS AND RESULTS

Now I am not clear, looking back over the last nine months, that the order of urgency between measures of recovery and measures of reform has been duly observed, or that the latter has not sometimes been mistaken for the former. In particular, though its social gains are considerable, I cannot detect any material aid to recovery in the NRA. The driving force which has been put behind the vast administrative task set by this act has seemed to represent a wrong choice in the order of urgencies. The act is on the statute book; a considerable amount has been done toward implementing it; but it might be better for the present to allow experience to accumulate before trying to force through all its details.

That is my first reflection—that NRA, which is essentially reform and probably impedes recovery, has been put across too hastily, in the false guise of being part of the technique of recovery.

My second reflection relates to the technique of recovery itself. The object of recovery is to increase the national output and put more men to work. In the economic system of the modern world, output is primarily produced for sale; and the volume of output depends on the amount of purchasing power, compared with the prime cost of production, which is expected to come on the market.

Broadly speaking, therefore, an increase of output cannot occur unless by the operation of one or other of three factors. Individuals must be induced to spend more out of their existing incomes, or the business world must be induced, either by increased confidence in the prospects or by a lower rate of interest, to create additional current incomes in the hands of their employes, which is what happens when either the working or the fixed capital of the country is being increased; or public authority must be called in aid to create additional current incomes through the expenditure of borrowed or printed money.

In bad times the first factor cannot be expected to work on a sufficient scale. The second factor will only come in as the second wave of attack on the slump, after the tide has been turned by the expenditures of public authority. It is, therefore, only from the third factor that we can expect the initial major impulse.

Now there are indications that two technical fallacies may have affected the policy of your administration. The first relates to the part played in recovery by rising prices. Rising prices are to be welcomed because they are usually a symptom of rising output and employment. When more purchasing power is spent, one expects rising output at rising prices. Since there cannot be rising output without rising prices, it is essential to insure that the recovery shall not be held back by the insufficiency of the supply of money to support the increased monetary turnover.

THE PROBLEM OF RISING PRICES

But there is much less to be said in favor of rising prices if they are brought about at the expense of rising output. Some debtors may be helped, but the national recovery as a whole will be retarded. Thus rising prices caused by deliberately increasing prime costs or by restricting output have a vastly inferior value to rising prices which are the natural result of an increase in the nation's purchasing power.

I do not mean to impugn the social justice and social expediency of the redistribution of incomes aimed at by the NRA and by the various schemes for agricultural restriction. The latter, in particular, I should strongly support in principle. But too much emphasis on the remedial value of a higher price-level as an object in itself may lead to serious misapprehension of the part prices can play in the technique of recovery. The stimulation of output by increasing aggregate purchasing power is the right way to get prices up; and not the other way around.

Thus, as the prime mover in the first stage of the technique of recovery, I lay overwhelming emphasis on the increase of national purchasing power resulting from governmental expenditure which is financed by loans and is not merely a transfer through taxation, from existing incomes. Nothing else counts in comparison with this.

BOOM, SLUMP AND WAR

In a boom, inflation can be caused by allowing unlimited credit to support the excited enthusiasm of business speculators. But in a slump governmental loan expenditure is the only sure means of obtaining quickly a rising output at rising prices. That is why a war has always caused intense industrial activity. In the past, orthodox finance has regarded a war as the only legitimate excuse for creating employment by government expenditure. You, Mr. President, having cast off such fetters, are free to engage in the interests of peace and prosperity the technique which hitherto has only been allowed to serve the purposes of war and destruction.

The set-back American recovery experienced this past Autumn was the predictable consequence of the failure of your administration to organize any material increase in new loan expenditure during your first six months of office. The position six months hence will depend entirely on whether you have been laying the foundations for larger expenditures in the near future.

I am not surprised that so little has been spent to date. Our own experience has shown how difficult it is to improvise useful loan expenditures at short notice. There are many obstacles to be patiently overcome, if waste, inefficiency and corruption are to be avoided. There are many factors I need not stop to enumerate which render especially difficult in the United States the rapid improvisation of a vast program of public works. I do not blame Secretary Ickes for being cautious and careful. But the risks of less speed must be weighed against those of more haste. He must get across the crevasses before it is dark.

The other set of fallacies, of which I fear the influence, arises out of a crude economic doctrine commonly known as the quantity theory of money. Rising output and rising incomes will suffer a setback sooner or later if the quantity of money is rigidly fixed. Some people seem to infer from this that output and income can be raised by increasing the quantity of money. But this is like trying to get fat by buying a larger belt. In the United States today your belt is plenty big enough for your belly. It is a most misleading thing to stress the quantity of money, which is only a limiting factor, rather than the volume of expenditure, which is the operative factor.

It is an even more foolish application of the same ideas to believe that there is a mathematical relation between the price of gold and the prices of other things. It is true that the value of the dollar in terms of foreign currencies will affect the prices of those goods which enter into international trade. In so far as an overvaluation of the dollar was impeding the freedom of domestic price-raising policies or disturbing the balance of payments with foreign countries, it was advisable to depreciate it. But exchange depreciation should follow the success of your domestic price-raising policy as its natural consequence, and should not be allowed to disturb the whole world by preceding its justification at an entirely arbitrary pace. This is another example of trying to put on flesh by letting out the belt.

CURRENCY AND EXCHANGE

These criticisms do not mean that I have weakened in my advocacy of a managed currency or in preferring stable prices to stable exchanges. The currency and exchange policy of a country should be entirely subservient to the aim of raising output and employment to the right level. But the recent gyrations of the dollar have looked to me more like a gold standard on the booze than the ideal managed currency of my dreams.

You may be feeling by now, Mr. President, that my criticism is more obvious than my sympathy. Yet truly that is not so. You remain for me the ruler whose general outlook and attitude to the tasks of government are the most sympathetic in the world. You are the only one who sees the necessity of a profound change of methods and is attempting it without intolerance, tyranny or destruction. You are feeling your way by trial and error, and are felt to be, as you should be, entirely uncommitted in your own person to the details of a particular technique. In my country, as in your own, your position remains singularly untouched by criticism of this or the other detail. Our hope and our faith are based on broader considerations.

If you were to ask me what I would suggest in concrete terms for the immediate future, I would reply thus:

CONSTRUCTIVE CRITICISM

In the field of gold devaluation and exchange policy the time has come when uncertainty should be ended. This game of blind man's buff with exchange speculators serves no useful purpose and is extremely undignified. It upsets confidence, hinders business decisions, occupies the public attention in a measure far exceeding its real importance, and is responsible both for the irritation and for a certain lack of respect which exist abroad.

You have three alternatives. You can devalue the dollar in terms of gold, returning to the gold standard at a new fixed ratio. This would be inconsistent with your declarations in favor of a long-range policy of stable prices, and I hope you will reject it.

You can seek some common policy of exchange stabilization with Great Britain aimed at stable price levels. This would be the best ultimate solution; but it is not practical politics at the moment, unless you are prepared to talk in terms of an initial value of sterling well below $5 pending the realization of a marked rise in your domestic price level.

Lastly, you can announce that you will control the dollar exchange by buying and selling gold and foreign currencies at a definite figure so as to avoid wide or meaningless fluctuations, with a right to shift the parities at any time, but with a declared intention only so to do either to correct a serious want of balance in America's international receipts and payments or to meet a shift in your domestic price level relative to price levels abroad.

THE FAVORED POLICY

This appears to me your best policy during the transitional period. You would be waiving your right to make future arbitrary changes which did not correspond to any relevant change in the facts, but in other respects you would retain your liberty to make your exchange policy subservient to the needs of your domestic policy—free to let out your belt in proportion as you put on flesh.

In the field of domestic policy, I put in the forefront, for the reasons given above, a large volume of loan expenditure under government auspices. It is beyond my province to choose particular objects of expenditure. But preference should be given to those which can be made to mature quickly on a large scale, as, for example, the rehabilitation of the physical condition of the railroads. The object is to start the ball rolling.

The United States is ready to roll toward prosperity, if a good hard shove can be given in the next six months. Could not the energy and enthusiasm which launched the NRA in its early days be put behind a campaign for accelerating capital expenditures, as wisely chosen as the pressure of circumstances permits? You can at least feel sure that the country will be better enriched by such projects than by the involuntary idleness of millions.

PLENTY OF CHEAP CREDIT

I put in the second place the maintenance of cheap and abundant credit, in particular the reduction of the long-term rate of interest. The turn of the tide in Great Britain is largely attributable to the reduction in the long-term rate of interest which ensued on the success of the conversion of the war loan. This was deliberately engineered by the open-market policy of the Bank of England.

I see no reason why you should not reduce the rate of interest on your long-term government bonds to 2½ per cent or less, with favorable repercussions on the whole bond market, if only the Federal Reserve System would replace its present holdings of short-dated Treasury issues by purchasing long-dated issues in exchange. Such a policy might become effective in a few months, and I attach great importance to it.

With these adaptations or enlargements of your existing policies, I should expect a successful outcome with great confidence. How much that would mean, not only to the material prosperity of the United States and the whole world, but in comfort to men's minds through a restoration of their faith in the wisdom and the power of government!

With great respect,
Your obedient servant,
J. M. KEYNES.

3

*The Economics of Public Works**

By SUMNER H. SLICHTER†

In a western state a railway bridge had been destroyed by fire and it was necessary to replace it. Two days later came the superintendent of the division. Alighting from his private car, he encountered the foreman of the bridge builders. "Bill," said the superintendent, and the words quivered with energy, "I want this job rushed. Every hour's delay costs the company money. Have you the engineer's plans for the new bridge?" "I don't know," said the bridge builder, "whether the engineer has his picture drawed yet, but the bridge is up and the trains is passin' over it."

The government in Washington is in the position of the railroad foreman who had to rush through an emergency bridge without plans —except that it has had to build many emergency bridges. No doubt some of the bridges which it has built should not have trains running over them very long. Possibly a few should not have trains running over them at all. In presenting this paper I may be compared to an engineer who appears with a blueprint after the emergency bridge is done and points out certain respects in which the bridge will not do permanently.

Until several years ago most proposals to alleviate depressions by expanding public construction contemplated simply long-range planning of public works. These proposals involved no ultimate change in the total volume of public expenditures but merely changes in the timing of the expenditures. It was assumed that a long-range program of public construction would be planned in the light of its cost and of the ability and the willingness of the community to bear the burden. Then it was proposed to concentrate construction as much as possible in periods of depression. Such a proposal is easy to defend, for it involves no ultimate change in the size of the government debt and no radical

* *American Economic Review,* Supplement, Mar. 1934, XXIV. Reprinted by the courtesy of the American Economic Association and the author.

† Harvard University.

effects upon the price structure. The government simply purchases less of certain materials and services at times when the rest of the community is buying more and it buys more of these materials and services at times when the rest of the community is buying less. Over a period of time, however, the volume of purchases by the government is presumably not altered. And although the government borrows to spend during depressions, it reduces its debt during booms so that in the long run there is no change in the government debt.

The present public works program is far more ambitious than mere long-range planning and fraught with far greater possibilities of both good and evil. The government is deliberately setting out to spend enough borrowed money on public construction to lift business out of the depths of the depression. Of course, the expenditures on public works are far from the entire recovery program, but they are predicated on the assumption that business needs this stimulus, and the magnitude of the expenditures is determined by the severity of the depression and by the amount of stimulus which business is assumed to require. Such a program may conveniently be designated a "market-supporting" program to distinguish it from the less ambitious proposals of long-range planning. You will appreciate at once that we are gambling with big stakes. If the program works, it may be regarded as practically costless for it will more than pay for itself by increasing production and employment. If it fails and we saddle ourselves with an enormous increase in the public debt without alleviating the depression, perhaps the community may feel unable or unwilling to pay the debt.

In this paper I shall not analyze in detail the specific program which the federal government has launched, but I shall examine the economics of programs of this general type rather than the economics of the long-range planning of public works. My discussion will fall into four principal parts. First, I shall discuss the need for supporting markets during depressions; second, I shall point out some of the limits to the usefulness of public works as a device for accomplishing this purpose; third, I shall indicate some dangers involved in public works programs of the market-supporting type; and, finally, I shall make some comparisons between public works and other methods of alleviating depressions.

I

Let me begin the analysis by expressing the conviction that there is urgent need of developing large expenditures which are not dependent on profit prospects and of dovetailing them with the expenditures which do depend on profit prospects. In no other way, short of abolishing production for profits, can the total volume of spending in the community be stabilized, because the spending which is governed by profit prospects is bound to fluctuate.[1] The instability of expenditures that depend on profit prospects is the result of a conjunction of circumstances; but the crucial one, however, is the fact that the demand for goods is not ready-made but depends in large measure upon the success of business men in discovering new ways of making money by changing products or processes or by enlarging operations. When business men discover an increasing number of such opportunities, expenditures rise and the demand for commodities and services increases. But if managers experience unusual difficulty in discovering new ways of making money, there is a shrinkage in the demand for capital goods and for the labor used in making and installing them. The drop in demand, however, is not confined to capital goods and the labor used in producing them. The reason is obvious. When employees in the capital goods industries lose their jobs and when the owners of plants in the capital goods industries receive smaller dividends, they must reduce their purchases of consumers' goods.

It is unnecessary to discuss the multitude of reasons why managers have varying success in discovering new opportunities to make money. Let me simply remind you that to assume that profit-making opportunities will be discovered at a constant rate is to assume, among other things, that technology will discover new products and new processes at a constant rate and that the new products and processes will bear a constant competitive relationship to the old products and processes—assumptions for which there is no warrant. It is theoretically conceivable that prices might be so flexible that the impact of a changing world upon the price structure would not alter the success of managers in finding new ways to make money, that no matter what changes occurred in the external world, prices would respond so promptly that profit prospects would always remain equally attractive. But although such fluidity of prices is conceivable, everyone knows that it is practically unattainable. Hence profit prospects vary and, as they do, the spending, production, and employment which depend upon them are bound to fluctuate.

Schemes for controlling credit and the relationship between saving and private investment offer some prospect of reducing the fluctuations in spending but they all leave undisturbed the fundamental fact that

[1] By stabilizing the volume of spending I do not necessarily mean keeping it constant in amount but simply free from fluctuations. Steady growth is merely one form of stability.

discoveries of new methods, new products, and new natural resources do not occur at an even rate. Consequently, there is little hope that fluctuations in the rate of interest alone will stabilize the prospect for profits. We are forced to the conclusion that unless spending which does not depend upon profits can be dovetailed with spending which does, millions of men are bound to be thrown into idleness every few years because business men fail to discover enough new opportunities to make money. Upon this fact rests the case for large programs of public works of the market-supporting type.

II

Before we examine the problem of stabilizing all spending, let us notice the magnitude of the undertaking. In 1932 debits to individual accounts were only about 40 per cent as large as in 1929. Allowing for the fact that cash payments fluctuated less than check payments, the volume of spending in 1932 was perhaps roughly half the volume in 1929. To offset such a precipitous drop in private spending would obviously require an enormous expansion of public buying. Now under favorable conditions a given outlay on public works may create a volume of private spending that is several times larger than the government expenditures on public construction. If the government expenditures, however, increase the total volume of spending, accelerate the reduction of excessive inventories and the repayment of indebtedness, and reduce losses and bankruptcies, their benefits may be far-reaching. By thus protecting the credit of firms, they will reduce the tendency of banks to force the liquidation of indebtedness. And by preventing business confidence from shrinking to the depths that it otherwise would, they will halt the tendency for business enterprises to postpone commitments and thus will tend to sustain the velocity of circulation.

But even allowing for the fact that a given outlay on public works under favorable conditions may have a very large effect upon the volume of private spending, it is obvious that an enormous program of public works would have been necessary to offset the drop in private spending between 1929 and 1932. Hence the possibility of stabilizing the total volume of spending by dovetailing public buying with private would appear to require a drastic reduction in fluctuations of private expenditures. The outlook for this is none too bright. Even in 1932 deposits subject to check were over two-thirds as large as in 1929. This indicates that rigid control of fluctuations of credit would not prevent enormous fluctuations in spending. Obviously, however, the achievement of stability through dovetailing presupposes drastic control of credit. The violence of fluctuations in private spending is due to the fact that credit expands at a time when the velocity of circulation is also rising. This suggests the conclusion that increases in the velocity of circulation should be offset by contraction of credit. But I do not believe this to be possible, for as long as we have a banking system of the present type, a quickening of business must produce simultaneously an expansion of credit and a rise in the velocity of circulation. Perhaps, therefore, the achievement of stabilization is incompatible with the retention of the present credit system.

The breakdowns in exchange which we call depressions have a dual nature. For one thing, they are reactions to maladjustments which develop between supply and demand. These maladjustments may develop in a vast variety of ways. Naturally, they all carry with them maladjustments in the price structure. For business to pick up, these maladjustments must in some measure be corrected. This means that there must be changes either in the prices or in supply and demand, usually in both. But although depressions are reactions to maladjustments, they are far from being simply corrective reactions. On the contrary, they are themselves a source of maladjustments, for the very drop in spending, which is the essence of depression, intensifies existing maladjustments and creates new ones. Furthermore, the prices which change first are not necessarily those which are most in need of being changed. In order to effect the necessary readjustments there is usually needed a drop in costs, but many cost prices are among the slowest to drop.

In so far as expenditures on public works halt the drop in the total volume of spending, they may reduce the tendency of depressions to create new maladjustments. As a general rule, however, it may be said that the construction of public works does not remove the fundamental causes which produce depressions.[2] Suppose, for example, that a depression occurs because technological discoveries have failed to provide enough new profit-making opportunities to maintain the demand for capital goods. The drop in the demand for capital goods produces unemployment and losses in the capital-goods industries, which, in turn, reduce the demand for consumers' goods and create unemployment and losses in the consumer-goods industries. All of this means a smaller volume of spending and a depression. The expenditures on public works may counteract in some measure the drop in private spending, but the

[2] Under some circumstances and within modest limits expenditures on public works may assist in removing the causes of the depression. For example, by helping to maintain the market for goods, the outlay on public works may assist enterprises in shifting out of industries which are overdeveloped into others which are not.

fundamental difficulty, which was the failure of technology to advance fast enough to maintain the demand for capital goods, has not been remedied. Of course, if the former rate of technological advance is promptly resumed, all may be well and public works will have served as a useful stop-gap in protecting the community from the consequences of fluctuations in the rate of technological discovery. But suppose that the previous rate of technological discovery is not promptly resumed. The country is unable to maintain a heavy outlay on public works indefinitely. When the expenditures cease, the depression may be resumed in full force and the country may find itself saddled with a heavier burden of debt and with the maladjustments which precipitated the depression still uncorrected.

Or suppose that a depression occurs because important branches of agriculture have become overdeveloped relative to manufacturing. If farmers are unable to buy enough manufactures, unemployment develops, with the result that the market for farm products shrinks and the overdevelopment of agriculture becomes worse. What is needed to get industry operating in a normal fashion is to restore the proper relationship between agriculture and manufacturing. Of course, expenditures on public works may be of temporary help in sustaining the demand for agricultural products and thus in cushioning the effects of the depression on agriculture, but they will not correct the underlying maladjustment. As soon as the public credit is exhausted or the willingness of the public to support the public works program ceases, the original maladjustment between manufacturing and agriculture will again make itself felt.

Public works programs, therefore, must be regarded as essentially palliatives rather than correctives. In view of this fact, is it wise to pledge public credit in huge amounts in an attempt to offset fundamental forces that are producing a decline in business? It is scarcely conceivable, for example, that even very large expenditures on public construction in the United States in 1930 or 1931 would have halted a depression which was the product of so many world-wide maladjustments and which was being made constantly worse by mistaken economic policies in many countries, including our own, and by critical political situations in several parts of the world. In considering the wisdom of spending large amounts on public works early in a depression for the purpose of halting it, one must recognize that governments, because of ignorance or political considerations, are likely to pursue some policies which aggravate rather than relieve the depression. The conclusion is inescapable, I believe, that until governments are far better able to avoid policies which aggravate depressions, the time to begin a large public works program is not early in the depression, but only after fairly unmistakable signs of recovery have begun to appear. In view of the doubtful value of many policies which are now being pursued to produce business revival, it is fortunate that we have embarked upon the present large construction program only after business the world over seems to have turned the corner and only after fundamental recuperative forces have become so strong that even serious administrative errors are unlikely to interrupt the recovery. Obviously, it is far safer to gamble with public credit on a rising market than on a falling one.

III

Up to this point my discussion has been based on the assumption that expenditures on public works, while not affecting the causes of depressions, would at least tend to mitigate their severity by increasing the total volume of spending. It is necessary, however, to consider the possibility that a large public works program may have the opposite effect—that it may aggravate the depression by diminishing the total volume of spending. Such a large part of all buying is controlled by private enterprises and such a small part by the government that only a small increase in the disposition of business men to postpone commitments would entirely offset a large increase in buying by the government.

There are several ways in which a large outlay on public construction may cause business enterprises to reduce their expenditures. In the first place, it may cause managers to regard the economic situation as too highly artificial. As long as they view the situations in this light, they are likely to be exceedingly conservative in planning private commitments. During a period of depression managements make plans for improvements, replacements, and expansion which they intend to carry out as soon as they feel reasonably sure that business has turned the corner. But the very fact that the government is generously supporting markets by large-scale buying makes managers uncertain whether a revival is due to recuperative forces or simply to the stimulus of government buying. And the larger the government expenditures the greater is this uncertainty. Consequently, a large government program, by preventing business men from recognizing promptly the beginning of revival, may prevent them from responding to it quickly.

In the second place, a rapid increase in the public debt may produce fear of ultimate inflation. True, this fear is not likely to arise in depressions of only moderate severity, but it is a real danger in extraordinarily severe depressions, particularly if the program of public works is not confined to the items which have been incorporated in a long-range plan but is of the market-supporting type. Under these circumstances, the action of Congress in authorizing large outlays may be interpreted by the public as merely the beginning of a still larger spending spree. Whether the community is right or wrong in its fears is beside the point. The point is that a large public works program of more or less indefinite magnitude in the face of rapidly shrinking public revenues is likely to arouse fear of inflation. This is important because the fear of inflation often has a deflationary effect. The fear of an inflation which will come, if at all, at an uncertain date in the future, may stimulate little immediate buying of commodities but it is likely to cause shifts from bonds to stocks and possibly some flight of capital. The depreciation in bonds may undermine confidence in the banks and produce a competitive pursuit of liquidity by them which makes them far more selective in granting accommodation and causes them to increase pressure on their slow accounts with the result that distress selling is increased and prices are weakened. Under such market conditions the volume of spending by business enterprises is bound to drop.

Finally, and in the case of most depressions most important, is the effect of a program of public works upon the price structure. Obviously it is impossible to spend large sums upon public construction without affecting certain prices. Consequently, whether public works are intended to peg prices or not, they are a form of indirect price pegging. Indeed, the fact that the effect on prices is largely unintended and unplanned is itself a source of danger. At the beginning of this paper I emphasized the fact that depressions are reactions to maladjustments between supply and demand which involve maladjustments in price relationships. Consequently, whether or not a program of public construction aggravates or alleviates a depression depends upon whether it reduces or magnifies the original maladjustments in the price structure. Now it does not necessarily follow that expenditures on public works will either increase or decrease maladjustments in price relationships, but it is highly probable that these expenditures will retard the very price changes which a revival of business requires. This is particularly true in case public construction is expanded on a large scale early in the depression.

What are the reasons for this conclusion? Depressions are a result of the fact that managers find fewer opportunities to make money by changing methods or expanding operations. Business emerges from depression when managers discover a sufficient number of new ways to reduce costs or to make money. Obviously this is very likely to require a drop in the cost of changing or expanding operations, particularly a drop in the cost of capital equipment and the labor used to install it. But it is precisely the prices which determine construction costs that are likely to be "pegged" by a large program of public building. This would be true even if the government bought everything at the lowest possible prices. It is even more true when the government makes some purchases at more or less arbitrary prices. This is well illustrated by the present public works program. The government is purchasing materials at the lowest possible price, but it is buying labor, which represents, of course, a large part of the total construction cost, at more or less arbitrary prices. In view of the fact that there is often no price for labor in the construction industry which may properly be regarded as a market price, the government is confronted with a difficult problem in fixing wages on construction jobs. The government has set a scale for skilled labor of $1.00 an hour in the South, $1.10 in the Middle states, and $1.20 in the North for skilled labor. In the South, union men have been striking to get $.75 an hour. In many places in the North, wages of the building crafts, even during the height of the building boom in 1928–29, did not reach $1.20. Now in the midst of perhaps the worst depression in our history, the government is paying wages which exceed the boom rates in many communities.[3]

As a matter of fact, however, I am not particularly alarmed at the probable effect of wages under the present public works program upon the revival of business. Fortunately the program has been initiated only after nearly four years of depression, after the prices of construction materials have had time to fall, after business men have had ample opportunities to discover many new ways of changing and enlarging their operations, and after a substantial shortage of some types of housing and equipment has developed. Consequently, although high wage rates on public works may discourage some private construction and even interfere seriously with the provision of cheap housing, they are not likely to have a disastrous effect upon recovery. I do, however, wish to stress emphatically the danger of pegging building materials and labor by an ambitious program of public works initiated early in a depression before these prices have had an opportunity to fall. By retarding a drop

---

[3] The rate of $1.20 an hour is often defended on the ground that Congress has limited the working hours on public works projects to thirty a week. If this be a justification for $1.20 an hour, let us be thankful that Congress did not limit the working week to fifteen hours which would presumably have justified a rate of $2.40 an hour.

in the prices which must fall in order for change and growth on a large scale to become profitable, a huge public construction program may seriously intensify and prolong the depression. The degree of harm is likely to be greatest, of course, following a boom, such as the last one, in which vigorous speculative expansion of private construction pushed up the prices of building labor and materials to high levels. For example, a large public works program in 1930, tending to peg building costs at 1928–29 levels, would have been disastrous.[4]

IV

Much of the foregoing discussion, as I have been at pains to point out, has little bearing on the present program of the government because this program was not started until after business had turned the corner. But the present program does raise interesting and important questions. Up to the present moment only about $150,000,000 of an authorized $3,300,000,000 has been spent. A substantial part of the three billions cannot be spent in the immediate future. It is entirely possible, however, that within the next year business will experience a revival as sharp and as sudden as that which occurred late in 1922 and early in 1923. In that event, competition by the government for men and materials in large amounts might easily stimulate an expansion of credit and a rise in prices which could not easily be controlled. And yet the government could not stop construction without exposing many half-completed projects to ruin. In an economic system such as ours, which is subject to pronounced and unforeseeable changes, government fiscal policy needs to be subject to quick reversal. Programs of public works tend to tie the hands of the government in reversing its fiscal policy and hence to weaken its ability to control booms. To a substantial extent, no doubt, the engineers can plan public works so that government expenditures can be temporarily reduced on short notice. This is an economic consideration of importance which should be given great weight in selecting and planning projects.

V

In view of the difficulties and dangers connected with large expenditures on public construction, it is pertinent to compare them with another method of dealing with unemployment; namely, unemploy-

---

[4] Public works are often urged on the ground that they are needed to help the capital-goods industries. In so far as they retard the resumption of private construction by pegging the prices of capital goods too high, their help to the capital-goods industries is temporary only.

ment reserves. In three important respects unemployment reserves appear to be superior to public works—or at least to very large programs of public works. In the first place, under most schemes of unemployment reserves the public credit is not ordinarily involved and the deflationary effects which accompany the fears concerning public credit are avoided. In the second place, the disbursement of unemployment benefits does not peg the prices of capital goods and thus tend to make a resumption of change and growth unprofitable. On the contrary, it affects primarily the prices of consumers' goods and, by supporting these prices, accelerates the time when a resumption of growth is advantageous. In the third place, the disbursement of unemployment benefits automatically diminishes as business improves. Hence there is no danger that these disbursements will be an inflationary influence during periods of revival.

In one important respect, however, public works appear to be superior to unemployment reserve plans of the type usually proposed. Public works which are financed by borrowing or by using idle government balances and which do not threaten public credit or raise construction costs too much may increase the total volume of spending in the community. But when unemployment benefits are paid by selling bonds from the reserve funds, they probably have little or no effect upon the total amount of spending. They simply transfer purchasing power from the bond buyers to the unemployed. In fact, large bond sales by the unemployment reserve funds when the bond market is weak may cause serious difficulties for the banks and for corporations with large maturities to meet and thus may be a powerful deflationary influence. This defect in unemployment reserve plans is serious and has received less attention than it deserves. Fortunately it can be removed by the simple device of depositing the reserve funds in the Reserve banks instead of investing them in government securities. In this way a real transfer of purchasing power from periods of boom to periods of depression will be effected. In addition, a powerful and automatic brake will be applied to the expansion of credit in times of boom and strong support will be given to the bond market during times of depression. Operated in this way unemployment reserves are superior to public works in every respect except possibly one. Public works create jobs directly as well as indirectly. Unemployment reserves do so only indirectly.

VI

In conclusion, let me summarize some of the results of the preceding analysis and make explicit several questions which it seems to raise. To begin with, there stands out the extreme difficulty of stabilizing an economy which is conducted for profit and in which the demand for goods depends in large measure upon the rate at which business men discover new ways of making money. In such an economy private spending is bound to fluctuate violently. In view of the many obstacles to using public spending to offset fluctuations in private spending, the achievement of stability must depend upon success in greatly reducing the fluctuations in private spending. For example, it would be folly to attempt to pledge public credit in sufficient volume to offset the enormous fluctuations in spending made possible by the present relatively uncontrolled credit system.

The analysis indicates that there is no sense in talking about public works in general terms because whether a program of public construction does more good than harm depends upon how it is planned and executed and under what conditions it is applied. Public works are subject to the important limitation that they support markets but do not remove the fundamental maladjustments which precipitate depressions. And, although I reject the view that unrestrained and uncontrolled liquidation is necessary to produce the price relationships which will permit a revival of business, I stress the fact that attempts to support the market for capital goods may defeat their purpose by keeping up the very prices which must fall in order to make a resumption of growth profitable. The danger is particularly great in case the public works program is of large magnitude and is started early in the depression. For this reason, as well as to avoid the deflationary effects which follow from fear of inflation, I conclude that public works programs of the long-range planning type, constructed on the basis of the ability and willingness of the community to bear the cost, are preferable to programs of the market-supporting type and that the construction of public works should not begin until the prices of capital goods have had an opportunity to fall. Indeed, public works might be used to induce a prompter fall in these prices. The government might predicate its willingness to expand construction by a given amount upon the willingness of building labor and producers of material to accept a given reduction in their prices.

These conclusions point to the further conclusion that public works are least valuable precisely when they are needed most. They may be of great help in accelerating the revival of business—when they are least needed—but they are of little use in the early stages of the depression when things are going from bad to worse. They may be of considerable help in mitigating depressions of moderate severity, but they are of little or no help in halting a drastic decline. For example, even a very large program of public construction would not have halted the avalanche of world deflation in 1931 and early in 1932, and, by undermining public credit, it might easily have added to the avalanche. Since public works are so obviously insufficient to meet the problems of depression, something else is needed. Unemployment reserves on a nation-wide basis would help, provided the financial administration were wise. They would be particularly useful in the early stages of depression when public works cannot be wisely initiated, but they would not be enough. Perhaps the only way to introduce reasonable stability into buying is to socialize a few major industries which are large consumers of capital goods. But this would not solve the problem if it resulted in too much support to the prices of capital goods—the very thing which needs to be avoided. Perhaps help would be derived from a constant tax on all industries to subsidize the production of capital goods during depressions. Or perhaps we should discard this industrial system which throws millions of men out of work whenever business managers have difficulty in discovering enough new ways to make money and should construct one which does not require the prospect of profit to keep it going. This may sound like a counsel of despair, but I confess a growing difficulty in seeing how a profit system can be satisfactorily controlled for the simple reason that the prospects for profit cannot be controlled.

4

*Federal Depression Financing and Its Consequences**

By HARLEY L. LUTZ†

Like any great emergency, the depression involved an increase of public spending and presented the problem of choice as to the methods of providing the funds. It is now a matter of history that little time was spent in canvassing the alternatives, which were, obviously, the cash basis versus borrowing. The assumption was made that because all taxation is burdensome, its increase under depression conditions would therefore retard recovery. There was apparently no realization that many of the things to be done in connection with, and as a result of, the loan policy would retard recovery fully as much as more taxation would have done. Nor was there any concern over the ease with which the lavish use of credit leads to its abuse, and to a disintegration of the normal processes of democratic government.

This paper will deal with the kind of depression tax policy that might have been used and with some of the effects of the loan and tax policy that has been pursued.

A DEPRESSION TAX POLICY

A cash basis, balanced budget policy was by no means an impossibility for the Federal Government during the depression. Resting on increased taxation such a policy would have required, however, a very different set of assumptions from those which underlay the program that was actually followed.

First, it would have involved a far more limited view of the scope of necessary government activity. The most important emergency task undertaken during the depression was to provide relief. No one starved, but in every other respect relief was not well handled. Had the relief

* *Harvard Business Review,* Vol. XVI, No. 2, Winter, 1938. Reprinted by courtesy of the *Harvard Business Review* and the author.

† National Association of Manufacturers, formerly Princeton University.

funds been provided by taxation, there would have been an immensely greater incentive to discover the causes of this burden and the best ways of terminating it, subjects toward which the attitude of government agencies has been one of indifference or even of hostility.

Under this restricted conception of the government task there would have been no room for costly experimentation. The loan method of providing funds seldom promotes prudence, and in the present instance it has apparently failed, in large measure, to stimulate even that degree of concern for the wisdom and social advantage of the things undertaken which may normally be expected of those who are spending other people's money.

Second, reliance on taxation would have required a reversal of accepted taxation methods. Since 1913 there has been increasing disposition to regard the income tax as a Federal prerogative, and as the most important feature of the Federal tax system. The Federal taxation resources have come to be measured and expressed more or less exclusively in terms of this tax.

But as applied in the United States, the income tax is essentially a prosperity tax. From a peak of $2,348,000,000 on incomes of the year 1928, its yield dropped to a low of $615,500,000 on incomes of the year 1932. This experience was deemed to have closed, quite conclusively, the case for any substantial increase of tax receipts, a position which seemed the stronger when the income tax yield did not respond actively to the successive advances of the rates.

Extreme variability of yield is inevitable under any tax which depends for its productivity chiefly upon large incomes. Such incomes are composed, in the main, of profits, and this share of the social income is highly variable. During the initial stage of a prosperity movement profits expand rapidly, because of the tendency for prices to rise at a faster rate than costs of production. In the depression phase of the economic cycle profits disappear entirely at many points, and their aggregate volume is greatly reduced.

The extent to which the Federal tax is dependent on the few large incomes is easily demonstrated from the published statistics of income. Table I is based on these data. The years chosen for this table reflect the major swings of all personal incomes. The proportion which the aggregate of the large incomes (i.e., $100,000 and above) bears to total personal incomes is small except for the years of marked prosperity. Even at their peak, in 1929, these incomes comprised only 17.6% of all personal income. Yet the proportion of the total tax is always relatively high. In 1929 this group of incomes supplied almost two-thirds of the entire tax on personal incomes, and at the bottom of the depression it supplied one-third of all such taxes.

In addition to being so definitely a prosperity tax, the great lag between tax collection and the period in which the income to be taxed is earned or received makes this tax quite unsatisfactory when quick revenue results are needed. For example, if business is good in the first half of 1937, it may be December, 1938, before all of the tax is paid on the profits from this business. In so far as corporations or individuals report on a fiscal year basis, it may be sometime in 1939 before the Treasury will get the final fiscal advantage from the good business done in the spring of 1937. Obviously the income tax, as operated in the United States, is not quickly responsive to a sudden need for additional revenue.

TABLE I

TOTAL INCOMES AND TOTAL TAXES IN THE PERSONAL INCOME BRACKETS $100,000 AND ABOVE FOR CERTAIN YEARS
(Amounts in millions of dollars)

Year	Total Incomes of $100,000 and More	Ratio to All Personal Income	Taxes on Incomes of $100,000 and More	Ratio to Taxes on All Personal Income
1917	1,606.5	11.7	361.5	52.3
1918	990.2	6.2	469.7	41.6
1921	463.0	2.3	202.2	28.1
1925	2,317.8	10.5	358.8	48.7
1929	4,368.2	17.6	653.4	65.3
1932	383.5	3.3	110.4	33.4
1934	419.8	3.2	179.9	35.1
1935	498.4	3.4	243.6	37.2

Source: *Preliminary Statistics of Income*, 1935, Tables 5 and 6 (containing summaries of data for each year since 1916).

Once the irregularity and fiscal inadequacy of the income tax during depressions are recognized, it remains to consider how sufficient revenue might have been obtained to keep the essential emergency functions on a cash basis. The experience of some of the states in this respect is illuminating. Crowded out of the income tax field by the growing Federal exploitation thereof, they turned to indirect taxes, and particularly to the sales tax. These taxes proved to be far more productive and dependable during the depression than the income tax. Had the Federal Government corrected some features of the income tax which contributed to the irregularity of its yield, and also broadened the Federal tax base by more extensive use of indirect taxes, there is little question that it could have obtained a revenue sufficient for all legitimate requirements of the relief program. In fact, it was only as there was extension of the indirect taxes that substantial stability was achieved in the Federal tax receipts.

The case against such a Federal tax policy for the depression was closed in advance by various arguments. Indirect taxes were and are opposed as being contrary to "ability to pay," and as not producing that state of mind in the taxpayer known as "tax consciousness."

The ability concept has a valid place in taxation theory, but it has been overworked and overpublicized. It has been invoked to support graduated and excessive taxation of business income, although ability is a purely personal attribute and it makes sense only when one is dealing with the relative tax burdens and obligations of individuals. Further, the assumption is frequently made that any kind of rate scale which a legislature may happen to set up is a correct application of the principle. The truth is that while the ability theory does justify progressive taxation of total personal incomes or total personal estates, it is so abstract and so general as to afford no clue whatever to the proper scale of rates.[1] Excessive rate scales, as well as those which rise too slowly may therefore be outright violations of the principle.

Considering ability, not as an abstraction but as a practical matter which covers such concrete details as paying the tax as well as the philosophy of the relation of the tax to the taxpayer's total income, we may find that administrative differences alter the case somewhat. Adam Smith might have objected to our reading his third canon in close conjunction with his first one. But if we take this liberty, in the search for a realistic conception of ability, we find that the indirect taxes rank well where the income tax is weak, just as this position is reversed when judgment is passed simply on the basis of the first canon.

The third cannon is: "The tax should be levied at the time and in the manner that is most convenient for the taxpayer to pay it." Convenience is the great virtue of the indirect taxes. Quarterly payment of income tax is a concession in that direction, but the indefinite number of small installments, characteristic of indirect taxes, is a perfect application of the principle. If we think of ability, not as meaning merely that one has had the income at some time and that the money to pay the tax has been in hand at some time, but also as meaning a minimum of financial embarrassment in meeting the successive tax installments as they become payable, then our former harsh judgments respecting the indirect taxes, based solely on their regressivity, seem to stand in need of some revision.

---

[1] This piece was written in the autumn of 1937. The writer's views on the doctrine of progressive taxation have changed completely since then and the foregoing sentence is not a correct expression of them.

Much nonsense has been uttered and written about "tax consciousness." The idea is that when the people have become tax conscious, they will at once demand more efficient and more economical government. This is only a pious hope. It rests on a naïve faith in human reactions that is largely unsupported by experience. Burdensome taxation of any sort, or a tax that is unpopular or deemed to be unjust according to the current view of equitable taxation, will produce a reaction. The direction of the force of this reaction is as unpredictable as that of dynamite. If it leads to an attack on the wastefulness of government, such result will be by chance only. Property owners should be tax conscious, according to the accustomed logic, yet they have done very little about the wastes of local government, simply as a result of knowing what their taxes are. Gasoline taxpayers have made no concerted protest against the wastes of highway construction, nor have income taxpayers banded together to protest Federal or state wastes.

It is well known that indirect taxes may develop tax consciousness, although the direction of the reaction is quite unpredictable. In New Jersey, consciousness of a sales tax led to its repeal and not to a demand for less costly government. The reaction against the eighteenth century English excise took the direction of clubbing and knifing the collectors, and of an immense satisfaction in the consumption of smuggled tobacco and liquors.

Again it is possible that the rigid theorists have overlooked something in always assuming the taxpayer to be ignorant of his indirect taxes. Quite possibly he is better informed than is commonly supposed, and on this basis he may prefer the greater convenience of indirect tax collection to the disadvantage of paying, in lump sums, other kinds of taxes which would bear a somewhat smaller ratio to his total income. He is certainly spared, under such taxation, what Adam Smith described as the "odious visits of the taxgatherer," and he may be wise in his acceptance of a somewhat higher tax, levied indirectly, as the price of his escape from these visits and their inevitable inquisition.

A further potent reason for not considering the cash basis method of financing the depression obligations, and the kind of taxation that would have been required to support this policy, was present but not expressly admitted. Such a program did not fit at all with the "soak-the-rich" doctrine that was, and is, so prominent a feature of current social philosophy. It would have been highly inexpedient, as a matter of political tactics, to offer a program of lavish spending and also to propose that it be financed by taxation methods which would have affected every one in some degree. It would then have been necessary to supply more lucid and convincing exposition of the reasons that warranted the liberality than would have been convenient in all cases. It was obviously more popular to lay all the blame for the misfortunes of the poor upon the misdeeds of the well-to-do and the rich, and to promise full redress by concentrating the taxation and the regulation upon these groups. The inconsistency of proposing to make everybody richer by making everybody poorer was never recognized.

THE DEPRESSION LOAN POLICY

While it would not have been impossible to formulate a reasonable relief and recovery program on a cash basis, supported by taxation, this was not done.[2] The advocates of large spending wanted to deal in larger sums than could have been provided in this way, and the advocates of taxation according to a narrowly construed ability principle objected to such broadening of the Federal tax base as would have established a reasonable relief program on a cash basis. Great efficacy was imputed to curious notions about the stimulating effects of depression spending, and many deceptive arguments were urged to prove that fiscal perfection was to be achieved through cyclical rather than annual budget balancing.

Self-deception took the form, also, of comparing the depression with a war, and of concluding that deficits were equally legitimate in both cases. The soundness of the major premise and of the analogy are alike open to question. It is by no means clear that every war should be financed by borrowing. This pernicious practice has done incalculable harm in the past hundred and fifty years. The device of public credit has been quite as responsible for endangering the peace of the world as the invention of gunpowder. Nevertheless, when war loans are used, financial experience counsels that every effort be made to tax the people to the limit.

It would be quite unfortunate to press too far the analogy between the depression and war, for another reason. A well-established fact of history is that no war has ever solved any problem, or accomplished any other result except the impoverishment of the people engaged in it. Today, with a sizeable business reaction under way, with the budget still a considerable distance from being balanced, with an enormous public debt, and with an indefinite future of crushing taxation in prospect, it

[2] England faced and dealt with a depression situation of considerable magnitude on virtually a cash basis. Cf. H. L. Lutz, "England's Financial Policy, 1928–1937," *Proceedings of the Academy of Political Science,* December, 1937.

becomes painfully clear that this war, if it really was one, has run true to form.[3]

The general facts of the depression borrowing are well known and may be passed over here. Attention may profitably be directed, however, to some consequences of the deficit policy which was supported by the large loans.

1. An immense debt principal has been created which, we must assume, is eventually to be repaid. Debt service requires taxation and it is now becoming clearer that the loan policy has not been entirely a clear gain. On paper it is possible to prove that taxation for domestic debt service is a mere transfer operation. In practice, the fact remains that the "stickiness" of taxes, the friction of high-geared and sometimes none too judicial tax administration, and the adverse psychology of heavy taxation are not altogether counterbalanced by the return flow of funds into another set of pockets.

2. A heavy load of debt management has been laid on the Treasury. To 1960, at least, the future bristles with debt maturities, many of which run into large figures. An imposing mass of floating and short-term debt must be handled during the next five years. The task of juggling these maturities will be a definite handicap if the future contains another serious emergency situation of any sort.

3. The circumstances of the borrowing have been such as to create an artificial situation respecting the public credit. The bonds and notes were not sold to the people, but to the banks and to institutional investors. The inactive condition of business established an abnormal price and yield structure for the government paper; that is, despite the low coupon rates, the net yield on these obligations has been even less.

This price and yield position is artificial in that it can continue only while the private demand for investment funds is relatively restricted. Unless good evidence can be produced o show that the interest rate can never again rise much above 2½%, it must be recognized that if and when such an advance occurs, it will automatically cause a recapitalization of the stipulated income from all fixed income obligations, including government bonds.

4. It has always been characteristic of Federal Treasury policy to assume that low interest rates and low investment yield on the government paper are normal phenomena. Many devices and expedients have

---

[3] Secretary of the Treasury Morgenthau, in his recent address before the Academy of Political Science, stressed again the point so frequently made a few years ago, to the effect that the government had been at war against the depression. This address may be found in the *New York Times* of November 11, 1937.

been tried in the effort to preserve this illusion.[4] In the present case it appears to have been assumed that the extremely favorable credit conditions of the depression must continue until the period of deficit financing ends, however long that may be. Accordingly, the government has become committed to the maintenance of easy money, low interest rates, and low investment yield, and to the manipulation of the market in order to preserve this status. When Federal bond prices softened in the spring of 1937, the Treasury and the reserve banks began to buy, ostensibly to preserve an "orderly" market. This interference with the course of the market did not serve to establish confidence, as later events revealed.

5. A fifth consequence has been a singularly inconsistent policy with respect to banking reserves and the credit inflation which excess reserves tend to encourage. On one hand, the reserve bank purchases of securities, and the earlier Treasury policy of buying gold, tended to pile up excess reserves. On the other hand, the Board of Governors of the Federal reserve system, in an effort to neutralize the effects of over-large reserves, made successive increases in the legal reserve ratios. The effect of the gold purchase policy on the reserves must have been apparent from the beginning, but it was not until December, 1936, that it was modified through the so-called "sterilization" order, which suspended the practice of replenishing the government's account after making gold purchases by delivering gold certificates to the reserve banks. Thereafter the gold was paid for by selling additional bonds or notes, an operation which tended to lessen the volume of reserves. The recent action, whereby $300,000,000 of gold was "de-sterilized," is a further indication of the government's intention to manipulate and influence the market, and the large quantity of free gold now on hand suggests the extent to which such action may be carried.

Another application of this policy is in the authorization to the Treasury to buy and sell Federal securities. Treasury purchases of securities in the course of debt retirement are entirely proper, as are Treasury sales of securities in the course of new or refunding financing. The blanket authority makes possible, however, open market operations having nothing whatever to do with the normal process of creating or retiring public debt, and hence for Treasury manipulation of Federal security prices and the volume of bank credit. The dangers flowing from such operations when they are inspired by the peculiar

[4] Cf. Robert A. Love, *Federal Financing* (New York, Columbia University Press, 1931), *passim.*

viewpoint which may at times prevail relative to the duty or the need of the Treasury are obvious.

6. The deficit policy has encouraged those who would dispense with the formality of issuing redeemable obligations and resort to more positive methods through currency inflation. In addition to the power, vested in the President and the Secretary of the Treasury, to require the reserve banks to buy a large quantity of Federal paper, thereby stimulating credit inflation through increasing bank reserves, the Thomas Amendment to the AAA of 1933 is still alive. Under this law, some $3,000,000,000 of Greenbacks may be issued. Nothing has been done, as yet, under this amendment, but it is always necessary to reckon with the currency inflationist pressure. No one takes Senator Thomas seriously enough to be greatly concerned over his perennial printing press schemes, but the matter may assume a different aspect in the minds of some because Senator Norris made a somewhat similar proposal not long ago. He was quoted in press dispatches of June 10 as saying that he intended to suggest the issue of paper money against the unobligated gold. The argument was that this would help the government balance its budget and pay its debts. In form, these bills would be gold certificates, but in substance they would be simply paper money, since they would not be redeemable to the private holder in gold. He was reported also to have said the following:

> It is a simple matter of currency expansion. The government owns the gold the same as I own my coat, and it has every right to use it to pay its debts.[5]

The Senator forgets that Germany, Russia, and various other countries began their disastrous post-war printing press inflation by assuming that they were engaging in a simple matter of currency expansion. It might be urged that there is no material difference between creating large-denomination gold certificates which are deposited in the reserve banks and creating small denomination certificates which are passed out to the public. The operation would be inflationary, either way, but the creation of inconvertible paper money with legal tender power, for the express purpose of balancing the budget, would have very adverse moral and psychological effects. Such results may be anticipated particularly because this step would come after a long period in which the budget has been badly unbalanced, and after a succession of promises regarding this balancing which, superficially, give an impression that vigorous effort has been made to achieve this condition. The use of

---

[5] *New York Times,* June 10, 1937.

paper money under such circumstances would quite probably be interpreted as an admission of inability to accomplish the balancing in any other way, and thus as the beginning of the end.

7. Finally, the loan policy has engendered too general indifference toward the state of the budget and toward the need of any expenditure reduction in order to balance it. This is a perfectly natural outgrowth of the manner in which the funds have been obtained. Credit inflation is so easy, so painless for all, and it produces such a soothing sense of unlimited financial resources, that it has lulled all but a very few into a false sense of security.

One of the worst results of the manner in which the depression requirements have been financed is the permanent effect of this policy on the level of public expenditures. The history of the Federal finances reveals that, after every great emergency expansion, it has been impossible ever to reduce the total expenditure to anything like the earlier amount. Heretofore, war has been the chief national emergency, and in every case our wars have caused permanently higher costs of government afterward.

The lavish depression spending has had the same effect. When the large deficit policy was decided upon, every one supposed that it would be but temporary, and that the budget would in time return to the Coolidge level as modified by the normal growth trend. Only a few realized that a temporary expansion of this magnitude would leave its permanent mark. In A.D. 2000 American taxpayers will still be feeling the effects of the "temporary" spending policy that was adopted in the 1930's.

SOME FURTHER CONSEQUENCES OF THE DEFICIT POLICY

The financial measures actually employed during the depression were not adopted simply because they represented anyone's judgment to the effect that they constituted, in the aggregate, the easiest and surest way of carrying the necessary load of public support until the storm had blown over. They were a product of other influences and views, and their fiscal effects were frequently subordinated to other purposes or ignored altogether.

For example, while there was no great pretense of using taxation to finance the increased public obligations, there was a considerable amount of tax legislation. The nature of this legislation suggests that the primary purpose was not to increase the revenue but to serve as an instrument of government regulation and control. During the years 1932 to 1936 inclusive, taxation provided less than half of the total spent. As in medieval times, it was once again a minor source of public funds.

On the other hand, there was much legislation in which taxation figured as a regulatory instrument. The production of cotton, tobacco, potatoes, coal, and other commodities was brought under government control, with a penalty tax to keep unruly producers in line. These laws were rejected by the courts, but another specimen, the Guffey Coal Act, has set up an impossible scheme of regulation for the soft coal industry, with a penalty tax that will make the operators glad to comply with the regulations.

The tax policy has degenerated, at certain points, to a very low standard of morality in its treatment of the taxpayer. Two examples only will be mentioned. One is the elimination of the net loss deduction, and the other is the restriction of capital loss deductions to $2,000 unless there have also been capital gains during the year. In both of these cases the government has taken the unsporting attitude, "Heads I win, tails you lose." Because of these provisions, the tax law has been aptly characterized as "jug-handled." A fair and honest arrangement would be one represented by a loving-cup rather than a jug. The taxpayer as well as the government deserves a handle to take hold of, else it will be a long time between drinks for the citizen.

The treatment of incomes, both individual and corporate, has been increasingly severe under the successive revenue acts, while the rates levied on estates (and the compensatory tax on gifts) have been frankly designed to destroy large accumulations as quickly as possible rather than to produce a regular flow of revenue from death duties over a long period. The most damaging aspect of excessive taxation of incomes and estates is its effect on the volume and the growth of the nation's capital fund. Indignation over the presumed, or established, unethical methods by which large estates and large incomes have been acquired has destroyed entirely the capacity to realize the social and economic contribution to the general well-being that is made by these accumulations as such. Resentment against individuals has been permitted to dictate severe reprisals against the economic system.

In consequence, tax rates have been set too high for the best revenue results, either in the present or in the long run. These rates keenly stimulate tax avoidance through utilization of every possible loophole in the law, and they tempt some to take the long chance of unlawful evasion. Such natural human reactions against oppressive taxation have been met by an increasingly suspicious and hostile administrative attitude, and with a disposition to cover with opprobrium those who have failed to maintain a sweet and sunny disposition under the tax lash.

Further, there has been complete disregard of the long-run effects of the current tax policy on the sources of supply from which the capital fund is supported and increased. It has been assumed that the taxes paid on large incomes or large estates do not affect the supply of capital since these taxes are paid in money while the capital apparatus consists of factories, machines, raw materials, ships, railways, and the like.[6] Obviously, there are as many of these productive goods after the tax is paid as there were before. Hence, it is said that the taxes have not diminished the nation's real capital.

This view regards only the immediate, and not the long-run, effects of the tax policy. It is true that when a large estate must be liquidated to pay the death taxes, buildings and machines do not immediately disappear. The securities representing equitable interests in these capital goods change hands, and apparently no damage has been done. It is equally true that when 50% or more of a large income is taken, the business which produced the income is not at once affected, nor is the taxpayer himself rendered entirely destitute by paying income tax at such rates.

It must be plain, however, that taxation of incomes and estates at the rates now imposed must curtail materially, if it does not wholly check, the flow of funds from present sources for the replacement and extension of the capital equipment. The assumption is prevalent that this capital equipment, having been once created, is a permanent and imperishable thing—hence the conclusion that only good can come from an equalizing tax policy which reshuffles the titles to this mass of supposedly permanent wealth. The truth is that the existing stock of tangible capital goods will soon wear out and disappear unless it is sustained and renewed by a perpetual flow of new investment. The important question then arises as to how the life blood of the nation's productive wealth is to be provided if the present levels of income and estate taxation are continued.

The available alternatives are none too promising. One is the government, and the socialist at once asserts that the state can and should own, maintain, and extend the capital supply. The only way by which the state can assure the necessary life blood of capital is through com-

---

[6] Cf. the following passage from the President's taxation message of June 19, 1935: "A tax upon inherited economic power is a tax upon static wealth, not upon that dynamic wealth which makes for the healthy diffusion of economic good." H.D. 229, 74th Cong., 1st Sess.

pulsory mass saving. This is being undertaken in Russia, where the ruling group decides how much of the nation's productive energy shall go into capital goods. Wages and prices are then adjusted so that the workers are just able to buy the quantity of consumers' goods that is allotted for production.[7] If the Russian experiment proves anything, it is that an autocracy can save and plan better than the mass of the Russian proletariat, but it proves nothing whatever as to the superiority of government over the individual in this country.

It is useless to expect that government saving can repair the damage being done by inordinate taxation, for the government cannot make ends meet, even after applying all that it takes from the rich to the current support of the poor. Furthermore, since the nature of this fundamental problem is not at all recognized in government circles, it is the more futile to expect that steps will be taken to repair damage which no one realizes is being done.

The second alternative is that the great number of those with small incomes will be able to supply the needed capital funds. This is quite unlikely, for in the past the task has required the contributions of those with large incomes as well as the amounts supplied by the marginal savers. The current taxation of personal incomes and estates is clearly a sacrifice of the future in order to gain a temporary and illusory advantage today. A similar sacrifice is being made in the treatment of business corporations, for the tax on undistributed profits is a device to compel the distribution of all earnings as they are earned, regardless of the wisdom or advantage of such distribution from the standpoint of the business as an economic enterprise. The flood of special dividends in 1936 refuted the charge that earnings had theretofore been withheld at the command and in the interest of large stockholders. Had the corporations generally been subject to the kind of manipulation that was alleged, they would have held back their profits as usual and have paid the extra tax, for the special dividends distributed were subjected to still higher rates of tax in the large individual returns. The full effects of this policy will be felt in the next severe depression, when productive operations, employment, and dividends will be even more irregular than they were in the last one, by reason of the depleted reserves. Needless to say, the public revenues will then suffer, likewise, in greater proportion.

Many features of the current tax policy appear to be deliberately framed to penalize and discourage risk-taking. They ignore the fact that

[7] Cf. L. E. Hubbard, *Soviet Money and Finance* (New York, Macmillan Co., 1936), *passim.*

enterprise is the core of the private economic system. In many other respects the tendency has been to undermine self-reliance, to encourage growing dependence on the government's bounty or wisdom, and to substitute bureaucratic red tape for individual resourcefulness and initiative. The tax policy definitely penalizes those who may not have succumbed to the demoralizing influence of paternalism, by appropriating a substantial share of the fruits of successful enterprise while leaving the risk-taker to bear the full burden of his losses. The government's true function of regulation should be that of pruning the exuberant and excrescent growths of enterprise, and not that of killing its taproot.

A second result, which may not unreasonably be traced to the fiscal policy, has been an inordinately greater propensity toward government regimentation of individuals and their private affairs. The supervisory activities of government have been expanding for some time, and their growing expense has been a moderate but universal factor in rising government costs. In the depression, the tendency received far greater impetus, and was given a definitely changed direction. The assumption has been encouraged that government planning and control are vastly superior to private control of enterprise.

The only correct diagnosis of this viewpoint is to call it government megalomania, a serious inflammation of the government ego. Its cause has been easy money. The Federal Government has created such enormous quantities of purchasing power through the manipulation and abuse of credit, and it has done this so easily, *apparently* so painlessly, as to produce an illusion of greatness. No one can talk of billions, legislate billions, spend billions, without developing an inner belief that he is a superman, that he knows best how other people should work and live and behave, and that he can run the world far better than anyone else.

Naturally, an administrative hierarchy which has become thoroughly accustomed to thinking and dealing in terms of billions would be impatient with the slow, clumsy, trial and error methods of democracy, which must always tolerate enough personal freedom to let people make mistakes. It is only natural, likewise, that this impatience should generate a strong urge toward personal government and away from any system which sets limits to the scope of government action. It likewise begets contempt for the fundamental theory underlying limited government powers, which is that unrestricted public authority cannot be reconciled with personal freedom. When government is subject to no restraints, the individual is necessarily subject to complete restraint. A regimented democracy is a fundamental contradiction of terms. The unspoken purpose back of the attack on the Supreme Court was to secure a sudden extension of Federal powers into fields and for objects which could not be approved as constitutional except by judges specially selected to give such a construction. Had it not been for the way in which it was decided to deal with the depression, this regrettable attack on the government system would never have been made, for there could not have occurred, otherwise, that inflation of government purposes which prompted the desire to circumvent the constitution in so flagrant a manner.

In summary, the depression financial policy has imposed upon American business two heavy burdens. One of these is taxation so extreme and so at variance with ordinary standards of good fiscal policy as to reveal a marked punitive element and purpose. The other is a regulation which goes much beyond the ordinary standards and purposes of state regulatory control and approaches regimentation. The root of both troubles has been in the system of deficit financing.

The business reaction has gone so far as to produce agitation, in and out of Congress, in favor of tax modifications. It remains to be seen how much will be done to correct the tax abuses that have been operative. No serious concern on this subject was expressed in the President's first message to the special session of Congress, which was assembled expressly to deal with some measures of stricter Federal control, namely, wages and hours, the farm subsidy, and the proposed regional districts. Nor was there anything, either in the message or in Mr. Morgenthau's recent address, referred to above, to show that concern is felt over the deadening effects of the whole regimentation policy.

This address was evidently designed to reassure business. The following passage, in particular, must have been so intended:

> The basic need today is to foster the full application of the driving force of private capital. We want to see capital go into the productive channels of private industry. We want to see private business expand. We believe that much of the remaining unemployment will disappear as private capital funds are increasingly employed in productive enterprises. We believe that one of the most important ways of achieving these ends at this time is to continue progress toward a balance of the Federal budget.

Under other circumstances this statement might have produced a greater effect than it did. In fact, it is simply a credo, a statement of beliefs and desires. It is faith without works, which has long been recognized to be barren. It will not be genuinely inspiring until it is implemented by definite assurances that another New Deal is to be dealt, this time from a deck which contains no Joker of punitive taxation and no "Jacks wild" of regimentation. The country and the budget alike need the full driving force of private capital in production. But capital cannot flow into production until the tax laws permit such movement without severe penalty, and it will not flow there until the prospects of extreme and arbitrary bureaucratic interference with the productive processes are removed.

5

*Fiscal Policy in the Business Cycle**

By GUNNAR MYRDAL†

Underbalancing the budget during a depression is not primarily a deliberate policy but a practical necessity. I would venture the statement that, with few exceptions, a budget never is, and never has been balanced in a depression. Depression, in modern society, causes a fall in all sorts of public income—rates of taxation remaining the same—and at the same time a rise in the bulk of public expenditure, especially for social purposes, standards of welfare policy remaining unchanged. The traditional, conservative reaction of the fiscal system to these influences by business on the budget is, as we all know, to raise the public income by increasing the rates of taxation, and at the same time to reduce expenditures as far as possible by lowering the standards of public activity. If the depression is at all serious, these measures for trying to make the two ends meet will, however, not suffice. The budget will not be balanced in the strict theoretical sense. That does not mean, however, that the budget cannot be presented as properly balanced. In fact, a very large part of the intricate art of budgetary technique in all countries was, and is even now, directed toward that task. And much of the irrational complexity of our budgetary systems is due to these attempts to present balanced budgets even when they are not balanced. Any budget has ample possibilities of concealed deficits in all its corners: hidden reserves which can be mobilized, incomes which can be accounted to an earlier year, costs which can be formally postponed without implying a real saving (e.g., payments due to pension funds and the like). It is this play with fictitious economies, branched out into all items of the budget to conceal an actual deficit from the general public and sometimes, also, from the legislators, which makes an economist feel so hopeless in dealing with budgetary matters. The same damage to clarity and rationality in budgeting is presented by the cor-

* *American Economic Review,* Supplement, Mar. 1939. Reprinted by the courtesy of the American Economic Association and the author.

† Economic Commission for Europe; formerly University of Stockholm.

responding attempts in good times to conceal an actual overbalancing of the budget by strengthening it in all its corners—which is also part of traditional "sound" budgetary policy.

The depression following the crisis of 1929 turned out to be so serious that even in the most respectable fiscal households the deficits could not be concealed by budgetary tricks of the traditional type. Furthermore, during this depression an almost world-wide deliberate fiscal deficit policy, motivated by the effects of the budget on the business situation, has been proposed and to some extent put in effect.

In most countries, including Sweden (which has served as the laboratory in working out certain of the conclusions which I shall present at a later stage of this paper), this policy was carried out only half-heartedly. Public works were generally begun too late; they were not prepared in advance and were, for this reason, delayed and scarcely aimed at the works which should have been selected before all others if a rational choice had been made. They were also usually of much smaller scope than would have been desirable. In countries where the state ordinarily carries on large productive enterprises it turned out to be quite difficult to induce the management of these public enterprises not to conform with the general business trend, but to increase public investment when private investment was shrinking. No country, so far as I know, has dared to carry out the expansionist policy even on the income side of the budget by actually decreasing taxation. On the contrary, taxation was generally raised, even such taxation on consumption and business as was certain to have deflationary effects. Monetary policy and trade policy were very often not regulated to conform to the expansionist objects of financial policy. But in spite of these and other shortcomings, a new fiscal policy has been inaugurated by which the old concealed-sin deficit budgeting during depressions not only achieved much greater magnitude, but was publicly confessed and actually turned into a virtue.

I will not stop to discuss the economic theory in back of this new expansionist fiscal policy, but only to make a few remarks in passing. It seems to me that very often this theory has been oversimplified by contrasting borrowing with taxation, thus neglecting a detailed discussion of the very different varieties of taxation. There are, however, taxes having effects more comparable to borrowing than to other kinds of taxes. Even on the expenditure side, a more detailed discussion of the different effects of various expenditures is called for instead of the broad statements commonly utilized in monetary theory. I would like further to point out that the question which has been so much discussed, particularly in this country, whether deficit spending has self-perpetuating effects and whether it, therefore, can be utilized as a start which then can be safely discontinued, has a very different impact depending upon whether the general trend of production and national income is unbroken as it is for instance in Sweden, or broken as in America; i.e., if we are dealing with a depression in the sense of a temporary setback or with a prolonged stagnation.

Business stagnation points to specific maladjustments in the structure of the economy and, therefore, calls for perhaps radical changes in the whole institutional framework of that economy. To my mind, it is an understatement detrimental to this much larger adjustment problem when this problem is dealt with in the euphemistic terms of business cycle policy. We are then apt to try to substitute symptomatic cures for the needed prophylactic treatment. The most that can be asked from fiscal policy in such a situation is that it procures the necessary breathing space for reforms attacking the deeper causes of maladjustment. The effect of deficit spending on the increase in private investment will naturally be much weakened if not reversed during a stagnation in which business confidence in the future is at a low point. Or to state it more specifically: If we are dealing with a predominantly capitalistic economy like America, where, in addition, public economic activity is by tradition very narrowly restricted, and public spending in profitable investment particularly limited; if, furthermore, that economy is experiencing an economic stagnation with business fluctuating around a trend of production reaching only two-thirds or perhaps one-half of its potential capacity; if, in such a situation, deficit spending, frustrated and driven into the very narrow channels remaining open to it, is utilized to uphold national consumption (and production) but the more fundamental causes of maladjustment are mainly left unattacked; then we should not be surprised if a decrease of public spending is immediately followed by a new downward turn.

In the following I am postulating that the trend of economic development is unbroken and that depressions are only temporary setbacks in a rising trend of production and national income. This assumption means that my conclusions are not directly applicable to the present situation in America. They will, however, have full bearing on the fiscal system set up as a standard to be realized within a better balanced economic development.

Without going further into the theory of business cycle policy, which is being dealt with at this meeting by other speakers, I take it for granted in the following argument that the general economic reasons for deficit spending during depressions are admittedly good. In addition to the common monetary argument of increasing total demand, there are also important, purely fiscal reasons for concentrating public expenditure in the years when costs are low, and for keeping tax rates at least constant if not decreasing them during depression years.

As I pointed out, the actual realization of this new fiscal policy showed serious shortcomings. In Sweden—where the depression turned into a revival as early as 1933 and where, since 1935, we have had a real boom bringing industrial production 50 per cent higher than the peak in 1929, which, in its turn, was 50 per cent above the peak of 1920—we have, during the last years, been reshaping our fiscal policy in order to avoid these shortcomings the next time. Part of this fiscal preparation for crisis has been to take precautions in order to avoid delay in setting the spending program in motion. An intensive inventory of possible public works in the field of public buildings, road construction, and municipal investments has thus been prepared. A general program for social housing has been worked out in some detail. The state production enterprises—railroads, power plants, post office system, mines, forest preserves, etc.—are urged to prepare yearly building programs for ten years in advance. They are asked to have available at all times technical and economic plans, ready for speedy action. The idea is that next crisis we shall not be caught unawares. The blueprints shall be at hand, the measures shall be decided upon in advance, and the government shall have only to press the button to set the machinery in motion. Meantime, state investment, which had already been planned and decided upon, was stopped during the boom period.

This aspect of the economic planning problem is certainly of the greatest importance. In this paper I am, however, passing it over to devote my main discussion to the reconstruction of the budget system. The shortcomings of the new fiscal policy as it has been tested out in various countries during the last depression are, to a considerable extent, to be explained by the fact that this policy was frustrated as a result of being pressed upon a budgetary system which had been built on principles contradictory to this selfsame policy. It is, therefore, just at present an important problem of economic engineering to construct a new scheme of legal and institutional regulations for the fiscal households: a set of fiscal formulas which at the same time guarantees to a satisfactory degree the "soundness" of public finances in the long run and allows enough flexibility from year to year for fiscal policy to serve its purpose among other measures to mitigate the fluctuations in business activity.

I must here desist from any attempt to discuss the concept of "soundness" of a fiscal system. So much must be said that there is nothing in the fiscal reality corresponding to a conception of absolute financial soundness with the implication that one fiscal system is "sound" and another "unsound." This notion can only be defined in relation to a particular fiscal household, and even then only in a relative sense. We have to make clear what we consider to be assets in a particular fiscal household. The trend of the net aggregate value of these assets minus public debts is, then, the measure of the relative soundness of a fiscal system; if this trend is lowered, the finances are somewhat less sound, and vice versa. The degree of soundness to be kept up in a system of public finances being the basic principle of fiscal policy, it must be established by a political decision. For stability in the system it is of the utmost importance that this principle be fixed and not changed in the short run as a concession to expediency.

It befits an enlightened democracy not only to make this fundamental decision explicit and to stick to it, but to base it not upon abstract stereotypes of definitions and the meaning of the terms, but upon an economic analysis in rational terms of the effects of a choice of one or another degree of soundness: effects on the trend of total capital formation, on income distribution, on the development during future periods of the tension between necessary taxation on the one hand, and possible expenditures on the other hand, and, last but not least, the effects on public confidence.

I want further to stress at the outset that soundness of public finance is a matter of the development in the long run. In principle there cannot exist any contradiction between the two postulated desiderata. Any degree of financial soundness in the long run is compatible with any amount of flexibility of the fiscal policy from year to year.

One of the obvious shortcomings of deficit spending during the last depression was, however, the adverse reaction of business confidence, which has too often restricted or even possibly reversed its stimulating effects. In itself it might seem astonishing that business is apt to react in this way. In a depression with falling demand, decreasing production, and increasing unemployment, there is temporarily a harmony of interests in society. Farmers, workers, businessmen—all should be interested in keeping up incomes, purchasing power, demand, production, employment, and prices.

If business, and public opinion more broadly, is afraid of a deficit spending program it must be because people fear a less sound trend of financial development in the long run. Could we, therefore, make some sort of arrangement giving guarantees for a corresponding overbalancing of the budgets in good times, the public confidence should be satisfied.

That would mean that the budget reaction to changes in business activity should be built on a fixed pattern, regulating deficits and surpluses in budget balancing. It must be admitted that the general public is quite right in feeling its confidence disturbed by rapid, unregularized changes within the field of budget policy, or, to state it in another way, by a fiscal policy which is not integrated and regularized into a system of long-range budget planning, but instead constitutes a break with acknowledged budgetary principles. We must, therefore, not only make a virtue of the sins but also incorporate them in the regular fiscal system in order to avoid the adverse confidence reaction.

The chief technical problem of fiscal policy in the business cycle is, therefore, to design formulas for public finance which, as part of the regular system, make room for deficit spending during depressions by securing the building up of corresponding surpluses in good years.

When insisting on the construction of a more rigid pattern of budget reaction to the business cycle of this sort, my argument is, however, not only the interest of realizing the chosen degree of soundness in public finances and the interest of preserving public confidence in the fiscal system. My conclusion from our practical experiences in Sweden, and from what I know of experiences gathered in other countries, is also that fiscal policy is rather a clumsy instrument in crisis policy when utilized as the mobile factor in fighting against depressive forces which change from month to month and from week to week. The most we can righteously request from fiscal policy is that it shall in a general and rather rigid way be adjusted to react contrary to the cyclical movements; it is certainly not a good instrument for taking care of the more individualized and concrete troubles of the day or the month. Other means must be found for dealing with them. But this day-to-day policy, broadly monetary policy, will have its way paved if the fiscal policy is built into a strong counter-cycle movement.

Finally, only by integrating the fiscal policy during depressions into a long-range scheme will it be possible to give deficit spending the magnitude actually indicated in the situation. I mentioned that, at least in countries where the Great Depression did not develop into a prolonged stagnation as in this country, the actual deficits have been very small when compared with brave theories—this is at least true of Sweden—and that in no country, as far as I know, has the courage been strong enough to induce a lowering of deflationary taxation; instead tax levies have usually been increased. This is all because the new policy is still in conflict with the basic principles of the budget system. Only by organizing it into a permanent budget system will a more courageous fiscal policy during depressions be possible.

The idea behind such a financial system, in which the budget reaction towards business fluctuations is diverted into a new pattern, more compatible with the desires of business cycle policy, must be not only to take away the irrational inducements to be too parsimonious during depression years, but also to make the budget situation seem difficult in boom years. Deficit spending must be accounted in such a way that it mortgages the otherwise ample resources of good years. The deficits ought, therefore, to be made ostentatiously visible, and a technique must be invented by which the deficits are carried forward until they are liquidated.

That is, of course, the big problem: how to tie the hands of governments and legislators in good times and hinder them from expansion beyond the trend at that time, but to be able to release their hands and spur them to action in depressions. If we want public finance to react as a counter-cycle, we must change the political psychology and give the state plenty of resources in depressions, but hold them back in booms. Such a change in psychology can be carried out by appropriate alterations in the institutional setup. We must, in financial as well as in monetary matters, try to come back to a reasonable degree of automatic reactions. But we must build up these automatic reactions so that they are better adapted to the needs of present-day society. It is not contradictory to ask the legislative body to create for itself, by enacting appropriate rules, new conditions for its own functioning. It is in fact a primitive democracy where the representation does not regularize its own action. The budget system in every country is such a more permanent regulation of the yearly fiscal action. The request is merely to change rules already existing into rules better adapted to their purpose.

After this very general discussion of the problems to be solved, I will continue with a very short description of the new Swedish budgetary system. I hope thus to avoid being too abstract and vague. Among the special conditions prevailing in Sweden at least two ought to be mentioned as of importance to the question of the applicability elsewhere of our new budget technique: after the severe depression Sweden enjoyed a real boom; this unbroken trend of economic development which gives us the right to deal with depressions as temporary setbacks also made it possible for us to redeem rapidly the extraordinary borrowing of the depression years. This, of course, was a more important factor in turning public confidence to modern rational budget principles than whole libraries of books.

We accepted as a start the time-honored idea that the formula for the soundness of public finance should even in future be to preserve intact the present net value of the state's income earning assets, over and above national debt.

We have even accepted—with certain adjustments to be discussed immediately—the equally time-honored financing principle that only profitable, self-liquidating investments could ordinarily be financed out of loans. This financing principle demarcates the capital investment budget. We now completely separated this capital investment budget from the running budget. In order to make this distinction clear we said that these two budgets should not hereafter be added together to make total budget sums. There is, indeed, no rational reason for adding together these two budgets; a private entrepreneur or an individual family household would never think of adding together its corresponding accounts.

The running budget contains, on the one hand, receipts from taxation, the yearly profits from productive state enterprises and other yearly state incomes, and, on the other side of the ledger, all sorts of ordinary expenditures which are not of the investment type, plus the writing off of the "productive" investment. The capital investment budget, on the other hand, is regularly financed by borrowed money —in so far as free capital out of sinking funds in the different "productive enterprises" is not available; i.e., in so far as the state is increasing investment over normal reinvestment.

The existence of a separate capital investment budget means, in itself, a considerable amount of regularized flexibility of fiscal policy within the business cycle. On the one hand, the state is free during depressions to expand its investments under this capital investment budget without increasing taxation at the same time. On the other hand, the yearly subtractions from the net profits earned by these investments for payments to the sinking funds mean the carrying out of an exact long-time balance. As the payments to sinking funds are made automatically and according to technical considerations, this long-time balancing is ordinarily to be considered well guaranteed. There has never been any doubt as to the permissibility of financing profitable investment in railroads, power plants, public utilities, etc., by loans. Financing them by taxation would rather have been considered an unnecessary burdening of the taxpayer.

It is obvious that the greater the proportion of a nation's productive and investment activity carried on in this way, directly by the state, the greater is the flexibility of fiscal policy in the business cycle and the more powerful is fiscal policy as a means of business cycle policy. The chief practical difficulty is that the managers of state enterprises are apt to react very much as managers of private enterprises. The management of state railroads, for example, is naturally most interested in investment when traffic is increasing and actually creating new needs. But the managers of the state enterprises ought to be more easily educated, and, in the last instance, they are under political control, which private investment is not.

Every enlargement of the scope of the capital investment budget will increase fiscal flexibility in the business cycle. With regard to the "soundness" of the financial system in the long run, there is, in theory, absolutely no difference if expenditures are carried over from the running budget to the capital investment budget, provided only that due provisions for sinking funds are established. For many reasons, and especially in view of making the budget principles understandable to the public, which always regards the budget as analogous to private bookkeeping—that this analogy is false does not matter—it seems advisable, however, to keep to the old convention that borrowing is only permissible to finance "productive," self-liquidating investments. But a number of expenditures can easily be made self-liquidating.

Thus, a public corporation, placed on the same level as the other productive enterprises of the state, was instituted to own and administer the state's public buildings, schools, post offices, hospitals, etc. The particular branch of administration has, thus, to pay to this corporation yearly rent for the use of its quarters. This rent is, of course, a yearly and ordinary expenditure on the running budget charged that particular branch of administration. The corporation, in its turn, utilizes its rent incomes for paying not only the upkeep of the buildings, but also interest and depreciation on the invested capital. The payment to the sinking fund is a matter of business routine and follows technical rules. This reform carries with it the added advantage of making the relative costs of different branches of public activity measurable and comparable with much more rationality and accuracy than was possible earlier when the various administrations were charged in the running budget with the costs of new buildings in the year, and only in the year, in which they happened to be built. In the present problem the reform means a greater flexibility in fiscal policy, because during a depression we can now expand our construction program for public buildings and finance it out of loans without breaking any budget principles and without endangering the soundness of finances in the long run. The burden on the running budget is thus automatically kept upon the same level even for the years when the building program is shrinking.

In the same way we are gradually transferring the social housing program to this capital investment budget in which yearly balancing is not a problem, and in which the long-run balancing of incomes and expenditures is automatically guaranteed by the technical depreciation rules. The state, through another state business corporation, makes loans on strictly business terms to communities and local nonprofit-making corporations and finances those loans from the capital investment budget. The very substantial housing subsidies from the state are kept distinctly separate; they are given in the form of yearly contributions from the running budget to the various local projects.

Nothing stands in the way of transferring the financing of the entire upkeep and construction of roads to another state business corporation. The taxes on automobile traffic are even now reserved for this purpose; these taxes, of course, flow most abundantly during boom years while the building work ought to be concentrated in the depression years. A better timing of investment would, however, be possible by turning over these automobile taxes to a corporation as a regular and guaranteed source of income. If it had these regular incomes this corporation would be able to finance the investment expenditures for new roads building from the capital investment budget. A technically appropriate amount of its yearly income has then to be paid into sinking funds for the depreciation of road capital.

But even with such important changes in the scope of the capital investment budget—which is the best form for an automatic budget structure securing long-range balancing while preserving flexibility from year to year—this capital investment budget will nevertheless be comparatively small. There is, therefore, need for still more flexibility. The method utilized in Sweden during the earlier depression was the usual one: first to conceal the deficit by exhausting certain funds and later, when that was no longer possible, to single out certain large items from the ordinary budget—all sorts of unemployment relief, public works of "unproductive" character, and agricultural subsidies—and finance them not out of taxes but by loans. We had, in other words, an emergency budget.

This method is, however, far from ideal. It is irregular; it breaks the budget principles and the budget unity. It further opens the door for certain very irrational influences upon fiscal policy. The minister of finance will, in spite of the extraordinary borrowing for the emergency items, find himself compelled to be most economical on the remainder of the running budget, at the same time as he must take pride in spending on the particular items selected for the extraordinary loan financing. He will further be hindered from decreasing deflationary taxation.

As the distinction between running budget and capital investment budget must be kept fixed and cannot be changed for temporary reasons of expediency, the rational solution must be to give up the old principle that the budget shall be balanced yearly and to make it a rule that the yearly budget shall be closed by a deficit or a surplus. During a depression a general deficit on the running budget should be allowed as part of the budgetary scheme. But it is then necessary to find the technical guarantees of subsequent overbalancing when the depression is over.

To create this guarantee it is stipulated that a deficit on the running budget shall never disappear from the budget before it is again made good. The deficit is transferred as a negative item to a special budget equalization fund which represents the continuity in public finances. This fund is made self-liquidating by the rule that one year's deficit shall be debited to the ordinary budgets during the next five years by one-fifth each year, that rule providing a maximum amortization term and, of course, not preventing the state from paying off the deficit in a shorter period. There is nothing to hinder a budget deficit during two or more subsequent years, but then the amortization to be paid to the equalization fund piles up. A budget surplus is not allowed to appear on the running budget before all deficits are paid.

In the last instance the guarantee of "sound finances" sought in this budgetary system is the openness with which a deficit is registered, and the institution of the equalization fund by which the deficits are carried forward until they are paid. It is, of course, part of the plan that the budget shall be worked out with scrupulous honesty and that all the customary tricks in traditional budgetary technique shall be forsaken.

This budgetary system makes it possible in the next depression to carry out a much bolder expansionist program without breaking the established budgetary principles. Large increases in investments in the state productive enterprises, in public buildings, in social housing and in roads can be carried out on the capital investment budget and in the ordinary way be financed by loans. The number of "unproductive" public works can also be increased on the running budget, and, which is still more important, there is no need to curtail ordinary expenditures, for the running budget is not supposed to be balanced at such a time. There is, then, for the same reasons, no need to raise taxes; but on the contrary, taxes, or particular varieties of taxes, considered to have deflationary effects may be lowered as part of the depression policy. The burden on the equalization fund will then be progressively increased. In the following boom a revised policy will be enacted by the principles instigated in this institution.

The ordinary maximum height of the equalization fund in a boom is fixed at only about 75 million kronor, which actually means that the normal height over a period of years will be very much under zero. Of course, in the Swedish financial situation in which the state has a capital wealth much in excess of the total national debt, there should have been no difficulty at all in starting the new system by creating a considerable positive fund. When we have, on the contrary, chosen to work with underbalances from bad years to be repaid during good years as the normal course of events, we have followed the pattern of the last depression. We have thought this to be more advantageous, as there is then no limit to the underbalancing during bad years. If we had constituted a positive fund it is to be expected that it would perhaps be exhausted in the very bottom of a depression, and that a further underbalancing could then (because of that), in a sensitive moment, create bad confidence reactions. It seemed better, therefore, to make a negative fund the normal thing right from the beginning. We thought, also, that the necessity of the repayment of accumulated deficits would be a stronger force toward consolidation during good years than merely the desirability of again building a fund which had been exhausted.

It may be asked: how shall it be ascertained that there is a depression and that a deficit is to be permitted? We have not correlated the working of the system to any specific index of employment or production. On the whole it is not very difficult to know when there is a depression, especially as Sweden obviously reacts to international crisis with a certain time lag. It is, of course, a harder test of economic knowledge and financial character to acknowledge that there is a revival and, therefore, when measures should be taken to strengthen the budget. It is actually in order to build up the character and courage of administrators that the use of the budget system is proposed to correct the accumulated sins of concealed deficits.

Finally, the point might be raised against this structure of fiscal reaction to various fluctuations, that it assumes normal business cycles with good times alternating the bad ones. It may be maintained that the system does not work if the trend should be broken into an economic stagnation interrupted by very short and weak revivals. The answer is that no financial system, and no political system, will long sustain such a development. Economic stagnation calls for perhaps radical changes of the whole institutional structure of an economy, including, of course, its fiscal system, but this reform cannot be carried out simply by fiscal policy. The budgetary system does, however, not exclude underbalancing for any number of years. The only effect will be that the deficits on the ordinary budget will then cumulate into huge sums.

6

The Federal Budget: Economic Consequences of Deficit Financing[*]

By B. F. HALEY[†]

Since 1930 the federal debt has increased about 175 per cent, from about 16.2 billions in 1930 to over 44 billion dollars in October, 1940. Economists probably differ somewhat in their appraisal of the seriousness of this increase; but all would agree, I believe, that such a rapid increase in the public debt has had, and must continue to have, economic consequences that warrant careful analysis. Particularly does the situation call for reconsideration and reanalysis in view of the certainty of still further increases in federal expenditures in connection with the National Defense Program, and in view of the dreary prospect faced by the United States of having to engage for years to come in an armament race, if not in war itself.

This enormous increase in the federal debt is of course one of the effects of the depression; more accurately, one of the effects of the particular methods employed by the Administration since 1933 in combating the depression. There is nothing new about deficits for governmental units in time of depression. In such periods it is to be expected that governmental receipts will decline, while expenditures fail to decline proportionately, or even increase. There is, however, a difference between a fiscal policy designed simply to alleviate the distress accompanying a severe depression and a fiscal policy designed to produce recovery through a deliberate unbalancing of the budget. The former policy is based on the assumption that the deficit is the lesser of two evils; the latter, on the assumption that deficit financing in such a period is a positive good. It is the latter policy which has been followed since 1933. The new aspects of our recent deficits have been their extraordinary size, for peacetime, and the complacency with which they have been incurred.

* *American Economic Review, Proceedings,* Feb. 1941, Vol. XXX, No. 5. Reprinted by the courtesy of the American Economic Association and the author.

† Stanford University.

They have been viewed as a necessary and important means of promoting recovery itself.

The term deficit financing will be used here to refer to this latter policy of promoting recovery through a deliberate unbalancing of the federal budget, a policy based on the expectation that a substantial excess of federal (income-increasing) expenditures over (income-decreasing) receipts will so increase consumers' incomes and demand that eventually there will be a more than proportionate stimulation of production activity, private employment and finally private investment.[1] It is the purpose of the present paper to examine the economic consequences of this program of deficit financing for the United States. For convenience the analysis will be divided into two main sections: (1) an examination of the effects of the spending program upon employment and income; and (2) a consideration of some of the more important effects upon our economy of the large public debt which has accumulated as a result of the spending program.

EFFECT OF THE SPENDING PROGRAM UPON EMPLOYMENT AND INCOME

Full consideration of the economic effects of deficit financing would involve many issues, only some of which are subject to reasonably satisfactory analysis. Among those issues which are important but which I cannot undertake to consider here are: (1) the extent to which the spending program has involved wasteful expenditure of labor and resources; and (2) the extent to which certain sections of the spending program have added to our ability to produce, and thus have contributed to the increase of national income for future generations.

Examples could easily be given of projects that have been wasteful; and other examples could be given of projects which should contribute in a substantial way to the increase in our national income of the future. It could be pointed out that, so far as the wasteful projects are concerned, much of the labor and resources so wasted would have been wasted anyway had they been left unemployed. And then it could be further pointed out that the waste which has occurred would have been avoided in large part if more attention had been given to long-range planning, if regional political considerations had not played their part, and if the

[1] For a statement of the multiplier doctrine and of the closely related but distinct conception of pump-priming, see: G. Colm and F. Lehmann, "Public Spending and Recovery in the United States," *Soc. Research,* 1936, III, 129–66; S. E. Leland, "Our National Debt," *Harvard Bus. Rev.,* 1937–38, XVI, 257–72; A. D. Gayer, "Fiscal Policies," *Am. Econ. Rev.,* Supplement, 1938, XXVIII, 90–112; J. M. Clark, "An Appraisal of the Workability of Compensatory Devices," *ibid.,* 1939, XXIX, 194–208.

need for immediate results had not been so great. But I must admit that I have no adequate basis for a thorough analysis of these two issues; consequently they will not receive further consideration here.

Attention will be directed in this section exclusively to the more immediate effect which the spending program has had upon the national income, employment, and private investment. How successful, as a recovery measure, has the program been?

First, there can hardly be any question but that the spending program has been in considerable part responsible for the increase in the national income which has occurred since 1933. The successive annual deficits of the federal government since that year have been accompanied by considerably greater annual increases in the national income in every year except 1938. Or, if the more precise and useful comparison is made between annual net "income-increasing" expenditures of the federal government and annual increases in the national income, the same conclusion follows.[2] It is a temptation to attribute the whole of the increase in the national income to the spending program, and to explain the response of the former to the latter by reference to the multiplier principle. It would be a mistake, however, to attribute the successive increases in the national income exclusively to the spending program, attractive though that simple explanation may be.

In the first place, if it be assumed for the moment that the greater part of the secondary effects of a given increment of government spending are enjoyed within a year, then the two variables to be compared are not the absolute amount of the net income-increasing expenditures and the increase of the national income, but rather the increase in the amount of government expenditures and the increase in the national income for each year. As Clark has reminded us, the stimulating effect of a given rate of government spending becomes exhausted when the national income has increased to that level at which a rate of saving (or "leakage" of other sorts) has developed equivalent to the given rate of government spending.[3] The appropriate multiplier relationship is that between annual increases in net income-increasing expenditures and annual increases in the national income.

Now when the successive annual increases in the amount of government expenditures are compared with the successive annual changes in the national income produced, it immediately becomes evident that in several of these years the increase in the national income was clearly disproportionate to the increase in federal spending. Take for example

[2] Gayer, *op. cit.,* pp. 97–102. Gayer's figures cover the period down to 1937 only.

[3] J. M. Clark, *op. cit.,* pp. 199–201.

the year 1935. In this year, according to Gayer's figures,[4] there was a federal net income-increasing expenditure of 3,154 million dollars; the national income produced in 1935 exceeded that of 1934 by 5,180 millions. But the net federal contribution in 1935 was no greater than it had been in 1934. With no increase in the rate of spending there developed a very substantial increase in the national income.[5] The conclusion is suggested, certainly, that circumstances other than the spending program had an important part to play in bringing about the increase in the national income in this particular year.

The same conclusion is suggested by an examination of the years 1931–33. In these three years the net federal income-increasing expenditures averaged 1,750 million dollars while the national income steadily declined.[6] Of course the explanation is obvious: the effect of the spending program in these years was more than offset by the decline that occurred in private investment.[7] This very explanation, however, serves to direct attention to the fact that the variations in the national income during the whole period under consideration must have been related to the variations in private investment as well as to the variations in public spending. And although the rate of private investment has certainly not been unaffected by changes in the rate of public spending, it has surely been affected by other circumstances as well. This clearly must have been true in the years 1931–33; it probably was equally true in the years since 1933.

With this conclusion in mind, take again the year 1935. In this year, it will be recalled, there was an increase of over 5 billion dollars in the national income while the net federal income-increasing expenditures showed no increase over 1934. But at the same time residential construction increased 465 million dollars, business construction 281 millions,

---

[4] *Loc. cit.*

[5] It may be argued that, since the stimulus of a given increment of spending is not limited to the year in which the spending occurs, some of the increase of the national income in 1935 may have been attributable to the increase in the rate of spending that occurred in 1934. This cannot be denied. However, it is highly improbable that such a delayed effect could have been an important circumstance underlying the substantial increase in the national income in 1935.

[6] Gayer, *loc. cit.*

[7] Kuznets' analysis of gross capital formation for these years shows a decline in business inventories, business construction, and the flow of producers' durable goods much more than sufficient to offset the effect upon national income of the net federal income-increasing expenditures. Furthermore, with the exception of producers' durable goods in 1933, each of the items declined in each of the years while net federal income-increasing expenditures, after increasing sharply in 1931, remained nearly stable in the two following years. See Simon Kuznets, "Capital Formation in the United States, 1919–1935," *Capital Formation and Its Elements* (National Industrial Conference Board), p. 35; Gayer, *op. cit.*, p. 107.

the flow of producers' durable commodities 591 millions, and inventories 19 millions as compared with 1934—a total increase in these important elements of private gross investment amounting to 1,356 millions.[8] It certainly would be unwise to attribute the whole of the increase of the national income to the federal spending program in a year in which there was no increment in the net federal contribution while there did occur a very substantial increment in private gross investment. Surely the same caution should be observed for the years since 1935. If there was a multiplier effect attributable to the government's spending program, there was also a multiplier effect attributable to the successive increments in the rate of private investment. Furthermore, although the rate of private investment has been discouragingly low since 1933, and although it has increased relatively slowly, yet the annual increases in the rate of private investment in some of these years compared quite favorably with the annual increases in the rate of government income-increasing expenditure.

The possible reply that such increase as did occur in the rate of private investment was itself stimulated by the spending program is not convincing. It is certainly not to be denied that the spending program should be given credit for some, possibly much, of the increase in the rate of private investment;[9] but there is some reason for believing that, even without a large spending program, the rate of private investment would have revived considerably during the years since 1933. As to how much it would have revived under other circumstances, it is useless to speculate. It is important, however, to stress the necessity for caution in attributing the whole of the increase in the national income to the spending program.

Yet even if it be granted that the increase which has occurred in the national income since 1933 is primarily attributable to the spending program, it must be concluded that the program has failed to produce the results expected of it. For it had been anticipated that the successive federal net contributions would not only increase incomes, the demand for consumers goods, employment in the consumers goods industries, and, somewhat later, private investment and employment in the capital goods industries but also that the rate of private investment would increase sufficiently rapidly and on a sufficiently large scale to make possible the gradual reduction and final elimination of the federal net contributions. In other words, the purpose was to "prime the pump," and

---

[8] Kuznets, *loc. cit.*

[9] The view that the spending program actually affected adversely the rate of private investment will be considered below.

then to withdraw, leaving the pump to do the work. But the pump has refused to be primed beyond the point of yielding a rather feeble trickle, and the government has had to continue its income-increasing expenditures on a large scale in order to prevent actual recurrence of a decline in business activity.[10]

There are several reasons which have been suggested for the failure of response of private investment. The most fundamental of these, I suspect, is the failure of businessmen to alter their long-term expectations upon the basis of an increase in the demand for consumption goods which they are convinced would continue only so long as government spending also continued.[11] A government spending program should favorably affect short-term expectations, at least as long as the program is continued, but unfortunately there is no reason to expect an equally favorable effect upon the long-term expectations of investors.

Second, renewed investment activity on any large scale is unlikely to result from increased consumption when there already exist inventories that are regarded as excessive and adequate plant capacity for considerably increased volume of production of consumers goods. In the three years 1933–35, Kuznets estimates that business inventories declined nearly 4 billion dollars, measured in 1929 prices, or over 2.6 billion dollars, measured in current prices.[12] This represents a very considerable volume of disinvestment, and indicates something of the slack which needs to be taken up, after consumption demand has increased, before investment is likely to respond.

Third, there should be mentioned the very considerable list of circumstances that have been responsible for the persistent pessimism of long-term expectations. One cannot help but believe that, even though the program of deficit financing had tended to make long-term expectations of businessmen more favorable to a renewal of private investment on a large scale, these other dreary aspects of the business situation would have overwhelmed any such tendency. The uncertainty of the in-

[10] Even though there were numerous other circumstances involved, the decline in the net federal contribution in 1937 surely had much to do with the recession of 1937–38. For an analysis of the complex of circumstances responsible for this recession, see S. H. Slichter, "The Downturn of 1937," *Rev. of Econ. Stat.*, 1938, XX, 79–110. While agreeing with Slichter's thesis that the drop in the federal net contribution in 1937 has been given too important a place in some of the explanations of this recession, I am inclined to attribute somewhat more importance to this circumstance than he does.

[11] Cf. J. M. Clark, "Effects of Public Spending on Capital Formation," *Capital Formation and Its Elements* (National Industrial Conference Board), pp. 62–63; P. M. Sweezy, discussion of a paper by A. Kahler, *Soc. Research,* 1939, VI, 230–31; D. T. Smith, "Is Deficit Spending Practical?" *Harvard Bus. Rev.*, 1939–40, XVIII, 38.

[12] Kuznets, *op. cit.,* pp. 34–37. During these same three years the net federal income-increasing expenditures totaled only about 8.2 billion dollars. Gayer, *op. cit.,* p. 107.

ternational situation, both politically and economically, the clear necessity for a long-period, painful readjustment of the structure of our agricultural industry, the uncertainty as to the future for private operators in the public utility industries, the unsettled and rapidly changing situation in regard to labor relations—all may be mentioned. In addition other more general aspects of the business situation have certainly played their part: First, the conviction on the part of businessmen that the Administration was determined to make political capital by maintaining an attitude hostile to business. Second, the whole aftermath of fear and uncertainty following upon the panic of 1933 has made businessmen cautious, hesitant to launch new and hazardous ventures and unwilling to tie up funds in long-term investments. Third, there has failed to emerge a wide range of opportunities for investment in new industries of promising scope or for profitable expansion of old industries. Altogether it is not surprising that private investment has failed to respond to the stimulus of public spending when long-term expectations have been dominated by such circumstances as these.

The question should be raised at this point, however, whether the failure of private investment to recover satisfactorily may not be attributable to the government's program of deficit financing itself. In support of this contention it may be argued that the program of large public expenditures has served to maintain wage rates and the prices of materials at levels that have discouraged the expansion of private business; that the waste characteristic of many of the projects has sapped business confidence; that the public borrowing of the government necessitated by the program has diverted funds from the private capital market; and that the threat of runaway inflation, of a future heavy burden of taxation, and even of a future breakdown of the federal credit have all served to increase businessmen's uncertainty as to the future and to discourage private investment.

It probably is true that the program of large public expenditures has played some part in creating a situation favorable to the maintenance of wage rates and prices of materials at relatively high levels. But the rise of wage rates is surely more closely related to the policies of the NRA, to later federal legislation with regard to labor, and to the virile and energetic efforts of organized labor itself, than it is to the size of the federal program of expenditures. The maintenance of prices of materials as well is certainly not unrelated to the influence of the NRA, and to the whole trend of development towards increasing control over price on the part of corporate business enterprise. There certainly has been no lack of funds available for investment in private issues because of the large public issues that have been made. Nor can one discern any clear evidence of the fear of inflation in businessmen's overt behavior, as distinct from their pronouncements, in the period since 1933, except possibly for a brief period in 1937. And the behavior of the government bond market certainly has not been such as to support the argument that private investment has been discouraged by fear of a collapse of government credit.

In a somewhat different category is the claim that the wastefulness characteristic of much of the spending has adversely affected business confidence. Several of the projects selected for development have clearly been ill-advised, and the failure of these particular projects has strongly colored businessmen's judgment of the whole spending program. They have found it correspondingly easy to believe that other projects, although socially justified, have been developed wastefully. Still other expenditures, such as those for relief, have produced no increase in the tangible wealth of the country. In short, it is quite likely that the way in which the money has been spent has had a bearing of some importance on the success of the spending program. How important this circumstance has been it is of course impossible to determine; unfortunately businessmen's own testimony on the matter is not very reliable. But it can hardly be denied that the spending program would have avoided such a possible adverse effect upon private investment if the projects could have been more carefully planned in advance, if less waste had been incurred in carrying them out, and if a greater proportion of the spending had been devoted to projects that would directly or indirectly tend to increase the national income of future years.

It is also possible, though not subject to proof, that the threat of increased taxation in future years, closely connected of course with the size of successive federal deficits, has played some part in adversely affecting long-term expectations. To the extent that this has been true, and to the extent that long-term expectations have been adversely affected by the belief of businessmen that much of the spending has been wasteful, it must be concluded that the spending program itself must share some of the responsibility for the slowness of recovery of private investment. The spending program has been, to some extent at least, self-defeating. But the opinion may be hazarded that this possible adverse effect of the spending program upon private investment has probably been of minor importance as compared with the more formidable list of circumstances recited above: the fact that businessmen have looked upon the program as temporary in character, and accordingly have refused to revise their pessimistic long-term expectations in the light of the program; the existence, particularly in the early years of the period under consideration, of considerable excess capacity and of large inventories; and, finally, the many seriously adverse circumstances that have persistently justified pessimistic long-term expectations.

The program of deficit financing has failed to produce lasting recovery fundamentally because of the failure of private investment to respond to the stimulus of increased consumption on a sufficient scale to permit gradual reduction of government spending.[13] Even though the current defense crisis had not developed, we probably should have had to continue the program of deficit financing for some time to come. We had the lion by the tail. With unemployment still at a high level and private investment still in a state of relative stagnation, reduction of expenditures and increase of taxation would have been a dangerous policy indeed.[14]

It follows that for some time to come, with the much larger expenditures contemplated under the defense program, continuing federal deficits must be expected. However, the problem is now in several respects a different one. In the first place, the annual net income-increasing expenditures under the defense program are likely to be substantially larger than those involved in the attack upon depression during the period since 1933. Furthermore, for several years at least, the annual increases in these expenditures are likely to be greater. Hence the multiplier effect upon national income and employment should be at least proportionately greater.

In the second place, any tendency which the former spending program has had toward discouraging private investment through adversely affecting business confidence will probably disappear almost completely in the case of the defense program. It is feed for the gristmill of the cynic that a large expenditure program for defense, when there is a strong conviction that such expenditures are imperative, may be expected to have little or no adverse effect upon confidence. The dangers of future inflation, of eventual collapse of the federal credit, of waste-

---

[13] The statement that the spending program has failed to produce lasting recovery is not intended to imply the generalization that under *all* circumstances a program of deficit financing must fail to produce lasting recovery. The general question involved unfortunately cannot receive attention here.

[14] Unless, of course, it is wrong to conclude, as I did above, that the policy of deficit financing itself has probably played a minor part in checking the increase of private investment.

fulness, of future burdensome taxation, of higher interest and wage rates and of higher prices of materials may, and probably will, actually be considerably more serious dangers than they were under the more moderate depression spending program. But businessmen, convinced of the supreme necessity for the program, will now pay little attention to these future dangers and threats of future burdens. Consequently the increased size of the new program is likely to have its full effect upon the national income and the volume of employment. The pump is more likely to be primed.

In the third place, we have good reason to expect the defense program to be continued on a grand scale for a considerable number of years—perhaps five, perhaps ten, perhaps even longer. Hence one of the principal difficulties which has beset the former deficit-finance program—the fact that the expenditures have been looked upon by businessmen as no more than a temporary stimulus—is now less likely to play a part. With five or ten or even more years of heavy government expenditures upon armaments in prospect, businessmen are more likely to revise their long-term expectations upwards and to be tempted by investment opportunities. Fear of the effects of expected higher taxes, an upward movement of wage and interest rates and in the prices of materials may tend to counteract this tendency somewhat; the development of actual, though moderate, inflation would probably accentuate it.

If it is assumed that a moderate upward movement of the general level of prices is permitted, that interest rates will be kept relatively low, that wage rates are permitted to rise no more than in proportion to the rise in the cost of living, then it would appear probable that the national defense spending program will have in the next few years a very favorable effect upon the size of the national income and the volume of employment. Whether it will affect the standard of living of the American people equally favorably is another question.

Meanwhile the federal debt will probably continue to increase at a fairly rapid rate for some years to come—perhaps even more rapidly than during the past nine years. It is appropriate, therefore, to devote the next section of this paper to an analysis of some of the effects upon our economy of this large and increasing public debt.

THE ECONOMIC EFFECTS OF THE LARGE PUBLIC DEBT

First it is important to review briefly the well-known proposition that a large public debt represents no direct burden for future generations, since future interest payments and repayments of principal will simply be transfer payments from taxpayer to bondholder.[15] To facilitate exposition, let period I refer to the period during which the extraordinary outlays are being made by government, whether for attack upon depression or for national defense; and let it be assumed that during this period the national debt is steadily increasing. Let period II refer to the period after the extraordinary outlays have ceased, or alternatively have come to be treated as ordinary outlays to be covered by taxation; the national debt is now assumed to be subject to periodic or steady reduction. Then clearly, from the point of view of society as a whole, the true direct burden of the outlays involved in period I is borne in the same period, and cannot be shifted to period II. Assume, for example, that the government makes outlays in period I from borrowed funds for the development of a public works project. Then the real cost of the project consists of the labor and other resources used for construction of the project, and this real cost can be borne only in period I, the construction period. Later, in period II, when receipts from taxation are employed to repay the bondholders, there occurs a transfer of disposable funds from taxpayers to bondholders; but this transaction can have no direct effect upon the total income for period II. The true direct burden remains upon the income for period I, in the sense that if the public works project had not been developed the labor and other resources could have been employed in other ways.

Of course, even in period I, the extraordinary outlays do not constitute a burden proportionate to the outlays involved when the economy is characterized by extensive underemployment of productive resources. Unemployed plant capacity and laborers are used instead of being permitted to go to waste. There are costs involved, of course, but in a sense many of these costs are "sunk" costs from the point of view of society.[16] Any public works or armaments produced with resources and men that otherwise would have been unemployed and thus lost to society are a net gain.

All of the discussion thus far has referred to the direct burden of the outlays and of the debt thereby incurred. But clearly there is also an indirect burden of the debt to be considered. For example, although it certainly is true that interest and principal payments in period II involve

[15] The proposition has been carefully examined by A. C. Pigou, *A Study in Public Finance,* Part 3, Ch. 1. In the brief review of the doctrine which is presented in this paper the assumption will be made that the debt is entirely domestic. The qualifications to the doctrine which have to be made when part of the debt is owed to foreign investors are well known to economists.

[16] From the social point of view, marginal user cost is very low. Cf. J. M. Keynes, *The General Theory of Employment, Interest and Money,* pp. 69–73.

simply transfer payments from taxpayers to bondholders, so far as the direct effect of reduction of the public debt is concerned, there may be an indirect effect of these transactions upon the size of the national income in period II, upon its distribution, and upon other aspects of the economy as well. It is this indirect effect which we usually have in mind when we refer to the heavy and oppressive burden of a large public debt.

For the purpose of analysis this indirect effect of the public debt upon the economy has a number of different aspects, each of which will be considered in turn: (1) the effect upon the distribution of income; (2) the effect upon the size of the national income; (3) the effect upon federal fiscal policy; (4) the effect upon the general level of prices; (5) the effect upon the banking system and the efficacy of techniques of credit control.

1. *The Effect upon the Distribution of Income*

Consider first the case of deficit financing in period I for the purpose of increasing income and employment during a severe depression. In this case there is little or no burden borne by those who purchase the government securities. Funds are not diverted from private investment or from consumption expenditures. If the purchases of securities are made by the banking system, there is not for this reason likely to be a corresponding contraction of other forms of bank credit.[17] If the purchases are made by individuals, the only sacrifice involved on their part, in most cases, is that of a very slight degree of liquidity, since most such purchases in time of depression are probably made from funds that would otherwise lie idle.

In period II, presumably a period of prosperity, reduction of the debt will involve a transfer of funds from taxpayers to security holders. Is it not possible that these transactions also may constitute no real burden—in this case, for the taxpayers? May not the spending program in period I result in such an increase in the national income in period II that the debt can be serviced and paid off without any increase in tax rates? Unfortunately no such neat and optimistic prediction can be soundly advanced. Once the deficit financing has come to an end the size of the national income (period II) will depend upon such circumstances as the marginal efficiency of capital, the structures of wage and interest rates, and the marginal propensity to consume in period II. If

[17] In the discussion which follows the assumption will be made that the expansion of credit arising out of large purchases of bonds by the banking system does not give rise to an inflationary rise in the general level of prices in period I. As long as there is considerable unemployment of labor and other resources this assumption is probably safe enough.

the expenditures of period I were qualitatively of a sort to increase the productivity of the economy, then this circumstance may contribute something to the size of the national income in period II. But in general all that can be predicted is that the national income probably will be larger in the latter period than in the former.[18] Probably tax rates will have to be increased in order to repay the debt.

In addition it should be noted that the security holders will be found mainly in the upper income groups and among the banking institutions. Consequently the additional taxation, even though it is highly progressive, will probably rest upon the lower income groups much more than in proportion to their holdings of government securities. For as Pigou has said, ". . . experience has never yet revealed a tax system graduated for increasing incomes anything like as steeply as loan subscriptions are likely to be graduated, at all events when the loan required is large."[19] Hence reduction of the debt in period II will involve transfer payments from the lower income groups to the upper income groups and to the banks.

But one must avoid the careless inference that debt repayment therefore of necessity involves a change in the distribution of income in favor of the upper income groups. It is true that the disposable income of the lower income groups will be reduced by the transfer payments; but it is also true that the disposable income of the upper income groups will similarly be reduced by taxation. Although the latter are money in pocket, having as a class received in cash for their securities much more than they have paid out in increased taxes, it does not follow that they have come off better than the lower income groups. Unless former security holders in the upper income groups look with equanimity upon impairment of their capital they cannot properly regard the cash received through redemption of their securities as an addition to disposable income.

Hence the process of repayment of debt does not in itself affect the distribution of income. The latter may be affected, however, by the nature of the additional taxation imposed for the purpose. For example, if the additional taxes make the tax system as a whole more progressive than it had been in period I, then this change may have an effect upon the distribution of income in period II. Disposable income must be lower in period II than it would have been if the debt had not been

[18] This almost follows from the definitions of the two periods. Presumably if the national income were not larger in period II than in period I repayment of the debt would not be undertaken.

[19] Pigou, *op. cit.*, p. 242.

reduced. How much lower it will be in different income groups as compared with one another will depend upon the nature of the tax system in period II.[20]

Although the process of repayment of the debt does not in itself affect the distribution of income, payment of interest on the debt in period II does have such an effect. Interest payments, like debt repayments, involve transfers of funds from the lower income groups to the upper income groups; but in the case of interest payments the outcome is not only a decrease in disposable income for the lower income groups but also an increase in disposable income for the upper income groups. Hence, since the additional taxation imposed is almost certain to rest upon the lower income groups more than in proportion to their holdings of government securities, transfer payments for interests on the indebtedness will tend to shift the distribution of income in favor of the upper income groups.[21]

Consider next the case of extraordinary expenditures in connection with an emergency national defense program. In contrast to the preceding case of deficit financing in time of depression, the national defense program may be financed either by borrowing or by increased taxation imposed contemporaneously with the increased expenditures, or of course by a combination of the two methods.[22] If the method of heavy taxation is employed, the effects of the program upon the distribution of disposable income will of course depend upon the nature of the increased taxation imposed. If the expenditures are large in any one year, the additional taxation, Pigou suggests, must be highly progressive, since the amounts required must be obtained in one way or another from the wealthy.[23] Hence the upper income groups are likely to be required to meet a greater proportion of the cost of the emergency defense program than they have been accustomed to meeting in the

[20] S. E. Leland suggests that the length of the period of repayment will have an important bearing upon the nature of the tax system in period II: "The longer the period the less likely is it that the debt will be paid by progressive taxation and the less steep is the progression likely to be." See his "Debt Retirement and the Budget," *Am. Econ. Rev.*, Supplement, 1937, XXVII, 81. Alzada Comstock was of the opinion in 1937 that an attempt to reduce the public debt would involve the levy of additional taxation that would rest largely on the lower and middle classes. "The Effects of a Federal Tax Program That Will Be Adequate for Substantial Debt Reduction," *Proceedings of the Thirtieth Annual Conference on Taxation under the Auspices of the National Tax Association* (1938), p. 386.

[21] If taxes should be increased in period I in order to meet increasing interest payments on the growing public debt, the same distributional effect would be operative in this period as well.

[22] Cf. Pigou, *op. cit.*, pp. 242–46. The analysis immediately following owes much to Pigou's presentation of the matter.

[23] *Op. cit.*, p. 243.

case of ordinary government expenditures. The distribution of disposable income may thus be altered in favor of the lower income groups during the period of the emergency expenditures when the annual amounts involved are large.

Pigou, however, clearly has in mind the case in which the lower income groups have little or no available margin upon which the government may draw. In a country in which the lower income groups do have some margin, the nature of the additional taxation imposed in time of emergency may be such that the whole system of taxation becomes less progressive than before.[24] For example, it may be regarded as important to prevent the increased taxation from discouraging productive activity, or it may be desired to obtain the maximum revenue. In either event the outcome from the point of view of distribution of income may be the reverse of that predicted by Pigou. The distribution of disposable income may be altered in favor of the upper income groups.

However, if part or all of the emergency expenditures are met by borrowing, the distribution of disposable income is almost certain to be altered in favor of the lower income groups.[25] The purchaser of bonds looks upon his outlay as an investment, and although he has good reason to look forward to an increase in his burden of taxes in period II he has no expectation that this future increase in taxes will be in proportion to his holdings of bonds. Hence, if he has a large income, his contribution through the purchase of bonds in period I is likely to be considerably larger than it would be if the necessary funds were raised exclusively through the levy of increased taxation. Conversely the lower income groups are called upon to make somewhat less of a sacrifice of disposable income in period I when the funds required are raised wholly or in part through borrowing than would be the case if the funds were raised through increased taxation exclusively.

The situation which develops in period II when the time comes to reduce the debt is precisely the same when the borrowing of period I was connected with an emergency defense program as when the borrowing was connected with a deficit finance program in time of depression; there is no occasion to repeat the analysis. In a sense the

---

[24] I am indebted to my colleague, E. D. Fagan, for the suggestion.

[25] Again the assumption is made that the purchases of bonds by the banking system in period I do not give rise to an inflationary rise in the general level of prices. In the case here considered, however, inflation may easily develop if borrowing is continued after full employment is approached and if bank credit expands in connection with the borrowing operations. In that event the well-known distributional effects of inflation will complicate the effects upon distribution to which attention is given in the text.

method of borrowing in period I makes it possible for those who constitute the lower income groups in period I to shift part of the burden of the outlays to those who will constitute the lower income groups in period II. The upper income groups finance the arrangement. Both interest payments and repayment of the debt will involve transfer payments from the lower income groups to the upper income groups in period II. So far as interest payments are concerned, since the additional taxation imposed is almost certain to rest upon the lower income groups more than in proportion to their holdings of securities, there will be a tendency for the distribution of disposable income to be shifted in favor of the upper income groups. In the case of repayment of the debt, the effect upon the distribution of disposable income will depend upon the degree of progression characteristic of the additional taxation imposed.

There are two other considerations to be mentioned, however. First, the payments to be made for service and liquidation of the debt in period II may extend over a longer period than the period of extraordinary expenditures. Hence the burden of transfer payments on the lower income groups in period II may be very much more bearable in any one year than would have been the burden of taxation for these same groups in period I if the program of expenditures had been financed exclusively by taxation.

Second, the national income may be larger or smaller in period II than in period I.[26] If it is larger, the burden on the lower income groups will be still more bearable.

In general it appears permissible to conclude that the accumulation of a large public debt will tend to affect the distribution of disposable income in the following ways: In the case of an emergency defense program which involves large expenditures the method of borrowing in period I permits the lower income groups to shift part of the burden to the lower income groups of period II. Therefore the distribution of disposable income in period I may be altered somewhat in favor of the lower income classes as compared with what it would have been if the method of taxation had been exclusively employed. But on the other hand interest payments on the growing debt in period I will tend to alter the distribution of disposable income in favor of the upper income groups. In period II interest payments will tend to operate in the same way, regardless of whether the debt has arisen as a result of depression spending or as a result of an emergency defense program. As

---

[26] In the case of the emergency defense program.

distinct from interest payments, the process of repaying the debt does not in itself affect the distribution of income in period II; whether one income class is affected less favorably than another will depend upon the nature of the additional taxation imposed.

2. *The Effect upon the Size of the National Income*

The effect upon the size of the national income of a government spending program has already been considered. The purpose now is to take up the effect upon the size of the national income of payments for interest on, or for the reduction of, the public debt. These payments, as has been pointed out, involve, in the main, transfers of disposable income from lower income groups to upper income groups, banks, insurance companies and similar investment institutions. These transfer payments in turn are likely to affect: (a) the propensity to consume; (b) the supply of funds for investment, and possibly also the rate of interest; (c) the marginal efficiency of capital. Through these variables the size of the national income will be affected.

In so far as there is a transfer of disposable income from the lower income groups to the upper income groups there is likely to occur some reduction in the propensity to consume. For since the marginal propensity to consume is higher for the lower income groups than it is for the upper income groups, the increased taxes paid by those with small incomes are likely primarily to affect their consumption. On the other hand, the interest payments received by security holders in the upper income groups are more likely to be saved than to be spent, and payments received in liquidation of their security holdings are almost certain to be saved and reinvested.[27]

The counterpart of the tendency toward a decrease in the rate of consumption is in general a tendency toward an increase in the funds available for reinvestment, particularly as the public debt is reduced. Individuals and insurance companies whose government securities are redeemed will now be in the market for other forms of investment opportunity and the supply of funds in the investment market will be increased. In the case of redemption of securities held by commercial banks, the immediate effect will be a reduction of deposits and an increase in reserve ratios. If there were already excess reserves, the net effect will be a reduction of outstanding bank credit; but if there were a demand for loanable funds or if the private securities market were attractive to the banks, there might simply occur a shift of bank funds

---

[27] Cf. Pigou, *op. cit.*, p. 82 n.

from government securities to private securities and loans with no reduction of outstanding bank credit.

The reduction in the government bond holdings of Federal reserve banks, however, will have a somewhat different effect. Member bank deposits, reserves, and reserve ratios will be reduced, and consequently the net effect in this case is more likely to be deflationary. If, however, there are already excess reserves, there need not occur a net contraction of bank credit. Of course Federal reserve policy can at the same time be so directed as either to accentuate or offset any deflationary tendency.

The net outcome with respect to the supply of investment funds would depend, of course, upon the relative amounts of securities redeemed for individuals, insurance companies, and commercial banks, on the one hand, and the Federal reserve banks on the other hand, with Federal reserve credit policy also to be considered. Since Federal reserve holdings of government securities are ordinarily a very small fraction of the total public debt, it would appear probable that the process of debt reduction would increase the supply of funds seeking investment and tend to lower the rate of interest.

The marginal efficiency of capital is also likely to be affected by both interest payments on the debt and the process of reduction of the debt. First, there is likely to be a favorable effect upon the long-term expectations of businessmen and investors when the public debt becomes stabilized or begins to decrease. In so far as long-term expectations had been at all adversely affected in period I by fears of inflation or of eventual collapse of the public credit, there should be an opposite, favorable effect upon expectations in period II.

On the other hand, the decrease in government spending, particularly if it has occurred rather suddenly, may have an adverse effect upon long-term expectations. This is a rather unlikely development since, it will be recalled, the spending program only under certain circumstances is likely to have favorably affected long-term as distinct from short-term expectations in period I.

More important is the possible effect of increased rates of taxation made necessary by either the necessity of meeting interest payments or the desirability of reducing the debt, or both. Of course it is possible that the national income may be sufficiently greater in period II than it had been in period I to permit payment of interest and gradual liquidation of the debt without any increase in tax rates. But if increased tax rates are imposed they may adversely affect the marginal efficiency of capital. Much depends upon the kinds of taxes employed, the exemptions allowed, and the degree of progression characteristic of the system. There is much work to be done by experts in taxation in designing the necessary changes in our tax system so that substantially increased revenue may be obtained with the minimum of adverse effect upon the marginal efficiency of capital.[28]

When all of these circumstances affecting the size of the national income are taken into consideration there appears some probability that large interest payments or payments in reduction of the debt are likely on balance to tend to affect adversely the size of the national income. A reduction in the propensity to consume will tend, at least in the short period, to reduce the demand for consumption goods and to affect businessmen's expectations adversely in certain sectors of the economy. At the same time, unless the tax system is very skillfully designed, the heavy burden of taxation may adversely affect the marginal efficiency of capital and discourage new investment. If at the same time ease of credit conditions and an increase in the supply of funds seeking investment lead to some decline in the structure of interest rates, the effect upon investment of a decline in the marginal efficiency of capital may be somewhat offset. However, the possibility appears very real that the net effect upon the national income may be depressing.[29]

3. *The Effect upon Federal Fiscal Policy*

The policy of incurring successive federal deficits during a period of severe depression should have as its counterpart the reduction of the public debt during the succeeding period of prosperity. When, however, the depression is prolonged, the limits to the increase of the public debt may be reached before the depression has come to an end. Or if this danger is avoided, it is possible that the succeeding period of prosperity may be too short or tax rates may not be raised sufficiently to permit reduction of the public debt to a low level again before the next period of depression necessitates further deficit financing. The outcome would be a steady increase of the public debt over the period of several business cycles until finally the public credit might become

[28] S. E. Leland, "Debt Retirement and the Budget," *Am. Econ. Rev.*, Supplement, 1937, XXVII, 75–85. Leland offers numerous suggestions for improvement of our revenue system with the above considerations in mind.

[29] But in any given period the effect of interest payments and payments in reduction of the debt on the variables considered above may be overshadowed by other circumstances affecting the propensity to consume, the supply of funds seeking investment, the rate of interest, and the marginal efficiency of capital. It is worth noting, for example, that debt reduction in England in the twenties probably held down the size of the national income somewhat in that period, while in the United States the reverse was probably true. See U. K. Hicks, *The Finance of British Government, 1920–1936,* pp. 340–42; J. M. Clark, *Strategic Factors in Business Cycles,* p. 99.

seriously strained. One of the indirect burdens of a large public debt consists, then, in the limitation which it may come to constitute on the scope of future fiscal policy. Eventually, a severe depression or a national defense emergency may find the federal government handicapped in meeting the crisis by an imminent limitation on its borrowing power.

The size which the public debt may reach before this danger becomes serious cannot be precisely defined. However, the more important elements which bear upon the matter can be stated. Some of these have already been considered above. First, there is the necessity of increased taxation as the debt increases; for if confidence in the public credit is to be maintained, tax revenue should be increased at least in proportion to increased interest cost on the debt. If at the same time that the debt increases the national income also increases, then the necessary increase in tax rates will be less than otherwise. But with every increase in tax rates there is the danger that the marginal efficiency of capital and the propensity to consume will be adversely affected, and that consequently the increase in the national income may be checked. The public debt may eventually become so large that a further increase in tax rates may decrease tax revenues by decreasing the national income.[30]

Much of course depends upon the nature of the tax system. Consequently it is not possible to set down the maximum ratio of the public debt to the national income upon the basis of an analysis of the maximum percentage of the national income that may be raised through taxation.[31] It is clear, however, that the upper limit of the public debt is related to (a) the size of the national income which can be attained with approximately full employment, and (b) the nature of the tax system, with particular reference to its effects upon the marginal efficiency of capital and the propensity to consume.

A further consideration, of course, is the rate of interest which the government must pay upon its indebtedness; the higher this interest

---

[30] "But it is extremely difficult to give any precise meaning to the concept of the limit of taxable capacity, except in the sense that powerful classes in the community may be unwilling to have particular taxes raised beyond a certain point and consequently withdraw factors of production under their control. It might perhaps be conceded that the limit has been overreached if it could be shown that the national income had been damaged as a result of revenue demands. Well-authenticated long-period examples of this are not unknown to history." U. K. Hicks, *op. cit.*, p. 232.

[31] However, Studenski ventures to state an outside limit: "It is very doubtful whether it is politically feasible for any national government to finance interest charges in excess of 15 per cent of the national income. . . . At a ratio of this sort the debt itself would be two and one-half to three times the size of the national income." P. Studenski, "The Limits to Possible Debt Burdens—Federal, State, and Local," *Am. Econ. Rev.*, Supplement, 1937, XXVII, 69.

rate the greater is the burden of the debt. A closely related difficulty is that of a rising rate of interest. For if, as the government makes successive issues, it must offer more and more attractive terms, the prices of earlier long-term issues are likely to decline. This development in turn is likely to have a bad effect upon the public's reception of the successive issues.

This difficulty suggests one further circumstance that has a bearing upon the problem: the intangible but important matter of public confidence in the government's ability to pay interest and eventually to reduce the debt, in the purposes for which the money is being spent, and in the government's ability to avoid an extreme inflation of prices.

Fortunately we began the depression in 1929 with a very small national debt, and as this debt has increased we have been able to keep the indirect burden of the debt relatively low through the maintenance of low rates of interest. It would be unwise, however, to continue to count on equally low rates of interest as production expands under the national defense program. Certainly it would be wise, as the defense program proceeds and as employment increases, to raise tax rates substantially, at the same time making such changes in the tax system as will minimize possible adverse effects of increased tax rates upon the expansion of production. As full employment is approached, tax rates should be raised to the maximum consistent with the maintenance of the maximum rate of production activity. Even though we may have no present reason to fear collapse of the public credit, if the present emergency should be followed by war, we should need to have our public credit position as strong as possible.

4. *The Effect upon the General Level of Prices*

The fear that the program of deficit financing during the depression would lead to a rapid, inflationary rise in the general level of prices was unjustified so long as a considerable proportion of these public expenditures served simply to finance a more orderly process of liquidation of private debts, and so long as there existed so much underemployment of men and resources. The real danger from such a program comes after recovery is well under way, from the potentiality for expansion of credit which exists in the form of excess reserves created during the preceding period of depression.[32]

With the immediate prospect of still larger public expenditures in connection with the national defense program, the possibility of a con-

[32] It is recognized that present excess reserves are to a very considerable extent attributable to the extraordinary inflow of gold which has occurred in recent years.

siderable rise in the general level of prices becomes greater. We are of course a long way from full employment, and so long as that is the case prices are not likely to rise greatly. Even so, if the defense program continues to expand, some rise of prices even in the present situation of employment is likely to occur. As we learned in 1937, there are so many individual prices which are subject to a considerable degree of control that even a mild expansion of production activity may well bring with it a corresponding upward movement of prices. This possibility is accentuated by the present relatively strong position of the labor movement. The upward movement is likely to be moderate, it is true, as long as so much unemployment of men and resources exists; but the development of bottlenecks in the defense industries may well quicken the movement.

If the national defense program comes to involve very large expenditures, as now appears quite likely, or if this country should be drawn into war, the danger of a rapid rise in the general level of prices will be greatly increased. With the existing excess reserves of the banking system and the potentiality that exists for an expansion of these reserves, the effective exercise of all the available means of credit control together with further increases of tax rates will be necessary to prevent an inflationary rise of prices as full employment is approached.

5. *The Effect upon the Banking System and the Efficacy of Techniques of Credit Control*

It is well known that a substantial proportion of the increase in federal securities since 1930 has been absorbed by the banking system, and the danger in this situation is generally well appreciated. The danger is twofold: a possible danger to the solvency of those banks heavily invested in governments, and a danger to the efficacy of credit control by the Federal reserve.

The danger to the solvency of the banks arises out of the possibility of a rise in interest rates and a fall in the prices of government bonds as business activity expands or as restrictive control upon further expansion of credit comes to be exercised in such a way as to raise interest rates. The danger is easily exaggerated, since it is probable that the banks have prepared for such a contingency by setting up appropriate reserves and by so distributing their maturities as to be able to avoid selling their governments in the market except in case of extraordinary emergency.[33] Of course if business activity expands rapidly under the

[33] It should also be noted that many of the securities held by banks are short-term maturities the value of which would be relatively slightly affected by a rise in interest rates.

stimulus of the defense program, the banks may find it worth their while to unload some of their governments in order to free funds for investment in more attractive opportunities. But if they were to do so, obviously the alternative investment would be sufficiently attractive to warrant the loss that would be taken on the sale of governments. Furthermore, as long as excess reserves are as ample as they are likely to be for some time to come, the banks could both hold their governments to maturity and invest funds in the newly developing opportunities.

The danger to the efficacy of credit control appears more real. For even though the central banking system does not need to fear the effect of a rise in the rate of interest upon the solvency of the banking system, there may be political considerations that would lead control authorities to hesitate to take steps that might result in lower prices for government bonds. Such a move would be highly unpopular with banks, insurance companies, corporations, and individuals that have become heavy investors in governments, and would be disturbing to public confidence in the government's credit. Hence one real danger of the present large public debt lies in the possible limiting effect that it may have upon the exercise of those instruments of credit control that might have the effect of raising the rate of interest.

6. *Conclusions as to Policy*

The preceding analysis of the indirect effects upon the economy of a large public debt yields certain suggestions with respect to policy in the present emergency:

a) The method of further governmental borrowing as a partial means of financing the national defense program has some justification as a means of lightening, for the time being at least, the burden of the program upon the lower income groups. But as full employment is approached and the danger of an inflationary rise of prices becomes real, every precaution should be taken to prevent the further purchase of government securities by the banks, or by individuals with funds borrowed from the banks.

b) As the public debt increases, tax rates should also be increased; and as full employment is approached the revenue from taxes should assume a much larger proportion of the cost of the defense program. In an emergency such as this there is much to be said for a tax system that is highly progressive. For as Pigou has said, ". . . there is a general feeling that, in a pre-eminent national emergency, the call from each should be for his *utmost* rather than for his *share.*"[34] But full consideration must also be given to the necessity of obtaining the maximum revenue without checking the increase of the national income, and without adversely affecting the marginal efficiency of capital, particularly in the defense industries.

c) If the national defense program comes to involve as large annual expenditures as now appear likely, measures may need to be taken, in addition to the increase of tax rates and the restriction upon the expansion of bank credit in connection with the purchase of government security issues, to prevent an inflationary rise in the general level of prices. Existing instruments of credit control should of course be used to prevent an excessive expansion of credit. But if the familiar instruments prove inadequate or if the use of some of these measures is made difficult because of the political consequences that might follow upon a decline of government security prices, then resort should be had to a rigorous rationing of credit, control of the private investment market, and, if necessary, direct regulation of the prices of key commodities, wage rates, and even the rationing of consumers goods.

[34] Pigou, *op. cit.,* p. 246 (Italics in original).

III. FISCAL POLICY AND INFLATION

7

Loans and Taxes in War Finance[*]

By O. M. W. SPRAGUE[†]

All great wars in modern times have been mainly financed by means of issues of paper money, government and bank notes, convertible and inconvertible, and by borrowing. Convertible paper money has narrowly limited possibilities and can only serve as an adjunct to other financial measures. The financial possibilities of inconvertible paper money, though more considerable, are also quite inadequate to meet the huge expenditures of a great war. Except as an extreme measure of last resort, paper money has therefore come to occupy a subordinate position in war finance. The accepted policy, one the effectiveness of which has been tested by much experience, is to issue paper money sparingly and to secure the bulk of the funds required for war by means of loans. It is commonly believed that if additional taxes are levied during the conflict, sufficient to take care of increasing interest charges, a sound and equitable financial policy has been adopted and that to meet even a small part of war expenditure currently from taxation is a counsel of perfection.

The limitations on the possibilities of paper money as the principal means of financing a war are due to its direct effect on prices. The amount of paper which must be issued is so great that it depreciates rapidly and soon becomes practically worthless. Borrowing has greater possibilities if the people generally subscribe to the loans. It does not necessarily and directly bring about an advance in prices, since a part of a stationary volume of the purchasing media of a country may be used over and over again, as it is secured by the government through successive loans. Changes in the volume of trade or in the rapidity of circulation of money may come during a war and occasion some change either upward or downward in the level of prices. A war will also inevitably cause violent changes in the prices of particular commodities.

* *American Economic Review, Proceedings,* 1917. Reprinted by the courtesy of the American Economic Association.

† Formerly Graduate School of Business Administration, Harvard University.

But in the absence of any increase in the volume of the purchasing media there would necessarily be no considerable rise in the level of prices, unless a country is fast approaching a condition of economic exhaustion.

It is not, therefore, absolutely inevitable that war finance based on borrowing should cause a general rise in prices. It is significant, however, that whenever governments have resorted to this policy prices generally have manifested a marked and continued upward tendency; though of course to no such degree as when the attempt has been made to finance war by means of issues of paper money.

War loans would not cause an advance in the level of prices if subscribers to the loans made payment entirely either with accumulated funds on hand or with savings made from current income during the period that the proceeds of each successive loan were being expended. In these circumstances the abnormally large demand of a government for goods and labor would be roughly offset by the curtailed demand of the people generally. But the funds secured by governments through war loans are never derived entirely from savings on hand or which become available while the proceeds of a loan are being expended. Voluntary saving is never sufficiently inclusive and rigorous. Even though greater economy is practiced by most people than in times of peace, subscriptions to successive war loans invariably exceed current savings. Many subscribers borrow from banks the funds required to meet their commitments, pledging other property and even the war loan itself. The banks adopt a liberal patriotic loan policy and also subscribe largely on their own account. These transactions, the borrowing from banks and the investments by banks, occasion expansion in the volume of credit, both in the form of bank notes and of deposits, and are the most potent single cause of the general advance in prices during periods of war. Purchasing power in the possession of the people is reduced by the loan, but not to the full extent of the purchasing power secured by the government. With this purchasing power the warring government enters the market for goods and labor in competition with its own citizens. The government demand is so insistent that it is not lessened by advancing prices. There is simply a more speedy exhaustion of the proceeds of the loan. On the other hand, the demand of the people for goods and labor is reduced in consequence of rising prices. Through this roundabout process a smaller part of the total current products of industry is consumed by the people in the ordinary ways of peace, and a larger part in the shape of military material of all sorts is secured by the government and consumed in the channels of war.

In the course of time, as the proceeds of a loan approach exhaustion, a larger proportion of the total volume of the purchasing media of a country gets back to the people. Another loan is then required unless the government is to resort to unlimited issues of paper money. The successful flotation of a new loan or the continuous sale of short-time obligations again provides a government with the means to enter the market in competition with its own citizens. This process of borrowing and spending can continue for an indefinitely long period if the people are prepared to make the necessary sacrifice of income, and provided also that not too great a part of what is subscribed to each loan consists of additional borrowing from or investment by banks, involving further credit expansion. In other words, a considerable part of each loan must represent savings, a sacrifice of current income on the part of subscribers; otherwise credit expansion will be so rapid as to threaten with collapse the entire credit structure in a fashion analogous to that which results from issues of paper money.

Even if there is an increase in voluntary saving during the course of a war, it is unlikely to be sufficient to counteract fully various influences tending toward a continuous upward movement of prices with each successive loan. With the progress of a long war the output of commodities of all kinds can hardly fail to undergo some diminution as more and more men are required for military service. No corresponding contraction in the volume of the purchasing media is, however, to be anticipated. On the contrary, as a means of facilitating the marketing of successive loans, a policy of continuous, even though moderate, credit expansion is practically certain to be adopted. An easy money market is a desirable, one may even say an essential, condition for carrying through the distribution of a government loan among investors. The process of marketing must be made as easy and simple as possible. Slowly expanding credit and the issue of short-term obligations which may be converted into long-time loans are most helpful devices. Credit contraction is naturally out of the question. Thus while the vital importance of strict economy is being everywhere urged, these easy monetary conditions enable many to satisfy their patriotic impulses by borrowing the funds which they subscribe to war loans, and at the same time postpone the sacrifice of accustomed luxuries and comforts to a more convenient season. Among those also who practice the most rigid economy there are many who subscribe by means of loans much more than they have been able to save. So far as the individual is concerned, future savings are invested in advance when he borrows in order to subscribe to government loans, but until he pays off his loans the arrangement commonly involves an increase in the volume of credit and so contributes to the advance in prices.

It is also to be noted that the initial advance in prices works against that general discontinuance of all unnecessary consumption in order to subscribe to war loans, which is needful if still further price advances are to be avoided. A war inevitably causes radical changes in many incomes. Those engaged in the production of articles for which there is an intense government demand secure exceptionally large wages and profits. Meanwhile the incomes of those engaged in a large number of other pursuits remain stationary or decline. Changes in income would be numerous even though the level of prices remained stationary. Both the number and extent of these changes are, however, much increased in consequence of rising prices. While the real income of the vast majority is reduced, that of a considerable number is enlarged in some instances to an extraordinary extent. These undeserved and temporary gains tempt many to extravagance in consumption. During the tragic course of the present war, the increasing readiness of the peoples of the warring countries to impose additional taxation is at least in part due to the desire to check positively indecent extravagance on the part of those whose incomes have been thus undeservedly increased.

All these conditions and tendencies have been present in the various belligerent countries during the present war. The crisis occasioned by the outbreak of the war, the readjustment of industrial activities, as well as the expense of mobilization, were in a large measure financed through the banks. In Great Britain, where checks are generally used, there was an unparalleled increase of credit in the form of Bank of England deposits. In continental countries there was an analogous increase in bank notes issued by the great central banks. As in the case of an ordinary financial crisis, this expansion of bank credit was a proper and effective means of meeting the sudden requirements occasioned by the outbreak of the war. Unlike the usual course of events following crisis, however, there was no contraction of credit after the period of initial strain had passed. On the contrary, the volume of credits has tended to increase from month to month. Rates for short-time loans have been maintained in the various European money markets in the neighborhood of 5 per cent throughout the war. In both France and Germany there has been something like a threefold increase in the note issues of the central banks of those countries, and in Great Britain a corresponding increase in the deposits of the Bank of England. Deposits in other banks in all the belligerent countries are also vastly greater than they were two years ago. In the meantime prices everywhere have advanced, the index number of the *Economist,* for example, registering an advance from 116.6 in July, 1914, to 153.2 in October, 1915, and to 217.1 at the end of November, 1916.

Borrowing as the principal means of financing a war, it will thus be seen, has some of the defects of paper money. Though not so directly nor to so great an extent, the borrowing policy is practically certain to involve a general advance in prices, which in turn increase the money costs of a war and also cause much undesirable variation in incomes. Against war finance based on borrowing there are, however, other and far more serious objections. It is manifestly unjust and inequitable because it gives not only to property acquired before a war but also to income received during its progress a far higher degree of consideration relative to life than is accorded to them in times of peace. In adopting the borrowing policy a government accepts in the field of finance the voluntary principle without qualification. Interest as a reward is offered at whatever rate is required in order to secure the necessary funds. An analogous situation would present itself if governments relying entirely upon voluntary enlistment offered successive increases in the pay of soldiers whenever the supply of volunteers was inadequate. When wars were waged by small professional armies, the appeal to economic motives was effective in securing an adequate number of recruits. Such appeals obviously would not provide the large armies engaged in modern warfare. Voluntary enlistment from patriotic motives has been tried, but its inadequacy as well as its lack of equality in sacrifice has been made apparent during the course of the present war. Compulsory service will certainly be the policy adopted by belligerent countries in all future wars. Immediate military exigencies will compel resort to this method of raising armies.

Conscription of men should logically and equitably be accompanied by something in the nature of conscription of current income above that which is absolutely necessary. The obligation that each citizen furnish the state in case of war a large portion of his current income manifestly would impose no more oppressive burden than the obligation of military service. To be sure, the pressing necessity which leads to compulsory service is absent since it is possible to finance a war by means of borrowing. Yet as a permanent war finance policy, borrowing has limitations which should exclude it from any comprehensive scheme of military preparedness. Modern wars are so enormously costly that a country which resorts to borrowing has not merely created for itself a difficult problem of taxation after the return of peace; it has also placed itself in a financial position which will make it exceedingly difficult to find the money to maintain and improve its military establishment in future years; it is also likely to find itself quite incapable of financing another war in the near future. Purely as a military measure, then, the conscription of income during a war should be adopted unless such a policy would prove in any way a serious obstacle to the effective conduct of hostilities.

The injustice of treating those who provide the funds for war purposes more generously than those who risk life itself will not be questioned. Consider for a moment the contrast under the borrowing method of war finance between a soldier in receipt of an income of $2500 before a war and his neighbor who remains at home in continued receipt of a similar amount. The civilian reduces his expenditures in every possible way and subscribes a total of $4000 to war loans. He is rewarded with a high rate of interest to which his soldier neighbor must contribute his quota in higher taxes if he is fortunate enough to return from the front. The contrast becomes still greater if, as often happens, the income of the stay-at-home increases during the war and if he is able to secure a superior position. On the other hand, the soldier often finds it difficult to secure a position as good as that from which he was taken at the beginning of the war.

But if borrowing as the principal means of financing a war is so evidently unjust, it is pertinent to inquire why this policy has been so generally adopted and approved. The explanation is in part found in a common misconception regarding the relative importance of the various sources from which the funds subscribed to war loans are derived. Not infrequently it seems to be supposed that war expenditure involves something like an equivalent devotion to war uses of capital and other wealth which were in existence before the outbreak of hostilities. To an audience of economists it hardly needs to be observed that in any event the greater part of war expenditure is derived from current income, most of which but for the war would have been devoted to the satisfaction of individual wants and so completely consumed.

Most of the capital and other property in existence within a country at the beginning of a war is not and cannot be converted into funds with which to prosecute the conflict. Property can, of course, be sold and the funds secured from the sale subscribed to war loans, but such transactions are merely transfers and do not increase the amount of funds within the country available for war purposes. Aside from the sale of securities in foreign countries and the exportation of gold and other valuables, a country cannot convert any large part of its past savings into uninvested funds. Modern warfare requires the use of a large part of the capital equipment of a country and it must therefore be maintained throughout the contest in a high state of efficiency. A part of the capital invested in a plant which cannot be employed for military purposes may, indeed, be idle because there is no demand for its products. Factories for the production of luxuries may be taken as an example; though it may be noted that during the present war some use has been found for nearly every variety of factory and workshop. Factories for which a use cannot be found may not be kept in repair during a war, and if it lasts long enough may fall into complete decay. The loss will be one of the costs of the war but will in no way contribute anything toward necessary military expenditure. Capital in the form of stocks of goods may gradually become available as the proceeds of sales are invested in government loans rather than in the replenishment of stock. Similarly, durable goods in the possession of consumers, such as clothing and furniture, may be made to last an abnormally long time and only absolutely necessary replacements may be made. In this way the accumulated possessions of the people may contribute to the conduct of a war, not by being used directly, but because they enable the people to devote a larger portion of income to war purposes than would be possible if at the beginning of the war their personal belongings were less abundant and durable.

In these various ways a considerable amount of funds for war purposes can be extracted from the capital and other property in existence before the outbreak of hostilities. A borrowing policy (aside from foreign loans), which should limit borrowing to antebellum wealth which might become available for new investments, would be entirely consistent with the equities of the situation created by war. But by far the lion's share of the funds subscribed to war loans is not derived from this source. It represents new savings from current income and the curtailment of individual consumption brought about by rising prices. If all these savings, and also the income which might have been saved but is in fact expended, were taken by the tax gatherer, it is certain that there would be slight need for domestic borrowing. Much of the preëxisting capital as it became available for new uses could be reinvested in those particular branches of industry in which additional facilities seemed to promise satisfactory returns.

General acquiescence in the policy of borrowing for war purposes is by no means to be attributed solely to misconceptions regarding the relative importance of the sources from which funds subscribed to war loans are derived. It is also commonly believed that by borrowing the burden of war costs is shifted from the present to future generations.

Such shifting is in large measure illusory. A burden can indeed be placed on future generations, but the generation conducting the war does not escape. A nation at the end of the war is poorer by the amount that its capital and other wealth is less than it would have been if there had been no war. This loss is inevitably greater if the borrowing rather than the taxation policy is adopted, because, as we have seen, borrowing does not reduce unnecessary consumption to the greatest possible extent.

Taking a community as a whole, a war debt is of course in no sense an asset. This would be evident enough if the ownership of the debt was distributed among the people in exact proportion to the additional taxes which they must pay in order to meet interest and sinking fund requirements. Owing to the manner in which the debt is in fact held, it alters to the disadvantage of the great majority of the people the distribution of the total income of the community. On the return of peace those who served in the armies will, generally speaking, enjoy a smaller share in the national dividend because they were deprived of the opportunity to earn income from which savings might be made for subscriptions to war loans. Large numbers of those who remain at home either because of a decline in their incomes or on account of advancing prices are also unable to save their quota of the war debts, and consequently find themselves in a less favorable position than at the beginning of the war. A fortunate and perhaps more thrifty minority become owners of the government debt and enjoy a rent charge on the income of the community which continues until the principal of their claim is returned to them.

There is one conceivable arrangement under which the burden of a war debt might be transferred entirely to future generations. If interest did not begin to accrue on the loans for twenty or thirty years after they were issued the generation conducting a war would escape. Even so, the immediate relief would be less than that which might be secured if the war were financed by taxation. Extravagant consumption would not be so completely curtailed and consequently to a somewhat greater extent the war would be financed from capital existing before the conflict which might become available for new investment during its progress. But this plan is obviously impracticable. Inasmuch as loans cannot be floated on a deferred interest basis the generation which conducts a war by borrowing must shoulder an increased burden of taxation for the benefit of those who were fortunate and prudent enough to subscribe to government war loans.

To war finance based mainly on borrowing there are, then, fundamental objections. During the years immediately following the conflict it impairs the ability of a country to keep up its military preparations, to say nothing of its power to undertake another war. It accentuates the redistribution of incomes during a war. It is unjust to all those who serve in the armies and also to many who remain at home. It enables a small section of the population to enjoy undiminished or enlarged incomes which are either expended extravagantly or become a claim upon the income of the community for an indefinitely long period in the future.

But although in all these ways borrowing as a means of financing a great war is most unsatisfactory, it has one advantage which cannot be questioned. It works. If a people are heartily in favor of a war, directly through the funds subscribed to loans and indirectly through the forced economy of those with stationary or declining incomes occasioned by rising prices, governments can secure command of a very large proportion of the labor force in a country and the use of much of its capital. Large armies can be formed and supported and enormous quantities of military supplies can be produced. Even though the burden is unevenly distributed, the transfer of labor and capital from the activities of peace to those of war is successfully accomplished.

It boots nothing, therefore, to dilate upon the equity and remote advantages of taxation over borrowing, unless it can be shown that by some other method the productive forces of a country can be as speedily transferred and as effectively exerted in the production of the large and varied supplies of material required in the conduct of a modern war. Equity would indeed sanction taxing away all income received during a war in excess of that which each citizen had received during the year preceding the conflict, and also so much of ordinary income as was not needed for absolutely necessary consumption. Taxation on this onerous scale would virtually eliminate the ordinary economic motives for effort and sacrifice. What would be the effect on production? There is no experience whatever on which to base a judgment. I venture to think, however, that no serious difficulties would be encountered when millions of men were fighting in the trenches during a great war in which a people believed that its vital interests were at stake.

In the first place, it may be stated with confidence that all the various considerations of which account must be taken in framing a permanent taxation policy have no bearing when it is a question of taxation for a limited period and for a specific purpose. Accepted canons of taxation and most economic principles have no application amid the conditions which develop during a great modern war. It is not necessary, for example, to take account of the effect of onerous taxation on saving and on the investment of capital. It is the avowed purpose of the state to secure through taxation all that can be saved. Onerous income taxes will not weaken the motive for maintaining the capital which was in existence before the war, because it will become the basis for the accustomed return to its owners upon the restoration of peace. In any event, whether the state borrows or taxes there will be less capital at the end of the war than at the beginning. But as we have seen, a greater part of the capital of the country is likely to be absorbed under the borrowing policy because it does not reduce individual consumption to the greatest possible extent.

It would seem at first sight that if no income could be saved for investment during a war serious difficulty might be encountered in securing the necessary additions to plants required for the production of munitions and other military supplies. Experience during the present war, however, proves quite conclusively that these requirements are too great and immediate to wait upon the slow processes of the adjustment of facilities of supply to demand working through prices and business profits. The warring governments have been obliged to undertake the erection or direct control of plants and the organization of production, not only of munitions but also of other indispensable articles. Much has of course been done by private enterprise but commonly under conditions which guaranteed against loss. Both these methods would be equally feasible even though there were no new savings available for investment. Within moderate limits, the cost of converting plant to war uses could be charged as at present to operating costs and not to capital account. Much capital also would become available for investment through the liquidation of capital in branches of industry unfavorably affected by the war. It would also be quite possible, and indeed this has happened during the present war, for governments to make advances of funds to private concerns for capital expenditure.

During a great war it would also seem that the chance of making large profits is not needed to secure persistent effort and readiness to assume business risks. Patriotic motives in the business and financial world even now in some degree take the place of ordinary economic motives, even though no strong appeal has been made to them. But it is also to be noted that business risks are far less than in times of peace even under conditions as they develop when a war is financed by borrowing, and these risks would be still further reduced if the taxation policy were adopted. In any event, the warring state takes a leading rôle in determining the direction of production. A large part of the total output of industry is in response to government orders. Those who supply the wayward demands of the few whose incomes have been increased by war do indeed incur serious risks. But if all income were heavily taxed there would be little or no demand of this character. Marketing risks would be reduced to a minimum, since virtually all the labor and capital of a country would be employed in producing articles of necessary consumption and military supplies.

Finally it may be observed that the evident justice of a policy under which no one would reap an economic benefit from a war, even though it might cause some relaxation of effort on the part of a few, would certainly stimulate the vast majority of people to greater efforts. In England, for example, during the present war, the large gains and extravagance of a few have caused serious discontent in labor circles, a grievance which was in some degree finally removed by means of the excess profits tax.

The abrupt curtailment of individual consumption which would come with the adoption of this taxation policy would occasion no serious disturbance in the labor markets. In all the warring countries it has been found necessary to utilize the labor of women to an unprecedented extent. The enormous number of men absorbed in the armies, together with the large government demand for goods, has much more than offset the reduction in the demand for labor in various peaceful pursuits.

More serious difficulties might be encountered by those having capital invested in the luxury trades. But thanks to the great variety of modern military requirements, a use can be found for much plant of this kind. It is reported, for example, that during the present war even candy kitchens and photographic studios have been utilized. Supplies of articles of luxury on hand can largely be disposed of in neutral markets. Moreover, the consumption of luxuries in a warring country would not be entirely discontinued if, as they properly should be, rates of taxation were so limited as not to occasion a serious change in the standard of life of any class in the community. During a great war it would be entirely equitable to tax far beyond the limit set by the standard of life, but practical considerations forbid. Taxation which would make necessary revolutionary changes might well occasion a greater loss in efficiency than would be offset by the gain in revenue. To take anything like half of incomes of say $3000 would be equitable, but it would involve changes in the manner of living which could only be made with the very greatest difficulty. On the other hand, to tax 50 per cent of incomes of $40,000 or 90 per cent of incomes of a million or more would still leave enough to permit in all essentials the maintenance of the standard of life to which the recipients of such incomes are accustomed.

It is of course impossible to determine in advance of experience just how far it would be possible to go in financing a war by taxes on income. Tentatively, and mainly for illustrative purposes, the following scheme of taxation may be suggested. All incomes, or at all events 90 per cent of all income, in excess of the average annual income received during the two years preceding a war should go to the state. This proposal simply involves an extension of the excess profits tax which has been adopted very generally during the present war. In addition ordinary income should be taxed "to the bone" but not beyond the point which would still leave every class of taxpayers sufficient income to maintain the essentials of its customary standard of life. Let us assume as a starting point a special war tax of 5 per cent on incomes of $1500, or perhaps $1200, of 10 per cent on incomes of $2000 and of 20 per cent on incomes of $5000. By successive stages the rates would be increased until 50 per cent of incomes of $40,000 and, let us say, all income in excess of $100,000 were taken by the state during the period of the war. These taxes would after all represent nothing more than patriotic citizens might be expected and urged to save and to invest in government loans under the borrowing policy of war finance. The imposition of these taxes would of course require a reorganization of all war charity, but the alleviation of much of the distress occasioned by war which is now left to private benevolence is properly a government function and could be far more effectively handled through its agency. In addition to taxes on income, special taxes on a few articles entering into general consumption should be imposed. A tax on sugar of five cents a pound, with correspondingly heavy taxes on tobacco and beverages, alcoholic and non-alcoholic, would presumably be sufficient for the purpose of reaching those whose incomes are too small to warrant resort to direct taxation. A high tax of say fifty cents a gallon on gasoline and on other articles of which enormous quantities are required for military use would also be advisable.

A war finance policy based on taxation presupposes that a country must have established and in operation highly developed income-tax machinery in time of peace, so that it may have at its disposal full information regarding the income of its citizens. It would also seem essential that the policy should have been carefully considered and that the people should have definitely decided in favor of its adoption as an integral part of its military program. It would indeed be highly advantageous to enact legislation authorizing the imposition of war rates of income taxation by executive proclamation upon the outbreak of hostilities. It might also prove advisable to provide that the tax rates to be imposed at the outset should be at half the rates which would become effective at the end of a period of six months of war. By that time the initial disturbance occasioned by the outbreak of war would have passed and it would be possible to judge with some certainty whether the country was engaged in a long and arduous contest.

This paper is primarily concerned with the underlying principles which should determine financial policy in time of war. But a few matters of less fundamental importance may be given passing consideration. As regards the proposed income taxes, a single annual collection would be unsatisfactory on fiscal grounds. The enormous payments to be made might seriously dislocate the banking machinery of a country. Monthly or quarterly payments would in large measure meet these difficulties. Payment of the taxes at frequent intervals would also reduce to a minimum loss of revenue from irresponsible individuals who otherwise might spend in extravagant consumption the funds which should have been set aside to meet the tax on their incomes. It would also be desirable to provide that tax payments might be made in short-time interest-bearing obligations of the government. Purchases of these obligations by those subject to income tax would provide a government with a reasonably steady supply of funds probably quite as effectively as under the present financial policy based on borrowing. In order to provide a comfortable working balance and to meet initial expenditures, a government loan at the beginning of a war would probably be necessary. Such a loan, absorbing uninvested funds accumulated before the conflict, would not run counter to the equities of the situation created by war.

War finance based on taxation has many advantages over either the paper money or the borrowing policy. One of these advantages, even though it is not the most important, may properly be given special consideration, because it would contribute much to the feasibility of the taxation policy. Both paper money and borrowing, as we have seen, are certain to bring about a general advance in the level of prices. It will, I think, be readily granted that a belligerent country which financed itself entirely (aside from foreign loans) by means of income taxes, supplemented by taxes on a few commodities, would experience little or no advance in the general level of prices. There would be no influence at work tending toward an increase in the total volume of its purchasing media. Surely not many would seek loans from banks for the purpose of maintaining accustomed expenditure, and banks certainly would not give favorable consideration to such loans. Prices in neutral countries would of course advance if they were resorted to for supplies on the scale witnessed during the present war. But it is one of the advantages of the taxation policy over borrowing, that it would greatly reduce the volume of goods imported to a warring country. Imports of luxuries would inevitably fall off. Moreover, owing to the smaller demand for luxuries produced at home, more labor would be set free for the production of necessaries and of military supplies, thus in turn reducing importations of such commodities.

The adoption of the taxation policy would not of course eliminate all changes in income during a war. It would, however, diminish the number of such changes and also confine them within narrower limits than is possible under the conditions of rapidly rising prices, which are found whenever a war is financed by means of paper money or borrowing. Comparatively stable prices would facilitate the execution of the income-tax policy in two ways. In the first place, the amount of excess profits as well as the number in receipt of such profits would be far less considerable than has been the case in past wars. And second, the special war tax on ordinary income would occasion less disturbance, since the necessary curtailment of expenditure would be more exactly estimated by the people generally if something like the accustomed level of prices were maintained. To those in receipt of stationary incomes of moderate size, it may be added, the proposed taxes would be less burdensome than the deprivation resulting from the rise of prices under the borrowing policy in the countries now at war.

The avoidance of rising prices is by no means the most important of the advantages to be derived from financing a war by taxation rather than by loans. There are indeed a number of other advantages which are of decidedly greater importance. To finance a war to the greatest possible extent currently from taxation is just. It would place all citizens upon an equal footing in so far as war conditions will permit. It would leave a country in far better position to make preparation for and to conduct future wars if they unhappily should come. The return to peaceful activities would be enormously simplified. Taxation would then be somewhat more burdensome than before the war, but the increase would be insignificant in comparison with that which must be borne if the borrowing policy is adopted. Moreover, the proceeds of the additional taxes would be used chiefly to relieve the families of those who were killed or the soldiers who were incapacitated during the war.

The danger that class antagonism may develop even to the point of revolutionary outbreaks would be eliminated. Finally the taxation policy would leave a country in a vastly better position for further industrial development, to compete in the markets of the world and above all to take up its social and other civilizing activities more nearly where they were interrupted at the outbreak of hostilities.

8

*The Behavior of Money National Income under Inflationary Conditions**

By ARTHUR SMITHIES†

The writer on inflation is fortunate in that his subject is generally well understood by economists, since its dramatic empirical manifestations leave little room for dispute as to the general conclusions to which theoretical analysis should lead. In this article, therefore, I shall content myself with setting up some simple models which I hope may be of assistance to the practical economist who is engaged in estimating the quantitative implications of an inflationary policy. Assuming that the government proposes to carry out a policy of applying a given proportion of the national income to war purposes by means of inflationary finance, it seems to me that the main questions that the economist should answer are: Has the inflation an upper limit, or will it continue indefinitely? What is that limit, if any? At what speed will the inflation progress?

I shall call the two methods by which I shall approach the problem the Keynesian method and the Tinbergian method.[1] Analyses based on the work of Keynes and Tinbergen lend themselves most readily to quantitative treatment and are, in fact, the types of analyses that are being most widely used at the present time. The Keynesian method is essentially the equilibrium method and enables one to give an answer

---

* *Quarterly Journal of Economics,* Nov. 1942. Reprinted by the courtesy of the *Quarterly Journal of Economics* and the author.

† Harvard University.

[1] J. M. Keynes, *General Theory of Employment, Interest and Money* (London, 1936); J. Tinbergen, *Business Cycles in the United States of America* (League of Nations, 1939), and elsewhere. Although my terminology inevitably does less than justice to the other distinguished workers in dynamic economics, Tinbergen has been preëminent in endowing dynamic models of the economy as a whole with empirical significance. I should like to enter a plea that those economists who consider themselves "non-mathematical" should not shun Tinbergen's work. Teaching experience has demonstrated to me that the essentials of his system can be mastered without difficulty by students who have had no more mathematics than some elementary algebra.

to the first two of the questions posed above. The more powerful method of Tinbergen is essentially dynamic and provides an answer to all three questions.

DEFINITIONS AND ASSUMPTIONS

I shall assume that the economy is initially in an equilibrium position of full employment. Real income, i.e. national income valued at the initial prices, Q is assumed to be incapable of further increase, and prices are unchanging. Gross money national income, Y, is divided into war expenditure, W, and consumption, C. War expenditure includes all expenditure by the Federal Government plus gross private investment expenditure. I have called this whole amount war expenditure, on the assumption that it will include no elements that can be eliminated during the period of the war. Consumption means consumption expenditure excluding all Federal taxation. Saving, S, will then include saving in the ordinary sense plus Federal taxation. On these definitions, therefore, war expenditure and savings are identically equal.

The average level of prices $P = Y/Q$. It is assumed that this average is significant, especially in the sense that it will represent adequately the prices of war goods (the objects of war expenditure) and consumption goods. I assume, in general, that changes in Y cause changes in P. Autonomous price increases, when decisions of producers to raise price result in an increase in income, are excluded except where expressly mentioned.

Our assumption that Q remains constant implies that it is always profitable to produce Q, and that this is independent of the behavior of wages. There is therefore no necessary unique relation between wages and prices. I shall assume, in general, that the wages bill, L, is related to P by a national wages policy (or the lack of it). I shall also assume, in general, that the adjustment of wages to price proceeds continuously, but we shall take notice of the possibility of discontinuous adjustments and autonomous wage changes.

The economy is assumed to be closed, in the sense that the value of imports does not increase as a result of the inflation. The value of exports above the value of imports is included in our definition of war expenditure.

It is assumed that throughout the inflationary process the economy is unaffected by changes in taxation, price-control, priorities or any other relevant policy.

We can now define an inflationary policy simply as a policy which aims at establishing war expenditure at a higher proportion of national income than is being saved at the initial equilibrium position. It will be noted that this definition is independent of the source of the funds expended by the Government. Any policy, whether financed by taxation, borrowing from individuals, or the printing of notes, is inflationary, provided that it initially increases war expenditure by more than it decreases consumption. This is not meant to imply that I do not consider the mopping-up of idle money a desirable policy as a safeguard against future panic expenditure; and we shall see later that an inflation financed initially by a progressive income tax will be more likely to have an upper limit than one financed by borrowing.

In the following sections we shall analyze the effects of an inflationary policy designed to maintain war expenditure at a given proportion of national income. The problems dealt with are therefore the problems of the operation of a full-fledged war economy, rather than those of the transition from a peace-time economy. The country is assumed to have reached the happy state of having solved its allocation and production problems, so that the problem resolves itself to one of finance. If this is borne in mind, the reader will have less difficulty in accepting some of the assumptions, especially as to wages and prices, on which the analysis of this paper is based.

THE KEYNESIAN METHOD

This analysis can be most easily presented by means of a diagram (Fig. 1). Let national income be measured horizontally, and war expenditure and saving vertically. Then let *OA* be the initial equilibrium value of income, *Q*. This will be determined by the intersection of normal[2] propensity to save line, *ODB,* and the rate of war expenditure, *OC.* The propensity to save line is determined by the taxation system, which we shall assume to continue to remain in force, and by the desire of the economy to save in the ordinary sense.

Now suppose at prevailing prices the Government proposes to increase *W* to *OE* and to maintain it at the proportion *OE*/*OA* of *Y*. Then for any value of *Y,* the money value of *W* will be given by the line *OG.*

Let *BH* represent the normal marginal propensity to save out of national income above its initial value, *OA.* There is, of course, no reason to believe that the slope of *BH* will be equal to the slope of *BO,* since increases of *Y* up to *OA* involve increases of real income, while increases beyond *OA* represent merely an inflation of money values. By "normal value" I mean the marginal propensity to save that will be

[2] The meaning of the term "normal" is explained in the next paragraph but one.

eventually established for any level of income that remains constant for a sufficient period of time. It has been frequently pointed out[3] that under the impact of additional war expenditure the marginal propensity to save is temporarily increased, and it is only after time has been allowed for the multiplier effect to work itself out fully that the marginal propensity to save returns to its normal level. In fact, it is this distortion of the marginal propensity to save that, if nothing else does,[4] will ensure the identity of war expenditure and saving at every point of time.

Conditions for the eventual outcome of the inflation may now be deduced from the diagram. If the slope of *BH* is greater than that of *OG*, the inflation may eventually come to an end; for a level of national income exists at which the normal savings of the economy are

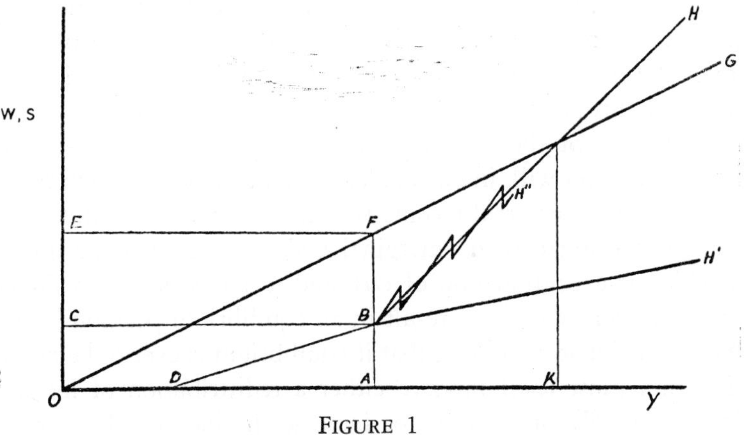

FIGURE 1

equal to the amount of war expenditure. Such a situation is depicted in Figure 1. A new equilibrium is established at income *OK*, and the average price inflation that has occurred above the initial price level will be *AK/OA*. If the slope of *BH* is equal to, or less than, that of *OG*, the inflation will go on indefinitely; there will be a widening gap between war expenditure and normal savings, which must be bridged by abnormal savings induced by the ever increasing rate of war expenditure. We can, therefore, formulate the following rule: An inflation will have an upper limit, if the proportion of war expenditure to national income is less than the marginal propensity to save out of inflated income. Otherwise it will continue indefinitely.

It will be readily perceived that our solution so far is incomplete.

[3] E.g., Keynes, *op. cit.,* p. 23; also my "Process Analysis and Equilibrium Analysis," *Econometrica,* Jan., 1942, p. 30.

[4] This equality may also be maintained as a result of other significant, but not necessary, lags in the system.

We have proved that there exists a possible upper limit to the inflation, but we have not shown that this limit will be approached in all circumstances, or, if not all, in what circumstances. In fact, the methods we are employing in this section provide no solution to this problem. We shall see, however, in the next section that in our present problem it does happen that the existence of an economically possible equilibrium in general implies convergence to it. The chief danger of this not being so lies in the possibility of anarchical panic spending as the inflation gets under way, which may cause the system to overshoot the equilibrium mark.

The magnitude of the upper limit, if it exists, is determined, as may be seen from the diagram, by the proportion of war expenditure to national income, the average propensity to save out of the initial value of national income, and the marginal propensity to save out of inflated income. The determination of the first two of these factors is beyond the scope of this paper, but the last we have now to discuss.

If the desire of the economy to save depends on its real income alone, the inflation will, in our model, have no effect on the proportion of income saved, since real income is assumed constant. In this case the normal propensity to save (marginal and average) will be given by *BH′*, which is a continuation of *OB*, and it is obvious from Figure 1 that the inflation will never result in an equilibrium position being attained. It is evident, therefore, that if equilibrium is ever to be attained, the inflation must itself produce either a redistribution of income in favor of relatively high savers, or increase the individual's propensity to save out of a given real income, or both.

The most important distinction to be made when considering the distribution of incomes in this connection is the distribution between wage-earners and non-wage-earners. I shall assume, as Tinbergen does, that changes in the relative shares of these groups are the main distribution factors affecting the propensity to save. A redistribution in favor of non-wage-earners will increase the propensity to save and *vice versa.* In our present model the distribution of income will then depend on the relation of wages to prices. Redistribution of income within the non-wage-earners group, notably between the fixed income group and equity owner, while of great social importance, is probably of secondary significance from the point of view of its effect on the propensity to save.

The main factor affecting the individual's propensity to save out of an inflated money income seems to me to be the incidence of the progressive income tax. We can assume that increases in the proportion of income to be paid as income tax will be borne partly out of consumption. An increase in money incomes will automatically increase the proportion paid as income tax and, consequently, will increase the propensity to save. It is for this reason that an inflationary movement financed by income taxation is less serious than one financed by borrowing. The former process must come to an end somewhere, since, if the wage rate went up to $5,000,000 a year, at least 80 per cent of the national income would go to the tax collector. I do not know of any empirical studies of this problem, but my guess is that the income tax effect alone should not be relied on to stop an inflation within reasonable limits. The argument of this paragraph only holds without qualification in so far as income tax payments are made, or provision is made for them, without a time lag. Otherwise the speed of inflation may be sufficiently great for the lag to have a greater effect in reducing the propensity to save than the progressiveness of the tax system has in increasing it.

The incidence of policies of selective price control and rationing may be changed by inflationary conditions, but I know of no *a priori* reason why they should. These policies are of course of great importance in determining the initial average propensity to save, but I shall assume that they do not produce changes in that propensity under inflationary conditions.

In view of these considerations, I assume that the behavior of wages in relation to prices is a major factor affecting the propensity to save, so that the slope of the line *BH* depends largely on wage policy; and if my assumption is correct, we reach the unwelcome conclusion that a policy that succeeds in maintaining the level of real wages throughout an inflation will ensure its indefinite continuance. On the other hand, if money wages are frozen at any level, the inflation will eventually come to an end, provided that the ratio of war expenditure to income is less than the marginal propensity to save of non-wage-earners.

If wages are adjusted to the cost of living discontinuously, rather than continuously, our diagram can easily be adapted to meet the situation. Suppose it is known that when prices have risen to given levels, certain wage increases will occur, but otherwise wages remain constant. On our assumptions as to the determination of prices, such a rise of wages will have no direct effect on prices, but will redistribute income in favor of wage-earners and so cause an abrupt drop in the propensity to save, which will then increase as prices increase and the distribution of income moves against wage-earners. This situation is shown by the zigzag line *BH″* in Figure 1.

We now go to the third question posed above: what will be the speed of the inflation? Although, as I said above, our analysis thus far does not enable us to deal with this problem quantitatively, we can at least list the relevant considerations here. The speed of inflation will depend on the significant lags in the system. That there are significant lags is obvious; for, if there were not, prices under an inflationary stimulus would move to their upper limit instantaneously, or if there were no such limit, the whole price system would immediately evaporate. That these results do not ensue is due to lags; and the more lags there are and the greater their length, the slower will be the speed of inflation. The lags that are of chief importance are the following:

(1) The lag, to which we have already referred, between the initial impact of an increment war expenditure and the establishment of the marginal propensity to save at its normal level. The length of this lag is associated with the income velocity of money, and its length depends in the main on the lag between the earning of profits and their distribution. The operation of this lag will certainly prevent the inflation proceeding with infinite speed; but it must be remembered that once an inflation gets sufficiently under way, people will make every effort to shorten or even reverse the lag. The magnitude of the German inflation is largely a monument to their success. This is where panic expenditure enters the picture.

(2) The lag between the prices that determine the rate of war expenditure and that expenditure. It seems that whatever its practical importance, this lag is conceptually necessary for an understanding of the dynamics of inflation. That is, prices determine the amount of war expenditure. If it is assumed that prices and war expenditure are simultaneously determined, it is possible to obtain absurd results. The causal sequence should run prices → war expenditure → prices rather than prices ⇄ war expenditure. To be consistent with our assumption that the Government obtains for war purposes a given fraction of the national income, we should assume that the prices that it actually pays are those that determine the amount of its expenditure.

(3) The lag between prices and wages. Whatever wage policy is adopted, it is probable that it can only be given effect with some lag; so that wages may depend not on present but on past prices.

Before concluding this section, we must consider briefly the possibility of price and wage changes that are determined by factors exogenous to our model. The model assumes a causal sequence income → prices → wages, but it is also necessary to consider the possibilities: (1) wages → prices → income; (2) wages → income → prices; and

(3) prices → wages → income. To simplify the discussion I shall assume that the model is in equilibrium. All the assumptions previously made as to the working of the model are retained, except in so far as they are abrogated by this discussion. I shall assume initially that the propensity of the economy to save depends exclusively on the distribution of income between wage-earners and non-wage-earners.

(1) Suppose wages increase by 10 per cent, and producers increase price by 10 per cent, then the economy will be again in equilibrium. If prices are increased by more than 10 per cent, income will be redistributed in favor of non-wage-earners and the propensity to save will be increased. If full employment is to be maintained, prices must fall until they are 10 per cent above their original level. If producers raise prices by less than 10 per cent or not at all, the situation can be maintained, but since income has been redistributed in favor of wage-earners, the propensity to save has been reduced, and consumer demand has risen; producers can continue to raise prices and sell their whole outputs until prices are 10 per cent above their original level.

(2) If wages rise by 10 per cent, but prices are initially unchanged, the propensity to save will be decreased, income will increase and prices will rise until they are 10 per cent above their initial level. The difference between this case and the last one is that, whereas in that case we assumed that producers fixed their prices at a certain level in response to the wage change, in the present case prices are determined by income.

(3) This case differs from case (1) only in that the initial autonomous change is a change of prices. A rise of wages is, however, more likely to produce a corresponding rise of prices than a rise of prices is to produce a corresponding rise of wages; and furthermore, even though producers may not spontaneously raise prices in response to wage increase, the increase in demand will induce them to. But there probably are no forces of equal strength tending to ensure a rise of wages in response to a rise of prices. Hence while an autonomous rise of wages is likely to produce a corresponding rise of prices, an autonomous rise of prices is likely to be untenable, since, for it to be effective, wages must increase correspondingly.

If we assume that saving is increased by a rise in prices, our conclusions must be modified: a given percentage rise of wages will require a somewhat smaller percentage rise of prices in order to reëstablish equilibrium.

Autonomous changes of wages or prices may, of course, be superimposed on inflationary processes of the type described by the model. This naturally impairs the use of the model for predicting the upper limit of an inflationary process, but, even so, its use for determining whether such a limit exists will not be affected.

THE TINBERGIAN METHOD

In this section the model will be subject to the assumptions that have already been made, but we shall not consider autonomous price and wage changes. We shall now formulate a system of relations giving effect to those assumptions, and these relations will be assumed to be linear.

W is proportional to *Y*, or, what comes to the same thing, to P. Thus

(1) $$W = \alpha Y,$$

where α is the fixed proportionality factor. This relation may operate with a lag. Thus

(1*a*) $$W = \alpha Y_{-1}$$

The subscript indicates the value of *Y* one unit of time ago, the unit of time being so chosen. In what follows I shall assume for simplicity that all the lag periods are of equal length. This assumption is, of course, not necessary for the application of the method.

Consumption is the sum of

(1) Wage-earners consumption C_w, which depend on *L*, i.e.

$$C_w = \epsilon_1 L + \delta_1$$

(2) Non-wage-earners consumption C_n out of a constant income, which depends on non-wage-earners income *Z* in a similar way, i.e.

$$C_n = \epsilon_2 Z + \delta_2.$$

In these relations ϵ_1 and ϵ_2 are necessarily positive and less than unity; and we assume $\epsilon_1 > \epsilon_2$. Since the income tax effect will tend to decrease the proportion of non-wage-earners' money income consumed, and the redistribution effect, if any, of the inflation will tend to increase their real incomes, we conclude that non-wage-earners will consume a decreasing proportion of the increasing money incomes, so that $\delta_2 > 0$. Wage-earners will be subject to the income tax effect probably to a lesser extent; and to the extent that income is redistributed against them, their real incomes will fall as their money incomes increase. Hence δ_1 may be positive or negative.

(3) A term to take account of consumption being abnormally low, as a result of the time required for the multiplier to work itself out. As was said above, this effect is felt chiefly in non-wage-earners expendi-

ture, and its strength may be assumed to depend on the rate at which Z has been increasing over the last unit of term. Thus are added a negative term to our formula for C_n : $-\beta(Z - Z_{-1})$.

Thus we have

$$C = \epsilon_1 L + \delta_1 + \epsilon_2 Z + \delta_1 - \beta(Z - Z_{-1}). \tag{2}$$

Since we may assume that, however fast Z increases, C_n will increase to some extent, we conclude $\beta < \epsilon_2$.

Wage changes depend on changes on prices. Thus letting L_0 and P_0 be the initial values of L and P, we may write

$$\begin{aligned} L &= L_0\left(1 + \lambda\frac{P - P_0}{P_0}\right) \\ &= L_0\left(1 + \lambda\left(\frac{Y}{Q} - 1\right)\right) \\ &= L_0(1 - \lambda) + \frac{L_0\lambda}{Q}Y. \end{aligned}$$

Thus we may write

$$L = \gamma Y + \eta \tag{3}$$

or if prices are adjusted to wages with a lag

$$L = \gamma Y_{-1} + \eta. \tag{3a}$$

It may be assumed that $0 \leqq \lambda \leqq 1$, so that $0 \leqq \gamma < 1$; $\eta \geqq 0$.

In addition, we have the following identities:

$$Y = L + Z \tag{4}$$

$$Y = C + S \tag{5}$$

$$W = S \tag{6}$$

These relations represent a closed system, and by a process of elimination a linear difference equation in any one of the variables may be found. The most convenient variable for our purpose is Y. We shall consider in order the solutions obtained by using the systems of relations (*a*): (1), (2), (3), (4), (5) and (6); (*b*): (1*a*), (2), (3), (4), (5) and (6); (*c*): (1*a*), (2), (3*a*), (4), (5) and (6). The most convenient method of elimination is to express both sides of equation (6) in terms of Y.

From system (*a*) we get:

$$Y[1 - \epsilon_1\gamma - \epsilon_2(1 - \gamma) - \alpha + \beta(1 - \gamma)] - Y_{-1}\beta(1 - \gamma) - [\eta(\epsilon_1 - \epsilon_2) + \delta_1 + \delta_2] = 0 \tag{7}$$

From system (*b*):

$$Y[1 - \epsilon_1\gamma - \epsilon_2(1 - \gamma) + \beta(1 - \gamma)] - Y_{-1}[\alpha + \beta(1 - \gamma)] - [\eta(\epsilon_1 - \epsilon_2) + \delta_1 + \delta_2] = 0 \tag{8}$$

From system (c):

(9) $$Y(1 - \epsilon_2 + \beta) - Y_{-1}[\epsilon_1\gamma - \epsilon_2\gamma + \alpha + \beta(1+\gamma)] + \beta\gamma Y_{-2} - [\eta(\epsilon_1 - \epsilon_2) + \delta_1 + \delta_2] = 0$$

In considering these equations, we are interested in knowing whether there exists an economically possible equilibrium position for the systems they represent, and whether, for any initial value of income, this equilibrium position will be approached.

Equilibrium is reached if income attains a constant value, and its value Y_E is obtained by dropping the subscriptions and solving for Y. For each equation we thus obtain

(10) $$Y_E = \frac{\eta(\epsilon_1 - \epsilon_2) + \delta_1 + \delta_2}{1 - \epsilon_1\gamma - \epsilon_2(1-\gamma) - \alpha}$$

Since the numerator is positive, Y_E will be positive if, and only if, the denominator is positive. Since only positive values of Y are economically possible, the condition we require is that the denominator is greater than zero. That is

(11) $$\alpha < 1 - \epsilon_1\gamma - \epsilon_2(1-\gamma)$$

Differentiating (2) with respect to Y, and assuming $\beta = 0$

(12) $$\left(\frac{dC}{dY}\right)_N = \epsilon_1\frac{dL}{dY} + \epsilon_2\frac{dZ}{dY}$$

where the subscript N indicates the normal propensity to consume. Differentiating (3) and (4) with respect to Y and substituting in (12)

$$\left(\frac{dC}{dY}\right)_N = \epsilon_1\gamma + \epsilon_2(1-\gamma).$$

Thus for (11) we may write

$$\alpha < 1 - \left(\frac{dC}{dY}\right)_N$$

That is

$$\alpha < \left(\frac{dS}{dY}\right)_N$$

which was the result achieved in Part II. It will be recalled that we stated in Part II, that one of the determinants of Y_E is the average initial propensity to save. This is consistent with formula (10), since that propensity determines δ_1 and δ_2.

We turn next to the question whether, assuming the equilibrium position defined by (10) exists and is economically possible, it will in fact be approached by our dynamic system, starting from any arbitrary initial position.

Equations (7) and (8) are linear first order difference equations of the form

$$AY - BY_{-1} - D = 0 \qquad A, B, D > 0$$

For such a system to converge to its equilibrium value, it is necessary and sufficient that $|B/A| < 1$.

By substitution from (7), we get, in respect of system (*a*), for B/A, which we shall denote by y

$$(13) \qquad y = \frac{\beta(1-\gamma)}{1 - \epsilon_1\gamma - \epsilon_2(1-\gamma) - \alpha + \beta(1-\gamma)}$$

It is seen immediately that, if (11) is fulfilled, this ratio is positive and less than unity. For system (*b*), we get by substitution from (8):

$$(14) \qquad y = \frac{\alpha + \beta(1-\gamma)}{[1 - \epsilon_1\gamma - \epsilon_2(1-\gamma)] + \beta(1-\gamma)}$$

The quantity enclosed in square brackets in the denominator is the normal marginal propensity to save, which is positive. Hence the whole ratio is positive, and is less than unity if (11) is fulfilled.

Equation (9), representing system (*c*) is a second-order linear difference equation of the form

$$AY - BY_{-1} + CY_{-2} - D = 0 \qquad A, B, C, D > 0$$

Whether this system converges to its equilibrium value depends on whether the absolute values of the roots y_1 and y_2, of the quadratic equation:

$$(15) \qquad Ay^2 - By + C = 0$$

are less than unity in absolute value. The roots of this equation will be real and positive if its discriminant, $B^2 - 4AC$, is positive. By substitution, and bearing in mind that $\epsilon_1 > \epsilon_2 > \beta$, it may be seen that this discriminant is positive. This being so, the roots will be less than unity if $A - B + C > 0$, and from (8), it follows at once that this condition will be fulfilled.

Thus we see that on our assumptions in all three cases, if an economically possible equilibrium position exists, the system will converge to it. Otherwise the inflationary movement will be "explosive."[5]

[5] In system (*a*), it may be seen from (13) that y may, if condition (11) is not fulfilled, be negative and of absolute value less than unity. In this case the model would yield convergent fluctuations of Y about a negative equilibrium value. This strange result

We turn next to the question of the speed of inflation. If, as we have assumed, the system is in equilibrium, and has been for one unit period for systems (*a*) and (*b*) and for two unit periods for system (*c*), Y at any integral value of t is given by the following formulas:

For systems (*a*) and (*b*):

$$Y(t) = (Y_0 - Y_E)y^t + Y_E \tag{16}$$

For system (*c*):

$$Y(t) = (Y_0 - Y_E)\frac{(1 - y_2)y_1^{\,t} - (1 - y_1)y_2^{\,t}}{y_1 - y_2} + Y_E \tag{17}$$

Since y in (16) and y_1 and y_2 in (17) are positive, these equations will determine an approach to equilibrium, or a departure from a negative equilibrium value of income of a non-cyclical character. The speed of the inflation, with given starting and final equilibrium points, will depend in (16) inversely on y, and in (17) inversely on y, and directly on y_2, where $y_1 > y_2$. From (13), (14) and examination of the roots of (16), it is seen that the speed will depend inversely on ϵ_1, ϵ_2, γ and α and directly on β; and it will also be seen that system (*b*) is slower than system (*a*), and system (*c*) slower than system (*b*). That is, the addition of the lags tends to slow the process of inflation.

We should now reconsider our assumptions to take account of the possibility of panic buying, which may be indulged in by those who have idle funds or who are in a position to speed up the expenditure of current income—mainly non-wage-earners. I therefore suggest that we can take account of panic buying by considering its effect on decreasing the value of β, and it follows from what we have said that this will increase the speed of inflation, until finally it approaches infinity, that is, equilibrium is reached, or the price system evaporates, instantaneously; but our conclusions as to the conditions under which the system will converge remain undisturbed.[6] But this argument does depend on the assumption that panic spending depends uniquely on the rate of increase of income. As we said above, the panic could be anarchical, and plausible postulates could be made under which the effects of panic would prevent equilibrium being reached.

---

is, I believe, a result of the faulty causal relation, $W \leftrightarrows Y$ implied in system (*a*). System (*a*), however, in general yields sensible results and is of use for studying the operation of the β factor in an otherwise lagless system.

[6] It will be seen from (13), (14) and (15) that negative values of β sufficiently great in absolute value may produce movements of a cyclical character about the equilibrium position, but such values of β are greater than those required to reach equilibrium instantaneously, and so need not be considered, since in fact the speed of an inflation is always less than infinite.

It may be instructive to apply our method to a numerical example, which is intended to be wholly fictitious, and which has been constructed so as to produce a convergent situation.

Let $\alpha = .40$, $\epsilon_1 = .80$, $\delta_1 = 5$, $\epsilon_2 = .30$, $\delta_2 = 10$, $\beta = .20$, $Y_0 = 100$, $L_0 = .50$, $\lambda = .60$, $\gamma = .30$, $\eta = .20$.

By applying condition (11), it will be seen that the system will approach a possible equilibrium value; and, from (10), we have

$$Y_E = 167.$$

For system (*a*), equation (15) will give

$$Y(t) = 167 - 67 \times (.48)^t.$$

For system (*b*), equation (15) will give

$$Y(t) = 167 - 67 \times (.78)^t.$$

For system (*c*), equation (16) will give

$$Y(t) = 167 - 67(1.24 \times (.82)^t - .24 \times (.08)^t).$$

The initial rate of inflationary expenditure will be the difference between the rate of war expenditure and the rate of saving for $Y = 100$. This will be 10.

CONCLUSION

Although I have no illusions about the possibilities of accurate economic prediction, I do believe that models of the type constructed in this paper can at least provide a surer guide to the implications of an inflationary policy than mere unsystematic speculation. As regards policy, I cannot see that an inflation that does not approach an upper limit has any constructive purpose. It must be stopped, and the difficulty of stopping it increases as the inflation continues. On the other hand, an inflation that has an upper limit that is considered to be socially tolerable may be considered a constructive means of implementing a policy designed to increase the real burden of a progressive income tax or to impose a levy on wage-earners or both.[7]

[7] This paper was completed before the wide extensions of price control and rationing announced by the President on April 27, 1942. Unfortunately the problem of inflation does not seem to have been reduced to one of merely academic interest, and the problems that have been dealt with here are still of great immediate importance. Rather than encumber the paper by introducing policies of price control and rationing explicitly into our models, I am adding this note to show the effects of those policies in terms of our analysis.

If *all* prices are fixed, national income is necessarily fixed if production is constant. Equilibrium exists either because a propensity to save that is equal to the desired rate of war expenditure has been established independently of the commodity controls, e.g. by taxation, or the commodity controls themselves compel or induce the economy to save the requisite proportion of their incomes. This latter effect may be produced either by price control together with a rationing policy or the automatic rationing provided by the price control itself in conjunction with increasing supply prices.

If incomes are increasing, that implies that the price control is not complete; e.g. the price of soldiers' services may not be fixed. In such a situation our analysis of inflation is still relevant, and commodity controls can be taken into account in the following way. First, the price control system will affect the proportion of money national income at which war expenditure must be maintained in order to obtain the desired proportion of real income for war purposes; that is, it will affect the slope of the line *OG*. Second, the relation of wage rates to the average level of prices will be affected. If, for instance, the cost of living rises less rapidly than the average level of prices, this will tend to make wages rise less rapidly than without price control, and so income will be redistributed in favor of high savers, and the propensity to save of the whole economy will be greater; that is, the slope of *BH* will be increased. It is here, incidentally, that the chief importance of controlling farm prices lies. Third, price control and rationing will affect the propensity to save of individuals in so far as their aggregate purchases are limited. Fourthly, shortages of particular commodities, especially durable goods, in conjunction with imperfect substitutability, may induce people to save rather than spend their incomes on the commodities that are available. Such figures as are available for 1942 suggest that the main part of the burden of limiting inflation has been borne by the price control and shortages.

9

Postscript on War Inflation: A Lesson from World War II[*]

By *WILLIAM J. FELLNER*[†]

War and post-war inflation have now developed to a point at which it seems worth while to inquire into the policies by which the rise in the cost of living could have been avoided. The available data permit a rough evaluation of orders of magnitude. They also permit a comparison of the effects of certain hypothetical measures with the effects of the policies actually adopted.

Most of what is contained in this paper leads up to the proposition that a linear (that is to say, proportionate) income tax of about 10 per cent, applied to all income without exemption and superimposed upon the income tax structure that actually prevailed, would presumably have prevented the formation of any appreciable inflation potential. Given such a tax, and given the direct controls necessitated by specific shortages, it would not even have been necessary to use war bond "drives" as a further means of reducing the demand for goods. However, it would of course have been necessary to prevent such wage increases as might start an inflationary process even in the absence of a pre-existing excess of demand over supply (that is to say, even in the absence of an "inflation potential"). In arriving at this proposition, we shall reconsider certain elements of the theory of war inflation.

THE CONCEPT OF THE INFLATION POTENTIAL, *EX ANTE* AND *EX POST*

Before defining a concept, it is useful to indicate briefly the purpose it is intended to serve. Concepts of the inflation potential should express the excess demand (at given prices) which *tends* to produce a rise in the price level and which in the absence of specific counter-inflationary

* *American Economic Review,* Mar. 1947. Reprinted by the courtesy of the American Economic Association and the author.

† Yale University; formerly University of California.

measures, actually produces such a rise. Even a crude quantitative appraisal of the inflation potential presupposes that we limit our concern to the "primary" pressure on the price level because the magnitude of the secondary "cumulative" tendency, which develops if the primary pressure is not suppressed, depends largely on unpredictable psychological reactions. Besides, for considerations relating to policy, the primary pressure frequently is the more significant magnitude,[1] although complete information concerning the effects of policies could of course be obtained only if both the primary and the cumulative forces could be estimated accurately. Furthermore, it should be realized that in a well-organized war economy the size of aggregate output depends mainly on the productive capacity of the economic system; and that, given the size of aggregate output, the pressure on the "cost of living" (or, generally speaking, on the price level of consumer goods and services) can be appraised more easily than the pressure on the price level of all goods and services. The so-called consumption function, in spite of all its crudeness, is a more dependable relationship than are the relationships existing between private investment demand and other measurable quantities. In addition, for the period to be considered, the pressure on the cost of living is a particularly significant concept because the monetary pressure against which the consumer-goods controls operated was not merely an important determinant of the effectiveness of these controls but also a significant determinant of the effectiveness of many producer-goods controls. Therefore the inflation potential will here be defined with respect to the pressure on the cost of living. It will express merely the primary pressure.[2]

We may now proceed to the definitions. By the *ex ante* inflation potential, as applying at some "present" date to a subsequent period,[3] we will mean the following: The excess of what the public, given its income during the subsequent period, *would like to spend on consumer goods,* over the supply of consumer goods during the period, where income, demand and supply are valued at "present" prices. In other words, the *ex ante* inflation potential is calculated on the hypothesis that prices remain unchanged and it explains why prices do not in re-

[1] E.g., a non-inflationary policy would attempt to eliminate or to suppress the primary pressure.

[2] The concept of the inflation potential, as defined in the subsequent paragraphs, is not identical with concepts suggested in some of the earlier writings on the subject, but it is similar to some of these. Cf., mainly, Walter A. Salant, "The Inflationary Gap," *Am. Econ. Rev.,* June 1942, Vol. XXXII, No. 2, Pt. 1, pp. 308–13; Milton Friedman, "Discussion of the Inflationary Gap," *ibid.,* pp. 314–20; G. W. Ensley and Richard Goode, "Mr. Warburton on the Gap," *Am. Econ. Rev.,* Dec. 1943, Vol. XXXIII, No. 4, pp. 897–99.

[3] All periods to be referred to in this article are clock-time periods.

ality remain unchanged, unless the inflation potential is suppressed.

The *ex ante* inflation potential either is suppressed by direct controls —in which case it expresses itself in an abnormally high savings ratio —or it results in a rise in the cost of living. If part of the *ex ante* potential is suppressed and another part translates itself into a price rise, the inflation potential becomes different *ex post* from what it was *ex ante.* The *ex post* inflation potential is the excess of what the public *would have liked to spend on consumer goods* during a completed period at the actual income level of the period, over the supply of consumer goods at actual prices (that is, over the actual value of consumption). The *ex post* inflation potential is that part of the *ex ante* inflation potential which was suppressed, *i.e.,* sterilized in the hands of consumers, by direct controls. It does not contain that constituent of the *ex ante* inflation potential which, in the course of the period, translated itself into an inflationary process, because this constituent of the *ex ante* potential reflects itself *ex post* in the actual consumption expenditure rather than in a difference between what the public would have liked to spend and what it actually did spend. There exists the further difference between the *ex ante* and the *ex post* magnitude that the former is calculated at base period prices and the latter at the actual prices of the period. But this further difference loses its significance if the inflation potential is expressed as percentage of disposable income, because income, consumption, and the inflation potential are "inflated" in roughly the same proportion. The main difference is this: part of the *ex ante* potential is "unloaded" into an inflationary process and does not *ex post* appear as a "potential" but as actual consumption. Deflating the *ex post* potential does not recapture this constituent. In deriving the *ex ante* potential from the *ex post,* it is necessary to add a factor expressing that part of the *ex ante* inflation potential which gave rise to the price increase that took place during the period.

These concepts of the inflation potential are of course not free from complications. The difficulties enter mainly through the phrase "what the public would like to spend (or would have liked to spend) on consumer goods." During the period that will be considered here, an extensive system of direct controls was in effect. It may be argued that the existence of these controls has reduced not merely actual expenditures but also the desire of the public to spend. To the extent to which it has done so, the controls have prevented not merely an inflationary process (by suppressing an "inflation potential") but they have also prevented the very formation of an inflation potential.

The size of the inflation potential is important even if direct controls are taken for granted, because a high inflation potential reduces substantially the effectiveness of direct controls. The magnitude of the "political" pressure against price and wage ceilings, as well as the significance of illegal transactions, depends very largely on the size of the inflation potential, that is, on *how* profitable it is for certain groups of the population to have the regulations in question changed or to circumvent them. A strictly non-inflationary fiscal policy would have taxed away the entire *ex ante* inflation potential of recent years. Yet, in consequences of *specific* shortages, direct controls would be needed during major wars and in post-war transition periods even if no inflation potential were allowed to develop. The inflation potential is merely an aggregative concept, measuring the pressure against the general price level (or cost of living) whenever the fiscal policy is not strictly "non-inflationary." Consumer controls, if they are effective, prevent the usual effects of this pressure on the price level. In addition, they may to some extent genuinely induce the public to more thrift and to this extent eliminate the pressure rather than merely render it ineffective. This is the source of the conceptual ambiguity mentioned in the preceding paragraph.

An alternative way of expressing the ambiguity in question is this. The foregoing definition of the inflation potential is equivalent to saying that it amounts to disposable income[4] minus "genuine" savings minus aggregate supply of consumer goods (*ex ante* or *ex post,* as the case may be), where savings are "genuine" if they are *not the product of certain controls* which interfere with the free spending of money. The *ex ante* potential is measured by the savings, other than genuine, that would be required to avoid any increase of the cost of living whatsoever; the *ex post* potential is measured by the savings, other than genuine, which actually were required to avoid a greater increase of the cost of living than took place during the period. Here the ambiguity enters through the italicized phrase "not the product of certain controls." For example, during the war, part of the money the public could not spend on automobiles became genuine savings. The public would have tended to save part of this money even if the *other* goods had not been subjected to controls (such as rationing and price control). Consequently, the pressure against which the other controls operated was not augmented by the full amount of these automobile savings. It might be objected that, on the other hand, the automobile controls themselves had to operate against the pressure arising from the desire to spend on

[4] Disposable income in the sense used by the Department of Commerce, that is, income payments minus personal taxes.

automobiles. Yet during the greater part of the period under consideration, the controls applying to the automobile industry were not of such a nature that the magnitude of the amount the public would have liked to spend on cars was a significant determinant of the effectiveness of these controls. The same is true of durable consumer goods in general, and, even more generally, of goods that, through production controls, were taken completely off the market (or so nearly so that the question of the effectiveness of rationing and price control lost its significance for these goods).

This difficulty will be assumed away *initially* by interpreting "genuine savings" as the amount of savings that would accrue at a given income level if the goods "normally" purchased at such an income level were available. The hypothetical savings in question are the "normal" aggregate propensity to save for the income rate in question (not augmented by such items as the automobile savings just considered). We disregard for a moment the limitations of the concept of the propensity to consume but we will return to them shortly. Thus calculated, the *ex post* inflation potential is $\alpha y - c$, if y is the disposable income of the period, α the "normal" average propensity to consume for the income level y, and c the value of the consumer goods purchased during the period. It is thereby assumed that the difference between disposable income times "normal" average propensity to consume, on the one hand, and actual consumption, on the other, measures, *ex post,* the savings enforced by the direct controls, and indirectly also the pressure against which the system of consumer controls operated.

It follows from what was said that the *ex ante* inflation potential cannot be derived by the process of deflating y and c for the price increase which took place during the period considered. By deflating the potential we would arrive at a magnitude that would be approximately the same in relation to the deflated disposable income as is the undeflated magnitude $\alpha y - c$ in relation to the undeflated y. The main difference between the *ex ante* and the *ex post* inflation potential is that the former includes that part of the potential which was "unloaded" into price increases and which therefore *ex post* does not appear in the form of a "potential." Consequently, in estimating the *ex ante* inflation potential, it is necessary to add to the *ex post* potential the equivalent of the actual price increase during the period. Yet, unfortunately, the price increase that took place during a given period cannot be translated into the corresponding constituent of the *ex ante* inflation potential without making arbitrary assumptions as to the length of time it took the unsuppressed fraction of the *ex ante* potential to unload itself into an inflationary process. It may be assumed, however, that if prices rose X per cent *during a year,* then the corresponding (unloaded) constituent of the *ex ante* potential was less than X per cent of the available yearly supply of goods. This seems a legitimate assumption because an *ex ante* potential amounting to X per cent of the available supply would presumably have resulted in a price increase of X per cent in *less than a year.* The yearly price rise of X per cent presumably was the result of a smaller unsuppressed potential at the beginning of the year which resulted in a smaller price increase in less than a year, which in turn contributed to creating a somewhat increased potential at that time, and so on. If, therefore, for a given year the *ex post* potential is measured by $\alpha y - c$, the *ex ante* potential for that year was greater by a margin, which, in relation to c, presumably was less than the percentage price increase.

A more precise formula would make the *ex post* inflation potential equal to $(\alpha - \beta\gamma)y - c$, where β means that fraction of y which "normally" would be spent on goods which, through production controls, are taken completely off the market,[5] and γ means that fraction of β which, given these production controls, the public genuinely desires to save additionally, rather than spend additionally on *other* goods. β depends directly on the nature of wartime production controls and indirectly on substitutability conditions in the production processes (such as the relationship between automobile and tank production). γ depends on substitutability conditions on the demand side (that is, on the degree to which liquid assets and alternative consumer goods, respectively, are substituted for the consumer goods which have disappeared from the market).

Using expressions such as the foregoing should not be interpreted to imply that consumption is a function of income exclusively. The magnitude of the various propensities denoted by Greek letters may very well depend on further variables not appearing explicitly in these formulae (*e.g.,* on the supply of money). With the actual methods of war finance, these other variables assumed magnitudes that probably tended to increase α beyond the value derived from pre-war experience. But the tax to be considered in the following pages would have reduced the magnitude of these other variables. Consequently, we will make no explicit allowance for them. This means assuming that under the tax in question the relative quantitative significance of the other vari-

[5] Or "practically" completely, so that the question of the effectiveness of consumer controls loses significance for these goods.

ables[6] would not have changed to such an extent as to affect the crude orders of magnitude with which we will be concerned. On the basis of the available figures, it is possible to lend this assumption plausibility with respect to the supply of money, which probably is the most significant other variable.

Furthermore, the expression $\alpha y - c$ will be used initially instead of the theoretically more satisfactory expression $(\alpha - \beta\gamma)y - c$ because it is difficult to evaluate $\beta\gamma$ numerically and because, after arriving at an initial numerical estimate, it will be necessary to make rough allowances also for another factor. This other factor bears on the difference between the intended and the statistical propensity to consume.

THE MAGNITUDE OF THE TAX THAT WOULD HAVE BEEN REQUIRED

In the years 1942, 1943, 1944, and 1945, individuals consumed the following percentages of their disposable incomes: 74.1, 73.3, 71.7, and 75.0, respectively. The "normal" average propensity to consume may have amounted to about 0.9. A slightly higher figure would be obtained by extrapolating the income-consumption regression line calculated by the Department of Commerce for the period 1929–41.[7] But only about 0.9 results if years such as 1937, 1939, and 1940 are taken in isolation, and this is more indicative because the war years were years of high employment, while the period 1929–40 includes several years of severe depression. The gap between 90 per cent, on the one hand, and the percentage figures appearing in the opening sentence of this paragraph, on the other, expresses the *ex post* inflation potential of the different years, as a percentage of the disposable income of the same year. Therefore, in these years the *ex post* potential may be estimated at between 15 and 18 dollars for every 100 dollars of disposable income.

In spite of the subsequent revision of income-consumption figures by the Department of Commerce, it does not seem necessary to change this estimate.[8] If, however, the war had required reducing consumption in

[6] That is, their quantitative significance in relation to income.

[7] *Survey of Current Business,* Apr. 1942.

[8] The purpose of the first paragraph of the present section in the text is to support the numerical statement on the *ex post* potential at the end of the paragraph. Since the publication of the article, the income-saving estimates quoted in the paragraph have been revised by the Department of Commerce, partly because of changes in the scope of concepts, and partly as a consequence of procedural changes. According to the revised estimates, the saved proportion of disposable income is smaller both in "normal" periods of high activity and during the war years. About 5 per cent seems to be a reasonable estimate for normal periods of high activity, and 20 to 25 per cent for the period of belliger-

general below pre-war levels (as was not the case), then it would presumably have been appropriate to use a somewhat higher estimate of the normal propensity to consume, because in this event the war period would have shared one characteristic with a period of cyclical contraction, in addition to having shared many characteristics of boom periods. In recessions and depressions, the average propensity to consume normally rises, partly because individuals reduce their desired rate of saving in a higher proportion than their rate of consumption. However, given the actual conditions during World War II, the foregoing estimate, which puts the *ex post* potential at 15 to 18 per cent of disposable income, seems appropriate.

The *ex ante* potential must have been greater because part of it got unloaded into an inflationary process and therefore does not appear in the *ex post* potential. The cost of living index rose by about 9 per cent in 1942, 3 per cent in 1943, 2 per cent in 1944, and 2 per cent in 1945. In addition to this rise, such phenomena as quality deterioration, the disappearance of cheap brands, and illegal transactions also were in the nature of price increases, so that the "true" rise of the cost of living undoubtedly exceeded the figures just given. Yet, as was pointed out earlier, the unsuppressed inflation potential, by which the *ex ante* magnitude exceeded the *ex post* for a yearly period, presumably was distinctly smaller in relation to c (and also in relation to y) than the ratio in which prices actually rose. The initial conclusion, to be qualified presently in several respects, is that the *ex ante* inflation potential—which a strictly non-inflationary policy of war finance would have eliminated—was in the order of 20 per cent of disposable income (probably slightly less). This figure is derived by adding to the 15–18 dollars per 100 dollars of disposable income a factor accounting for the actual price increase. If from Pearl Harbor on, about 20 per cent of *all* disposable income had been taken away by *further* taxation, no inflation potential would have developed. (With $\alpha = 0.9$, a tax of 20 per cent would have eliminated an inflation potential of 18 per cent, considering that the tax would have reduced savings as well as consumption.)

There are, of course, many reasons why such an estimate must be regarded as very crude, and no attempt will be made to appraise all these reasons. Yet it should be emphasized that the two most obvious, and probably strongest, reasons call for downward correction.

---

ency. The difference, which is the *ex post* potential, continues to lie between 15 and 20 per cent—closer to 15—as suggested in the text. Also, the ratio for 1941 continues to be about 5 per cent higher than our "normal," as is suggested on page 145. After V-J Day, the ratio declines markedly from its war level, as suggested on page 146. (Cf. the 1951 National Income Supplement of the *Survey of Current Business,* p. 151.)

In the first place, the $\beta \cdot \gamma$ factor, considered on pages 142–43, calls for correcting such an estimate downward. The numerical significance of this factor may easily have been in the neighborhood of 5 per cent of disposable income. For, in the good years of the period preceding the war, the expenditure on durable consumer goods used to be in the order of 10 per cent of disposable income, and expenditures on durable consumer goods are not the only ones entering into β. Consequently, even if γ should have been less than 0.5, $\beta \cdot \gamma$ may have been in the neighborhood of 5 per cent of disposable income.

Secondly, even aside from this, the "normal" average propensity to consume may have been lower during part of the period in question than is the figure derived from the pre-1941 experience (that is to say, α may have fallen short of 0.9). There is no reason to assume that in the long run the average propensity to consume should decline markedly with rising income, because such a decline does not seem to have occurred over a period of one-half of a century during which the national income in constant prices increased fivefold.[9] Yet in 1941 the average propensity to consume was at the unusually low level of 0.84, which in terms of our concepts must be considered a "normal" value[10] for that year because no direct consumer controls were in effect in 1941.[11] The low propensity to consume of 1941 may have been a consequence of the rapid rise in income during the year, in consequence of which consumers "did not have time" to adjust their consumption expenditures to the new income level before the year was over. In fact, the relative significance of the defense sector in the economy grew considerably during the year. The cost of living rose about 10 per cent from the beginning to the end of the year, and an inflationary process of this kind always works in such a way as to give the government[12] consistently the advantages of the "first move" in the competitive bidding for resources which reflects itself in the inflationary process. Consequently, the "normal propensity to consume"—*i.e.,* the propensity to consume in the absence of consumer controls—is lowered (in the *ex post,* statistical sense[13]). Now, if after 1941 the actual controls had been in effect and,

---

[9] Simon Kuznets' estimates are the main source for this statement. For detailed references and discussion, see the present writer's *Monetary Policies and Full Employment* (Berkeley, University of California Press, 1946), Ch. 3 and appendices.

[10] Or almost so.

[11] Except for the restrictions of consumer credit adopted in the fall of that year.

[12] Or the first spenders of the "new money," regardless of who they are. In the models of the monetary over-investment theories, the investing entrepreneurs are the first spenders.

[13] In other words, the *ex post* propensity to consume falls short of the *ex ante,* because of the familiar concept of "forced savings."

in addition, the inflation potential had been taxed away, conditions would have remained partly similar to those of 1941, so far as the "normal propensity to consume" is concerned. It is true that the "forced savings" would not have been produced by an inflationary process. But income, and at the same time the relative significance of the war sector in the economy, would have increased considerably through 1943,[14] and the increase in income would have been initiated by the expansion of war production, with consumers lagging behind the government.

During the war the propensity to consume was reduced also by the war bond drives. But we are assuming that in the hypothetical non-inflationary war economy there would have been no such drives in addition to the tax here discussed, although the public would have been free to buy government securities to the extent to which it genuinely desired to buy them. Consequently, no allowance will be made for a smaller propensity to consume under this heading.

We have seen that from 1942 through 1945 the *ex ante* inflation potential could be estimated at roughly 20 per cent, or slightly less, of disposable income, by a method which disregarded at least two important factors. One of these factors (the durable goods savings) may well have reduced the 20 per cent to 15 per cent, and the order of magnitude of the second factor (of the consumption lag just considered) may also have been several per cent. The second downward correction—which was in the order of 5 per cent in conditions such as existed in 1941—ceased to be important after 1943, when war production reached its top level. The first downward correction, for durable goods savings, tends to turn gradually into negative (*i.e.,* into an upward correction) for the post-war transition period, when the public *would like to spend* on durable consumer goods not merely the "normal" fraction of its income but also part of the previously accumulated savings. But for the period following V-J Day, the original (uncorrected) figure for the inflation potential is considerably less than 20 per cent (for the last quarter of 1945 only about 7 to 8 per cent,[15] and for the first half of 1946 around 4 per cent). Consequently, the following generalization seems permissible for the period beginning with Pearl Harbor: The "crude" method, disregarding the durable goods savings and the consumption lag, leads to the assumption that the inflation potential amounted to almost 20 per cent of disposable income during the war; it seems

---

[14] As they actually did.

[15] In the last quarter of 1945 net savings of individuals amounted to 17.5 per cent of disposable income. In the first quarter of 1946 they amounted to 12.9 per cent and in the second quarter to 14.1 per cent of disposable income.

reasonable to assume that the two downward corrections, for the factors disregarded by the "crude" method, were in the order of 5 to 10 per cent of disposable income; during the early phases of the reconversion period the crude figure was less than 10 per cent but, instead of being corrected downward, it needs to be corrected upward for the pent-up demand.

During the war, a strictly non-inflationary policy of war finance would therefore have taxed away additionally[16] about 10 to 15 per cent of disposable income, with somewhat different percentages in different subperiods. In 1941, the necessary rate of taxation would presumably have been smaller. There was no price control or rationing in effect during that year, and practically the entire *ex ante* potential translated itself into price increases. The cost of living rose about 10 per cent, and it seems very likely that a *yearly* increase of this size results from an initial inflation potential of smaller size. For the earliest phase of the post-war period (*i.e.*, for the last quarter of 1945), the rate required for strictly non-inflationary financing may have been somewhat smaller than the wartime rate.

It would not have been reasonable, however, to attempt "strictly non-inflationary financing" in the foregoing, somewhat dogmatic sense. As may be seen from the preceding analysis, the inflation potential can even now be reconstructed only by rather crude methods. The methods by which it could have been estimated beforehand would have involved some additional sources of error, although it is very likely that *ex ante* estimates, say, from quarter to quarter, would have resulted in figures of the same order. Wartime estimates were not subject to all limitations of the post-war projections because during the war full utilization could be postulated. The information available to the authorities would have rendered possible the evaluation of the correct order of magnitude of the inflation potential, but no more than this. It can hardly be contested that a slight deviation in the inflationary direction would have been less harmful than a deflationary pressure. The latter would have made it more difficult to raise the rate of aggregate output rapidly and significantly, and it also would have impeded the process of post-war readjustment very considerably. Consequently, a reasonable policy would have preferred to err slightly on the inflationary rather than on the deflationary side, all the more because direct controls would have been necessary at any rate to cope with the problem of *specific* shortages. A small or moderate *general* (over-all) upward pressure on prices would have been kept down effectively by the system of controls. It is submitted

[16] That is, in addition to the taxes that were in existence.

therefore that a correct *ex ante* evaluation of the data would have made it desirable to superimpose on the actual tax structure some measure such as a proportionate income tax, applying to all incomes without exception, and amounting, on the average, from 1942 on, to about 10 per cent of disposable income. This would have corresponded to slightly less than 9 per cent of income before personal taxes (except in 1942 when it would have corresponded to about 9.5 per cent).

Correct evaluation of the *ex ante* inflation potential of 1941 should have resulted in adopting a distinctly smaller tax of this nature at that time. An ideal policy would have varied the tax rate from time to time, but a comparatively small rate for 1941[17] and a rate of 8–9 per cent (on income before taxes) for the entire period of belligerency would probably have accomplished the desired objective. If the reader should feel uneasy about our downward corrections and if he should feel that a tax of about 20 per cent (corresponding to our initial crude estimate) might have been needed for closing the gap, he should take into consideration that the line of argument of the concluding sections of this article would be the same even if the required tax had been in the order of 20 per cent of disposable income. But the downward corrections are justified. A small additional tax in 1941 and an additional tax approaching 10 per cent (on income before taxes) during the war would have made it possible to hold the cost of living, although a small (but sterilized) inflation potential would probably have remained in the background of developments. As for the future, it is obvious that a reasonable post-war tax policy would have to be flexible and that it should be capable of changing the effective rate on short notice. It so happens that during the war this would not have been absolutely necessary.

Some economists might maintain that not merely a small but a significant inflation potential was required in order to be released at the appropriate time and to offset the deflation potential to be expected for certain phases of post-war economic development. In my opinion, the answer to this is that a deflation potential calls for expansionary fiscal policies when it develops and not for creating and suppressing a significant inflation potential many years earlier. The idea of creating and suppressing an inflation potential beforehand and of releasing it in the right moment rests on two main assumptions. The first is that it is possible to suppress a large inflation potential completely, or almost so. The second is that it is possible to release the inflation potential in the

[17] This does not mean, however, that in 1941 the yield of such a tax would have been small as compared to the yield of other taxes. It is merely maintained that the rate would have been small as compared to that of the subsequent years.

appropriate period and thereby to go a long way towards offsetting the deflationary tendencies of that period. The first of these assumptions already has proved thoroughly wrong, and so will the second in due time. Inflationary tendencies call, among other measures, for a rate of taxation that reduces the inflation potential to a manageable size; and deflationary tendencies call, among other measures, for expansionary fiscal policies absorbing the deflation potential. Not to take the appropriate measures in either of these two types of situations is a mistake, and it is unreasonable to expect that these two mistakes will cancel each other.

PROPORTIONATE TAXES COMPARED WITH PROGRESSIVE TAXES AND WITH INFLATION

In the foregoing pages the "required tax" was conceived of as a proportionate income tax, applying to all incomes without exception, and superimposed on the taxes that actually have been in effect. Clearly, there is nothing in the reasoning that could not be made to fit tax schemes of a different sort. There exists, however, a good reason why it seemed preferable to state the conclusion in this form. It is (almost) "obviously" and "unequivocally" true that the avoidance of inflation by such a tax would have been preferable to the actual degree of inflation. The possible counter-arguments, which will be mentioned briefly, would be quite unconvincing. The question of whether the avoidance of inflation by additional progressive taxes would have been preferable to the actual degree of inflation would, however, raise controversial issues.

A proportionate income tax with no exemption possesses distinctly objectionable features, *but they all are shared by inflation, and inflation possesses additional objectionable properties.* From the point of view from which a proportionate income tax is bad, that is, from the point of view of social equity and the so-called ability to pay, a rise in the cost of living is certainly no better. From a 1939 base, the cost of living index rose by about 6 per cent through 1941, by 17 per cent through 1942, by 24 per cent through 1943, by 26 per cent through 1944, by 29 per cent through 1945 (yearly averages). By August, 1946, the rise had reached 45 per cent and by October it had reached very nearly 50 per cent. The cost of living index disregards phenomena such as the deterioration of quality, the disappearance of inexpensive brands, violations, etc., and it seems, therefore, legitimate to conclude that the "true" rise in the cost of living must by now surely have exceeded 50 per cent (perhaps by a considerable margin). The dollar has lost about one-third of its value, if measured by the cost of living, and distinctly more if measured by wholesale prices. It would be difficult to argue that on the grounds of social equity a proportionate income tax in the order of 10 per cent (of disposable income) since 1942, and a considerably smaller tax in 1941, would have been worse than such a degree of price inflation. On the contrary, a proportionate income tax at least leaves relative positions unaffected, while the redistribution of income under price inflation strongly favors those belonging to well-established power groups. The argument would be no weaker if we had concluded that a tax of 10 to 15 per cent (corresponding to the full inflation potential) would have been required, or if we had concluded that a tax approaching 20 per cent would have been needed, corresponding to the inflation potential crudely calculated, without the appropriate downward corrections. But, in reality, such high rates would not have been required.

When a proportionate income tax is introduced (and price inflation is avoided), everybody's disposable money income[18] declines for a given aggregate real output, although of course the money value of the gross national product (GNP) and that of the national income remain unchanged. At the same time, the money value of the government contribution to the GNP increases. The aggregate GNP and national income increase in monetary terms only if (and in the proportion in which) aggregate real output rises as a consequence of increased input of resources or increased productivity per unit of input. On the other hand, if the expansion of the government sector is brought about by an inflationary process (and tax rates are not increased), the money value of the GNP, that of the national income, and also that of disposable income, rise even for a given aggregate real output. The increased money income is injected into the system at some point in such a way that the changed pattern of income distribution shows no stability whatsoever, and then the population "fights out" the question of how this distortion should be eliminated by "adjustments." If the economic efficiency of the system were not affected by this procedure, aggregate real output and aggregate real consumption would be the same as under taxation, yet the distribution of income would be more "fortuitous"; or it could be viewed as being hastily "revised" in a series of struggles which take place in an acute emergency, and in which, therefore, well-organized power groups find it particularly easy to bring pressure to bear effectively. It might be objected that strategic power groups could insist on such a "redistribution" in an emergency even if the relative distribution pattern remained initially unaffected (as under a proportionate income tax). Indeed, to some extent they probably would. But it is highly

[18] That is, everybody's income after personal taxes.

probable that incentives for a struggle over redistribution would be much weaker in these circumstances than when large flows of money income are injected into the system at arbitrary points, where according to generally accepted value judgments they produce substantial distortion. As a consequence, not only is it unlikely that the inflationary method would result in a distribution pattern that would have been considered equitable *a priori* had it been subject to conscious planning, but the economic efficiency of the system as a whole can scarcely remain unaffected by the struggle in question. Aggregate real output and all its constituents, including the output of the war industries and of the consumer goods industries, is very likely to be reduced by the fight over adjustments. Moreover, an inflationary process—even if it does not reach "astronomical" dimensions—undoubtedly increases the danger of a subsequent serious setback.

It may therefore safely be concluded that the *superimposition* of a proportionate income tax, of the order of magnitude previously discussed, upon the taxes actually in existence would have been "preferable" to the actual degree of price inflation. The same would be true even if all our downward corrections were considered inappropriate and if close to 20 per cent were regarded as the necessary degree of additional taxation, although this certainly would be an extreme position. It is, however, impossible to make an equally clear-cut statement on whether it would have been "good" or "bad" to *substitute* proportionate (linear) taxes for part of the progressive taxes in existence,[19] or whether it would have been "good" or "bad" to supplement the existing taxes with *further* progressive taxes.[20] If the inflation problem alone is considered, then a tax is the less effective the more progressive it is. For example, with a sufficiently progressive, instead of a linear additional tax, it would have been necessary to tax away additionally more than the roughly 10 per cent of disposable income previously calculated in order to "close the gap." In the higher income groups, taxation partly reduces savings rather than consumption, so that progressive taxes increase the α factor of our formula. One-sided emphasis on the inflation problem makes progressiveness in general appear to be undesirable. The same is true of a one-sided emphasis on the problem of incentives. A tax affects incentives the more unfavorably, the more progressive it is, that is to say, the more disproportionately it reduces marginal earnings. On these grounds alone, a strong case could be made against progressiveness in general, in a setting in which the maintenance of effective demand

[19] That is to say, to make the existing tax structure less progressive.
[20] That is to say, to increase the progressiveness of the tax structure.

does not give rise to difficulties. On the other hand, a very strong case can be made *for* progressiveness on the grounds of social equity and thereby also in terms of the morale of the population. There are real issues involved in this complex of problems and it is impossible to state with general validity (*i.e.,* without expressing a very definite value judgment) that a given degree of progressiveness is preferable on balance to a higher or to a lower degree. One gets much closer to a "purely logical" proposition (which "should not be controversial") by stating that a proportionate tax of the magnitude here considered would have been preferable to the approximately 50 per cent increase in the cost of living that actually has occurred. For the rise in the cost of living also performed the functions of an income tax and certainly those of a nonprogressive one!

It should be admitted that even this proposition is not (strictly speaking) purely logical, although it comes very close to being so. In the first place, a person may have predilections for certain well-organized groups in the economy—on either side of the "fence"—and he then may feel that the distribution pattern actually established under more or less controlled inflation is more to his taste than would be the case under sufficient taxation. In fact, one of the main reasons why in major wars taxation always is insufficient is that too many powerful groups have a good *a priori* chance of improving their relative position under an inflationary process, as compared to their would-be position under sufficient taxation. But it is difficult to see how a disinterested person should have a preference for the "inflationary" distribution as against a "planned" pattern; and it need not be futile to stress the logic of the case because "selfishness" in the foregoing sense is not the only reason for failure to tax adequately in inflationary periods. Another reason is the incomplete understanding of the issues involved. It is perhaps not unreasonable to assume that the attitudes towards the problem of taxation and of inflation would have been different, had it been realized what the order of magnitude of taxation was by which all or most of the actual degree of inflation could have been avoided.

A second possible objection relates to the problem of incentives. Even a linear additional tax would have raised marginal as well as average tax rates, although it would have raised marginal rates by no more than average rates. The effects of taxation on incentives consist of a favorable and an unfavorable constituent. The former is produced by the fact that it is necessary, in consequence of the tax, to work more, or to undertake a greater amount of risky investment in order to earn a given income; the unfavorable constituent arises as a consequence of the burden placed on the reward for additional effort. The unfavorable constituent becomes the more important, the more progressive the tax is (provided the problem of maintaining effective demand may be disregarded for some period). It would be difficult to forecast even the algebraic sign of the total effect of a proportionate tax. It is very unlikely, however, that an additional tax of the magnitude here considered would have had a stronger unfavorable effect on incentives than did the uncertainty concerning the nature and the timing of adjustments in the framework of the actual inflationary process. A minor qualification should be made. If such an additional tax had been in effect, some reduction of the surtax rate would have been necessary in the highest income groups in order to avoid taxing these groups at a marginal rate of about 100 per cent or more. Or, alternatively, the tax could have been levied on income after (other) taxes.

A POST-WAR PROBLEM

This paper has been concerned with the bearing of fiscal policies on the problem of war and post-war inflation. A brief remark will now be made concerning the validity of certain elements of this reasoning for "normal" periods of expansion and contraction. Some elements of the analysis could be made to fit the usual developments during the cyclical process; others could not.

The main point that remains true, even for "normal" periods, is that an *ex ante* inflation potential[21] calls for higher taxes, while an *ex ante* deflation potential calls for tax reductions and—if the deflation potential is substantial enough—for consumer subsidies. It is, of course, possible to substitute other expansionary monetary policies[22] for tax reductions and consumer subsidies, but the other monetary measures are either less effective or inferior in certain respects (although possibly superior in others) and it would therefore be highly desirable to combine them with those here considered. Measures other than those of a "monetary-fiscal" character are also very important, but we are not concerned with them here. A flexible tax policy is a promising means of

---

[21] However, normally it seems preferable to apply these concepts to the aggregate level of output rather than merely to the output of consumer goods because the aggregate level of output cannot be regarded as "given" (i.e., as determined by considerations lying outside the framework in which the estimate is made), except when full utilization may be taken for granted.

[22] Such as credit policies and mainly compensatory public works (possibly also producers' subsidies). It also is possible to substitute other measures for anti-inflationary tax increases; but in a period with a large stock of idle balances, these other measures (mainly credit policies) would be very little effective.

reducing economic instability.[23] A reasonable degree of flexibility could, however, scarcely be accomplished without maintaining the "pay-as-you-go system" and without the possibility of adjusting tax rates in, say, quarterly intervals. The difficulties standing in the way of such adjustments are political in nature. The necessary measure of flexibility cannot be accomplished without some delegation of power on the part of Congress—possibly to a committee of its own, rather than to the administration.

There is little hope that the adjustment of tax rates to changing business conditions could be accomplished without undue delay, if each adjustment raises the problem of the desirable degree of progression. Chances would seem to be better for accomplishing flexibility by adding to, or abating from, the basic progressive tax rates a linear (nonprogressive) element. The basic structure could then stay in effect for the entire fiscal year, while the special linear tax or refund, possibly even linear subsidy, would be adjusted to business conditions in shorter intervals. A recent suggestion to adjust the "first bracket" income-tax rate in quarterly intervals[24] belongs, generally speaking, in the category of measures just discussed. However, adjustment of the "first bracket" rate contains an implicit element of (changing) progression because the present income tax does not apply to incomes below the exemption limits. This kind of change in the degree of progression would not make it politically more difficult to achieve flexibility, although it would, of course, make for a smaller aggregate effect per given percentage change in the rate. We considered a tax without exemption because the tax was compared with inflation which operates with no exemption limits.[25]

[23] There exist at least two reasons why cyclical fluctuations can be reduced but cannot be *eliminated.* In the first place, in normal times *ex ante* estimates of the gap are too undependable—more so than in a war economy for a short period ahead. After an initial interval of deflationary developments, it is wise to take a chance on antideflationary policies, and the analogous statement holds of inflationary deviations, but policy of this sort will merely mitigate, not eliminate, the cycle. Secondly, eliminating minor recessions—that is, guaranteeing full employment *de facto*—would result in chronic inflationary pressure because of concerted wage-and-price raising activities. Only a comprehensive system of direct controls could cope with these pressures, and such an apparatus would considerably reduce the efficiency of the economy.

[24] Committee for Economic Development, *Jobs and Markets* (Research Study) (London and New York, McGraw-Hill, 1946), pp. 74–76 and 121.

[25] Except perhaps in that the very lowest income groups consume relatively more of the items the prices of which were held more successfully during the war than the cost of living in general.

10

*Fiscal Policy, Military Preparedness, and Postwar Inflation**

By HASKELL P. WALD†

Toward the end of World War II there appeared a rash of articles on the general theme of alternative budget policies for achieving full employment in the postwar period.[1] The objective of these studies was to analyze the implications of different methods of varying government expenditures and revenues in order to secure an addition to total public and private outlay sufficient to absorb any manpower resources that otherwise would have remained idle.

It is interesting to translate these studies into the postwar inflationary setting. The requirements of national defense, international reconstruction, and related governmental programs placed Federal spending on a rising curve at a time when manpower and important raw materials and manufactured goods were in relatively tight supply. In such a situation the need was for a tax policy which would be consistent with general price stability and minimize the necessity for economic controls

* *National Tax Journal,* Mar. 1949. Reprinted by the courtesy of the National Tax Association and the author.

† International Program in Taxation, Harvard University; formerly National Security Resources Board.

[1] For example, see: R. A. Musgrave, "Alternative Budget Policies for Full Employment," *Am. Econ. Rev.,* June 1945, XXXV, 387–400, and Board of Governors of the Federal Reserve System, "Fiscal Policy, Stability, and Full Employment," in *Public Finance and Full Employment* (Washington, 1945); N. Kaldor, "The Quantitative Aspects of the Full Employment Problem in Britain," Appendix C in W. H. Beveridge, *Full Employment in a Free Society* (New York, 1945); M. Kalecki, "Three Ways to Full Employment," Part 3 in Oxford University Institute of Statistics, *The Economics of Full Employment* (Oxford, 1944); A. H. Hansen, "Three Methods of Expansion through Fiscal Policy," *Am. Econ. Rev.,* June 1945, XXXV, 382–87. Among the more recent analyses of the subject are: T. Morgan, *Income and Employment* (New York, 1947), pp. 218–23; P. A. Samuelson, "The Simple Mathematics of Income Determination" and R. I. Bishop, "Alternative Expansionist Fiscal Policies," in *Income, Employment, and Public Policy,* Essays in Honor of Alvin H. Hansen (New York, 1948). For a useful, simplified statement, see P. A. Samuelson, *Economics* (New York, 1948), Appendix to Ch. 18. An early treatment of the problem is H. M. Somers, "The Impact of Fiscal Policy on National Income," *Canadian Jour. Econ. and Pol. Sci.,* Aug. 1942, VIII, 364–85.

which are distasteful to the private economy. To the extent that the additions to government spending were not being fully offset by reductions in the private sector, the result was an intensification of inflationary pressures.

One's first reaction is to state that the answers to the fiscal-policy problem in such a setting are the opposite of those obtained under less-than-full-employment assumptions. Whereas loan-financed expenditures have the largest "leverage" factor, if the possibility of an unfavorable reaction on private investors is ruled out, such expenditures would be least appropriate when there is no slack in the economy; and tax-financed expenditures, particularly those financed by taxes which are most effective in restraining private investment and consumption spending, would be most appropriate.

These generalizations are valid, but they go too far in simplifying what is basically a difficult problem in reconciling competing demands for limited resources. In the first place, a tax-financed expenditure program ordinarily will still have an income-generating effect, and thus will intensify demand pressures; as a general rule, both a careful selection of tax measures and a sizable budget surplus are necessary if the tax-induced cut in private spending is to offset the income-increasing effect of added government spending. Secondly, a variety of considerations may militate against relying solely on tax policies to curb the inflationary impact of increased spending for defense and related activities.

The purpose of this article is to illustrate certain fundamental principles of fiscal-policy determination in an inflationary setting in which military preparedness is a prime objective of national policy. In the attempt to simplify the presentation and extend the analysis beyond the realm of theoretical reasoning, certain hypotheses are relied upon which must be subjected to further testing before they can be used as a basis for policy determination. Nevertheless, it is obvious that progress in clarifying broad policy principles is an important first step in the direction of formulating sounder tax policies. Moreover, the difficulties of deriving estimates of the economic effects discussed below should not be exaggerated; crude statistical approximations often can serve as useful policy guides.

REQUIREMENTS FOR NONINFLATIONARY FINANCING

It is easy to lose sight of the fact that the expansionary effects of an increase in government purchases of goods and services are not neutralized merely by a dollar-for-dollar increase in tax revenues, even though the individuals who pay the incremental taxes have consumption and savings habits which are identical with those of the recipients of incremental government expenditures.[2] Since the effect of the revenue-expenditure process is to transfer purchasing power from taxpayers to recipients of government expenditures, it is true that aggregate private demand remains unchanged as long as the consumption demand of the payers and payees is the same. In the meantime, however, government purchases will have increased, with a consequent rise in national production or, if the economy had already been operating at maximum rates, with a consequent rise in prices and some redistribution of output.[3]

Under the simplified assumption of a revenue-expenditure process which is neutral in its distributional aspects, therefore, the multiplier (which relates the tax-financed increase in government expenditures, as the multiplicand, to the increase in total outlay) is exactly one when there is a balanced increase in expenditures and taxes. If a full employment situation already prevails, the addition to government expenditures becomes, on balance, a dollar-for-dollar addition to the inflationary pressure in the economy, even though the budget balance is undisturbed. Without recognizing this relationship, we miss the chief reason why the fiscal policy aspects of military preparedness in the postwar economy are not as simple as they first seem.

There is nothing mysterious about the income-creating effect of a balanced budget. Government spending for goods and services adds directly to the value of the gross national product; it enters the national product on the "first round," so to speak. Tax collections, on the other hand, do not enter until the "second round."[4] Taxes are paid in part from funds that otherwise would have been saved, so that the amount subtracted from gross national product falls short of the amount of additional revenue. Private disposable income, consumption, and savings are unchanged, however, since it is assumed that the effects of taxing

[2] This point is ably developed by Henry C. Wallich in "Income-Generating Effects of a Balanced Budget," *Quart. Jour. Econ.*, Nov. 1944, LIX, 78–91. Samuelson refers to this proposition as the "balanced-budget theorem" and presents several explanations (see "The Simple Mathematics of Income Determination," *op. cit.*, pp. 140–42). The effects of time lags in the income-expenditure process are ignored in the present presentation. For most problems this is not a serious oversimplification, although it would still be important to allow for such lags when making policy decisions.

[3] Throughout this article the references to government expenditures apply only to purchases of goods and services, i.e., transfer payments are excluded.

[4] It may be noted that government transfer payments, such as social security benefits, also enter on the "second round." Thus, raising taxes and transfer payments simultaneously will not have any multiplier effects (apart from the effects of redistribution among income classes).

and spending are of an offsetting character. What is added that is new is the expansion of the government sector.

The analysis might be extended a step further by taking into account the impact of the new expenditure and tax programs upon the level of private investment. Let us suppose that the added government spending stimulates an expansion in private investment and that the tax deterrent effects on investment incentives are of no consequence. The additional investment would then have a magnified effect on aggregate private outlay, and on what might be thought of as the "inflationary gap," because of the respending of the resultant increase in consumers' income. Conversely, a negative effect on investment would ease the inflationary pressure by more than a dollar-for-dollar reduction.

Given the decision to finance an increase in the government's budget in a manner which would not add to total public and private demand and thereby aggravate a pre-existing inflationary situation, either private investment or consumption, or both, must be curtailed in an amount equivalent to the added government expenditure.[5] There are analytical advantages in formulating the requirements for a noninflationary fiscal policy in algebraic terms in order to determine the general nature of the taxes that would need to be levied or the magnitude of the budget surplus that would be called for. This is done in the appendix accompanying this article. The implications of the algebraic analysis for policy formulation are illustrated in the following examples.

Example 1. No Increase in Taxes

Under what is generally considered to be the most inflationary budgetary policy, the stepping up of government spending for goods and services would not be accompanied by any increase in tax rates. The additional spending would be financed through loans or through a reduction in a pre-existing budget surplus.[6] In such a situation the addition to aggregate public and private outlay would be (1) the original

[5] This is a minimum acceptable objective for a noninflationary fiscal policy. If fiscal policy is to make a positive contribution to an anti-inflation program, it should curtail private spending by more than the addition to government programs. Moreover, because the above statement is in terms of aggregates, there is an implicit assumption that resources will flow freely from one activity to another. Thus, it overlooks the risk of intensifying inflationary pressures in particular sectors of the economy, which is, of course, a real risk under postwar conditions.

[6] In the interest of simplifying the presentation, no allowance is made at this point for the fact that part of the additional spending would be automatically covered by the higher yield of existing taxes as total income is raised.

increment of government spending, plus or minus (2) the change in private investment spending, plus (3) the sum of the familiar chain of respendings of successive portions of the resultant increases in consumer income.

In theory, the economic impact of an increase in government purchases should be the same whether it is financed by borrowing or by reducing a budget surplus. In practice, the two courses may differ in their effect on business investment decisions; supposedly, the likelihood of an adverse effect on private investment would be greater if the budget were placed in the red than if merely the surplus were reduced. This difference would doubtless be less now than in the 'thirties when the bogey of deficit financing had greater influence.

Aside from a psychological reaction of this sort, it might be asked whether a loan-financed expenditure program would reduce private spending through its effects on the availability of funds. One would not expect an outcome of this sort in the postwar economy, however, since the supply of liquid assets is redundant by most standards.[7] The effect of government borrowing on the availability of bank credit cannot be of any real significance as long as banks are able to secure reserves at will by selling government securities in a guaranteed market; nor should the effect on the availability of nonbank funds be of serious concern since government borrowings flow back to the economy as the money is spent. Only in a situation where a government borrowing campaign is specifically directed at stimulating small savings or at diverting funds from other spending purposes is it likely to contribute to an anti-inflation objective. Of course, to the extent that government securities are sold to banks, quite the opposite result is achieved insofar as there is an inflationary expansion of the money supply.

A negative change in private investment would tend to offset the effects of the additional government spending. The increase in personal incomes generated by the expenditure program would be reduced and the net effect on consumer expenditures would be correspondingly diminished.

In the postwar situation, however, it seems more realistic to expect the induced change in private investment to be a positive magnitude, since additional government spending for military and related programs tends to bolster the general business situation. Thus, government spending would be augmented by larger private investment and the chain of consumer respendings would be correspondingly inflated.

---

[7] See the author's article, "The Expanded Money Supply and Economic Activity," *Survey Current Bus.*, May 1946, pp. 8 ff.

An original outlay of, say, $5 billion for government programs, plus, for example, a $2 billion expansion in private investment, might well wind up as a $21 billion addition to aggregate demand.[8]

Aside from any stimulative effects on private investment, a policy of increasing the expenditure side of the budget without levying additional taxes would still be highly inflationary as long as the slack in the economy is maintained at a minimum. The 3 to 1 ratio serves as a rough indicator of the magnitude of the expansionary effect on total public and private outlay.

Example 2. Balanced Budget

A more orthodox budget policy would call for tax increases in line with the increase in government expenditures. It has already been demonstrated that this would not necessarily be a noninflationary policy; in all likelihood, it would still have inflationary effects. Nevertheless, the balanced budget approach would be a decided improvement over loan financing because (1) the stimulative effect on private investment would tend to be smaller and, in some cases, the effect might well be negative, and (2) the new taxes would absorb income available for consumer spending.

In order to analyze the balanced-budget approach in further detail, it is desirable to treat separately the investment and consumption effects. Clearly, if private investment is curtailed, either because the new taxes reduce the incentive to invest or absorb funds that would otherwise have been invested, a negative multiplier chain becomes operative and the inflationary effect of the government outlay tends to be offset. Under balanced-budget conditions, the consumption-reducing effects of higher taxes would be an additional influence in this same direction. A complete offset would thus be possible, even though the decline in investment were substantially smaller than the increase in the government budget.[9] Under the loan-financing case just considered, these two opposing changes would need to be about equal in size.

In the event that the effect on private investment is negligible, the

[8] The multiplier of 3 which is used in this and succeeding examples is the approximate value derived from the national income and product statistics for the 1929–1940 period. It is used only for illustrative purposes; more refined calculations would be necessary to determine its applicability to the postwar situation. As noted in the appendix, this particular formulation of the multiplier is a variant of the definition which is generally adopted. It can be defined as the reciprocal of one minus the ratio of consumer expenditures to gross national product minus tax payments.

[9] See section 5 in the appendix for an algebraic formulation of the necessary relationships.

inflationary effects of the balanced-budget approach will hinge on the extent to which the tax-financed expenditure program is neutral, stimulative, or repressive in its effects on consumption. It would be neutral if the individuals who pay the additional taxes have the same consumption and savings habits as the recipients of the incremental expenditures. It would be stimulative if the taxpayers as a group spend less, on the average, than the recipients of the expenditures, and repressive if the reverse were true.

A neutral financing policy would leave total consumer spending unchanged, although aggregate public and private demand would be raised by the original amount of government spending. This is the general case, already described, where the multiplier is one, despite the absence of loan financing. A stimulative policy would raise consumer spending and a repressive policy would lower it.

It is the latter possibility which suggests another opportunity for noninflationary financing, namely, the possibility of adopting a tax policy which results in a redistribution of income from high-consuming (low-income) to low-consuming (high-income) groups. The requirements for a noninflationary financing policy of this type are illustrated in Table 1. Three assumptions are involved in these computations: (1) the incremental expenditures and taxes are in balance; (2) private investment outlays are unchanged; and (3) the multiplier is 3. The reader is referred to the appendix for the algebraic formula underlying the computations.

In brief, the problem is to devise a tax program which will curtail consumption by a larger amount than the new government expenditures will add to it. According to the computations summarized in the table, if one-fourth of the new expenditures will be reflected in increased consumer spending, then 58 per cent of the new taxes must be paid at the expense of such spending. And if the former fraction is raised to three-fourths, then the tax-induced decrease in consumption would have to be even larger than the revenue yield.

What is the likelihood of the occurrence of any of these combinations of figures? On the expenditure side, it may be noted that if government purchases are subject to the same proportion of "leakages" into corporate and consumer savings as are the purchases for the economy as a whole, a value of .67 would be indicated as the proportion which will be reflected in increased consumer spending. This value, of course, corresponds to the crude multiplier of 3 which has already been used.

On the tax side, we are faced with the problem that the impact on savings and consumption will vary substantially with different types of taxes. Even for a regressive tax, however, a significant proportion will still be paid out of savings. The Federal Reserve survey of consumer

TABLE 1

ILLUSTRATIVE REQUIREMENTS FOR A NONINFLATIONARY FISCAL POLICY UNDER THE BALANCED-BUDGET ASSUMPTION*

Proportion of Added Government Expenditures Which Will Be Reflected in Increased Consumer Spending	Necessary Distribution of Source of Added Tax Payments	
	Decrease in Consumption	Decrease in Saving
0.25	0.58	0.42
0.50	0.83	0.17
0.75	1.08	−0.08

* Balanced-budget assumption applies only to the new expenditure program. The multiplier effect of consumption respending is assumed to be 3. No allowance is made for effects on private investment.

finances indicated that about 9 per cent of money income was saved in 1947.[10] This figure, however, is not a satisfactory guide to the problem at hand, for certain obvious reasons: (1) the 9 per cent figure is an *average* propensity to save and is below the *marginal* propensity, which would be more applicable to the problem at hand; (2) the 9 per cent is weighted down by sizable negative savings for a large group of consumers; (3) there is a difficult problem of making allowance for time lags in the adjustment of consumer spending and saving to a new tax. If the marginal propensity to save by income groups is used as a guide to the impact of a new tax, the available statistics suggest that a tax which is distributed among income groups in proportion to the amount of money expenditures for consumption would be paid out of savings to the extent of 20 to 25 per cent in 1947. For a less regressive type of tax, the proportion paid out of savings would be substantially higher.

These statistical approximations illustrate the difficulty of formulating a noninflationary financing policy within the framework of a balanced budget, unless reliance is placed upon the adverse effects on private investment. With a stimulative effect on private investment, the balanced-budget framework would be intolerable from the standpoint of inflation control. Only a tax surplus could provide the necessary fiscal offset.

[10] See *Fed. Res. Bull.*, June, July, and Aug. 1948, XXXIV.

Example 3. Budget Surplus

Still a third budgetary course is provided by the possibility of levying additional taxes which will more than pay for the incremental expenditures. If the surplus thus created is sufficiently large, the inflationary impact of the expenditure program could be checked. The important variables to be considered in this example are (1) the effect on private investment, (2) the character of the expenditure program, which will determine the induced effect on consumption, (3) the kind of taxes levied, and (4) the amount of revenue obtained.

With respect to the first of these, the opportunity for a decline in private investment which would compensate for the additional government purchases would ordinarily be greater the larger the increase in taxes. New taxes will affect both investment incentives and the availability of funds. From this standpoint, therefore, the budget surplus approach offers distinct advantages as a method of noninflationary financing.

The mathematical formulation followed in the preceding example provides a means of illustrating consistent combinations of values for the remaining three variables, given the objective of a noninflationary policy. These values are shown in Table 2. For example, if it is estimated that one-half of the added government expenditures will reappear as additional consumer spending, the required amount of additional taxes (expressed as percentages of the added government expenditures) would be:

333 per cent, if one-fourth of the new taxes were paid at the expense of consumption;
167 per cent, if one-half the new taxes were paid at the expense of consumption;
111 per cent, if three-fourths of the new taxes were paid at the expense of consumption.

The final figure in the second row of the table suggests that a surplus would not be required in this situation, provided that the taxes induced a dollar-for-dollar reduction in consumer spending—a wholly unrealistic proviso. The general rule, of course, is that the more repressive the tax policy adopted, the smaller the required surplus. These computations, however, do not allow for any adverse effects on private investment. Such effects, of course, would lower the tax requirements.

Certain combinations of figures in the table apply to a neutral expenditure-taxation policy, i.e., a policy which involves expenditures and taxes with equal proportionate effects on consumer spending. In these cases, the amount of taxes required to check the inflationary pressure of added government expenditures would range downward from 233 per cent of the amount of added spending, if the expenditures and taxes had only a small relative effect on consumption, to 144 per cent if the effect were substantial. This illustrates a point made at the outset of this paper, namely, that a financing policy which is neutral in its distributional aspects might still be inflationary, unless it were associated with a sizable budget surplus.

TABLE 2

ILLUSTRATIVE REQUIREMENTS FOR A NONINFLATIONARY FISCAL POLICY: NECESSARY RATIO OF ADDED REVENUES TO ADDED EXPENDITURES*

Proportion of Added Government Expenditures Which Will Be Reflected in Increased Consumer Spending	Ratio of Revenues to Expenses, Assuming That Proportion of Added Taxes Paid at the Expense of Consumer Spending is as Follows:			
	0.25	0.50	0.75	1.00
0.25	2.33	1.17	0.78	0.58
0.50	3.33	1.67	1.11	0.83
0.75	4.33	2.17	1.44	1.08

* Computations assume that the multiplier effect of consumption respending is equal to 3. No allowance is made for effects on private investment.

SELECTION OF APPROPRIATE POLICY

Two separate decisions are involved in the process of formulating an appropriate policy for financing additional government expenditures in a period of high employment and general pressure on the price level: (1) How should the necessary contraction in aggregate private spending be distributed between consumption and investment? (2) What is the best means of accomplishing this objective? By way of explanation it should be noted that the first question refers to the net result of the combined revenue-expenditure program that is adopted, rather than merely to the tax-induced contraction in private spending. The second question should be interpreted so as to embrace both the types and rates of taxes and the various nontax instruments of government economic policy.

There is a simple reason why a decision on the first question is more likely to recommend that the cut be made in consumption rather than in investment. With consumption running at an annual rate of about $180 billion and gross private domestic investment at $40 billion, an expansion of, say, $5 billion in the government program would necessitate a less than 3 per cent contraction in consumption and a 12.5 per cent contraction in investment. On the other hand, one must take account of the more volatile nature of investment spending; changes in consumption spending are typically associated with larger relative changes in investment.

Basically, of course, the decision should depend on where there is more "fat" in the economy, in the consumption or in the investment sector. This consideration also seems to recommend the consumption sector to bear the brunt of the contraction in private spending, although investment in recreational facilities and the like should not be ignored as a candidate for curtailment. In a period of high income and employment there is bound to be considerable leeway for reducing consumer spending without encroaching upon essential living standards. Moreover, both the requirements of national security and the desirability of filling the void which is the legacy of the lean investment period of the 'thirties and the late war years point to the need for continued high investment volume. Consumer spending for durable goods, including residential construction, represents another area where there is a backlog to be worked off.

An additional set of factors, however, weighs heavily on the opposite side of the scale. The inflationary forces have been considerably stronger in the durable goods area of the economy than in the nondurable goods area. Since a stepped-up defense program has its heaviest impact in the former sector, it might be argued that the anti-inflation objective would be best served if the offsetting reduction were made in private spending for durable goods.

If it were agreed that this were the most desirable approach to adopt, then a strong case could be made for relying upon nontax measures. It would be extremely difficult to devise a tax which would have its primary impact on durable goods spending for less essential purposes and at the same time satisfy other criteria for desirable revenue measures. A system of selective excise taxes would appear to have much to recommend it from the standpoint of deterring certain types of purchases, but it would also have important drawbacks such as its limited revenue potentialities, the impossibility of differentiating according to essentiality, the difficulty of taxing secondhand goods, and the high tax rate that would be needed for goods where demand backlogs are large. A program for allocating raw material supplies and rationing production among the more essential users could accomplish the desirable objective in a much more effective manner.

A system of direct controls would make possible a selective curtailment of outlays for producers' plant and equipment, whereas tax measures would have haphazard effects. There would be no certainty that a tax which impinged upon investment incentives would not shut off some of the more urgent plant expansion and modernization programs.

It should be stressed that an anti-inflation program which focused on the curtailment of business and consumer demand for durable goods need not conflict with the various considerations favoring continued large additions to the nation's stock of such goods. There would not be any conflict provided the curtailment program did not interfere with the achievement of maximum production of these goods. As long as productive capacity and materials supplies are deficient at some stage of production, government intervention might serve a useful purpose in channeling output to the high priority users.

The task of curtailing general consumer purchasing, on the other hand, might well be relegated to the individual income tax. The selection of an acceptable pattern of normal and surtax rates always is a difficult one involving the amalgam of social and political considerations entering into income distribution problems. To the extent that it is decided that the reduction in spending should be made largely at upper-income levels, the excess of revenues over expenditures that would be needed to effect a given reduction in consumer spending would be considerably larger than if a less progressive rate structure were selected. This is readily apparent from the pattern of revenue-expenditure ratios shown in Table 2. This requirement illustrates the well-known conflict between anti-inflation objectives and tax progression. A revenue surplus, however, would do more than restrain the immediate inflationary forces, since it would offer long-run advantages in the form of lower carrying charges on the public debt.

A variety of other taxes, such as the corporate income tax, might well have a place in the financing program. Whether or not such taxes are needed as direct anti-inflation measures, they offer possibilities of satisfying various social, political, and fiscal objectives. It may be noted that taxes which are desired for the latter reasons might have an important though indirect effect on the inflation problem. Higher corporate income taxes, for example, have been proposed as a means of slowing down the wage-price spiral, on the ground that the existence of large after-tax profits has lent support to wage demands. To counter this proposal it is argued that a higher tax would weaken employer resistance to wage demands, since the government would in effect pay a large share of the new wage bill. Arguments of this sort involve human more than economic relationships. Their relevance to tax policy formulation should not be minimized.

Finally, one should not overlook the purely fiscal objective. It is a cardinal principle of public finance that a tax program to cover current requirements and debt retirement should always be pursued as vigorously as is consistent with the effective operation of the economy.

APPENDIX[1]

The necessary conditions for financing an increase in government expenditures for goods and services in a manner which will not add to total public and private outlay may be formulated in simplified algebraic terms in the following manner:

$$E + k(I + aE - bT) = 0$$

where

E is the additional government expenditure on current output;
I is the induced change (positive or negative) in private investment;
a is the marginal propensity to consume (out of income after taxes) of the recipients of E;
T is the additional tax revenue (from existing and new legislation);
b is the marginal propensity to consume (out of income after taxes) of those who pay T;
k is the multiplier applicable to a change in private expenditures on consumption or investment, based upon the marginal propensity to consume (out of income after taxes) for the community as a whole.

This equation states that the net effect on aggregate public and private spending will equal (1) the original addition to government purchases, plus (2) k times the change in investment, which may either be positive or negative, plus (3) k times the induced change in the consumption spending of those who receive additional income, minus (4) k times the induced change in the spending of those who meet the increased tax bill. In order to satisfy the equation, the terms must balance out to zero.

An advantage of formulating the problem in the above manner is that it permits a differentiation between the marginal propensity to consume of the community at large, which underlies k, and the respective propensities (a and b) of the groups whose incomes are directly affected by the governmental programs. Of particular importance for the present problem is that this formulation makes it possible to contrast alternative tax policies.

Since the values of E and aE are assumed to be positive, the offsetting influences can have their source either in a negative change in I or in the value of bT. Should the change in I be positive, the burden of offsetting the expansionary influences would rest solely with bT. The value of the latter term depends upon the type of taxes imposed, since b would ordinarily be different for different taxes, and upon the amount of revenue that is obtained. Various simplified non-inflationary financing policies may be illustrated.

1. If sole reliance for counteracting the stimulative influence of additional government spending is placed on a negative change in I, so that $T = 0$, the equation will be satisfied if the reduction in private investment equals the increase in the government program, provided that the marginal propensity to consume of the recipients of government payments equals the marginal propensity

[1] The algebraic presentation in this appendix is an adaption of R. A. Musgrave's equations in "Alternative Budget Policies for Full Employment," *Am. Econ. Rev.*, June 1945, XXXV, 387–400.

to consume of the community at large. In algebraic terms these conditions[2] are $I = -E$, and $a = \frac{k-1}{k}$. In addition, of course, $T = 0$. The proof of this proposition can be demonstrated by substituting the required values for a and T in the original equation and solving for I, as follows:

$$\begin{aligned} E + k\left(I + \frac{k-1}{k}E\right) &= 0 \\ E + kI + kE - E &= 0 \\ kI &= -kE \\ I &= -E \end{aligned}$$

2. It follows from the above that if tax revenues rose so that bT were greater than zero, I could be smaller than $-E$. In the simplified case where $I = 0$, a non-inflationary policy would be possible if $bT = E$ and the marginal propensities to consume of the recipients of government payments and of the community at large are equal (i.e., $a = \frac{k-1}{k}$). Substituting for I and a and solving for bT, we obtain the following:

$$\begin{aligned} E + k\left(\frac{k-1}{k}E - bT\right) &= 0 \\ E + (k-1)E - kbT &= 0 \\ E + kE - E - kbT &= 0 \\ -kbT &= -kE \\ bT &= E \end{aligned}$$

Of necessity, b must be less than one. The preceding equation, therefore, demonstrates the need for a tax surplus in the assumed situation. The surplus requirement also is considered in 4 below.

In the event that there is a divergence between the respective propensities of the recipients of government payments and of the community at large, the necessary condition for bT is:

$$bT = \frac{E}{k} + aE$$

3. Under the balanced budget approach, where $T = E$, whether or not the financing policy is inflationary will hinge on the induced change in investment and on the values of a and b. If the further simplification is made that $I = 0$, then it will be necessary for b to exceed a by an amount equal to the reciprocal of k. By substitution,

$$\begin{aligned} E + k(aE - bE) &= 0 \\ E + kE(a - b) &= 0 \\ a - b &= -\frac{1}{k} \\ b - a &= \frac{1}{k} \end{aligned}$$

[2] The relationship between a and k is derived from the familiar proposition that the multiplier must equal the reciprocal of 1 minus the propensity to consume; that is, $k = \frac{1}{1-a}$. Solving the equation for a gives the expression in the text.

The balanced budget requirement, in other words, is not sufficient to insure a noninflationary policy.

4. Conversely, a "neutral" expenditure and tax program, in which the new taxes were so designed that the tax-induced curtailment of consumption exactly counterbalanced the stimulus to consumption generated by the additional government spending, would not be sufficient, even though taxes and revenues were held in balance. For example, if $a = b$ and $I = 0$, a tax surplus $(T - E)$ of the following magnitude would be necessary:

$$E + k(aE - aT) = 0$$
$$-kaT = -E - kaE$$
$$T = \frac{E}{ka} + E$$
$$T - E = \frac{E}{ka}$$

In the above case, the requisite surplus would be smaller, the larger the values for k, a, and b. Where $a = \frac{k-1}{k} = b$, it can be readily shown that the above result is equivalent to that obtained in 2 above.

5. Under the joint assumptions of a balanced budget $(T = E)$ and a "neutral" expenditure and tax program $(a = b)$, realization of the objective of noninflationary finance would require a negative change in investment in an amount equal to the reciprocal of the multiplier times the added government expenditure. By substitution,

$$E + k(I + aE - aE) = 0$$
$$E + kI = 0$$
$$I = -\frac{E}{k}$$

6. Finally, the situation might be examined where there is a stimulative effect on private investment as well as on consumption. The result in such a case is the same as if government spending were raised by the amount of the additional investment, provided that the simplification is made that government spending and investment outlays are equally stimulating in their effects on consumption. For example, if

$a = \frac{k-1}{k}$, then,

$$E + kI + (k-1)E - kbt = 0$$
$$E + kI + kE - E - kbT = 0$$
$$I + E - bt = 0$$
$$bt = E + I$$

The preceding examples are in the nature of limiting cases which are designed to illustrate various methods of approaching the problem of designing a noninflationary financing policy. In actual practice, of course, a wide range of intermediate policies would be possible.

11

*The Economic Reports of the President and the Problem of Inflation**

By FRANK WHITSON FETTER†

The first Economic Report of the President, called for by the Employment Act of 1946, appeared in January 1947, and the fifth and most recent Report appeared in January 1949. These Reports have received unusually widespread public attention. The reprinting in a popular priced trade edition of the first three, and more recently of the five Reports[1] has made the full texts readily available and has contributed to a careful study of them in college classrooms and by economists, bankers, business men and just plain citizens. It is true, as the Council of Economic Advisers points out in its Introduction to the reprint of the first three Reports, that "the ultimate judgments entering into the Economic Reports to the Congress rest with the President," but the general public as well as economists believe that most of the technical analysis represents the professional opinion of the Council. It is therefore especially incumbent on economists to subject the Reports to a more searching criticism with respect to their economic analysis than would be warranted in the case of the ordinary public document originating in Congress or in the Executive Branch.

The Reports on two major points have taken a position with which most American economists would agree: the need to curb inflation, and (in the first three Reports) the desirability of not reducing taxes until a substantial surplus is assured and the inflationary situation is under

* *The Quarterly Journal of Economics,* May 1949. Reprinted by the courtesy of the *Quarterly Journal of Economics* and the author.

† Northwestern University.

[1] *The Economic Reports of the President.* Introduction by the Council of Economic Advisers. (New York, Harcourt, Brace & Co., 1949). All citations are to the 1949 reprint. In this reprint a new pagination is used after the 1949 Report, and hence citations to the 1949 Report are marked I, and citations to earlier Reports are marked II.

The individual reports were also published as House Documents and as separate Government Documents.

control.[2] After tax reduction was enacted over the President's veto early in 1948, the two subsequent Reports continued to stress the importance of a budgetary surplus and to urge a selective tax increase.[3]

The fact that on the question of tax reduction professional economic opinion was opposed to the consensus in Congress and in business and financial circles quite understandably would make many economists feel that the earlier Reports had analyzed correctly not only the seriousness of the inflationary danger in the period covered but also the nature of the forces back of price movements. But more critical reading of the Reports fails to support the favorable first impression. Not only do they, in particular the earlier ones, have many statements about the price situation that in effect run contrary to their expressed fears about inflation and the inflationary dangers in tax reduction, but some of the economic analysis of the price situation is open to serious question.

A comparison of the Report of January 1947 with that of a year later reveals much less concern over inflation in 1947 than in 1948. In fact, the first Report when considered as a whole, despite some general statements about the dangers of inflation and the evils of high prices, gives the impression that production and employment were in a precarious situation, maintained only by the temporary forces of domestic and international investment. In the face of an increase in 1946 of nearly twenty per cent in the cost of living, and of over thirty per cent in food prices and in wholesale prices, the whole trend of the discussion is on the necessity of maintaining a high level of monetary expenditure. This is illustrated by the analysis in Part V, "Favorable and Unfavorable Factors in 1947,"[4] where the forces that might hold up prices or send them still higher are classed as "favorable," and those that might keep prices from going higher or might lower them are classed as "unfavorable." "To maintain maximum production and employment in 1947 it is desirable that business investment be at an annual rate of at least equal to the annual rate prevailing in the last quarter of 1946."[5] Exports in 1946 "played an important role in the maintenance of domestic production, employment, and purchasing power and may be expected to do so this year."[6] The availability of "abundant aggregate funds including ample bank credit" is a "clear element of strength" in business demand.[7]

That economists at the end of 1946 should have misjudged the nature of the price developments in the next two years is understand-

[2] Jan. 1947, II, p. 34; July 1947, II, pp. 61, 67, 85, 99; Jan. 1948, II, pp. 122, 163.

[3] July 1947, II, p. 257; Jan. 1949, I, p. xxiv.

[4] II, pp. 21–28.

[5] II, p. 24.

[6] II, p. 44.

[7] II, p. 27.

able. Few if any economists have a perfect record of prediction. But an examination of the analysis in both the 1947 and 1948 Reports suggests that the misjudging of the situation was not simply the misplaced emphasis or the bad timing that can upset the predictions of even the ablest of economic analysts, but was inherent in the fallacious conception in the Reports of the nature of inflationary and deflationary forces in the modern economy. In the January 1948 Report the inflationary danger is given more prominence,[8] and the Midyear Report of 1948 states that "we are in the very midst of gathering inflationary forces." "The favorable factors" of the 1947 Report—consumer demand, business demand, exports, and an easy credit situation—have eighteen months later become part of the "interacting processes making for continued inflation."[9] However, insofar as the 1948 Reports represent a more realistic appraisal of the price situation, the realism results largely from being faced by the facts of a continuing upward movement of prices rather than from a re-examination of the analysis of the previous year.[10]

In brief, the Reports of 1947 and 1948 suffer from four analytical errors:

1. The assignment of a very minor role to, and in places the almost complete ignoring of, the increase of the money supply as a factor in the inflationary picture, and the repeated implications that rising prices are due in large part to the unreasonable action of business men and of labor leaders.
2. An assumption that the volume of production and employment has an almost 100 per cent correlation with money payments, even in a period of practically full employment.
3. The failure to recognize that, in a period of practically full employment, capital formation and foreign investment must of necessity reduce the product available for consumption.
4. An unwarranted alarm over the recent decline in the purchasing power of per capita disposable income, as a result of the failure to recognize that a basic reason for the decline in real disposable income has been the impact of domestic and foreign investment demand, and of an increasing propensity to consume, on the price structure.

NEGLECT OF MONETARY CAUSES OF INFLATION

The shortcomings of the Reports on this point are ones of emphasis rather than of complete neglect, for even in the early ones there are

---

[8] II, pp. 157–60. [9] II, p. 255.

[10] In the 1949 Report, following the small drop in a number of price indices in the closing months of 1948, there is a shift in emphasis to the monetary basis of inflation, with the result that the economic analysis in this Report is free from some of the defects in the earlier ones.

references to monetary and credit conditions.[11] Not until the January 1948 Report, however, is the monetary situation discussed as an important factor related to inflation,[12] but neither in that discussion nor anywhere else previous to the January 1949 Report is there any reference to the great expansion in the monetary supply since 1939. The 1949 Report says that money and credit "increased enormously during the war,"[13] but up to that time nothing in the text of the Reports would give the reader any inkling of the fact that currency in circulation in 1947 was over four and a quarter times what it was eight years before, or that demand deposits adjusted and currency combined were three and a half times what they were eight years before.

The reader of the Reports gets the impression that the heart of the problem of inflation is in the attitude of business men and labor leaders. These men are repeatedly exhorted to be reasonable. The first Report lectures business and labor on the virtues of moderation.[14] The second Report points out that the President, after the abandonment of price control, had "urged businessmen to resist inflationary pressures or temptation and to make voluntary price reductions wherever possible;" and gives similar advice to labor about wage increases.[15] The January 1948 Report reiterates the theme, urging business men to "hold the line against price increases and reduce prices wherever they can," and preaching that "labor should be moderate in its wage demands, mindful of recent experience which demonstrates the impossibility of registering real gains in an inflationary spiral."[16] In the 1948 Midyear Report, with what seems like unintended irony in view of the alarm shown in that Report over inflation, we are told that "many leaders in both industry and labor can be applauded for the conscious restraint they have exhibited in their pricing policies and wage demands."[17]

RELATIONS OF MONETARY PAYMENTS TO PHYSICAL PRODUCTION AND EMPLOYMENT

On this point passages can be found to support almost any view, but the dominant theme, particularly in the earlier Reports, is that physical production and employment move up and down in almost exact relation to money payments. In the first 1947 Report appears the categorical statement: "The volume of employment and production in any given period depends upon the volume of expenditures."[18]

---

[11] Jan. 1947, II, p. 10.

[12] II, pp. 164–66. In the January 1947 Report, "ample bank credit" had been mentioned under the heading of "favorable factors in business demand," II, p. 27.

[13] I, p. xix. [14] II, pp. 31, 32. [15] II, pp. 89, 96.

[16] II, p. 168. [17] II, p. 255. [18] II, p. 14.

Foreign sales in 1946 "played an important role in the maintenance of domestic production, employment, and purchasing power and may be expected to do so this year."[19]

The Midyear Report for 1947 is on the defensive in the matter of the export surplus, but the emphasis is on the quantity of goods available for the consumer rather than upon the price consequences, although there is a reference to foreign buyers' contribution to the "upward pressure on prices."[20] Instead of praising the export surplus as a stimulant to production, as was done six months earlier, the point is now made that "it is easy to exaggerate the degree of deprivation" for home use.[21] In itself this is a correct statement, but it contributes to the misleading picture that foreign demand in 1947 had its impact largely upon production and not upon prices. In the 1948 Report there is a further shift in emphasis, and the Report states that exports in the first half of 1947 "had an important bearing upon the total levels of employment and production and upon the level of prices."[22] It is certainly open to question, however, whether exports had an appreciable effect upon total production and employment, particularly in view of the fact that in the case of many manufactured and agricultural products, exports simply deprived domestic consumers of part of an output which was at a maximum.

RELATION BETWEEN CONSUMER INCOME, CAPITAL FORMATION, AND FOREIGN AID

The first Report stresses the point that appears in subsequent ones, namely, that per capita real "disposable income" (personal income after taxes), after rising in 1944 to more than 50 per cent above the 1935–39 average, had fallen slightly in 1945 and 1946, and that only by a substantial reduction in savings (from 28.3 per cent of disposable income in 1944 to 9.5 per cent of disposable income in the last quarter of 1946) and by an increase in installment credit had it been possible for consumers to purchase the same quantity of goods and services as before.[23] The January 1948 Report observes that, with the further decline in the real income of consumers in 1947, consumption "was maintained by liquidation of past savings, a reduction of the saving out of current incomes, and the extensive use of consumer credit,"[24] and the 1949 Report points out that in 1948 there was

[19] II, p. 44. As "purchasing power" is defined in the Reports in real terms (II, p. 10), this statement would appear to mean that in this period of virtually full employment the product available to the American economy was greater as a result of our large exports.

[20] II, pp. 70, 111. [21] II, p. 111. [22] II, p. 144. [23] II, pp. 21–25.

[24] II, p. 131.

no appreciable gain in consumer per capita real income despite a rise in total national output.[25]

When an economy reaches approximately full employment, particularly if there is a decline in overtime work and a stoppage of production through strikes, it is not surprising that less goods will be available for consumers, if business is to increase capital plant and if we are to have a large export surplus, whether that export surplus be financed by credits, gold shipments to the United States, or a drawing down of dollar balances. The economic miracle of the years 1940 to 1944, of rising real per capita disposable income in the face of a diversion of a large proportion of production to ends other than consumption, requires for its accomplishment the stage property of a large volume of unemployment at the start of the performance. The Reports seem to miss this point and to consider the development of the years 1940 to 1944 as a normal feature of the American economy even in a state of full employment. They have an almost mystical belief that any decline in real per capita disposable income is a threat to economic stability, regardless of the cause of the decline.

Insofar as consumers, by reducing their rate of savings, by borrowing, or by drawing on past savings, refuse to adjust their consumption to their reduced real disposable income, the effect must be either that goods are diverted from investment to consumption, or that the allocation to consumption is unchanged but on the basis of higher prices, or that there is some combination of these effects dependent upon the various price, income, and supply elasticities. As a result of the combination of a belief in the normality of an increase in per capita real disposable income, and the assumption—perhaps not recognized explicitly but nevertheless basic to much of the analysis—that the problem of the inflationary years of 1946 and 1947 are much the same as the problems of the 1930's, the Reports are confused as to the significance of this rising propensity to consume, and as to its desirability in the period covered. This confusion is illustrated by the discussion in the January 1948 Report where the "survey of consumer income and expenditures during 1947 points to two causes for concern:" the contribution to "inflationary pressure," and a reduction in "the real purchasing power of consumers to the point where it will not be adequate to take the consumers' share of the national output at present prices when certain abnormal demands are reduced and when the rate of consumer saving cannot be further reduced."[26]

[25] I, p. xix. [26] II, pp. 136–37.

THE PROBABLE CONSEQUENCES OF A DECLINE IN DEMAND FROM DOMESTIC CAPITAL FORMATION AND EXPORT SURPLUS

The authors of the Reports have got themselves into a vicious circle of their own creation on this whole problem of the relation of consumer purchasing power, investment demand, and export surplus to prices and employment. In individual passages, particularly in the 1948 Reports, the influence of these demands upon prices is recognized,[27] but the significance of this inflationary impact is never integrated into the analysis. The inflationary effects of increased expenditures of a temporary type are regarded as non-reversible. The thesis of the Reports seems to be that although an increase in money payments from domestic capital formation, export surplus, and a high propensity to consume may raise prices and distort previously existing price relations, a decline in capital formation, a smaller export surplus, and a lower propensity to consume will not bring a downward movement of any individual prices. Given these assumptions, the conclusion of course follows that a slackening of demands from these three sources must result in depression and unemployment. The real issue is whether the Reports' approach to the problem is a realistic one, or one that will contribute to a solution of the problem of readjustment with the slackening of these demands.

Repeatedly the point is made that if these special demands fall off, consumer income cannot absorb output at existing prices,[28] but with the exception of one statement in the 1949 Report,[29] I find nothing that suggests that the end of these special demands will bring any pressure toward a readjustment of price relations, much less that forces of the market will actually bring about such a readjustment. The position of the Reports on such an adjustment seems to be that business men should become more reasonable or that the government should take more vigorous action against inflation, and not that there are forces in the market which would make such an adjustment likely.[30]

I would not minimize the reality of the problem of adjustment of production and of prices with a decline in the demand for individual products. A sound economic policy must not only obviate drastic de-

[27] II, pp. 157–58. "The inflationary impact of spending was strong in all fields—capital expansion, exports, and consumption." The same idea appears in the Midyear Report for 1948, II, p. 255.

[28] Jan. 1947, II, pp. 20, 30–31; July 1947, II, pp. 90, 92, 101, 108; Jan. 1948, II, pp. 119, 125, 137, 149, 195; Jan. 1949, I, pp. xvii, xxi.

[29] I, p. xvii.

[30] Jan. 1949, I, p. xxi; Jan. 1947, II, pp. 20, 21, 30, 31; July 1947, II, p. 88.

creases in total money payments, but it should also recognize that in some areas the prices of individual products will decrease in response to a decrease in money payments, and that the extent of these price decreases, and the area over which they operate, is to some degree dependent upon governmental policy. The failure of the Reports to recognize this twofold nature of the problem of adjustment to changing monetary demand, and their consequent assumption that unemployment must be the result of any decrease in money payments—except as prices are reduced from causes that apparently are not connected with the decrease in money payments—has resulted from their circular reasoning on the relationship between the various parts of the national product.

The Reports from the beginning have performed a public service in stressing inflationary dangers and in pleading for the unpopular policy of maintaining high taxes. They contain much excellent economic analysis, but the thinking of the authors is permeated with the idea that real disposable incomes of consumers must rise, regardless of other developments, and much of the discussion is shackled to the fears of deflation and mass unemployment. The neglect of the monetary basis of inflation, the attempt to make business men and labor leaders personally responsible for inflation, and the repeated assumption that the impact of demand changes is almost exclusively upon production and employment rather than upon prices, results in an unbalanced picture of the forces of inflation and of deflation.

The Reports raise for economists the larger question as to the use and the limitations of logical analysis as a basis for prediction and as a basis for the formulation of public policy. The dominant thought in them is Keynesian, in the broad sense of the body of doctrine that was inspired by the *General Theory.* Underlying most of the analysis is the basic assumption that changes in aggregate demand have employment effects rather than price effects, and that a steady increase in consumer purchasing power is essential to economic stability with full employment. A great deal of the controversy of the last thirteen years over consumption, savings, investment, aggregate demand, and employment, that is associated with the name of Keynes, has been a battle of logicians. Interpreted with perspective, the fruits of this controversy have contributed greatly to the understanding of the monetary economy. Yet those on both sides of the argument have all too frequently taken the view that logic could settle public policy. Many ardent Keynesians, acutely conscious of the fact that they have discarded the conclusions of Ricardo and his followers, apparently do not realize that their conceptual approach is almost identical with that of Ricardo and of other great figures of the classical tradition: there are economic laws which when mastered tell us how the economic system behaves at all times.

In the later 1930's the Keynesian approach seemed to many economists—and certainly to a great majority of younger economists—a more satisfying explanation as to how the modern economy had behaved in the last few years than was anything found in classical economics. What was all too frequently forgotten, or greatly underestimated, was that the validity of either approach depends in large part on such shifting factors as the current psychology of consumers, the nature of the pricing practices affecting individual products, and the existing investment situation. In view of this situation, economic theory, if it is to be useful for prediction, must be considered as a hypothesis whose applicability in any particular situation depends upon the changing human reactions to particular monetary impulses. A failure to recognize the limitations of pure analysis, and the assumption that conditions in 1946 were much like those in the early 1930's have been the basic shortcomings in the Reports' discussion of inflation and employment.

12

*How to Pay for the War**

By JOHN MAYNARD KEYNES

THE CHARACTER OF THE SOLUTION

Even if there were no increases in the rates of money-wages, the total of money-earnings will be considerably increased by the greater number of insured men engaged in the services and in civilian employments, by overtime, and by the movement into paid employment of women, boys, retired persons and others who were not previously occupied.

It will be shown in the next chapter, what is fairly obvious to common sense, that in a war like this the amount of goods available for consumption will have to be diminished—and certainly cannot be increased above what it was in peace time.

It follows that the increased quantity of money available to be spent in the pockets of consumers will meet a quantity of goods which is not increased. Unless we establish iron regulations limiting what is to be sold and establishing maximum prices for every article of consumption, with the result that there is nothing left to buy and the consumer goes home with the money burning his pocket, there are only two alternatives. Some means must be found for withdrawing purchasing power from the market; or prices must rise until the available goods are selling at figures which absorb the increased quantity of expenditure—in other words the method of inflation.

The general character of our solution must be, therefore, that it withdraws from expenditure a proportion of the increased earnings. This is the only way, apart from shortages of goods or higher prices, by which we can secure a balance between money to be spent and goods to be bought.

Voluntary savings would serve this purpose if they were sufficient. In any case voluntary savings are wholly to the good and limit to that extent the dimensions of our problem. No word should be said to dis-

* Chapter II of *How to Pay for the War* (New York, Harcourt, Brace, 1949). Reprinted by the courtesy of Harcourt, Brace.

courage the missionary zeal of those who campaign to increase them or the self-restraint and public spirit of those who make them. Nor is there anything in the plan which follows to make voluntary personal economy useless or unnecessary. I aim at a scheme which will achieve the bare minimum; and by the time it has been qualified by practical concessions nothing is more likely than that it will fall short of the bare minimum, and will not be sufficient by itself. Every further economy in personal consumption beyond what is prescribed will either ease the position of some other consumer or will allow an intensification of our war effort.

But the analysis of the national potential and of the distribution of the national income, which will be given in the next two chapters, shows clearly enough how improbable it is that voluntary savings can be sufficient. Those who allege otherwise are deceiving themselves or are victims of their own propaganda. Moreover, many people would, I think, welcome a prescribed plan which indicates to them their minimum duty; and those who feel moved to do more can rest assured that their effort is not useless. A minimum plan will not close the way to the voluntary self-sacrifice of individuals for the public good and the national purpose, any more than our system of taxation does. The nation will still need urgently the fruits of further personal abstention—always bearing it in mind that some forms of economy are much less valuable than others. But I also reckon it a merit of a prescribed plan that it reduces for the average man the necessity for a continuing perplexity how much to economise and for thinking about such things more than is good. An excessive obsession towards saving may be more useful than lovely; it is not always he who decides to save who makes the real sacrifice; and public necessity may sometimes become an excuse for giving full rein with self-approval to an instinct which is also a vice.

The first provision in our radical plan (Chapters V and VI) is, therefore, to determine a proportion of each man's earnings which must be deferred;—withdrawn, that is to say, from immediate consumption and only made available as a right to consume after the war is over. If the proportion can be fixed fairly for each income group, this device will have a double advantage. It means that rights to immediate consumption during the war can be allotted with a closer regard to relative sacrifice than under any other plan. It also means that rights to deferred consumption after the war, which is another name for the National Debt, will be widely distributed amongst all those who are foregoing immediate consumption, instead of being mainly concentrated, as they were last time, in the hands of the capitalist class.

The second provision is to provide for this deferred consumption without increasing the National Debt by a general capital levy after the war.

The third provision is to protect from any reductions in current consumption those whose standard of life offers no sufficient margin. This is effected by an exempt minimum, a sharply progressive scale and a system of family allowances. The net result of these proposals is, to increase the consumption of young families with less than 75*s.* a week, to leave the *aggregate* consumption of the lower income group having £5 a week or less nearly as high as before the war (whilst at the same time giving them rights, in return for extra work, to deferred consumption after the war), and to reduce the aggregate consumption of the higher income group with more than £5 a week by about a third on the average.

The fourth provision (Chapter VIII), rendered possible by the previous provisions but not itself essential to them, is to link further changes in money-rates of wages, pensions and other allowances to changes in the cost of a limited range of rationed articles of consumption, an iron ration as it has been called, which the authorities will endeavour to prevent, one way or another, from rising in price.

This scheme, put forward in the light of criticism and after further reflection, is more comprehensive than the plan for deferment of income which I proposed in the columns of *The Times* last November. Nevertheless this original proposal is the lynchpin of the whole construction, failing which the rest would be impracticable. Without this proposal the cost of family allowances would aggravate the problem of consumption by increasing it in one direction without diminishing it in another; and would merely make the progress of inflation more inevitable. The same is true of an iron ration at a low price. Unless we have first of all withdrawn the excess of purchasing power from the market, the cost of subsidising consumption will lead the Treasury deeper into the financial bog. But if a deferment of earnings is agreed, the whole construction stands solid.

A general plan like this, to which all are required to conform, is like a rule of the road—everyone gains and no one can lose. To regard such a rule as an infringement of liberty is somewhat silly. If the rule of the road is imposed, people will travel as much as before. Under this plan people will consume as much as before. The rule of the road allows people as much choice, as they would have without it, along which roads to travel. This plan would allow people as much choice as before what goods they consume.

A comparison with the rule of the road is a very fair comparison. For the plan is intended to prevent people from getting in one another's way in spending their money.

IV. FISCAL POLICY AND THE NATIONAL DEBT (MONETARY POLICY)

13

*The Implications of Fiscal Policy for Monetary Policy and the Banking System**

By JOHN H. WILLIAMS†

I

One of the most striking facts about the development of fiscal policy in the past decade is that while it grew out of monetary policy and was designed to supplement and strengthen it, fiscal policy has ended up by threatening to supplant monetary policy altogether.

The emphasis on central bank control was carried to great heights in the late twenties and early thirties. Failures to achieve adequate control were ascribed to the shortcomings of the central bankers rather than to any weaknesses inherent in the method of control. But as the great depression deepened, despite the fact that the easy money policy was carried to lengths unprecedented in this or any other country, the conviction grew that whatever might have been the defects of central bank policy, the main trouble lay in the inadequacy of this method, by itself, to control investment and the level of output and employment.

Fiscal policy was designed to supplement monetary policy in two ways. First, if an easy money policy would not, by itself, sufficiently induce investment, this object could be achieved by creating new community income through budgetary deficits. In this sense, fiscal policy could perhaps be regarded from the beginning as a substitute for central bank policy. The analysis of income-creating expenditures has been the chief preoccupation of fiscal theory. In the pump-priming version of the theory the emphasis was laid on the power of deficit spending to stimulate private investment. In the later versions it was placed on the

* Delivered at a joint session of the American Economic Association and the American Statistical Association at their annual meetings in New York on December 28, 1941, and published in the *Proceedings of the American Economic Association,* March 1942. Reprinted by courtesy of the American Economic Association and the author.

† Harvard University.

need for compensating, by means of public expenditures, for chronic tendencies toward over-saving and under-investment.

But throughout the analysis attention was also given to the ways in which fiscal policy could make central bank policy more effective. Monetary analysis had been directed increasingly toward the role of the rate of interest as the controller of investment. Until Keynes's *Treatise on Money* appeared in 1930, the main emphasis had been on control of the short-term rate. That short-term credit was the only proper concern of banking and of monetary control was an idea deeply rooted in the history of banking theory. It appeared to follow, for example, from the commercial loan theory of bank assets, which had its roots in the controversies of the banking and the currency schools in the first half of the nineteenth century, but which had persisted with such vitality as to dominate the philosophy and many of the basic provisions of the Federal Reserve Act. While the theory was never lived up to entirely in banking practice, short-term assets played the predominant role in banking changes and it was through them that adjustments were made to changes in the reserve position of the banks. The result was a high degree of sensitivity in short-term open-market rates. Historical charts of interest rates show that until recent years short-term rates fluctuated widely above and below the long-term rates; and some of the older economic treatises insisted, though I think with much exaggeration, upon the constancy of the long-term rate as indicating a persistent natural tendency of saving and investment to equalize at an unchanging rate of interest.

Since the first World War revolutionary changes have occurred in American banking. The post-war boom of 1919–20 was a great blow to the commercial loan theorists, for it was an inventory boom and found its banking expression primarily in excessive commercial loan expansion. It was followed by important changes in financial practice, whereby business became increasingly its own banker so far as working capital was concerned. Commercial loans diminished. By 1929 commercial paper eligible for rediscount was only 12 per cent of total earning assets, and by 1932 only 8 per cent. In the stock market boom of the late twenties, we saw the enormous increase in security loans both for the banks' own account and for the account of others. Out of this experience came the grant of authority to the Reserve System to control the stock market use of credit. This was a fundamental, indeed a revolutionary, development in monetary policy, away from the traditional over-all quantitative control of the supply of money toward the control of a specific use of money.

But the greatest change which has occurred in banking since the Reserve System was established has been in the growth of bank investments. This growth began in the first World War when the banks, with the aid of the new Reserve System, bought government securities for their own account and made loans to finance purchases by the public. That this change in the composition of bank assets was not merely a temporary war-time change was indicated by the fact that as the Federal debt was reduced during the twenties, the banks did not reduce their holdings of government securities. Then followed, beginning in 1931, the continuous series of budget deficits to the present day. The Federal debt, direct and guaranteed, has risen from $15,922,000,000 on June 30, 1930 to $54,747,000,000 on June 30, 1941, and the holdings of Federal government securities by the commercial banks have risen from $4,981,000,000 to $20,098,000,000. At the present time investments, mainly in government securities, comprise about 57 per cent of total earning assets.

As this great change occurred in bank assets, the theory of assets underwent important changes. The commercial loan theory came in for closer scrutiny and some of its fallacies were revealed, though not, I think, without leaving in it an important kernel of truth. Attention was directed toward what was called the "monetary theory" of bank assets, by which was meant that changes in *any* type of assets affect the quantity of deposits and currency, which in turn was held to produce economic changes. The implication was that what kinds of changes occur in the *composition* of bank assets is immaterial.

As bank investments have increased, long-term interest rates have shown increased sensitivity to changes in bank reserves, and the emphasis in monetary theory has shifted to the need for controlling the long-term rates, as more effective for the control of investment, income, and employment than control merely of the short-term rates. It was in connection with the long-term rate of interest that fiscal policy was expected to strengthen central bank policy. The appearance of excess reserves came as a distinct shock to many monetary theorists in the early thirties. Much of previous monetary theory had been built on the assumption that the banks would always be loaned up. But it became unmistakably clear, as bank reserves expanded, that bankers were interested in the quality as well as the quantity of their assets and rather than assume undue risks would hold their reserves idle. It was at this point that monetary policy and fiscal policy joined hands. The financing of deficits, combined with pressure through reserves, affords an avenue for expansion of bank assets and deposits accompanied by a decline in interest rates. In addition to the new money thus created, government borrowing provides an outlet for old deposits which might otherwise remain idle rather than assume the risks of investment in depression. Theoretically, the decline of interest rates would begin in the market for short-term securities, but as the short-term rates declined, the banks would reach out for longer maturities. The fall in the rate on government securities would spread to other investments and loans, attracting both bank and non-bank investors, until after a transition phase of refunding of old securities the new issues market would be affected and a stream of new investment set in motion.

As we look back over the period since 1932, when the excess reserves and large-scale deficits began, we can see that the only part of this expectation that failed to materialize was the revival, to an adequate extent, of private investment. Though the excess reserves were not used up, bank assets, mainly in government securities, greatly expanded, and the expansion of bank deposits was greater than in any previous period in our history. By 1939 demand deposits and currency were over 50 per cent greater than at the peak of the boom in 1929. As bank reserves and the money supply expanded, the rates on long-term governments and on the better-grade corporate securities fell to the lowest levels in the history of this or any other country,[1] and the rate on short-term governments declined to practically zero.

II

My concern is with the implications of these developments for the future of banking and of monetary policy. There is no denying that we have had the most tremendous experiment in history with the easy money policy. It should be said that the scale on which the experiment occurred was not intended. The conscious, deliberate policy of creating excess reserves by central bank operations lasted only through 1932 and 1933. The enormous increase of reserves which occurred thereafter was due mainly to gold inflow and to a much less extent to the silver purchase policy. But it should be added that for some time the authorities were not unsympathetic to the continuing expansion of excess reserves and the decline of interest rates which accompanied it. The gold sterilization begun in December 1936 and the raising of reserve requirements in 1936–37 were not intended to reverse the easy money

[1] The most nearly comparable period is that of the late 1890's and early 1900's, when interest rates also fell to very low levels. The conditions, however, were hardly comparable. The securities which sank lowest were those baring the national banknote circulation privilege. Moreover, the national debt was then very small.

policy, though they did indicate a judgment that there would be no further advantage, and a growing balance of disadvantage, if the growth of excess reserves were allowed to proceed unchecked.

Of special significance were the events which accompanied these attempts to reduce the excess reserves. For a short period in 1937 there was something resembling a government bond panic. One can readily appreciate the apprehension which was felt. Selling of government securities by the banks at a time when the government debt was still increasing could have highly deflationary effects. It would mean that non-bank investors would be called upon to buy not only the new securities being issued but also the old securities being sold by the banks; and this process would have to take place at a time when the volume of deposits, by reason of bank selling, was contracting. Actually the net amount of selling by the banks, and the effects of the selling, were exaggerated in the current discussions. If we look at the full year from June 1936 to June 1937, during which the changes in reserve requirements occurred, what broadly happened was that New York City banks sold securities while the interior banks bought. But in the crucial first half of 1937 both classes of banks made net sales. The net contraction of bank holdings of governments was about a billion dollars, and interest rates advanced by about a half per cent. The episode revealed once more, as the bank holiday had done in 1933, that the peculiar vulnerability of New York, which had been responsible for our money panics prior to the creation of the Reserve System, still remains a problem, and one that takes on an added significance now that bank assets consist to such a large extent of securities subject to fluctuations in market price. The country banks met the increased reserve requirements mainly by drawing upon their balances with their city correspondents. Their excess reserve position remained but little affected, while the New York banks were subjected to the double pressure of meeting their own increased reserve requirements and providing reserves for the country banks.

The fact that the raising of reserve requirements was followed by the new depression of 1937–38 caused some persons to place the responsibility for the depression upon the Reserve policy, while others ascribed it mainly to the fact that for a brief interval in 1937 the Federal budget came into balance. Though in my judgment neither of these developments was a major cause of the new depression, the conjuncture of circumstances had important effects upon the further development of ideas with regard to both fiscal and monetary policies. The gold-sterilization policy was dropped, the reserve requirements were moderately reduced, and the Reserve System's newly developed function of "maintaining orderly market conditions" for government securities took on added significance. As for the banks, some said that the new depression, coupled with the disappearance of any near prospect of resumption of monetary control, had "saved the banks." While there was, of course, much exaggeration in this view, it did point to a growing awareness of the new elements of instability which the combination of excess reserves and government deficits had introduced into the banking system. The selling crisis was shortlived. Gold continued to pour in, the growth of excess reserves was resumed, the banks resumed their buying of government securities, and the prices of the securities steadily rose to new all-time highs, with some minor setbacks such as that on the outbreak of the war in 1939 and on our own entry into the war in 1941.

Much the most important change, for our present subject, that occurred as a result of the new depression in 1937 was the change in fiscal theory. The conviction grew that we were faced with something more than cyclical recovery from a major depression. The emphasis shifted from pump-priming to the need for deficits as compensation for long-run structural changes in the economy, changes which were held to be due to chronic tendencies toward over-saving and under-investment and which were said to call for deficits that might be permanent or at any rate should be continued so long as under-employment prevailed.

I had been, and still am, sympathetic to the alliance between central bank policy and pump-priming. They do not differ from each other in purpose or in general analysis of the problem. Both are aimed primarily at cyclical variations on the assumption that aside from such movements the economy can be self-sustaining. Properly managed, they could be mutually reinforcing. In recovery from depression the deficits might play the larger role, both by creating new income directly and by helping to implement an easy money policy. In a boom monetary policy could play an important and perhaps even the predominant role. A contraction of bank reserves, especially if coupled with some direct controls such as those over stock market and instalment credit, can exert powerful effects upon investment, output, and employment, provided excess reserves are not too large to prevent central bank contact with the money market. With budget surpluses in boom offsetting deficits in depression the problems of bank holdings of government securities would not exist, or at any rate would not reach serious dimensions.

Whether the pump-priming policy could be successful is another question. It was really never tried. There is no evidence that the Administration, as distinct from some persons within it and some economists offering advice from the outside, ever had a conscious interest in fiscal policy as an instrument of recovery prior to the new depression in 1938. Government spending was primarily for relief and was regarded mainly as the unavoidable accompaniment of unemployment until recovery could be achieved by other means. I have been inclined to agree with those who hold that relief expenditures do not reach down far enough into the economic process to afford much leverage. Public works expenditures, if they could be adjusted to the business cycle, would probably be more effective, and military expenditures also would probably have a greater stimulating effect, even in peace-time. Now that our military expenditures are likely to remain large, for improvements, replacement, and maintenance even after the initial expansion has been completed, we may have in such expenditures, so far as they can be adjusted to business cycle changes, a significant instrument of control of economic fluctuations. A further important consideration is that if pump-priming is to be seriously attempted in the future, it must be done in an atmosphere that is favourable to "business confidence" and must give attention to the other economic conditions, including the behaviour of costs and prices and the effects of taxation on investment as well as on consumption, which bear upon the revival of output and employment under private enterprise.

The difficulties for banking and for monetary control grow not out of pump-priming but out of the long-run spending policies. The question which I raise is whether a large and growing public debt which continues to be financed to a large extent by the banking system does not make impossible a general monetary policy and deprive us of the power to vary the interest rate and the money supply as instruments of control of economic fluctuations.

That such a control is not feasible in war appears to be amply indicated by the fact that all the countries at war, not only totalitarian Germany but democratic England, Canada, and our own country, are pursuing an easy money policy, notwithstanding the fact that the money supply is redundant and interest rates are at or near their record lows. This is a situation without precedent in the history of wars. Prior to the first World War there would probably have been general agreement that to control inflation we should place reliance upon monetary controls first, fiscal controls second, and direct controls last. Even in the last war Treasury financing was done at rising rates of interest, though there was little or no deliberate effort to impose restraints upon monetary expansion. But in the present war the policy is frankly one of easy money. With this policy I am entirely in accord. A restrictive monetary policy is not feasible or desirable so long as the government is the principal borrower and the banks must be relied upon to do a large portion of the lending. The restraints imposed upon inflation must come mainly through direct controls and through taxation. That the possibilities of financing war by taxation may be limited, however, would appear to be indicated by the fact that in England, whose war effort absorbs some 50 per cent of national income, less than 40 per cent of the war expenditures are met by taxes. Our need for borrowing will undoubtedly remain large. It is, of course, desirable that this financing should be done as much as possible outside the banks, but unless and until other sources of funds can be proved adequate it would be the height of folly to prevent bank buying of government securities.

III

Under war-time conditions we shall probably have to bow to this necessity. But what are the implications of an indefinitely prolonged continuance of large-scale public borrowing thereafter? This question breaks down into a number of aspects, such as the future of interest rates, of the volume of deposits, the condition of the banking system, and the future course of excess reserves and monetary policy.

One of the main lessons to be drawn from our experiences of the past decade is that it is possible to overdo an easy money policy. It is a curious fact that though fiscal policy grew out of the recognition that pushing down the interest rate does not adequately achieve a revival of investment, output, and employment, the emphasis upon low interest rates was carried over not only into the pump-priming policy, where it rightly belonged, but also into the long-run "compensatory" fiscal theories, which in one version rest upon the assumption of chronic oversaving, and in another upon the assumption that in a mature economy private investment *cannot* be adequate, however stimulated. Doubtless the explanation is that even under these assumptions it is desirable to do everything possible to stimulate private investment.[2] Great emphasis was placed by Keynes in his *General Theory* on the need for reducing the interest rate. His thesis is that since, by reason of risk and other factors affecting "liquidity preference," we cannot push the interest rate below a certain minimum, we must use deficit spending (or taxation) to fill the gap between saving and investment.

The question raised by our experience, however, is whether too

[2] Another consideration may be the cost of carrying the public debt, but this is surely a very minor point with those who hold these theories, since they repeatedly take pains to demonstrate that the economic cost of public debt is slight.

much emphasis has not been placed upon the interest rate as a cost of investment and too little upon it as an inducement to invest. Interest is but one of the costs of investment and is unlikely in most cases to be the controlling one, even though it is more important in long- than in short-time investment. But there is also the viewpoint of the lender. When the interest rate falls very low there may be inadequate inducement to invest out of income, or even to keep capital invested. This is, one must admit, not altogether a simple question. We must recognize, for example, that some kinds of institutions have increased their investments, even at falling interest rates, when they have been under pressure to invest and could find safe investments. As already described, it was the pressure of excess reserves, combined with the need for earnings as interest rates declined, that induced the banks to invest in government securities. One could cite too the increase of investments of the insurance companies, also under heavy pressure to invest premiums and maintain earnings. But such facts do not prove that the aggregate of investment would not be greater if interest rates were higher. And when the theoretical problem posed is that of idle saving, is this not the proper question? One of the most striking aspects of our experience during the thirties was that the unprecedentedly large increase in the volume of deposits and currency which resulted from the combination of excess reserves and deficit financing was offset by an equally great decline in the velocity of money. There is no precedent for this experience, on such a scale, in all preceding monetary history. The explanation of it is probably complex. One important cause may well have been the "lack of confidence," quite apart from the interest rate, on which the business and financial world so much insisted during the period of New Deal experimentation. But it may well have been due also to the fact that the interest return from investment was not high enough to overcome "liquidity preference."

That an easy money policy can be overdone is indicated also by the fact that when interest rates fall to very low levels deflationary stresses and strains appear in the economy which are directly attributable to this decline. A wide range of institutions and individuals dependent upon fixed income-yielding investments suffer losses of income whose effects upon their ability and willingness to invest further, their sense of security, and even their ability to maintain consumption, work directly counter to the purpose of the easy money policy. If the low interest rates did actually achieve an adequate recovery of investment, output, and employment, these adverse effects could perhaps be dismissed as part of the necessary cost of a successful monetary policy. But when rates reach such a low level that they accomplish little or nothing further to stimulate investment, from the side of demand for capital, while impairing the ability of some important income groups and institutions to invest or even to consume, the easy money policy has overreached itself.

There have been suggestions in recent years, and some of them have come from fiscal theorists who in the past have been most insistent upon low interest rates, that it may be necessary to subsidize some classes of interest receivers, by devising special government security issues at higher coupons than the prevailing open-market rates. There could be many candidates for such subsidies long before interest rates reached Joan Robinson's suggested zero.[3] Recently one or two of the leading insurance companies have announced an advance in premium rates to offset the decline of yield upon investments.[4] Savings banks have had to cut their interest payments to a very low level. Universities and other endowed institutions have had to cut their budgets. We are told that in England it is frankly recognized that the government must sustain the banks by borrowing at rates high enough to cover bank expenses, and that the same subject has aroused some interest in Canada.

One of the chief difficulties of an easy money policy, when it is implemented or accompanied by large government borrowing, is that it becomes increasingly difficult to reverse the policy. This, as I have sought to show, has been the main implication of our own experience of the past decade. And it is the main reason for the suggestions that we may have to make a list of exceptions to the application of the policy. The larger the public debt and the greater the continuing need of the government to borrow and spend, the greater are the hazards for the Treasury and for the banking system that are involved in any reversal of the policy. For the Treasury it would mean financing at rising rates of interest, which means not only a rising cost of borrowing, which by itself might not be decisive though increasingly important as the debt expands, but also an increasing worry that the market may develop an inclination to hold off and wait for better terms and so have increasingly to be coaxed or threatened. To the banks it would mean increased earnings on new issues, but losses in market values upon old ones. The result is that even when there may be general agreement that interest rates have gone too low and that it might have been better to stabilize them

[3] *Essays in the Theory of Employment,* p. 255: ". . . when capitalism is rightly understood, the rate of interest will be set at zero, and the major evils of capitalism will disappear."

[4] See *New York Times* editorial, "Easy Money and Insurance," Nov. 22, 1941, suggesting special Treasury issues for insurance companies.

at some earlier time when they were higher, there is always a strong presumption in favour of stabilizing at the current level, if not indeed of allowing them to go still lower. To put rates up would mean to throw the main burden of adjustment upon the banking system and the Treasury. That such a policy would be unwise in wartime seems generally to be recognized, but the problem would be no different in time of peace if the same facts as to size and distribution of the public debt and the continuing need for public borrowing prevailed.

One further important aspect of an extreme easy money policy, implemented by excess reserves and public borrowing, is that the effects are different upon different rates of interest. In the debates about monetary policy in the late twenties and early thirties one of the points most emphasized by those who doubted the adequacy of interest rate control[5] as a means of controlling investment, output, and employment was that there was not one rate of interest but many, and that the differences in their behaviour greatly complicated the task of central bank control. One complication was a perverse cyclical variation, such that when the rates most subject to monetary control were falling in depression and rising in a boom in response to central bank policy, other rates were rising and falling in response to expectations of income affecting risk. Owing to such factors as defects of market organization, inertia, local or regional customs, and the importance of personal relations between lender and borrower, many interest rates were largely insensitive to quantitative monetary controls, which affected mainly the open-market rates of the large financial centres. Looking back at our experiences of the past decade, we can see how uneven the effects of the easy money policy have been. Great gaps have been opened up in the interest rate structure. At one extreme short-term open-market rates, prior to the recent decline in excess reserves, had been reduced to virtually zero. Such low rates as have prevailed for Treasury bills and other high-grade short-term paper serve no useful purpose and reflect nothing other than the abnormality of excessive bank reserves. Were such rates more nearly in line with longer term rates, as used to be the case, banks would be under less pressure to reach out for longer maturities to maintain earnings, and one of the main dangers of banking instability would be removed. At the other extreme some other interest rates, such as mortgage rates and the general level of customer loan rates outside the larger centres, have been largely insensitive to excess reserves and have tended to remain rigid at relatively high levels. For these reasons the interest

[5] See my paper, "The Monetary Doctrines of J. M. Keynes," *Quart. Jour. Econ.,* Aug. 1931.

rate discussion has entered a new phase in recent years, with a growing recognition that rates may be both too low and too high at the same time, the low rates accomplishing nothing further to stimulate investment while causing injury to many institutions and individuals, while the high rates may still retard investment in some directions. There has been growing recognition also that this kind of problem calls for new methods of attack to supplement the traditional central bank methods. I have not touched upon the government lending agencies, which are the subject of Professor Jacoby's paper on this programme.[6] But one major question in the part which such agencies can play in carrying into important areas of credit the effects of monetary policy. A closely related question, and one of great importance, I believe, for the future of monetary policy, is whether such agencies, exercising as they do important monetary powers, ought not to be tied more definitely than at present into the organization of monetary control.

IV

There remains the implications of fiscal policy for the future of the banking system. We must distinguish between what has already happened and the long-run effects of large-scale, long-continued government borrowing from the banks. As regards our experience thus far, it is easily possible to exaggerate the adverse effects. The banking system has shown a high degree of adaptability to the revolutionary changes in bank assets. Each period of unsettlement since 1937 in the government security markets has been met with greater calmness. The banks have made progress in so arranging their portfolios as to be able to hold longer-term securities through periods of temporary market stress. They have also developed some sources of new earnings and of service in meeting the credit needs of the community. Looking back to the bank holiday of 1933, we can see that the banking system has made decided progress. Outside the large cities bank earnings have been well maintained, and even in such centres, where the fall in open-market rates would naturally be most strongly felt, the decline has not affected the soundness of the banks. But there may be more serious earnings problems during the war period. In the thirties the decline of interest rates was in part offset by reduction of expenses. But with the rise of taxes, wages, and other costs incident to war there is some danger that the banks may be more seriously pinched.

Some other effects of long-run government borrowing from the

---

[6] Neil H. Jacoby, "Government Loan Agencies and Commercial Banking Agencies," *Am. Econ. Rev.* Supplement, Mar. 1942, pp. 250–60.

banks may be more serious than the effect on earnings as that has thus far developed. Bank buying of government securities increases bank deposits. The growth of deposits has two important aspects. One is the monetary aspect. I have always been dubious about the effect of an increase in the supply of money, taken by itself, upon money-spending and thus upon output and employment. It is a permissive rather than an activating factor. There was a time, in the late twenties and early thirties, when such a suggestion was vigorously combated, but now the pendulum may have swung too far in favour of this view. Granted that money supply has only a passive influence unless other factors are present to stimulate its use, it is not prudent to add continuously to a money supply which already is greater, both absolutely and in relation to volume of output and employment, than at any previous time in our history. But this is the logical implication of long-continued government spending, combined with excess reserves, unless the financing can be done outside the banking system.

At least equally serious are the implications of a long-continued large-scale growth of bank deposits for the capital position of the banks. Already there has been a marked reduction in the capital-deposits ratio, particularly in the centres where bank buying of government securities has been heaviest. It is true there have been some important offsetting changes. The margin of safety which capital is supposed to afford depends not merely upon the quantitative excess of total assets over deposit liabilities but also upon the soundness and the liquidity of the assets. From this point of view excess reserves are themselves an important factor in bank safety, since they constitute a buffer which protects the banks from being forced to liquidate assets to meet withdrawals of deposits. It is in this way that the presence of excess reserves has enabled the banks to reach out for government securities of longer maturity as the rates on short-term assets have declined. It is true also that the very fact that banks now hold government securities in large amounts means that the quality of their assets has improved. In these respects it can correctly be argued, as some bankers have done, that a smaller capital-deposits ratio is needed than used to be the case. But some of the implications of this line of argument I find disturbing. It implies, for example, that excess reserves will continue to be needed indefinitely, or as long as bank assets continue to consist of government securities other than short-term securities. It implies also that as deposits and government security holdings expand and the margin of capital over deposits becomes thinner, it will be less and less possible for banks to increase their other assets, except for those which likewise involve a minimum of risk. Finally, it implies that the function of the Reserve System would be more and more that of preserving stability in the government bond market and less and less that of exercising monetary control. Moreover, if the banking system is to become more and more a mechanism for providing funds to finance government expenditure, and a mechanism the preservation of whose stability becomes increasingly a matter of concern to government, could not the ultimate reaction of the public be that such a mechanism should be a public rather than a private institution? It would not need a disturbance on the scale of the bank holiday of 1933 to develop this conviction. Of course, if bank capital could be increased correspondingly with bank deposits, the problem of the capital-deposits ratio would be solved. But falling interest rates and earnings do not encourage investment in bank capital, and maintaining dividends in the face of reduced earnings is not a remedy. If capital were provided by government agencies, the implications of eventual government ownership would be strengthened, and suggestions of government subsidies to sustain earnings would point in the same direction.

V

The obvious solution of many of the problems I have discussed would be to finance government spending outside the banking system. That we have had to rely so heavily upon the banks is indeed the great paradox of deficit spending. Why should this need to be the case, if, as the theory maintains, the condition of under-employment which the spending is to correct is due to over-saving or under-investment? Why should not the saving itself finance the deficits? In Kahn's early article on the multiplier this part of the logic of the process was expressly recognized. He pointed out that there should be no problem of money supply. The deficit spending needed to maintain full employment would be precisely equal to the leakages out of income.[7]

It could be argued that the saving might remain idle and thus need to be offset by new money from the banking system. But this is business cycle analysis. It is appropriate to the pump-priming theory, which is cyclical and assumes no increase of either money supply or public debt for the cycle as a whole. But in the long-run "compensatory" fiscal theory business cycle influences play no part. There is no ground for assuming variations in either the quantity or the rate of use of money, except for the long-run tendency with which the theory is concerned,

[7] R. F. Kahn, "The Relation of Home Investment to Unemployment," *Econ. Jour.*, June 1931, pp. 174, 189.

which is the tendency for a part of income to be saved and not invested. As I have said and as Kahn clearly expected, it is the function of public spending, by the theory's own logic, to absorb this saving and restore it to the income stream.

In what may be regarded as an effort to adapt the theory to business cycle changes and the problem of war-time expansion, it has been suggested that government expenditures should be financed by a combination of borrowing from banks, borrowing from non-bank sources, and taxation, in this order, the emphasis shifting forward as output and employment increase and the danger of inflation becomes greater. As a fiscal programme for war-time expansion, starting from a state of underemployment, this is the right pattern. But as I said earlier, it does not seem probable that we shall be able, at any stage of our war financing, to avoid a substantial amount of borrowing, or to avoid doing a considerable part of it from the banks.

It has been suggested that the financing of deficit spending in the thirties gave evidence of conforming to this pattern. From 1933 to 1936 bank holdings of government securities substantially increased, but from 1936 to 1939 they were about stationary. This fact, however, affords no proof that bank investment diminishes as output and employment expand, unless the expansion is accompanied by monetary control. The period 1936–39 is the one I described earlier. That bank holdings for the period as a whole did not increase was due to the selling of securities by the banks in 1936–37, when excess reserves were reduced by the raising of reserve requirements. When the pressure was removed by further gold inflow, abandonment of gold sterilization, and a moderate reduction of reserve requirements, bank buying of government securities was resumed. The question I raised was whether in the light of that experience it will be feasible to exert monetary pressure on the banks so long as their holdings of governments remain large and the need of large-scale borrowing continues.

Since 1939 the banks have greatly increased their holdings, both absolutely and in relation to the increase of the public debt. In 1930–39 they took 36 per cent of the increase in the Federal debt. In the two years from June 30, 1939 to June 30, 1941 they took 47 per cent.[8] This increase has occurred, moreover, at a time when the need for borrowing outside the banks has received much emphasis and an organized effort has been launched to attract the nation's savings. Such an effort takes time to plan and to gain its full momentum. Probably now that we are actually at war the non-bank part of our borrowing will substantially increase. But nothing in our experience thus far indicates that it is possible to finance large-scale, long-continued public borrowing without considerable dependence on the banking system.

I do not regard the monetary and banking difficulties which I have discussed in this chapter as necessarily decisive arguments against large-scale deficit spending, indefinitely prolonged. My principal doubts about such a policy rest on other grounds. I am not sure that with careful handling some of the banking difficulties might not be removed or considerably lessened. One way might be through lessening the dependence upon excess reserves. This is in part a matter of altering bankers' psychology by re-creating the willingness and the habit of resorting to the central bank to meet temporary changes of reserve position. In the past year, mainly through cessation of gold inflow and the expansion of deposits and currency, the excess reserves have been greatly reduced. It seems certain that within the next year bank reserves will need to be increased. If, however, advantage could be taken of the present circumstances to

---

[8] NET CHANGES IN HOLDINGS OF FEDERAL GOVERNMENT OBLIGATIONS, *DIRECT AND GUARANTEED*
(In millions of dollars)

June 30 Dates‡	Total Outstanding Interest Bearing Securities*	Holdings					
		Federal Agencies and Trust Funds, and Federal Reserve Banks	Commercial Banks		Mutual Savings Banks	Insurance Companies†	Other†
			Central Reserve N.Y.C. Member Banks	All			
1916–19	+ 24,262	+ 391	+ 645	+ 4,390	+ 660		+18,800
1919–30	− 9,312	+ 1,142	+ 464	− 162	− 150		−10,200
1930–40	+ 31,952	+ 7,944	+4,339	+11,571	+2,590		+ 9,900
1940–43	+ 91,598	+11,988	+8,401	+35,906	+2,180	+ 6,600	+34,900
1943–46	+129,106	+31,389	+1,759	+31,642	+6,210	+12,200	+47,800
1933–35	+ 9,610	+ 1,736	+1,258	+ 5,243	+ 820	+ 1,600	+ 200
1935–37	+ 8,697	+ 1,686	− 179	+ 1,839	+ 850	+ 2,400	+ 1,900
1937–39	+ 4,871	+ 2,327	+ 854	+ 1,138	+ 650	+ 900	− 100
1939–41	+ 9,411	+ 2,241	+2,784	+ 4,398	+ 386	+ 1,200	+ 1,100
1941–42	+ 21,770	+ 2,590	+1,282	+ 6,315	+ 465	+ 2,100	+10,300
1942–43	+ 62,955	+ 8,256	+5,337	+26,048	+1,399	+ 3,900	+23,400
1943–44	+ 61,587	+12,474	+2,270	+15,973	+2,016	+ 4,200	+26,900
1944–45	+ 55,707	+12,734	+1,335	+15,638	+2,282	+ 5,400	+19,700
1945–46	+ 11,812	+ 6,181	−1,846	+ 31	+1,912	+ 2,600	+ 1,200
1946–47	− 13,381	+ 1,769	−3,034	−14,147	+ 674	− 300	− 1,400
1947–48	− 5,065	+ 2,433	−2,126	− 5,258	− 169	− 1,900	− 200
1948–49	+ 653	+ 501	− 59	− 1,089	− 316	− 2,400	+ 3,900
1949–50	+ 4,441	− 1,455	+ 5	+ 2,681	− 96	− 700	+ 4,000
1950–51	− 2,347	+ 7,779	−1,793	− 6,933	−1,333	− 2,800	+ 900
1951–52	+ 4,028	+ 3,300	− 228	+ 2,431	− 660	− 1,400	+ 400
1952–53	+ 7,090	+ 5,066	−1,541	− 2,640	− 48	+ 200	+ 4,500

* Since holdings of insurance companies and "other" investors have been rounded to the nearest 100 million, the changes do not add to the totals shown.

† Prior to 1932 holdings of insurance companies were included in "other holdings."

‡ Prior to June 1946 these figures were based on an ownership series compiled by the Board of Governors of the Federal Reserve System which has been discontinued. From June 1946, figures are based on the series currently published in the *U.S. Treasury Bulletin.*

create in our banking system the conditions which now exist in England and Canada, where there is assurance of an easy money policy supported by ample bank reserves but without large excess reserves, that would be a long step toward removing some of the abnormalities that have developed in the past ten years. Reduction of excess reserves would mean, as we have seen in recent months, that short-term interest rates would rise, removing or lessening one of the important gaps in the interest rate structure. With short-term rates higher, banks would be under less pressure to invest in long-term government securities, and we might approach more nearly a logical division of the government security market, with the banks holding the short-term securities and non-bank investors the long-term public debt. Such a distribution of the debt would lessen the dangers now involved in temporary fluctuations in government security prices, and might permit again some use, under peace-time conditions, of a general monetary control.

I do not think, however, that this change will be easy to bring about. And it would still remain true that the larger the public debt becomes, the harder it will be to avoid the kinds of difficulties I have described. The real solution, and the only logical one, would be to finance deficit spending outside the banking system. For the advocates of large-scale, long-continued public spending this seems likely to become a major challenge. My own belief is that the monetary and banking difficulties raised by public spending constitute an added reason for seeking correctives for secular defects in our economy in other directions, including taxation—though I am convinced that as yet our knowledge of the economic effects of taxation is not very great—and for using deficit spending primarily for business cycle changes.[9]

[9] I have not revised this paper or attempted to bring it down to date, since to do so would run easily to the length of another paper. It should be read in the context of the period in which it was written. I have, however, brought down to date the Table on page 200.

14

*Is a Rise in Interest Rates Desirable or Inevitable?**

By LAWRENCE H. SELTZER†

A view that is vigorously voiced by some respectable students of monetary and fiscal policy,[1] and one that is fearfully shared by many less articulate but responsible bankers, economists, and business men may be outlined roughly as follows:

(1) The extremely low level of interest rates that has prevailed in the United States during the war has forced the banking system to absorb huge quantities of government securities because the latter could not be sold to bonafide investors at the prevailing low rates. The result has been a vast increase in the amount of currency and bank deposits outstanding, and the consequent creation of a grave menace of inflation.

(2) The level of interest rates has been artificially depressed and maintained by Federal Reserve policy and is bound to rise substantially before long. Federal Reserve policy will have to be reversed and interest rates raised sharply if we are to prevent the development of drastic inflation; and interest rates will soar anyhow if inflation comes. In short, substantially higher interest rates are inevitable, whether these are brought about by inflation itself or by the government's attempts to avoid it.

(3) An immediate tightening of the money market and increase in interest rates, accompanied by the funding of most of the federal debt into long-term obligations, would constitute an effective attack against the inflationary danger. At higher interest rates the public could be expected to save more and to use much of its idle currency and bank deposits to buy back governments from the banks. Excess currency and bank deposits would thereby be extinguished.

---

* *American Economic Review,* Dec. 1945. Reprinted by the courtesy of the American Economic Association and the author.

† Wayne University.

[1] See Benjamin M. Anderson, "Inflation Control and Treasury's Borrowing Policy," *Commercial and Financial Chronicle,* October 18, 1945, Vol. CLXII, No. 4430; and "The Road Back to Full Employment," in *Financing American Prosperity* (a symposium; P. T. Homan and F. Machlup, eds.) (New York, Twentieth Century Fund, 1945), pp. 44–52.

Because some such structure of thought exists in the minds of many economists and business men—although some of them only fear that it *may* be correct—it should be useful to subject these views to critical analysis. This is done in the following pages. At the outset, however, I think it well to summarize my net position: I agree that the present situation holds inflationary possibilities. I disagree with the foregoing diagnosis of the underlying cause. I doubt the effectiveness of the proposed remedy. I disagree with the view that a substantial rise in interest rates is inevitable.

I. CHARACTER OF THE EXISTING DANGER OF INFLATION

The existing inflationary danger is due to the combination of a vast increase in the quantity of liquid assets possessed by the public and great shortages of desired goods. The liquid assets are of three kinds: currency, bank deposits, and government securities. The gross deposits of Federal Reserve member banks on June 30, 1945 were 3.3 times those of mid-1929, and about 2.3 times those of mid-1940. The amount of currency in circulation was six times that of 1929 and 3.4 that of 1940. And in addition, between June 30, 1940, and June 30, 1945, individuals, business firms, and state and local governments had added approximately 80 billion dollars of highly marketable or redeemable federal securities to their holdings. The total of currency, bank deposits, and government securities held by the general public at the middle of 1945 (excluding the holdings of the federal government, banks, and insurance companies) was more than three times the amount held five years earlier.

Great shortages now exist not only in consumers' goods but also in business inventories, housing, and business equipment. The combination of such shortages and the public's possession of enormous liquid assets is favorable to price rises because it may induce the public to increase its spending faster than additional civilian goods become available. If the public decides to go on a buying spree, it has the means to do so.

The increase in liquid assets does not make a marked inflation inevitable, however. There is no mechanical relationship between the amount of currency, bank deposits, and other liquid assets owned by the public and the price level or price movements. Idle currency and idle bank deposits do not bid up prices. Someone has to spend to do this. The amount of cash and other liquid assets possessed by the public constitutes only one of the factors that influence the rate of the public's spending. The state of its confidence or expectations about the future, and the value it places upon the convenience and security of a high level of liquid assets, are also important.

The increase in private spending may be moderated by the continuance of rationing and other direct controls, and by caution induced by cancellations of government orders, reconversion unemployment, etc. Further, the rate at which the desired supplies of civilian goods become available will be important in determining whether and how much prices move up. The increase in private spending may conceivably be fully offset by the combination of a sharp decline in government outlays and a rapid expansion in the output of civilian goods and services.

II. ONLY HEAVIER TAXATION COULD HAVE PREVENTED THE GREAT GROWTH IN THE PUBLIC'S LIQUID ASSETS

The only kind of fiscal policy that could have prevented a great growth in the public's liquid assets during the war would have been taxation drastic enough to balance the wartime budgets. When current income is taken from the people in taxes, the transaction is complete. A tax receipt does not add to a man's liquid assets. But any kind of government borrowing, whether it be long- or short-term, from individuals or from banks, and at low or at high interest rates, increases private wealth and private ability subsequently to increase spending.

The primary function of a tight money market and high interest rates is to discourage and curtail borrowing. But the only really large borrower during the war has been the United States Government, and no practicable rise in the level of interest rates would have reduced its wartime borrowing and spending. Regardless of interest rates, the amount of military expenditures was limited primarily by the country's ability to produce; and there is no reason to believe that Congress would have imposed heavier taxes if the long-term rate of interest had been 3½ instead of 2½ per cent or one-year money had commanded 2½ instead of ⅞ per cent. There was no need to tighten the money market for the purpose of restricting credit extension to business because priorities, rationing, and inventory controls removed the incentives for unnecessary borrowing by business.

A higher rate of interest would not have slowed down the growth of the public debt nor the growth in the public's liquid assets.

III. THE INCREASE IN CURRENCY AND BANK DEPOSITS LARGELY REFLECTS THE PUBLIC'S DESIRE TO HOLD ITS SAVINGS IN CASH

Many persons make the mistake of assuming that the sale of government securities to the banking system and the consequent increase in currency and deposits measure the extent to which savings have been deficient. They ignore the conspicuous fact that numerous savers prefer to accumulate sizable amounts of their savings in the form of currency and bank deposits. Savings were greatly stimulated during the war by the rise in incomes and by the limitations upon the supplies of desired goods. But much of the saving was done by persons unused to the purchase of securities. These people naturally put only a portion of their surpluses into Treasury Bonds, and kept the remainder in cash. Others, remembering what happened to the prices of Liberty Bonds after the last war, were afraid of price losses in the case of marketable securities, and of the possibility, often baselessly rumored, that the government might refuse to redeem the Savings Bonds on demand. Many other people expected the war to end at any time and wanted to keep their funds instantly available. Besides these factors, the great growth in output, payrolls, and taxes during the war increased the ordinary needs for currency and bank deposits for use in day-to-day transactions and as pocket and till-money reserves.

The sale of securities to the banking system constitutes our principal means of creating currency and deposits to supply all such increased demands. In addition to the bank purchases needed to enlarge the supply of money for transactions purposes, the banks, in effect, bought large amounts of government securities in lieu of the savers who preferred to hold cash. The current savings of the public are not necessarily one bit less when they take the form of bank balances and currency rather than government securities.

IV. THE POSSESSION OF LARGE AMOUNTS OF GOVERNMENT SECURITIES BY WEAK OR UNWILLING HOLDERS CAN ENCOURAGE INCREASED SPENDING JUST AS MUCH AS CASH

It is true that the ordinary investor finds government securities less liquid than currency and bank deposits and is more likely to hang on to them than to keep inactive cash. But the difference between a man's holdings of cash and governments is only one of degree. This is particularly true when governments are sold in very large amounts to all classes of the public, including investors whose surpluses are only temporary and who do not ordinarily invest in securities. The governments are then widely regarded as potential cash. After World War I a considerable part of the Liberty Bonds previously purchased by corporations and individuals was quickly sold and the proceeds spent. Even many experienced and customary investors feel that they make a less permanent commitment when they buy governments than when they buy corporation bonds and stocks. In fact, nearly all investors are likely to feel and act as though their liquid assets are expanded when they first add to their holdings of government securities. The result is that even when a recent purchaser of them does not actually sell his governments, he feels that his holdings of them reduce his needs for cash reserves and place him in a position to spend his current income and his cash balance more freely. This increased feeling of liquidity exists wherever the new holdings are not regarded as permanent.

If the Treasury had pursued a high interest rate policy from the outset of the war, most of the existing inflationary danger would nevertheless exist. Higher interest rates might have induced the public to put more of its savings into Treasury obligations and less into currency and bank deposits. The extent to which this would have been brought about by a 3½ per cent instead of a 2.5–2.9 per cent long-term rate is debatable. But in any event, the increase in what most of the public regards as its liquid assets would have been no less. Larger amounts of bonds would be held by wage earners, salaried employees, and business corporations as only temporary holdings to be turned into cash and used for goods as soon as the latter became available.

An interest rate that was high enough to cause the public to prefer more Treasury Bonds to bank deposits when goods were unobtainable would not necessarily be high enough to cause the public to keep the bonds after these goods became available. Our experience during World War I provides a good case in point. The Treasury then paid 4¼ per cent for long-term money as compared with high-grade corporate bond yields averaging between 3.3 and 4 per cent in 1900–13, and 4.05 per cent in 1916–17. Giant Liberty Bond rallies, reinforced by the availability of virtually unlimited bank credit for the financing of Liberty Bond purchases, resulted in a wide distribution of the bonds among individuals and business corporations. The direct sales of Treasury securities to banks were relatively much smaller than in World War II.[2] But when goods again became available and the patriotic pressures of wartime were no longer operating, thousands of investors reverted to their previous patterns of spending and saving. In the two years immediately following the end of hostilities, wartime purchasers

[2] Extension of bank credit to finance bond sales to individuals and corporations was relatively greater in the First World War than in the Second. Everyone was encouraged to "Borrow and Buy," and the banks liberally financed Liberty Bond purchases by their customers, whereas this was discouraged during World War II. In addition, relatively larger amounts of bank credit were required to finance manufacturers awaiting payments from the Treasury. The speedier payments during World War II, including large amounts of advance payments, have had the effect of substituting Treasury borrowing from banks for bank loans that would otherwise have been made to corporations.

dumped millions of dollars worth of the bonds on the market at large discounts. High yields did not keep these investors from cashing their bonds. The average yield on United States Government Bonds rose to 4.63 per cent by January 1919, to 4.93 per cent by January 1920, and reached 5.67 per cent in August 1920. The commercial banks expanded their holdings of governments by about 2 billion dollars or approximately two-thirds, between the middle of 1918 and the middle of 1919.

V. THE USUAL CONDITIONS FOR AN EFFECTIVE USE OF TIGHTER MONEY ARE NOT PRESENT

A substantial tightening of the money market—which means both a sharp reduction in the availability of credit and a marked rise in interest rates—has been the chief weapon of the central banking authorities against an inflationary boom. Even in the absence of deliberate action by the authorities, it has usually occurred in the later stages of a boom because of the growing shortage of credit. In either case there is little doubt that it has tended in the past to restrict or halt inflationary booms, though not always promptly.

Nevertheless, I am forced to conclude that any moderate or tolerable use of this mechanism on an over-all basis would be of very limited effectiveness in the present situation and would be capable of introducing extremely adverse complications of its own.

Tightening the general market can be very effective against an inflationary boom based upon short-term speculative borrowing. The ability of speculators to continue to bid prices up and to accumulate greater inventories usually depends upon their ability to expand the scale of their borrowing. When the central banking authorities tighten the money market by limiting the growth of or actually reducing the reserves of the commercial banks, the latter are forced to refuse accommodation to new would-be borrowers and/or to reduce the credit extended to established customers; and in this process interest rates rise in reflection of the diminished supply of credit. Both the increased cost of borrowed funds, and, more particularly, the diminished availability of credit, force borrowers to liquidate portions of their inventories and to curtail the scale of their commitments in order to reduce their debts. The speculative markets, which are highly sensitive to the cost and availability of bank credit, are normally the first to be affected, but the pressure to liquidate and to reduce debts eventually spreads out in many directions. A period of liquidation and contraction displaces the boom.

But these usual purposes of a tightening of the money market have no direct relevance to the present situation:

(a) The principal user of bank credit, the United States Government, will not be moved by the appearance of higher interest rates to reduce its demands for accommodation. Unlike individual business borrowers, the government would not find it possible to respond to a higher interest rate by paying off any considerable part of its borrowings with the proceeds of inventory liquidation, etc. Nor would any practicable increase in the rate of interest cause Congress to reduce government expenditures and increase the scale of taxation sufficiently to make early large reductions in the public debt.

(b) The unprecedentedly large amount of currency and bank deposits now owned by the business and consuming public is mostly owned outright. The owners do not owe large offsetting sums to the banks. They do not need to renew loans at the banks to keep their cash. In effect, they own unborrowed "excess reserves." Their ability to spend for business and consumption purposes is therefore insulated in considerable degree against the effects of tighter money. Only *borrowers* need to pay the higher rates and face the credit curtailment of a tighter money market.

(c) But ample credit accommodation may nevertheless be needed by some businesses to facilitate reconversion and rising production. Even though industry as a whole appears to have abundant liquid resources, the distribution of them may be spotty. To expand bank credit to enable various enterprises to make disproportionately large increases in civilian output would be anti-inflationary rather than inflationary in its net effects. An over-all restrictive credit policy, on the other hand, would be capable of impeding the growth of output of such enterprises without being highly effective against the undisciplined spending of the huge unborrowed cash balances.

(d) The expansion of consumers' credit might conceivably be checked somewhat, but this type of credit is far better regulated directly and by itself, as under the existing wartime method. It does not lend itself well to regulation by a general tightening of the money market. The consumers' demand for credit is relatively insensitive to ordinary changes in interest rates, and the supply of consumers' credit is likely to remain abundant in the face of curtailment elsewhere. The cost of money to the merchant, finance company, or bank extending the credit accounts for only a modest and sometimes tiny fraction of the gross charge paid by the customer. The gross margin of profit is therefore great. It represents heavy overhead costs as well as variable costs and profits. A strong motive therefore exists to provide abundantly for consumer credit by outbidding competing uses to the extent necessary. The record of this type of credit since 1929 has been so satisfactory from a risk standpoint that the larger consumers' finance companies could doubtless increase substantially the sale of their obligations, secured by installment contracts, to individuals with idle bank balances if the banks themselves curtail their own takings of them. The nominal volume of bank deposits would not be enlarged if this were done, but an increase in spending would be just as effectively financed.

VI. THE SECONDARY RESTRICTIVE EFFECTS OF A MODERATE TIGHTENING OF THE MONEY MARKET ARE NOT LIKELY TO BE SUBSTANTIAL UNDER PRESENT CONDITIONS

Granted that a general tightening of the money market under present conditions would not operate through its usual effects upon borrowers, would it not moderate inflationary tendencies significantly by curtailing spending in other ways? Higher interest rates might exert such effects

(a) by promoting greater saving of current income and accumulated cash balances by both consumers and business;

(b) by discouraging the sale of government securities from the public to the banks and the further expansion of bank credit in the process; and

(c) by inducing the public to use part of its idle currency and bank deposits to buy governments.

Let us examine each of these possibilities:

(a) It seems safe to say that moderately higher interest rates would not significantly influence the public to reduce its spending either from current income or from accumulated cash balances. In the short run the amount saved from current income is predominantly determined by habits, institutional practices, the amount and distribution of income, and the availability of desired goods. Consumers do not decide to do without washing machines or automobiles or more clothing because the rate of interest obtainable on government bonds rises from 2½ to 3½ or 4 per cent. Their disposition of their wartime accumulations of liquid assets between consumption spending and retention as investments will also be largely governed by factors other than the rate of interest.

Nor would a moderate rise in interest rates be likely to curb business spending materially. Corporations with big cash balances and bright business prospects are not apt to be induced by this development to stop replenishing inventories or remodeling plants, and instead, to hang on to their cash or to buy government securities with it. Nor would they be moved to pay out noticeably less of their profits in dividends to stockholders. The only ones that would be appreciably affected would be those owing short-term debts to the banks. Even these would be induced to curtail their spending significantly only if the amount of bank credit available to them were curtailed, for a rise in interest costs would mean a negligible increase in total costs for most business enterprises. And banks have lots of low-yield short-term governments that they could sell or fail to replace at maturity in order to get funds with which to maintain and even increase the relatively modest amount of bank credit now extended to business.

(b) It may be argued that a rise in interest rates, by depreciating the market value of government securities, putting some of them below par, would at least have the effect of discouraging holders from selling them and spending the proceeds or lending the latter for new real investment or consumption by others.[3] Since the banks would presumably have to absorb much of such liquidation, any reduction of it would lessen the further expansion of bank credit.

An examination of the distribution of ownership of government securities throws serious doubt on the possibilities in this direction. The distribution as of June 30, 1945, is outlined in the following table.

Much the greater part of the holdings of individuals would seem to be relatively insensitive to this influence. Of the 59 billion dollars of governments held by individuals on June 30, 1945, 41 billions, or 70 per cent of the total, consisted of Series E and other United States Savings Bonds.[4] The holders of such bonds can suffer no depreciation in price by reason of an advance in open market interest rates because their bonds are redeemable at fixed prices on demand. (The redemption values of Series G Savings Bonds decline slightly during each of the first twenty-one semi-annual periods to reflect the relatively excessive interest disbursement made currently.)

Moreover, significantly higher and rising yields are already provided for holders of Savings Bonds to induce them to retain their holdings to maturity. A man who has held his E bond for three years is already offered a yield of 3.58 per cent for the remaining period to maturity; at five years, the yield to maturity is 4.01 per cent; at six and one-half years, 4.36 per cent; etc. The corresponding yields for F bonds are

[3] See, for example, H. S. Ellis, "Economic Expansion through Competitive Markets," in Homan and Machlup, eds., *op. cit.*, pp. 143–44.

[4] Including Treasury Tax and Savings Notes.

3.07, 3.27, and 3.31 per cent, and for G bonds, 3.13, 3.32, and 3.34 per cent. No additional stimulus for the retention of Savings Bonds would be provided, therefore, by a moderate rise in interest rates unless the whole schedule of yields on outstanding Savings Bonds were raised, and even then the psychological deterrent against selling out at a loss would be absent.

OWNERSHIP OF THE FEDERAL DEBT, JUNE 30, 1945*

	Billions of Dollars	Percentage of Total
Individuals		
E Savings Bonds	29	11.3
A–D, F, G Savings Bonds, Tax and Savings Notes	12	4.7
Other securities	18	7.0
Total	59	22.8
Other non-bank investors		
Federal agencies and trust funds	25	9.7
State and local governments	5	1.9
Insurance companies	23	8.8
Mutual savings banks	10	3.7
Other corporations and associations	30	11.8
Total	92	36.0
Commercial banks	84	32.7
Federal Reserve Banks	22	8.5
Total, all holders	257	100.0

* Includes direct and guaranteed obligations; figures for distribution among holders are based upon estimates of the Treasury Department contained in the Treasury Bulletin. Slight discrepancies between the detailed figures and the totals are due to rounding.

So far as individuals are concerned, then, the psychological deterrent to selling out at a loss and spending the proceeds would be confined to the 30 per cent of their holdings—7 per cent of the total debt—that is in the form of marketable securities. And the *marketable* securities held by individuals are held mainly by members of the upper income groups who are less likely than holders of E bonds to liquidate for the purpose of increasing their current spending.

Price depreciation as a deterrent to the sale of government securities would appear to offer no greater promise of effectiveness in the case of business corporations. Treasury Savings Notes, which account for about one-third of the aggregate of Treasury obligations held by business corporations, may be cashed at fixed prices on demand and therefore could suffer no depreciation from a rise in market yields. Nor would corporate holdings of Treasury certificates of indebtedness and other short-term obligations be greatly affected. A moderate depreciation in market price would not be highly effective against sales of even 2's, 2¼'s, and 2½'s by manufacturing and mercantile corporations intent on financing reconversion and expansion. Investment companies might be induced to hold on to more governments rather than to switch them into other securities, and the same might be true of a portion of the holdings of state and local governments; but little more than this could be expected.

A better case for the effectiveness of price depreciation in deterring liquidation of government securities can be made for the holdings of insurance companies and commercial and savings banks. The men who manage the investments of these institutions, aware that the contractual interest income and principal repayment of federal obligations are perfectly safe, can be expected to be reluctant to sell such securities at a loss, and thereby appear to confess errors in judgment. But this reluctance competes with and is often overcome by stronger opposing considerations, such as the availability of attractive yields on new business loans or home mortgages, or the credit needs of established customers. Tax considerations, moreover, commonly provide a positive stimulus for the realization of book losses by these institutions. By reducing the institution's taxable income, a realized loss on the sale of securities enables it to enlarge its after-tax net income, to retain a larger sum for investment, and therefore to increase its subsequent investment income.[5] In short, the reluctance of institutional investors to realize a capital loss on government securities is a highly qualified one that often yields to other considerations. Finally, we may note that the prices of short-term securities are not greatly affected by a moderate rise in interest rates and that the commercial banks, in particular, held large amounts of such securities at the end of 1945: $31 billion of Treasury obligations becoming due or callable within one year, constituting 37 per cent of their total holdings of government securities, and $56 billion of Treasury obligations becoming due or callable within five years, constituting 67.5 per cent of their holdings of government securities.

On balance, the prospective effect of a moderate depreciation in market values as a deterrent to the sale of government securities and the spending of the proceeds is not impressive.

(c) Moderately higher interest rates might have some influence in inducing the public to use part of its idle currency and bank deposits

[5] See, for example, the annual report of the Irving Trust Company of New York for 1953. It is noteworthy that in 1953, a year marked by exceptionally wide movements in both directions in the prices of government securities, the total of losses, charge-offs, and transfers to reserve accounts on securities by all banks insured by the FDIC substantially exceeded the total of their recoveries, transfers from reserve accounts, and profits on sales of securities in that year or any of the preceding five years.

to buy additional governments. The purchases might consist of new Treasury issues or securities bought from the banks. The effect would be either to reduce the amount of currency and deposits or to lessen the increase that would otherwise take place.

How large an effect of this character would be produced by a moderate rise in interest rates cannot be confidently predicted. There have been no comprehensive empirical studies of the responsiveness of investment to changes in interest rates, so far as I am aware. In the early part of 1937, when an increase of one-third in member bank reserve requirements took effect, superimposed upon a previous 50 per cent increase in the preceding year, and when sitdown strikes were occurring in the automobile industry, and bank loans were expanding, the average yield of all Treasury Bonds not due or callable for twelve years or more rose from 2.46 per cent at the beginning of the year to 2.83 per cent early in April. The yield of nine-months Treasury bills went from .32 to .67 per cent, and the average yield of 3–5 year Treasury notes, from 1.13 to 1.65 per cent, in the same period. The member banks reduced their holdings of government securities, direct and guaranteed, by 856 million dollars in the first six months of the year and by an additional 318 millions in the second six months. Insurance companies and mutual savings banks increased their holdings of governments during the year by approximately 1 billion dollars, and the Federal Reserve banks by 134 millions, accounting for substantially all the bank liquidation. (Non-member commercial bank holdings were virtually stationary.) Non-bank investors, however, absorbed the whole of the 1,168-million-dollar increase in the interest-bearing public debt held outside of federal agencies and trust funds.

Interest rates declined thereafter and by the end of the year were little above those of the beginning. (The Treasury bill rate went much lower.) Bank holdings of government securities continued to decline during the first six months of 1938. For the eighteen months of declining bank holdings as a whole, the net decrease of 1,292 millions in the governments held by commercial banks was more than absorbed by the 1,440 millions taken by insurance companies and mutual savings banks. The 600-million-dollar net increase in the interest-bearing public debt held outside of federal agencies and the Federal Reserve banks was taken wholly by non-banking purchasers of non-marketable securities and by insurance companies and savings banks. There was no net increase in the holdings of marketable Treasury securities by noninstitutional investors for the eighteen months as a whole.

It is possible to draw the inference from the figures for the first half of 1937 that the non-bank demand for governments might be somewhat, though not impressively, responsive to a moderate rise in yields, though little weight can be placed upon the evidence of a single short period. The sharpness of the price decline in governments attracted a considerable amount of speculative buying motivated by the hope of profit from price recovery rather than by the larger investment yields as such. A new plateau of higher yields would soon lose the demand from this quarter. Actually, the holdings of marketable governments by non-institutional investors in June, 1938, were back to the level of December, 1937.[6] The 2.90 per cent yield on United States Savings Bonds, on sale continuously since 1935, offered a higher return for moderate amounts of investment funds than the highest yields reached in the 1937 decline, and still does. The limits of $7,500 (issue price) annually on Series A-D Bonds, issued between 1935 and 1941, and of $3,750 on the present Series E, have probably constricted the flow of funds into these issues from wealthy individual investors, although we must not lose sight of the common practice of widening the effective limits by the purchase of the maximum amount annually in the names of each of several members of a family. Since 1941, Series F and G Savings Bonds, yielding 2.53 and 2.50 per cent, respectively, have been available up to $100,000 (issue price) annually for the combined series ($50,000 in the calendar year 1941) for each investor. These considerations are relevant mainly for the motivation of individual investors and ordinary business enterprises. Institutional investors, with short-period exceptions, tend to invest their funds at the going rates just about as fast as they come in. In the absence of better evidence than is now available, we cannot count on more than a modest, if any, responsiveness of investment to a mild rise in yields.

If the reserve position of the banks were made so tight that they could absorb no more governments, sales would continue to be made by some parts of the non-bank public to other parts. The accompanying rise in yields could not be relied upon to slow up spending. Those who insisted upon selling in order to spend would merely acquire and use the previously inactive balances of those who purchased their securities. And even if a moderate amount of bank balances were actually destroyed by being used to purchase governments from banks, the rate of current spending would not be likely to be reduced materially. The idle or less active balances of depositors would be the most apt to be converted. Few persons or business enterprises would feel poorer or

[6] Board of Governors of the Federal Reserve System, *Banking and Monetary Statistics* (Washington, 1943), Table 149, p. 512.

markedly less liquid for having converted part of their cash into government securities. The net effect might be mainly that depositors would turn over their remaining cash balances more rapidly than before, with no significant curtailment in their rate of spending. That is how we used to finance our spending when interest rates were higher and cash balances smaller. The high rates on short-term investments—2 per cent was frequently obtainable on demand deposits—and the short supply of cash relative to income, price level, etc., provided nearly everyone with a distinct inducement to minimize his idle cash, but the volume of spending was not correspondingly, if at all, reduced because the remaining cash balances were turned over more rapidly. With very low interest rates and a greatly enlarged supply of cash, this inducement disappeared. Much of the increase that has taken place in currency and bank deposits in recent years has been "absorbed" in the maintenance of larger idle balances. A reduction in the size of these idle balances would by no means force a reduction in spending. And it is spending, not the nominal number of dollars outstanding, that bids prices up.

The various considerations cited in the foregoing have led me to conclude that a moderate rise in interest rates, reflecting a moderate restriction of bank credit, would be ineffective for precautionary purposes, and would be ineffective as an attack even upon the actual development of an inflationary rate of spending if the latter did not owe much to an expansion of direct bank lending to business or of new capital flotations.

Yet even a moderate rise in interest rates would be very unsettling and capable of quickly getting out of control. Once the movement became well started, no one would know in advance that it would be confined to moderate proportions (unless this were officially announced, in which case much of the efficacy would be sacrificed). All anyone could be sure of was that the long-established policy of low or declining interest rates had been withdrawn. Disorderly selling in considerable volume might develop, necessitating large-scale market support by the Federal Reserve System to avoid sharp price declines.

VII. A SHARP RISE IN INTEREST RATES WOULD BE DANGEROUS

While a moderate rise in interest rates, reflecting a moderate restriction in the availability of credit, would be likely to be ineffective in curtailing the aggregate rate of spending, a sharp and substantial rise—say, to a level of 5 or 6 per cent for governments—would be another matter. Such a rise might well dampen inflation both because of the effects of the rate rise as such and because of the degree of credit restriction it would reflect. It is also capable of having the opposite result, however, if the rise were widely interpreted as reflecting upon the credit of the federal government. A rise of this magnitude would by no means be impossible for a temporary period, even in the absence of deliberate policy. Such a rise could readily occur if the bond market were permitted to become demoralized by a curtailment of member bank reserves and were not supported against the panicky selling of banks and others. But a radical rise in interest rates would be highly dangerous on several counts:

(a) There is the danger just noted that it would be widely interpreted as reflecting upon the credit of the federal government, with the result that the fear of inflation, and therefore the possibility, would be accentuated. On a 5 per cent yield basis our 2½ per cent long-term Treasury's would be selling in the early and middle 60's; our 2¼'s, in the early 70's; and even an 8-year 2 per cent would be selling nearly 20 points under par. For large parts of the public, such discounts would not be interpreted merely as a reflection of a tighter money situation, but as strong evidence of the impaired credit of the government. The totals of our public debt, currency in circulation, and bank deposits are now so strikingly greater than ever before as to be capable of lending color to ill-founded rumors and interpretations conducive to a loss of confidence in the currency. In short, although the net effects of a radical rise in interest rates would more probably be distinctly deflationary, as noted in the next paragraph, the risk of an undisciplined opposite reaction, arising from a loss of confidence in the Treasury and the currency, would be real.

(b) There is great risk that the deflationary effects of a radical rise in interest rates might be so severe as to throw the whole economy into a crushing business depression. Such a rise would cause drastic depreciation in the market values of all types of securities. It is six years since Aaa corporate bonds have yielded more than 3 per cent, or long-term U.S. governments more than 2½ per cent. A rise in yields to the neighborhood of 5 to 6 per cent would play havoc with institutional portfolios. It is no doubt true that if the rise were "permanent," the earning power of banks and other institutions would be correspondingly increased and that the enhanced earning power, viewed rationally, would far more than compensate for the shrinkage in asset values, as has been pointed out recently by Paul A. Samuelson.[7] But who could

[7] "The Effect of Interest Rate Increases on the Banking System," *Am. Econ. Rev.*, Mar. 1945, Vol. XXXV, No. 1, pp. 16–27.

say how long the new level would last, or that a particular bank would not be forced to realize heavy capital losses? Moreover, bankers and their customers, and indeed the public as a whole, live by the established bookkeeping conventions, which adjudge an enterprise insolvent if the market value of its balance sheet assets is less than the market value of its balance sheet liabilities. Even if valuation conventions, generous lending, and other procedures by the Reserve banks and federal agencies succeeded in insulating the formal balance sheets of banks and insurance companies from the effects of the price declines, disrupting shifts of deposits from small and medium-size to big banks, stimulated by fear, might well take place, as they did in 1930–33, and public suspicion of the solvency of financial institutions generally incited. Stock prices would decline sharply, with damaging effects upon business confidence and the opportunities for corporate financing.

(c) The political repercussions of a radical rise in interest rates could easily be destructive of our existing machinery for credit control. In view of the whole new framework of thought stressing the long-run desirability of low interest rates, which has gained widespread adherence since 1929, and of the importance of low interest rates to various public programs and to farmers and home-owners, and of the consequences of a sharp rise in interest rates to financial institutions and to the budgetary problem of the federal government, I can think of no important group in the country that could be expected to support a policy of permitting or bringing about such a rise. With a public debt that will shortly approximate 275 billion dollars, an increase of 2 per cent in the level of interest rates would mean the prospect of an ultimate increase in interest costs to a total of more than 11 billions a year. Both Congress and the Executive could be expected to combat strenuously any such prospect and would be likely to interfere with the powers or personnel of the Federal Reserve System in the process.

(d) So long as the greater part of bank earnings is derived from interest on their government securities, the banks would get into an increasingly vulnerable political position as interest rates rose. Already there is considerable criticism on this score. The net profits of the member banks in 1944, 649 million dollars, were substantially larger than in any previous year and about two-thirds larger than in 1941. The increase was due primarily to the growth in their holdings of United States securities. The rate of net profits on their capital accounts rose from 6.7 per cent in 1941 to 9.7 per cent in 1944, when it was nearly as high as in the previous peak years of 1919–20. Their earnings from securities more than doubled between 1941 and 1944.

The average rate earned by the banks on securities in 1944 was about 1.5 per cent.[8] The wartime boom in bank earnings differs from that in many other industries in that the supporting conditions will not disappear with the end of the war—the earning assets of the banks will continue at substantially their present level or will increase. Further, reductions in corporate income and excess profits taxes are capable of adding sizable additional amounts to bank earnings.

VIII. THE PROBLEM IS NOT YET SOLVED

In pointing out the reasons why a rise in interest rates would be ineffective if we succeeded in confining it to moderate proportions, and clumsy and dangerous if we allowed it to become substantial, I do not mean to suggest that a problem does not exist or that nothing can be done about it. A problem does exist, or rather two related problems: the broader problem of inflation, and the narrower problem of the government bond market and the relationship of the banking system to it.

(*a*) *The inflation problem*

I think I have sufficiently indicated that the inflation problem confronting us in the early post-war period is primarily a problem of controlling the rate of spending of already-existing, unborrowed funds owned by the business and consuming public. A moderate rise in the rate of interest on borrowed funds does not attack it effectively and may get out of hand.

The problem may at some time also become one of restraining an undue expansion of bank lending to business. But in this case, too, it is difficult to see how a moderate use of the traditional kind of overall credit restriction could be expected either to be adequately effective against the particular target at which it was aimed or to avoid adverse and possibly long-lasting effects upon other types of credit. Such overall credit restriction would not be likely to be highly effective against an expansion of direct bank loans to business so long as the banks possess large amounts of government and other highly marketable securities which they can liquidate to replenish their reserves when necessary. The initial effect, at least, would be apt to be felt most in the bond market, particularly the government bond market.

Similarly, moderately tighter credit, with moderately higher interest rates, would hardly offer the most appropriate remedy for an inflationary movement that obtained its chief impetus from the federal deficit.

[8] *Federal Reserve Bulletin,* May 1945, pp. 429 *ff.*

What is primarily needed in such a situation is diminished governmental spending or greater taxation or both, rather than tighter money. Whether the deficit is financed by bank credit or by non-bank purchases of securities is of some importance but is not decisive.

If inflation should actually get under way, other weapons would be more appropriate and effective in the circumstances now existing than a tightening of the money market. Among these methods are the prompt balancing of the federal budget; the accumulation of budgetary surpluses in the Treasury's account with the Reserve banks or their use to retire Treasury securities held by the Reserve or commercial banks; aggressive promotional efforts by the Treasury for the retention and continued purchase by the public of Savings Bonds; the continuance, but on a permanent legislative basis, of the present type of Federal Reserve control over installment credit, with such tightening or loosening as seems appropriate to changing circumstances; an increase in the Reserve System's margin requirements on securities even above the present 75 per cent requirement for new purchases, and the application of the higher requirements to the carrying of old accounts; recommendations by the Reserve System to the President and to Congress to slow down the operations of the government's various promotive credit agencies; and, if the war powers are sufficiently prolonged, priorities requirements and price controls might be usefully continued in a few fields.

(*b*) *The government bond market*

Independent of the broader problem of inflation, but related to it, is that of preserving an orderly market for government securities, and the proper policy to pursue in this connection with respect to bank holdings of government securities. The reasons why this problem might become acute are noted in the next few paragraphs, and the general character of the probable attack on it is indicated in the concluding paragraph.

(1) *The market will face considerable redistribution of ownership and additional offerings.* Now that the Japanese war has ended, the market for government securities may be subject to great, if temporary, strains at any time. The demand will lose the force of the patriotic motive operating in wartime and the powerful support flowing from the near-absence of competing investments. Selling pressure, on the other hand, will appear from many quarters. Many business corporations will liquidate their holdings or fail to replace them as they mature in order to obtain funds to replenish depleted inventories or reconvert

plants or exploit new developments. Many individual and institutional investors will reduce their holdings of governments as new issues of higher yielding corporate securities become available. Many holders of War Savings Bonds will turn in their bonds for cash in order to buy automobiles, household furniture, houses, etc. Various banks may wish to sell some of their holdings in order to increase their loans to business.

Moreover, the ending of hostilities has not stopped the Treasury's need for net additional borrowing. We shall face the costs of policing occupied territories in Europe and Asia, of extending aid in the reconstruction of various European countries, of demobilization, and of possible domestic reconstruction programs. The Treasury will doubtless be able to meet some of its maturities, redemptions, and new money needs by letting its cash balances run down, by liquidating surplus war materials and properties, and by using net receipts of the old-age, unemployment, and other trust funds. But on net balance it is likely to face heavy cash deficits for some time.

The market will have to withstand, therefore, both a considerable redistribution of the outstanding debt and substantial additions to it.

(2) *We cannot rely upon new savings to absorb all offerings promptly.* Over a period of several years the investment demands of insurance companies, savings banks, trustees, and individual investors might conceivably absorb all of the liquidated, refunding, and new securities without a significant rise in interest rates and even with a further fall. But these regular investors are not usually in a position to anticipate their future needs far in advance. Their investment funds come to them in relatively small amounts every day through receipts of premiums, interest, dividends, rents, savings deposits, etc. At any one time they can put into the market only their current receipts and perhaps a small amount of previous receipts, for they do not ordinarily carry large idle balances.

(3) *Only limited support can be expected at first from the war-created cash balances.* With the war ended, the individuals and business enterprises with large cash balances are mainly those whose very preference for cash over securities during the war was principally responsible, in the last analysis, for most of the wartime sales of government securities to the banks, and, correspondingly, for the increase in the total amount of currency and bank deposits outstanding. For if these savers had been willing to buy governments during the war, smaller amounts would have been sold to the banks, and correspondingly smaller additions to currency and bank deposits would have oc-

curred. It is not likely that many of these holders of cash balances will suddenly decide to shift into governments.

Undoubtedly, many of them will be content with smaller balances when priorities and other restrictions on production are lifted. Substantial amounts of cash are now held idle by their owners only because the desired types of goods cannot be had at present but are expected to become available in the not-distant future. As civilian goods become increasingly available, we can expect these holders to spend much of their balances promptly for the replenishment of inventories, deferred repairs and replacements, and for new producers' and consumers' goods. In these cases the cash balances will get into new hands, and to the extent that the successive new owners likewise have pressing desires for goods and services, the balances will be quickly transferred again and again. Unless developments occur to make the owners prefer the maintenance of the wartime levels of cash balances to additional goods or income-yielding securities, efforts to spend or invest the unneeded amounts will persist. If prices and/or output do not rise sufficiently in this process to take up the slack in cash balances, the excess will tend more and more to get into the hands of persons and institutions readier to buy government securities than the previous holders of the funds. But this will take time.

(4) *The middlemen's services of the commercial banking system will be sorely needed.* In the immediate situation, the middlemen's services of the commercial banks will be sorely needed. Without their intermediation, disorderly and damaging fluctuations in bond prices might easily occur even if underlying conditions remained favorable. For the commercial banks perform services in the government bond market similar to those of dealers and jobbers in other fields in cushioning the effects of sporadic offerings and purchases. They constitute the largest block of immediate purchasers and of wholesalers and retailers of government securities.

But the banks are loaded up with ordinary governments, and in the absence of special stimulation they may not be eager to add large amounts to their holdings immediately. In fact, instead of supporting the market, the banks may at times themselves generate sharp waves of selling either because they fear higher interest rates or to free reserves for commercial lending. The Federal Reserve System will be faced with the dilemma that over-all quantitative restriction of member bank reserves will damage the bond market, but liberal provision of member bank reserves in support of the bond market may lead to undesirable credit expansion.

(5) *Strong Federal Reserve support of the bond market seems inevitable.* In this situation I do not see how the Federal Reserve authorities can decide otherwise than to do everything they can to support the government bond market. The Treasury's influence would certainly be expected to be exerted powerfully to this end, for apart from any theory respecting the continuous desirability of low interest rates, the Treasury will be facing large new and refunding issues for many years to come. The Treasury's maturities of public marketable issues alone during the next five years aggregate 80 billion dollars and during the next eight years they amount to 123 billions. A declining bond market would create difficulties for the refunding operations. Moreover, the tax increases needed to meet even a moderate rise in interest costs, superimposed upon the heavy taxes that will be required for other purposes, would meet great resistance, for they would create additional burdens for the lower income groups and further damage to business incentives. An increase of only one per cent in the average rate of interest would add a greater sum to the federal budgetary requirements than the total receipts from individual income taxes in any year between 1925 and 1940. The same tax increases that might be tolerated if adopted expressly for temporary periods to combat inflation, with the proceeds available to reduce the public debt, might be intolerable if levied to meet advances in the interest cost of a deadweight debt. In this atmosphere, the Federal Reserve authorities should not find it difficult to persuade themselves that inflation controls can be exercised more directly and more effectively through other channels. And this, I have argued, is actually the case.

The technical problem confronting the Reserve authorities will be to provide abundant member bank reserves for support of the bond market and yet to prevent these reserves from being used for excessive expansion of bank credit for other purposes. This problem can be attacked by selective credit controls, as previously mentioned, possibly including the use of special Treasury securities for banks,[9] in conjunction with other governmental measures to control the rate of spending.

[9] See Lawrence H. Seltzer, "The Problem of Our Excessive Banking Reserves," *Jour. Am. Stat. Assoc.*, Mar. 1940, Vol. XXXV, No. 209, pp. 24–36.

15

On Debt Policy[*]

By H. SIMONS[†]

I have never seen any sense in an elaborate structure of federal debt. The national government must, of course, provide and regulate the currency—a task it has never faced. It may perhaps, on some occasions, properly borrow money; that is, open-market operations are a convenient, traditional, and perhaps desirable temporizing means of currency regulation.

On the other hand, it is essentially improper and undemocratic (Schachtian) to confuse issues by proposing and using a miscellany of debt forms. In wartime and in peacetime we should issue currency and (or) bonds. We should never disguise currency as bonds or conversely. Moreover, every issue of bonds should be primarily an announcement of prospective tax increases. (The converse here is not valid, since debt retirement may and should proceed secularly, at least if bonds are outstanding in excess of the amounts necessary to facilitate open-market measures.) Bond issues are properly a means for checking incipient inflation and are, like currency issue, a means especially well suited for prompt action by administrative rather than by legislative action.

Bonds, as the antithesis of money, here denote consols or perpetuities, that is, obligations without *either* maturities or "call" features. In the good financial society bondholders could liquidate only by open-market sales; the Treasury could sell only one interest-bearing debt form and only by open-market sale; and it could retire such debt only by paying the current, free-market price. (There would, of course, be no bonds save those of the Treasury or, at least, no trading of private debts on organized exchanges; but sane government finance obviously need not wait for sane reform in private corporate finance.)

There is little hope for sound monetary-fiscal policy under representative government if our representatives persist in confusing every-

---

[*] *Journal of Political Economy,* Dec. 1944, Vol. LII, No. 4. Reprinted by the courtesy of the *Journal of Political Economy.*

[†] Formerly University of Chicago.

body, including especially themselves, by issuing moneys, practically moneys, and near-moneys under other names. Trying to steer a path between phobias about paper money and terror of high interest costs, they create only fiscal bedlam and intolerable monetary uncertainty.

The community is now almost persuaded, on Treasury authority, that it can, with the same dollars, buy ammunition to make things hot now for Germans and refrigerators to keep things cool later on at home. Economists may be less credulous; but their relevant persuasions cannot be said to have escaped the confusion which bad fiscal practice invites. It is indeed difficult for anyone to think quite straight about equipment-trust certificates issued to pay either for war materials or for food distributed to the unemployed.

The issues here come to focus upon the problem of interest rates. Should the Treasury offer better interest terms to its lenders now? What interest rates should be offered after the war, when and if we clean up an awful mess of debt by consolidations and refundings. If wartime borrowing, like wartime (non) taxation, is beyond repair for the duration, postwar financial measures cannot yet be dismissed as unalterably determined wrongly by momentum or political habit. Neither may one concede the impotence of academic opinion or the certainty that its influence will again be predominantly wrong at the crucial time.

One merit of these strictures about debt form is that, if sound or if provisionally accepted, they largely answer our interest problem by indirection. Borrowing or refunding via consols must mean higher interest rates; we must pay people something to give up the liquidity features of their near-moneys. If we will not pay taxes to stop inflation, we must at least pay interest!

It should not be inferred, however, that the devices proposed will necessarily increase the interest burden, real or nominal. Confining bond issues to consols, we must pay higher rates, to be sure; but we need not pay higher rates on so large a debt. Retiring short-term and redeemable issues, we may then safely have more debt in a noninterest-bearing form; indeed, we should certainly need more money to prevent deflation if we dispensed with moneys disguised as bonds. Indeed, there is even less sense in the Treasury's paying interest on demand or time deposits than in permitting banks to do so (whether in cash or in kind).

Come at in this way, the postwar problem (if not war finance!) becomes readily intelligible and discussible. Our federal debt should be refunded promptly and totally into currency and consols. In other words, we should remedy as rapidly as possible our wartime mistakes as to debt forms. (Our sins of omission taxation-wise cannot, unfortunately, be corrected so easily, if at all. Inflation will prove largely irreversible—although much may be said for stabilizing the indexes rather than the realities, that is, for deflating back to where the indexes tell the truth instead of revising the indexes so that they promptly cease lying when peace comes.) Some people evidently think that, having done everything wrong during the war, we should or must go on doing it all wrong afterward. I find little use for the hypothesis that error becomes truth merely by long or consistent practice.

This leaves the question of how much near-money should be converted into real, honest money and how much into consols. The answer is simple in principle and amenable to determination by experiment. It is only a matter of implementing monetary stabilization, that is, of doing what is necessary to stabilize some sensitive and reliable price index. The major variable, namely, private investment, is largely an independent variable for fiscal or monetary policy—assuming that thrift is not undermined by extreme inflation and internal disorder. Investment is largely a matter of the fundamental security of property, including security against monopolies, labor and other. Another major variable is postwar banking policy, especially as to reserve requirements or permitted devices of corporation finance. (It would certainly clear the air, however, if banks as owners of federal debt were offered simply a two-way choice between "unsupported" consols and fully supported currency.) Finally, there is the relation between federal tax revenues and expenditures.

The rule for policy as to consols and currency, that is, for *composition* of the debt including money, is simply stabilization of the value of money. Converting money into consols is an anti-inflation measure; converting consols into money is a reflationary or anti-deflation measure; and that is that. The problem becomes difficult or complicated only on the assumption that measures taken in other areas of policy will simply prevent stabilization, regardless of debt policy. Considering the amount of debt available to be monetized, the real problem here is uncontrolled inflation. Until this whole game is hopelessly lost, however, it is the business of debt policy to assume that it will *not* be lost and to *stick* to *its* appropriate anti-inflation measures *whatever the interest cost.* Above all, it should both assume and imply that the Treasury intends to *stay* in business, not just for ninety days or ten years but indefinitely, and issue its obligations accordingly.

Simple debt management would almost certainly improve policy and action in other areas. If Congress and the executive could finance expenditures only by taxation, by currency issue, or by borrowing, each in its most straightforward form,[1] we might expect really responsible behavior not only in these matters but in expenditure as well. Currency issue, as I have argued elsewhere, is both a more effective and politically a safer means of reflation or inflation than is (that compounding of opposites) inflationary borrowing, if only because the process and its possible abuses are generally understood. It would be hard politically to pursue obviously inflationary finance in the midst of actually inflationary conditions. Moreover, it would be politically more difficult to hold taxes down or expenditures up if the obvious cost was borrowing at open-market consol rates—with "danger" of having to pay through the nose later on to retire the current consol issues. On the other hand, it would be conveniently difficult to advocate or to pursue a scheme of combating deflation by selling *consols* to private issuing agencies (banks). The case for currency issue instead of indirect deposit creation would be very clear.

Many readers will have recorded their categorical dissent from our proposals because these all imply a price-index rule or guide for policy. I persist in the notions that stabilization of the value of money, however unrealized, is the only rule or principle of monetary-fiscal policy we have ever had, that it is the only rule really available to a demo-

---

[1] The proper tax form, as I shall argue elsewhere, is a holeproof personal income tax, with a high and stable basic rate, with a variable exemption level, and, of course, with extensive source collection.

It is interesting to speculate, in this connection, on how the democratic process would work if currency, instead of debt, were the residual element in fiscal policy or practice. Normally, of course, Congress makes appropriations and levies taxes, leaving the Treasury to cover deficits by borrowing under generous, elastic, and routine authorizations, or to utilize any surplus for debt reduction. Suppose this practice were reversed, i.e., that all legislation regarding sale or purchase of debt (consols) were mandatory, like tax legislation, and that all deficits or surpluses were handled automatically, under broad, permissive, continuing authorizations, by issuing or retiring currency. It is arguable that, if issue powers were really confined to the government (i.e., with 100 per cent or ceiling reserves), this scheme would produce more responsible fiscal policy than the prevailing one.

What we are really proposing, of course, lies in between. There would be no borrowing authorizations save for consols; i.e., the Treasury would have no freedom or discretionary power with respect to maturities, and possibly none as to nominal interest rates. Subject to that limitation, however, and a mandate to stabilize a price index, the Treasury would have generous or unconfining authorizations for both currency issue and borrowing. Revenue surpluses or deficits would then determine the decrease or increase in the aggregate of currency and consols; while the necessities of price-level stabilization would determine changes in the relative amounts of currency and consols. Excessive expenditure relative to taxes would then reflect itself in the increase of consols or, with an inordinate amount outstanding, in failure of a proper debt-reduction program. A mass electorate may be expected to understand the virtues of price-level stabilization and the need for conserving borrowing powers against the contingency of war or, during wars, against the contingency of very long war. It might, with a simple debt structure, recognize practices which jeopardized or sacrificed these objectives and effectively threaten the political future of leaders who indulged or espoused such practices.

cratic society, and that only by recognizing and by accepting this rule explicitly can legislatures be made responsible financially or business be spared intolerable monetary uncertainty. Be that as it may. One may, I presume, reject price-level stabilization without embracing its opposite. Opponents, in the main, do not advocate maximum instability or total monetary uncertainty. Rather they recommend crossing bridges when we come to them, that is, trusting to the authorities of the moment, or crossing, bridge or no bridge, and finding the bridge afterward if we did not drown. Consequently, it may be of interest to see what kinds of measures are consistent with stabilization and what kinds are not, since no one is proposing to go squarely in the opposite direction. The important fact is that so many people are actually proposing measures or stressing considerations which lead where no one wants to go.

Let us first belabor those numerous folk who, while applauding, condoning, or just not discussing the size of our debt, insist on keeping down its interest burden. The company is numerous, distinguished, and highly placed, both in government circles and in academic esteem. There is, to be sure, a grain of wisdom in their solicitude. First, the Treasury should never offer its issues on such terms that radical rationing measures are required; bonds should not be distributed like postmasterships. Second, the government should never raise interest rates by promoting, by encouraging, or by tolerating expectations of price inflation. These propositions about exhaust the truth in a mountain of foolishness. The truth assay is really very low.

Subject to these obvious reservations, the Treasury should seek always to pay as much interest as possible. (There may be impurities here, but I have not found them.) This merely amounts to saying that it should pay enough interest to prevent inflation. On the other hand, as a corollary, it should also always issue as much money as can be issued without raising the price level. Thus, it should simultaneously maximize the rate of interest payment and maximize the amount of noninterest-bearing issue, subject to the same condition, namely, a stable price level or index.[2]

Since it is difficult to argue about axioms, I shall attempt only some elenctic remarks. First, if one *wants* to minimize the nominal interest cost, one may best resort to paper money. It is admittedly improper to issue additional currency when inflation is under way. By the same token, it is wrong to issue short maturities or, indeed, any debt form save that furthest removed from the pure-money category. In such

[2] These references to "maximizing," and others which follow, are perhaps polemic extravagances, for the "conditions" alone imply determinate amounts.

circumstances issue-yields will normally vary directly with maturities. Consequently, when we want to stop inflation, we should maximize interest rates; we should mop up money not with other moneys slightly disabled but with money contracts as much unlike money as possible. Conversely, stopping deflation, we should issue not near-moneys but the real thing without disabilities; and, issuing it, we should displace not near-moneys but as-far-from-money-as-possible moneys.[3]

During actual or imminent deflation, on the other hand, it may be better to borrow at short term than at long term; but it is best not to borrow at all, that is, to issue merely currency, not only for the desired immediate effect but also for long-term safety and minimal national misunderstanding. Borrowing is an anti-inflation measure, not a proper means for financing reflationary spending. Borrowing is properly a means for curtailing purchasing power, private and governmental. To use it for injecting purchasing power is (to repeat a figure I have used elsewhere) like burning the fire engines for heating purposes when there is an abundance of good fuel to be had free.[4]

To repeat, the right way to lower interest costs is to issue paper money—which sometimes is and sometimes is not a proper thing to do.

Let us now argue obliquely from another direction, namely, from the standpoint of the Treasury as central bank (which it alone should be). Here is the one aspect of the traditional monetary-fiscal pattern which has been mainly correct—indeed, the only one where perverseness has not prevailed. It is naturally also the phase of action with respect to which orthodoxy is most nearly sound. It is generally agreed

[3] For merely monetary purposes, of course, open-market operations should be conducted with equities, not with money contracts at all. Only a collectivist, however, may intelligently offer this counsel of monetary perfection. With ultimate control lying in revenues and expenditures, the strong case for any open-market measures lies where there is an interest-bearing debt requiring some management in any case. There is little reason, in an economy where government is already surfeited with (misused) monetary powers, for admiring the collectivist state for its still larger powers.

[4] It does not follow that debt should never be retired during prosperous years, though it certainly should be retired more slowly at such times, and not at all unless inflation is otherwise fully under control. If tax rates are properly sustained and increased during prosperous years, open-market operations may properly show a balance of purchases even at such times. In depression or deflation, debt retirement should reach its maximal rate, as part of a deliberate program of monetizing bonds. For the good future, retirement of our huge war and pre-war debt will be a continuous process at varying rates, not a matter of alternate forward and backward steps. There will be no more sense in sustaining the aggregate amount than there was in acquiring it in the first place. If our democracy again becomes responsible financially, our bonded debt will fall at least as rapidly after this war as it did during the twenties. Borrowing power must be carefully conserved, if only against the inflation contingencies of our next (first) total war. Unused borrowing power and a record of fiscal good faith (which it is still our opportunity to initiate) are now grossly undervalued relative to an army and navy; but I will lay my bets for the future of an America which protects internal unity and morale by real fiscal prudence.

that the Treasury, at least in disguise, should sell bonds to banks in boom times and buy them during severe deflation. This obviously means, in general, seeking to maximize capital losses over time, concentrating purchases at bond-price peaks and concentrating sales at the lows.[5] (Why such inherently lossful responsibilities were ever delegated to private corporations, I have never understood.)

Surely it is logically or heuristically permissible to treat such capital losses as part of the cost of servicing the debt. Indeed, in an institutionally well-ordered democracy, based on systematic dispersion of power, it would probably seem silly to regard them otherwise. One of the costs of living with near-moneys, even though they be no nearer than consols, lies in the necessity of forever buying them dear and selling them cheap, as monetary stabilization necessitates. Even if we evade the responsibility of rapid secular amortization, we must always be prepared to give money freely for bonds when they are most valuable and to take money for bonds when they are least valuable.

Thus, we may charge that proponents of minimal "controlled" rates on our federal bonds are inconsistent unless they also propose to reverse traditional rules about open-market operations. Surely the formal interest burden could be diminished or offset budgetwise if "perverse" rules of Federal Reserve practice were "put straight," if Reserve Bank capital-gain profits were recaptured, and if the revenues thus smartly obtained were used instead of taxes to pay bond interest! There should be no trouble in selling the scheme, for it only involves asking the Reserve banks to make more money and to follow accepted Treasury practice instead of attempting to stabilize prices—which, behavior notwithstanding, they have always denied trying to do and certainly have not the power to do. Indeed, even for intelligent people, it may seem wise to do everything wrong consistently, since the shortest political route to thesis may involve going all the way to antithesis first.

It is now fitting to pass comment on some minor variants of the antithesis. Some people, while commending and condemning mildly a little bit of everything in practice, have steeled themselves to accept postwar refunding into longer if not indefinite maturities but still lack the fortitude to accept possible high costs of debt retirement. Thus, they veer toward a consol form for the bondholder but leap back toward money for the Treasury via wide or indefinite "call" options. Here the inconsistency noted above is just reversed. The advocate of call features, while accepting higher interest rates, seeks to avoid the illusory misfor-

[5] The losses, of course, may properly be minimized by avoiding instability, i.e., by making stabilization measures really effective.

tune of contingently high bond prices. Escaping one horn of a spurious dilemma, he impales himself on the other; or, in a better figure, he avoids Charybdis by smashing upon Scylla.

The proper way to avoid high prices for retired debt is to avoid deflations, that is, to maintain private investment and reasonably attractive alternative investment outlets for private funds. Labor and patent monopolies, among others, may make this difficult to achieve by monetary measures; but debt policy should do its best willy-nilly and stick to its price-level guns. If we must have deflations and high consol prices, the more the government has to pay for its debt the better. Surely it does not aggravate the task of monetizing debt to have opportunely high bond prices! With effective monetary stabilization and the sustained prosperity which it would assure in a free-market economy, there would be no wide sweeps in bond prices. But it will do no good, and some harm, to control this monetary thermometer when the task is one of stabilizing the monetary temperature. Even penny-pinchers should not complain if the community asks high prices to exchange its bonds for non-interest-bearing obligations and makes this conversion harmless by its increased demand for socially costless liquidity.

We are asking people now to buy war bonds which it is here traditional to default on substantially, via inflation—and with only optimists expecting a small default this time. Against this near certainty and the enduring risk of further wild inflation, there is the relatively small chance of nominal gain through eventual decline of interest rates. This remote favorable contingency the call feature is designed to remove! Save for indefinite forced lending (and do not suppose there will ever be none of it), call features can only raise the interest rate[6] and, besides, create an implied obligation to support the market, that is, to convert bonds into money at the worst times, if not, indeed, to make them really money all the time.

We have proposed, to repeat, that our debt be wholly and promptly converted into currency and consols, in whatever proportion is requisite for price-level stabilization. Such action, as already intimated, would place banks in a quandary. They would be loath to take consols, because of the loss of liquidity. They would be loath to take currency because of the loss of interest revenue, unless permitted to compound the currency by their own expansion of investments and deposits. The proper answer here is as simple as it is remote from our thinking or from our likely actions. Those institutions which choose cash should find their

[6] The captious critic will note here an exception to my general rule about maximizing interest rates!

reserve requirements radically increased thereby (to or toward 100 per cent)—and should find their revenues in service charges. Those which choose consols should find their equity requirements increased (also ultimately and ideally to 100 per cent)—and should thereafter become largely or exclusively investment trusts. Thus, we only repeat proposals for the 100 per cent reserve scheme—for which I still have no great enthusiasm save as part of a gradualist program whose objective is recognized (and consistently pursued) as gradual reduction and ultimate denial of borrowing and lending powers to all corporations, especially as regards obligations of short term.

Misguided fiscal practice and unguided institutional evolution have placed us in a foolish quandary. Seemingly, we cannot afford prosperity or full peacetime employment because they would render our banks insolvent and increase interest costs of our federal debt! Conversely, one way to keep our banks solvent and our interest costs at a low level is to render private investment so unattractive, and property so insecure, that people will be glad to hold money and deposits in preference to real assets and delighted to buy money in an interest-bearing form. The dilemma again is wholly spurious, save for those who deplore increase in reserve requirements of banks (or our reluctance to accept collectivism). The government, instead of worrying about interest costs, should covet the large revenues which high prosperity and high interest rates bring along—while always eschewing, of course, the too easy route of deliberate or permitted price inflation, which must sometime produce astronomical interest rates if not eschewed. Let us pray for the highest interest rates consistent with monetary stability—for the highest possible "real" marginal efficiency of capital. Prosperity need not prove insufferable or disastrous.

There is urgent need for reducing discussion of monetary and fiscal problems to simple, common-sense terms. Our financial system is becoming simply too elaborate and too complex for the political system within which it operates. Both private financial institutions and fiscal practice are too complicated for government by law; that is, they are not sufficiently amenable to effective control through the democratic process of action out of discussion and deliberation. Needless complexity in the private financial structure is the heritage of bad policies in the past and should gradually be corrected and removed. Needless complexity in government finance can and should be dealt with by prompt, thoroughgoing measures.

Taxation, expenditure, pure debt, and pure money are, along with price level, quite intelligible conceptions. If institutional borrowing and, especially, institutional issue were exclusive governmental prerogatives, and if these governmental prerogatives were exercised only in the most straightforward way, both economists and the public might quickly and wisely distinguish between proper uses and abuses and, thus, democratic government might adhere to sound fiscal-monetary policies. The proper first step is simplification of our federal debt.

16

Liquidity Preference and Monetary Policy[*]

By JAMES TOBIN†

The contention of this paper is that the demand for cash balances is unlikely to be perfectly inelastic with respect to the rate of interest, and that policy conclusions which depend on the assumption that the demand for cash balances is interest-inelastic are therefore likely to be incorrect. First, the relationship between monetary and fiscal policy recommendations and assumptions concerning the interest-elasticity of the demand for cash balances will be examined. Second, the argument of Dr. Clark Warburton, whose "Monetary Theory of Deficit Spending" implicitly depends on the interest-inelasticity of the demand for cash balances, will be considered. Third, the position of Professor William Fellner, who explicitly makes and defends the same assumption, will be reviewed. It will be held that this assumption leads Professor Fellner into a theoretical dilemma which can be escaped only by abandoning the assumption, and that Professor Fellner's reasons for believing the demand for cash balances to be interest-inelastic are inadequate. Finally, a statistical relationship between the demand for cash balances and the rate of interest will be presented; this relationship, though admittedly not conclusive, is difficult to reconcile with the hypothesis that the demand for cash balances is interest-inelastic.

I. RELATIONSHIP BETWEEN ASSUMPTIONS AND POLICIES

Questions of policy often serve to expose with clarity differences in theory. In the field of monetary theory and policy, two crucial test questions are:

1. Will expansion of the money supply by methods which do not directly generate income—e.g., open market purchases—lead to an expansion of money national income?

* *Review of Economics and Statistics,* May 1947. Reprinted by the courtesy of the *Review of Economics and Statistics* and the author.

† Yale University.

2. Will expansion of income-generating expenditures financed by methods which do not increase the money supply succeed in increasing money national income?

At the level of static aggregative theory, the answers to these questions of policy depend on the views held with regard to the shapes of three functions: the "L" function, expressing the demand for cash balances as a function of the rate of interest; the "I" function, expressing investment demand as a function of the interest rate; and the "S" function, expressing the supply of current saving as a function of the interest rate. Naturally, the demand for cash balances, investment, and saving are functions of variables other than the interest rate; most important, the demand for cash balances, saving, and perhaps also investment are functions of the level of money income. But it is the nature of their partial elasticities with respect to the rate of interest which is the major issue.

The relationship between views on the interest-elasticities of these functions and views on the two test questions of monetary policy are summarized in Table I.

TABLE I

Interest-Elasticities	Effectiveness of Monetary Policy Alone (question 1)	Effectiveness of Income-Generating Expenditures Alone (question 2)
(A) "L" function perfectly inelastic, implying either "I" function not perfectly inelastic, or "S" function of positive elasticity, or both.	Effective (constant velocity of money)	Ineffective
(B) "L" function elasticity between 0 and ∞, *and* either "I" function not perfectly inelastic or "S" function of positive elasticity or both.	Effective, but Less than (A)	Effective, but Less than (C)
(C) (a) "L" function perfectly elastic, regardless of other elasticities, or (b) "I" & "S" functions perfectly inelastic, regardless of "L" function.	Ineffective	Effective (complete leverage effect)

A. To assume that the "L" function is perfectly inelastic means that no change in the price of securities, i.e., in the interest rate, will induce substitution of money for securities, or vice versa. Changes in the money supply must therefore be absorbed entirely by substitution between goods and money. An addition to the money supply must result in an equivalent increase in the demand for cash balances, so that the additional money will be willingly held. Since no additional money will be willingly held as idle balances, i.e., in place of securities, the demand for cash for working balances must increase enough to absorb all of the additional supply. Money national income, which determines the demand for working balances, must rise until the cash required to handle it has increased as much as the money supply. There are two explanations of the process by which money national income is thus increased, one naive and the other sophisticated.

The naive explanation merely notes that if M is increased, the community will have unwanted cash holdings and will seek to spend them until increased spending has restored the desired relationship between their incomes and their cash balances. The implicit proposition in regard to the community's decisions to spend money on goods is simply that whether total spending, including investment and consumption, exceeds, equals, or falls short of current money income depends directly on whether actual cash balances exceed, equal, or fall short of required cash balances.

The sophisticated explanation arrives at the same result, but does not rely on a doubtful direct relationship between consumption and investment decisions and the size of cash balances. Instead, investment and consumption expenditures are assumed to depend on the level of income and on the interest rate. Adding to the quantity of money creates unwanted cash balances which will be used to bid up the price of securities and lower the interest rate. Reduction of the interest rate induces an increase in spending, by encouraging investment or by discouraging saving. The expansion of income proceeds until all the additional money is required for working balances, since the decline in the interest rate cannot induce the public to hold larger idle balances. It is clear from this explanation that since the "L" function is perfectly inelastic with respect to the interest rate, then either the "I" function or the "S" function must not be interest-inelastic. Otherwise there would be no mechanism to restore equilibrium between the demand and supply of money.

On either explanation, the conclusion is that an increase in the quantity of money is a sufficient condition for the expansion of money national income. How great this expansion is depends only on the relationship between money national income and requirements for working cash balances. This relationship is usually taken to be a constant ratio, changing only slowly over time. The ratio is determined by the degree of synchronization of income and expenditure periods, the extent of business integration, and other institutional or customary arrangements. The velocity of money, the reciprocal of this ratio, is consequently a constant.

An increase in the quantity of money is also a necessary condition for an expansion of money national income. There can be no increase in money national income unless additional money is made available to support the higher value of transactions. It follows that added business investment (an upward shift in the "I" function) or government spending, financed by means which do not expand the money supply, cannot expand money national income. For the additional transactions involved in such spending will decrease the ratio of cash balances to money national income, and the community will endeavor to restore the desired ratio by reducing its other spending in order to acquire larger balances. Since the supply of money has not increased, this process will continue until the reduction of spending has cut income to its original level. The initial addition to business or government spending is offset by equal reductions in other spending. The sophisticated explanation of the same process would be that the attempt to obtain additional balances to support the initial increase in spending raises the rate of interest. But, since no rise in the interest rate will induce dishoarding, no addition to working balances can be obtained in this way. Therefore the rise in the interest rate must continue until enough consumption and investment expenditure is discouraged to offset completely the initial increase in spending, leaving the level of money income unchanged.

B. If the demand for cash balances is not completely inelastic with respect to the rate of interest, part of an addition to M will end up in idle balances. The added money will be used to bid down the rate of interest, and the lowering of the rate of interest will make the community willing to hold larger idle balances. So long as either investment or the propensity to consume is favorably affected by a lowering of the interest rate, there will also be an increase in money income. But since there is some increase in idle balances, the increase in money national income cannot be proportional to the increase in M; V cannot be considered a constant. On this set of assumptions, monetary expansion alone can increase money national income but not so effectively as under (A).

Similarly, on this set of assumptions, an increase in spending without any increase in M can succeed in expanding income. The additional transactions demand for money will raise the interest rate, and this rise in the interest rate will induce the community to hold smaller idle balances. Greater working balances are thereby made available to support a higher money national income. The increase in spending will increase national income, but not by the full leverage effect because the rise in the interest rate will cause a partially offsetting decline in other spending.

C. Under the third set of assumptions, purely monetary policy is impotent. An increase in the quantity of money merely piles up in idle balances; it requires no reduction in the rate of interest to induce the public to hold them. Or, if the rate of interest is reduced, investment and consumption expenditure are both insensitive to the reduction. In either event, there is no expansion of income. On the other hand, an increase in spending can be supported entirely by balances otherwise idle. Either these balances can be obtained for transactions purposes without a rise in the rate of interest, or, if a rise in the interest rate occurs, it has no effect on other spending. The initial increase in spending, therefore, will increase national income by the full amount of its leverage effect.

II. WARBURTON'S "MONETARY THEORY OF DEFICIT SPENDING"[1]

Dr. Warburton does not explicitly recognize that his "Monetary Theory of Deficit Spending" depends on the special assumption that the demand for cash balances is perfectly inelastic with respect to the rate of interest. But a mere statement of his propositions will suffice to show that they belong in category (A) discussed above. His main contentions can be summarized as follows:

1. The value of the gross national product is the product of the quantity of money and a circular velocity of money. For various reasons, outlined in the article, the circular velocity is gradually decreasing. Aside from this secular trend, V is a fairly stable quantity determined by the habits of payments of the community.[2] Therefore, fluctuations in GNP can be explained largely by changes in M.

2. Deficit spending is one of a number of techniques by which M may be increased. Deficit spending, like the other techniques, increases GNP by the amount of the increase in M associated with it times the circular velocity of money.

3. Net increases or decreases in total debt, whether public or private, need not imply changes in GNP if only the monetary authority keeps M increasing at a rate which just offsets the secular decline in V.[3]

---

[1] *Rev. Econ. and Stat.,* 1945, XXVII, 74–84. See also his reply to this article, "Monetary Velocity and Monetary Policy," *Rev. Econ. and Stat.,* 1948, XXX, 304–14; my "Rejoinder," *ibid.,* 314–17; and his rebuttal, "Monetary Velocity and the Rate of Interest," *ibid.,* 1950, XXXII, 256–57.

[2] This view of the stability of V is emphatically reaffirmed by Warburton in his Reply to H. W. Arndt's Comment, *Rev. Econ. and Stat.,* 1946, XXVIII, p. 92.

[3] These propositions raise the incidental problem of controlling the quantity of money independently of the volume of public and private debt and of public and private deficit

It might be expected that such propositions would be buttressed by arguments in favor of the assumption that the demand for cash balances is perfectly inelastic with respect to the interest rate. No such arguments are presented. Dr. Warburton does present a correlation of gross national product with the quantity of money, after the quantity of money is corrected for his geometric secular decline in velocity. But this "secular" decline in velocity can be interpreted in a manner completely contradictory to Dr. Warburton's thesis. During most of the period, interest rates were declining; and at the extremely low rates of the 1930's the demand for cash balances may be so elastic with respect to the rate of interest that almost indefinite quantities of cash will be willingly held idle. This is what seems to have happened to the additions to the money supply during that decade. If this interpretation is correct, the only result of following Dr. Warburton's advice to keep the quantity of money increasing fast enough to offset the "secular" decline in velocity would be to accelerate the decline in velocity itself.

III. FELLNER'S "MONETARY POLICIES AND FULL EMPLOYMENT"[4]

Professor Fellner examines thoroughly and supports ably the theoretical assumptions on which his policy conclusions are based. Indeed his ultimate recommendation, with which adherents of any of our three positions could agree, is a combination of fiscal and monetary measures. The surest method to expand national income is government deficit spending financed directly or indirectly by borrowing from the central bank.

Professor Fellner believes that the "L" function is inelastic with respect to the rate of interest; consequently he is pessimistic concerning the results of deficit spending unaccompanied by an increase in the quantity of money. In fact, he is one degree more pessimistic concerning deficit spending than Dr. Warburton. For he suspects also that banks' demand for reserve balances as a percentage of their deposits

spending. In particular, M must be expanded at a rate sufficient to compensate for the decline in its rate of use, while total debt either remains unchanged or indeed is retired. Although Warburton emphasizes the breadth of his conception of monetary policy, most methods of monetary control would be unavailable to him since they involve direct or induced changes in public or private debt.

[4] Berkeley, University of California Press, 1946. Only Part 3, pp. 137–235, is considered here, and in particular Chapters 5 and 6. This excellent book covers a wide range of other topics. See also his reply to this article, "Monetary Policy and the Elasticity of Liquidity Functions," *Rev. Econ. and Stat.,* 1948, XXX, 42–44. I agree with Professor Fellner that the corner of an L-shaped liquidity function would represent an "impasse," from which both income-creating and money-creating policies would be required to raise the level of activity.

is inelastic with respect to the rate of interest.[5] This means that no rise in the interest rate will suffice to induce banks to permit their deposits to increase unless their reserves are increased. For this reason, Professor Fellner has hope only for policies which increase bank reserves at the same time that they increase the quantity of money.

The chief issue remains the elasticity of the "L" function. Even if banks behave in the manner Professor Fellner fears, this would prevent deficit spending financed by methods which do not increase bank reserves from being effective only if the "L" function is perfectly inelastic. Banks' insistence on a certain reserve ratio merely places selling bonds to commercial banks as a means of deficit financing on the same footing as selling bonds to individuals. Both become methods of increasing income-generating expenditures without changing the quantity of money. They will fail, as shown in section I, only if the demand for cash balances is perfectly inelastic with respect to the interest rate.

For different reasons, Professor Fellner is less optimistic than Dr. Warburton concerning the effectiveness of monetary policy alone. He believes that the "L" function is inelastic and he concurs with the usual agnostic assumption that the "S" function is perfectly inelastic with respect to the interest rate. The "I" function he takes to be interest-elastic; he is logically compelled to do this, because at least one of these three functions must be interest-elastic. But in times of underemployment he fears that the "I" function has shifted so far to the left that even at a zero interest rate the volume of investment would be insufficient to restore full employment. This is the "Fellner impasse."[6] Deficit spending alone—without monetary expansion—cannot break through it. Because the "L" function is inelastic, increased demand for transactions balances will raise the rate of interest until an equal amount of private investment is discouraged. Monetary expansion alone cannot break through it. The rate of interest will fall, but even if it falls to zero it will not stimulate enough investment to bring full employment. The only escape Professor Fellner can find is the combination of fiscal and monetary expansion which is his chief recommendation.

The "Fellner impasse" is a position of disequilibrium. The supply of money exceeds the demand. Equality of the money supply and demand is supposed to be restored, after an increase in the supply, by an increase in the demand for idle balances due to a reduction in the interest rate or by an increase in requirements for working balances due to an expansion of money income. Professor Fellner permits neither

[5] P. 183 and pp. 200–206.   [6] Pp. 180–86.

of these equilibrating factors to operate. There is no increase in demand for idle balances because the "L" function is perfectly inelastic. There is little increase in the requirements for working balances because the "I" function is insufficiently elastic. The pertinent question to ask Professor Fellner at this point is: Why does not the excess supply of money drive the interest rate down far enough—to zero or below if necessary—to stimulate sufficient investment to absorb the excess money into working balances? This is the way out of the impasse which his own theory indicates, provided he sticks to the bitter end with the assumption that the "L" function is inelastic. The implausibility of that assumption could not be better dramatized. For surely at zero interest rates no one would be willing to hold securities rather than idle money balances. As the interest rate approached zero, more and more securities would be sold. In other words, the demand for cash balances would become elastic.

If it is admitted that the rate of interest cannot, for these reasons, fall to zero no matter how much money is poured into the system, then the postulate that the "L" function is perfectly inelastic has been discarded in favor of the Keynesian doctrine that at low positive rates the demand for cash balances approaches perfect elasticity. The "Fellner impasse" becomes the "Keynesian impasse," case (C) in Table 1. The "Keynesian impasse" is, unlike the Fellner version, a position of equilibrium; the demand for money is equal to the supply because at the minimum rate of interest an indefinite amount of cash will be held in idle balances. The "Keynesian impasse" can of course be escaped by deficit spending, with or without monetary expansion.

If Professor Fellner sticks to the assumption that the demand for cash balances is interest-inelastic, his "impasse" can be avoided simply by expanding the quantity of money. He cannot then stick to his conclusion that monetary expansion will be unsuccessful in raising the national income. If he abandons the assumption, the way out of his "impasse" is deficit spending, whether or not it is accompanied by monetary expansion. He cannot, in this case, maintain that deficit spending, unless it is financed by the central bank, will fail to increase national income.

Professor Fellner is led into this dilemma by his theory of interest.[7] Just as his "impasse" is a condition of disequilibrium, his theory does not determine an equilibrium rate of interest. The interest rate, in his theory, is determined by the equation of the demand and supply of

[7] Chapter 5, especially pp. 140–52 and 166–73.

loanable funds. The demand schedule is the sum of the "I" function, which is interest-elastic, and the "L" function, which is interest-inelastic. The supply schedule is the sum of the "S" function, current saving, and "M," new money, both of which are taken as interest-inelastic. The interest rate is determined, then, by the condition that $I + L = S + M$.[8] This is not a sufficient condition for equilibrium of the system or of the interest rate. Equilibrium requires the additional condition that $I = S$, (or, what amounts to the same thing, that $L = M$). So long as this condition is not satisfied also, the level of income will change. Change in the level of income will influence at least two of the determinants of the interest rate: saving (S) and the demand for additional cash balances (L), and therefore change the interest rate.

On Professor Fellner's assumptions, the equilibrium interest rate would be determined as shown in Chart 1. In part A of Chart 1, S and L are represented as functions of income (Y). New money (M) is given by the decisions of the monetary authority. The level of income Y_0 is determined by the equality of L and M_0; it must be such a level that all the new money is absorbed into new working balances. At income Y_0, an amount S_0 will be saved. In part B of Chart 1, S_0 is shown, and I gives the schedule of investment with respect to the interest rate. The interest rate i_0 is determined by $I = S_0$. This presentation makes it clear that any level of Y can be achieved by creating enough new money. Professor Fellner's "impasse" arises when the amount of saving—e.g., S_1 from income Y_1 based on new money M_1—exceeds the amount of investment which will be forthcoming even at zero interest rates. Here, on Professor Fellner's assumptions concerning the functions, equilibrium requires a negative interest rate. The failure of monetary policy to produce zero and negative interest rates can be explained only by departing from the assumption that the "L" function is perfectly inelastic with respect to the interest rate and, indeed, attributing to the "L" function perfect or near perfect interest-elasticity at very low rates.

Professor Fellner's reasons for believing that the "L" function is inelastic with respect to the interest rate follow:

1) In Keynesian theory, the reason given for the high (negative) elasticity of the demand for money at low rates of interest is that "speculators" believe that the rate of interest will rise and therefore prefer to hold cash rather than securities. According to Fellner, "it is not convincing to argue that the expectation of a 'return to normalcy' of interest rates produces substantially increased hoarding at lower-than-normal

[8] Pp. 168–71. Figure 22, p. 170.

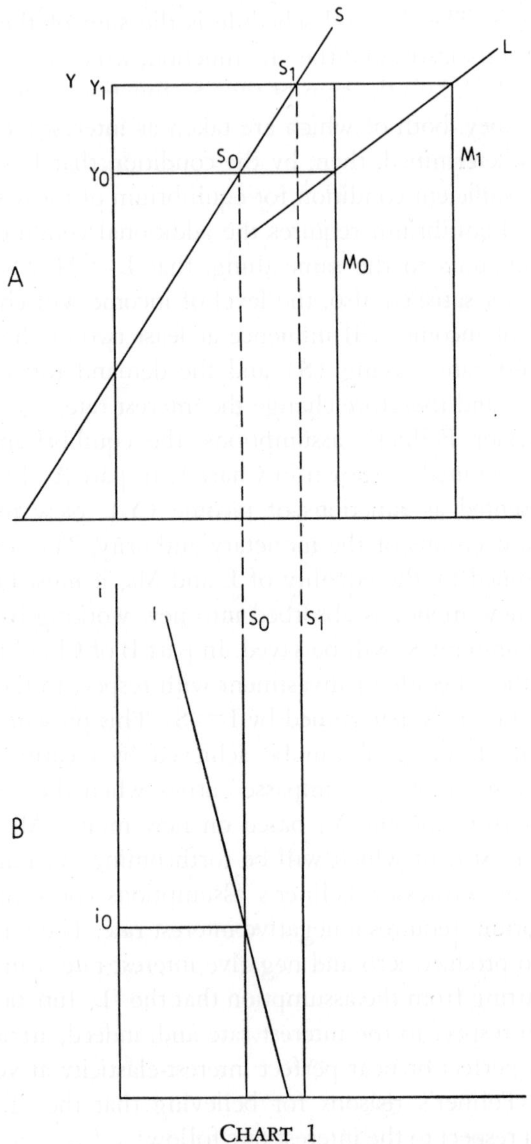

CHART 1

rates. If the expectation of a return to normalcy is strong enough to produce significant phenomena it is likely to produce a recovery to previous levels of the main economic variables . . ."[9]

2) Therefore, idle balances should be regarded as being mainly contingency (or precautionary) balances rather than speculative balances. But contingency balances, according to the *communis opinio* of

[9] P. 149.

economists including Keynes, are insensitive to interest rate changes.[10]

3) "Moreover, the occurrence of (unfavorable) contingencies itself may appear to be more probable if interest rates rise, and it may appear to be less probable if interest rates decline, because interest rates enter into the costs of enterprise. Consequently, it is not only true that the interest elasticity of contingency hoarding is likely to be small, but the algebraic sign of this elasticity could sometimes even be 'inverse.'"[11]

These points will be discussed in turn:

1) It is true that Keynesian theory emphasizes "that the demand for liquidity rises when interest rates decline because (1) the likelihood of a rise in interest rates . . . increases; and (2) at the same time, the compensation for bearing the risk of declining capital values is reduced."[12] Professor Fellner finds the first of these two reasons unconvincing. But either one of them alone is sufficient to justify an "L" function of negative elasticity and of high elasticity at low interest rates. Even if the risk of a rise in interest rates is no greater at low rates than at high, the compensation for bearing that risk approaches zero as the interest rate declines. Keynes, it is true, emphasizes strongly the increased liquidity preference of speculators at interest rates below what they consider normal and safe. Their psychology in this regard is quite compatible with the holding by a different set of individuals of pessimistic views concerning the profitability of real investment. But the case for a highly elastic "L" function at low interest rates does not depend on that psychology.

2) Keynes included precautionary balances in his M_1 (working balances), dependent not on the interest rate but on income. Professor Fellner correctly points out that precautionary balances have more in common with speculative balances (Keynes' M_2). For if there were no uncertainty in regard to future interest rates, contingency reserves would be held in interest-bearing assets rather than in cash. So long as there is a possibility of a rise in interest rates, even though such a rise is not expected more strongly than a fall, the interest rate is a relevant factor in determining the allocation of contingency reserves between cash and securities. Some skepticism is justified, therefore, regarding the *communis opinio* of economists that the demand for contingency cash balances is inelastic with respect to the interest rate. The effect of the reduction in the compensation for illiquidity applies here just as in the case of speculative balances. In addition, individuals or firms holding

[10] Pp. 146–51.

[11] P. 148.

[12] P. 141.

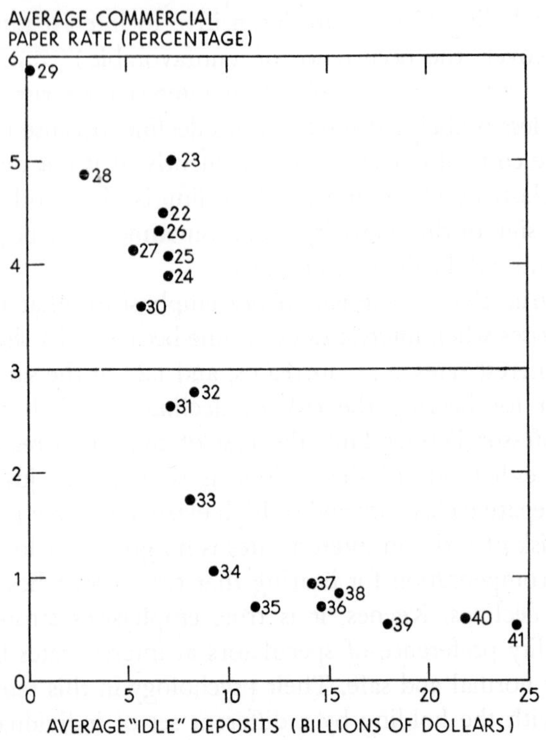

CHART 2.—RELATIONSHIP BETWEEN AVERAGE "IDLE" DEPOSITS AND AVERAGE COMMERCIAL PAPER RATE, ALL COMMERCIAL BANKS, 1922–41

contingency reserves differ from speculators in their attitude toward risk; in the case of contingency reserves, the disutility of the chance of a loss from a rise in interest rates is more likely to overbalance the utility of the chance of an equal capital gain. Even if the holder of a contingency reserve views a rise and fall in interest rates as equally likely, the chance of a rise may impress him more seriously. The lower the interest rate, the smaller the rise in it which will decrease the capital value of an asset enough to wipe out the yield. Uncertainty concerning the future of interest rates, whether or not a rise is considered more probable than a fall, is sufficient to make the risk of illiquidity seem greater the lower the rate.

3) Professor Fellner's ingenious argument for an inverse relationship between the demand for money and the rate of interest relies on the effects of higher interest rates as higher costs to the entrepreneur. The reasons for doubting that interest is a significant factor in cost calculations are familiar from discussions of the role of the interest rate in investment decisions.

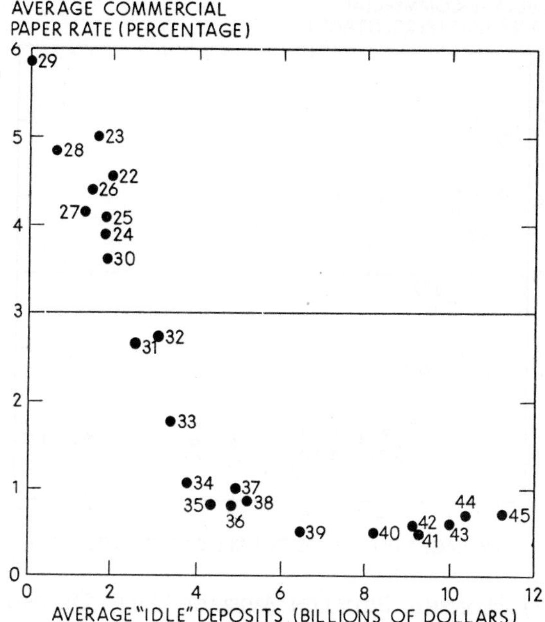

CHART 3.—RELATIONSHIP BETWEEN AVERAGE "IDLE" DEPOSITS AND AVERAGE COMMERCIAL PAPER RATE, NEW YORK CITY BANKS, 1922–45

IV. RELATIONSHIP OF "IDLE" BALANCES TO SHORT-TERM INTEREST RATE, 1922–45

Theories cannot be proved or disproved by statistics, but the statistical evidence at least suggests that the demand for cash balances is not perfectly inelastic with respect to the interest rate. In an attempt to discover the statistical relationship between idle deposits and the short-term interest rate, estimates of average "idle" deposits were computed for every year from 1922 to 1941 inclusive, and for subsequent years where comparable figures were available. Separate calculations were made for all commercial banks, for New York City banks only, for banks in 100 centers outside New York, and for Chicago banks only. In all cases the highest transactions velocity of deposits occurred in 1929.[13] To estimate the deposits in each year required for transactions purposes, total debits to demand deposits for each year were divided by the 1929 velocity. The result was subtracted from the actual average demand deposits for the year to obtain "idle" deposits, money which was not necessary to support the volume of transactions. This procedure results

[13] Board of Governors of the Federal Reserve System, *Banking and Monetary Statistics* (1943), Table 55, p. 254.

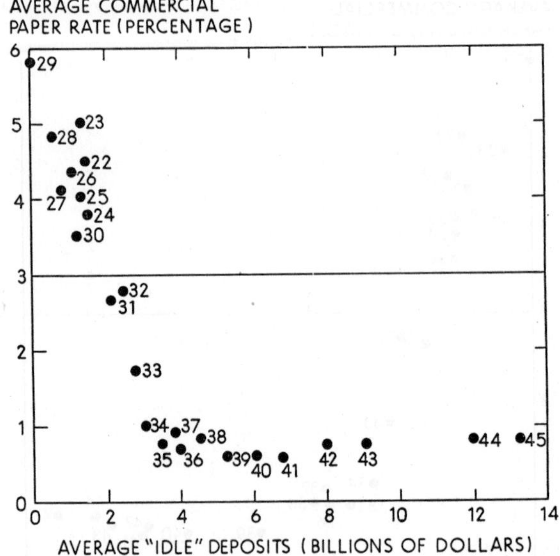

CHART 4.—RELATIONSHIP BETWEEN AVERAGE "IDLE" DEPOSITS AND AVERAGE COMMERCIAL PAPER RATE, BANKS IN 100 CENTERS OUTSIDE NEW YORK CITY, 1922–45

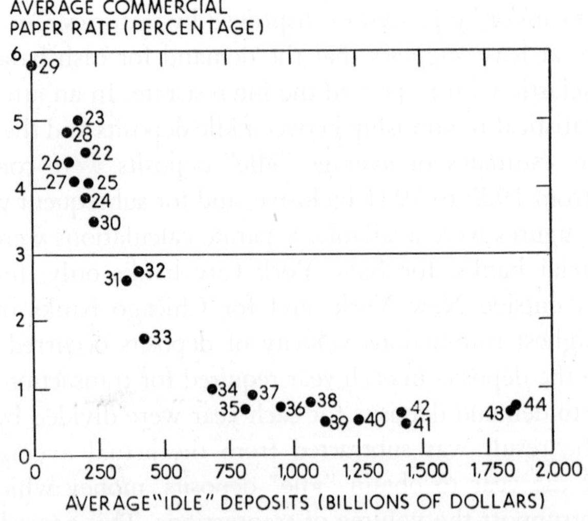

CHART 5.—RELATIONSHIP BETWEEN AVERAGE "IDLE" DEPOSITS AND AVERAGE COMMERCIAL PAPER RATE, CHICAGO BANKS, 1922–44

in arbitrarily defining "idle" deposits for 1929 as zero. Average "idle" deposits so computed are plotted against the average rate on prime commercial paper in Charts 2–5. The simple relationships shown can, on the whole, be improved by elimination of a downward secular trend in the commercial paper rate, but this has not been done. Even without such improvement, the relationships are of the general form postulated by liquidity preference theory.[14]

[14] The same conclusions can be reached by direct correlation of the transactions velocity with the short-term rate of interest. This has been done for English statistics by Kalecki, "The Short-Term Rate of Interest and the Velocity of Cash Circulation," *Rev. Econ. and Stat.*, 1941, XXIII, 97.

17

Monetary-Fiscal Policy Reconsidered[*1]

By G. L. BACH[†]

The need to make explicit the institutional and theoretical assumptions underlying the use of monetary-fiscal policy has been emphasized by postwar experience. On the one hand, we economists have failed to predict adequately the need for stabilizing policies or to prescribe satisfactory policies to maintain relatively full employment without inflation. On the other, as has recently been emphasized,[2] it seems disconcertingly likely that, instead of guaranteeing full employment without inflation, in a free society monetary-fiscal policy may well guarantee inflation without full employment because of the upward income pressures of monopolies and organized political power groups. Nevertheless, co-ordinated monetary-fiscal policy remains probably the most hopeful single weapon that we have against instability of the traditional business-cycle type and against the waste of secular unemployment.

This paper represents an attempt to clarify this problem by re-examining briefly the assumptions on which effective monetary-fiscal policy must rest. It falls into two parts: (I) a suggested framework of certain fundamental assumptions on which any workable monetary-fiscal policy for the proximate future apparently must be built and (II) a tentative suggestion as to the type of policy arrangements toward which this reconsideration seems to point.

To give substance to the concept of "effective" monetary-fiscal policy, a dual measure of success is adopted. We want continuous, reason-

* *Journal of Political Economy,* Oct. 1949. Reprinted by the courtesy of the *Journal of Political Economy* and the author.

† Carnegie Institute of Technology.

[1] I am indebted to W. W. Cooper and O. H. Brownlee for helpful suggestions.

[2] See, e.g., M. W. Reder, "The Theoretical Problems of a National Wage-Price Policy," *Canadian Jour. Econ. and Pol. Sci.,* Feb. 1948; M. Friedman, "A Monetary and Fiscal Framework for Economic Stability," *Am. Econ. Rev.,* June 1948; M. Bronfenbrenner, "Postwar Political Economy: The President's Reports," *Jour. Pol. Econ.,* Oct. 1948; and Bach, "Monetary-fiscal Policy, Debt Policy, and the Price Level," *Am. Econ. Rev., Proceedings,* May 1947.

ably full useful employment (say, a floor of 3–4 million under unemployment in the United States), and a reasonably stable price level (excluding prices of productive services which could rise steadily with increasing productivity). Moreover, this dual goal, at least in the United States, must be achieved with minimal interference with the freedom of the individual through direct controls.[3] However unreasonable this double goal, subject to the individual freedom constraint, may appear to the economic theorist, it is what people want. And they are unlikely long to be satisfied with less. Perhaps the goal is impossible, but at least we need to measure policy against it.[4]

I. WHAT ARE VALID BASES FOR MONETARY-FISCAL POLICY?

If the nearest possible approach to effective monetary-fiscal policy is to be achieved, it is essential to be clear as to the theoretical and institutional bases, or assumptions, on which policy can *realistically* be founded. I have suggested six below, without pretense of precision or finality of judgment, in each case indicating briefly what would be the "ideal" assumption on which completely effective policy could be built. The assumptions could be listed quite differently, but this arrangement focuses attention on certain institutional factors which seem to me to deserve major attention. Assumption 1 deals with the efficacy of monetary-fiscal action, assuming that the "correct" policies are utilized; the others deal primarily with our ability to prescribe and carry out the "correct" policies at the proper time.[5]

1. *The Limited Efficacy of Monetary-Fiscal Policy*

To assure effective monetary-fiscal policy, monetary-fiscal action would have to be able to control within a narrow range (say, ±5 per cent) the level of national money income or gross national product, assuming that we knew just when to take how much of what policy action and could take it without delay or threat of negation from private pressure groups and monopolies in the economy. In fact, it is not clear that national money income could be so controlled even under these ideal conditions. The repeated "real" shocks from technological

[3] On this basis the present note is concerned with the possibilities of monetary-fiscal policy in a society in which extensive direct controls over wages, prices, etc., are excluded except as temporary expedients. See also n. 16.

[4] This statement of goals neglects the international aspects of the problem. A goal of maximum contribution to stability of the international economy, or to exchange stability, might be added, if this is desired; but much greater difficulty is faced here in obtaining a consensus as to the specific end desired.

[5] As listed, the assumptions are not entirely mutually exclusive.

change, international politics, weather conditions, etc., may exert strong destabilizing pressures. The very process of economic growth appears to involve basic "real" irregularities and bunchings which exert enormously strong pressures on the level of total spending. A shifting internal structure of costs and prices may exert pressures on total investment and consumption hard to offset by monetary-fiscal measures alone. The highly volatile and crucial nature of inventory investment is now widely recognized.

For the policy-maker, recognition of such limitations on the efficacy of monetary-fiscal policy even under ideal conditions emphasizes the need to focus on checking major swings in income rather than aiming at every minor fluctuation. It also emphasizes the short-sightedness of permitting excessive preoccupation with the details and niceties of particular policies to stand in the road of their acceptance if they promise useful performance on a broader level.[6] If we try to achieve more than "reasonable" stability of national money income with monetary-fiscal policy, pending better diagnoses and acquaintance with our tools, we are likely to be using a hammer when only a scalpel will do, with greater instability the result of our excessive zeal.

2. *Imperfect Wisdom in Analysis and Prediction*

For effective results the monetary-fiscal authority or rule must be able to analyze current developments and predict the future course of incomes, employment, and prices sufficiently well to provide the basis for forming the policy decisions required to achieve assumption 1. If the "authority" approach is used, the crucial assumption is that experts are (can be) wise enough in analysis and prediction to provide the necessary basis for the formulation of successful monetary-fiscal policy measures. Evaluations of the expertness of the experts in this area will vary. On the evidence as I see it, the record is unconvincing. Outside the obvious case of inflationary wartime pressures generated by wartime financing, it is hard to recall a single important cyclical turn in the last quarter-century when economists have been conspicuously successful forecasters; our record in recognizing promptly major changes in direction is not much better. And, unfortunately, in spite of steadily improving data and analytical and statistical techniques, we now seem to be doing not a great deal better than we did ten or twenty years

[6] For example, the objection to "price-level stabilization" that precisely the right index cannot be found to stabilize, and to "maintenance of full employment" that we cannot sharply define full employment, may become of relatively minor importance under this criterion.

ago. Passing over the unfortunate experience of the post–V-J Day predictions, even since 1946 the profession has been widely split during one of the major inflations of our history as to whether we should be acting vigorously to check inflation or preparing to fight depression just around a very near corner.[7]

The "rule" approach, which utilizes a single guide to policy (e.g., some price index or the level of national money income), avoids some of this problem by taking a major guide which will presumably call for action only when the need is clearly demonstrated. But, here again, no evidence is available to support the adequacy of such a guide on more than a very general basis, and it is not clear that small variations in such an index might not be seriously misleading.

To the policy-maker this means that any workable policy must be able to operate on highly imperfect signals for action. It must be susceptible of quick reversal. It must be such as to minimize the human dangers of seriously erroneous prediction in the imperfect state of our knowledge. If we are too slow, the dangers are patent. But if we are too fast, they may be almost as great. On smaller swings a strong monetary-fiscal cure may, through severe reversal of a minor movement, easily be worse than the disease—and the problem is, How shall we tell in advance whether the disease really needs strong medicine? Contrary to standard prescription, very prompt, vigorous action to check incipient booms and recessions may be the least wise policy. "Wait a little and see before trying anything drastic" comes more readily from the present state of our analysis and prediction possibilities.

3. *Imperfect Wisdom in Policy Formation*

To ferret out incipient inflation or deflation is not enough. Once these developments are recognized, the authorities must know what to

[7] It is true, of course, that the argument from history may not be completely convincing. Economists in the past have had to use data and techniques inferior to those available now. And one may point to this or that economist or method that has successfully called one or more turns or has correctly predicted no turn; the "modern" method always looks best when we view the current scene, for obvious reasons. Perhaps X or Y has really hit upon a reliable method of prediction, but caution and the record suggest that we wait for better proof before being convinced that it is so (cf. Everett Hagen, "The Problem of Timing Fiscal Policy," *Am. Econ. Rev., Proceedings,* May 1948; and Leo Barnes, "How Sound Were Private Postwar Forecasts?" *Jour. Pol. Econ.,* Apr. 1948, Vol. LVI.

It should be recognized, moreover, that successful performance would require not only quick ability to recognize important developments but also the courage to make analyses boldly as a basis for national policy. Many an economist who is willing to call the turns with confident precision from his ivory tower has developed a surprising degree of "iffiness" when put into a position of recognized responsibility for national policy. Not only is it human nature to want to be right before millions of people, but any responsible predictor must always remember that serious failure in only one or two crucial predictions may well discredit himself, the profession, and the whole monetary-fiscal approach.

do and how much of it. If a recession appears, is a combination of a \$3 billion bank-financed deficit and \$1 billion of open-market purchases about what is needed? Will this prove to be the force that restores the waning inflation, or will it prove grossly inadequate to check the cumulative downswing? Here, again, I think we must admit that we are not quite sure, in using most of the generally discussed tools of monetary-fiscal policy (open-market operations, government-expenditure policies, particular tax changes, etc.), whether we are swinging a sledge or only a hammer.[8] Thus a double danger looms up—that we may overshoot the mark and seriously reverse mild inflations or deflations or that we may do too little and let almost irresistible cumulative sweeps get well under way.[9]

Given our lack of clear empirical evidence or convincing deductive conclusions as to the potency of various monetary and fiscal measures under varying conditions, sound policy must be built to minimize the importance of this uncertainty. This points strongly in the direction of policy arrangements that somehow minimize the danger of serious "wrong guesses" and that permit quick adjustments in case the estimate of either the situation or the policy results turns out to have been wrong.

4. *The Likely Importance of Lags*

To achieve goal 1, the time lag between the need for stabilizing action and the stabilizing effect of the action taken must be so short that national income does not vary outside the limits of tolerance.[10] The aggregate lag between the need for action and the stabilizing effect of action taken has three components: (*a*) the lag between need for action and recognition of this need; (*b*) the lag between recognition and taking action; and (*c*) the lag between action and its stabilizing results.

---

[8] Witness the amazing disagreement among economists as to whether substantial central-bank open-market sales in the United States were too powerful a weapon to risk using against the recent inflation or such an unimportant weapon that the likely anti-inflationary effects did not justify even a small rise in Treasury interest costs or other minor disadvantages.

[9] Witness, respectively, the role of fiscal policy in 1937 and the post–V-J Day inflation and 1929–32 deflation.

[10] In one sense this assumption would make assumptions 1 and 2 unnecessary. If the lag were short enough (say, only one week), how correct our predictions are on the need for action and on the results of different policy measures would not matter much, since we could always experiment, with the chance of altering policy in another experiment next week before things could get badly out of hand. Actually, fulfilment of this condition would not alone handle the problem, since it presumes that the legislature and the public would be willing to suffer with a policy which continually and unpredictably rocked the economic boat from side to side, even though the rocking seldom threatened complete capsizing.

Extended discussion here of these lag components would be superfluous.[11] I think it is fair to say that, with our present analytical techniques and empirical information, we must be reconciled to a substantial lag on component *a.* On component *b,* it is conspicuously true that getting action on fiscal policies is slow business. Congress' recalcitrance on fiscal matters has driven many an economist to dismay; central-bank action can be much more prompt, once the need is agreed on. But lag component *c* reverses this advantage. We suspect that the stabilizing impact of fiscal policy (especially expenditure variations) can be strong and prompt, since it bears directly on the income stream and (probably) on consumer and business outlays; but the lag between monetary action and its impact is one of the great unknowns of the profession. Over all, therefore, there seems to be no apparent way, given present knowledge and institutions, in the United States at least, to eliminate a substantial *and unknown* aggregate lag in the application of stabilizing forces to unstabilized situations.

The policy implications of the lag problem are similar to those of point 3 above—a more flexible machinery for altering the government's net contribution to the income stream and policy formation aimed at minimizing trouble from errors attributable to wrong-guessing on the length of the lag.

5. *The Difficulty of Obtaining Adequate Delegation of Power*

For effective policy, adequate power must have been delegated to the monetary-fiscal authority to take whatever monetary-fiscal action is required to achieve point 1. This is true whether the basic plan is for a discretionary authority or for a "rule," since even under the rule the problem of implementation remains to be handled on at least a semi-discretionary basis.

Extensive (though far from complete) legislative delegation of monetary power to the central bank has been orthodox for many decades, and no major reversal of this situation appears imminent.[12] But to assume Congressional renunciation of direct control over the power to tax and the power to spend, except possibly for some delegation of authority over timing of prearranged programs, appears to have little relevance to reality. Formulation of a workable monetary-fiscal policy

[11] Cf. the more complete analysis of Friedman, *op. cit.,* esp. pp. 254–58.

[12] Government ownership of central banks has generally left effective control to the executive branch of the government. Yet in the United States it is significant that the major point on which Congress has rebelled at giving more adequate monetary powers to the Federal Reserve System is where their powers begin to infringe on the federal budget through raising interest costs.

must recognize the stubborn fact of Congressional prerogatives. There appears to be little point for the foreseeable future in schemes that rest on an administrative authority delicately manipulating tax and expenditure rates, on the basis either of discretionary decisions or of a simple, definite rule. The problem is to devise a workable monetary-fiscal policy consistent with substantial legislative maintenance of present fiscal prerogatives, looking hopefully toward a better day in the future.

6. *The Basic Importance of Monopolies and Other Income-Power Groups for Monetary-Fiscal Policy-Making*

For effective policy the monetary-fiscal authority must operate without irresistible pressures from special interest groups (business, labor, agriculture) seeking to place their welfare above that of the general public. Furthermore, there must be no other, nonofficial, contesting groups able, in fact, to control the level of income, employment, and prices counter to the authorities' policies. The importance of income-seeking power groups and monopolies as a barrier to full employment without inflation has been increasingly recognized in the past few years.[13] Thus no elaborate restatement of the problem is required. The essential difficulty is (*a*) that organized labor, business, and other major power groups are now likely to exert strong expansionary pressure on governmental monetary-fiscal decisions, even when inflationary forces are strong, and (*b*) that upward income and price pressures by these groups cannot be effectively resisted by a government whose monetary-fiscal guide is (openly or apparently) the maintenance of "full employment," so that repeated wage and price demands are increasingly likely to produce a stair-step or cumulative, fiscal-policy-aided inflation. Such inflationary pressure, moreover, may persist in the absence of anything like full employment.[14]

In such a setting it is clear that the monetary-fiscal authority is by no means unchallenged as "the" monetary-fiscal authority—organized labor and business have virtually as much control over the level of employment and prices as does the official authority. The parallel to trilateral oligopoly in the market place is close; the levels of employment and prices are indeterminate and governed by trilateral bargaining, with a strong presumption of upward-moving prices as money-income disputes are adjudicated upward at the expense of relatively

[13] See the references noted in n. 2 of this paper.

[14] Recognition of the importance of this force, therefore, of course does not necessarily imply the absence of intermittent periods of "recession" or "depression" or of intermittent weakening of prices and wages in such periods, such as have commonly occurred in "business cycles."

fixed incomes. Actually, of course, society is far from being so simple, and there are many smaller power groups rather than three giants. Yet this simplified analogy has enough realism to be unpleasantly suggestive for the future. And the present monetary-fiscal policy-making procedures (the committee system in Congress and generally diffused monetary-fiscal responsibilities) provide an ideal opportunity for pressure groups to advance special interests without ever exposing the real issues to the public gaze.

The crux of the matter is that the issue of income distribution (money and real) is shifted from the traditional textbook fragmented market place to a politico-economic arena in which the monetary-fiscal authority may be only one of several powerful groups. As long as none of the nongovernmental power groups believes that the monetary authority will bail out unemployment or falling sales by expansionary monetary-fiscal policy, the fear of going "too far" and of inducing unemployment and depression is likely to moderate the struggle for income position and power. This seems clearly to have been the important restraining force to date. But, once the enormous potential power of monetary-fiscal expansion is widely recognized and its use generally accepted, the pressure groups will have little to lose from intermittent or continuous efforts to improve their individual income positions through wage-price pressures in the market place and through direct pressures on government for income-raising measures (e.g., farm income parity and the Guffey Coal Act). In a modern "democratic" state, it would be a remarkably insulated and politically insensitive monetary-fiscal "authority" indeed that would consistently permit the development of unemployment rather than expand purchasing power (and raise prices) to maintain total output and employment.

The implicit neat separation in much of economic theory between distribution theory and monetary-fiscal theory can hardly be accepted as useful in the world of today, where politico-economic power groups are rampant and the potential expansionary power of monetary-fiscal policy is increasingly recognized. In a stand against inflation the monetary authority becomes, in effect, the protector of the income of a particular social group—the unorganized fixed income-receivers who are relatively helpless to protect their real income share against raids. In permitting higher prices with higher wages to maintain employment, the authority's weight is thrown the other way in the income struggle.

Advocates of a monetary "rule," as distinct from a discretionary "authority," argue that by adopting one stated, unambiguous guide to policy this problem can be kept within bounds. But this solution is disarmingly simple. First, the rule must somehow be adopted. In such a legislative struggle the major organized income groups can be counted on to look out for their own interests. But at least the argument would be open to all to see, and the chance of subordination of the "public good" to pressure-group interests (as so often occurs in the day-to-day making of *ad hoc* decisions) would be minimized. Second, once a monetary-fiscal guide-rule is adopted, it will face the same income-group pressures as do "authority" approaches. A price-level stabilization policy, on the one hand, would insist on reasonable protection for the fixed-income groups against their more powerful competitors,[15] but at the risk of intermittent or constant unemployment if power groups press or hold wages or prices above the levels consistent with full employment at the fixed price level. By removing the "safety valve" of price inflation, a price-stabilization rule would focus the income-power issue on maintenance of the price-stability rule rather than on the *ad hoc* decisions of the authorities; it would not remove the issue. On the other hand, "full employment" (superficially the most appealing) cannot be the rule upon which to face the income–power-group issue, since with a full-employment guaranty the compromise of inflation through assured monetary-fiscal expansion is always available to resolve conflict.

What monetary-fiscal policy can be built on this conflict-ridden foundation? In a vain endeavor to escape the dilemma, most economists still prescribe the standard discretionary authority whose role is deftly to obscure the fact of conflicting income claims behind the veil of money (with just a little inflation where necessary) and so to keep the various income-seekers happy. That this scheme has worked as well as it has as long as it has can but amaze most economists. But the struggle for power and income appears to be swelling in intensity, and the war lesson that government deficit spending can, if necessary, create almost any amount of purchasing power in the market will not soon be forgotten. Under these circumstances, a discretionary authority that aims at fooling most of the people most of the time must prove self-delusive as a long-run policy, helpful as it may be in compromising explosive conflicts until a more fundamental solution can be devised.[16]

[15] The once popular policy of "neutral money" (commodity prices falling apace with increasing productivity) would guarantee an even better position to fixed-income groups, assuring them a share of the fruits of technological progress that they would not obtain under commodity-price stability.

[16] The other major alternative is the use of extensive direct controls over prices, wages, materials, real investment, etc., to reconcile the aims of full employment and price stabilization by holding down monopoly and pressure-group wages and prices directly. As indicated at the outset, this note does not deal with such policies. But one may note in passing the remarkable naïveté involved in believing that powerful interest groups will passively

In a democracy where major power groups clash, no policy can long stand which does not command a substantial consensus from the citizenry. Ultimately there can be no continuing rule or authority beyond the strength that it commands through popular support. As a temporary expedient, "outbargaining" the various groups of the public may work satisfactorily for the monetary authority; but without a "religion" of money on which to anchor (often unreasoning) public confidence and support, the policy is self-doomed. As Henry C. Simons has eloquently put the core of the issue:

> The modern test of truth [in public policy formation] is simply voluntary rational consensus. . . . The good, progressive moral order must rest on intelligent consensus and on much the same kind of free, critical discussion as is involved in scientific inquiry. The social processes of a free society are, if not infallible, the only reliable means to moral truth and the best means to security under law.[17]

In the end, Simons must be right. Democracy's greatest danger and its most pressing problem—the compromise of conflicting interests of minority power groups—can ultimately be faced and settled only on the grounds of a working voluntary consensus. Whatever the temporizing expediencies that may seem (and be) so important for the day, this is the direction in which monetary-fiscal policy must ultimately point if the current income struggle is not to destroy the hopes so widely held for a stabilizing monetary-fiscal policy. A workable system of monetary-fiscal policy in a democracy must be one in which wages (income claims generally) *are,* in fact, sufficiently stabilized to permit full employment without inflation, under the impact of a voluntary consensus of support for the stabilization plan.

II. THE ESTABLISHMENT OF POLICY ON VALID ASSUMPTIONS

If the preceding analysis is substantially accepted, the implications for policy formation are relatively clear. Stated in somewhat different order, workable monetary-fiscal policy must:

a) Minimize the chances of serious human errors in analysis and action prescription, giving substantial weight to the uncertainties involved

b) Minimize the aggregate lag between the need for stabilizing action and the stabilizing effect of the action

---

let themselves be so restrained unless they are substantially convinced of the equity of the entire plan. Where direct controls over wages and prices would work effectively in peacetime they are likely not to be seriously needed.

[17] *Economic Policy for a Free Society* (Chicago, University of Chicago Press, 1947), pp. 8–9.

c) Be operative without much additional delegation of monetary-fiscal power by the legislature to administrative authorities

d) Concentrate on maintaining stability of income within reasonable limits rather than attempt to offset all minor fluctuations

e) Be able, at least as time goes on, to command widespread moral support and thus serve as an effective compromise ground for the conflicting income-power groups prevalent in the modern economy (in other words, serve to remove the income struggle to grounds other than the exertion of pressure on monetary-fiscal policy).

To design monetary-fiscal policy in accordance with such realistic specifications is the task which economists face if they are to provide relevant counsel. The following paragraphs outline briefly, for suggestive purposes, one possible two-part policy approach that might satisfy the specifications reasonably well, at least until the basic assumptions alter because of improving prediction techniques, changing legislative attitudes, lessened minority-group power, etc. The suggestion involves attempting to combine certain major advantages of two previously suggested approaches—"built-in flexibility" and a monetary-fiscal "rule"—while dropping certain aspects of each that seem unworkable in the light of the specifications suggested.

Built-in Flexibility

Specifications *a* and *b* point to the need for an "automatic" policy—automatic in indicating promptly the need for action and in prescribing the action to be taken. A policy so oriented has been widely discussed under the names "full employment budget balance" and "built-in budget flexibility."[18] Under this proposal the desired volume of government expenditures on goods and services is determined on non-cyclical grounds. Then a tax system, relying heavily on taxes sensitive to income changes and calculated to finance this volume of spending at, say, a 95 per cent full-employment income level, is devised and enacted by the legislature. Regardless of cyclical business fluctuations, the tax rates and government spending on goods and services are then left untouched, except for periodic adjustments to allow for changes in the proportion of its real income that society wants to channel through the government. Under these circumstances a drop in income will lower tax yields and produce an automatic deficit as expenditures are maintained. The deficit will be financed by creation of new (central or commercial bank) money,

[18] The most concise, complete, and theoretically explicit proposal is Friedman's (*op. cit.*). Earlier proposals were made by B. Ruml and H. C. Sonne, *Fiscal and Monetary Policy* ("National Planning Association Pamphlets," No. 35 [1944]), and the Committee for Economic Development, *Taxes and the Budget* (1947). Friedman's statement is the basis for the text comments here.

automatically producing an expansionary pressure through both fiscal and monetary channels. A rise in income above the 95 per cent employment level will have the reverse effect, creating a surplus which will simply be destroyed (used to repay bank debt). This will be deflationary on both fiscal and monetary fronts.

In its most "automatic" form,[19] this proposal includes a predetermined plan to expand transfer payments (especially unemployment insurance) if income falls below the prescribed level. It also includes 100 per cent reserve banking, so that the total money supply could and would change only with changes in the government deficit or surplus—i.e., only with changes in the level of national income above or below the prescribed 95 per cent employment level. Thus discretionary monetary-fiscal decisions would be eliminated completely, except for the periodic decision as to the desired full-employment level of government spending on goods and services and as to the corresponding tax structure. The system would be automatically self-stabilizing. It would avoid the dangers of human errors in prediction and policy formulation; it would be essentially foolproof against mistaken results counterdirectional to those needed; it would provide flexibility as to direction and amount of action—all without appreciable risks of error.

Such a policy of built-in flexibility would also be reasonably compatible with specification *c.* Though it would restrict continuous legislative changes in tax and expenditure policies, at least it would involve no delegation of additional fiscal-monetary power to administrative authorities. Whether members of Congress in the United States or parliamentary bodies elsewhere could be convinced of the case for such a scheme for stability is rather doubtful. Certainly, they are not very likely to tie their hands completely with such a plan. Still, steps in this direction would be helpful, and the general principle of only infrequent determination of "full-employment" expenditure and tax levels might gradually be "sold" to legislators.

The big difficulty with the plan, as its proponents and critics have readily agreed, is that its built-in flexibility may not be powerful enough to prevent ruinous depressions or inflations. The built-in stabilizers will work continuously and in the right direction, but there is no guaranty that they will hold fluctuations within any prescribed limits.[20] Thus to

[19] As suggested by Friedman, *op. cit.*

[20] On the other hand, most of the technical criticisms of the plan on this score (e.g., R. A. Musgrave and M. H. Miller, "Built-in Flexibility," *Am. Econ. Rev.,* Mar. 1948) appear to have underrated its potentialities because of their failure to recognize the self-correcting forces inherent in a deflation-period rise (inflation-period fall) in the real value of cash balances and other liquid assets. For a more complete analysis of this aspect of the

pin complete support on such a policy could hardly be advocated; its advocates all admit that, if really serious fluctuations should nonetheless develop, reinforcing discretionary measures would probably be wise.

Moreover, once the legitimacy of throwing over the automatic policy in time of "serious stress" is generally recognized, the policy's usefulness for our specification *e* is very limited. Genuine, unswerving popular support for such a complex, indirect policy could hardly be expected. It provides little basis for formulation of stable business and consumer expectations. The scheme has little appeal as a "religion of money" or as a direct compromise ground for conflicting income interests except to professional economists and intellectuals. Unfortunately, they are not the critical groups for this problem.

A Monetary-Fiscal "Rule"

If we start our policy search at the other end—with our specification *e*—attention is focused on the need for a simple, appealing policy that can command widespread support and (if possible) understanding. Only such a policy can hope to resist the ominous monopoly, minority-group income struggle, by clarifying the issues and thrusting the income contest back into the market place or into open, visible political issues as the minority groups seek such special arrangements as farm and wage parity.

Price-level stabilization is, as I have argued at length elsewhere,[21] as far as I can see the only available policy rule from which there seems to be much hope on this fundamental problem. Obviously, "full employment" per se cannot be used if avoidance of inflation is taken seriously. A stable dollar and a stable cost of living could provide a reasonable basis for stabilizing the creeping or stair-step inflation that promises to characterize a society effectively cartelized in wide sectors of industry, labor, and agriculture. No one can reasonably expect self-restraint from any one group when there is no guaranty that other groups will not capitalize on this self-restraint. It is only on the basis of some eminently reasonable, understandable "stabilizer" (basis for compromise) that real hope for an income truce can rest—not that income conflicts can be eliminated but that they can be confined to a reasonably manageable

problem see Don Patinkin, "Price Flexibility and Full Employment," *Am. Econ. Rev.*, Sept. 1948, esp. pp. 547 ff.

[21] *Op. cit.*, and "Rearmament, Recovery, and Monetary Policy," *Am. Econ. Rev.*, Mar. 1941; see esp. pp. 37–41 of the earlier article, which argues that the theoretical differences between price-level stabilization and other monetary "rules," such as stable income per capita, are slight but that price stabilization presents very strong advantages on institutional and "practical" grounds.

area in the market or in open political struggle, where the raid of any minority group must stand the test of legislative action and public opinion. We cannot expect to destroy or completely transform economic and political power in the modern world. In a democracy such as ours the main goal must be the stabilization of a set of "rules" within which the power conflicts can be resolved with a minimum of disruption and violence.

The specific hope of price-level stabilization is that labor, business, and agriculture could be convinced of the wisdom and equity of a "reasonable" truce on the basis of a stable price level—that on the basis of a firm guaranty against over-all price and income deflation they could be persuaded that wages and incomes can rise only with increasing real productivity, once full employment is reached, and that competitive income pressures thereafter inevitably mean either unemployment or inflation. If this recognition could be achieved *and* if public support for the stable-money plan could be attained (as should not be difficult after the painful oscillations of the past two decades),[22] then public opinion, mobilized behind a price-level stabilization policy, could exert enormous pressure on monopoly or political power groups seeking special gains at the obvious expense of others in the community and of the general stabilization program.[23] Complete agreement would not be needed, only a workable consensus. Our basic political constitutions were adopted and are maintained as working compromises of sharply conflicting interests; scarcely any law or administrative practice commands absolute unanimity. Reasonable agreement among reasonable men is the essence of liberty and democracy.

But price-level stabilization, too, has serious failings. Its full implementation would require extensive Congressional delegation of fiscal power to the administrative authority; its signals for corrective action would probably be only moderately satisfactory as to timing; it might in practice be excessively occupied with correcting small variations in the price index; it prescribes no implementative measures. Clearly, this policy would conform only moderately well to our basic specifications, great as are its potential advantages under *e.* It is weakest where auto-

[22] The strongly ingrained popular belief that the inevitable result of inflation must somehow be deflation, currently quite apparent among both labor and business groups, should not be overlooked as an important factor in building up popular support for any price-level stability scheme, whether the belief is rational or not.

[23] A. P. Lerner has suggested that price stabilization be combined with a national wage policy under which arbitration procedures would use as a compulsory guide prescribed rates of wage increases consistent with general price stability ("Money as a Creature of the State," *Am. Econ. Rev., Proceedings,* May 1947). This would, he feels help to clarify the rights and responsibilities of the various income groups under such a plan.

matic budget flexibility is strong; strongest where the flexibility plan is weak.

Built-in Flexibility and Band Stabilization

What we need for a workable monetary-fiscal policy is some plan that combines the "technical" advantages of the built-in budget flexibility approach with the basic politico-economic promise of price stabilization. In fact, the two approaches turn out to have a remarkable degree of complementarity. A joint policy might well operate, with reliance on the principles of built-in flexibility, as long as some acceptable price index did not vary outside, say, a band of 90 to 110.[24] Thus all smaller fluctuations, on which a rigid price-stabilization rule with discretionary implementation would risk erroneous performance, would be handled within the relatively foolproof built-in flexibility plan. But if a really serious recession or inflation should nevertheless develop, driving the price index sharply up or down, at the prescribed limits an automatic signal for reinforcing discretionary policy would be given. At this point, it is important to notice, directional errors from discretionary policy are quite unlikely, since the recession or inflation is already well developed, and at this point reinforcing policy is clearly desirable on its own merits.[25]

With these "technical" advantages, the combination would also retain the major advantages of price stabilization as a basic monetary truce, subject to a "reasonable" degree of flexibility that would presumably appeal to both laymen and professional economists. The substantially stable price level guaranteed would provide a reasonable basis for stable monetary expectations. And to attain all this, Congress would not be called upon to delegate any monetary-fiscal powers not already delegated. It would be asked only to return to a full-employment-level balanced-budget policy (so near to fiscal orthodoxy), except when the price-level guide clearly indicated the need for major countercyclical action. At that time, Congress could be trusted, if ever, to enact budget policies with the right general effect.[26] Once the price index was back

---

[24] One might argue that the *rate of change* of prices rather than the level would be the appropriate indicator of when the bounds of tolerance were passed. Thus one might say that, whenever prices rose or fell more than 1 per cent monthly for three months, the limits of tolerance were passed. But the gains from such superiority, however real, appear to bulk small against the loss of directness and simplicity involved.

[25] The main problem would arise if prices tended as a standard matter to bump along against the top of the band.

[26] When the signals are this unambiguous, delegated power in the hands of an administrative body would be preferable in terms of quick, efficient utilization of monetary-fiscal measures. Moreover, with an administrative body deputized to use monetary-fiscal

within bounds, the need for discretionary countercyclical budget policy would be past, as evidenced by an unambiguous policy guide. Congress would thus be asked to violate—and would be publicly justified in violating—the canons of "sound" fiscal policy by conscious budget unbalance only under the emergencies evidenced by very substantial price (and income) fluctuations. Lastly, appropriate emphasis would be placed on the problems of handling minor and major fluctuations; an attempt would be made automatically to offset small fluctuations, but discretionary protection would be reserved for major fluctuations.

Moreover, such a two-part policy would lend itself to gradual, "reasonable" introduction. Except for 100 per cent reserve banking, all the basic ideas in the plan are commonplace and probably acceptable in at least a general way to both professional economists and laymen.[27] No one wants sharp inflations or deflations; no one in his senses believes that we can prevent every minor business fluctuation through monetary-fiscal policy; no one likes the idea of continuous unpredictable changes in tax rates and government expenditure policies. Yet most people are now reconciled to the moderate use of fiscal-monetary policy to combat business fluctuations; and most people would like to see countercyclical monetary-fiscal policy further "out of politics" than it is now. Most important of all, power groups are with us to stay, politically and economically; and most individuals at heart do, I think, want to stand firm for the public welfare against damaging group income raids, if only they can see clearly what is the public good and what raiding is being attempted by minority groups.

The policy outlined is a far from perfect plan. Its main purpose is to suggest directions along which fruitful policy development may lie, combining realism as to politico-economic institutions with reasonable conformity to the dictates of monetary-fiscal theory. Few policy proposals that require a revolution for their introduction are proximately useful. A Congressional resolution accepting the principle of moderate

policy freely to bring the index back within the allowed limits and specifically responsible for this function, there would be less danger of Congress' continuing to try actively to act countercyclically after built-in flexibility should again take over. As W. W. Cooper has emphasized ("Some Implications of a Program for Full Employment and Economic Stability," *Pol. Sci. Quart.*, June 1948), a large, bicameral legislature such as Congress is an innately inefficient body to do the actual governing of the economy; rather, it can efficiently make only the general rules of government and maintain a close investigative check on the actual governing activities of the administrative branch of the government. Still, Congressional countercyclical action under the conditions specified in the text should promise substantial improvement over the present "ruleless" arrangements.

[27] And the plan would be workable, though less automatic, with the present fractional reserve banking system. The major portion of the 100 per cent system gain could be attained at reserve requirements substantially below 100 per cent.

built-in flexibility plus the intention of holding the (some) commodity price level within some moderate range such as 90–110 of "normal" is not at all difficult to conceive. One of this policy's greatest advantages is that its very simple, homely aspects which might obtain greatest popular and governmental support are those which are, in fact, steps in the right direction as seen by the professional economist.

18

*Integrating Debt Management and Open Market Operations**

By ROBERT V. ROOSA†

A great deal of ground has been covered by debt management and credit policy over the past year, both in terms of events and of the printed word. The Treasury-Federal Reserve "accord" of March, 1951, has given credit policy an opportunity to begin to demonstrate in the market place many of the potentialities which these purely personal and unofficial remarks of mine might otherwise have been trying to demonstrate here in the simpler, but far less convincing, medium of the hypothesis and the syllogism. A provocative and persuasive review of the part that credit policy has played in shaping recent events has been presented by Woodlief Thomas, in his paper on "Recent Experience with Monetary-Fiscal Measures." Soon many of you will also be reading each other's contributions to the important symposium being conducted by a special Congressional subcommittee, and there, too, much will have been added to the literature on credit policy and on the central role which purchases and sales of government securities by the Federal Reserve banks (under direction of the Federal Open Market Committee) occupy in giving that policy a promising measure of effectiveness.

In view of all this, I shall not attempt to boil again what will soon be an old pot. While further analysis of the influences and the limitations of credit policy as a contracyclical device is certainly still needed, and while the process of reshaping and reappraising will no doubt continue as long as these meetings are held, the greater relative need now is to look at the other side of things—at the problems for debt management that arise from pursuance of a flexible program of credit control. Con-

* *American Economic Review,* May 1952, Vol. XLII, No. 2. Reprinted by courtesy of the American Economic Association and the author. This paper was prepared in December, 1951.

† Federal Reserve Bank of New York.

siderations of debt management held credit control in shackles for so long that there is now a dangerous tendency to forget that there were, beneath the array of shibboleths that so many critics have been exposing over the last several years, some good and fundamental economic reasons for the original imposition of constraints upon credit policy at the outset of World War II and for some part of the hesitancy in removing those constraints following the war. The controversy brought on by the overlong delay in removing the arbitrary features of those constraints has fostered an implication that, once the political questions of jurisdiction were resolved, the economic implementation of co-ordination between debt management and credit policy could be a straightforward, simple matter. That is not the case.

Co-ordination, or integration, will pose problems during any phase of credit control, from ease, through neutrality, to restraint. But the tough, knotty problems arise during a period of restraint on the general availability of credit, when interest rates in the market are rising. This paper will be focused almost exclusively on those most troublesome problems. It will not, however, discuss the conditions of a state of all-out war, although much of what follows should have a bearing upon the design of a war finance program that aimed to minimize both wartime inflationary pressures and a postwar inflationary aftermath.

After a brief summary of the principal obstacles to smooth integration, this paper will take up several possible alternative approaches toward overcoming them. The outcome should be at least to suggest that no simple, nor single, solution can be found. A continuing succession of compromises between the objectives of debt management and credit policy will probably be unavoidable, but wider discussion of the possible bases for compromise should help to assure the greatest practicable fulfillment of both sets of objectives. In passing over the administrative side of Treasury-Federal Reserve relations and in ignoring the need for co-ordination among these two agencies and the activities of all other arms of government, I do not mean to imply that the problems remaining in those areas are unimportant. It merely seems to me that the substantive problems of integrating debt management and open market operations are difficult enough to deserve separate study.

I. THE NATURE OF THE UNDERLYING DILEMMAS

There has been increasing recognition, in recent years, of the fact that debt management should be exercised with a view to over-all economic conditions—that it is not enough merely to pursue a program that assures temporary lodgment of the outstanding public debt. However, the opposite side of this shield must be continued recognition of the fact that the Treasury does have to lodge all of the debt somewhere. Consequently, despite its awareness of a need for credit restraint, the Treasury cannot itself take steps in furtherance of that restraint which entail any appreciable risk of the failure (substantial undersubscription) of a new money offering or of an unusually large attrition (i.e., cash redemption) on a refunding or an exchange offering. The limits of elasticity that the Treasury might safely allow are probably subject to some range of variation, as will be suggested at a later point in this paper, but the Treasury certainly will always want to feel assured that it can place in the market the greater part of any offering designed in reasonable conformity with the prevailing pattern of market prices. There are two kinds of obstacles to successful Treasury financing which may become serious in their proportions during a period of credit restraint: one arises from the influence of investor expectations in a competitive market and the other arises from the magnitude of the market operations which the Treasury must attempt to undertake.

The Influence of Expectations

Declining securities prices (rising rates of interest) during a period of credit restraint may cause investors to defer the commitment of their funds while awaiting the movement of market yields to still higher levels. Investor motivations of this type led to the near failure of two important Treasury offerings in October, 1942. It was this narrow escape which compelled a final crystallization of the plans that had been developing for some time to rely on price support through the subsequent war years while Treasury new money borrowing continued on an enormous scale. The support techniques developed were probably unduly rigid, and the added complications created by fixed support so paralyzed credit control that eventual abandonment was essential. Nonetheless, in greater or lesser degree, the reluctance of investors to commit their funds to any given security issue during a period of rising interest rates will always present a problem to a debt management program. It is difficult to convey the pervasiveness and seriousness of this dilemma in brief, simple language; the fact that it literally haunts those who are associated with the government security market, however, is unquestionable. At the very least, this dilemma affects significantly the types and maturities of securities which the Treasury can expect to market successfully.

The Problem of Size

A government debt which amounts to one half of the total fixed-interest indebtedness outstanding in the economy can be kept continuously lodged only through the use of a wide range of security issues, reaching all principal classes of investors and extending into all segments of the maturity structure of the total debt. Three corollaries may be drawn from this fact. First, the active trading interest in any single government security at a given point of time is often relatively "thin"; and the supplementary absorptive capacity of the government security dealers, who "make a market" for all types of government securities through standing offers to buy or sell in reasonable amounts for their own account at quoted prices, must be measured in the aggregate in millions rather than billions. Second, in comparison with the size of the usual current active interest in any single sector of the market, the amount of each Treasury offering must be relatively large. That is, at whatever maturity the Treasury chooses to place a new offering, the dollar amount of that offering will be very large in comparison to the usual flow of funds available at a given time within the selected maturity sector. Third, any refunding operation must take out of the market a very short-term security which the market has shown itself willing to hold and replace it with a new security that must be at least several months (if not years) longer in term.

The question then is whether, despite the existence of a well-organized market, itself sensitive to changes in the prices at which securities are available, the Treasury can expect to sell successfully its refunding or new money issues without strong outside help. This help would presumably have to correspond, in effect, to a vast underwriting service capable of carrying the offering while it was being wedged gradually into investor portfolios over a period of some duration after the date of issuance.

The market mechanism does, to be sure, provide a possible way out. By facilitating a series of trades among holders of all different types of outstanding government securities, as well as facilitating the sale of such securities to investors with currently investible funds, the over-the-counter market brings together all potentially available funds into a single pool. And that pool will then include all investors who consider the terms of the Treasury offering attractive, whether those investors were currently in possession of investible funds or whether they had to obtain such funds by selling other securities out of their portfolios to investors who preferred these other securities to the new offering announced by the Treasury.

Despite the usual smooth and effective functioning of the market mechanism in bringing about the greatest possible convergence of funds at the point in the market to which the new Treasury security is being directed, the Treasury cannot be fully certain that the magnitude of these funds, after they have been assembled, will be sufficient to meet the Treasury's needs. This is a kind of gamble that a borrower as large as the Treasury of the United States must face under any conditions, whatever the current state of credit policy. But so long as the Treasury, in designing its offering, takes into account not only the current level of market yields but also the weight which the new security will add to the particular sector of the market in which it is being placed, skillful debt management will normally assure a satisfactory subscription—unless interest rates should be rising at the time of issuance under the pressure of a general tightness in credit availability. Thus it is the combined influence of the large volume of any single Treasury offering in relation to the current flow of funds in the market at a given time, taken together with the influence of expectations mentioned above, which makes the problems of debt management so much more difficult when credit policy is aimed at restraint.

The Possibilities for Reconciling Successful Debt Management with Effective Credit Restraint

The obstacles to smooth integration between debt management and credit policy during a period of restraint arise out of the nature of a free market and the necessary magnitude of the Treasury's borrowing operations. So long as the market remains free and the public debt large, it is doubtful that there can be a simple resolution of the dilemmas just described. There are, however, four possible approaches to a workable compromise between the necessities of debt management and the objectives of credit restraint. Each of these four approaches represents a different degree of "give and take" as between the accepted aims of debt management and credit policy. The first of these, while recognizing that rigid, continuous support of the government security market could lead only to nullification of any attempted credit restraint, would accomplish integration through the use of "stabilizing purchases" of government securities from time to time. In effect, government security prices would be pegged at least part of the time, but the pegs themselves would be adjusted at intervals to major changes in credit conditions. Credit policy would be effected within the limits permitted by those pegs. The second approach would aim at insulating a large proportion of the government debt from the action of the market, in the hope that credit policy might then be exerted freely upon the private sector of the credit structure. The third would attempt to allocate "spheres of influence," such as depending upon the Treasury to protect the prices of its securities through trading on its own account while the Federal Reserve pursued an independent course of action aimed at influencing member bank reserves and general credit availability. The fourth would call for a wide range of flexibility in debt management operations, with the maturities and rates of interest on new (or refunding) offerings continuously adapted to changing credit conditions.

All four of these approaches have been reflected in some form at various times in the actual implementation of policy during the postwar period. No doubt, any doctrine of debt and credit policy which eventually emerges out of the experience following the accord of March, 1951, will find some place for one or more of the aspects of each of them. Whatever that outcome may be, however, a review of each will at least provide a convenient method of focusing attention upon some of the challenging issues that must be faced in attempting to achieve co-ordination between government debt operations and the national credit policy.

II. THE "PEGGED MARKETS" APPROACH TO INTEGRATION

If it were possible to ignore the effect of debt management upon general credit and economic conditions and if control over the volume of credit and the creation of money were not important, direct support of government security prices by the central bank could clearly provide an answer to the dilemmas described above. The actual marketing of the debt would always be accomplished with certainty. But that is a familiar story. The question here is whether some modification of this approach might not also be capable of providing the Treasury with the certainty it requires, while allowing credit policy to express itself. There are three different degrees of such a compromise approach which should be distinguished: market support, market stabilization, and market orderliness. The use of these terms has certainly not become standardized; any one of the three terms is often used to cover the meaning intended here for the others. Before discussing each of them separately, the usage intended for each in the present paper will have to be indicated.

Market Support, Stabilization and Orderliness

For the purposes of this paper, market support means the pegging of floor prices for government securities of all maturities (except perhaps the very shortest). The term will be further limited here to mean that the actual levels of these floor prices may be changed at infrequent intervals in response to major adjustments in the credit outlook. The transition from one pegged yield curve to another would be accomplished swiftly, so that no damaging expectations concerning Treasury offerings could be expected to backfire against the Treasury. The market would be assured that any given set of pegs, once established, would be kept in place for a considerable period of time.

By contrast, market stabilization would imply only that the central bank should hold prices relatively constant in the sector of the market to which a current Treasury offering was being directed. Interest rates would generally be free to move for some period of time between major Treasury financing operations. There might be both a broad and a narrow interpretation of stabilization. The broad would imply that purchases in the relevant sector of the market would continue from the original date of a Treasury announcement until the sale or exchange had been consummated and, if necessary, for some time thereafter in order to allow a suitable time for "market digestion" of the offering. No precise dates could be set upon this broad interpretation since the duration of the stabilizing purchases would depend upon the rate at which any given offering moved out into relatively firm hands. The narrower or stricter interpretation of stabilization would mean the setting of relatively firm bid prices from the date of the Treasury's initial announcement until the subscription books were closed, with an occasional possibility of "when issued" trading by the central bank until the date of actual issuance of the security.

Central bank purchases for the purpose of maintaining orderly market conditions would have only an indirect bearing upon the reception of any specific Treasury new offering by the market. Instead, orderliness would be preserved throughout the market for government securities by preventing unduly large day-to-day price reactions as a consequence of small purchase or sale offers at a time when no corresponding sales or purchases were forthcoming. System purchases or sales might be limited to a single issue, with the market itself carrying through the influence upon others, or the System's orderly market transactions might be made directly in several issues. The rationale of such orderly market operations would arise from the fact that wide price swings on the basis of very thin activity might possibly set off cumulative reactions that would carry market prices and market activity far beyond the magnitude that could be expected to be maintained over time on the basis of underlying supply and demand conditions. Shielding investors in government securities against the risk of capricious price movements would encourage a wider measure of continuous participation in the market. That result would be helpful to credit policy by widening the active trading base, but would not prevent the System from backing away under heavy selling pressure. It would be also of benefit to the Treasury by helping to broaden ownership of the outstanding debt; but it would not attempt to limit price movements reflecting real changes in the supply of or demand for credit.

These attempts at definition, it should be stressed, have not been blessed by official sanction in any quarter. They represent only my own handiwork in constructing crutches upon which the argument of the present paper can lean.

Support with Adjustable Pegs

The proposal to use adjustable supports, which can be changed in response to major credit developments, represents a serious misreading of the basis upon which an effective credit policy rests. Actually, the case for credit policy which has been evolving from the many-sided discussions of the past several years does not attach particular significance to any given level of interest rates. Credit restraint can be maintained so long as interest rates are free to move. It is the uncertainty of future rate movement which makes it possible for credit restraint—at least in some circumstances—to become effective, while resulting only in fractional changes in interest rates; and it can even be effective at times without causing any noticeable change in actual market yields. This analysis of the means through which credit becomes tightened has been summarized in the replies recently submitted by the Federal Reserve Bank Presidents to the Patman Subcommittee, which will be published shortly, and need not be developed at length here.

Of course, a sudden downward adjustment in support prices, or pegs, would have the immediate, temporary effect of tightening credit, as holders of outstanding government securities found themselves faced with capital losses, the magnitude of which would depend upon the maturity of the obligations they held. But so long as the new curve remained pegged, with yields ascending gradually from the shorter-term to the longer-term obligations, the passage of time would begin to bring about a rise in the market price of fixed-interest obligations that would soon offset, for the nearer term securities, the absolute amount of the capital loss implied by the rate increase. The capital loss deterrent would thus become weaker with each passing month. Within a short time, a substantial volume of debt would be available for sale without appreciable penalty at the supported prices being maintained by the fixed purchase bids of the Federal Reserve System. In an important measure, the initiative for the creation of fresh reserves would then shift to market investors, as an inevitable consequence of System support of a fixed yield curve. Recognition of that fact might cause a support effort to rely on maintenance of a horizontal yield curve. In that event, the phenomenon just described would not occur. The effect of supporting a horizontal yield schedule, however, would be to place government securities of all maturities on a common yield basis and to hold them there regardless of the relative short- and long-term preferences of the market. In effect, all government debt would become short-term debt. It can scarcely be argued that a government debt equal to one-half the debt of the total economy could all be kept lodged in short-term form. The debt monetization that would accompany such an approach to pegging would be frightening. That type of pegging could only be contemplated during a period of total war, with compulsory direction of investments and ironclad physical controls over production and spending.

On the other hand, so long as a sloping yield curve were to be frozen, the phenomenon of "playing the pattern of rates" that characterizes any firmly supported market would re-emerge. And the consequences of this kind of abuse, which eventually forced the abandonment of rigid support the last time, would begin exerting the same kind of pressure again.

Market Stabilization for Specific Offerings

The broad interpretation of stabilization purchases would, in effect, assure investors that they could not possibly better their return until some appreciable period after the given offering had been placed, and even that relatively distant prospect of possibly greater yield would be uncertain. Moreover, the free availability of Federal Reserve credit during the period of the Treasury's offering would provide sufficient funds for the kind of underwriting operation that was described above. Since most of the large investors whose combined actions dominate the course of the market have contractual (or actuarial) income requirements to meet, their long-term investible funds cannot remain out of the market for any extended period (nor in highly liquid short obligations bearing relatively low yields). A relatively long period of market stabilization might be expected, therefore, to assure the maximum attainable commitment of investible funds to any given offering, either through the direct attraction of those funds or through the indirect mobilization of those funds by means of a chain of switches among holders of other securities within the market. But the hazards for credit control under this approach would be relatively great.

During a period of general restraint when inflationary forces presumably would be strong, alternative demands for credit would also be strong, and holders of any securities in the range affected by the Treasury's offering could have assurance of new funds, obtainable on their own initiative, for use in expanding the flow of credit to the private sector of the economy throughout the relatively long period of the System's stabilizing operations. The narrower interpretation of stabilization—a relatively brief period of stabilizing bids, with bids limited to only one or at most very few issues and with the duration of the bids subject to some uncertainty—would present relatively little threat to the continuation of credit restraint. Funds released to the market might be reabsorbed at the time through sales of other securities more remote from the area in which the new offering was to be placed, or in any event could be reabsorbed fairly readily within a few weeks after the Treasury's books were closed. The question here would be whether the protection offered to the Treasury's marketing operation would be adequate. Investors could feel assured that nothing could happen in the market to disrupt their calculations during the actual offering period, and that would exert some influence upon them, but the fear of an early resumption of further tightening (with the implication of rising yields) might persuade them to "sit this one out."

From the standpoint of credit policy, in the sense in which that policy has been developed and refined in the recent literature and through the recent actions of the Federal Reserve System, only the narrower approach to stabilization would seem acceptable. It is partly for that reason that attention has also been given to such proposals as those for insulation of the government debt from the market, or the use of the Treasury's own funds to support its obligations in the market, or the development of more diversified and variable techniques for management of the Treasury's marketable debt. Each of these approaches will be considered shortly.

The Maintenance of Orderly Markets

By preventing capricious movements of market prices, in a market so extensive that occasional air pockets are unavoidable, orderly market purchases or sales can certainly make a useful contribution toward maximizing investor participation in the government security market. As already noted, that contribution will be of indirect benefit both to the System's sustained use of open market operations as the principal instrument of credit policy, and to the Treasury's ability to keep all of its debt placed within the market. There can be little question that orderly market operations of the type described in this paper should be continued. There is little ground for hope, however, that they can contribute materially toward a resolution of the fundamental dilemmas to which this paper is addressed.

III. INSULATING THE GOVERNMENT DEBT FROM THE MARKET

Proposals for insulating the government debt from the market, in order to allow credit policy a wide range of freedom in influencing the availability of credit to the private sector of the economy, have often been presented as panaceas for the kind of difficulty just described. Insulation might be attempted in two ways: by freezing bank holdings of short-term government securities into a required secondary reserve of some type or by putting most of the debt (except that of shortest term) in nonmarketable form. A required secondary reserve of government securities would probably only succeed, however, in locking up the intramarginal holdings of the banks, leaving effective credit policy dependent upon the System's use of open market operations at the active margins where bank or nonbank holders of short- or long-term government securities attempt to switch out in favor of other uses for their funds. Perhaps Professor Seltzer intends to provide an answer to reservations of that sort. But I have not yet seen such an answer, and consequently this paper will pass quickly to insulation of the second type: placing a major portion of the government debt in nonmarketable form.

The price of a nonmarketable (but redeemable) government security would not be subject to fluctuation. Consequently the Treasury's marketing difficulties, which arise from the risks of changing market prices, would apparently be by-passed completely. The flaw in the elegance of this analysis is that even nonmarketable debt must be sold to investors who have the alternative of placing their funds in the freely fluctuating private market. It would thus appear that nonmarketable debt could only be initially sold, and the Treasury thereby provided with the advantages of insulation, if the nonmarketable debt were to bear a yield near the top of the range of practicable fluctuation in other investment outlets (after allowance for a differential adjustment for credit risk).

Limitations on the Use of Nonmarketable Debt

The price of insulation would thus seem to be extremely high. The Treasury would find itself paying an interest yield, not only during an inflationary period, but at other times as well, in excess of the highest yield at which market obligations might be placed. Fiscal prudence would scarcely permit that kind of approach. But the proponents of nonmarketable debt have suggested an answer to that difficulty. Since the transition to a debt consisting largely of nonmarket obligations must inevitably be gradual, much of the nonmarketable debt could be placed in periods when interest rates were at moderate or low levels. While substantial amounts of Treasury borrowing in this long-term form might not be attempted in the trough of depression, in order to avoid any semblance of competition with the private credit market then in need of great encouragement, there would be many other periods when nonmarket debt might successfully be sold at interest yields somewhat above the current market, while not excessive in an absolute sense. Then, the proponents would argue, once investors had become lodged in nonmarketable securities they could not, or would not, get out to return again into the free sector of the credit market.

There are several practical questions concerning this prescription. For one, most of the large-scale investors are alert enough to the need for retaining flexibility of action, in order to take advantage of improving market yields, to avoid initial purchase of an obligation clearly designed to be a trap. Thus a nonmarketable obligation which did not contain some kind of redemption feature would probably be passed over by most investors, and the Treasury would be left holding an empty bag. If, however, a redemption feature is included, initial subscriptions might be somewhat greater, but serious risks would then be created both for debt management and credit policy.

Here, again, the freshness of recent experience provides a ready substitute for detailed explanation. The Series F and G bonds, for example, built around a redemption schedule which provides heavy penalty against early encashment and high yield for holding over the later years, were initially sold in very large amounts during the war. Part of their attractiveness came from the fact that their average interest yield was above that obtainable on most other savings outlets for the private individual. Yet as interest rates have risen under the interacting pressures of credit restraint and inflationary credit demand, sales of these savings bonds have declined; redemptions have increased.

All forms of outstanding savings bonds and notes have been a net drain upon the Treasury over the past year. In fact, the redemption schedules of the savings bonds now outstanding actually constitute schedules of "peril points." Whenever prevailing yields in the market rise appreciably, as they must if the accelerating impetus of credit expansion is to be checked during an inflationary period, the nonmarketable debt begins to fall in upon the Treasury for redemption. It has been insulated from the market only for the period when insulation was not particularly needed, either from the standpoint of Treasury cash operations or from the standpoint of credit policy. Once the time has arrived for insulation to furnish its protection, the nonmarketable debt becomes a drain upon the Treasury's cash, and the resulting risk that the Treasury may have to borrow in a form that will intensify inflationary pressures becomes greater.

Nonmarketable Securities for Small Savers

This is not to suggest that there is no place for the savings bond in a well-diversified Treasury financing program. Such an instrument can serve two important purposes. First, it provides the small saver or investor with a certain alternative to the risks of market price fluctuation. Since many small savers cannot undertake the close study required for successful investment in a fluctuating market, they may well be satisfied with a security that pays them a relatively high yield when market rates are low, even though it does not pay them a higher yield when market rates are rising under inflationary pressure. As a way of protecting the small saver against the kind of disheartening decline in government security prices that bewildered so many individual investors after World War I, the savings bond can make an important contribution. As a second consideration, by providing a safe haven for the small saver's funds, this instrument gives the Treasury access to an important source of real savings, widening the direct participation in holding of the Treasury debt. With a debt of the present magnitude, it is important that every possible pool of investible funds be reached by the Treasury through an instrument best suited to the investors who compose each of these pools.

It is doubtful whether more than token holdings of savings bonds can find a place in the diversified portfolios of the market-wise and market-sensitive institutional investors, whose combined resources represent the greater share of the nation's supply of savings and investible funds. To the specialized staffs of portfolio managers in these institutions, market price fluctuations are the "stock in trade."

The Threat to Flexible Credit Policy

So far as credit policy is concerned there is another great risk introduced by the existence of a large outstanding volume of redeemable savings bonds. The threat of the peril points imbedded in the redemption schedules is not only a potential drain of Treasury cash but also a threat that the utilization of the cash obtained through net redemptions will further aggravate the difficulties of controlling the over-all supply of investment funds through credit restraint. At a time when restraining measures might lead to a further rise in interest yields (although a precise effect upon yields is never the specific objective of credit restraint), the central bank may be reluctant to proceed. For if interest rates in the market should rise above the peril points for any sizable volume of the nonmarketable bonds outstanding, the release of funds through Treasury redemption of large amounts at the initiative of the holders might seem a greater evil than that of postponing further direct measures of credit restraint. Paradoxically, then, the nonmarketable debt might be kept insulated only because credit policy has ceased to meet its full responsibility. Instead of freeing credit policy, the nonmarketable debt would have placed a new kind of strait jacket upon it, as confining in its ultimate effect as a program of outright central bank support for the prices of marketable government securities.

In passing, note should be taken of the latest innovation in the design of nonmarketable debt instruments. That is a nonmarketable bond which, although not redeemable, is convertible into a marketable note of short or intermediate term. That kind of instrument is intended, in effect, to provide a flexible redemption schedule. In times of credit tightness, market yields on the convertible note would be well above the coupon rate. Anyone wishing to get out of the nonmarketable bond, in response to rising yields in the market outside, would find, on converting his nonmarketable bond into the marketable note, that he could sell the note in the market only at a substantial penalty. The penalty would continue to increase as credit tightened further. It may be that an instrument of this type offers a possibility for successful insulation of some part of the government debt from the current market, although the related impact on the market for notes would raise serious new problems. These possibilities certainly deserve further study, but the present writer is unable to comment further upon them in the space of this paper.

On balance, it would appear that an attempt to insulate a substantial part of the debt from the market would probably fail, so long as investors are left with freedom of choice. But even if a way could be found, credit policy would then be deprived of one of its most important new opportunities. For decades, the effectiveness of central bank control over credit availability has been impaired because the channels through which that control reached the long-term market were devious and indefinite. Instead of retreating from the opportunities now provided for making credit policy effective through open market operations in the long-term sector, the rewarding course should be to develop methods for assuring successful placement of an even greater volume of long-term marketable debt.

IV. DESIGNATING SEPARATE SPHERES OF INFLUENCE

Up to this point, Treasury operations have been considered solely from the viewpoint of the issuance and management of the public debt. The Treasury is also, in its capacity as agent or adviser for the various government trust funds and investment accounts, an important investor in its own obligations. The Treasury could potentially, through the funds and accounts which it administers, become a much larger investor in its own outstanding marketable securities than the Federal Open Market Account. Moreover, in addition to the investment potential of the various funds and accounts, the Treasury could be given wider power to purchase its own securities in the market out of budgetary receipts.

In recognition of the vast amount of unused Treasury possibilities for direct trading in the market, the suggestion has been made from time to time that the Treasury should accept full responsibility for maintaining the kind of market conditions that it considers satisfactory from the viewpoint of its own requirements. With the Treasury carrying this responsibility, the suggestion would then be that the Federal Open Market Account should operate solely with regard to prevailing credit conditions and the need for limiting or increasing bank reserves. The central bank would thus, presumably, be freed of the dual responsibility which has created so many difficulties in the past. There is an appealing ring of simple, straightforward logic in this suggestion. But, like most solutions intended to cut through to the roots of a problem in a single blow, the easy simplicity of this one is deceptive. Nonetheless, while practical obstacles and considerations of principle would prevent successful segregation, a brief review of these difficulties does suggest that greater use could be made of the funds and accounts along lines already established.

Can the Treasury Obtain Funds for Stabilizing Purchases When the Funds Are Needed?

The fact that the Treasury administers a large volume of investible funds does not in itself assure the Treasury that it can have an adequate supply of free funds available at any time for the uncertain volume of purchases that would have to be made in assuring stable markets for every offering. The net cash proceeds of the funds and accounts now flow into the Treasury's current cash budget; if any of these proceeds are to be held in idle balances for use in market stabilizing operations or eventually lodged in further net acquisitions of marketable debt through such operations, the Treasury must find a corresponding amount of additional funds for its current budgetary requirements. In over-all effect, the Treasury will have to obtain greater revenues through taxation or add to its own direct borrowings in the market in order to make funds available for the purpose of stabilizing market prices. The paradox will be that the Treasury can most readily set aside funds for market stabilizing purposes when it currently enjoys a cash surplus; yet in such periods, the use of a Treasury surplus to build up idle balances at the Federal Reserve banks or to retire maturing debt held by the Federal Reserve banks could itself serve as a useful limitation upon bank reserves.

Thus, at a time when the Treasury would be best able to stabilize the market for its own outstanding securities, a more direct use of the Treasury's cash receipts in an anti-inflationary manner would actually reduce the need for decisive measures of credit restraint through the Federal Open Market Account. Conversely, if the Treasury were not accumulating a current cash surplus during an inflationary period, there would be an even greater need for vigorous credit restraint through the System's open market operations. In order to carry out an independent program of market stabilization at such a time, the Treasury would have to obtain the necessary additional funds by selling other marketable securities out of the existing portfolios of the accounts or by redeeming special issues held by the accounts and selling new issues of other types of securities that were in demand in the market. That is, at the very time when the System Open Market Account was refusing to buy, or perhaps selling, in the interest of credit restraint, the Treasury would also have to place additional securities in some sectors of the government security market in order to obtain the funds needed for protecting the particular sector of the market that was most under pressure. The conflict between credit restraint and the stabilizing of markets for purposes of Treasury borrowing might thus be further aggravated.

The Risks of Conflicting Operations

In a period of inflationary expansion, the Federal Reserve could be expected to back away from any sale offers arising in the market, whether or not it was making an effort to sell securities out of its own portfolio. The Treasury, meanwhile, might find it necessary to make stabilizing purchases in the market. The resulting see-saw influence upon bank reserves and the prices of government securities would produce conditions of such uncertainty that the Treasury's market might well be spoiled, while the Federal Reserve System might find the same uncertainty mounting to such heights that it could not successfully make all of the offsetting sales that would be needed if the freshly created reserves were all to be reabsorbed. If there were to be any resolution of the conflict before this deplorable extreme had been reached, that resolution would depend upon agreement and understanding between the Treasury and the System. It would essentially be an agreement of the same nature that would have been required in reconciling Treasury borrowing requirements with the objectives of credit policy if the Treasury had not assumed responsibility for "protecting" its own market. Recognition of this fact does not, however, rule out the possibility for use of the cash available in the Treasury administered funds and accounts in a manner that may supplement or reinforce the day-to-day efforts of the Federal Open Market Account itself to operate on the basis of a reasonable compromise between these objectives.

Co-ordination Instead of Separation

In general, the Treasury's objective in the past in administering the funds and accounts has been to avoid or to minimize interference with the activities of the Federal Open Market Account when purchasing suitable securities with any funds earmarked for investment in the marketable sector. But there may well be room for a change of degree, or emphasis, in the customary investment procedures of the Treasury's funds and accounts. Instead of neutrality, interrupted by infrequent direct purchases aimed at influencing an unusual market situation, the approach might be that of continued readiness to provide funds (as available) for co-ordinate use along with the System's funds for any temporary phase of market stabilization. The trust funds and accounts might also expect to come into the market to relieve institutional investors of holdings temporarily acquired at a time of compelling Treasury need for funds, as the sustained carry of those holdings at relatively low yields begins to impair the ability of such institutions to satisfy their actuarial income requirements. The prerequisites for such action would be understanding and co-operation between the Treasury and the System; and there could be no reliance upon a simple formula for "sharing the work." Continuous compromises would have to be developed, case by case.

V. INCREASING THE FLEXIBILITY OF DEBT MANAGEMENT

The conflict between credit restraint and maintenance of market conditions favorable to Treasury financing does not arise in the market as an "all or nothing" phenomenon. It affects the type of financing and the proportion of new money or refunding offerings accepted readily by the market. A fairly substantial response can be expected to any Treasury offering reasonably adjusted to current conditions, and so long as some investors are willing, it should be possible to increase the degree of response through further development of debt management techniques. Investor reluctance in the face of restraint will probably be greatest while memories of pegged markets are still fresh. Eventually, a free market should in some measure embody in its current prices the discounted effects of expected future variations in interest yields.

While the heavy responsibilities of debt management preclude frequent or extensive experimentation and justify a certain gingerliness in espousing any innovation that resembles a mere "gadget," the Treasury should be able to aim its long-range program at reducing the area of conflict between debt management and credit restraint, and may also be able to consider changes in the design of its offerings or in its offering techniques for meeting specific situations from time to time.

Reducing the Area of Conflict

For the longer run, one great potentiality for reducing the conflict lies in the development of a governmental fiscal policy focused on the maintenance of economic stability. If fiscal policy could follow the course laid out for it in the economic literature, Congressional expenditure and revenue measures would, in their combined effect, provide the Treasury with a substantial cash surplus whenever inflationary pressure became strong. In that happy state, the Treasury would then have no occasion to borrow new money in a tightening credit market; occasionally large cash redemptions on refunding offers could be met without impinging on the Treasury's cash needs for current expenditures; and the residual funds remaining in the Treasury's balances, after expenditures and attrition had been met, could be devoted selectively to retiring debt held by the Federal Reserve banks in order to maintain pressure on bank reserves. In an important degree, it is the apparent inability of the real world to approximate that ideal which creates the need to develop other approaches for integrating debt management and credit restraint.

The Treasury could also help to minimize collisions between debt management and credit restraint over the long run ahead by pursuing a vigorous program for funding the debt and by carefully spacing the maturities of that portion of the debt which remains in short-term form. At present, the proportion of the outstanding marketable debt which passes through the market for refunding each year is approaching one half. The passage of time forces upon the Treasury a continuous shortening of the outstanding debt. Any success over the long run ahead in reducing the proportion of short-term debt would not only lessen the burden of refunding during an inflationary period by virtue of the smaller amounts coming due but would also permit the Treasury in a period of market disturbance to place its then current offerings in the short-term market without risk of overloading. That would also coincide with investor preferences for temporary liquidity in such periods. If, in addition, the portion of the debt regularly allotted to the short-term sector could be carefully spaced in maturity, there would be more room for flexibility in credit policy during the intervals while the Treasury was out of the market. Recent partial efforts to cluster one-year debt around quarterly maturity dates suggest a promising line of development.

During periods of credit tightness, debt management would presumably have to give particular emphasis to the weight which a given new offering will place upon the sector of the market in which it is to be lodged. This is not a simple matter in practice because unduly rich coupons would, in the language of the market, "throw the existing debt out of bed." One way to help limit the unloading of outstanding securities by investors switching into an attractive new offering might be to place such offerings, where possible, at wide vacant spaces in the maturity distribution of the outstanding debt.

As the procedures of debt management become adapted to the conditions of a flexible credit market, it is also possible that some of the more or less arbitrary criteria of successful financing can be modified. Perhaps present views concerning the admissible attrition on a refunding offering are unduly narrow as a result of the long acquaintance with supported markets. The fundamental test would seem to be whether or not the Treasury is able to obtain the funds needed to meet its contractual obligations. So long as the Treasury can meet an unexpectedly poor response to a given issue by re-entering the market with another, perhaps placed in a different sector, and so long as temporary advances from the central bank are available in the extremity of a momentary cash shortage, the Treasury should be able to meet this underlying test with a somewhat broader definition of satisfactory response to given offerings than has been judged necessary in recent years.

Variation in the Design of Treasury Offerings

The range for flexibility in the design of Treasury offerings extends over the three essential characteristics of any given security: its marketability, its maturity, and its coupon (or interest) yield.

The principal investor groups are geared to sensitive adjustment among the yield opportunities afforded by marketable securities. For this reason and because credit policy may gain in effectiveness by reaching such investors directly through open market operations in long-term government securities, the bulk of the Treasury debt should probably always be placed in marketable securities. For a comparable reason, which deserves further elaboration than space permits here, it is doubtful whether issues of longer-term bonds in the future should be ineligible for bank purchase, except possibly during a war when deficits may have to be financed to a considerable degree by bank credit and special arrangements may be needed. At any other time, the processes of refunding or exchange within the market reduce the arbitrary segregation of bank restricted issues to a mere fiction. Alert bank examination will, in any event, prevent bank acquisition of such securities in excess of the prudent limits dictated by the nature of each bank's liabilities. And the issuance of Treasury securities can be better handled if all classes of market investors are permitted to enter initial subscriptions, even though many may merely serve as temporary underwriters pending ultimate resale to other investors over time. The risks which must be most closely guarded are those which arise in permitting banks to make payment by credit to a Treasury account on their own books.

So far as the maturity of Treasury obligations is concerned, the increasing importance of institutional investors and their own development of very long-term lending techniques for serving the private sector of the economy suggest that the Treasury might successfully use bonds of longer term. The longest issues in the Treasury list now run sixteen years to call, or twenty-one to maturity. The Treasury might open up an important source of funds, even during a period of restlessness in market rates, by reaching out beyond to thirty, forty, or perhaps even fifty years. Following some experience with this approach, it might be able eventually to consider the use of "consols" and thereby possibly place some portion of its indebtedness in a form that would never require refunding. With a debt of the present magnitude, that further type of diversification might well be justified. Another technique, suitable for a period of credit restraint, would be to widen the gap between call date and maturity date on a long-term issue, thus providing the Treasury with a hedge against a marked decline in long-term rates at some distance in the future while giving investors the assurance of a relatively high yield for the period to call date. Other variations of this approach have been suggested; some of them would make the call feature conditional upon market prices reaching a specified premium. While suggestive, these more particularized devices run the risk of being too narrowly designed to meet the problems visible today without possessing the range of general adaptability that may be needed over an uncertain future.

Setting a coupon which will be attractive to the market without unduly disturbing the holdings of outstanding securities is a challenging assignment. The successful development of the auction method in connection with Treasury bills suggests that an extension of this technique to obligations of somewhat longer term might provide the Treasury with a means of letting the market decide the precisely suitable yield, in relation to alternative uses for funds. Another approach to that same end, which would be applicable in the case of longer-term issues, might be for the Treasury to indicate the general nature of a forthcoming offering well in advance and await market reaction to that announcement before setting its specific terms.

The Treasury's Techniques in Offering Its Securities

Many of the Treasury's offering methods are imposed upon it by the present organization and composition of the government security market. While there is nothing sacrosanct about the nature of that market and while it does have shortcomings, the relevant question is whether any other alternative set of market arrangements would correct those shortcomings without creating other more serious defects. Such an examination, if it is ever to be made, must proceed under high auspices and be conducted with the aid of skilled technicians. The suggestions made here presume continuance of the existing form of market organization.

Given that type of market, the possibility must always be kept open for efforts by the central bank to provide some measure of price stabilization. So long as the market has assurance that a backstop may be put in place from time to time, no unusual repercussions would follow the actual appearance of occasional stabilizing purchases. The market is, however, so sensitive and the competition among dealers is so keen, that any attempt to define specifically the conditions on which stabilizing purchases might be made would unavoidably lead the active interests in the market occasionally to work against the System Account, and thus against the joint aims of debt management and credit policy.

In addition to stabilization purchases of an undefinable magnitude, for the purpose of maintaining market conditions suitable for the placement of Treasury offerings, several innovations might be considered in the Treasury's detailed offering techniques. One question concerns the time period allowed between the date of original Treasury announcement of actual terms and the date for opening the Treasury's subscription books, as well as the interval between the date set for the closing of the Treasury's books and the date on which the subscription must actually be taken up. In general, the shorter these intervals the less will be the conflict between any purchases specifically aimed at market stabilization and the System's attempts at credit restraint. As already suggested, however, in the case of longer-term offerings, the Treasury might under some circumstances wish to make a broad indication of its plans well in advance of setting the specific terms in order to permit the market to provide some guidance to the selection of adequate terms and to permit investors to arrange their investment plans.

The Treasury may also have to find a way to compete directly against the heavy commitment backlogs of the large institutional investors. Of course, the extensive use of private commitment arrangements may be in part an outgrowth of "pegged market thinking," and as greater flexibility appears, investors may be less anxious to commit in advance a large proportion of the funds they expect to receive. Should commitments continue on a substantial scale, however, they would indicate an investor willingness to tie up long-term funds at attractive terms despite the intervening fluctuations of the market. The Treasury might then find a way to share in those forward commitments. One possibility would be to offer a security for which payment could only be made in installments spread over several months or calendar quarters. The Treasury might also be able to vary its offering arrangements, and perhaps minimize the risks of miscalculating investor response in some situations, by using a package offering of several issues, thereby spreading the impact of a given operation over several sectors of the market.

None of the possible innovations in design or in offering techniques can receive here the attention they deserve; nor is this paper intended as an unqualified endorsement of them. Perhaps enough has been said, however, to justify the suggestion that further wide-ranging study of such possibilities should eventually be able to provide debt management with a measure of flexibility that is at least consistent with a genuinely flexible credit policy, and may also at times actually reinforce the influences exerted on general credit availability by the System's open market operations.

VI. CONCLUSION

The market sensitivity arising from the large size and wide distribution of the public debt and from the increased channeling of investment funds through the portfolios of institutional investors has created a fresh opportunity for exerting effective credit restraint through the open market operations of the Federal Reserve System. The developments which have provided credit control with this opportunity have, at the same time, intensified the problems confronting debt management in assuring lodgment of the debt during periods of credit restraint. Both the opportunities for credit policy and the problems for debt management are inevitable results of the fact that investment decisions remain free while placement of the large public debt is imperative. Any attempt to strike through the dilemmas addressed in this paper by resort to methods of compulsion in lodging the public debt would undercut the fundamentals of this country's financial structure. Perhaps such a question may at some time have to be faced; but the attempt here has been to suggest that a wide range of possibilities remain open for compromise between debt management and credit restraint within the framework of a market responsive to free investor decisions.

While rigid support of government security prices, even if the support levels could occasionally be changed, would eventually result in the nullification of attempts at credit restraint, there would appear to be good reason for the central bank to exert a limited stabilizing influence on market prices from time to time. So long as there is no adherence to a rigid formula for stabilization and so long as the market is aware that stabilization is provided on a case-to-case basis, the actual duration and volume of such purchases may not be a substantial deterrent to sustained credit restraint during an inflationary period. It is also possible that closer co-ordination between the Treasury and the System Account may result in placing a somewhat greater proportion of the burden of stabilization purchases on the Treasury administered funds and accounts, thereby also permitting any needed stabilization to be accomplished with funds currently obtained from the income stream or the market rather than funds newly created by the Federal Reserve. Insulation of a major part of the debt from the action of market forces would seem an impossibility, so long as investors' decisions remain free and the principal investors remain keenly sensitive to fluctuating yields. Nonetheless, by providing some savers with an attractive nonmarketable security, the Treasury can keep one of the more volatile groups of investors out of the marketable sector of the outstanding debt. In addition, the Treasury should be able to develop a wider range of flexibility in programing its financing, in order to meet the competition of the market and to help in realizing the important potentialities of a contracyclical control over credit availability. From among the alternatives discussed here, it should prove possible to find workable methods for keeping the debt continuously placed in the market, while debt management and credit policy alike aim to minimize any threat to economic stability arising from the credit structure of the economy.

V. FISCAL POLICY AND STABILITY

19

*Alternative Budget Policies for Full Employment**

By RICHARD A. MUSGRAVE†

During the thirties fiscal theorists were interested primarily in the effects of deficit spending, that is, changes in over-all income resulting from an *increase in public expenditures* above the level of tax yields. Recently, attention has been drawn to an alternative approach to deficit finance under which the deficit is brought about by a *reduction of tax yields* below the level of expenditures. Both techniques may be considered at the same time and be combined with other approaches not directly concerned with the size of the deficit. The level of private consumption and investment expenditures may also be affected by adjusting the *kind* of taxes and public expenditures included in the budget totals, and under certain conditions public expenditures may provide for a net addition to national income, even though there is no deficit and the level of private expenditures does not increase.

Adjusting the level of expenditures relative to tax yields is thus only one among several approaches. If fiscal policy is to provide for a given dollar addition to the national income, this may be accomplished through a number of alternative budgets, providing for varying tax, expenditure and deficit totals and for varying revenue and expenditure structures.[1]

---

* *American Economic Review,* June 1945. Reprinted by the courtesy of the American Economic Association and the author.

† University of Michigan; formerly with the Division of Research and Statistics, Board of Governors of the Federal Reserve System. The views he expresses are his own and not necessarily those of the Board. A. G. Hart, E. E. Hagen and J. Mosak have made helpful suggestions on an earlier draft of this note but share no responsibility for its shortcomings.

[1] See, for instance, Alvin Hansen, *Fiscal Policy and Business Cycles* (New York, Norton & Co., 1941), pp. 182–83, and Hansen and Perloff, *State and Local Finance* (New York, Norton & Co., 1944), pp. 244–46; A. P. Lerner, "Functional Finance," *Soc. Research,* Feb. 1943, Vol. X, No. 1; H. C. Wallich, "Income Generating Effects of a Balanced Budget," *Quart. Jour. Econ.,* Nov. 1944, Vol. LIX, No. 1; N. Kaldor, "Quantitative Aspects of the Full Employment Problem in Britain," Appendix C in William Beveridge, *Full Employment in a Free Society* (London, Allen & Unwin, 1944); and B. Ruml, *Na-*

I

The interrelationships between the major variables of budget policy may be presented in a simplified form, somewhat similar in nature to the statement of monetary variables in the equation of exchange. Suppose that with a given federal budget over-all income falls substantially short of the potential output at full employment. What adjustment in the budget can be made to raise income to the full employment level? Any adjustment in the budget will do which meets the condition

$$G = E_1 + k[\alpha(E_1 + E_2) - \beta T] + kI \qquad (1)$$

where

- G is the required increase in income
- E_1 is the *additional* public expenditure on currently produced goods and services
- E_2 is the *additional* public transfer expenditure
- T is the *change* in tax revenue (+ or −)
- α is the marginal propensity to consume (out of income after tax) of the recipients of additional government expenditures
- β is the marginal propensity to consume (out of income after tax) of the taxpayers meeting the changed tax bill
- I is the induced change in private investment expenditures (+ or −)
- k is the multiplier applicable to an extra dollar of private expenditures on consumption or investment, based upon the community's marginal propensity to consume out of income after tax and independent of a given tax rate

Expression (1) shows that, for the budget adjustment to be successful, the required increase in income must be matched by the proposed increase in public expenditures on currently produced goods and services plus the resulting net increase in private consumption and investment expenditures. These variables will be examined briefly.

The *required increase in income,* or G, is the gap between the income which is realized "in absence" of an active fiscal policy—defined, for purposes of this discussion, as a situation where the budget is balanced at a minimum level—and the income that can be reached at full employment. For the gap to be filled without a change in public expenditures or tax yields (allowing, however, for reduced tax rates), there would have to be an autonomous increase in private investment or consumption by an amount equal to G/k.

tional Fiscal Policy and the Two Super Budgets (Charlottesville, University of Virginia, 1941).

The *increase in public expenditures on currently produced goods and services* or E_1 is the first leverage factor. E_1 is here written as a separate term, distinct from E_2, because real expenditures on currently produced goods and services are in themselves a direct addition to national income. Transfer expenditures make no such direct addition; they enter into national income only when respent by private income recipients.[2]

An increase in public expenditures on currently produced goods and services will thus result in a *net* addition to over-all income unless offset by reduced private expenditures. Suppose the government spends $100,000 on a soil conservation project and increases taxes to cover the cost. The national income will then be increased by public expenditures of $100,000. Now suppose that those paying $100,000 of additional taxes reduce their consumption expenditures by $50,000 while those receiving $100,000 of additional income payments from the government increase theirs by $50,000. As a result, the level of private consumption expenditures is unchanged. Assuming private investment to be unchanged, the $100,000 worth of soil conservation is a net addition to national income.[3] For private consumption expenditures to remain unchanged, in this illustration, there must be no lag between the public outlay on the conservation project, the reduction in the taxpayer's consumption expenditures and the increase in consumption expenditures of the project workers; that is to say, there must be an increase in income velocity. If there is a lag in the public disbursement of the additional tax yield or in the respending of the additional income received by the project workers, the direct contribution of the real public expenditure may be offset in part or fully by reduced private expenditures, measured in the second term of expression (1). If such lags apply, this result may be avoided if the initial public outlay is financed out of credit or taxes drawn from idle balances. For purposes of present analysis, we assume that no lag exists.[4]

The *increase in private consumption expenditures,* resulting from adjustments in public expenditures and taxes is the second leverage factor. The total increase is equal to *k* times the initial net increase. The

---

[2] Pigou defines as "exhaustive" or real expenditures those expenditure items which involve surrender of real resources and are made to secure the production of goods and services. Placed on a current basis, this definition meets our requirements although there are numerous border-line cases. See A. Pigou, *A Study in Public Finance* (New York, Macmillan Co., 1929), p.19.

[3] This, of course, involves the assumption that public projects, valued at cost, can be added on to privately produced goods, valued at market price. For present purposes this assumption is accepted.

[4] *Cf.* H. C. Wallich, *op. cit.,* p. 81.

initial net increase, in turn, equals the initial increase in expenditures by those receiving additional income from the government minus (or plus) the initial decrease (or increase) in expenditures of those paying additional (or reduced) taxes. The initial increase in expenditures by those receiving additional government payments is defined as $(E_1 + E_2)$, *i.e.*, the marginal propensity to consume (α) of those receiving the additional payments, times the total increase in public expenditures, including transfer as well as real expenditures. The initial decrease (increase) in expenditures of taxpayers is defined as $\pm\beta T$, *i.e.*, the marginal propensity to consume (β) of those who meet an increased (decreased) tax bill, times the *change* in tax yield, $\pm T$.

It is a major point of this analysis that E_1, the initial public expenditure on current produced goods and services, is singled out as the first term, while the multiplicand to which k is applied is defined to include the initial increase in *private* expenditures only.[5] This permits us to differentiate between the marginal propensity to consume of income recipients in the economy at large, which underlies k, and the marginal propensity to consume of those who receive additional income from the government (α), or of those who meet a changed tax bill (β).[6] This is of considerable advantage. During a depression period, for instance, fiscal planning calls for taxes which are drawn from taxpayers whose marginal propensity to consume is low relative to that of income recipients as a whole, and for expenditures going to recipients whose propensity to consume is high relative to that of the community as a whole. The opposite tends to hold during a period of inflation. If the specific propensities of taxpayers and expenditure recipients are not allowed for, *i.e.*, the marginal propensity to consume of all groups is assumed to be the same, the number of variables is reduced.[7] However,

---

[5] No double counting is involved by including E_1 as a separate first term, because the multiplicand to which k is applied in the second term includes only such fraction (α) of $(E_1 + E_2)$ as is initially respent.

Alternatively, E_1 might be omitted as a separate term, in which case k would apply to $(E_1 + E_2)$ as a whole and E_2 would be deducted in the first round.

[6] As pointed out below, α and β also differ from the community's propensity to consume upon which k depends in that they refer to consumption of particular groups, whereas the latter refers to consumption of the community at large.

[7] We have in this case $\alpha = \beta = \frac{\gamma}{\quad}$ where γ is the community's marginal propensity to consume after tax and t is the marginal tax rate. In this case $k = \frac{1}{1 - \alpha}$ and expression (1) reduces to:

$$G = \frac{E_1 + \alpha(E_2 + E_1 - T) + I}{1 - \alpha}$$

For a discussion of the relationship between multiplier and tax rate see Paul A. Samuelson, "Fiscal Policy and Income Determination," *Quart. Jour. Econ.*, Aug. 1942, Vol. LXI, No. 4, p. 584.

this simplified formulation of the problem is not very useful for our purpose since it implies the assumption that resulting changes in consumption expenditures are independent of the *type* of public expenditure or tax adjustment. Only changes in revenue or expenditure totals are accounted for and thereby an important part of the problem is assumed away.[8]

The marginal propensities to consume of those receiving additional income from the government (α) or of those meeting a changed tax bill (β) are weighted averages. They greatly depend upon the kind of policy by which adjustments in the expenditure or yield levels are brought about. The α applicable to transfer expenditures may exceed or fall short of the α for real expenditures. Thus, if the additional expenditures are relief payments, α may be close to one; if they are for debt redemption, α may be close to zero. If the expenditures qualify for inclusion in E_1, it is likely that α will fall somewhere in between these extremes. Similarly, if the change in tax yield is in sales tax yield, β may be close to one; if the estate tax yield is involved, β may be close to zero. The β applicable to the corporation tax depends upon its incidence. To the extent that the tax is reflected in higher prices or lower wages, β will be relatively high; to the extent that the tax is reflected in reduced dividends, β will be less, and where the tax is reflected in the retention of less earnings, β will be equal to zero. By defining the revenue item as $\pm\beta T$, the implicit assumption is made that the β applicable to borrowing is equal to zero. This assumption is not entirely realistic, even for the case of depression borrowing, but is made to simplify the problem.

The *change in tax yield,* or $\pm T$, includes all changes in yield, whether due to changes in the tax base (brought about by increased consumption, investment and public expenditures) or to changes in tax rates. When government expenditures $(E_1 + E_2)$ increase and the tax rate remains unchanged, T will be positive since a part of the additional income received from the government will be returned to the Treasury in taxes. Having defined T is this way, α is defined as the marginal propensity to consume out of income *after* tax but is applied to $(E_1 + E_2)$, the full initial addition to private income, *before* allowing for additional taxes. In other words, with respect to the term $\alpha (E_1 + E_2)$ it is assumed that no additional taxes are paid by the re-

[8] Ideally, we should apply different *multipliers* to $E_1 + E_2$ and T respectively, instead of assuming different marginal propensities to consume in the first round of private spending, while applying the general multiplier thereafter. But this is impracticable. Within the limitations of any multiplier analysis based upon the marginal propensity to consume of the community as a whole, the formula should give a reasonably good approximation.

cipients of the additional government payments. The fact that additional taxes are paid by this group and that the net increase in their expenditures falls short of $\alpha\ (E_1 + E_2)$ is allowed for in deducting βT, where T covers all additional tax yield.

Changes in tax yield are here considered the primary planning factor, the necessary changes in tax rates being determined by the changes in yield and income. The opposite approach could be taken but would be less useful.[9] As a matter of fiscal planning, yield adjustments are the primary objective and changes in tax rates the means to accomplish them. In planning rate adjustments to bring about the desired change in yield, secondary changes in yield due to changes in the level of income and hence in the tax base must not be neglected. As a matter of legislation, action is taken in terms of rate adjustment but the final purpose is adjustment of tax yields.

The change in yield, or T, may be positive or negative, depending on whether the yield provided for in the adjusted budget falls above or below the initially assumed level. T is equal to zero if the yield level is unchanged. It should be noted that $\pm T$ refers to increments or decrements in tax yield only, so that βT does not allow for changes in private expenditures brought about by changing the sources from which the initially assumed amount of tax yield is drawn, as, for instance, by changing from excise to income taxes.[10]

The *multiplier* k is here applied to initial changes in private expenditures on consumption or investment. It is based on the marginal propensity to consume of the community at large, not on α or β which reflect the consumption habits of certain groups only. Usually, k is based on the community's marginal propensity to consume out of income *before* tax and thus allows for leakages from additional tax payments, in this paper it is based on consumption out of income *after* tax. Since the multiplier is based on the community's marginal propensity

[9] An alternative approach would be to define α as the propensity to consume out of income before tax and T as such addition to tax yield as results from an autonomous increase in tax rates only, excluding such additional yield as results from an increase in the tax base. The net result, in terms of the addition to total income, would be the same for both approaches.

[10] The lower the initially assumed yield level, the less serious is this defect. At the cost of some complication it may be remedied by adding another term to expression (1).

The difficulty might be avoided by redefining G to be the deficiency in income on the assumption of a zero (rather than a balanced minimum) budget. This would have the advantage of making T identical with the over-all yield level, so that changes in the β for the total tax yield would be accounted for. But this would be more than offset by the disadvantages of this approach, in particular (a) it would pose the altogether unrealistic problem of having to estimate G for the assumption of zero public expenditures and (b) it would exclude the analysis of budget adjustments involving a reduction in tax yield.

to consume out of income after tax, k will remain constant when tax rates fall and/or when tax rates rise. This avoids considerable difficulties which can only be mentioned here. If, for instance, expenditures are increased to sustain a higher level of income and the tax *rate* is held constant, the initial increase in expenditures must be sufficiently high to allow for the fact that tax yields will be increased at the higher level of income and the deficit be smaller. This is allowed for in our formulation of the problem where the deduction term βT will be positive. If, instead, the tax *yield* is held constant, this leakage will not be present and T will be equal to zero. However, the implied reduction in tax rates means that the marginal propensity to consume out of income before tax payments will be larger at the higher level of income. Under our definition k remains unaffected by such changes.

The final leverage factor is kI, the change in private expenditures on investment and consumption due to $\pm I$, the *induced change in private investment.* It is not related to changes in E_1, E_2 or T in any simple multiplier fashion as is the case for consumption expenditures. Specifically, I is defined to include both such changes in investment as may accompany *any* over-all increase in income, brought about by fiscal or other policies, and such changes as may result from the impact of quite *specific* revenue or expenditure policies. If fiscal policy can be successful in assuring a high and stable level of income, this very assurance will undoubtedly contribute to a higher level of private investment. Also, private investment may be stimulated directly through developmental programs such as power development, urban redevelopment and so forth. Well-selected reductions in tax rates may give further incentives to private investment. On the other hand, higher tax rates, public expenditures which compete with private enterprise and psychological repercussions of an increased budget or of a rising debt may work in the opposite direction.

II

The interrelationship between the contribution of the budget to over-all income and the major variables of budget policy may now be illustrated with reference to hypothetical post-war magnitudes. The quantitative results, of course, are illustrative relationships, not forecasts or policy data. Like the equation of change, our formula presents questions rather than answers, but it may serve as a "table of contents" for some functional relationships involved.

For purposes of these illustrations the familiar concept of gross national product may be used as the over-all measure of income, even though theoretically the net product would be the better concept. The gross national product for the year 1950 is widely estimated at about 200 billion dollars under conditions of full employment. Now suppose that the outlook at the close of 1949 indicates a prospective gross national product of 170 or 180 billions only, both estimates being based on the assumption that the federal budget is balanced at a level of 10 billions.[11] This exceedingly low initial budget level is assumed for analytical reasons, not because it is felt that expenditures could or should be reduced that far. Under such conditions, what adjustments in the budget can be made that will raise total income by 30 or 20 billions for the two assumptions respectively?

In answering this question, attention will be concentrated on three variables: the size of the budget, the size of the deficit and the consumption impact of the tax structure. First we shall consider the required level of public expenditures if given amounts of deficit are incurred and then the required size of the deficit if public expenditures are at given levels. In both cases the results will be observed for varying values of β.

SIZE OF REQUIRED BUDGET AS A FUNCTION OF THE DEFICIT AND TAX STRUCTURE

It will be convenient to make certain substitutions in expression (1) as follows: *E,* the total increase in expenditures may be written

---

[11] The underlying situation might be as follows:

Given a balanced federal budget of 10 billion dollars and a similar budget for state and local governments, consumers' expenditures corresponding to a gross national product of 200 billions might amount to 142 billions. With real public expenditures of 17 billions, the remaining quota for private investment would be 41 billions. Assuming housing expenditures of 4 billions, growth in inventory of 2 billions, net exports of 2 billions, business replacement expenditures of 8 billions and net business investment of 10 billions, a deficiency of 15 billions would remain. With net business investment of 15 billions, the deficiency would be 10 billion dollars.

Assuming a multiplier of 2, the gross product would settle at 170 or at 180 billions respectively. Consumers' expenditures might then be at about 127 or 137 billions respectively, the remainder in both cases being 17 billions of public real expenditures and 26 billions of investment. This disregards a further fall in income due to reduced private investment.

If investment declines with the level of income, as it most likely will, the gap between realized and full-employment income might be much above the 30 or 20 billions here assumed, but similarly, when the level of over-all income was raised through an appropriate fiscal policy, there would be a corresponding increase in private investment and income and, in choosing 30 and 20 billions as our gap illustrations, this *"income-induced"* effect on investment (as distinct from investment effects caused by specific revenue or expenditure measures), *has been omitted.* If it is assumed that the "income-induced" drop in investment as income falls is the same as the "income-induced" rise in investment as income increases, the autonomous increase in expenditures needed to close the gap may be estimated correctly while neglecting the "income-induced" changes in investment in both directions.

for $(E_1 + E_2)$; rE may be written for E_1, where r is the fraction of additional budget expenditures in the form of real expenditures; E minus D may be written for T, where D is the deficit. Because the effects of specific revenue and expenditure policies upon private investment cannot be appraised without a much more detailed analysis, they will be neglected in the following illustrations *and the term kI in expression* (1) *will be omitted.*[12] Specific investment effects will be reconsidered in the concluding paragraphs. Solving expression (1) for E, we have

$$E = \frac{G - k\beta D}{r + k(\alpha - \beta)}. \tag{2}$$

To concentrate on the more important variables, let us assume constant values for r, k and α. Values of .75 for r, 2 for k, and .70 for α may be reasonable.[13] Substituting in (2) for the larger of the two gap assumptions, *i.e.*, for a gap of 30 billions, we have

$$E = \frac{30 - 2\beta D}{2.15 - 2\beta}. \tag{3}$$

To obtain total budget expenditures, the initially prevailing expenditure amount of 10 billion dollars is added to E; if E is equal to zero, total expenditures are equal to 10 billions. Similarly, if the level of tax yield, or $E + 10 - D$ falls below 10 billions, tax yields are reduced from their initial 10-billion level.

Proceeding from these assumptions, Table I shows the size of the budget total required to raise over-all income by the deficiency G if selected values of D and β apply. For each combination in the table, the required increase in expenditures (E) is obtained by deducting 10 billion dollars from the budget total. The required change in tax yield (T) is obtained by deducting 10 billions from the yield total, *i.e.*, from the total budget minus the deficit. The results are shown for values of G equal to 30 and 20 billions. The table is to be read like a

[12] While the investment effects of *specific* revenue or expenditure measures are thus not covered, our definition of the initial income deficiency implicitly allows for "income-induced" changes in investment. (See the preceding n. 11.)

[13] The community's marginal propensity to consume out of individual income after tax is assumed at 4/5. Allowing for such factors as changes in corporate savings and in transfer expenditures, this might make for a multiplier estimating very conservatively of 2. The α for public real expenditures is assumed at 2/3, that is, somewhat below the 4/5 applicable to *individual* income after tax, since allowance must be made for such factors as corporate savings and changes in transfer payments. The α for transfer expenditures is assumed at .8. If r is assumed at .75 this gives a weighted average for the combined α of .7. As noted before, this simplified analysis does not allow for the fact that k varies with implicit changes in the tax rate.

mileage chart. It shows, for instance, that with a deficit of 5 billions and a β equal to .6, an increase in expenditures from 10 to 35 billions would be required under the 30-billion gap assumption.

Moving *down* each column, Table I shows that, for low levels of deficit, the required budget will be the larger the higher the value of

TABLE I

REQUIRED SIZE OF BUDGET UNDER ALTERNATIVE FISCAL POLICIES[a]
(In billion dollars)

β[b]	Deficit—Billion Dollars												
	0	1	3	5	7	9.3	10	13	13.9	15	16	18	20
	G = \$30 Billion[c]												
0.	23.9	23.9	23.9	23.9	23.9	23.9	23.9	23.9	23.9	23.9	23.9	23.9	23.9
0.2	27.1	26.9	26.5	26.0	25.5	25.0	24.9	24.2	23.9	23.7	23.5	23.0	22.6
0.4	32.2	31.6	30.4	29.3	28.1	26.7	26.3	24.5	23.9	23.3	22.7	25.6	20.3
0.5	36.1	35.2	33.5	31.7	30.0	28.0	27.4	24.8	23.9	23.0	22.2	24.0	—
0.6	41.6	40.3	37.8	35.3	32.7	29.8	29.0	25.1	23.9	22.6	21.4	18.8	—
0.7	50.0	48.1	44.4	40.7	36.9	32.6	31.3	25.7	23.9	22.0	20.1	—	—
0.9	95.7	90.6	80.3	70.0	59.2	47.9	44.3	28.9	23.9	18.6	—	—	—
	G = \$20 Billion[c]												
0.	19.3	19.3	19.3	19.3	19.3	19.3	19.3	19.3	19.3	19.3	19.3	19.3	—
0.2	21.4	21.2	20.7	20.3	19.8	19.3	19.1	18.5	18.3	18.0	17.7	—	—
0.4	24.8	24.2	23.0	21.9	20.7	19.3	18.9	17.1	16.6	15.9	—	—	—
0.5	27.4	26.5	24.8	23.0	21.3	19.3	18.7	16.1	15.3	—	—	—	—
0.6	31.0	29.8	27.3	24.7	22.2	19.3	18.4	14.6	13.5	—	—	—	—
0.7	36.7	34.8	31.1	27.3	23.6	19.3	18.0	—	—	—	—	—	—
0.9	67.1	62.6	51.7	41.4	31.1	19.3	15.7	—	—	—	—	—	—

[a] Effects of *specific* revenue and expenditure policies on private investment are disregarded.
[b] Fraction of marginal tax dollar reflected in reduced consumption expenditures.
[c] Deficiency in income if budget were balanced at 10 billion dollars.

β, whereas for high levels of deficit the opposite is the case. At the deficit level of 13.9 billions for the 30-billion gap assumption (9.3 billions for the 20-billion gap assumption), the size of the required budget will be the same for all values of β. This must be the case because at that point E is equal to D so that T or $E - D$ is equal to zero.[14] Since the tax yield remains unchanged, the value of β does not matter. If the deficit falls short of 13.9 billion dollars, it appears that $E - D$ is positive, *i.e.*, tax yield must be increased above the initial level because required expenditures are relatively high and the deficit is relatively small. If the deficit exceeds this figure, $E - D$ is negative, *i.e.*,

[14] With T equal to zero (and neglecting kI), expression (1) becomes $G = rE + k\alpha E$. Substituting $G = 30$, we obtain $E = 13.9$. Adding the initial expenditures of 10, we have total expenditures of 23.9. Deducting initial taxes of 10, we have $D = E = 13.9$. Similarly, for $G = 20$ we have $D = E = 9.3$.

the tax yield can be reduced from the initial level because required expenditures are relatively low and the deficit is large. While the change in yield is upward, the budget must of course be the larger the heavier the pressure of the additional taxes on consumption. If a reduction in tax yield occurs, this will be the more stimulating and hence the budget may be smaller the heavier the prior burden of the tax yield upon consumption.

Moving down the deficit columns, the required budget figure ($E + 10$) is carried to the point at which the size of the budget falls to the level of the corresponding deficit. Combinations which would require a smaller budget are not very meaningful and are indicated in Table I by dashes.[15]

Moving *across* each row, Table I shows how the required budget will be the smaller, for any positive value of β, the larger the deficit. If β is equal to zero, the required size of the budget will be the same for all values of D since there will be no difference between tax and deficit finance. Moreover, if β is equal to zero, the required budget level will be the same as in the preceding case where the budget level was the same for all values of β.[16] By increasing D for the higher values of β we again reach a point at which the entire budget is deficit financed and beyond which a further increase in the deficit would be meaningless.[17]

---

[15] Given any level of deficit, the limiting value for β is that for which the entire budget can be deficit financed. Thus with a deficit of 16 billion dollars for instance, the limiting value for β may be found by substituting $E + 10 = 16$ in expression (3). We then obtain

$$6 = \frac{30 - 32\beta}{.75 + 1.4 - 2\beta} \quad \text{or} \quad \beta = .855.$$

For smaller values of β and a deficit of 16 billions, hoarding of deficit-financed funds would be required to avoid inflation.

The relationship between E and β for $D = 16$ is determined by

$$E = \frac{30 - 32\beta}{2.15 - 2\beta}$$

for values of $\beta \geqslant .855$.

[16] In both cases, expression (2) reduces to

$$E = \frac{G}{r + k\alpha}.$$

[17] Given any level of β the limiting value for D is again where $E + 10 = D$. Assuming $\beta = .6$ and substituting in expression (2), we have

$$D - 10 = \frac{30 - 1.2D}{2.15 - 1.2},$$

or $D = 18.37$. For larger values of D and a β of .6, hoarding of deficit-financed funds would again be required to prevent inflation.

The relationship between E and D for $\beta = .6$ is determined by

$$E = \frac{30 - 1.2D}{.75 + 2(.7 - .6)}$$

or $E = 31.58 - 1.26D$ for values of $D \leqslant 18.37$.

Table I, obviously, does not provide us with ready-made prescriptions for post-war budget policy. A number of arbitrary assumptions are involved and, most important, effects of specific tax and expenditure policies upon private investment are neglected.[18] It will be of some interest, however, to consider what ranges of Table I may be relevant and what, if any, significance the results may have for post-war fiscal policy.

The value of β will undoubtedly depend upon the amount of tax yield relative to the level of income. If the tax yield were very small, say 5 billion dollars out of a gross national product of 200 billions, β might be held to a very low level; a very substantial part of the tax yield might be obtained out of middle to high bracket income taxes. But if the tax yield were to be larger, say 10 or 15 billions, this would be more difficult. If the yield were 20 or 25 billions a substantial burden on consumption would be inevitable. A β of close to .5 might be the best that can be expected for a 20-billion-dollar level. If the level of tax yield were still higher, say 30 billions or more, β would hardly be below .6 and possibly substantially more.[19]

If this is the case, the currently popular proposition that full employment can be readily reached through a large balanced budget may be dismissed as of little practical interest. Assuming a β of .6, the balanced budget needed to fill the 30-billion gap would be about 42 billions; for a β of .7, the result would be 50 billions, levels of expenditure which would seem out of question for the peacetime economy. If, as is altogether likely, such an exceedingly high level of taxation should depress private investment below the assumed level, the required budget would be still higher, which in turn might depress private investment still further and so on. The result might be expected to be more favorable if a higher value for α is assumed. Thus, with α equal

---

[18] Note, however, that in choosing our gap illustrations we have excluded the more or less *automatic* changes in private investment which accompany general changes in over-all income. See, however, notes 11 and 12 above.

[19] In an unpublished study on the "Impact of the Personal Income Tax on Savings," I have estimated the impact of alternative income tax rate structures upon savings and consumption at a high and low level of yield. While the results of this study are based on rather inadequate information as far as the consumption impact for *any one* rate schedule is concerned, they do give some idea of the differential impact obtained under various rate schedules.

For a yield of 16 billion dollars at a national income of 140 billions, the impact upon consumption is estimated at 43 per cent, assuming rates in effect in 1944, at 30 per cent assuming a maximum degree of progression and at 50 per cent assuming a flat rate (however, with 1944 exemptions). For a higher yield level the impact on consumption would be substantially higher. Assuming such proportionate increase in the 1944 rates as is necessary to raise the yield to, say 30 billions (which might correspond to 40 billions at the higher income level here assumed), the ratio would be well above 50 per cent. If excises were relied upon, the average ratio would, of course, be substantially higher.

to .9 and β equal to .6 the required budget would be 32 billion dollars instead of 45 billions, but only on the assumption that r remains at .75. This, however, is unlikely, since the increase in α to .9 would require that almost all the additional expenditures be for cash subsidies to low income consumption. If we allow for this and assume r to fall to .1, while keeping α at .9, the required budget rises to 53 billion dollars, or above the level required under the initial assumption. More reliance on consumption subsidies, therefore, does not render the "large and balanced" budget approach more feasible.

SIZE OF REQUIRED DEFICIT AS A FUNCTION OF THE EXPENDITURE LEVEL AND TAX STRUCTURE

There is much to be said in favor of an alternative approach under which the desired size of the budget is taken as the independent variable, while the size of the deficit is obtained as a function of the predetermined expenditure level and of the best possible value for β. If this approach is taken, expenditure planning will be guided more largely by considerations of resource allocation and there will be less need for "made-work" projects. To illustrate this approach, expression (2) might be rewritten as

$$D = \frac{G + Ek(\beta - \alpha) - rE}{k\beta} \tag{4}$$

Retaining r at .75 and α at .7, we have, for the 30-billion-dollar gap assumption,

$$D = \frac{30 + E(2\beta - 2.15)}{2\beta} \tag{5}$$

Table II shows the required levels of deficit corresponding to selected levels of public expenditures ($E + 10$) and values of β. Again the results are shown for both the 30-billion and the 20-billion gap assumptions and again Table II is to be read like a mileage chart. Thus for the large gap assumption and a budget of 28 billions (where $E = 18$), the required deficit is somewhat below 11 billions if β is equal to .6.

The general picture provided by Table II is very similar to that of Table I. Moving *down* each column we now find that the required deficit will increase or decrease with a rising value of β, depending on whether the adjusted yield falls above or below the initial level, *i.e.*, whether T is positive or negative. Again the required deficit is the same for all values of β when E is equal to D so that the level of tax yield is unchanged.[20] Moving *across* each line, we now find at all values

[20] The explanation is similar to the preceding case, see n. 16 above.

of β that the required deficit is the larger the smaller the size of the budget.

Again certain combinations of E and β are ruled out because they imply either (a) an excess of deficit over total expenditures or (b) a negative deficit. In the case of (a) we have a situation where the pro-

TABLE II

REQUIRED SIZE OF DEFICIT UNDER ALTERNATIVE FISCAL POLICIES[a]
(In billion dollars)

β[b]	G = 30[c]				G = 20[c]			
	Total Budget Expenditures							
	28	23.9	20	15	28	20	19.3	15
0.....	*	d	—	—	*	*	d	—
0.1.....	*	13.9	—	—	*	2.5	9.3	—
0.2.....	*	13.9	—	—	*	6.3	9.3	—
0.3.....	3.5	13.9	—	—	*	7.5	9.3	—
0.4.....	7.1	13.9	—	—	*	8.1	9.3	—
0.5.....	9.3	13.9	18.5	—	*	8.5	9.3	14.3
0.6.....	10.8	13.9	17.1	—	2.4	8.8	9.3	12.7
0.7.....	11.8	13.9	16.1	—	4.6	8.9	9.3	11.6
0.8.....	12.6	13.9	15.3	—	6.3	9.1	9.3	10.8
0.9.....	13.2	13.9	14.7	—	7.6	9.2	9.3	10.1
0.95....	13.4	13.9	14.5	15.0	8.2	9.2	9.3	9.9
1.0.....	13.7	13.9	14.3	14.72	8.7	9.3	9.3	9.6

For explanation of asterisks and dashes, see text below.
[a] Effects of *specific* revenue and expenditure policies on private investment are disregarded.
[b] Fraction of marginal tax dollar reflected in reduced consumption.
[c] Deficiency in income with balanced budget of $10 billion.
[d] If $\beta = 0$, it is a matter of indifference whether the budget is tax- or loan-financed. Hence, the deficit may assume any value between zero and total budget expenditures.

posed increase in expenditures is relatively small, so that a decrease in tax yield is required to obtain the necessary leverage. The heavier the consumption incidence of the initially obtained tax yield, *i.e.*, the higher β, the more stimulus is provided by a dollar's worth of tax reduction and hence the smaller is the required tax reduction or necessary deficit. If the β of the decrement in tax yield falls to a certain point, the required deficit will be so large as to necessitate the repeal of all taxes. If β is still smaller, we have the situation indicated by dashes in Table II, where the scheduled increase in expenditures is insufficient to provide the required leverage, even though the entire budget is deficit financed.[21]

[21] For the case of the 20-billion budget and the large gap assumption, expression (5) reduces to

$$D = \frac{10\beta + 4.25}{\beta}.$$

The minimum value below which β must not fall is reached where D is equal to $E + 10$ or 20; at this point β is equal to .425. If β is smaller, the required deficit exceeds the level of expenditures, *i.e.*, the scheduled increase in expenditures is insufficient to provide the necessary leverage even though the entire budget is deficit financed.

The leverage cannot be increased further without raising expenditures, and this is not possible because a given budget level is assumed. With respect to (b) the opposite situation prevails. There the scheduled increase in expenditures is relatively great, so that tax yields must be raised to avoid inflation. The lower the value for β, the higher will the increase in tax yield have to be and the smaller is the permissible deficit. If the β of the increment in tax yield falls to a certain point, it will be necessary to balance the entire increase in expenditures with increased tax yield, so that D is equal to zero. If β is still smaller we have the situation indicated by asterisks in Table II, where the scheduled increase in expenditures is too high to avoid inflation, even though a balanced budget is retained.[22]

Table II indicates that, within the range of feasible adjustments, the size of the required deficit may be considerably reduced, or the extent of permissible tax increase be considerably increased, if β can be held to a low level. Taking the 28-billion-dollar budget, for instance, the necessary deficit for the large gap assumption will be 7 billions if the β for the additional taxes can be held to .4 and nearly 12 billions if the β rises to .7. For the small gap assumption the same budget can be balanced only if β can be held down to .52. But whatever their relative impact upon consumption, all additions to tax yield are more or less restrictive. As shown in Table II, the size of the deficit will have to remain the major variable of budget policy if the initial gap in the level of over-all income is large, whether the deficit be brought about by raising expenditures more than tax yields, as under the large budget assumptions, or by raising expenditures while lowering tax yields, as under the small budget assumptions.

Specific revenue and expenditure effects on investment are included in expression (1) but have been neglected in its experimental application to possible post-war magnitudes. Since the picture might be quite different if such effects on private investment are accounted for, this greatly limits the usefulness of our illustrations. The effects of fiscal policy upon private investment are a complex matter and sufficiently familiar to render any brief enumeration superfluous; a detailed discussion would greatly exceed the limits of this paper.

---

[22] For the case of the 28-billion-dollar budget and the large gap assumption, expression (5) reduces to

$$D = \frac{18\beta - 4.35}{\beta}.$$

The minimum level below which β must not fall is now reached where D is equal to zero and hence β is equal to .24. If β is smaller, the formula indicates a "negative deficit," *i.e.,* tax-financed hoarding is required to forestall inflation.

Even cursory examination of the problem suggests, however, that private investment is likely to be the lower, *at any given level of total income,* the higher the level of taxation and (with the exception of stimulating developmental programs) the larger the government budget. If the initial deficiency in over-all expenditures is large, we have seen that the balanced budget approach will require exorbitantly high levels of expenditures and taxation, both of which will tend to depress private investment. If, as a result, private investment expenditures are depressed, budget figures even higher than those shown in Table II are needed. If the unfavorable reaction of private investors is violent, tax-financed additions to expenditures when carried beyond some point may well lower rather than increase the over-all level of income.

All this points to the conclusion that a substantial deficit will be needed unless we succeed by non-fiscal means to narrow down the initial deficiency in the over-all expenditure level to much below the illustrative figure of 30 billion dollars used in the preceding discussion. If a large deficiency remains to be filled through fiscal measures, after other policy approaches have been exhausted, it will be neither desirable nor feasible to make expenditures sufficiently large to balance the budget at full employment. Instead, a thoroughly worth-while expenditure budget should be provided including expended social security and adequate developmental programs stimulating to private investment, but excluding made-work projects.[23] On the basis of such an expenditure program the level of taxation should then be set sufficiently low to leave such deficit as the economic situation may require in the average year. After the budget is thus adjusted to the longer-term needs of the economic situation, short-term variations in underlying conditions and localized relief needs remain to be met by a flexible expenditure program and an elastic tax system, including flexible income tax rates.

[23] This principle, of course, does not indicate whether the budget should be large or small. It merely requires that long-run expenditure planning should be considered primarily a matter of resource allocation rather than of employment creation.

20

"Model-Building" and Fiscal Policy*

By ALBERT GAILORD HART†

A number of recent writings on fiscal policy[1] draw important policy inferences directly from "models" showing hypothetical values for the main components of the national product. These "models" on examination turn out to be equilibrium positions of systems of static relationships, of much the same sort teachers of economics have been accustomed to use in the classroom—with the important difference that in classroom discussions concrete magnitudes need not come in question, whereas these fiscal-policy model-systems are aimed to give a realistic quantitative picture.

These model-systems are set up on the hypothesis that the major components of the national product are determined by the scale and character of the government's fiscal operations—in a setting, of course, of relationships among the components expressing other economic

* *American Economic Review,* Sept. 1945. Reprinted by the courtesy of the American Economic Association and the author.

In addition to the general debt to the literature indicated in my footnotes, I wish to acknowledge obligations arising from conversations and correspondence with K. E. Boulding, M. G. de Chazeau, Nancy Dunlap, W. J. Fellner, M. V. Jones, L. Klein, T. Koopmans, J. Marschak, R. A. Musgrave (whose article in the *American Economic Review* prompted this article), P. A. Samuelson, T. L. Smith, and T. O. Yntema—none of whom, however, shares responsibility for any errors the article may embody. [At the time of writing this article I inadvertently omitted the name of Jacob Mosak from the list of those whose criticisms helped in the preparation of my article. Dr. Mosak was generous not only with the use of unpublished materials, but with specific written criticisms, in the light of which I rewrote the article in a way which I (but not, I fear, Dr. Mosak) regard as a great improvement.]

† Columbia University; formerly Committee for Economic Development.

[1] See in particular National Planning Association, *National Budgets for Full Employment* (Washington, March, 1945); "Forecasting Postwar Demand" (papers by Morris Livingston, Arthur Smithies and Jacob Mosak, in *Econometrica,* Jan. 1945); Appendix C by Nicholas Kaldor in William Beveridge, *Full Employment in a Free Society* (New York, Norton, 1945), pp. 344–401; and R. A. Musgrave, "Alternative Budget Policies for Full Employment," *Am. Econ. Rev.,* June 1945, Vol. XXXV, No. 3, pp. 387–99.

The present discussion is not aimed to cover the "projections" of the national product accounts through the transition period which are being worked out in various quarters. These have of course a related economic logic, differing chiefly in being tied to immediately antecedent history at one end and in dealing with the shortest of short-run effects.

forces.[2] The system may be thought of as involving four classes of magnitudes:

(1) "Active variables"—government expenditures; revenues (or rates and exemptions) of various taxes; and other magnitudes which may be thought of as directly controllable by government.

(2) "Passive variables"—the components of national product (consumption, investment); of private income (wages, profits, etc.); of disposal of income (consumption, individual savings, etc.); in principle also prices.

(3) Cumulative variables, reflecting the resultant of action of the above variables over time—chiefly the stock of money and the stock of capital goods.

(4) "Parameters"—the quantitative characteristics of the relations among the variables, determining (for example) the shape of the marginal-propensity-to-consume function, the relations of investment to taxation and to other product components, etc.

The model-builders seem to operate with a more or less explicit set of algebraic equations (or of equations and diagrams) relating these magnitudes; but their publications do not lay much stress on the equilibrium concepts involved, and in general are of limited usefulness to the reader who wishes to try the effect of putting variant assumptions through the analytical machine.

It is not my purpose to discredit this approach. As will appear shortly, I feel that the recent model-systems are in some respects seriously misleading; and that, with all improvements, such systems cannot bring us as near the threshold of policy recommendations as their sponsors seem to think. But the drawbacks of operating with such model-systems have to be weighed against the drawbacks of trying to get on without them. There has to be some sort of explicit forecast of the intensity of the economic forces with which fiscal policy has to deal, and of the responsiveness of the economic system to fiscal measures. On the whole, it seems safer to begin by setting up an equilibrium system such as these model-systems embody, continuing by considering factors it cannot adequately handle, rather than to plunge directly into the full complexity of economic forces.

The thesis of this article is that the discussion has now reached a stage for a more careful survey of the limitations of the "models" approach, and of ways to improve it and to use its results more fruitfully. It will be argued:

(1) That the recent model-systems tend to neglect factors of great importance for policy, and to make inefficient use of available evidence—primarily as

[2] This way of viewing the problem emphatically does not commit the model-builder to the assumption that government fiscal policy is the only motive power in the economy. It merely brings a particular set of variables into the foreground for closer study.

the result of failure to be explicit about the relations of static to dynamic systems;

(2) That the drawbacks of these systems can be overcome in good part by more explicit recognition of their logical character, and fuller use of devices for mapping out the field of possibilities;

(3) That development of model-systems must not lead us to overrate the certainty of our forecasting, to overrate the possibilities of forestalling economic difficulties, or to underrate the necessity of adapting policy rapidly to circumstances as they develop.

I. DEFECTS OF RECENT MODEL-SYSTEMS

The recent systems of models, though originating with a number of different workers, all represent rather similar points of view—substantially, the point of view of Sir William Beveridge's *Full Employment in a Free Society,* which in turn represents an application of Keynesian insights. I feel, therefore, that no major violence is done by treating them as products of a school, and putting criticism in terms of the tendencies of that school; though the examples brought forward under this implicit assumption of joint liability may be mildly unfair to some of the group. My main complaints are:

(1) Confusion of impact effects of economic changes with long-run effects;

(2) Inadequate recognition of cumulative factors;

(3) Underemphasis on elements in the structure of the economy which tend to generate fluctuations of activity and prices;

(4) Careless use of assumptions of ignorance;

(5) Formulation in terms which make it needlessly hard to try variant assumptions and to confront assumptions with evidence;

(6) Underemphasis on intangibles.

In the main, these are consequences of failure to be explicit about the limitations and peculiarities of a static approach.

Impact versus Long-Run Effects

The equations, tables and graphs which embody the model-systems here under discussion are formulated in terms of the *levels* at which the variables (government expenditure, revenues, consumption, investment, etc.) stand, without explicit reference either to *rates of change* or to *immediately previous levels.*[3] Consequently they must be taken as formally static, representing equilibrium situations (either at full employment or with under-employment) which would be found if the

[3] Such "dynamic" elements are of course brought in to some extent in the discussion surrounding these model-systems.

"active variables" were held constant[4] for several years on end. This does not commit the model-builders to dealing only with the ultimate effects of keeping the "active variables" constant forever and a day; but it does seem to make their model-systems incapable of handling the impact effects of sudden changes. Where different sets of values for the levels of the "active variables" are dealt with in the same model-system, therefore, such a system can describe the effects of *holding one set constant rather than another,* but not the effects of *having just shifted from one set to another.*

This logical limitation is not explicitly faced by the model-builders in question. In consequence, we tend to find a mixture of assumptions appropriate for static analysis with assumptions appropriate for dynamic analysis of impact effects. For example, Dr. Mosak[5] uses a formula for corporate profits before taxes which shows them as varying by 23.6 per cent of any variation in gross private national product,[6] derived by a regression of undeflated figures for 1929–1940. The base period of course reflects not experience with under-employment equilibrium but experience with sharp fluctuations—with a period in which low-income years were years previous to which activity had been much higher, and high-income years were years previous to which activity had been much lower. Had the "active variables" been held constant until the "passive variables" leveled out in an under-employment equilibrium, equilibrium ratios of profits to income would surely have varied much less than the regression suggests. Similar considerations apply to Dr. Mosak's corporate savings series: the negative figures he shows for low values of gross national product would not be compatible with any equilibrium, and the gradient is uncomfortably steep.

The effect of confusing impact and long-run effects on corporate savings estimates is seen in extreme form in Nicholas Kaldor's comparison[7] of actual 1938 with a hypothetical 1938 which would have existed had a full-employment policy then been in effect. He puts actual 1938 output at £4,675 million, with net savings of £440 million (9.4

---

[4] All variables may be supposed "deflated" to remove the effect of price-level changes; changing productivity may be thought of as reflected in some sort of smooth-acting growth factor; and population changes may be taken care of either in the growth factor or by reduction of variables to a per capita basis. "Constancy" of the variables can thus be construed in terms of a growing rather than a stationary economy if desired; what it precludes is chiefly oscillation.

[5] *Econometrica, loc. cit.*

[6] I.e., gross national product minus product arising in government, and minus indirect taxes.

[7] For Great Britain, in 1938 prices. The figures given here are from William Beveridge, *op. cit.,* pp. 350, 353, 355, 359.

per cent); had there been full employment he estimates that the product would have been higher by £500 million and net savings by £120 million (24 per cent of the difference in output), of which no less than £75 million is attributed to additional undistributed profits (net of tax). As Kaldor himself points out, the "difference between the average and marginal profits (and in particular the high proportion of marginal profit going to undistributed profits) are chiefly responsible . . . for the increase in savings, following on an increase in incomes, being so much larger than the proportion of savings in total income."[8] The total difference in profits, distributed and undistributed, is put at £255 million, before taxes, or 51 per cent of the difference in product. No specific adjustment period is indicated; but to attribute half the product difference to profits smacks of a sudden change rather than a difference in equilibrium levels. On the investment side, however, Kaldor explicitly limits himself to long-run effects. Instead of the £360 million actually invested in 1938, he writes for his hypothetical full-employment 1938 £400 million, "not meant as an estimate of what private investment would have been in 1938 if output had suddenly been raised to the full employment level, but rather as an indication—not unreasonable in view of the general prewar experience—of what the normal annual private investment outlay could have been expected to be under a continuous full employment policy."[9] Kaldor's model system thus confronts an impact effect (estimated at £120 million) on savings with a long-run effect (estimated at £40 million) on investment. This mixture of assumptions manifestly is the primary reason for the wide gap in the forecast net balance of private savings and investment at full employment, and consequently for the large scale of fiscal adjustments shown[10] as necessary to execute a full-employment policy.

The illustration just given relates primarily to undistributed corporate profits, or "corporate saving." Failure to distinguish sharply between impact and long-run effects also has much to do with the high estimates of the marginal propensity to save among individuals, which are standard equipment in the recent model-systems. It must of course be recognized that there is profound uncertainty as to post-war savings patterns, and that the unexpected readiness of the public to save during the war registers at least a possibility that full-employment income levels would lead to ratios of individual savings to disposable incomes far above those previously experienced. But the inter-war regressions of

[8] *Ibid.*, p. 353.
[9] *Ibid.*, p. 361.
[10] *Ibid.*, p. 363.

consumption on disposable income on which the model-makers rest their case are *prima facie* the record of years of sharp fluctuations (not of a range of equilibrium levels of income each maintained for some time) and hence are not entirely relevant. Both the characteristics of the inter-war period and the apparent stability of the proportion saved over the long period 1879–1928[11] have led at least some of the model-builders to think in terms of an upward trend in consumption, operating irrespective of income.[12] This "trend" must be construed as reflecting the upward drift of the standard of living. But why is there an upward trend in the standard of living? Basically, most economists would probably agree, because as incomes rise people recognize "needs" which they previously kept under when they were too poor to have any chance of satisfying them. Accordingly, this upward trend in living standards should probably be regarded as part of the response of consumption to income.[13] In a static system, therefore, it might be more appropriate to show a marginal propensity to save from disposable income slightly

---

[11] This is based on the stability of net capital formation (roughly the sum of individual and corporate saving, with the former predominating) as a percentage of net national product (roughly equal to disposable income) as shown by Simon Kuznets, *Uses of National Income in Peace and War* (New York, 1942), and the fact that such fluctuations as appear do not seem to be linked with the rate of growth of income. By decades, Kuznets shows:

Decade	1879–88	1889–98	1899–1908	1909–18	1919–28	1929–38
NCF as % of NNP, current dollars	10.4	12.0	11.3	11.3	10.8	3.1
Outlay per consuming unit as % of previous decade	—	107.0	128.2	115.7	134.7	98.7

[12] Such an upward trend is included in the consumption-income relation used by Smithies (*Econometrica, op. cit.*, p. 6), and in the relation derived by L. J. Paradiso which is used in the National Planning Association pamphlet (*op. cit.*, p. 79).

[13] A very interesting discussion of this issue is presented by P. A. Samuelson in his paper on "Full Employment after the War," in S. E. Harris, ed., *Postwar Economic Problems* (New York, McGraw-Hill, 1943), pp. 32–37. Samuelson prefers to say that the consumption function has an upward drift through time rather than that the long-run elasticity of consumption with respect to income exceeds the short-run elasticity; but the only explanation of the drift he offers is an "enlarged scale of wants." He denies "that there is any guarantee that the upward shifts of the consumption schedule will be at a rate rapid enough to keep up with our productive potential; especially if the war and a prolonged period of depression keep us from knowing what we are missing in the way of new good things of life, so that our consumption 'requirements' increase more slowly than our productive requirements" (p. 33).

In short, Samuelson does seem to recognize that in a very long-run sense the upward trend of standards is an adaptation to income. But he would apparently not advise model-builders to assume that their model-systems are dealing with a long enough run to make a very low marginal propensity to save appropriate.

Professor Alvin H. Hansen, on the other hand, is inclined toward the view that the percentage of income consumed is stable through time. See his *Fiscal Policy and Business Cycles* (New York, Norton, 1942), p. 233, also pp. 236–38.

above 0.10, in preference to the coefficients of 0.20 and upward which seem to be appropriate in dealing with year-to-year changes.[14]

Cumulative Factors

The model systems under study make no explicit allowance for cumulative factors. While it is somewhat dangerous to read interpretations of omissions into other people's work, I am inclined to venture that these omissions are intentional. The possibility that the accumulation of capital goods may damp investment is a standard part of the Keynesian background from which these model-systems spring; but since this is ordinarily taken as a bearish factor, its omission from consideration is presumably intended as a precaution against overstating the case for "stagnation" which the model-builders are developing. The possibility that accumulation of money and other liquid assets may stimulate consumption and investment is presumably left out of account as part of the general reaction against the quantity theory of money.[15]

There is a great deal of doubt as to the correct weight to be assigned to these factors; but as will be argued presently, this is no excuse for assuming they should carry no weight. The presumption is that the United States as well as Europe will come out of the war with a serious deficiency of housing and of many types of business facilities, as well as other durable goods, relative to high-employment volumes of activity and income. The problem of fiscal policy depends partly on the size of this deficiency, partly on the rate at which post-war net capital accumulation proceeds, and partly on the sensitivity of the demand for new durables to their accumulation—all matters which ought to be brought into the open as part of the problem the model-systems are designed to treat, however poor the evidence is for estimating them.

On the monetary side, experience since 1929 certainly justifies a reaction against the quantity theory of money and related doctrines; but it is possible that the reaction is going too far. Admittedly, it is hard to unravel the net effects of monetary changes. Through peace and war, however, the year-to-year changes in the supply of money and money

---

[14] I am myself on record (*Rev. Econ. and Stat.*, Aug. 1942, p. 104) in favor of writing a marginal propensity to save disposable income at 25 per cent. This was in a very different context, however: my object was to make a maximum allowance for the degree to which "normal" savings adjustments could be counted on to mitigate the wartime inflation problem.

[15] *Cf.* P. A. Samuelson's omission of the stock of wealth from the list of variables affecting saving (*op. cit.*, p. 36) explicitly on the ground that this influence is "relatively minor in importance."

substitutes have been in the same direction and of the same general magnitude as changes in expenditures.[16] While it is possible that this fact merely reflects the parallelism of the money supply with other factors of much higher causal importance, it is equally possible that this parallelism has caused part of the influence of money to be attributed to other factors. The deficits which the model-builders here under discussion think may be necessary are large enough to build up the public's liquid holdings by upwards of 5 per cent per annum, so that variations in these holdings are likely to be substantial enough to count. Both the peculiarities of the early post-war years and the effects of a long series of substantial deficits (or surpluses) can be adequately analyzed only by procedures which treat monetary influences as at least potentially important.

Fluctuations

The temptation to underrate the fluctuations problem is one of the most serious consequences of overconfident use of equilibrium models. It is true, of course, that the success of a full-employment policy implies a rather small amplitude for fluctuations of total activity, since intense depressions are supposed to be banned. But this does not settle the issue. Fluctuations in the *intensity and direction of the "spontaneous" forces* in the economy with which policy must deal are not ruled out by pronouncing the words "stable full employment" as an incantation. Avoidance of fluctuations in total activity implies success in offsetting (or using) fluctuations in these forces through policy action.

These tendencies to fluctuation are very likely to be serious not only during the demobilization period but for a decade or more beyond. In an economy which had been stable for some time, it might reasonably be assumed that the "damping" tendencies most econometric workers believe in would have largely eliminated this problem. But for the visible future we shall not be living in that kind of economy. We are coming out of a period of unprecedented fluctuations in both the scale and the composition of the national output. In consequence the composition and age-distribution of our physical wealth and the various parts of our labor force will call for changes in the composition of current output and the fields to which new workers are to be guided. Furthermore people's expectations will be unstable. A static model-system cannot express these forces making for fluctuations; and this limitation must always be kept in mind in using such a system.

---

[16] *Cf.* C. Warburton, "Monetary Expansion and the Inflationary Gap," *Am. Econ. Rev.,* June 1944, Vol. XXXIV, No. 2, p. 305. Minor exceptions to the parallelism of year-to-year movements appear in 1926–27 and 1928–29.

Assumptions of Ignorance

It is always a puzzle how to deal with causal relationships which are known to exist, in the absence of adequate quantitative knowledge. The literature under discussion in this paper shows a tendency to cut the Gordian knot by ignoring the relationship—plainly an unsatisfactory remedy.

The chief relations involved are those determining the volume of private investment. We find Kaldor, for example, writing the same figure for private home investment outlay under all the circumstances represented by his alternative "Routes to Full Employment," despite the fact that tax revenues range from £460 million in Route III up to £1710 million in Route II—a range of 24 per cent of the assumed full-employment national output.[17] It is scarcely conceivable that such a difference in taxes should have negligible effects upon investment. Admittedly, it is hard to justify any specific numerical coefficient linking investment with revenue. But a coefficient of zero is as much a specific numerical coefficient as any other—and any coefficient reflecting a negative correlation would surely be more defensible.

Some sort of recognition must plainly be given to the effect of activity on investment—both the components of gross capital formation reflecting replacement of goods worn out, and net investment. At this point Kaldor simply writes investment at £400 instead of £360 million, as we have seen;[18] since this is a net figure, the implied increase in gross capital formation is greater by whatever increase in depreciation is involved. Musgrave[19] operates with an assumption of a full-employment level of investment when defining the initial deficiency in income, with the consequence that neither the character of the potential under-employment equilibria nor the effect of the compensating fiscal-policy adjustments is explicitly mapped out.

Mosak and Smithies[20] protect the reader by treating the *amount of investment required to balance the national product accounts* as a residual in their calculations, and inviting the reader's own judgment as to the attainability of the required amount under the assumptions made. This frank treatment of an area of ignorance by leaving part of the model-system incomplete has much to commend it; but of course it still leaves the problem of what the undefined relations are actually like.

The evidence on the effect of activity on investment is very unreli-

---

[17] Beveridge, *op. cit.*, p. 363.

[18] See above, p. 311.

[19] *Am. Econ. Rev.*, Vol. XXXV, No. 3, pp. 387–99.

[20] *Econometrica, loc. cit.*

able for statistical reasons,[21] and there is a wide range of possibilities. Clearly for each particular firm, pressure of productive activity upon facilities (so that new facilities are needed to permit handling more business, lower costs on existing business, or both) is a necessary if not a sufficient condition for investment in equipment, buildings, etc. At first glance this may seem to be merely a question of impact effects. But a sustained high level of activity means both more rapid wearing out of existing facilities and a wider field for cost-reducing installations, so that a long-term effect of activity on investment must also be accepted. The likelihood of a substantial effect is sometimes ruled out on the ground that unless investment is insensitive to activity the combined effect of activity on consumption and investment may be so strong as to yield models that are highly unstable or even "explosive"—*i.e.,* not tending to find any other equilibrium position if pushed upward or downward from an original equilibrium. If we postulate a high degree of stability, we must infer that activity affects saving a good deal more strongly than investment. But the postulate should not command too much confidence. In the first place, the economy is not highly stable on the record. In the second place, most changes in the "active variables" of policy have probably been reversed before their consequences have been fully worked out.[22] In the third place, some of the "dynamic" elements neglected in a static model-system probably have important stabilizing effects.[23]

Another field in which assumptions of ignorance must be handled gingerly is that of foreign trade. In short-period analysis, the best way to manage this problem would probably be to analyze the effects of activity on imports and exports separately and combine the results into

[21] See the discussion between L. Klein and M. Ezekiel in *Econometrica,* 1943 and 1944.

[22] Followers of Keynesian doctrines should bear in mind that the degree to which national income exceeded depression-trough levels during the 1930's was not perfectly correlated with the size of the deficit; cumulative effects of the early deficits may explain how the deficits of $3.6 and $3.7 billion in the fiscal years 1939 and 1940 came to be associated with much higher national incomes than the $3.8 billion deficit of fiscal 1935.

[23] The following comment on this point of view, made in a letter from Professor P. A. Samuelson, seems to me to sum up very well the opposing view: "Hart's remarks concerning the empirical validity and analytical fruitfulness of assuming an 'unstable' system are interesting and *logically* tenable, but to me [P.A.S.] unconvincing. The historical record shows fluctuation—not necessarily explosive instability. To assume that multiplicands will conveniently vanish or reverse themselves so as to keep things finite is either gratuitous or involves implicitly considerations of a wider system which is 'stable.' Mathematically, the introduction of lag or delayed effects simply changes the requirements of stability; it does not preclude the 'necessity' for stability. In a really unstable system, all intuitively sensible results tend to become exactly reversed, especially on the (quite irrelevant!) comparative statistical level. Finally, an unstable system is really not to be desired even by optimists, because the knife cuts both ways."

an estimate of the foreign balance. The same procedure might also be appropriate for long-period analysis aimed to show the requirements which domestic employment policy may impose on foreign trade and international currency policy. But if the objective is to show the framework within which domestic employment policy must operate, in terms of potential under-employment or full-employment equilibria, it does not make sense to assume that there will be a foreign balance larger than can actually be financed.[24] In any model-system representing long-run relationships, it must be supposed that imports and exports will balance—if we include in both totals service transactions as well as security purchases. Only if it can be shown that a higher level of activity favors a larger export balance on security account does it make sense to assume an increased "leakage" through foreign trade as higher levels are achieved. My provisional inclination is toward making just such an assumption of ignorance as I have been criticizing above, and assuming the foreign balance to be independent of the level of activity—clearly a dangerous assumption, in need of review—for purposes of model-building.

The effect of income levels on income distribution is another critical area of ignorance. Mosak[25] operates with a set of equations based on undeflated figures for 1929–40, which for reasons argued above in relation to profits are probably useless for gauging the difference between potential equilibrium positions; these equations imply some increase of inequality at higher national product levels. Fortunately, *marginal* propensities to consume, etc., are apparently less variable over the income scale than the averages; so that any assumption over a fairly wide range will give about the same model-system.

Formulation of Relations

As the recent model-systems are formulated, it is far from easy for a reader who finds the answers disconcerting to make up his mind how far he is confronted with the results of assumptions he is unwilling to accept, and how far with the results of assumptions he is willing to accept but has not previously worked through to conclusions. There is still a great deal of room for ingenuity in developing ways to map out the effects of variant assumptions about the underlying parameters of the system.

From this standpoint, it is particularly awkward to pack up a number

[24] Kaldor (*op. cit.*, p. 363) writes an impossibly heavy import balance in his standard set of models, but offers an alternative set (p. 365) with no adverse balance.

[25] *Econometrica, loc. cit.*

of assumptions in a single assumed "multiplier," as Musgrave does.[26] The multiplier in the strict sense of the reciprocal of the marginal propensity to save is itself a fairly complex concept, since savings from corporations as well as individuals have to be allowed for. Musgrave's assumed value of 2 for the multiplier in question indicates that he is dealing with a variant concept; and any such variant is bound to be still more complex.[27] The reader is on much more secure ground if multiplying factors are treated as derived magnitudes rather than elementary assumptions.

Another weakness in the formulation of the recent systems is a tendency to treat significant variables in ways which prejudge policy questions. This is partly a question of omitting variables from the list. Omission of the stocks of money and of durable goods was discussed above; the difficulty of fitting interest rates into the list of variables creates additional temptations to underrate monetary possibilities. There is also the question how variables are classified. In Kaldor's model-system, for example, corporate savings are treated rather casually as a passive variable which must be expected to respond to changes in active variables of fiscal character. On the face of his figures, however, policies designed to act via corporate savings might under British conditions be very potent. It would be easy to add to his four "Routes to Full Employment" a fifth under which the national product of 1938 could have been brought to a full-employment level, without changes in government revenue and expenditure, by securing the disbursement of part of the net corporate savings.[28]

---

[26] *Am. Econ. Rev., Vol.* XXXV, No. 3, pp. 387–99.

[27] For illustrations of such variants and their derivation, see the Appendix to this article.

[28] According to Kaldor's figures (*op. cit.*, pp. 355, 359) undistributed profits in 1938 were £330 million, of which taxes took £98 million, leaving £232 million net of tax. With a rise of output by £500 million, net savings would have risen by £120 million, of which £45 million is net individual saving, against a rise of £40 million in investment. What is required, then, is a corporate savings policy which would have caused such savings to fall instead of rising—by enough to offset the £5 million excess of added individual savings over added investment, *plus* any rise in net individual savings arising from the implied increase in dividends. If we put this induced rise in net individual savings for illustration at ¼ the rise in dividends, a policy which would bring undistributed profits (net of tax) to an even £200 million at full employment would have done the trick. This would have implied additional profit distribution of £107 million, net of tax (since undistributed profits net of tax in Kaldor's full-employment model appear as £307 million), raising individual net savings from £253 to £280 million, but cutting total net savings at full employment from £560 to £480 million. The permitted £200 million of undistributed profit would still have been 3.6 per cent of national income at full employment, as against 4.5 per cent in actual 1938! With less unreasonable assumptions about the proportion of additional product going to profit, a still more modest adjustment might have done the trick.

Misunderstandings arise very easily out of the mere form in which the results of model-systems are arranged. For example, the final stage of Dr. Mosak's analysis appears in his tables in the following form (abbreviated here to save space):

Assumed level of gross national product (billion)	$150	$160	$170	$180	$190	$200
Mosak estimates of amount of government expenditure plus private gross capital formation required to use part of GNP not attributed to consumption:[29]						
1. With 1944 taxes, except no excess-profits tax	$ 59.3	64.6	69.9	75.3	80.6	85.9
2. The same, except individual income tax at 1941 rates and exemptions	$ 52.7	57.3	62.1	66.8	71.6	76.3
3. The same, except corporate and individual income tax at 1940 rates, etc.	$ 49.8	54.1	58.4	62.7	67.1	71.4

The figures in the range near supposed full-employment levels, at the right, being enormously higher than any reasonable estimate of investment, it might appear that unless there is something wrong with the arithmetic we should plan for enormously expanded income-supporting government expenditures. Had the revenue data been summarized in parallel form, however, the inference might have been different; results are as follows:

Assumed gross national product (billion)	$150	$160	$170	$180	$190	$200
Mosak estimates of revenues of all government bodies, excluding social security:[30]						
1. With 1944 taxes, except no excess-profits tax	$ 37.4	40.3	43.4	46.6	49.6	52.8
2. The same, except individual income tax at 1941 rates and exemptions	$ 28.9	31.0	33.3	35.6	37.7	39.9
3. The same, except corporate and individual income tax at 1940 rates, etc.	$ 24.4	26.2	28.0	30.0	32.0	34.1
Amount of *government deficit* plus private gross capital formation "required":[31]						
1. With 1944 taxes, except no excess-profits tax	$ 21.9	24.3	26.5	28.7	31.0	33.1
2. The same, except individual income tax at 1941 rates and exemptions	$ 23.8	26.2	28.8	31.2	33.9	36.4
3. The same, except corporate and individual income taxes at 1940 rates, etc.	$ 25.4	27.9	30.4	32.7	35.1	37.3

[29] *Econometrica, op. cit.,* Table 3B, lines 12–13, and 3C, line 14.

[30] *Econometrica, ibid.,* Table 1, line 3; Table 2, lines 5–6; Table 3B, lines 2–3, 5; Table 3C, lines 4–5.

[31] By subtraction from the foregoing.

Comparison of the figures shows that the situations calling for astronomical government expenditures to sustain employment are off the map as far as policy goes. A federal, state and local tax revenue of $52.8 billion at full employment would be desired only in one of two contingencies: (1) if the public demanded government expenditures, for the sake of benefits from those expenditures other than sustaining employment, of roughly this magnitude; or (2) if with much lower government expenditures experience showed that a large government surplus and rapid debt retirement did not interfere with prosperity. If experience showed a large deficit to be necessary, public policy would inevitably move toward it largely by lowering taxes rather than solely by raising expenditures. In short, the reader's eye should move downward as it moves to the right along the table of "required" amounts of government expenditure plus private gross capital formation—and if Dr. Mosak's prognosis is correct, on down to lower levels of taxation than the table shows—rather than simply straight across the line, if he is to form a just impression.

Intangibles

Unavoidably, model-builders have to leave *"in ceteris paribus"* a number of factors of "economic climate" which may vary sharply enough to affect significantly the working of the private investment process. Examples are labor policy, monopoly policy, and the general social climate of approbation or disapproval toward entrepreneurs and their activities. I can see no way to bring these factors inside a numerical framework; but I have an impression that the model-builders whose work I am discussing are giving them less than adequate recognition both in sizing up the historical record and in drawing policy inferences from their models.

II. PROPOSALS FOR IMPROVED MODEL-SYSTEMS

As was pointed out at the beginning of this article, there is no excuse for stopping with negative criticisms of existing model-systems. Such systems are a useful tool of policy analysis; the question is how to improve them.

Possibilities of Dynamic Model-Systems

The defects just analyzed trace largely to the attempt to derive static relations. Obviously, then, one possible remedy is to try to derive "dynamic" systems of relationships, in which the timing of the events that the variables measure is taken into account. Methods for such an analysis have been developed by the school of econometric workers following Tinbergen; and the Cowles Commission is pushing research along these lines. In principle, a realistically correct system of relationships of this type would provide a much better guide than any static system since it would show the consequences of following any specified path of policy from a specified date onward. A static system could of course be derived from it by solving the equations on the assumption that successive values of the active variables were all equal (or differed only by a growth coefficient).

Merely to wait for the completion of this econometric analysis, however, is not a safe reliance. In the first place, policy questions will not wait, and the job may prove a long one. In the second place, one must not exaggerate the gains from its formal completion. For technical reasons, such a dynamic analysis is limited to a rather small part of the total mass of available evidence. Its time span is limited by the fact that some key series run out not many years in the past. In view of the limited number of observation years, of the high inter-correlation among the various series which might be used, and of computation difficulties, the list of variables recognized explicitly has to be held down, and cannot take in all those of importance for fiscal policy problems. Furthermore, it is always likely in such a statistical operation that the apparent weights of different variables in "explaining" the changes under study will be misleading because one variable "picks up" weight which properly belongs to another highly correlated variable. Still further, it is likely that the effects of changes in the active variables, as distinct from the effects of differences in their levels, might be rather drastically altered by the adoption of a strong fiscal policy.

The suggestions which follow are aimed at patching up static systems of the general type discussed earlier in the paper, rather than at developing a fully dynamic system.

Classification of Variables

A general scheme of classification of variables was suggested at the beginning of this article. The list of "active" variables, supposed subject to change by positive policy action, should include as a minimum:

- Expenditures by government bodies on "real" goods and services;
- "Transfer payments" (relief, social security benefits, etc.) for which no services are received;
- Corporate profits taxes;
- Other business taxes (excise, property, etc.);
- Personal taxes (perhaps itemized by types).

No way to express these variables is ideal for all purposes. The tax variables, in particular, are somewhat awkwardly expressed by revenues, but hard to express in any other way. Public policy, of course, operates in the first instance on tax rates and exemptions rather than on tax revenues; and for such purposes as explaining the behavior of private investment it is primarily rates which are relevant. On the other hand, tax revenues lend themselves much better than rates to being summed up by indices which can be manipulated conveniently in a model system; and revenues rather than rates come in question in most of the relations determining consumption. On the whole, it probably is best to think of revenues as the variables,[32] while keeping track of the way in which revenues would vary, at different rate levels, if product levels were modified.

As "passive" variables, it is appropriate to list at least:

Private consumption;
Private investment (gross or net);
Income payments;
Disposable income;
Individual savings.

It may be appropriate to list separately various components of consumption, investment, and income payments. Two items seem to be in a doubtful group—to be listed as "active" variables for analyzing some policy possibilities, but as "passive" for others:

Corporate savings (gross or net of depreciation, etc.; if the latter, depreciation should appear separately among the passive variables);
The foreign balance (unless treated as part of investment).

Beveridge and Kaldor appear to regard private investment as an active variable—*i.e.*, set in amount by state decisions;[33] but this point of view does not seem to extend to American discussions. As already mentioned, the stock of money and the stock of durable goods should appear as cumulative variables.

Structure of Relations

The system of relations among these variables must necessarily include the accounting equations (more strictly, identities) which result from the fact that most of the active and passive variables are components of national product and expenditure. The system must

[32] Note that the effects of changes in government expenditure, investment, etc., "other things equal," may be strongly affected by the question whether tax rates or tax revenues are taken as part of those "other things."

[33] Beveridge, *op. cit.*, pp. 177–78, 349.

also include several equations (or if preferred, diagrams) reflecting economic influences, thought of as relations in under-employment or in full-employment equilibrium. As a minimum, there must be relations:

(1) Showing consumption as a function of:
Transfer payments,
Other income payments,
Personal taxes, and
Money stocks;

(2) Showing investment as a function of:
Activity, measured by gross national product or major components (it is algebraically convenient to use consumption plus "real" government expenditure, less business taxes other than corporate profits taxes),
Current depreciation, etc.,
Current net corporate saving,
Corporate profits taxes,
Personal taxes, and
Stocks of capital goods;

(3) Showing net corporate savings (if not treated as an active variable) as a function of:
Activity, measured as above,
Corporate profits taxes, and perhaps
Personal taxes.

This structure is capable of expressing substantially all the relationships contained in the recent model-systems (besides other relationships now left between the lines), in a form that permits testing the effects of varying assumptions about the three major functional relations as well as varying values of the active variables. On the other hand, it stops far short of making all the relevant variables explicit. In particular, it leaves "impounded in *ceteris paribus*" the factors which govern the proportionate share of different groups of income recipients in income payments, the foreign balance, relative prices, and interest rates; and it is not capable of tracing out the path of adjustment in case of any quick change in the active variables. A picture of "moving equilibrium" can be built up by expressing the cumulative variables in terms of successive values of the related active and passive variables (the stock of capital in terms of cumulative capital formation less cumulative depreciation; money chiefly in terms of cumulative deficits), and by introducing trend factors into the basic equations; but there should be no pretense that this is a subsitute for full dynamic treatment.

Admission of Evidence and Handling of Uncertainty

At least pending completion and audit of "dynamic" statistical studies, we can scarcely avoid imitating the builders of the recent model-systems, and piecing together impressions of the parameters of the system from scattered sources. Generally speaking, the relations in which we are interested are such that a statistical "regression analysis" for part or all of the inter-war period is a sensible way to assemble at least part of the evidence. But as will be seen from the criticisms of a number of such analyses which are offered earlier in this paper, there is a good deal of doubt as to the possibility of finding out much about the effects of *levels* of the various magnitudes in question from the record of the inter-war period, in view of the prominence of *fluctuations* during that period.

There seems to be no room for a testing of such a static model-system as a whole by "fitting" it to past periods and checking its hindcasts. Unfortunately the instability of the inter-war period was such that the only period in which levels rather than fluctuations may have been dominant was 1926–28. It might be reasonable to require that a model-system set up for the post-war should "fit" 1928. But in view of the probability that trends were important, this test is too easy; any system can be made to "fit" by apparently reasonable trend allowances.

The art of handling such a system is to try to make reasonable allowances for uncertainty about such magnitudes as the marginal propensity to consume by inserting a whole battery of alternative assumptions in succession and attempting to map out the field of reasonably likely equilibrium positions. As was noted above, the recently published model-systems are deficient in this respect. They allow for alternative values of the active variables; but they are stated in terms of single-valued assumptions regarding the basic relations listed above, except for some contemplation of alternatives for private investment.

General Character of Results

My own attempts at model-building have not yet reached the point where I am satisfied with my map of possibilities, and in any case would require too much space and too much technical analysis for publication here.[34] But some sketch of preliminary results seems in order here.

To begin with I conclude tentatively that to estimate even within 10 per cent the level of gross national product corresponding to a given

[34] A technical analysis is in preparation with a view to possible publication elsewhere; and some figures are given in the Appendix to this paper.

set of active variables is likely to be very difficult. All the uncertainties of the situation are compounded at this point. The presence and strength of a tendency for the standard of living to adjust to income; the presence and strength of an influence of "excess liquidity" on consumption and investment; the strength of the influence of activity on investment; the presence and intensity of a long-run shortage of real capital relative to post-war labor force and income levels—all are very deeply uncertain, and all are highly relevant. It cannot be disproved that there is a possibility of under-employment equilibrium, at levels so low as to mean very serious unemployment.[35] But neither can it be disproved that there is a possibility of equilibrium at full employment with a relatively orthodox fiscal pattern.[36] Not until we have at least a few years of post-war experience can we expect to make good estimates of this sort.

On the other hand, it appears that we can estimate a good deal more definitely the effect of a marginal billion of budget deficit or surplus on the equilibrium position. As so often happens in economics, there is a better basis for forecasting the *differential effect* of preferring one policy to another than for forecasting the *absolute effect* of either. My tentative conclusion is that an extra billion of deficit corresponds to at least an extra 5 billion dollars added to the equilibrium gross national product, and perhaps 10 billion or more. This may be roughly checked from Mosak's figures above.[37] It follows that we can plan on the as-

[35] This may be seen from the figures based on Mosak given in the text above, p. 319. At a \$150 billion level of GNP (which at the assumed 1944 prices means very heavy unemployment), a balanced governmental budget of around \$30 billion (calling for 1944 business taxes and 1941 personal taxes, plus about \$1.2 billion of additional revenue) would leave a need of \$23 billion of private investment, which might very possibly not be forthcoming. These figures seem to me to have a pessimistic "slant," but are definitely not off the map of possible outcomes.

[36] With relatively low (1940) taxes, Mosak shows \$37 billion of private investment needed to give a \$200 billion GNP with a balanced budget. This is no larger relative to GNP than the investment of the best years in the 1920's, but does look to be past the range of reasonable likelihood as an equilibrium (rather than a peak) position for the post-war. Adjustments to correct Mosak's pessimistic "slant" on the items of the calculation, however, suggest about \$31 billion for required private investment, which is not at all out of the range of possibilities so far as I can see.

[37] Looking at the revenue-estimate part of the table on p. 319 above, the \$31 billion figure for \$160 billion of GNP in line 2 (with 1941 income tax rates) would correspond to revenue in line 3 (at 1940 income tax rates) of \$31 billion at about \$185 billion of GNP. If private investment were the same in both cases, government expenditure would have to go up by (\$35.1 + 32.7)/2–\$26.2, or about \$7.7 billion for a \$25 billion rise in GNP. On the other hand, Mosak's model-system provides for a \$1 billion drop in the Social Security deficit between these points, so that the net rise in governmental deficit is only \$6.7 billion if investment is constant. A 5/1 ratio between added GNP and added deficit is therefore obtained if the added \$25 billion of GNP (coupled with a sharp tax cut) can generate a difference of as much as \$1.7 billion in private gross capital formation.

sumption that a change of a billion or two in the government surplus or deficit is quite large in terms of its long-run effects; impact effects, however, are a separate problem. If the period in question is long enough or the size of the surplus or deficit great enough to affect the quantity of money significantly, effects may be greater.

III. POLICY USES OF MODEL-SYSTEMS

If we could suppose that a model-system could give a perfect forecast —not only of equilibrium positions but of transitional reactions taking effect at stated dates—such a system could provide substantially all the needed data for fiscal policy. We should simply have to ask our model-system what would happen under different policies, and advocate that policy (or cluster of alternative policies) under which the outcome would be satisfactory.

The only trouble with this pipedream is the imperfection of foresight. The mere fact that the recently published model-systems (as well as that developed in connection with this paper) are static testifies that they are incapable of guiding policy in this way. Furthermore, as already indicated, the parameters determining the locus of equilibrium positions are subject to great uncertainty. What use have we for a forecasting machine whose results must be regarded in advance as uncertain?

The answer is, of course, that policy cannot allow itself either to become a slave to a particular forecast or to be paralyzed by uncertainty. Because our foresight is imperfect, we must be in a position to adapt policy as circumstances develop. But to say this does not get us around the necessity of making some advance commitments in the light of such foresight as we can muster.

Essential Advance Commitments for Monetary-Fiscal Policy

The main advance commitments which seem to be unavoidable may be listed as follows:

(1) Scale of routine operations of government;
(2) Scope of subsidies, social security benefits, and other transfer payments;
(3) Range of socialized or semi-socialized industries constituting the field for public investment;
(4) Structure of the revenue system (types of taxes, etc.);
(5) Standard tax rates and exemptions;
(6) Advance preparation for manipulation of revenues and expenditures;
(7) Provision for control of the money supply, and for manipulation of that supply through public debt operations, central bank policy, etc.

The models help primarily toward solution of the first five questions; the last two turn chiefly on the amplitude of fluctuations likely to arise from "dynamic" factors, and secondarily on the probable error of forecasts of equilibrium positions.

Other factors bearing on the first three questions suggest that, for all government bodies combined, expenditures below 25 billion dollars (probably below 30 billion) are out of the question; on the other hand, if it were not necessary to limit the size of deficits to avoid inflation, other considerations would not maintain any large volume of taxes. Mosak's figures suggest that, with taxes completely abolished, only about 45 billions of government expenditure plus private investment would be required to fill out a full-employment national product.[38] It follows that tax cuts are definitely capable of generating any deficit conceivably needed (unless for a temporary emergency) without any "abnormal" government spending at all and that, even if deficits are limited only to avoid inflation, all public spending proposals need to be justified as worth the levying of otherwise avoidable taxes of roughly the same dollar amount. The alleged necessity of planning for gigantic outlays does not follow from the models; if this claim of necessity can be defended, it must be not merely in terms of the likelihood that a deficit will be needed, but in terms of some combination of superior effects on long-run productivity, higher priority in terms of immediate enjoyments by the public, or superior flexibility for meeting dynamic shifts, as compared with tax cuts.

There does seem to be a pretty strong case against the possibility of maintaining prosperity with a large budget surplus continued over a long period of time. The case rests, on closer analysis, on the assumption that the effects of war-accumulated liquidity on consumer and business expenditure will not pull savings for long below "normal" percentages of income. But the likelihood that we may need to operate in the range from a 5-billion-dollar surplus to a 5-billion-dollar deficit seems very strong. This implies, in regard to questions (4) and (5) that we cannot afford not to maintain the structure of a really powerful tax structure—though we may be able to use it a good deal below capacity.

---

[38] The effect of dropping all taxes, in Mosak's $200 billion model, would be as follows:

Eliminating $16.4 billion of business taxes would raise "private gross product" from $166.6 to $183.0 billion;

Eliminating $6.6 billion (or more) of corporate taxes as well would raise "national income after corporate taxes" from $166.5 billion (or less) to $189.5 billion, and income payments from $166.5 (or less) to about $182 billion;

Eliminating $7.8 billion (or more) of personal taxes as well would raise disposable income from $149.4 billion (or less) to $182 billion, and consumption from $128.6 billion (or less) to $155 billion.

Flexibility

The initial commitments should include provision for flexibility to cope with surprises in the short run—before we have either had time to adjust the basic structure of the fiscal system or even to determine whether the deflationary or inflationary drifts we are experiencing are deep-seated enough to justify such an adjustment.

How far it is desirable to build automatic flexibility into the system (as by extending current tax payments or social security), or how far it is desirable to set up machinery for swift changes in tax collections, transfer payments or public works depends on our estimates of the degree to which we may be surprised by future developments despite all foresight. Such estimates cannot be derived from static models. As was indicated above, the model-builders in their pre-occupation with equilibrium have tended to push into the background the whole question of economic fluctuations. If the whole problem were simply how to keep on operating a stabilization system with twenty years of successful stabilization behind it—which seems to be the problem Beveridge and many of his disciples set themselves—this consideration might be unimportant. But between us and this happy state lies not merely the immediate post-war transition but a much longer period during which the reverberations of past fluctuations and the public's willingness to speculate in ways which imply the failure of stabilization may be very troublesome. My feeling is that an adequate fiscal-monetary system for this stage of economic stabilization should be able within six months to arrest—better, of course, to reverse—the effects of a 5-billion-dollar drop in the annual rate of private investment. But this is a provisional finding, subject to revision as relevant evidence turns up.

Contingent Policy

The school of economists from which these model-systems spring seems to feel that the only lesson economists need to convey to the public is that government spending can remedy depressions. Certainly it would be irresponsible at this stage of the nation's history to pooh-pooh the deflation danger or the usefulness of deficits (if not necessarily of spending) to correct it if and when it strikes. For while deflation may not be a continuous threat, we can certainly not hope to get through the next ten years—probably not through the next five—without confronting strong deflationary pressure at some stage.

Particularly in view of the strong political pressures against continuation of effective price control, however, it would be irresponsible to overlook the inflationary dangers in sight for the transition. Furthermore, it would be also irresponsible to overlook the likelihood of a fairly prolonged post-war plateau if the transition from war to peace goes well. Such a one-sided view may not only contribute to inappropriate policies during the years in question but also interfere with the application of anti-deflationary policies when needed. If we persuade the public now that it should put all its vigilance into watching for the deflationary wolf, an inflationary experience would be terribly misleading to public opinion. By the time the boom gave way and the wolf became really dangerous, the public might have made up its mind he did not exist. The deflationary wolf is real; but he may not be the nearest peril. It is the business of the economic profession to convey that there are inflationary contingencies and deflationary contingencies; that there are policies appropriate to each; and that there are ways to plan the initial commitments of policy which leave us in a position to meet either contingency.

APPENDIX

It is impossible within the scope of this article to present a full-dress discussion either of the mathematics of model-systems or of the empirical magnitudes involved. But at least a sketch should be presented here to give the reader an impression how far my disagreements with the model-builders referred to above are concrete. For brevity, I have limited my direct comparisons to Dr. Mosak's model-system.

My disagreement is on two fronts: (1) I believe the basis on which Mosak (and also several of the other model-builders) set up their relations is likely to give a misleading impression as to the rôle of government expenditures in a full-employment policy; and (2) I believe the assumptions as to concrete magnitudes adopted by Mosak are off at one edge of the field of reasonably likely values, giving an extremely pessimistic forecast of the functioning of the private economy in a form that suggests it is a middle-of-the-road forecast.

BASIS OF PRESENTATION: THE MULTIPLIER PROPER

The dispute over the basis of presentation may most easily be visualized in terms of a family of "multiplier" concepts. In a nutshell, a Keynesian "multiplier" shows the ratio between a change in the level of national product and the change in the level of "offsets to saving" which is necessary to sustain it. Since saving is assumed to be higher when incomes are higher, and "offsets" must equal saving, the amount of offsets needed per unit of added GNP may be inferred if we know how much saving will rise per unit of added GNP. If we think in terms of a billion dollar increment of GNP, the "multiplier" is a fraction with a numerator of unity and a denominator which is *either* the sum of the increments of individual and of corporate (*ex post*) saving *or* the sum of the offsets provided by business and government—*i.e.,* the sum of the increments of investment and of government deficit. (Since we are thinking in terms of GNP, we may think of both savings and investment as *gross* of depreciation and related accounts, but of savings as *net* of dis-savings by individuals outspending their incomes and by corporations paying dividends out of surplus.) In algebraic notation, if we write E for government expenditures, T for tax revenues, I for private gross capital formation, the multiplier is $d(GNP)/d(E-T+I)$.

EXPANSION FACTOR IMPLICIT IN MOSAK ANALYSIS

Dr. Mosak's point of view may be paraphrased as follows: Of any increment of GNP, only a fraction becomes an increment of consumers' disposable incomes, the remainder being absorbed by "leakages"—chiefly increments of taxes and corporate savings. Of the increment of disposable income, only a fraction is spent, since part is saved. If (say) 3/8 of the increment of GNP goes in "leakages" and 1/5 of the remaining 5/8 is saved, then only half of any increment in GNP can be accounted for by added consumption. If a balanced budget for federal, state and local governments combined would lead to an under-employment equilibrium with GNP at $130 billion, to continue the illustration, this could be raised to $200 billion only by adding $35 billion to the sum of government expenditure and investment. This twofold expansion represents a magnification factor similar to the multiplier as above defined except that the denominator lacks the term for taxes; the factor is to be written $d(GNP)/d(E+I)$. If tax rates are constant, taxes will of course move parallel to GNP, so that this factor by definition must be less than the Keynesian multiplier.

This approach to the problem implies a very curious sort of fiscal policy. In terms of the hypothetical illustration of the preceding paragraph, getting up from an under-employment equilibrium at $130 billion to a full-employment equilibrium at $200 billion implies an increment of $35 billion in the sum of investment and government expenditure, of which the lion's share is to be assigned to government expenditure. But it also implies a rise in revenues of the order of $15 billion. The implied program is to raise tax-financed government expenditures from $25 to (say) $40 billion, deficit-financed expenditures from zero to (say) $15 billion, a raise of (say) $5 billion in private investment making up the remainder of the $35 billion increment in the sum of investment and government expenditure, and consumption rising $35 billion. Assuming that experience demonstrated that a balanced budget yielded the $130 billion under-employment equilibrium, it is hard to imagine who would advocate this sharp rise in tax-financed expenditure.[1]

LEVERAGE FACTORS

As a guide to the problem of fiscal policy, it would be more useful to present results of analysis on a different basis, in terms of what Dr. Hansen calls "leverage factors."[2] If deficit-financed government expenditure and consumption are

[1] I can see no reason to differ with the finding of the model-builders (Musgrave, *Am. Econ. Rev.*, Vol. XXXV, No. 3, pp. 387–400; Beveridge, *op. cit.*, pp. 262–63) that the theoretical possibility of eliminating a "deflationary gap" by having a very large balanced budget would call for so large a budgetary adjustment that it could never become a practical counsel.

[2] *Fiscal Policy and Business Cycles* (New York, Norton, 1942), p. 264.

both at a higher level, both depreciation and net capital formation may be expected also to be higher; and when the change in deficit is thought of as the "active" factor, it is natural to regard the higher investment as a by-product. The "leverage factor" is to be calculated by *reducing* the denominator of the "multiplier," so that it becomes $d(GNP)/d(E-T)$. The leverage factor must therefore *exceed the multiplier.* In principle, different leverage factors must be recognized for deficits arising from added expenditure (if desired, classified by type), or reduced tax revenue of any of the major sorts.

CONCRETE DIFFERENCES

In principle, all these variants of the multiplier concept lend themselves to calculation from any given set of assumptions about "leakages," marginal propensities to consume, influences of output upon revenues, etc. As was indicated above, my impression is that Dr. Mosak and the other model-builders whose work is discussed in this paper have introduced a marked pessimistic slant into their underlying assumptions. My reasoning on the chief items of the calculation is indicated in the text. The following tables tie these items together in terms of the three multiplier concepts just discussed.

We may conclude that:

(A) Under 1944 taxes, the multiplier proper is over twice the expansion factor which sums up Dr. Mosak's analysis, and the leverage factor substantially larger again. These differences widen as assumptions on consumption and investment grow more optimistic.

(B) While under 1944 taxes, the Mosak expansion factor is only 24 per cent larger on the "moderately high" than on the "moderately low" assumptions, the multiplier is 60 per cent larger, and the leverage factor 135 per cent higher. The economic potency of deficit financing, at the margin, is thus substantially affected by the actual size of leakages, marginal propensity to consume, and investment sensitivity; and accordingly we must take it as decidedly uncertain.

(C) *On these assumptions* refusal to tolerate a "leakage" through net corporate savings would substantially raise the multiplying factors.

(D) Similar conclusions hold under 1940 income taxes; though the effect of lower income taxes in favoring savings lowers somewhat the multiplier proper and the leverage factor.

A SAMPLE OF CONTINGENT CALCULATIONS

As indicated in the text, my view is that a satisfactory handling of these questions involves formulating sets of relations in algebraic form, solving the resulting equations, and working out the consequences of variations over the field of likely values in the parameters expressing marginal propensity to consume, etc. There is space here only for a sample of the results.

Suppose the basic relations are given by:[3]

[3] *C* denotes consumption expenditure.
TP denotes transfer payments.
RE denotes "real" government expenditures.
I denotes gross capital formation (investment).
CS denotes corporate saving, gross of depreciation, etc.
CT denotes corporate profits tax revenue. (*Cont.*)

TABLE I

ESTIMATION OF MULTIPLYING FACTORS—TAXES AT 1944 LEVELS EXCEPT FOR REPEAL OF EXCESS PROFITS TAX

"Slant" of Assumptions, Expressed in Terms of Resulting Multiplier	Extremely Low	Mosak[a]	Moderately Low	Moderately High	Extremely High
Marginal rates of change (per unit of GNP except as noted under G):					
(A) Tax revenues: 1944 taxes, except for repeal of excess profits tax	0.32	0.31	0.30	0.28	0.26
(B) Depreciation, reserves, etc.	0.03	0.02	0.02	0.02	0.02
(C) Net corporate saving	0.04	0.05	0.02	0.01	0.01
(D) Decline in foreign trade balance	0.04	0.01[b]	0.02	0.00	0.00
(E) Sum of (A) through (D): Total leakages	0.43	0.39	0.36	0.31	0.29
(F) (1-E) Residue after leakages	0.57	0.61	0.64	0.69	0.71
(G) Marginal propensity to consume *per dollar of additional disposable income*	0.77	0.80	0.83	0.89	0.91
(H) (F) × (G) Marginal propensity to consume additional GNP	0.44	0.49	0.53	0.61	0.65
(J) (1-H) Reciprocal of Mosak expansion factor	0.56	0.51	0.47	0.39	0.35
(K) (F) × (1-G) Marginal individual savings	0.13	0.12	0.11	0.08	0.06
(L) (E) − (A) Leakages other than taxes	0.11	0.08	0.06	0.03	0.03
(M) (K) + (L) Gross private savings: reciprocal of multiplier	0.24	0.20	0.17	0.11	0.09
(N) Marginal domestic gross capital formation	0.03	0.05[b]	0.04	0.06	0.08
(P) (M) − (N) Reciprocal of leverage factor	0.21	0.15	0.13	0.05	0.01
Computed multiplying factors:					
(Q) 1/(J) Mosak expansion factor	1.8	2.0	2.1	2.6	2.8
(R) 1/(M) Multiplier proper	4.1	5.0	5.9	9.4	11.0
(S) 1/(P) Leverage factor	4.7	6.6	7.7	18.0	—
Adjusted multiplying factors with corporate savings constant:					
(Q′) Mosak expansion factor	1.9	2.1	2.2	2.7	2.9
(R′) Multiplier proper	4.8	6.2	6.6	10.0	12.0
(S′) Leverage factor	5.6	8.9	8.9	27.0	—

[a] Based on range from $150 to $200 billion of GNP.
[b] No magnitudes suggested by Mosak; midpoint of "moderately high" and "moderately low" adopted.

$$(1)\quad C = a + b(TP) + c(RE + C + I - CS - BT - CT) - d(PT) + e(M);$$

$$(2)\quad I = f + g(RE + C - BT) + h(CS) - i(PT + CT) - jZ;$$

$$(3)\quad CS = k + m(RE + C - BT) - n(CT).$$

BT denotes other business tax revenue (chiefly excise and property).
PT denotes personal tax revenue.
M denotes stock of money.
Z denotes stock of durable goods.
Small letters denote parametric constants.

TABLE II

ESTIMATION OF MULTIPLYING FACTORS—INDIVIDUAL AND CORPORATE INCOME TAXES AT 1940 LEVELS, OTHER TAXES AT 1944 LEVELS

"Slant" of Assumptions, Expressed in Terms of Resulting Multiplier	Extremely Low	Mosak[a]	Moderately Low	Moderately High	Extremely High
Marginal rates of change (per unit of GNP except as noted under G):					
(A) Tax revenues: individual and corporate income taxes at 1940 rates and exemptions; other taxes at 1944 rates	0.20	0.19	0.19	0.17	0.16
(B) Depreciation, reserves, etc.	0.03	0.02	0.02	0.02	0.02
(C) Net corporate saving	0.04	0.04	0.02	0.01	0.01
(D) Decline in foreign trade balance	0.04	0.01[b]	0.02	0.00	0.00
(E) Sum of (A) through (D): Total leakages	0.31	0.26	0.25	0.20	0.19
(F) (−E) Residue after leakages	0.69	0.74	0.75	0.80	0.81
(G) Marginal propensity to consume *per dollar of additional disposable income*	0.77	0.80	0.83	0.89	0.91
(H) (F) × (G) Marginal propensity to consume additional GNP	0.53	0.59	0.62	0.71	0.74
(J) (1 − H) Reciprocal of Mosak expansion factor	0.47	0.41	0.38	0.29	0.26
(K) (F) × (1 − G) Marginal individual savings	0.16	0.15	0.13	0.09	0.07
(L) (E) − (A) Leakages other than taxes	0.11	0.07	0.06	0.03	0.03
(M) (K) + (L) Gross private savings: reciprocal of multiplier	0.27	0.22	0.19	0.12	0.10
(N) Marginal domestic gross capital formation	0.03	0.05[b]	0.04	0.06	0.08
(P) (M) − (N) Reciprocal of leverage factor	0.24	0.17	0.15	0.06	0.02
Computed multiplying factors:					
(Q) 1/(J) Mosak expansion factor	2.1	2.5	2.6	3.5	3.8
(R) 1/(M) Multiplier proper	3.7	4.6	5.3	8.5	9.7
(S) 1/(P) Leverage factor	4.2	6.0	6.8	17.0	43.0
Adjusted multiplying factors with corporate savings constant:					
(Q′) Mosak expansion factor	2.3	2.7	2.8	3.6	3.9
(R′) Multiplier proper	4.2	5.4	5.8	10.0	12.0
(S′) Leverage factor	4.8	7.4	7.6	26.0	—

[a] Based on range from $150 to $200 billion of GNP.
[b] No magnitudes suggested by Mosak; midpoint of "moderately high" and "moderately low" adopted.

This is of course not the only possible linear approximation to such a set of relations; but I think its form is not unplausible.

Suppose now we try to measure the "leverage factor" for *RE* upon *GNP*, in terms of possible values of the constants *c* (marginal propensity to consume income payments) and *g* (marginal propensity to invest net receipts of business from sales to non-business buyers). We must of course adopt suppositious values for the parameters h and m (which are the only two parameters other than c and g which under these assumptions bear upon this leverage factor); we may write h (marginal propensity to invest gross corporate savings) as 0.50, and m (marginal propensity of corporations to save net receipts from non-business buyers) as 0.05. The leverage factor then works out as follows:

c	0.78	0.80	0.82	0.84	0.86	0.88	0.90	0.92
g								
0.00	4.3	4.7	5.1	5.7	6.5	7.2	8.4	10.2
0.01	4.5	4.9	5.4	5.9	6.8	7.8	9.1	11.1
0.02	4.7	5.1	5.7	6.4	7.2	8.4	10.0	12.4
0.03	4.8	5.4	6.0	6.8	7.8	9.1	11.1	14.0
0.04	5.1	5.7	6.4	7.2	8.4	10.0	12.3	*
0.05	5.4	6.0	6.7	7.7	9.1	11.0	13.9	*
0.06	5.6	6.3	7.2	8.3	9.9	12.2	*	*
0.07	5.9	6.7	7.7	9.0	10.8	13.6	*	*
0.08	6.3	7.2	8.2	9.7	11.9	*	*	*
0.09	6.6	7.5	8.8	10.6	13.3	*	*	*
0.10	7.0	8.0	9.5	11.6	14.9	*	*	*

* Denotes over 15.0.

As indicated above, the range of c from 0.83 to 0.89 may be taken as likely, and the range of g from .04 to .06, giving leverage factors from about 6.8 to about 14. This calculation is somewhat more refined than that in the tables earlier in this Appendix, allowing for influences via corporate savings, etc.; but it will be observed that these limiting values match roughly with those obtained in the previous table.

The algebra of this model-system shows rather similar leverage factors for all the fiscal active variables upon GNP. The general order of magnitude of all these leverage factors is given by cr when r is a factor equal to $\frac{1}{1 - c - cg + cm - chm}$; and while the coefficients of cr and the terms not containing cr differ somewhat from variable to variable, the differences roughly cancel out.

21

Multiplier Effects of a Balanced Budget[*]

By TRYGVE HAAVELMO[†]

I. INTRODUCTION

It has commonly been argued that public spending, to be a remedy against unemployment, must be *deficit* spending and not spending balanced by an equal amount of taxes, since, in the latter case, the government would only be taking back with one hand what it gives with the other. One necessary qualification of this statement is, of course, well known, namely, that taxes corresponding to an equal amount of public spending may lead to a redistribution of incomes which, in turn, may lead to a higher level of national consumption at a given level of private investment. The effect of such redistribution, however, depends essentially on whether or not there is any substantial difference in the marginal propensities to consume, as between the various income groups. If, for example, the propensity-to-consume function of the individual is a linear function of personal income the marginal propensity to consume will be constant for all levels of income, and there could be no redistribution effect (unless the redistribution had an effect on private investment).

In this latter case it might then be thought that public spending balanced by an equal amount of taxes would have no effect upon total income and employment in the society (apart from a possible effect, indirectly, on the propensity to invest). This commonly made conjecture is, however, false, as has already been pointed out by several writers on the subject.[1] In a situation with unemployment and idle resources

* *Econometrica,* Oct. 1945, XIII. Reprinted by the courtesy of the Econometric Society and the author.

The author expresses sincere thanks to Professor J. Marschak for many helpful suggestions.

† Universitetets Socialekonomiske Institutt, Oslo.

[1] See, e.g., P. A. Samuelson, "Full Employment after the War" in *Postwar Economic Problems,* S. E. Harris, ed. (New York, 1943), p. 44. (*Cont.*)

there is a definite employment-creating effect of public outlays even when the are fully covered by tax revenues. And this is true quite apart from whatever other effects the taxes and the expenditures might have on the distribution of income or on the behavior of consumers and investors.

Although this idea is not a new one, there still seems to be much need for a rigorous theoretical analysis of the whole subject. The existing literature is not altogether clear on the matter. Mr. Kaldor, for example, in discussing the possibility of full employment under a balanced budget, explains the matter as follows:

> Full employment could be secured, however, by means of increased public outlay, even if the State expenditure is fully covered by taxation—for the reason that an increase in taxation is not likely to reduce private outlay by the full amount of the taxes paid. It may be assumed that all taxes have some influence on the savings of the individuals on whom they fall; taxes which fall on the poor have a relatively large effect on consumption and a relatively small effect on savings; with taxes paid by the rich it is probably the other way round. Hence an increase in public expenditure will cause a net addition to the total outlay of the community even if it is covered by taxation; . . .[2]

This statement would seem to convey the idea that taxes equal to public expenditure can create employment only to the extent that they cut down on people's savings. This is not correct. We shall show below that public expenditures covered by taxes have an employment-generating effect which is *independent* of the numerical value of the propensity to consume.

Hansen and Perloff, in their comments on the same subject, write as follows:

> . . . Moreover, an increase in useful governmental expenditures (the initial expenditure being financed by borrowing) will tend to raise the national income even though subsequently financed from consumption taxes. Thus, when additional government expenditures are paid out to the public, the income receipts of individuals are increased. If, now, subsequently a consumption tax is imposed equivalent to the enlarged income, it follows that private expenditures after taxes remain as before. The Gross National Product is increased by the amount of the

A. H. Hansen and H. S. Perloff, *State and Local Finance in the National Economy* (New York, 1944), pp. 245–46.

N. Kaldor, "The Quantitative Aspects of the Full Employment Problem in Britain," Appendix C in William H. Beveridge, *Full Employment in a Free Society* (New York, 1945), pp. 346–47.

Henry C. Wallich, "Income-generating Effects of a Balanced Budget," *Quart. Jour. Econ.,* Nov. 1944, LIX, 78–91. (My attention has been drawn to this important article which I had not heard of at the time when my manuscript was submitted for publication. Mr. Wallich's paper, I am sure, deserves more extensive comments than those I had occasion to add to the present article.)

[2] Kaldor, *op. cit.,* p. 346.

new government spending while private expenditures remain the same. Thus in this case the total Gross National Product (governmental expenditures plus private expenditures) is enlarged roughly by the amount of the new expenditure but not by a magnified amount.[3]

Here the final conclusion, namely that expenditures covered by taxes will raise income (and employment) by the amount of the tax, is correct. The assumption of the initial expenditure's being financed by borrowing is, however, unnecessary. Indeed, if this assumption were necessary, the conclusion would not hold in the second year, the third year, etc., since then current expenditure would equal current taxes.

Mr. Wallich, in his recent article dealing directly with the subject discussed here, has reached the same conclusion as Hansen and Perloff. He has a clear illustration in terms of a numerical example. His more general discussion of the "reason why," however, might perhaps give rise to misunderstandings. He writes, in part:

> The reason why national income can increase in this instance, without an increase in investment and without a redistribution of income from the higher to the lower income groups, is that the additional income financed by the Government does not give rise to new net saving. It is true that the previously unemployed will save part of their new income, but an equal volume of savings of the initially employed is absorbed by the additional tax. Since the two groups are assumed to be similar, the savings of one are offset by the reduction in the savings of the other. [Footnote omitted.] By absorbing part of originally existing income and respending it in its entirety, the Government prevents some fraction of this amount from being saved, as it otherwise would be. . . .[4]

If investment is assumed to remain constant it seems unnecessary to prove that saving remains constant. What is needed is a rigorous proof that under these circumstances total income will actually rise as a result of the taxation and spending. For this purpose the argument that the government spends income that otherwise would have been partly saved is dangerous as it might lead to the false belief that the higher the propensity to save for the public the larger the effect of the fiscal policy discussed. As already mentioned we shall see that this is not the case.

The whole matter may in fact be stated much more simply as follows: Let us use the words "net income" to designate the sum of incomes at the individuals' disposal after they had paid the taxes. The words "gross income" will mean the sum of individuals' incomes before taxes. Gross income is thus the sum of earnings made by individuals in

[3] Hansen and Perloff, *op. cit.*, p. 245.

[4] Wallich, *op. cit.*, p. 80.

producing goods and services: it is equal to the money value of goods and services produced, either for private or for public needs. Thus while the demand of private people for goods and services depends on net income, their employment depends on gross income. Extra public expenditure covered, simultaneously, by taxes can obviously be added to the existing gross income in such a way that it will leave the people with exactly the same amount of net income, and hence will leave the private demand at exactly the same level as before the tax was imposed (provided the tax policy does not lead to a change in the distribution of net incomes and, thereby, to a change in the marginal propensity to consume of the society as a whole). But, while the government collects the tax money without any direct compensation to the individual taxpayer, the government requires goods and services from the public in return for money expenditures. Now, if there were already full employment before the tax was imposed, the result would be that the public as a whole would have to work partly for the government *instead* of working for their own direct benefit. Then they could not pay the taxes by working more. If, however, there is a sufficient amount of idle manpower and resources the amount of employment and productive services required by the government will come forth in *addition* to what is wanted by the private sector of the economy. The gross income, i.e., the money value of all goods and services produced (for private as well as public needs) will have increased, although the net income has remained unchanged. In fact, from an employment point of view, the result for the society as a whole will be exactly the same as if the government had ordered idle manpower and resources to work without any direct compensation.

In the following we propose to give a more accurate demonstration of this simple conclusion.

II. THE SIMPLEST CASE: A LINEAR CONSUMPTION FUNCTION

The assumption of a linear consumption function is of particular interest here, since, in that case, as already mentioned, no multiplier effect can result from a redistribution of incomes. This simplifying assumption, therefore, allows us to isolate whatever "pure" multiplier effects might be generated by public spending balanced by taxes.

We shall use the symbol r to denote gross individual money income, while $\bar{r}$ will denote gross average individual money income, and R gross total national money income. (Throughout this study we shall assume that there are sufficient unused manpower and resources available to justify the assumption of a constant level of prices. We shall further assume that we are dealing with a "closed economy.") Since we shall be interested in comparing incomes before and after imposing a certain income tax we shall indicate by r_0, $\bar{r}_0$, and R_0 the individual, average, and total income, respectively, *before* any tax is imposed, while r, $\bar{r}$, and R will be used to denote the same income concepts (gross, i.e., including taxes paid) after a certain income tax is imposed. The total number of individuals, N, is assumed to remain constant.

We assume that the private consumption expenditure, $u(r_0)$, of an individual having the net income r_0 is given by

$$u(r_0) = ar_0 + b, \tag{2.1}$$

where a and b are positive constants $(0 < a < 1)$. Then, whatever be the income distribution, the average consumer expenditure $\bar{u}$ is given by

$$\bar{u} = u(\bar{r}_0) = a\bar{r}_0 + b \tag{2.2}$$

and the total consumer expenditure of all the individuals, $U(R_0)$, is given by

$$U(R_0) = aR_0 + Nb. \tag{2.3}$$

Let V denote total private investment. In all that follows we shall assume V to remain constant. The average investment V/N, then also a constant, we shall denote by v. Total national income R_0 (= total consumer and investment expenditures) is then defined implicitly by

$$R_0 = aR_0 + Nb + V, \tag{2.4}$$

which gives

$$R_0 = \frac{Nb + V}{1 - a}. \tag{2.5}$$

If now a tax totalling T dollars is imposed on incomes, and the tax money is fully spent by the government, the resulting total gross national income, earned in the production of goods and services for both private and government use (= consumer expenditure + private investment + government spending) is defined implicitly by

$$R = a(R - T) + Nb + V + T, \tag{2.6}$$

which gives

$$R = \frac{Nb + V}{1 - a} + T. \tag{2.7}$$

Comparing (2.5) and (2.7) we have the following:

THEOREM I: *If the consumption function is linear, and total private investment is a constant, a tax, T, that is fully spent will raise total gross national income by an amount T and leave total private net income and consumption unchanged. And this holds regardless of the numerical value of the marginal propensity to consume, a.*

The result obtained may also be expressed as follows: If the government spends T dollars and at the same time covers this expenditure by taxes, the multiplier effect, per dollar spent, will be equal to 1.

This, of course, does not mean that the net income and consumption of every single individual necessarily remain the same after the tax has been imposed. For the tax is a certain loss of net income to every individual while the gain from the government expenditure is only an average gain. The individual gains might differ widely.

From (2.7) it follows that by making T sufficiently large one can reach a full-employment level of R. It is interesting to consider the *rate* of taxation that such a full-employment policy might require. Let λ be the tax rate imposed on R. [The distribution of the taxes as between the various individual incomes is here irrelevant, owing to the assumption (2.1).] Then we have

$$R = aR(1 - \lambda) + Nb + V + \lambda R \tag{2.8}$$

or

$$R = \frac{Nb + V}{(1 - a)(1 - \lambda)} = \frac{R_0}{(1 - \lambda)}. \tag{2.9}$$

In other words, a tax rate of, say, 50 per cent will double the total gross income that existed before the tax was imposed.

In the preceding analysis it has of course been assumed that the various services and benefits which the government is able to provide through the spending of the tax money are not counted by the individuals as a part of their consumption or their savings. This assumption is necessary in order to consider a and b as independent of the tax. The government might no doubt provide such services and benefits in return for the taxes that, in particular, the demand for private savings would be reduced. The government might, on the other hand, provide goods and services that would cover a certain part of regular consumer needs. If, as a result of the tax and spending policy, the propensity to consume were changed from a to, say, $a(\lambda)$ then, instead of (2.9), we would have

$$R_1 = \frac{R_0(1 - a)}{(1 - \lambda)[1 - a(\lambda)]}. \tag{2.10}$$

If $a(\lambda) > a$, $R_1 > R$; if $a(\lambda) < a$, $R_1 < R$.

It would no doubt take a considerable amount of research to obtain actual information on the influence on consumers' behavior of the various types of services and benefits provided directly or indirectly by the government. But such a study might be well worth while.

III. MORE GENERAL CASE: NONLINEAR CONSUMPTION FUNCTION

We shall first study the effect of a proportional income tax imposed on all individual incomes, the total tax revenue being spent by the government. Since we assume that the consumption function might be nonlinear we shall have to make some additional assumptions about the behavior of the income distribution through this process of taxation and public spending. The usual simplifying assumption is that "the income distribution remains unchanged." Taken literally, this assumption makes little sense, since a "constant income distribution" would mean that the total (or average) income as well as all other parameters of the distribution would have to remain constant at one level. Usually, what is meant is that, if the average income varies, the income distribution will be subject only to a proportional stretch or squeeze.

Let $\Phi(x)$ denote a certain relative frequency distribution where the average of x is equal to 1, and let us assume that the ratio $r/\bar{r}$ is distributed as x, for all values of $\bar{r}$. The distribution of r will then be

$$\Phi\left(\frac{r}{\bar{r}}\right)\frac{1}{\bar{r}}, \tag{3.1}$$

i.e., the distribution will belong to a parametric class defined by the form Φ, and the parameter $\bar{r}$. We shall assume here that the structure of the economy is such that the income distribution always must belong to this class.

Let r_0 denote individual incomes before the tax is imposed, and let us assume as before that the average investment per individual, v, is a given constant. Further, let the consumption function be $u(r_0)$. Then the average income, $\bar{r}_0$, is given by

$$\bar{r}_0 = \int_0^\infty u(r_0)\,\Phi\left(\frac{r_0}{\bar{r}_0}\right)\frac{1}{\bar{r}_0}\,dr_0 + v. \tag{3.2}$$

If now a proportional tax rate λ is imposed, the resulting gross average income, $\bar{r}$, is defined by

$$\bar{r} = \int_0^\infty u[r(1-\lambda)]\,\Phi\left(\frac{r}{\bar{r}}\right)\frac{1}{\bar{r}}\,dr + \lambda\bar{r} + v. \tag{3.3}$$

If we denote the net income, namely $(1-\lambda)r$, by r_t, and the average of r_t by $\bar{r}_t$, this relation may be written as

$$\bar{r}_t = \int_0^\infty u(r_t)\Phi\left(\frac{r}{\bar{r}_t}\right)\frac{1}{\bar{r}_t}\,dr_t + v. \tag{3.4}$$

Comparing (3.2) and (3.4) we see that the implicit definition of $\bar{r}_0$ by (3.2) is identical with the implicit definition of $\bar{r}_t$ by (3.4). Hence, if this definition is unique, we have

$$\bar{r}_t = \bar{r}_0, \qquad \bar{r} = \frac{\bar{r}_0}{1-\lambda}. \tag{3.5}$$

We therefore have

THEOREM II: *If the income distribution has the property of always remaining within the class defined by* (3.1) *the effect of a proportional tax, fully spent, will be exactly the same as if the propensity-to-consume function had been linear, i.e., private net income and consumption remain unchanged while gross national income rises by the total amount of the tax, and this result is independent of the form of u.*

We have studied the particular case of a proportional tax rate because this seemed the most reasonable assumption in connection with the assumption that the income distribution always must belong to the one-parameter class (3.1). But the particular assumption about a proportional tax rate is not essential. If the assumption is made that also the distribution of net income, r_t, always must belong to the same parametric family of the type (3.1) then our results will follow without making any separate restrictions upon the manner in which the taxes are collected and spent. For we can then write down the equation (3.4) directly. This equation defines $\bar{r}_t$ as a function of v independently of the size and the distribution of the tax. We must, therefore, have $\bar{r}_t = \bar{r}_0$, and $\bar{r} = \bar{r}_0 +$ the average amount of tax. This gives us:

THEOREM III: *If the structure of the economy is such that it maintains a constant "relative" distribution of net incomes whatever the tax is, then the average net income will be the same as before the tax was imposed, while total gross income will increase by the total amount of the tax.*

It might perhaps be worth while in this connection to point out that the assumption we have made about the income distribution is *not* exactly equivalent to saying that "all incomes change in the same proportion." For let $\Phi(r_0/\bar{r}_0)/\bar{r}_0$ and $\Phi(r_t/\bar{r}_t)/\bar{r}_t$ be the income distribution before and after imposing the tax, respectively. Then these two distributions are only the *marginal* distributions of the two variables r_0 and r_t. The knowledge of these two distributions does not uniquely determine the *joint* distribution of r_0 and r_t. If, for example—and only as an illustration—the two distributions were normal distributions, the correlation coefficient would still be free to take any value from -1 to $+1$. The practical meaning of this remark is that a study of the income distribution before and after the introduction of a tax will not fully reveal the eventual "reshuffling" that the individual income receivers might have been subject to as a result of the tax and spending policy of the government.

* * *

It would of course be interesting to study the effects of more general forms of tax rates and more general forms of respending the tax money. Such an analysis, however, would take us into a general discussion of the effects of a redistribution of incomes, and that was not our objective. We only wanted to demonstrate that a "balanced budget" has a direct multiplier effect, with a multiplier equal to 1, in *addition* to whatever (positive or negative) effects there might be from a redistribution of income.

22

*Monetary Policy**

By LLOYD W. MINTS†

My contention will be that general economic equilibrium and a high level of employment can be maintained by means of monetary-fiscal policy, and without highly variable expenditures by the federal government. However, if this end is to be attained we shall have to give more heed than heretofore to the need for protecting the freedom of the market from encroachments by both business men and laborers. A simple governmental policy of laissez-faire is indefensible in an enterprise economy, since if the government is purely passive private groups will then not fail to take advantage of the opportunity to impose monopolistic restrictions of various kinds on the community. Such restraints will mean not only outright reduction of output, but also a rigid price structure. Unless we have a fairly flexible price system a dynamic economy will be subject to an inordinately high level of frictional unemployment, and unless we also have monetary stability it will be subject to intolerable fluctuations in employment.

In what follows I shall include only incidental reminders of the need for free markets and price flexibility, but I should like to emphasize the fact that these factors are of equal importance with monetary stability if we are to have a stable economy and a high level of employment.

MONETARY STABILITY

A depression is initiated by a decline in aggregate demand. Whether this decline is caused by a reduction in the quantity of money, or by an increase in liquidity preferences, is a matter of secondary importance, although, if it were always the former, the problem of maintaining demand manifestly would be simplified. It also does not matter greatly

---

* *Review of Economics and Statistics,* May 1946, XXVII. Contribution to "A Symposium on Fiscal and Monetary Policy." Reprinted by the courtesy of the *Review of Economics and Statistics* and the author.

† The University of Chicago.

whether the initial decrease in demand comes from a lessened demand for consumers' or for capital goods. In fact, it is probable that it usually and predominantly originates in the market for producers' goods, although it is quite likely that there should be a concomitant decrease in the demand for durable consumers' goods. In any event, however, the important thing is the decline in aggregate demand, and the consequent reduction of employment and income. The initial disturbance and decline in income promptly produce an adverse effect on expectations, which further reduces aggregate demand. The worsening conditions of business result in a decrease in bank assets, and thus the quantity of money is reduced. These forces continue to interact upon each other, with the effect of progressively deepening the depression.

If we had a definite, announced monetary policy, based upon legislation and firmly accepted, and if Congress provided ample means of implementation, there would be no reason why aggregate demand should continue to decline after an initial disturbance. On the contrary, aggregate demand could be quickly restored by monetary-fiscal measures, if not by mere expectations of such measures, and thus nothing more than a minor recession in business activity need ever arise.

Any one of a number of possible guides to monetary action would be about equally acceptable. We might either increase the quantity of money at some constant rate, roughly equivalent to the rate of increase in output, stabilize an index of the price level, stabilize per capita money incomes, or follow some similar rule. In any case aggregate demand could be maintained. Stabilization of a price level index is most familiar; it is simple; it is definite; and it would require that changes in velocity be offset. Everything considered, it is probably preferable to any of the alternatives. In what follows, therefore, I shall assume that a price index is to be the guide to monetary action.

Granted a reasonable degree of flexibility of prices (absence of monopoly), a decline in aggregate demand will be reflected promptly in a fall in the price level. It follows that if we stabilize the price level, under competitive conditions, aggregate demand will be sustained, and thus unemployment will be kept to tolerable levels. If a given increase in the stock of money does not raise aggregate demand to the desired level, there is nevertheless some larger increase that will, and there is no serious obstacle to as great additions to the stock of money as may be required—or to subsequent subtractions, if the need for large additions proves temporary.

Unemployment can be kept to tolerable levels by monetary measures under even the most extreme conditions of high liquidity preferences and low investment opportunities. If the marginal efficiency of capital were zero, and if the propensity to save and liquidity preference were extremely high, it would still be feasible continuously to maintain aggregate demand, and thus a high level of employment, without any public investment whatever. As a portion of the public saved and hoarded, which would be the same thing as a constantly rising demand for money, new money would be injected into the system. Thus the demand for additional money would be met. The desired effect would be achieved whether the new money went exclusively to savers or to non-savers, although in practice it would go to both.

If it went to the savers a somewhat larger injection of money would be required than would be the case if it went to the non-savers, since the savers, being those with higher incomes, would have a more rigid propensity to consume. Nevertheless, it is inconceivable that the marginal propensity to consume would be zero even for the savers, if we consider them as a group, although it might be for some individuals. If the savers who received the additions to their cash balances spent, on either consumers' or producers' goods, any small portion of an increment to their cash, the problem could be solved. To be sure, if the marginal propensity to consume were very low, and if none of the additional cash were spent on producers' goods, the necessary additions to the quantity of money would be large, but these circumstances would constitute no bar to success. It is hardly likely, however, that the savers would permit their cash balances to rise indefinitely without turning to investment in some measure so long as the prospective rate of return was in excess of zero.

If the new money went to the non-savers, which is to say, to the lowest income groups, it is preposterous to suppose that consumption would not increase markedly. To the extent that it did go to this group, the program here outlined would bring about a redistribution of real income in favor of the lower income groups. This fact has perhaps been overlooked because a period of inflation has unfortunate effects on the distribution of income. Thus, even though the economy were in an extreme position of "maturity," aggregate demand could be maintained by using all resources for the production of consumers' goods. This situation could continue indefinitely, and without any rise in the level of prices.

Actually, it is hardly conceivable that a technique for increasing the stock of money could be found that would make it possible to increase the cash balances of only the lower income groups. It is also highly improbable that any western industrial nation has reached the degree of "maturity" wherein employment could be maintained only by devoting all resources to the production of consumers' goods; but these are matters of secondary importance if the preceding analysis is correct.

To me it seems evident that, given monetary stability and an absence of restrictive practices on the part of industry and labor, opportunities for investment will be plentiful at rates of return which will not lead to liquidity preferences greatly in excess of those prevailing before 1929. If this is true it means that no large continuous increase in the stock of money would be necessary, although a relatively small secular increase would probably be required so long as the volume of output continues to grow. Minor variations in the rate of injection of money might be required to offset variations in the propensity to hoard, although it is at least conceivable that such fluctuations would be virtually non-existent in the absence of disturbances originating in the quantity of money. It is more likely, however, that changes of such magnitude in the propensity to hoard will occur as to require some variation in the rate of addition to the stock of money; and occasional withdrawals might become necessary. In any case, I am convinced that the problem is not of greater magnitude than these statements suggest. However, even though secular stagnation is neither present nor imminent, a program of price level stabilization would actually avoid more than frictional unemployment if such conditions should develop.

While the numerous current attempts to estimate postwar income, savings, and private investment under conditions of full employment are of some interest, they have little necessary relevance to the problem of public policy. The estimates may be made by able men, as many of them are; they may represent a close approximation to the truth; and they may superficially appear to be very alarming; but nevertheless they should not in fact disturb us. Whatever the magnitude of the difficulty shown by these estimates, it can be managed by an appropriate monetary-fiscal policy; or, rather, there is in fact no serious problem if only we will adopt a reasonable monetary policy and vigorously oppose the development of monopolistic restrictions. (The really serious problem is that of restraining the growth of monopoly; and a successful attack on this problem is as much necessary to the success of a program of maintaining employment by means of federal expenditures as to the policy which I am defending.)

Free markets and monetary stability are not so much remedies for unemployment as they are essential conditions for the functioning of an economy of private enterprise. Given these conditions, autonomous responses to disturbances will ceaselessly operate to maintain a close approach to general equilibrium. A high level of employment will be the incidental but certain result. Unless we provide these conditions, there is no point in attempting to encourage private investment by means of a suitable tax structure, by devices for increasing the volume of foreign investment, or by other remedial measures currently urged upon us. I am wholly in sympathy with such measures as these, but they are minor (though important) refinements in the constitution of a competitive system, whereas free markets and monetary stability are part of the essential framework.

IMPLEMENTATION

Opinion is not unanimous concerning the best means of purposively adding to, or subtracting from, the quantity of money in circulation. During the nineteenth century and approximately the first third of the twentieth, the theory was developed that this could be done by means of changes in the rate of interest, induced by a central bank. This theory runs to the effect that changes in the central bank discount rate and open market operations will affect the market rate of interest, but particularly the rate charged by the member banks. If a lower rate is made effective, business men will increase their borrowings from the banks, and thus the quantity of money, in the form of bank deposits, will be increased.

There is some tendency to believe that the events of the thirties have proved that central bank policy is ineffective. This contention is entirely unwarranted. Not sufficiently vigorous action was taken by central banks, and particularly not by the Federal Reserve System, during the early thirties to warrant any simple inferences from the actual course of affairs of those years. The Reserve Banks did, indeed, reduce their rediscount rates promptly after the panic of the autumn of 1929; but the reduction thereafter was only gradual, a rate of 1½ per cent at the New York Bank not being reached until May 1931. Moreover, and this is of more importance, open market operations were not employed on a scale sufficient to increase the reserves of the member banks, despite the fact that the volume of circulating medium (deposits and hand-to-hand currency) was actually declining. Meanwhile, the wholesale price index declined from 96 (1926 = 100) in September 1929 to 73 in May 1931. Although the Reserve Banks purchased large volumes of government bonds in 1932 and again in 1933, the reserves of the member banks had increased by October 1933 by only an inconsequential amount. The price index declined to its low point of 63 in May 1933, and the volume of money dropped to a low level in the summer of 1933 which was 25 per cent below that in 1929. In the light of these facts one cannot say that the Federal Reserve System made any serious attempt to maintain the quantity of money in the early thirties. We therefore are not justified in asserting that the course of events during those years has proved the inadequacy of conventional central-bank measures.

Nevertheless, I believe the critics of central banking are right, even though the reasons for their conclusions are not acceptable. It takes time for a central bank to make its rate policy effective in the market, and in the short run the demand for funds, particularly short-term funds, is inelastic. Under these circumstances, the cumulative forces of a depression are likely to operate so much faster than a reduction of bank rate that a situation will be reached in which pessimistic expectations will overwhelm the effect of the lowest rate of interest which it is feasible to obtain.

Open market operations by a central bank may have an influence in the desired direction, both because they will induce changes in the rate of discount and because they will directly affect the size of the cash balances of the public. The latter effect will be the more immediate of the two, and it is likely that it would be sufficient to maintain substantial stability of the price level when disturbances were minor in character. Nevertheless, open market operations immediately affect the cash balances of only a small proportion of individuals and corporations, and consequently they are unlikely to be sufficiently effective, in the presence of severe disturbances, to serve as a sole reliance for the implementation of monetary policy.

The doctrine of central bank control fell into disrepute during the thirties, although some few men continue to have faith in it—notably R. G. Hawtrey. In place of it there has arisen the belief that only by means of fiscal policy can adequate control of the quantity of money be had. I subscribe to this later point of view.

The case for implementation of monetary policy by way of the fiscal operations of the national government does not rest exclusively upon skepticism concerning the effectiveness of the operations of a central bank. The final monetary authority is and must be the legislature, and it is therefore impossible to provide a politically independent agency for the management of the monetary system. If Congress is convinced that the policies followed by some supposedly independent agency are undesirable, it will and should intervene.

One of the traditional fears of the American public is that of "political" or "arbitrary" interference with the currency. This attitude ignores the fact that the fiscal operations of the national government unavoidably have monetary consequences. Such an attitude leads to failure on the part of the government to adopt and carry through a rational monetary policy. The major difficulty in governmental control of the monetary system lies in the fact of limited knowledge of monetary matters on the part of the public and of governmental officials. The tradition against political interference serves to absolve the officials of responsibility for their actions which in fact have monetary significance, and to prevent the development of the requisite knowledge upon which a rational monetary policy can be based.

The Secretary of the Treasury is in effect the agent of Congress in carrying out the directions of the latter in fiscal matters, and the federal finances may, and at times do in practice, become the major factor in determining the quantity of money in circulation. Budget deficits and surpluses, the shifting of the working balances of the Treasury between the member and the Federal Reserve Banks, and the borrowing and redemption operations of the Treasury, all have monetary significance. Since these matters must be managed by a financial department of the government, it follows that it is impossible to create a monetary agency that either is independent of Congress or, without an intimate association with the Treasury, has exclusive control of the quantity of money. This means that if there is a central bank it must be a second monetary agency, and monetary policy must therefore be implemented by two agencies, each independent of the other, but both deriving their authority from Congress.

Monetary policy consists of regulating the quantity of circulating medium in accordance with some criterion. To have two agencies with power to change the volume of money will in all probability lead, at times, to conflict, indecision, irresponsibility, and failure to follow any rational policy. The only reasonable conclusion seems to be, therefore, that the powers of the Board of Governors of the Federal Reserve System and certain powers of the Secretary of the Treasury should be lodged in some one agency. In this way, responsibility to the extent of the powers delegated by Congress would be centralized; and this agency could not escape responsibility on the grounds that it had less than full authority within the limits of the powers so delegated.

While there is now agreement among a large proportion of economists to the effect that monetary stability can be obtained only through directing fiscal policy to this end, there is much disagreement concerning the kind of policy that should be pursued. (1) There are those who would rely upon either a high or variable volume of federal expenditures for achieving full employment. (2) There is a second group who would also rely on fiscal policy, but who would both minimize and substantially stabilize the volume of federal expenditures. They would vary tax collections in such manner as to produce deficits and surpluses and thus to change the quantity of money in accordance with some predetermined criterion of policy, such as an index of the price level. It is this policy which I am defending.

Manifestly, deficits and surpluses can be produced by stable revenues and variable expenditures, by variable revenues and stable expenditures, or by a combination of these two methods. The second of these methods is distinctly preferable to the first, and also to the third—with minor and improbable exceptions. Either variations in tax liabilities and collections, or the promise of such variations, can be obtained within a short period of time. If the monetary agency were given authority, within prescribed limits, to vary exemption levels under the income tax, the volume of tax collections could be greatly changed within a short time. This is particularly true since we now have "current" collection, largely at source. This method is simpler than variation of expenditures, and it could be brought into operation more quickly.

Implementation of monetary policy by means of variable federal expenditures would require the central government to undertake construction work or other projects which would largely redound to the benefit of local communities. One need consider only the log-rolling incidental to legislation for the improvement of rivers and harbors to deter one from urging an expansion of the activities of the federal government in comparable directions.

An expansion of the volume of public expenditures merely for the purposes of monetary policy would mean that the aggregate of such expenditures would be larger than otherwise would be the case. This fact would increase the area within which the public authorities would determine the allocation of resources, in other words, the ends of economic activity. We defend political democracy in part because it permits the will of the majority to prevail, but in this one respect a competitive economic system has more to commend it. In a system of free markets the desires of even very small minority groups are duly registered, and the appropriate amount of resources is devoted to their satisfaction. I do not mean to imply that the technique of the market can be applied to political affairs, or that this criterion alone can serve as the final basis for an appraisal of democracy or of private enterprise; but it does suggest that we should not resort to political control in areas where the mechanism of the market will function, unless there are overwhelmingly strong reasons for so doing. Since simpler means are available, implementation of monetary policy is not one of those reasons.

I am by no means opposed to public investment that is clearly required to promote the general welfare. I would merely urge that projects for the expenditure of public funds should be decided upon in view of their merits, independently of the requirements of monetary policy, and that, having been so decided upon, their volume should be substantially stabilized.

The administration of monetary policy requires that all monetary powers delegated by Congress be centralized in a single agency. For this purpose a Monetary Agency should be established. The powers of the Board of Governors of the Federal Reserve System, as well as certain powers of the Treasury Department, should be given to this agency. The agency should acquire all the outstanding stock of the Federal Reserve Banks; it should be given the power of varying the exemption levels under the income tax law within prescribed limits; it should be given such powers as are delegated by Congress to determine the maturity of, and rates of interest on, government bonds; it should be given the power to determine the division of Treasury balances between the member and Reserve banks; and it should be given large powers to buy and sell government bonds in the open market. Finally, it should be explicitly charged by Congress with responsibility for maintaining stability of a wholesale price index, the technical problem of constructing the index to be left to the agency.

Since this agency would have little discretionary power, it would have little need for deliberation or determination of policy. It could and should, therefore, be small. Under the circumstances a board of three men would seem to be appropriate. Preferably the Secretary of the Treasury should be ex officio a member and chairman of the board. If he were not, then the chairman should be a member of the cabinet, in order that he might represent the administration in fiscal matters before Congress. All members of the board should be appointed by the President.

This board or agency would operate in somewhat the following manner. Let us assume that the index is to be stabilized at 100. It would hardly be likely that any action to change the quantity of money would be required if it rose to 101 or fell to 99. There might be some doubt if it rose to 102 or fell to 98, but without much doubt action should be taken if it rose to 103 or fell to 97. Just where these limits of tolerance should be placed might have to wait upon experience. If, for example, the index fell to 97, the Monetary Agency would immediately enter the open market and purchase government bonds. The volume of purchases could not be prescribed in advance, although experience in time should furnish some guide. In this matter, therefore, some discretionary authority would have to be granted to the agency. In any case, however, purchases would continue until the index rose to 100. Contrariwise, the agency would sell if the index rose to 103, although it might be wise to discontinue sales at 101. There would be need for a secular increase in the quantity of money; consequently, a continued change in the quantity until the index reached 100 would probably be less desirable in the downward direction than the upward. These are matters upon which no very definite statements can be made; we would have to rely upon an accumulation of experience for satisfactory guides to action.

How effective open-market operations would be we cannot say, since no central bank or governmental agency has ever given them an adequate test. (Our experience in 1923–24 and 1927 is at best inconclusive.) It would be my hope, however, that they would be sufficient to bring the index back to "normal" after a minor disturbance, or if the decline in the index were due to technological improvements or a secular increase in the volume of transactions. In any event, if the decline were not halted in a very short time, exemption levels under the income tax would be raised. The deficit thus created would afford opportunity to inject additional money into circulation. If the decline still were not halted—but I am convinced that it would be—it would become necessary for Congress to pass legislation providing for a further raising of the exemption level beyond that which the agency had been authorized to make. In an extreme case, it is conceivable that the tax rates themselves would have to be reduced.

Maintenance of price level stability would be powerfully aided by the spontaneous action of the public under conditions wherein it was generally understood that the government would take energetic steps to maintain substantial stability of a price index at some announced level. The program might have some rough going for a few years following its inauguration if there chanced to be serious disturbances, but as the public gained familiarity with, and confidence in, the policy it would to an increasing extent become self-maintaining. It is probable that after the first few experimental years had passed success would be achieved more easily than at first one might suppose.

The federal budget is not likely to be less than 15 billion–20 billion dollars per annum for many years to come. This amount of money could therefore be added to the system each year by the device of reducing tax collections to zero. It may be doubted, however, that a complete elimination of taxes on the wealthy would be desirable, or indeed, that any reduction in the tax collections from the higher income brackets should be made. However, a deficit of 10 billion dollars could easily be achieved, and I am convinced that far less than this amount would be ample to maintain a price index if action were taken promptly when the index had declined sufficiently to indicate the need for an addition to the stock of money. Furthermore, with the huge public debt now outstanding, vast additional sums could be put into circulation merely by purchasing government bonds in the open market. In fact, the public debt could be entirely eliminated in less than fifty years, merely by retirement of new money to the extent of the (probable) secular need for increase in the quantity of money. However, to achieve this result, interest on the debt would have to be paid in large part out of tax revenues, and the banks could not be permitted to make further additions to the stock of money.

This program would permit resort to borrowing by the national government only as a means of withdrawing money to be impounded when inflation threatened. Contrariwise the government would buy securities in the open market only as a means of adding to the stock of money, and thus combatting deflation. So long, therefore, as the secular advance in transactions continued, this policy would operate to decrease the amount of the federal debt. Such a debt policy would be precisely the opposite of the recommendations of those who would borrow to finance federal expenditures. The latter policy would lead to a continuous rise in the debt in an expanding economy. When deflation threatens, the need is for more money, and that being the case money, not bonds, should be issued; and when inflation is imminent, money should be withdrawn. All bond issues should be consols, since they would fluctuate more in price than short-term government issues and hence would be less acceptable than the latter as a substitute for cash in "cash" balances. If we borrow on short term, we give the lender a security that is almost as liquid as cash itself, and the result must be to increase velocity in some measure. Likewise, if short-term governments were bought in the open market, the security withdrawn would be only slightly less liquid than the cash received for it, and consequently the antideflationary effect would be less than would be the case if consols were bought.

Briefly, consols should be bought and tax collections reduced in the face of deflation, and consols should be sold and tax collections increased when inflation threatens.

While the federal budget and debt clearly will be adequately large for the purpose of adding to the stock of money for many years to come, we should not ignore the possibility that at some more distant date the debt may (should) be eliminated and the budget reduced to a figure below 15 billion dollars. I believe that, even with a budget as low as 5 billion, we could prevent deflation by a reduction of tax collections. This, however, is by no means certain, and we should therefore consider what other means might be used under these circumstances.

If there were no debt to be monetized, and if tax reductions were insufficient to meet the need for additional money, it would become necessary in some way to increase the outlay of the federal government. This, of course, could be done by means of an expansion of public works, and while some expansion of this kind should not be a cause for great concern under conditions wherein it would be neither permanent nor large in amount, it nevertheless is desirable, for the reasons already given, to avoid resort to this device if possible.

On grounds of monetary effectiveness, the most attractive device, by a wide margin, is a manufacturers' or retail sales subsidy. Whereas a sales tax is regressive, the relative benefits of a sales subsidy would be inversely related to the income of the purchaser. Such a subsidy would at the same time reduce the purchase price of commodities to buyers and add to the stock of money. Since it would apply to all consumers and since the subsidy could be made large if necessary, an enormous addition to the stock of money could be made within a short period of time. A large proportion of the additional money would go directly to those with the lower incomes; and inasmuch as their marginal propensity to consume is high, it could be confidently expected that most of the new money would promptly be offered for goods and services. While success in maintaining aggregate demand would not depend upon a high marginal propensity to consume, such conditions would require a smaller addition to the stock of money than would be needed with a low marginal propensity to consume. This fact leads to the conclusion that a sales subsidy would have to be neither high nor long continued in effect.

The drawback to a sales subsidy lies in the fact that it would be difficult to administer. This is true of a sales tax, and would undoubtedly be true in substantially the same measure of the subsidy. However,

I am doubtful that in this respect it would be significantly worse than a program of public works; and since it could be instituted and withdrawn more promptly, it would offer some advantage over the latter program.

A publicly announced program such as I have outlined would in a significant degree be self-enforcing, once the public became convinced that it was to be rigorously followed. Under the conditions of the past, it was reasonable to assume that if the price level declined to some extent this fact would lead to unemployment, a decline in bank loans and consequently in the quantity of money, and a further decline in prices. The wise thing to do, therefore, was to stay off the market, either in the hope that still better bargains could be had in the future, or in the fear that adverse developments would give rise to a need for cash. If it were generally known that vigorous action would be taken to combat a decline in the price level, and if it were believed that this effort would be successful, it would then be reasonable to re-enter the market. Such a development would bring about the desired result of restoring aggregate demand before any addition to the quantity of money had actually taken place.

I can see no avoidance of the conclusion that, granted an absence of an undue upward pressure on monopolistically controlled prices, including wage rates, stabilization of the price level would maintain fairly continuously a high level of employment. To deny this is to assert that additional money in unlimited amounts would be hoarded in its entirety. Some hoarding of the new money there might be; but, so long as any portion of it was spent, the program could attain a high degree of success. Much hoarding would simply require a larger addition to the stock of money.

That there would be a complete elimination of unemployment or of fluctuations in employment is out of the question. If some important industry was confronted with a drastic decline in the demand for its output, it would not be practically possible to bring about the necessary adjustments in the economy so quickly as to prevent some increase in unemployment. Nevertheless, by means of an addition to the cash balances of the public, if it should become necessary, the maintenance of aggregate demand could be assured, and thus there would be other industries which would find the demand for their products rising. In this way, the reallocation of resources would be facilitated, even though it could not be made instantaneous. Under these circumstances no widespread depression would occur. In a changing economy readjustments are constantly necessary, and frictional unemployment of some minimum amount is therefore unavoidable. This is a problem, however, which cannot be solved by monetary means. It requires flexibility of prices, information available to the public, particularly to workers, concerning the regions and industries in which additional workers are in demand, and geographic and occupational mobility.

It is as much a governmental function to provide the means to a minimization of these obstacles to mobility as to maintain conditions of monetary stability. To say, therefore, that some fluctuating minimum of frictional unemployment is unavoidable as a practical matter, is not to say that governmental policies should not be adopted which are directed toward reducing this minimum to a low level. Monetary stability would aid in reducing frictional unemployment only in that it would, through the maintenance of aggregate demand, insure that when the demand for labor declined in one region or industry it would correspondingly rise in others.

As nearly as I can discover, the essential differences between those who propose a policy of price level stabilization by means of variations in tax revenues and those who favor federal expenditures—either in fluctuating amounts to prevent variations in employment, or in continuously large amounts to avoid the effects of what is believed to be a condition of economic "maturity"—are (1) a difference as to the size of the federal budget which is deemed necessary, (2) a decided difference concerning stabilization of the price level, and (3) a difference concerning either the desirability or possibility of maintaining an essentially competitive organization.

The defenders of public expenditures in effect desire a relatively large federal budget. Explicitly they assert that this is necessary to maintain employment, but there seems frequently to be implicit in their discussions a feeling to the effect that the central government should do more than it now does by way of direct investment to promote the general welfare. The proponents of price level stabilization, on the other hand, are opposed to federal centralization if not to reduction of the area within which the market decides the allocation of resources, and to handing these decisions over to authorities. Nevertheless, they of course concede that there is some amount of public expenditure which is highly desirable, and which should be undertaken quite independently of the requirements of monetary policy.

It is my impression that those who would implement monetary policy by means of a variable volume of federal expenditures would subscribe to the view that stability in the price level is desirable. They look upon this matter, however, as a secondary consideration. They would presumably call it a desirable end, but not a sufficient means of achieving the more important goal of a reasonably high level of employment. In any case, they for the most part ignore the question, and they enormously underemphasize the importance of monetary stability. They do not, therefore, provide any definite means for maintaining this stability, or indeed, of surely avoiding a very marked degree of inflation. Those who would stabilize the price level assert that a stable price level is the evidence that aggregate demand is maintained, and that therefore nothing more than frictional unemployment will appear.

Those who would rely upon variable federal expenditures for maintaining employment have little to say concerning the need for free markets. Their position therefore is problematical. The truth is, however, that avoidance of rigidity in the presence of downward pressure on prices, and of undue upward pressure, but particularly the latter, is as necessary to the success of their program as to that of a policy of price level stabilization. An attempt to maintain employment by means of public expenditures can lead only to endless inflation if product and labor monopolists are given a free hand. They will constantly raise their prices above the equilibrium level, and, if the monopolies themselves are to be undisturbed, the only possible means of meeting, or rather, of attempting to meet, the difficulty will be to raise the level of expenditures and increase the quantity of money. This action will lead to further price increases by the monopolists, and thus inflation will proceed. To be sure, for a short time immediately following the inauguration of the public expenditures program, constantly increasing tax collections or borrowing from the nonbanking public might prevent rising prices, but taxes and borrowing would soon reach levels beyond which they could not be increased.

The above program pertains to the long-run. It does not have particular reference to the immediate postwar monetary conditions. During the reconversion period it is somewhat problematical what the nature of the monetary problem will be. There are those who believe that deflation is likely, while there are others, including myself, who believe that for some time inflation will remain the greater danger. If deflation develops it can be opposed in the manner I have suggested above. If, on the contrary, inflation threatens, somewhat different weapons may be required to combat it.

The existing large cash balances of the public and the enormous amount of near moneys in the form of government bonds may well lead to a level of spending so high as to bring about a serious inflation, providing nothing is done to prevent such a development. The means of preventing a postwar inflation, however, are readily available, if only we will use them. Taxation at a level that will yield a surplus, and the destruction of money to the extent of this surplus, is, of course, the logical device. Nevertheless, it is not our sole resource.

It would be a simple matter to enforce a reduction of bank assets and consequently of deposits. This could be done either by refunding the short-term government debt now held by the Reserve Banks at rates of interest which would induce the public to buy the refunding issues, which should be long-term (preferably consols), or by raising the required reserve ratio for the member banks. This latter measure should be used, however, only for the purpose of raising the ratio permanently to a level higher than now prevails; that is to say, raising and lowering the reserve requirement should not become a permanent instrument for the implementation of monetary policy.

The institution of a policy of price level stabilization at any other time than one of general equilibrium and a fairly high level of employment would present some difficulties. The program could not be started at a time of a large amount of unemployment, since such conditions require, as a practical matter, both an increase in the quantity of money and some rise in the price level as a means of restoring employment. If an act were passed providing for stabilization of the price level while these conditions prevailed, it would be necessary to give some discretionary power to the Monetary Agency during the period of reemployment.

23

*Taxes and the Budget: A Program for Prosperity in a Free Economy**

By THE COMMITTEE FOR ECONOMIC DEVELOPMENT†

"What will this mean to me?" is the first question that the average man asks when he thinks of taxes or government expenditures. It is natural for us as individuals to consider federal government finance as it affects us directly in terms of the taxes we ourselves pay, the government services we ourselves enjoy, and the government bonds we ourselves own. But the real importance of government finance lies not in these things. It lies in the consequences for all of us of the taxes *everyone* pays, and in the effect upon us of the *total* government debt and the *total* government expenditures.

Government financial policy benefits or hurts us all by the way in which it helps to answer the following questions:

What are our prospects for steady employment and income?
What are the risks that inflation will reduce the buying power of our income and our savings?
Will we have the opportunity to enjoy during our lifetime a continuing improvement of our standard of living such as our parents and grandparents knew in theirs?
Will we and our children have the opportunity for continued enjoyment of the blessings of a free society?

These are vital questions. They constitute the fundamental tests by which government financial policy and action must be judged. This policy statement explains the connection between government finance and economic progress, freedom and stability and presents a program to serve these objectives. The program consists of two related parts: a) budgetary policy to set the proper relation between government expenditures and government receipts, and b) tax policy to raise the

* Part I. Reprinted by the courtesy of the Committee for Economic Development.

† A Statement on National Policy by the Research and Policy Committee of the Committee for Economic Development. 1947.

necessary revenues in the ways most appropriate to the objectives. Economic stability and progress in a free society require sound public policy not only in taxation and the budget but also in other areas—including money and credit, management of the debt and labor-management relations. These subjects and others are now being studied under the CED Research Program. The recommendations of this policy statement are offered as part of a rounded program of government and private action which must be developed for a solution of our basic economic problems.

Government Financial Policy, High Employment and Stable Prices

The level of employment and prices is governed largely by the total demand for goods and services. Total demand is the combined amount that individuals, businesses, governments and foreign purchasers are willing and able to buy. Both "willingness" and "ability" are essential. No amount of money or credit or income would be large enough to assure adequate demand if individuals and businesses were not willing to use it for consumption or investment. There must be ability to buy—but ability to buy does not alone create demand.

When total demand exceeds the output that can be produced with the available materials, labor and equipment—as it has since the start of the war—prices rise, and we suffer the now-familiar evils of inflation. When total demand is inadequate to buy the output that would be produced by a fully employed labor force—as it was in the 30's—we have depression, unemployment and falling prices. *An essential condition for high employment and stable prices is reasonable stability of total demand at an adequate level—which means a steadily rising level of demand as our productive capacity grows.*

The level of total demand is the composite product of millions of individual decisions to spend or invest which are made by consumers, businesses and governments. The federal government cannot possibly control these decisions, and a system in which the government tried to exercise such control would be intolerable to freedom-loving people. But the government cannot help influencing these decisions that affect total demand through its taxes, expenditures and borrowing—its fiscal policy.

A major factor in the decisions of individuals and businesses to spend or invest is the amount of income they have available. In collecting taxes the government subtracts from the available income of individuals and businesses. On the other hand, federal expenditures add to the incomes available for private expenditure. By its policy with respect to the amount and timing of these subtractions from and additions to private income, the government inevitably influences the separate decisions of millions of individuals.

Many of the decisions that enter into total demand are based not so much upon current available income as upon the prospect for future earnings. This is particularly true of business decisions to invest—to launch new products, to build new plants, to buy new machinery. The question here is whether the investment seems likely to yield to the investor a return sufficient to compensate for the risks and costs involved. In these decisions federal tax policy—especially through the rates and character of taxes on profits—bears a heavy weight.

The size of the public debt, its form, and who holds it also are important factors affecting individual and business expenditure. For instance, if the government sells savings bonds to the public, and uses the proceeds to retire bonds held by the banks, individuals will have less cash and are likely to buy less.

In addition to influencing private demand in these various ways, the government directly controls another large part of total demand—its own demand for goods and services. The federal government is by far the largest single employer of labor and purchaser of supplies. Although government expenditure should decline, it will remain large enough to have a great influence upon the adequacy of total demand.

Fiscal policy is not a panacea for all the problems of maintaining high employment and price stability. Even perfect stability of total demand, if it could be achieved, would not eliminate all fluctuations in employment or the general level of prices. Nor can fiscal action by itself achieve complete stability of total demand. Since we are dealing with the independent decisions of millions of separate units—in a free economy this will always be true—fiscal policy cannot completely iron out fluctuations in total demand. The picture of an all-wise expert precisely manipulating the keys of the fiscal instrument to produce a perfect harmony of stable demand is sheer, and dangerous, fantasy. But if we manage our fiscal affairs as well as we know how, duly recognizing their impact on employment and prices, we shall be contributing much more than ever before to a continuing high level of economic activity. And if we supplement this with intelligent behavior in other fields, such as money, banking and foreign trade, we may reasonably expect to maintain a high level of productive employment.

Fiscal Policy and Economic Progress

During the past century, the real output produced by an hour's work in the United States has approximately doubled in each generation. This rapid—unparalleled—growth of productivity has been a major source of America's strength. It has meant more than a continuous improvement of the material welfare of the American people. Every sector of the population has been able to look forward to further improvement simultaneously with other sectors, and not at the expense of other groups; economic progress has been important in reducing potential friction among groups. Moreover, America's lead in productivity on two occasions has enabled a non-militarist democracy to overcome the armed challenge of militarist dictatorships.

Two essentials for economic progress are: *a*) *the willingness of individuals to devote effort, imagination and capital to increased production, more efficient production and the production of new things, and b*) *the supply of capital ready to move into the frontiers of economic development.* In the United States both of these factors have been abundant. The American system has held forth the chances of large rewards to persons who would turn their efforts or funds to economic development. This *chance* for large rewards was the driving force behind countless ventures. Many of them failed but large numbers succeeded, in smaller or greater measure, and pushed upward the curve of economic progress. The profits from the successful enterprises constituted a large flow of capital into the hands of venturesome, energetic, imaginative persons willing to risk this capital in further development. The point is not merely that we had a large supply of savings; the savings were attracted to participate in the *risks* of economic enterprise.

Today our economy faces a new situation. Except in war or its aftermath, we have never endured taxes as high as we now face. This means that federal taxes will be taking a much larger proportion than ever before of the income that must provide the incentives to individual enterprise and the sources of private capital investment. We cannot hope to return in the near future to tax levels as low as those before the war. But we must do our utmost to reduce taxes by economy in government expenditure, and we must distribute the remaining burden in the ways least damaging to progress.

Fiscal Policy and Freedom

Fiscal policy, because of its effects upon employment, prices and progress, has a direct relation to the preservation of our freedoms. There is danger that if we fail to achieve the goals of stability and progress by methods appropriate to a free society the public may turn to measures of control inimical to freedom without realizing their consequences. It is not only our own freedoms that are at stake. The world looks to the United States for a demonstration of the ability of a free society to solve its basic economic problems.

There is another vital way in which fiscal policy affects the survival of a free society. A free society must have a competitive, decentralized economy. In such an economy the power of any individual to make decisions affecting the welfare of others—decisions as to prices, wages and output—is limited by the existence of actual or potential competitors in the market.

Essential to a competitive economy is "A climate in which new, small and independent business can be conceived and born, can grow and prosper . . . If the opportunities for new business are destroyed or otherwise disappear, a system of free enterprise will atrophy."[1]

A tax system that discourages new and independent business and arrests the growth of established businesses therefore is a threat to a free economy and a free society. The present tax system does this. It bears most heavily upon those characteristics most likely to be associated with newness, independence, growth and competitive vigor in business. It erects a barrier to the success of businesses that are especially risky, that have widely fluctuating earnings, or that are highly dependent upon internal financing. By creating a tax system that will be fair to all businesses we can contribute greatly to the vitality of our free society.

I. BUDGETARY POLICY

In Section II of this Policy Statement we shall offer recommendations for raising the necessary government revenues in the most appropriate way. In the present section we shall consider the requisites of a budgetary policy—a policy with respect to the relation between total government revenues and total expenditures—to achieve the basic objectives we have outlined.

The Principles of Budgetary Policy

Four considerations are of supreme importance in the development of budgetary policy:

a) *Federal finance should help to make fluctuations in total demand less severe, and thus aid in stabilizing employment and prices.* When total demand exceeds total supply and inflationary conditions prevail, the effect of federal finance should be to restrain demand. When total de-

---

[1] William Benton, "The Economics of a Free Society," CED Supplementary Paper, *Fortune,* Oct. 1944.

mand is low, when unemployment is high and prices falling, the effect of taxation and expenditure should be to stimulate demand.

b) *Budgetary policy should serve to restrain unnecessary government expenditure and to stimulate efficiency in government.* Everyone agrees that economy in government is important. But the *achievement of economy* requires that our *belief in economy* be effectively directed against the particular pressures that always will be found in support of particular expenditures. Budgetary policy can be an effective force for economy if we harness the legitimate and specific interest in lower taxes to the general interest in economy. Every proposal that would expand government functions should pass the test of society's willingness to pay for it in taxes.

c) *Budgetary policy should provide for the reduction of the public debt under conditions of reasonably high employment and production.* The interest charge on the debt now accounts for about ten per cent of our federal tax load. Surely we cannot think that these taxes are burdenless because we pay the proceeds to ourselves in interest. The deterrent effects of high taxes upon risk-taking and incentives to effort are not at all offset by the payment of interest on government debt; interest on the government debt is not the kind of income that is most important to reward or stimulate private effort or enterprise.

d) *Budgetary policy should recognize that it takes a long time to make most fiscal decisions and achieve their effects, and that the present state of our ability to forecast economic fluctuations is still very low.* Any fiscal program that relies for its success upon prompt response and adjustment to known economic changes through a series of separate decisions, or upon accurate forecasting of future fluctuations, invites failure.

There are some particular measures that can be initiated so quickly and, if necessary, reversed so promptly that they involve only short and relatively safe forecasts. But success in the year-to-year operation of most elements of fiscal policy requires that minimum reliance be placed upon forecasting economic fluctuations.

What's in the Budget?

Before we can decide on budgetary policy, it is necessary to make clear what we mean by "the budget."

There are two "budgets" of the federal government officially compiled and in current use. These are the administrative budget and the consolidated-cash budget. The administrative budget does what the budget system was first created to do—to enable the Congress and the

President to control the expenditures and operations of the hundreds of agencies that constitute the federal government. It does this by stating in detail the funds appropriated to each agency and purpose, the obligations incurred for expenditure under each of these heads, and the amounts spent out of each fund, including amounts paid or transferred to other accounts. Beyond this administrative function, this budget, together with its supplementary statements, serves another purpose. It presents an accounting statement of the financial relations of the various federal agencies, corporations and trust accounts to the public and to each other.

The other budget—the consolidated-cash budget—is designed for quite a different purpose. It shows the government's financial transactions as they affect the whole economy—the expenditures that absorb goods and services or add to private incomes, the receipts that subtract from private incomes, and deficits or surpluses that add to or subtract from the public's holdings of money and government bonds.

The dollars that affect demand are the dollars paid to or taken from the public, not the dollars transferred from one government account to another. Therefore, in the consolidated-cash budget all transactions between one part of the government and another are excluded. And since the transactions that are significant for total demand are those that involve receipt or payment of money, this budget is on a "cash" basis. All cash transactions between the government—and this includes all government agencies, corporations, and trust accounts—and the public are shown. It excludes all transactions not involving payment of money to the public or receipt of money from the public.

The recommendations of this policy statement are framed throughout with reference to the consolidated-cash budget.

In recent budget messages of the President a statement of the federal accounts on a consolidated-cash basis has been utilized as supplementary information to make clear the relationship of federal financial operations to the economy. The consolidated-cash budget has also been used in the President's Economic Reports as the significant representation of the economic effects of federal finance. In its policy statement, "Fiscal Policy to Fight Inflation" (September, 1946), the Research and Policy Committee of CED based its quantitative recommendations on this budget. Other business organizations and non-governmental groups concerned with the impact of federal finance upon the economy have turned increasingly to the picture shown by the consolidated-cash budget. A few illustrations will show the nature of the distinction between the two budgets.

Because the consolidated-cash budget excludes all intra-government transactions, it does not show as an expenditure the transfers from the general government accounts to, for example, the trust accounts set up for the operation of the social security system. Such transactions are important to the administrative budget for recording the status of the various accounts in relation to each other. But the transfers are not transactions with important current economic effects.

At the same time, there are billions of dollars of receipts and expenditures that appear in the consolidated-cash budget but are not included in the administrative budget. The outstanding case is the payroll tax receipts and expenditures of the social security system. Present legal and accounting relations between the general government and the trust accounts are best revealed if these transactions are shown separately from other receipts and expenditures. But if we want to weigh the effects of the budget upon private purchasing power, total demand, employment and prices, the budget must include these important collections and payments.

The "cash" character of the consolidated-cash budget is illustrated by the treatment of the issue and redemption of veterans' terminal leave bonds. For fiscal 1947 the administrative budget included as an expenditure about $2 billion to reflect the issue of these non-negotiable non-cashable bonds in that year. Their economic effect was small; in fact, terminal leave was paid in this form to prevent the payment from having inflationary consequences. The consolidated-cash budget did not include this item as an expenditure. In fiscal 1948, when about $1.5 billion of these bonds are being turned into cash, much of which will be used for consumption, the administrative budget shows no expenditure in this account. But the fiscal 1948 consolidated-cash budget does include this $1.5 billion payment because it is now actually being put into the hands of individuals as expendable income.[2]

The size of the net difference between the two budgets varies from year to year. Thus, in fiscal 1947, the surplus in the consolidated-cash budget was almost $6 billion larger than the surplus in the administrative budget. But, by contrast, official estimates are that the consolidated-cash surplus in fiscal 1948 will be $5.5 billion and the administrative surplus $4.7 billion—a difference of $800 million. (The indicated surplus for calendar 1948 is much larger.) Under some

---

[2] Similarly, the consolidated-cash budget shows interest on savings bonds as an expenditure when it is paid in cash, while the administrative budget includes the interest as it accrues. In both budgets taxes are included in receipts when collected, not when the liability accrues.

conditions the consolidated-cash surplus would be smaller than the administrative surplus. Many of the differences between the two budgets relate to the time at which various transactions are recorded; over a reasonably long period—say ten years—these differences would cancel out. At present, the most important *persistent* difference between the two budgets is in the treatment of the social security trust accounts. Over a ten year period, the consolidated-cash surplus would exceed the administrative surplus by approximately the amount of surplus in the social security accounts. If the social security system were set up so that its expenditures and receipts balanced over a moderate period, the average surplus in the consolidated-cash budget would be roughly the same as the average surplus in the administrative budget.[3]

The Three Alternatives in Budget Policy

There are three distinct alternatives in budgetary policy:

1. *The annually-balanced budget policy.* This policy attempts to keep government revenues continuously equal to or in excess of government expenditures, regardless of economic conditions.

2. *The managed compensatory budget policy.* Under this policy, attempts would be made to adjust tax rates and expenditure programs as often as necessary and to the extent necessary to keep employment or the national income steady at a high level.

3. *The stabilizing budget policy.* This policy is described herein, and advocated as the most practical method of achieving all the objectives of budgetary policy. Its basic principle is to set tax rates to balance the budget and provide a surplus at agreed high levels of employment and national income and thereafter to leave them alone unless there is some major change in national policy or condition of national life.

Annual Budget Balancing

The annual-balance policy cannot be made to work, and the effort to make it work accentuates inflations and depressions. With its inevitable breakdown fiscal policy becomes a mere day-to-day expedient.

This program requires that, whenever a decrease in the national income is forecast, tax rates must be raised or expenditures cut, or both,

---

[3] The consolidated-cash budget bears no relation to the "dual budget" or "capital budget" system sometimes proposed during the depression. These budgets called for division of government expenditures into two categories, one to include all expenditures that resulted in "capital assets," such as public buildings or dams. This system moved in exactly the opposite direction from the consolidated-cash budget, which seeks to present a unified picture of the transactions that have important economic effects, without regard to financial or functional differences.

to prevent a budget deficit. Whenever the forecast of higher national income promises larger surpluses, it not only permits but invites a cut in tax rates and a rise in expenditure programs. On the record, the program meant tax cuts in the prosperous 20's, and tax increases in the depressed 30's.

The implications of such a program are clear:

a) Tax rates and expenditure programs will be changed at times and in directions most harmful to high employment and stable prices. When incomes are low and unemployment is widespread, tax rates must be raised and government expenditures cut. In boom times the program welcomes tax reductions and new expenditures.

b) Annual budget-balancing policy does not in the long run promote government economy. The program allows a growth of public expenditure in boom times, without any increase of tax rates, even with a decrease in tax rates. The policy does not furnish steady pressure against the initiation of unnecessary expenditures; the pressure it does provide, to end entrenched expenditure programs in depressions, is certain to be ineffective.

c) The system dissipates the potentially large surpluses of good times and strives vainly for balance in bad times. In a fluctuating economy this program will not result in debt reduction.

d) To carry out the program requires a degree of accuracy in forecasting fluctuations in business activity that has not been achieved in the past and that is not possible now.

e) The program involves irregular and unpredictable variations of tax rates, with unsettling effects upon business and personal planning.

The Managed Compensatory Budget Policy

The theory of the managed compensatory budget is simple. Whenever employment is judged "about to be" below a high level, taxes should be cut and expenditures increased by the amount necessary to prevent the forecast from coming true. Whenever prices seem "about to be" above the proper level, tax rates must be raised and expenditures cut.

Dependence upon accurate forecasting of business fluctuations is even greater for the compensatory budget than for the annually-balanced budget. If forecasting is inaccurate, the compensatory budget could easily increase fluctuations rather than moderate them.

Like the annually balanced budget system, the compensatory program encourages increased expenditure programs without higher tax rates at some stage of the business cycle. However, whereas the annually balanced budget plan opens the door to new spending in boom times, the compensatory plan opens the door in depression—actual or forecast. In either case the effect upon government economy is likely to be the same—periods of rapid increases in spending, followed by futile efforts at retrenchment and a generally excessive upward drift of expenditures.

If the managed compensatory system is to make any progress towards reducing the debt, it must count upon creating large surpluses in prosperous periods by raising taxes and cutting expenditures. But expenditures resist downward change and taxes resist upward change. In the present state of economic forecasting, it will always be possible to make out a plausible case that depression is around the corner. Such a prediction will permit both unpleasant alternatives to be avoided, since under the managed compensatory theory the forecast of depression requires lower tax rates and higher expenditures. This system offers no realistic hope of debt reduction.

Under this plan, as under the annual-balance plan, tax rates are subject to frequent and unsettling changes.

The Stabilizing Budget Policy: What It Is

The key to a program that will promote stability, government economy and debt reduction without requiring impossible accuracy of forecasting business fluctuations is this:

Set tax rates to balance the budget and provide a surplus for debt retirement at an agreed high level of employment and national income. Having set these rates, leave them alone unless there is some major change in national policy or condition of national life.

Tax *rates,* by themselves, do not determine how much revenue will be collected. The *rates* merely say, for example, that revenue will be $9 per gallon of liquor sold, $38 per $100 of corporate profits, $50 per $100 of individual taxable income within a certain bracket, and so on. How much will be collected with these rates depends upon the amount of liquor sold, the amount of corporate profits, and the amount of individual incomes. Since all of the important elements of the tax base are closely related to the national income, collections under any system of unchanging tax rates will be larger as the national income rises and smaller as the national income falls.

Some kinds of government expenditures also tend to vary automatically with economic conditions. Unemployment compensation payments are the outstanding case. When unemployment rises these payments also rise, and when unemployment drops the payments decline. In addition, some expenditures—such as public works—may be advanced or held back to meet changing economic conditions within the limits of an agreed total expenditure program.

With tax rates set to yield a moderate surplus at high-employment national income, larger surpluses will result when the national income is above that level. At lower national incomes the surplus will be smaller and below some point there will be deficits.

Under this system, surpluses arising when national income goes above the standard high-employment level should not be used to increase expenditures. Likewise, a reduction of tax rates without a corresponding reduction of expenditures would be contrary to the policy, regardless of the *actual* surplus at the *actual* national income (subject to exceptions that will be stated below).

A direct consequence of the stabilizing budget principle is that fluctuations in the national income do not call for fluctuations in tax rates, or in expenditures except for the automatic response of some expenditure items. However, changes in tax rates or expenditures will be appropriate under some circumstances. If, for example, improvement of the international situation should lead to a substantial reduction in annual expenditure for defense, a lowering of tax rates would be appropriate. Similarly, if a new program is to be adopted that will substantially raise the annual level of federal spending, higher tax rates will be required.

Three exceptions should be noted to the general principle that tax *rates* and expenditures should only change up or down in step with each other:

1) With a growing population and rising productivity, the national income at high employment will gradually rise. Therefore, the yield of a constant system of tax rates at the standard high-employment national income will also slowly and steadily increase. This gradual increase of tax yield will permit, without higher tax rates, some gradual increase in normal government expenditure that may accompany the growth of the population and the national income. Moreover, as the economy grows into higher income levels, the amount of debt reduction consistent with high employment and stable prices may increase also; if so, the increased yield of the tax system should be retained for that purpose. Any readjustment of tax rates made possible by the long-time growth of the tax base should be made at reasonable intervals, say five years, in order to avoid the unsettling effects of annual rate changes.

2) From time to time an urgent need may arise for an extraordinary expenditure that is large in amount but known to be temporary. It would probably be undesirable to raise tax rates sharply in order to finance such expenditures currently, and then to cut tax rates when the expenditure ceases. A plan for meeting these expenditures over a somewhat longer period would therefore be appropriate. This plan might take the form of a smaller tax rate increase, extended over a longer period. If the expenditure is in the form of loans, the repayments may provide the source from which the expenditure will, in the end, be met. Whatever the plan for ultimately financing the expenditure, any im-

mediate inflationary consequences of the expenditure should be offset by anti-inflationary borrowing. Outlays under a program for foreign rehabilitation may fall within this exception.

3) The recommendations of this report are presented in the belief that, if they are combined with appropriate measures in other fields, economic fluctuations can be confined to moderate departures from a high level. Yet it would be foolhardy to ignore the possibility that we may again confront an economic crisis of great magnitude—either severe depression or major inflation. Some extraordinary action must and will be taken if such a crisis appears. An emergency Congressional reduction or increase in tax rates (perhaps with a fixed, automatic termination date) would then be one of the most effective and least dangerous of the available courses.

How the Stabilizing Budget Policy Works. The policy recommended here cannot be "adopted" and left to run without common sense and vigilance. Basically, we are presenting the principles that are important in making the decisions that must be made. The policy will not yield the results of which it is capable unless the principles are consistently followed and reasonably interpreted.

Any policy faces the danger that those responsible for administering it will not accept it or, giving lip-service to it, will seek to evade its intent. This is not a peculiarity of the policy recommended here. The first essential for the success of any policy is the existence of a *will* to carry it out. But it would be undue cynicism, unjustified by experience, to believe that reasonable adherence to principles is unattainable.

The policy of the stabilizing budget is more likely to be consistently followed than either of the alternative policies, simply because it is easier. It does not call for unachievable accuracy in forecasting economic fluctuations or impossible speed in action. It does not seek to impose an intolerable and unattainable increase of tax rates in the face of unemployment and shrinking income.

The enactment of the Legislative Reorganization Act in 1946 provides basis for confidence in the development of a determination by the government to carry out a policy such as is recommended here. The most important feature of the Act, from the standpoint of this program, is that it recognizes the need for a Congressional fiscal program as distinguished from a series of unrelated fiscal actions. This Act and the Employment Act of 1946 gave us for the first time Congressional mechanisms that begin to approach adequacy for formulating and executing a Congressional budget. These mechanisms need to be strengthened and improved. Particularly, responsibility needs to be centered upon the majority party to adopt a legislative budget and to follow it in appropriations and tax legislation. But at least a start has been made toward the development of new Congressional machinery that can make possible an integrated Congressional fiscal policy.

At present, the President submits to the Congress each year a budget of estimated receipts and disbursements under existing and proposed expenditure authorizations and tax laws. The four revenue and appropriations committees of the two Houses of Congress, acting jointly, then prepare a legislative budget. The committees present their recommended budget, including estimates of total receipts and expenditures, to the two Houses for adoption. When adopted, this budget serves as a guide to Congressional action on appropriations and taxes.

Aside from the improvements of this procedure that are needed to make *any* fiscal policy work, the stabilizing budget policy involves three changes from present practice:

1) The budget used by the President and the Congress in decisions on total receipts and expenditures should be the consolidated-cash budget, rather than the administrative budget.

2) Estimates of revenue yield from existing or recommended taxes should be based on a high-employment national income, rather than upon a forecast or arbitrarily selected national income.

3) The program recommended here suggests a standard to be followed by the President and the Congress in deciding upon the relation between total receipts and total expenditures. That standard is that the consolidated-cash budget should show a moderate surplus at an agreed high-employment level of national income. There does not now seem to be any standard generally accepted or consistently applied.

How the Stabilizing Budget Policy Promotes Economic Stability. The automatic change in tax collections and government outlays with fluctuations in the national income is an essential feature of the program recommended here. This kind of variation is precisely what is required if fiscal policy is to aid economic stability. When employment, production and prices rise, national income will rise. As the national income rises, tax collections will rise, taking more and more from the available income of the public. At the same time, outlays under such programs as unemployment compensation will fall. This process will restrain increases of demand and curb inflationary pressure. Similarly, the automatic decline of tax revenue acts to check a downward movement. When production and income drop, tax collections will fall too. Income after taxes will decline less than income before taxes. This will help to sustain production and employment. The stabilizing effect will be reinforced by an increase in unemployment compensation and other payments.

In other words, *with stable tax rates* variations in tax yields and outlays will tend to cushion variations in available incomes, after tax, and thereby to lessen fluctuations in demand and production. This is not new, but its importance has grown greatly since before the war for the following reasons:

1) Even with strenuous efforts for economy, federal taxes for some time will be much higher in relation to the national income than they were before the war.

2) Greater reliance upon the progressive income tax means greater relative change in tax collections with any change in national income. When a wage-earner goes on part-time work, for example, his consumption of tobacco, gasoline, and other commodities subject to excise taxation is unlikely to fall to zero, or even to fall in proportion to his loss of income. But his income tax is very likely to fall to zero and will certainly fall relatively more than his income.

3) The pay-as-you-go, withholding method of income tax payments has greatly shortened the time between a drop in an individual's income and the consequent reduction in his income tax payments. For most taxpayers, changes in income and changes in tax are simultaneous.

4) Unemployment compensation is new and has only recently begun to approach its potentialities as a stabilizing force. Unemployment compensation benefits under present laws would increase about $175 million per year for every million increase in unemployment, and this amount would be higher if desirable extensions of coverage and improvements of benefits were made.

These developments have given us an instrument, which, *if we allow it to operate,* will be a new, powerful force for economic stability.

The great advantage of the automatic corrective response of tax revenues and expenditures is this: *It does not depend for its stabilizing effect upon an impossible accuracy in forecasting economic fluctuations or an impossible speed in making fiscal decisions and taking fiscal action.*

Public Works and Conservation. It is probably now generally agreed that what can be done toward stabilizing the economy by varying the timing of public construction and conservation expenditures is fairly small, in relation to the total problem. But once its limitations are recognized, the programming of public works and conservation projects can make a valuable contribution. Both money and resources will be economized if the government, or any other public or private body with stable prospects, concentrates its building in periods when total construction activity is low. At the same time, this will make for the stability of the construction industry and indirectly of the whole economy.

Success in such a program will depend upon the quality of advance preparations. As far as possible, financial, engineering and administrative arrangements should be completed on a reserve of diverse projects to be started quickly when necessary. The scope of useful action will be expanded by coordination of federal plans with those of state and local governments.

There are two clear dangers in a federal program of this sort. First, attempts to apply the principle to projects involving a long construction period may result in federal construction in fact reaching its peak when other construction activity is high. Second, the counter-cyclical program can be made the excuse for commitments to continuing programs of a character, location and volume that are inappropriate for the federal government. These dangers can be avoided in a program of modest size, but their avoidance will require constant attention, both by the executive departments and the Congress.

How the Stabilizing Budget Policy Promotes Economy. No budget rule can be a substitute for a real interest in government economy and efficiency. But if interest in economy exists, adherence to sound fiscal principles can help restrain unnecessary expenditure. Under the program recommended here, a proposed increase of expenditures will require raising tax rates.[4] The social costs of particular undertakings will become sharply visible in the form of higher tax rates. It may then be possible to bring these costs properly into balance with the social gains of expenditure when decisions are made.

With the stabilizing budget policy, the close link between expenditures and tax *rates* will be kept at all stages of the business cycle. A high national income and an extraordinary surplus will not mean that additional expenditures should be assumed without an increase of tax rates. Nor will the fact that unemployment exists or is forecast justify the addition of new federal expenditures without higher tax rates, except perhaps in extreme circumstances.

The surest road to economy is to prevent the initiation of unnecessary expenditure programs. *No policy that invites or permits new expenditures at any stage of the business cycle merely because they appear painless to the taxpayer can hope in the long run to result in government economy. The really frightening possibility is that we shall oscillate between adherence to the annual balance principle in prosperity and belief in compensatory spending in depression. This could only mean an endless ascent to higher and higher government spending, both in prosperity and depression.*

---

[4] Certain exceptions to this principle have been noted (a) to the extent of the growth of tax yields with the rise of population and productivity, (b) for large temporary disbursements, and (c) for advancing the execution of public works and conservation in a time of depressed total construction activity.

How the Stabilizing Budget Policy Promotes Debt Reduction. Will adherence to the stabilizing budget policy in fact result in reduction of the debt over a reasonable period of time? The answer to this question depends upon two factors: the standard level of income at which the budget is set to yield a surplus, and the level of income that actually prevails. If the actual income level on the average exceeds the level at which the yield of the tax system equals the expenditures, the debt will be reduced. If on the average the national income falls short of this level, the debt will be increased. Budgetary policy alone—the determination of tax rates and expenditure programs—cannot assure debt reduction. It can only establish the conditions under which the debt would be reduced.

Tax rates could be set high enough to yield a surplus even at a very low level of national income. If this were done, the debt might be reduced despite the prevalence of large-scale unemployment. But, in this case, the budget would exert a repressive force upon the economy in depressed conditions, as it did in the 30's, and would itself contribute to unemployment and a low level of income. While such a program is conceivable, it is certainly not a satisfactory solution to the problem of the debt, and it is unlikely that such a program could survive the pressures that mass unemployment would create, as past experience has shown.

The policy recommended here is to set tax rates high enough to yield a moderate surplus at a high level of employment, and to utilize fully all appropriate means to assure that high employment is maintained. Such a program recognizes the interdependence of all aspects of economic policy.

A sound structure of taxes would be a major contribution to debt reduction under the program laid down here. Collecting the needed revenues in the ways that are least restrictive of private demand for goods and services will assist in the maintenance of high employment along with debt reduction. Other measures that would have similar effects include action in the field of money and banking, the management of the debt, farsighted policy by business and labor in their attitude towards technical progress and productivity, arrangements to improve the flow of savings into constructive investment, and many other instruments. These subjects are under study by the CED as part of its research program on high employment. From the work already done, we are confident that—with reasonably good sense—levels of employment can be maintained that will reduce the debt under this program.

The Committee recommends that tax rates be set sufficiently high to *yield a surplus of about $3 billion at a national income corresponding to employment of about 96 per cent of the labor force. With a labor force of the present size, this would mean a $3 billion surplus if unemployment is about 2.5 million. The budget would balance when unemployment is approximately 4 to 4.5 million.*

These precise figures cannot be rigorously defended against other figures in the same neighborhood and some adjustments may be indicated after the system has been in operation. However, the appropriate figures cannot be far away in either direction. Actual unemployment may, from time to time, lie below 4 per cent, as it does now; it probably cannot be much below this figure without serious inflationary pressure. With 4 per cent unemployment, most involuntary idleness is of the between-jobs variety. To set tax rates so that the budget yields a moderate surplus only at a higher income level would therefore mean that debt would be reduced only under conditions which it should be public policy to avoid. On the other hand, tax rates high enough to reduce debt at a much lower income level would put deflationary pressure on the economy, and promote unemployment.

The Management of the Debt

The Committee intends to issue a separate policy statement discussing the management of the debt. Here we wish to emphasize only that the success of the budget policy we are recommending will be strongly influenced by the effectiveness of debt management.

Most people regard the federal debt as a single undifferentiated total. They think of debt policy as simply using the surplus to pay the debt.

There are in fact many different kinds of federal debt—some held by the public and some held by banks, some long-term and some short-term, some marketable and some not. These different kinds of debt differ in their economic effects—such as their effects on inflation and deflation. With the debt at its present size the differentiations are extremely important.

The problem of debt management is to choose the kind of debt to retire when there is a surplus, and the kind of debt to issue when there is a deficit or when outstanding debt matures. These choices must be made with an understanding of their economic effects if we are to have both high employment and continuous debt reduction.

What Price Level?

Selection of the standard national income at which a surplus of a specified size is to be developed requires the selection of a price level, just as it requires the selection of an employment level. There is a fundamental difference, however, between selection of the employment level and selection of the price level. There are some employment levels, defined as percentages of the labor force, that are definitely better than others. It is better that 96% of the labor force should be employed, than only 80%. One does not have such a gauge for the price level. The virtues or defects of any particular price level are matters of relationships—relations to past price levels, to existing wage levels, and to foreign price levels, and the relations of particular prices to each other.

Probably the most important consideration in the choice of an initial price level is that the price level taken should be consistent with the maintenance of stable high employment. The lower the price level used in calculating the standard national income, the higher the tax rates that will be required. If the price level chosen is too low, the necessary tax rates may so restrict total demand as to make high employment impossible. A process of gradual adjustment may be needed before a tenable price level is determined.

There are great advantages in not changing the assumed price level once the system is in operation. The standard national income, in terms of which tax rates are set, must be simply and objectively determinable. This will be much easier if the same price level is used year after year. Moreover, certain kinds of change in the price level basis would defeat the stabilizing force of the system. For example, an inflationary increase in prices, with employment at a high level, should not be the signal for raising the *assumed* price level. To raise the assumed price level would lead to reducing the required tax rates and thus would feed the inflation. These presumptions do not rule out the possibility that under some conditions revision of the price level basis may be appropriate. But recognition of the value under most conditions of keeping that level stable would restrain arbitrary increases. It would help counteract the temptation that will always exist to raise the assumed price level in order to rationalize popular but economically injurious tax reductions.

24

Built-In Flexibility[*]

By R. A. MUSGRAVE *and* M. H. MILLER[†]

I

The essence of compensatory fiscal policy lies in adjusting the level of government receipts and expenditures so as to stabilize total income (and employment) in the economy. This requires an increase in expenditures and a reduction in tax revenue during periods of deflation and a decrease in expenditures and increase in tax revenue during periods of inflation. Such compensatory movements may be brought about by properly timed changes in expenditure programs and in tax rates, but to some extent they occur automatically. Certain public expenditures, such as unemployment benefits, are geared to move in a countercyclical fashion. Similarly, tax yields under given statutory rates will fluctuate with changes in the national income since the size of the tax base usually varies directly with the level of income. Recently, the automatically compensatory movement of tax revenues—generally referred to as "built-in flexibility"—has received increasing attention. The purpose of this note is to appraise its importance as a stabilization device.

II

The magnitude of the automatically compensatory adjustment will depend of course upon the dollar change in tax revenue resulting from a given dollar change in the national income, that is, upon the "marginal tax rate" and the problem might be formulated in terms of this marginal rate.[1] There is, however, a more detailed and for our purposes more useful way of stating the problem. The fiscal planner, from year to year, is confronted with setting an "average tax rate," that is, a rate

* *American Economic Review,* Mar. 1948. Reprinted by the courtesy of the American Economic Association and the authors.

The authors are indebted to Mr. Alfred Sherrard for his helpful suggestions and criticisms in the preparation of this note.

† University of Michigan and the Johns Hopkins University, respectively. Both formerly of the Board of Governors of the Federal Reserve System.

[1] For a statement of the problem in terms of the marginal rate see note 2 below.

which will raise the desired amount of tax revenue at the expected level of income. This total revenue can be raised by various combinations of statutory rates and tax sources, and different combinations will result in tax systems which possess different degrees of sensitivity of yield in response to changes in income. It is the selection of one of these combinations and of the rates necessary to produce the desired yield from the expected level of income that determines the extent of "built-in flexibility" or the marginal tax rate for the system as a whole. Consequently, the degree of flexibility will be analyzed in this note in terms of the level of taxation (average tax rate at the expected level of income) and the sensitivity to changes in income of the selected combination of tax sources.

To measure the effect of "built-in flexibility," it is useful to start with a simplified model which assumes that public expenditures are fixed and wholly for goods and services, that all taxes are in the form of a personal income tax, that there are no corporate savings in the economy and that the level of investment is independent of taxation. The expression for the *change* in income between two periods may then be written as

(1) $$\Delta Y = \Delta I + c\Delta Y - c(r_1Y_1 - r_2Y_2)$$

where ΔY equals $Y_1 - Y_2$ or the change in income from the first to the second period and ΔI equals $I_1 - I_2$ or the change in investment; (c) is the marginal propensity to consume out of disposable income which is assumed to remain constant; and (r_1) and (r_2) are the *average* rates of tax in the two periods.

The income elasticity (E) of the tax yield (T) is the ratio of the percentage change in tax yield to a given percentage change in income and may be expressed as

(2) $$E = \frac{(\Delta T)Y_1}{(\Delta Y)T_1}$$

Solving for ΔT and substituting the result for $(r_1Y_1 - r_2Y_2)$ in equation (1) gives

(3) $$\Delta Y = \Delta I \frac{1}{1 - c + cE\dfrac{T_1}{Y_1}}$$

and by substituting (r_1) for $\left(\dfrac{T_1}{Y_1}\right)$ we obtain[2]

[2] Expressing the relationship in terms of the marginal tax rate or (m) equation (1) is rewritten as

(4) $$\Delta Y = \Delta I \frac{1}{1 - c(1 - Er_1)}$$

As a convenient measure for the compensatory effectiveness of "built-in flexibility" we may then write

(5) $$\alpha = 1 - \frac{\Delta Y}{\Delta Y_a}$$

where ΔY refers to the change in income in the particular tax system under discussion (with its specific positive value for Er_1) and ΔY_a refers to a system where (E) is set equal to zero. That is, $\frac{\Delta Y}{\Delta Y_a}$ is the ratio of the decline (or increase) in income in the particular tax system under analysis to the decline (or increase) in income if the system had no "built-in flexibility"; and (α), which is one minus this ratio, is the *fraction of the change in income which is prevented because of the existence of "built-in flexibility."* If $\alpha = 0$, there is no built-in flexibility; if $\alpha = 1$, built-in flexibility is perfect, *i.e.,* total income remains unchanged.

Substituting (4) in (5) we have

(6) $$\alpha = 1 - \frac{1 - c}{1 - c(1 - Er_1)} = \frac{cEr_1}{1 - c + cEr_1}$$

Given the community's propensity to consume, (α) will thus vary directly with (r_1) and (E), the level of taxation and the income elasticity of the selected combination of tax sources. But "built-in flexibility" can never be so effective as to eliminate all change in income. However high the values for (E) and (r_1), (α) will be less than one in any economy whose propensity to consume is less than unity. As a practical matter, of course, (Er_1) could not exceed 1, that is a marginal tax rate of 100 per cent. At this extreme (α) would be equal to (c) and the investment multiplier would be fully offset (equation 4). The change in income before tax would be limited to the change in investment and income after tax would be stabilized.

In interpreting the concept (α) as here developed, it should be noted that (c) is not a variable in the same sense as (E) or (r_1). While the numerical value of (α) will increase as (c) increases, the absolute

---

(1a) $$\Delta Y = \Delta I + c\Delta Y - cm\Delta Y$$

and solving for Y,

(1b) $$\Delta Y = \Delta I \frac{1}{1 - c(1 - m)}$$

which of course is the same as (4) above because $(E) = \frac{m}{r_1}$.

amount of the remaining change in income will also be larger (equation 4). Consequently (α) has relevance only for comparing the effect of different tax systems in a single economy, all of whose other basic relations (including the value of [c]) are held constant.

III

Turning now to a consideration of the magnitude of (α) for various tax structures under ordinary conditions, the assumptions in the simplified model must be revised to take account of transfer payments, excise taxes and most important, corporate savings and taxes.

The introduction of transfer payments presents no particular difficulties. They may be handled either by introducing into equation (1) a new term which expresses consumption out of transfer payments or they may be treated as "negative taxes" reducing (r_1).[3] By extending the analysis in this fashion a new equation (4) may be derived which allows for "built-in flexibility" on both the revenue and expenditure sides of the budget.

The introduction of excise taxes raises no serious difficulty if they can be thought of as paid out of consumer expenditures, that is, as personal income taxes assessed on an expenditure basis. This procedure permits a measurement of their contribution to the flexibility of the tax structure but it does not account for the complications arising from the fact that excise taxes are reflected in the price level of output. These complications, however, do not bear significantly upon the major argument here developed and can be neglected for simplicity's sake.

Corporate profits and corporate income taxes may be introduced with a minimum of complication by treating corporations as unincorporated businesses. Total income is then defined as personal income plus corporate profits before tax (but after dividends which are already included in personal income) and (c) becomes the marginal propensity to consume out of disposable personal income plus retained corporate profits. The values for (E) and (r_1) would apply to the tax system as a whole, and (α) would measure the effect of "built-in flexibility" on the entire private sector of the economy.[4]

---

[3] For the simplest case where transfer expenditures are assumed constant, the decline in (r_1) would be offset by an increase in the value for (E) leaving (Er_1), the marginal tax rate, unaffected.

[4] The redefinition of (c) as the propensity to consume out of disposable income plus retained corporate profits has the disadvantage of making (c) more subject to changes in (Y) and more dependent upon the particular tax structure in use. Thus (c) will be lower if the corporation tax is lower and changes in the corporation tax share in total receipts will affect the value of (c). To a lesser extent, the same problem arises with respect to differences in the consumption impact of, say, highly progressive income taxes and highly re-

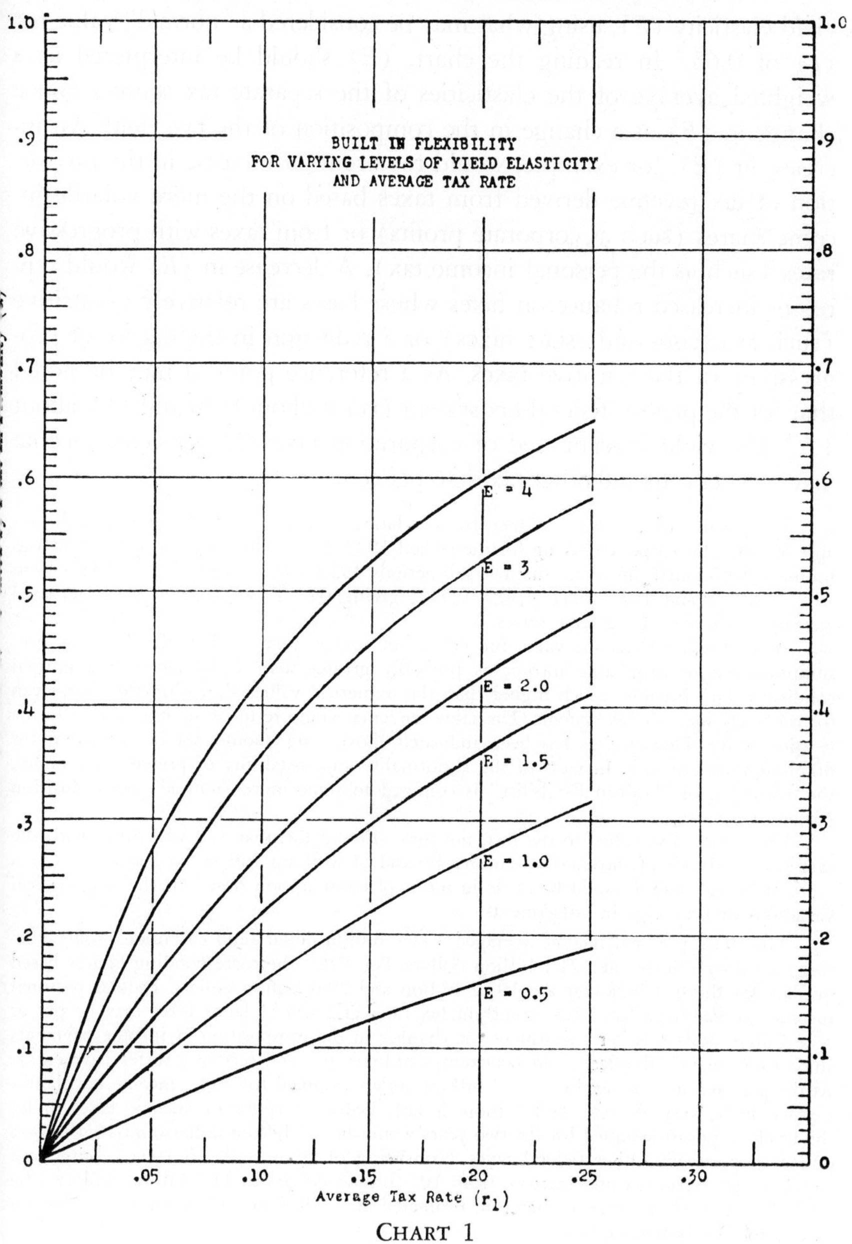

CHART 1

Chart 1 shows the value of (α) for the United States under normal conditions at various levels of tax yield (r_1) and for various degrees of

gressive spending taxes. For a fuller discussion of the implications of the differences in the consumption impact of various taxes see R. A. Musgrave, "Alternative Budgets for Full Employment," *Am. Econ. Rev.*, June 1945, Vol. XXXV, No. 3, p. 387.

yield elasticity (E), using what may be considered a "normal" value for (c) of 0.65.[5] In reading the chart, (E) should be interpreted as a weighted average of the elasticities of the separate tax sources and a change in (E) as a change in the composition of the tax yield. An increase in (E), for example, would represent an increase in the proportion of tax revenue derived from taxes based on the more volatile income shares (such as corporate profits) or from taxes with progressive rates (such as the personal income tax). A decrease in (E) would represent increased reliance on taxes whose bases are relatively insensitive (such as excises and estate taxes) or a reduction in the degree of progressivity of the sensitive taxes. As a reference point, it may be noted that for the present federal tax system (r_1) is about 0.20 and (E) about 1.5.[6] The yield is composed of corporation taxes 24 per cent; income taxes 50 per cent and other taxes 26 per cent.

---

[5] This value of (c) was obtained by correlating total net private saving with disposable income plus corporate saving for the period 1929–1941. This thirteen-year period was found to be divided into three distinct sub-periods 1930–1932 ($[c] = 0.74$); 1933–1936 ($[c] = 0.63$); and 1937–1941 ($[c] = 0.54$), giving 0.65 as an average. All data used were from the new Commerce series.

At the present time, the value for (c) is, of course, very much higher and for consumption out of disposable income is probably greater than 1. Under such abnormal conditions (α) becomes much higher than the numerical values shown on the chart even for relatively inelastic tax systems. The same tendency would result if an acceleration factor is allowed for. However, as has been indicated above, (α) should not be compared for different values of (c). In view of the abnormality and instability of present (c) values, the discussion of "built-in flexibility" is confined to some more "normal" post-transition period.

Attention is also called to the fact, not here allowed for, that (c) will differ with the rate and amplitude of income fluctuations. Instead of working with a fixed value of (c) a more elaborate analysis could be made in terms of consumption functions showing cyclical variations or time lags in adjustments.

[6] In 1946, personal income averaged 177.2 billion dollars and corporate profits (before inventory adjustment) 21.1 billion dollars. For 1947, the corresponding figures based on data for the first half year are 197.2 billion and 29.0 billion dollars. Federal personal income tax *liabilities* for 1946 at current tax rates and size of labor force may be put at 17.8 billion dollars (after adjustment for changes in the composition of income payments since 1946, mainly the decline in tax-exempt military pay and certain transfer payments). At the personal income level of 197.2 billion dollars assumed for 1947, income tax liabilities would be very close to 21.5 billion dollars. Federal corporation income taxes under the levels of profits assumed for the two years would be 7.3 billion dollars and 10.4 billion dollars respectively. Other federal taxes (consisting of estate and gift taxes, excises and social security taxes) would increase from 10.7 billion dollars to 11.2 billion dollars. The total change in tax revenue is therefore estimated at 7.7 billion dollars, from 35.4 billion dollars to 43.1 billion dollars.

For measuring (E), "total income" should be defined as personal income plus corporate profits before tax (but after dividends which are already included in personal income) giving 220.0 billion dollars for 1947 and 192.7 billion dollars for 1946. On this basis, (E) for the present federal tax system works out to be 1.46. It may be noted that this estimate for (E) would not be too greatly affected by moderate errors in estimates of the level of tax yields under the assumed income conditions. An underestimate by as large an amount as 2 billion dollars (which is rather unlikely) would raise (E) to about 1.8.

The chart shows that for an (r_1) of 0.20 and an (E) of 1.5, (α) will be 0.358, that is, somewhat more than a third of the change in income due to a change in investment will be offset by "built-in flexibility" at that yield level. Should revenues be reduced uniformly by 50 per cent to an (r_1) of 0.10 without changing the composition of the yield, (α) will fall to 0.218. On the other hand, the effectiveness of "built-in flexibility" could be maintained at the lower level of yield by raising the average elasticity to 3.0.

IV

These preliminary considerations suggest that "built-in flexibility" may be an important factor in maintaining stability over the long run if taxes take a large proportion of income and if income elastic taxes are relied upon. But the analysis here provided lends no justification to the view now growing in popularity that "built-in flexibility" can do the job alone and that deliberate countercyclical fiscal policy can be dispensed with. The computations of the value for (α), despite their roughness, show that even under optimistic assumptions as to yield flexibility, the automatic movement of tax yields can not offset the major portion of a decline in income and employment.[7] Moreover, it should be noted that "built-in flexibility" cuts two ways: If it is helpful in cushioning the downswing in a depression, it also serves to delay the return to a full-employment level of income.

Actually there is every prospect that the value for (Er_1) will decline in the post-transition period. The level of (r_1) will be determined largely by average budget needs over the cycle. These will tend to decline as a per cent of income, although remaining higher than the pre-war average. It is unlikely that much can be done to offset the fall in (r_1) by raising (E) through qualitative changes in the tax structure or its composition. In fact it is probable that (E) will be lowered somewhat as the tax system is modified to reduce the impact on "investment incentives."[8] The flexibility of the tax system might be increased if pro-

---

[7] Changing levels of unemployment benefit are the major item of flexibility on the expenditure side of the budget. If these are taken into account and using present rates of benefit payments, the value for (d) might be raised by from 5 to 10 points. The results would thus not be changed greatly.

[8] Much will depend upon what happens to the corporation tax rate and the share of the corporate tax in total receipts. Reduction of the corporate share in taxes will reduce (E) but reduction in the corporate rate applicable to dividends only would reduce (E) less than an equivalent reduction in the present uniform rate on profits because of the greater stability of dividends in comparison with total profits.

The value for (E) will also be decreased if weight is shifted from the personal income tax to the estate tax and if present exemption levels are maintained while upper surtax bracket rates are reduced faster than lower bracket rates. In the other direction, decreased

vision was made for automatic adjustments in tax *rates* with changes in income but this could hardly be called "built-in flexibility" in the usual sense of the term. Rather, it is a way of applying deliberate countercyclical adjustments in the rate of taxation and expenditures. Such adjustments must remain the primary reliance of fiscal policy when it appears (as it most certainly will) that the actual level of fluctuations passes tolerable limits.

---

reliance on excises would tend to raise (E) somewhat. To the extent that the various adjustments described are successful in raising the average level of investment and hence income over the cycle, this will tend to compensate for decreased flexibility as well as lessen the need for deliberate countercyclical adjustment.

25

The Government Budget and the Nation's Economic Budget[*]

By GERHARD COLM[†]

I. FROM GOVERNMENT BUDGETS TO NATIONAL ACCOUNTS

Traditional public finance policy used the government budget as its main tool of guidance. The government budget states the needs that are to be met by government expenditures and the means by which these expenditures are to be financed. Historically, the budget served two purposes: (1) it was designed to aid in the formulation and execution of government expenditure and financial programs; (2) it was designed to enable the parliament to control and supervise the financial operations of the government—it was the instrument by which the legislative "power of the purse" could be exercised. Most of the literature and debates concerning government budgets and budgeting stressed these two aspects up to perhaps a decade ago.

Stimulated by the experience of the Great Depression of the thirties and of the Second World War, a new aspect of government budgeting was developed more recently—the relationship of government budgets to the national economy. The *economic* role of government budgets was first emphasized when various nations struggled to get out of the depression. It was discovered that the government, by loan-financed or even tax-financed expenditures, can bolster the nation's active purchasing power and thereby contribute to the recovery of business activities. Various methods for measuring the economic effect of government expenditures were proposed and used in an experimental fashion. In the United States the terms "government net contribution" or the government's "net income-creating expenditures"[1] were used for measuring

* *Public Finance,* III, 1948. Reprinted by the courtesy of *Public Finance* and the author.

† National Planning Association; formerly Council of Economic Advisers, Executive Office of the President.

[1] See, for example, Alvin Hansen, *Fiscal Policy and Business Cycles* (New York, 1941).

the amount of income the government creates through its expenditures in excess of the income it absorbs through taxation.

An attempt to measure the impact of the government budgets on the economy by one such figure was obviously insufficient. Critics pointed out that government expenditures may add to the purchasing-power of consumers but at the same time unfavorably affect business investment. Also, there is not only an impact of government budgets on the economy, but an impact of the economy on the budgets which is neglected in the "net contribution" approach.

The search for an adequate measurement of the economic implications of budgetary policy was paralleled by a search for new principles of public finance. Annual balancing of the budget was no longer regarded as the supreme principle of budgeting; the conviction grew that government budgets, in their expenditure, tax and borrowing policy, should be directed towards making a contribution to a balanced economy. No concrete principle was developed for budgetary policy that could take the place of the simple and clear principle of budget balancing. But there was a groping for new modern budgetary principles and for statistical budgetary statements that could be used as practical guides of policy.

The Second World War brought a test of the new budget principles that had been sought. If during the depression it was good financial policy to create additional incomes through government spending, then it was good budget policy during the war to collect more taxes in order to counteract the inflationary pressure. As during the depression estimates were prepared to measure the desired anti-deflationary or "reflationary" effect of government budgets, so during the war estimates of the "inflationary gap" were made to show the amount of purchasing power that should be absorbed by taxation or additional saving.

The conscious use of fiscal policy as an anti-inflationary measure was the most significant difference between World War I and World War II financing. It was a first and positive test of a budgetary policy conducted in consideration of its effects on the flow of income and purchasing power. The war years also brought a remarkable progress in the official use of statistical tools needed for a fiscal policy of that character.

In Great Britain it brought forth the White Papers on National Income since 1941,[2] and in the Federal Budget of the United States, and more recently in the President's Economic Reports, it brought forth

[2] See, e.g., "National Income and Expenditures in the United Kingdom," 1938–1946. Cmd. 7099 (London, 1947).

statements on the Nation's Economic Budget.[3] Of course estimates of national income have been made for many decades. These documents are significant, however, because both in Great Britain and the United States they were released as official background for the formulation of fiscal and budgetary policy. They dramatize the adoption of new principles of budgetary policies and show that a new presentation of facts for guidance of such policies is needed.

While the depression and war experience demonstrated that budgetary policies can be a very powerful instrument in influencing the economy as a whole, combating deflationary or inflationary tendencies, these same experiences also proved that budgetary policy cannot do the whole job.

The American experience during the depression showed that government net spending did increase purchasing power in accord with theoretical expectations but failed to induce business investments and a self-supporting prosperity.

A wartime tax policy sufficient to offset all inflationary pressure would have had to be much more drastic than it actually was. In all probability it would have curtailed incentives to work and hurt more than promoted the war effort. Thus a compromise had to be made between the use of tax policies and direct controls for the stabilization of the economy. Irrespective of whether or not the best possible compromise between tax policies and other controls was made, it can be stated that relying exclusively on fiscal controls would not have been possible without serious harm to war production. The lesson to be drawn is that fiscal policy is an extremely potent instrument but cannot be used like a faucet that can be turned on and off to stabilize the economy as a whole.

Suggestions were made to replace the principle of budget balancing by the principle of requiring a fiscal policy designed to restore balance in the economy. On the basis of the depression and war experience, a more cautious formulation is preferred and it is demanded only that budgetary policy should *contribute* to a policy designed to balance the economy. Budgetary policy can only be one among several devices for that end.

The presentation of the Government Budget and the Nation's Economic Budget that was first included in the President's Budget Message of January 1944 portrayed developments in each of the major sectors

[3] In the Appendix a table of the Nation's Economic Budget is shown as an example of the type of presentation used in the messages and reports of the President of the United States.

of the economy, the household, business, government, and international relations. Such a statement can be used as an instrument for the appraisal of budgetary policies as well as other policies designed to affect economic conditions. These other than fiscal policies include, for instance, measures designed to influence prices, wages and profits, business investment, foreign trade, and many other policies carried out either by the government or by business, labor and other organized groups.

Budgetary policies are now recognized as one group among other groups of devices for promoting a balanced expansion of the economy. As guidance for such a policy, a system of national economic accounting is needed. Government transactions are just one of several accounts combined in the whole of the Nation's Economic Budget.

II. NATIONAL ECONOMIC BUDGETS: FORECASTS AND OBJECTIVES

The United States official statements which were referred to in the first section present national income and expenditure data for the most recent past. Strictly speaking, they are National Economic Accounts rather than National Economic Budgets. They are used, however, for drawing conclusions for the formulation of economic and fiscal policies for the future. In the published documents the projections into the future are made in the form of textual narrative rather than in figures. It is clear that these figures are presented as a basis for appraising "current and foreseeable trends," as the Employment Act of 1946 requires. In this respect denotion of these national accounts as "budgets" is an adequate expression of the way in which they are used and may be further developed.

For the formulation of fiscal and other economic policies, it would be very useful if national economic budgets for the future could be presented in the same way in which government budgets present estimates for the future. An earlier version of the "Full Employment Bill" provided that the President, at the beginning of each session of Congress, should transmit to the Congress (1) an estimate of a national economic budget objective under conditions of full employment for the ensuing year; (2) a national economic budget forecast estimated under the assumption that then existing legislation and policies would be continued; and (3) in case that there is a gap between the objective and what would be likely to happen under existing legislation and policies, a recommendation for legislation and policies, particularly government expenditure policies, needed to achieve the objective. These three elements of a national economic budget were retained in the Employment Act of 1946 as finally adopted, but the language no longer makes exact quantitative forecasts obligatory. The law, as enacted, requires statements by the President on (1) "needed levels of production, employment and purchasing power," (2) "current and foreseeable trends in the levels of employment, production and purchasing power," and (3) recommendation of a program of economic policies and legislation necessary for accomplishing the objective. Statements are no longer limited to the "ensuing year," leaving the possibility for longer-range programming. An appraisal of "foreseeable" trends does not necessarily involve quantitative forecasts. Such appraisal may very well envisage several alternative circumstances.

Another significant change in the final version of the Act was that government expenditure policies were no longer singled out, as in the original bill, as the final means for assuring continued full employment; the present Act simply refers to programs of economic policies. Nevertheless, the U.S. Employment Act does recognize that the determination of economic objectives and an appraisal of "foreseeable" trends are essential to furnish bases for the formulation of programs of economic policy and for the success of a full employment policy. These programs are to be recommended to the Congress by the President in the Economic Reports, which have to be prepared with the aid and assistance of the Council of Economic Advisers.

I do not propose in this article to deal with the many complex technical problems involved in the determination of economic objectives and the appraisal of foreseeable trends. In both respects much work has been done in the United States, as well as in other countries, during recent years. Economic forecasting yielded some encouraging results during the war, but official estimates made in the United States for the reconversion and postwar period proved erroneous to a considerable extent. The attrition of industry, the intensity of consumer backlog demand, and the need of foreign countries were underestimated.

Today economists, at least in this country, have much less confidence in their ability to make economic predictions than they had a few years ago. Much work is being done to improve methods of economic analysis and to provide more factual information, e.g., on business intentions and consumer attitudes. Studies of this sort, particularly carried on in Canada[4] and the United States,[5] are likely to improve our ability in economic forecasting.

In the United States, much of the economic forecasting is done by

[4] See "Forecast of 1947 Investment by Canadian Business," Department of Reconstruction and Supply (Ottawa, 1947).

[5] See "National Survey of Liquid Asset Holdings, Spending and Saving," particularly Part 3: "Prospective Spending and Saving," sponsored by the U.S. Board of Governors of the Federal Reserve System (Washington, D.C., 1946). More studies of the same character have been published in the *Federal Reserve Bulletin.*

private business economists and private business consultant services. There is, however, a considerable degree of exchange of views between private and government economists.

It is likely that business forecasting in turn will have a growing influence on business itself. In recent years some studies have been made for the first time as to the manner in which widely circulated pessimistic or optimistic forecasts did affect the behavior of businessmen. It is probably due to such influences that the psychology during the present boom is somewhat different from that of earlier boom periods. This is a field in which much more observation and analysis are needed before a conclusive appraisal of these influences is possible.

While work devoted to improvement of our ability to forecast is being carried on, economic policy must be formulated in full recognition of the fact that short-run forecasts are at best very uncertain. This uncertainty makes it all the more necessary to provide for legislative and administrative arrangements that permit quick adjustments in policy in case economic conditions change. Interesting proposals have been made, particularly with respect to a more flexible fiscal policy, but the present political and psychological conditions are not particularly favorable for their adoption.[6] Still it remains true that the less confidence we have in our ability to make reliable predictions, the more necessary it becomes to provide for an adjustable economic and fiscal policy.

Recently, increasing emphasis has been placed on the establishment of long-range economic objectives and long-range economic programs. It is likely that we are better able to analyze economic resources and resource use than the exact timing in economic fluctuations. After some pioneering before[7] and during the second World War,[8] the Twentieth Century Fund has issued a monumental volume entitled *America's Needs and Resources* which outlines attainable economic objectives for

---

[6] For a proposal of a more flexible expenditure policy, see, for instance, the book by the former U.S. Budget Director, Harold D. Smith, *The Management of Your Government* (New York and London, 1945), p. 96 ff. Problems of a flexible tax policy are discussed, for example, in Alvin Hansen, *Economic Policy and Full Employment* (New York and London, 1947). An interesting specific legislative proposal was made by Senator Wayne Morse on the floor of the U.S. Senate (see *Congressional Record* for July 11 and 12, 1947).

[7] See Edwin G. Nourse and associates, *America's Capacity to Produce,* and Leven, Moulton, and Warburton, *America's Capacity to Consume* (Washington, D.C., Brookings Institution, 1934).

[8] See National Planning Association, *National Budgets for Full Employment* (Washington, D.C., April 1945); and the U.S. Bureau of Labor Statistics study *Patterns for Full Employment, 1950* (Washington, D.C., 1947).

1950 and 1960. This is not the place for appraising or criticizing the methods and results of this volume. It is mentioned only as a promising contribution to the effort to provide more adequate background information for guidance in formulating long-range economic and fiscal policy.

An analysis of long-run trends, even more than a short-run analysis, must of necessity include assumptions with respect to future policies and an appraisal of the effect of such policies. This leads economists to analyze what is to be expected in a given situation if given lines of government policy and business and labor policy are followed, and what results may be expected in case other policies are followed. In the establishment of economic objectives and in national economic budgeting, very interesting experiments are being carried out by a number of countries.

III. NATIONAL ECONOMIC BUDGETS IN COUNTRIES WITH DIFFERENT ECONOMIC SYSTEMS

It is of great interest to compare the use made of national economic budgets in countries which have basically different economic conditions. National economic budgets have been formulated in recent years in the Netherlands,[9] Norway,[10] France,[11] Great Britain,[12] and Sweden.[13] The Paris Report of the Committee of European Economic Cooperation, of September 1947, might be regarded as a first step in the direction of international economic programming or budgeting.

Economic plans have, of course, been developed in all countries with a fully regulated economy, like Soviet Russia. It is obvious that a country with a socialized economy needs a plan. It is also obvious that a country that allocates scarce raw materials, equipment and limited imports to various purposes of industrial use needs a system of priorities. Such a system can be administered only on the basis of a plan that states economic objectives. Thus there were some more or less formalized national economic objectives established in all war economies. It seems much less certain why it should be necessary to establish economic objectives in a country like the United States in which most wartime

[9] Central Planning Bureau of the Netherlands, *First Memorandum on the Central Economic Plan 1946 and National Budget 1947* (The Hague, 1946).

[10] Norwegian Ministry of Finance, *Om masjonalbudsjettet 1947, St. meld. nr. 10, 1947.*

[11] In connection with the Monnet Plan.

[12] *Economic Survey for 1947,* Cmd. 7046 (London, 1947).

[13] *Sveriges Utrikeshandel Efter Kriget Meddelanden frau Konjunktur-Institutet* B: 7 (Stockholm, 1947).

controls have been abandoned and where greatest reliance is placed on free enterprise.

Economic objectives in a fully regulated economy are determined by political decisions. They may be changed later or the administration may fail to live up to the plan. Nevertheless, these plans are not guesses but orders. Even in formulating plans for a communistic country, a certain element of guesswork is necessary to the extent that some freedom of choice is left to consumers, or to workers to choose their jobs. To a large extent, however, consumers' and workers' preferences will be made to comply with the plan by means of price and tax determination or by direct controls, if necessary.

In countries that adhere to the principle of free enterprise but in which war or postwar scarcities make allocations and the establishment of priorities for allocations necessary, a greater amount of guesswork enters the establishment of objectives than in countries with a fully regulated economy. The economic objectives incorporate what, under assumed circumstances, consumers are likely to demand and what enterprises are likely to invest. Since presumably not all consumer demands and business intentions to invest can be executed because of scarcities, those are selected which have the highest degree of social and economic priority. But except for that part of the program that is to be executed by direct government operation, the objectives are based on a selection of anticipated consumer and business decisions. This is even more true in countries in which decisions with respect to business investments are not influenced by government compulsory allocations of materials but only by voluntary agreement between an official agency and the investing public and private enterprise. This is the case in Sweden.

The establishment of economic objectives in an economy of predominantly free and competitive enterprise, as in the United States, assumes largely the character of *conditional forecasts.* We ask: *If* we have full employment, what will be the aggregate of production and income; and if we have full employment production and income, what will consumer demand and business investment be? Even in a predominantly free enterprise economy there are, of course, certain vital areas which are regarded as government responsibility. These areas include not only the conventional functions of government, but also areas left mainly to private activity in which certain standards of desirability are emerging, such as those related to nutrition, health and medical care, housing, and development of natural resources.

With respect to these government functions or functions of private activities influenced by government measures, the objectives reflect anticipated policy decisions rather than forecasts. There is, however, no assurance that the sum total of expected consumer demand, plus expected business investment, plus government operations will approximate the aggregate full employment production target.

At this point the analysis of objectives suggests the need for action programs that will influence, either directly or indirectly, consumer demand, business investment or government operations. These action programs may be of a fiscal nature, may affect the market relations of prices, costs and profits, or may be any other private or public economic measure.

The final step of the analysis consists in a new computation of the nation's economic budget under the assumption that such action programs of an economic or fiscal character will be adopted. It will often be useful to make the computation under assumption of various courses of action.

Thereby the national economic budget objectives can provide perspective for public and private decisions and yardsticks by which to measure success or failure of public and private performance. This is quite different in character from the corresponding plans in many European countries. These plans, to a larger extent, are of an "imperative" character, although the imperative character applies also in these countries only to certain segments of the economy. All the national budgets mentioned here have elements of both the imperative and the orientation character, but the relative importance of these two characteristics differs between the various types of national economic budgets.[14]

Thus the establishment of economic objectives becomes an essential basis for a rational formulation of economic and fiscal government programs. It also enables business to consider its own expansion programs in the perspective of targets for markets, production and capacity. The same applies, even though to a somewhat lesser degree, to farmers, labor and other groups. Such economic objectives can be used effectively only if the people have confidence in the validity of the estimates. This requires cooperation between the government and the various groups in the economy in the preparation of the estimates. The people must have confidence too that the economic objectives will be approximated by the forces of the market if possible, and that these forces in turn will be influenced and supplemented by government programs if necessary.

---

[14] These terms are suggested by André Marchal in "Le plan français," *Kyklos,* Vol. I, Fasc. 2 (Bern, 1947).

APPENDIX

The Nation's Economic Budget

(In billions of dollars, seasonally adjusted annual rates, current prices)

	October–December 1946			January–June 1947		
	Receipts	Expenditures	Excess (+) or Deficit (−)	Receipts	Expenditures	Excess (+) or Deficit (−)
Consumers:						
Income after taxes	167.0	—	—	169.6	—	—
Expenditures	—	154.9	—	—	158.0	—
Saving (+)	—	—	+12.1	—	—	+11.6
Business:						
Undistributed profits and additions to reserves	14.2	—	—	19.1	—	—
Gross domestic investment	—	30.4	—	—	29.5	—
Excess of receipts (+) or investment (−)	—	—	−16.2	—	—	−10.4
International:						
Net exports of goods and services	—	5.2	—	—	10.0	—
Net expenditures on foreign account (−)	—	—	−5.2	—	—	−10.0
Government (Federal, State, and local):						
Receipts from the public	57.1	—	—	58.2	—	—
Payments to the public	—	48.7	—	—	53.2	—
Excess of receipts (+) or payments (−)	—	—	+8.4	—	—	+5.0
Adjustments:						
For Government receipts from abroad	−.1	—	−.1	−.8	—	−.8
For Government transfers abroad	—	−3.1	+3.1	—	−7.6	+7.6
For Government domestic transfers	−17.5	−17.5	—	−18.1	−18.1	—
For statistical discrepancy	−2.1	—	−2.1	−3.0	—	−3.0
Total gross national product	218.6	218.6	0	225.0	225.0	0

26

*Federal Expenditure and Revenue Policy for Economic Stability**

By THE NATIONAL PLANNING ASSOCIATION†

INTRODUCTION

Although our economic system accords a dominant role to private enterprise, government expenditures and receipts have now reached a scale that makes them crucially important factors in our national welfare. In 1949, with a gross national production of 250 billion dollars, the Federal Government is spending more than 40 billions, while Federal, state, and local governments together are spending around 60 billions.

Government programs of this size make it more than ever desirable that every dollar of government expenditures be used as efficiently as possible. We are not rich enough to afford waste of resources by government any more than by anyone else.

It is equally important that the expenditure and revenue programs of government, in their formulation and execution, be consistent with the progress and stability of the private economy. The fiscal policy of the government must make useful positive contributions to the maintenance of high levels of employment and income—the goals declared in the Employment Act of 1946 to be a national objective.

Government affects business through both sides of its budget. Payments to government employees, bond holders, veterans, the aged, and the needy all constitute income that can be used to buy consumption goods from business; government procurement affords a direct market for business. On the other side of the budget, taxes capture funds that consumers might have spent or that business firms might have invested in improved facilities. Taken by themselves, tax collections tend to shrink the market of private business, contract employment, and lower

* Reprinted by the courtesy of the National Planning Association.

† A statement drafted and unanimously approved by the NPA Conference of University Economists, September 16–18, 1949, Princeton, New Jersey.

prices; just as, taken by themselves, government expenditures tend to expand the market for business, increase employment, or raise prices.

It is not only the size of revenue and expenditure that counts; their composition must also be considered in any appraisal of the effects of government policy. The economic effects of a billion dollars collected in the form of income taxes will be different from those of a billion dollars collected in excise taxes. Spending to build roads may stimulate private investment in automobiles, trucks, and garages; there are other forms of expenditure that may have adverse effects on private investment. Rationally or irrationally, government spending and taxing may greatly affect the climate within which families and businesses make their decisions.

THE PRINCIPLE OF AN ANNUALLY BALANCED BUDGET

The traditional goal of fiscal policy was to secure a balanced budget in every single year. But that objective has now proved impracticable and, besides, has serious disadvantages in principle. There is not even a clear or unique concept of "budget" to which the requirement of balance could be applied. For instance, in *the regular budget,* bookkeeping transfers to the social security trust account are classified as expenditures. As a result of this, that budget may show a deficit at a time when *the cash budget* shows an excess of receipts over outgo. But even the cash budget may not be adequate to portray the effects of fiscal policy; taxes may have their impact when tax liabilities are incurred rather than when payment is made; purchases may have their impact when contracts are entered into rather than when disbursements are made. However, where a single budget concept is used in economic analysis bearing on stabilization policy we prefer the cash budget to any available alternative.

Compared to the full span of the business cycle, a year is a short period of time. To insist upon a balance in every single year is certainly undesirable and to attain it is probably impossible. To attempt to raise tax rates every time there is a decrease in national income will only result in discouraging private consumption and investment at a time when these are most in need of expansion; on the other hand, to try to eliminate a tax surplus by cutting tax rates or expanding government activities would serve to increase inflationary pressures at a time when they are already acute.

If the budget were balanced in good years as well as bad, there would have to be either big fluctuations in expenditure programs or severe and perverse changes in tax rates. To vary expenditures in this manner would disrupt the essential services provided by government. Applied to military expenditures, it would mean a large defense program in boom years and a small defense program in depression years. This is both ineffective and wasteful. Government would be increasing its employment of resources when they were scarce and cutting down on their use when they were abundant. This, of course, would aggravate the fluctuations in private business.

THE PROBLEM OF CONTROLLING GOVERNMENT EXPENDITURES

Annual budget balancing is, thus, both difficult in practice and unsound in principle. But one great merit it does have: it provides a yardstick by which legislators and the people can scrutinize each activity of government, testing it both for efficiency of operation and for its worthwhileness in terms of cost. Every government program undertaken has to be paid for in a clear and unequivocal sense. The Legislature and the Executive are required to justify additional taxes equal to the cost of any new program. This is a principle every citizen can understand. If dropping the principle of annual budget-balancing were to mean dropping all restraints to unwise and inefficient expenditure, grave damage would be done to our economic and political system.

Were expenditures divorced entirely from the need for taxation, political opposition to extension of the government's expenditure programs would largely disappear. The scale on which the public sector absorbs resources would grow beyond what was really desired by the people as a whole; sooner or later the country would find itself in a state of chronic inflation. Such inflation is a sign of weak government and comes from eagerness to spend without a willingness to tax. Accordingly other general principles, other habits of thought and of action must be set forward to insure the standards of judgment and the self-discipline of government's activities and to do better what the principle of annual budget policy attempted—though imperfectly—to accomplish.

Experience shows that business activity has its ups and downs. There is thus a strong case for countercyclical fiscal action—surpluses in good times and deficits in bad. If we do not adopt such a policy deliberately we are likely to be forced into an imperfect version of it through the pressure of events. One of the major questions for the future is how such a policy can be administered with the restraint and efficiency that is supposed to be achieved through the balanced budget rule. If a flexible policy is to win acceptance, it must not be used as an excuse to introduce expenditure or tax programs that cannot be justified on their merits. Boondoggling should have no place in a rational fiscal program.

We doubt whether it would be possible, or even desirable, to rely exclusively on fiscal action to offset fluctuations in private business. That course could easily involve changes of impractical magnitudes in taxes and expenditures; it would mean placing excessive reliance on one measure for achieving economic stability and growth; it would involve problems in forecasting beyond the reach of present knowledge and techniques.

We can, however, reasonably expect that the budget be formulated in the light of economic judgment available that takes full account of the actual course of events and should contribute to economic stability rather than aggravate instability. In view of uncertainties, part of the planning process should be preparation for quick adaptation of fiscal operation to changing circumstances. Certain automatic devices for bringing remedial forces quickly into play are in a stage where they deserve consideration.

GUIDES TO FISCAL POLICY IN NORMAL TIMES

When the economy is prosperous and stable and there is no clear-cut reason to expect a change in any particular direction, the objective of policy should be to adapt the budget to changes in the Government's requirements but to leave its economic impact on total employment and purchasing power unchanged. This could be approximately achieved if newly planned increases or decreases in expenditures were to be matched with corresponding changes in planned tax receipts. The net expansionary or contractionary effect of the budget would then remain roughly the same. Thus, in conditions of continued prosperity, a modified version of the balanced budget rule could be used as a guide: taxes should grow or shrink corresponding to desired changes in expenditures. Thus proposed increases in expenditures would be exposed to the traditional test of whether they are worth their cost in terms of taxes.

However, if recent events and the outlook for the near future pointed, on balance, toward unemployment and deflation in the private sector of the economy, then budgetary changes should be made in the direction of producing a moderately expansionary effect. New government expenditure programs should still be considered on their merits, but the additional taxation that in prosperous times would accompany them should now be deferred. Taxes that are deferred in these circumstances should be put into effect as soon as that can be done without impeding recovery. There should be no delay in making the tax reductions warranted by any reductions in government expenditures; and if expenditure requirements are expected to decline in the future, anticipatory tax reductions could be enacted.

On the other hand, if the weight of the evidence appeared to be on the inflationary side, the opposite policy should be followed. The rule that increased expenditures should be accompanied by increased tax yields should be rigidly followed. Tax reductions that would normally be in order should be deferred; and tax increases should anticipate expected increases in expenditures.

GUIDING PRINCIPLES IN TIME OF ACUTE RECESSION OR BOOM

Where there is a definite expectation, justified by events, of serious recession or inflation, more strenuous fiscal measures would be called for, and the policies described above should be supplemented by emergency fiscal action.

In the event of severe recession, it is not only politically necessary, but economically desirable to provide additional employment projects that can be started and ended quickly. Temporary tax relief should be given in order to stimulate private spending and employment. Other incentives for private investment, such as guarantees, should be considered. There can be no social or economic justification for allowing mass unemployment to persist for extended periods at a time when there is abundant need for roads, schools, hospitals, and other useful objects of public expenditures. However, we recognize that there are difficult questions of extent and timing connected with any such program. An overambitious government program may impede the course of recovery in the private sectors of the economy by dislocating resources and delaying needed price adjustments. On the other hand, a program that was over-cautious could needlessly fail to advance recovery by not stimulating the demand for the products of private industry. Much skill and judgment are required to move from depression to stable prosperity. We must not rely on the private economy, unaided by government action, to perform that task. The Government must not shirk the responsibility placed on it by the Employment Act, and fiscal policy is one of the most promising instruments it possesses.

On any occasion when serious inflation is in prospect, emergency measures would be needed to curtail expenditures and increase taxation. Wartime and postwar experience provides convincing evidence that the political obstacles to a fiscal policy adequate to combat inflation are so great that there is little practical danger of going too far. The survival of a relatively free and stable price system depends heavily on our willingness to fight inflation by fiscal methods.

A policy that helps to maintain stable prosperity will be no more likely in practice to result in an upward trend in the national debt than one that does not. The course of events may in fact be such that stabilization requires steady reduction in the debt. Budgeting surpluses to fight inflation will provide for the reduction of the public debt in a helpful rather than a painful fashion. Surpluses are not feasible in times of depression. They are desirable where the private economy is strong enough for the Government to tax more than it spends without causing unemployment. The private economy is not likely to possess this strength if Government policies aggravate rather than offset business fluctuations.

ADDITIONAL POSSIBILITIES FOR A FLEXIBLE FISCAL POLICY

While we consider these guides for budget policy essential to a stabilization program, the annual budget cannot, in the nature of things, be based on precise forecasts; nor can it be expected to compensate for sudden and short-run fluctuations in business that occur within the period of its operation. Even though the budget can and should be amended in the light of changing circumstances, the legislative process is necessarily too cumbersome to make delicately timed adjustments in fiscal policy. Therefore, we consider whether further flexibility can be achieved by two devices which may be called "automatic flexibility" and "formula flexibility."

"Automatic flexibility" means a tax system such that revenue under a given set of tax rates will fall sharply if unemployment develops, and rise sharply in the opposite case of inflation; and expenditure programs under which increased outlays arise from increased unemployment.

"Formula flexibility" means a system under which pre-announced tax cuts and upward revisions of spending programs will come into force if unemployment exceeds a certain figure or production falls below a certain level, and pre-announced changes in the opposite direction if price indexes rise at more than a certain speed.

AUTOMATIC FLEXIBILITY

Automatic flexibility is exemplified by the unemployment compensation system. If unemployment increases, employers' contributions at once decline, while the unemployed begin almost immediately to draw more in benefits. Thus the Government finds itself automatically taking less money out of the public's pockets and putting more in.

There are now many such flexible elements in federal taxes and revenues; and they have greatly increased in importance with the growth of the budget. Besides the unemployment compensation system, there is, for example, substantial automatic flexibility in personal and corporate income taxes.

Automatic flexibility can slow down and perhaps halt a decline of activity or a rise of prices; it can give time for restorative forces to come into play, but it will not, by itself, pull activity back to a full-employment level or restore prices to a pre-inflation level.

We feel strongly that the existing automatic flexibility makes an important contribution to economic stability, which should not be frittered away, as it would be, for instance, by rigid application of the annual-balanced-budget rule. But we do not believe it prudent for policy to regard automatic flexibility as more than a first line of defense; more must be done to cope with serious economic fluctuations.

FORMULA FLEXIBILITY

The enactment by Congress of rules under which tax rates, and perhaps of rules under which expenditure programs, will shift in certain contingencies specified in advance is a possibility that deserves further exploration. For example, the period during which unemployed workers can draw unemployment compensation might be extended according to a flexible schedule based on the volume of unemployment. The withholding rate under the personal income tax for any calendar quarter might rise by a stated amount above a standard rate whenever, say, the index of retail prices has increased by over a certain amount in the preceding 6 months. The withholding rate might be lowered whenever standard indices of production and employment drop below stated levels or trends.

The question of formula flexibility shades off into the question of granting to the Executive wider discretionary authority than it now possesses to initiate changes in the timing or extent of the fiscal program. This raises difficult issues of political principle and administrative responsibility. We can here do no more than call attention to them.

CONCLUSION

In this statement, we have confined ourselves to fiscal policy of the Federal Government. But, while essential, that is only one element in a stabilization policy. The policies of state and local governments can make useful contributions within their more limited spheres. Monetary and credit policies including debt management must play an active role in their own right and must be properly coordinated with fiscal policy. All necessary measures must be taken to preserve and stimulate competition. Supported by such measures, Federal fiscal policy offers the best prospect of achieving sustained prosperity within the framework of our existing economic system.

27

*The Problem of Economic Instability**

By

EMILE DESPRES *MILTON FRIEDMAN*
ALBERT G. HART *PAUL A. SAMUELSON*
DONALD H. WALLACE†

This report is about the problem of economic instability in peacetime in the United States—how to avoid mass unemployment and major fluctuations in the price level while maintaining steady growth in production. It was written in 1949, before military action in 1950 transformed the immediate goals of the economy of the United States. It does not deal with problems of economic mobilization and economic stabilization for war, partial or total, although some of the basic facts and analysis presented here are fundamental for wartime economic problems, as well as for those of peacetime.

The report is addressed primarily to the interested public, not to economists. Its purpose is to tell them what economists do and do not know about the problem of economic instability. Its preparation and publication reflect the belief that there is a body of technical knowledge in economics that has a great deal to contribute to the formation of intelligent policy on economic stability.

This is a brief report dealing with complex and complicated problems. The details, refinements, and qualifications needed in their work by experts in economic analysis or administration would be out of place

* This is a report prepared under the auspices of the American Economic Association. It is not, however, an official utterance of the Association which by provisions of its Charter will not "commit its members to any position on practical economic questions."

† This report was prepared by a subcommittee of the Committee on Public Issues of the American Economic Association. Members of the subcommittee were Emile Despres of Williams College, Milton Friedman of the University of Chicago, Albert G. Hart of Columbia University, Paul A. Samuelson of the Massachusetts Institute of Technology, and Donald H. Wallace of Princeton University, chairman.

here. Economics can best serve the public only if its useful conclusions can be briefly and simply explained.

This report endeavors to explain the nature of the fluctuating economic pressures which stabilization policy must offset, remove, or divert into useful channels, and to present economists' thinking about policy measures helpful in stabilization and about the problem of building a coherent program. While economists are not unanimous about stabilization problems, the committee which drafted this report believes that there is a broad consensus which the report reflects. Important professional disagreements are also noted, however, and the range of opinions within the committee is wide enough to make it likely that a large share of such disagreements have been located.

This report has been prepared under the auspices of the American Economic Association. It is not, however, to be considered an official utterance of the Association which by provision of its Charter does not "commit its members to any position on practical economic questions."

I. OBJECTIVES

Price and Employment Objectives

Domestic economic stability has two major objectives—sustained full employment, and stability of price levels. The importance of full employment was underlined by our experiences in the 1930's, and has been formally recognized in the Employment Act of 1946. The importance of price-level stability, already widely understood before the war, has been emphasized by our experiences in the 1940's.

Full employment means that qualified people who seek jobs at prevailing wage rates can find them in productive activities without considerable delay. It means full-time jobs for people who want to work full time. It does not mean that people like housewives and students are under pressure to take jobs when they do not want jobs, or that workers are under pressure to put in undesired overtime. It does not mean that unemployment is ever zero. People are unemployed for a time while changing jobs. Full employment is the absence of mass unemployment. By this standard, employment was full, and probably overful, most of the time during the years 1943–48.

Price-level stability means the absence of any marked trend or sharp, short-term movements in the general level of prices. Marked shifts in *relative prices* of individual commodities, reflecting changes in consumer preferences, or in conditions of production, are however, entirely compatible with a stable average *price level*—in fact, most economists favor both price-level stability and flexibility of relative prices.

The desirability of full employment is obvious: unemployment means waste of potential output and hardship for the unemployed and their dependents. The desirability of price-level stability is, perhaps, less obvious. But, on the one hand, any large price drop is almost sure to be accompanied by serious unemployment. And, on the other hand, inflation, though pleasant for some people, hurts those whose dollar incomes do not increase or increase less than living costs; and also sharpens conflicts of economic interest and impairs the group consensus necessary for solving national problems.

The Relation of Stability to Other Objectives

Economic stability is but one among a number of widely accepted objectives for social policy. To some extent the attainment of economic stability is likely to promote other objectives as well. But some measures to promote stability may to some extent conflict with them; hence, it must be borne in mind that economic stability is not desired at all costs.

Three other objectives—peace, progress, and freedom—call for special mention, by reason of their importance and their close relation to economic stability.

The strengthening of peaceful and democratic institutions in the rest of the world depends, much more than most Americans realize, on the maintenance of prosperity in the United States. If depressions in the United States undermine the markets of other countries, or if for reasons of domestic policy we do not let imports flow in freely, the prosperity of other countries will be endangered. Instability in the United States is thus likely to generate economic and political reactions abroad that will endanger the preservation of peace.

Progress involves change, reorganization of economic resources, replacement of the old by the new. A dynamic, progressive economy is one in which new techniques are constantly being developed and introduced, new products are seeking to attract public favor and replace old products, new firms are challenging the old. Such an economy cannot be completely stable. Adaptation to change takes time and involves friction, with resulting dips or jogs in production and employment. On the other hand, willingness to venture into new lines and to develop new products and processes is greatly hindered if individuals and business firms must devote a considerable part of their energies and resources to adjusting themselves to substantial fluctuations in the general level of economic activity.

The essence of freedom is the exercise of free choice by individuals with respect to a wide range of their activities—in the economic sphere, a large measure of freedom in choice of goods to consume, of occupations to follow, of ways of investing or using property. Freedom in these respects implies freedom to experiment, and to change one's mind. It also implies that individuals can and will make mistakes. It thus implies change, which in turn forces adaptation to change. On the other hand, marked economic instability creates conflicts and hardships, sets group against group and produces dissatisfaction with the existing structure of society. Thus it may undermine the basic consensus on which freedom and democracy rest.

The Institutional Setting

Americans live today in a society with a large measure of personal freedom, a great deal of private enterprise, and a great deal of government activity. This report treats the problems of economic stability in this kind of mixed society. It assumes that, while government will continue to undertake much economic activity directly and to control private activity in many ways, the bulk of our people will be employed by private business or be self-employed; and that decisions on what to consume, where to work, how to use property, and what and how much to produce will be governed primarily by incentives affecting the people making them, rather than by directives from government. At present the great majority of Americans—including the writers of this report—desire this kind of institutions. Hence this report does not treat proposals for effecting economic stability by extensive government directives requiring economic units to do certain things and forbidding them to do other things.

II. THE HISTORICAL RECORD

Section II gives some main facts of the historical record of instability. Section III presents some basic ideas which, with the facts of Section II, form the basis of the discussion of policy measures in Sections IV–VII.

Economic instability has been chronic in America, as in other advanced economies. Price records, going back to colonial days, show at least one sizable swing each decade. Production records, going back to the Civil War, show numerous depressions and booms of output, few long stretches of full-volume production. The records of employment and unemployment, fragmentary until recent years, confirm this picture of instability, as far as they go.

This record of instability is frequently analyzed in terms of "business cycles." In depressions we find a phase of "revival," a few months in which many prices and much non-agricultural employment and output turn upward. Then comes a phase of "expansion," sometimes lasting for years, with output high or rising, and with prices high or rising, or both. Eventually comes a phase of "recession," occasionally dramatic, when within a few months many prices and output and employment in many industries turn downward. This is often followed by a phase of "contraction," with further declines of output, employment, and prices.

Depressions

In the Great Depression of the 1930's with its mass unemployment, output was for a decade far below what our labor force and plant could produce. The total loss of output that could have been produced and was not has been estimated as running into the hundreds of billions of dollars—comparable to the volume of output that went into the waging of World War II. But this depression was not our first long and deep depression. There were dismal years after 1837, and the depressions of the 1870's and 1890's were protracted and severe.

Besides these major depressions, sharp minor slumps appear in the records for 1884–1885, 1904, 1908, 1914, 1920–1922, and 1937—not to mention such dips of output as 1924 and 1927, which were picked up in the seismographic records of the business-cycle analysts, but did not involve serious and prolonged unemployment.

It is not necessary first to be prosperous in order to have a slump of output. A depression-within-a-depression can happen, and did happen in 1895–1898 and 1937–1938.

Inflations

Full-blown inflation—a price rise which is widespread, rapid and carries prices to a peak 50 per cent or more above the starting point—has happened in American history only during and after wars. Our only inflations of this sort were linked with the Revolution, the War of 1812, the Civil War, World War I and World War II. (The Mexican War and Spanish-American War did not subject the United States to enough strain to generate inflation.) However, there have been periods of sustained though less severe price rise during peacetime. For example, between 1899, a year of recovery, and 1909 wholesale prices rose by one-third.

Sustained Prosperity

The economic records show few periods of sustained prosperity. Between the big depressions of the 1870's and 1890's, the decade of the 1880's was mostly prosperous, though it contained also a two-year slump with a panic in 1884. Prosperity also reigned in most of the years 1899–1913 although there was a panic in 1907, and brief, sharp slumps in output occurred in 1904, 1908, 1911, and 1914.

The interwar years exhibit the longest record of sustained prosperity, as well as the worst recorded depression. The years 1923–1929 were on the whole years of prosperity. The setbacks of 1924 and 1927 never became serious.

Some Important Characteristics of Business Cycles

Some of the most important uniformities found by study of business cycles are the following:

1. Prices and production, outside of agriculture, ordinarily rise and fall together, instead of moving in opposite directions.
2. Total expenditure on durable goods fluctuates by a greater percentage than spending on non-durable goods. Total private spending on capital goods (plant, equipment, housing, and the like) fluctuates by a greater percentage than consumption expenditure.
3. Total output and employment fluctuate by a much larger percentage in *durable-goods* industries than in *non-durable-goods* industries. For instance, auto production is more unstable than gasoline production, house construction than the renting of rooms.
4. Total output and employment fluctuate by a much greater percentage in construction and capital equipment than in consumer goods.
5. Current expenditure on business inventories fluctuates by a greater percentage than total sales.
6. Large changes in total output and employment or in the price level are normally accompanied by large changes in the same direction in the volume of money, *i.e.,* currency and bank deposits, and a change in the velocity of circulation of money.
7. Some prices are highly flexible, others highly rigid. Price rigidity centers in manufactured goods, price flexibility in farm products and foods.
8. Total profits fluctuate by a much greater percentage than other types of income.

The lack of uniformity found in some key characteristics of business cycles is equally significant:

1. The *length* of cycles, averaging about 3½ years, varies widely. For example, counting from trough to trough we find a 5-year cycle in 1927–1932, from peak to peak an 8-year cycle from 1929–1937. On the other hand, 1919–1922

and 1920–1923 were 3-year cycles, and shorter ones have been observed. So we can never tell where we are in the cycle by counting months elapsed since some past event.

2. The *amplitude* of cycle swings is very irregular. The down-swing of 1923–1924, for example, reduced manufacturing output about a tenth; that of 1937–1938, by nearly half. So we cannot count on any particular amplitude as "normal." Moreover, the evidence is not clear whether as time goes on cycles are becoming more or less severe.

3. Expansion in some cycles brings output up to a full-employment level and holds it there for some time, as in 1925–1927. In other cycles, expansion leads only to a "submerged peak," with unemployment still heavy, as in 1895 and 1937. There is evidence that in full-recovery cycles building construction characteristically contributes heavily to the expansion, while in submerged-peak cycles it does not.

4. No two cycles are exactly alike in the relative rôles played by different factors such as commodity prices, security prices, inventories, foreign loans, or construction. Inventory building and commodity price speculation characterized the boom of 1919–1920 followed by a price collapse. Stock market speculation and foreign loans were important elements in the boom preceding the 1929 decline.

5. Numerous attempts have been made to use our knowledge about uniformities in business cycles to "forecast" the future course of business activity. Economic forecasting has not developed to the point where it is a reliable guide for national policy. Even identification of phases of the cycle as they happen, or soon afterward, is far from easy.

In making use of our knowledge of the past we must be careful to give adequate weight also to our knowledge of the present. Changes in political or economic circumstances or in our institutions make older experience partly obsolete. The record suggests that in peacetime our economy is usually less susceptible to inflation than to depression. But the tremendous government requirements on production in "cold war" and the backlog of demands on the "social security state" are new elements that may create inflationary pressure for some years to come. Moreover, the increased power of organized labor added to the power in business and in farm organizations may introduce an inflationary bias.

If we do not have much more difficulty with inflation, it will probably be because world political tension eases and backlogs of demand prove less urgent than they now look; in that event, we may have to make adjustments to a serious decline of private investment and government purchase of goods and services within a few years. Indeed, some economists fear that such a decline might usher in a protracted period in which large unemployment would be chronic, unless overcome by extensive government programs. Other economists see a danger of both chronic unemployment and a persistent inflationary tendency combined.

III. BASIC IDEAS

Study of business fluctuations has yielded, in addition to the historical knowledge just sketched, a large amount of useful analysis. Together, these two kinds of knowledge afford an adequate basis for framing stabilization policies that can avoid both severe unemployment and severe inflation. The job of this section is to outline some of the ideas most useful in analysis of business fluctuations. First, however, we should dispose of some common misconceptions.

There is a widespread impression that economists disagree so much that they can give no sound guidance on policy. This is erroneous. There is, indeed, a good deal of disagreement, but it is much less than it seems to outsiders. Economists do not spend much time talking or writing about the large part of their subject matter on which they agree. As in all branches of learning, professional discussion relates chiefly to advancing the frontier of knowledge, where controversy and criticism are indispensable for progress; and the part of the discussion most likely to catch the attention of journalists is whatever happens to be least good-tempered or most extreme, rather than most fundamental. Moreover, many disagreements are merely about how to formulate findings which all accept, or about the relative quantitative weight of factors whose importance nobody denies. Again, many differences of opinion among economists on public policy reflect differences in philosophy rather than in economic analysis as such. This does not mean that their views are to be disregarded. The essence of democracy is to permit different opinions on public policy and to provide means of selection and compromise that enable adoption of workable policies and programs in the face of differences. Moreover, disagreements among economists help to mark out the areas where future developments and effects of policy are peculiarly uncertain, and thus show points at which policy must be kept flexible to permit adaptation as a situation develops.

A second misconception is contained in the proposition that effective stabilization policies can be designed only if we understand fully all the causes of fluctuations. Partial knowledge can be very useful for deciding how to act. People need not know just what causes cloud bursts, or just when they will occur, in order to use their knowledge of the course of floods to design safeguards against flood damage. In economics people need not know, for example, just what makes the volume of construction contracts change from time to time, in order to design arrangements to safeguard us against a general economic collapse when construction shrinks. More complete knowledge is, of course, worth seeking in order to improve the design of policy, but as we go along we can effectively use what we do know.

A third misconception is that inability to forecast coming economic changes accurately leaves us helpless in the grip of events. Present limitations on forecasting, and lack of complete understanding of causes, do make it impossible to treat economic instability solely by use of "preventive medicine." This is not to say, however, that it is impossible to tell when the economy is really sick and may get worse unless curative measures are taken; or that it is impossible to design effective cures. We can, in fact, diagnose real trouble soon enough to treat it. And, although we may not be able to prevent mild recessions or inflations, we do know enough to design policies that can keep them from developing into prolonged periods of mass unemployment or violent inflations.

Classes of Expenditure and Decisions

Substantial changes in total expenditure in the whole economy mean substantial changes in total employment or in the price level, or in both.

In studying the course of fluctuations or analyzing policy proposals, economists commonly break down the total expenditure into four main headings: (a) consumption expenditure; (b) domestic private investment spending (or "capital formation") on new buildings, equipment, and additions to inventory; (c) government expenditure on goods and services; and (d) net foreign balance, representing the balance of all the goods and services we sell the rest of the world over what they sell us (an item which may, of course, be positive or negative in any given year).

Each of these major expenditure classes can be further subdivided. These divisions and subdivisions group together expenditures which rest on similar types of *decisions.*

Consumption expenditure represents use of income by households for direct enjoyment. Sub-groupings run in terms of the durability of the things bought. Services and perishable commodities involve little forward-looking calculation. At the other extreme, the buying of new houses is regarded as a business-type of decision and classified with investment. Other durable-goods buying is moderately forward-looking, but is classed as consumption rather than investment.

Domestic private investment represents spending by business of undistributed profits, cash assets or proceeds of new security issues or bank loans to buy additional goods for business use. Its main components are purchase of new plant and equipment, additions to inventories, and purchase of new housing.

Government expenditure on goods and services includes payment for services of government employees and purchase from private business of supplies, equipment, buildings, etc. (including, for example, goods bought under the Marshall Plan). In addition, government makes outlays for interest, veterans, Social Security benefits, and the like, where the government does not get currently produced services or commodities in exchange. These are called "transfer payments," and are treated essentially as taxes with a minus sign.

Decisions To Produce and To Buy

Except for the limited sector of direct government employment, output and employment are set in the first instance by private decisions. Business decisions to produce rest largely on the selling market created by non-business purchasers—consumers, the government, and foreigners—and on the buying markets in which materials, property, labor. and funds are obtained.

The amount of consumer expenditure depends largely on the incomes received by people from the proceeds of productive operations. In other words, households get income in the form of wages, salaries, dividends, etc., from business in return for providing services; and the business output of consumer goods and services is sold to households in return for expenditures out of this income. The simple circle of production-income-expenditure-production is, however, modified by saving of individuals and business enterprises and by business spending on plant and equipment and inventories. Business investment spending is forward-looking and is therefore influenced by many diverse factors, not only by the current state of business activity. The fiscal operations of government also modify the circle by taxation, which reduces taxpayers' disposable income, and by government payments such as salaries and "transfer payments" that constitute income for households.

The total stream of income, before taxes and including business profits not distributed to owners, can be shown as a matter of accounting to equal the total value of contemporaneous output, including items added to business inventory and plant and including government services valued at cost. But this is simply a bookkeeping identity following from the fact that what one consumer, business enterprise, or government agency treats as an expenditure is treated by some other unit as a receipt. In this bookkeeping sense any level of output, high or low, is potentially self-financing—that is, it sets up a flow of incomes out of which that amount of output *could* continuously be bought at current prices. It does not follow, however, that any existing level of output and employment *will* perpetuate itself—the record shows that it never has for long. For example, the accounting identity between income and value of output may reflect the unwilling acceptance of large inventory accumulations by businessmen in consequence of an unexpected decline in consumer expenditures. In this case, the identity conceals forces making for a decline in income. Or, the identity may reflect an unintended piling up of unused profits in the hands of businessmen in consequence of an unexpected rise in consumer expenditures. In this case, the identity conceals forces making for a rise in income.

Changes in total expenditure and income reflect changes in expenditure by some units in the economy. Total consumer expenditure can and may vary in relation to the flow of income set up by production for various reasons, such as a general change in the fraction of their income people desire to save, or a change in tax rates, or in government "transfer payments," or in dividend rates. Business enterprises may decide to increase or decrease expenditure on plant and equipment or on inventories because of changes in the business outlook, technological change, interest rate movements, or other factors. This will set in motion forces that tend toward increase or decrease in total expenditure and income in the whole economy. Changes in tax structures or in the level of government expenditures, and changes in our net foreign balance may also affect the level of total expenditure and income. Political changes abroad may lead to expansion or contraction of government outlays for military and foreign-assistance programs.

In general, a decision by any group to increase its expenditures in relation to its receipts is a force making for an expansion in aggregate expenditures and income, and to decrease its expenditures in relation to its receipts is a force making for a decline in aggregate income. Whenever the net effect of the decisions of consumers, business, and governments is to raise total expenditure and income there will be an increase in output and employment, or in the price level, or in all three—unless some decisions are changed. Similarly, when the effect is toward lower expenditure and income, there will be a decline in output and employment or in the price level or in all three—unless some decisions are changed.

The decisions by firms and households that make for expansion or contraction in total income are influenced not only by the flow of income but also by monetary factors: holdings of cash and of liquid resources (government securities and other securities easily cashed) and the cost and availability of bank and other credit. When firms and households regard the amount of cash and other liquid resources they hold as large relative to their total wealth, they will try to convert part into other forms of wealth; that is, spend more than they are currently receiving, thereby tending to increase total money income in the economy. Similarly, when it is relatively easy and cheap to borrow, firms and individuals who seek to make investments will find it easy to finance them and will thereby add to the upward pressure on income. Conversely, when firms and households regard the amount of cash and other liquid resources they hold as relatively small, they will try to spend less than they receive; when it is relatively difficult to borrow, investment will be discouraged; both of these will tend to reduce aggregate money income.

It follows from these considerations that one way to counter forces making for contraction is by monetary action designed to increase the amount of cash or other liquid resources held by individuals and firms and to reduce the cost and increase the availability of loans. Similarly, one way to offset any forces making for expansion is by monetary action designed to reduce the amount of cash or other liquid resources held by individuals and firms and to increase the cost and reduce the availability of loans.

With an upswing of business activity and rising prices, most borrowers look like better risks, and there is an expansion of bank financing of business and consumer buying. In a business recession the opposite occurs. This instability of bank credit is enhanced by the great elasticity inherent in a banking system with fractional reserves against deposit liabilities. The banks as a whole can, through their loan operations, create a quantity of purchasing power in the form of deposits equal to several times the amount of their reserves. With present legal reserve requirements and habits of the public with respect to holdings of pocket-book cash, the banking system can create new deposits equivalent to four or five times the amount of excess reserves. In a recession, banks may seek to increase their reserves as a fraction of their liabilities, thereby forcing a contraction in deposits, and conversely in an upswing. In addition, there are a number of factors that tend to increase reserves in business expansion when it would be desirable for them not to increase, and to decrease reserves in business recessions when it would be desirable for them not to decrease.

Expansion and contraction of bank credit is in part a reflection of business fluctuations. But most students of business cycles believe that for the reasons just cited, our banking system has an effect in amplifying these fluctuations, although there is wide disagreement on the quantitative importance of this factor. The great depression of the 'thirties was sharpened by credit contraction, and the postwar inflation of 1946–48 was heightened by credit expansion. Many economists regard our present banking system as an automatic destabilizer, unless effectively controlled.

Economists use the analytical tools outlined above to look for elements in the situation that can lead to expansion or contraction. They also rely heavily on the principles of national accounting to check the consistency of their reasoning. Explanations which have not been checked in this way for consistency are only too common—witness the theories underlying the Townsend Plan, "Thirty Dollars Every Thursday," Social Credit, and many other "schemes"—and would, if used, lead to gross errors in policy.

We can see the shadows of a good many future changes in components of the economy. The postwar boom in housing and automobiles will slacken sooner or later. Easing of international tension would allow armaments to diminish. Developments in atomic energy may some day induce a temporary bulge in capital investment expenditure. The object of stabilization policy is not to prevent all fluctuations in components, but to see that they offset rather than reinforce each other. Reduction of armaments or housing brings a shrinkage of income earned in those sectors, which threatens to induce cutbacks also in things we can then afford to produce in greater quantity, emergency needs having been partly met. The basic strategy of economic stabilization is to mitigate and offset the effect on total expenditure of changes, upward or downward, in particular sectors or components of the economy.

Room for Policy

As explained at the outset, this report excludes from consideration stabilization methods which, involving large assumption by government of the decision-making of households, of business firms, of labor, farm, and other groups, would negate basic freedoms. Also, it is plain that governmental decision-making of this sort would be clumsy and ineffectual. Even totalitarian governments which have no objection in principle to this type of "planning," find it necessary to decentralize most decisions to organizations with much the functions of our firms and households, and to guide decisions by "incentives."

Another conceivable method is to attempt stabilization by setting up organizations in each line of production and instructing each to stabilize its own sector. This may sound excellent for a moment, but it does not stand examination. Such a sector-stabilization organization, confronted with changes in the demand for its output, could not stabilize *both* its selling-price *and* its sales and output. The record of behavior of producer organizations suggests that they usually sacrifice output stabilization to price stabilization, or even to price boosting. Moreover, shifts in the *components* of output and the price level are often desirable. New products find their place by expanding their output, bidding up the prices of labor and other resources, and forcing down the prices and outputs of competing products. To stabilize the individual components of the economy, if we could do it, would be to throw away our prospects of progress and scrap the adaptive mechanism which facilitates progress.

Manifestly there is some room for groups and leaders, conscious of the stabilization problem, to modify their decisions in ways that will help to stabilize the economy. But since individual leaders are ordinarily in a relation of stewardship to others, their freedom to modify decisions in this way is limited. The primary responsibility for stabilization policy falls on government, particularly the federal government, and on public bodies such as the Board of Governors of the Federal Reserve System.

In a system where the great majority of workers are in private employment government stabilization policy consists primarily in altering the general economic climate so as to mitigate or offset developing fluctuations in private business. There is a wide variety of measures by which government can do this. Some of the more important are the following:

1. Change in the amount of tax revenue taken by government from incomes of individuals or businesses. Some change occurs automatically with change in incomes. Alteration of tax rates or of the design of the tax structure could give greater change.
2. Change in government contributions to the income stream through "transfer payments," such as unemployment compensation and farm income supports. Again some change occurs automatically but more can be obtained by change in the rates or structure of "transfer payments."
3. Change in amount of government expenditure on public works or on other things bought by government.
4. Change in the incentives to individuals by changes in tax rates or structure, or in the rates or structure of "transfer payments," or in the kinds of expenditure undertaken.
5. Change in the cost and availability of bank credit, effected through controls of the monetary authorities.

6. Change in the structure of the public's financial assets and liabilities brought about by monetary or debt management policy.

7. Influencing the business outlook by government pronouncements and prospects of future government action, thus affecting investment decisions or current scheduling of output and employment, or both.

8. Government influence on the price-making and wage-making machinery.

9. International economic policy.

IV. FISCAL POLICY

A. Strategic Principles for Fiscal and Monetary Policies

Sections IV and V discuss fiscal policy and monetary policy. In these fields economics provides some strategic principles for achievement of economic stability. The most important are:

1. Government tax revenue should be higher relative to government expenditure in periods of high employment than in periods of substantial unemployment.

2. Money and credit should be relatively tight in periods of high employment and relatively easy in periods of substantial unemployment.

These two principles are intended to counteract fluctuations in total money demand, thereby restraining price fluctuations and promoting stable, high employment. Whatever may be considered the "normal" or desirable level of government tax revenue and expenditure, and whatever may be considered the "normal" or desirable relationship between them—as far as these can be determined from considerations other than stabilization—tax revenue should be higher than this relative to expenditure in times of high employment and lower than this relative to expenditure in times of substantial unemployment. Whatever may be the "normal" or desirable monetary policies, including debt management—and these may be determined in part on the basis of considerations other than stabilization—money and credit conditions should be relatively tight in times of high employment and relatively easy in times of substantial unemployment.

These are principles of operational strategy. The Congress and the Executive can put them into operation.

Nearly all economists agree with these strategic principles of stabilization. Disagreements relate chiefly to tactics, *i.e.,* specific measures to put these strategic principles into operation.

B. Importance of Fiscal Policies of Governments

Despite the primary rôle of private enterprise in our economy, government expenditures and receipts have reached a scale that makes them a crucial influence on the way the private economy works. In 1949 when the national income was a little more than $200 billion, federal, state, and local governments spent about $60 billion. And there seems little prospect of a large decline in government expenditures in the foreseeable future. Plainly, government fiscal policies and their timing constitute one of the major influences on the state of employment, production, and prices, whether or not they are deliberately framed with that end in view.

Government affects business activity through both sides of its budget. Wages paid to government employees, interest paid to holders of government bonds, and payments to veterans, to the aged, and to the needy, all constitute income that can be used to buy consumption goods from business. Government procurement of goods is a direct market for business. On the other side of the budget, taxes capture funds that consumers might have spent, or that business firms might have spent on plant and equipment. Taken by themselves, tax collections tend to contract the market of business, and thus to reduce employment or lower prices; and government expenditures, taken by themselves, tend to expand the market and thus to increase employment or raise prices.

It is not only the *size* of revenue and expenditure that counts; their qualitative *composition* is also important. For example, the effects of "transfer payments" depend on who gets them and on what terms—for example, whether unemployment compensation goes largely to the poorest workers and whether payments are set so high as to discourage acceptance of job offers. Again, a billion dollars of taxes collected in one way may have different economic effects from those attending a billion dollars levied in another way, because incentives are affected differently. For example, when people must pay one-fifth or more of their extra earnings to the government, their decision as to whether to work longer or shorter hours may be influenced. To take another example, a particular treatment of business losses in the tax laws may affect people's willingness to venture their capital in new activities.

On the other side of the budget, spending to build roads may stimulate private investment in automobiles, garages, and trucks; some other types of public expenditure may have adverse repercussions on private investment. Some government spending and taxing policies may affect, rationally or irrationally, the psychological climate within which families and businesses make their decisions.

Fiscal measures for stabilization may be divided into three types: (1) those that are built into the fiscal system and operate automatically; (2) measures adopted in advance that are to go into effect promptly in certain specified contingencies; and (3) measures adopted only as the occasion arises.

C. *Automatic Stabilizers in the Fiscal System*

Since the prewar period the automatic stabilizing effect of federal fiscal operations has become substantial as a result of the increase in built-in stabilizers, including the pay-as-you-go principle, and the great expansion in the scale of the budget. Most economists consider the marked increase in automatic stabilizers a highly favorable development with respect to maintenance of economic stability.

When total income rises, the existing structure of federal taxes and expenditures tends automatically to increase government revenues relative to expenditures, and when total income falls, to increase expenditures relative to revenues. These changes tend to mitigate or offset inflations or depressions, in part at least.

On the spending side, unemployment compensation, relief, farm benefits, and the like tend to rise and fall with unemployment, and so to be higher in depression than in prosperity. Most other federal expenditures would not change much automatically with changes in the level of total income.

On the revenue side, tax receipts vary sharply in the same direction as national income. Revenue from the personal income tax, our largest single tax, varies directly with changes in national income, and in greater proportion owing to the "progression" in the tax structure. The next largest tax, that on corporate income, also varies in greater proportion than national income, since corporate income fluctuates more sharply than national income itself. Social security contributions from payrolls move roughly in proportion to national income.

We may summarize the automatic stabilizing influence of the 1949 federal fiscal system roughly as follows: in the absence of any offsetting action by Congress or the Executive, every drop of $10 billion in national income will lower taxes by something like $3 billion, thereby reducing by $3 billion an existing surplus or increasing by that amount an existing deficit. Similarly, every rise of $10 billion in national income will increase tax receipts by something like $3 billion thereby increasing an existing surplus by $3 billion or reducing an existing deficit by that amount. Moreover, these effects on the condition of the budget will be accentuated by automatic changes in expenditure. As explained above, every drop in national income will tend to raise federal government expenditure and every increase in national income will tend to lower it. Many economists think that some further increase in built-in automatic stabilizers is possible and desirable.

D. Needed: A Principle to Replace the Annually Balanced Budget

Automatic built-in fiscal stabilizers can be either supplemented or thwarted by explicit legislation and administrative action taken in response to changing business conditions. When high incomes cause tax collections to exceed expenditures, legislatures may destroy this automatic anti-inflation effect by cutting tax rates or by spending recklessly. Likewise, the automatic anti-unemployment effect of built-in stabilizers may be lost if, as happened in 1932, falling tax receipts in depression lead to reduced government outlay and higher tax rates. We cannot balance the budget annually and at the same time have a stabilizing fiscal policy—on this almost all economists agree. The tradition of an annually balanced budget calls for discretionary action from time to time that perversely cancels out the effects of the automatic stabilizers now built into the system.

Abandonment of the rule of an annually balanced budget necessitates adoption of other standards of budgetary policy to enable Congress and the electorate to determine when increases in expenditure call for increases in taxes and when decreases in expenditure can safely be balanced by decreases in taxes. Otherwise, there would be no check to waste and inefficiency, or to expenditures exceeding what the people really want, and hence no check to chronic inflation.

One important proposal is to aim at budget balance over a longer period. Nobody would advocate a *monthly* balance irrespective of seasonal changes; why should any special magic be attributed to a yearly balance irrespective of business-cycle changes? The so-called Swedish budget proposal is to balance the budget over a business cycle. Extra spending would call for extra taxes, but not necessarily for an equal amount of tax revenue in the same year. Budget surpluses in some years would cover the deficits of other years. Uncertainties about the length of the "cycle" and about the relative duration of depression and prosperity would, of course, create difficulties in application, but this proposal deserves serious consideration.

Another possibility is to preserve balance each year in a "target" or "normal" budget in which tax revenues, unemployment compensation and relief expenditures, and other items that must or should vary with business conditions, are always entered at the amounts they would be in a period of high employment and national income without inflation.

An increase in the general scale of government activities would then call for a tax rate increase, but a bulge of relief expenditures and a drop in tax revenue because of a business slump would not. Nor would an increase in tax revenue accompanying inflation call for a tax cut. Many economists believe this plan would be a marked improvement over the traditional annual budget balance rule. It would, however, present some difficult problems in application, particularly what levels of employment and national income would be the proper basis for the "target" or "normal" figures of tax revenues, relief expenditures, etc.

A third proposal is a modified version of the annual balance rule, applicable in periods when the economy is prosperous and stable and there is no evident swing toward depression or inflation. In this situation, newly planned increases or decreases in government expenditure would call for tax-rate changes to produce corresponding changes in tax revenue. Thus, proposed increases in government expenditure would have to meet the traditional test of whether they are worth their cost in terms of higher taxes. As far as it goes, this proposal would probably have the approval of most economists. But it provides no standards for appraisal of the existing relation of government expenditures and receipts, whether deficit or surplus, or for fiscal policy in periods of depression or inflation.

Some economists would dispense with any hard-and-fast rule or formula. They would vary total government revenue in relation to expenditure so as to exercise a stabilizing influence on the economy. They claim that it is not possible to say in advance whether such an approach would call for tremendous surpluses and public debt reduction in the years ahead or a predominance of deficit spending.

E. *Discretionary Stabilizing Action*

Some economists would place exclusive reliance on built-in stabilizers. They believe that these automatic stabilizers are very likely to reduce economic fluctuations to tolerable magnitudes; and they fear that discretionary government actions are likely to do more harm than good, owing to the defects of forecasting, the destabilizing influence of uncertainty about government action, and the political pressures to favor special interests. Most economists approve the greatest possible use of automatic stabilizers, but do not consider it prudent to rely solely on them. Hence they favor use of additional stabilizing measures if unemployment or inflation pass certain points.

The principal types of discretionary fiscal action for stabilization are: (1) changes in tax rates and tax structures; (2) changes in "transfer payments"; (3) changes in expenditure on public works; and (4) general expansion or contraction of government activities.

The stabilizing influence of the present federal tax structure could be increased by reducing tax rates during a slump in order to encourage business and family expenditure; and by raising tax rates when an excess of money expenditure is causing inflation. Tax exemptions could also be varied.

The same logic underlies proposals for increasing "transfer payments" in bad times: *e.g.,* increasing grants-in-aid by the federal government to help carry the local relief load. Some economists even go so far as to advocate that the government send checks to people broadside during times of mass unemployment. The possible abuses of such a program, and an aversion to giving people money they have not in some sense earned, explain the considerable skepticism toward this proposal and the wider approval of work relief as a means of providing incomes for those who cannot, for the time, be employed in private industry or on public works.

Shifts in the timing of construction of some public buildings, river improvements, power facilities, public housing, and the like, would do no great harm. The question is therefore raised whether such heavy public works cannot be hurried forward in case of a slump and slowed down in case of a boom, and thus used to temper economic fluctuations. In the past this sector of government expenditure has often behaved perversely, growing in prosperity and shrinking in slump. There would be widespread agreement among economists that the least that should be done is to correct this destabilizing tendency by a closer approach to regularization of government expenditure on heavy public works. State and local governments face real obstacles to such regularization of expenditure, but it may be possible to remove these in considerable degree by appropriate federal assistance programs or by other devices.

Some economists would go further and seek to increase heavy public works in depression and retard them in prosperity, particularly if the swings in economic activity should be fairly long in duration and substantial in amplitude. However, there seems to be a trend away from the earlier enthusiastic belief that this can go a long way, by itself, in stabilizing business activity. It takes so long to get public-works projects under way, even with a "shelf" planned ahead, that more accurate forecasting than we now have would be needed to guide the timing of such a program.

"Light" public works—road maintenance, earth-moving projects in relation to conservation and flood control, etc.—offer advantages in flexibility of expenditure and timing, and are regarded by many economists as an important part of a stabilization program.

Finally, the federal government could contract or expand the scope and scale of its activities. Few economists would favor the use of such changes to temper mild short-run fluctuations in economic activity. A larger number would use changes in the general level of government activities along with the other devices mentioned above to meet sharp or prolonged unemployment or inflation.

Whether discretionary action is to operate on public works and work relief expenditures, "transfer payments," or tax rates, or on the general level of government activities, two related problems must be solved: (1) Who is to have the authority to decide when action is to be taken and what kind of action is appropriate?; and (2) What criteria can and should this authority use in reaching its decisions? The second problem would be solved and the first would not be serious if we could forecast accurately for a considerable period ahead, since in that case it would make little difference where the authority was lodged. Different authorities would reach much the same decisions, and in any event, success or failure could be easily gauged and thus effective legislative control would be possible. The admitted impossibility of accurate forecasting makes both problems serious. Retention of authority by the legislature is almost certain to mean a substantial lag before action is taken. As a practical matter, the process of changing a tax law or expenditure program usually takes the Congress many months of hearings and debate. Moreover, each separate action is likely to become enmeshed in political controversy. On the other hand, delegation of authority means surrendering in some measure what have hitherto been exclusive prerogatives of the legislature and thus strengthens the executive arm of the government. It means, not the elimination of political pressures, but concentration of these pressures on an executive authority rather than on the legislature.

Difficulties of the sort just mentioned might be overcome in part by the device of advance enactment by Congress of statutes providing for changes in taxes, "transfer payments," or public works expenditures, and setting forth rules or standards for putting those programs into effect. For example, the law could provide that the withholding rate in the personal income tax be raised by a stated amount whenever an appropriate price index had risen by a certain amount in a defined period of months; and be lowered by a stated amount whenever standard indices of production and employment dropped below specified levels or trends. Again, the law could provide that the period during which unemployed workers could receive unemployment compensation be temporarily increased according to a standard index of the volume of unemployment. Another example is found in advance authorization for a specific program of public works, to be put into operation in accordance with changes in standard indices of production and employment and to be curtailed in accordance with changes in the same indices. Standards for application of these measures would have to be quite easily and widely understood. Congress could, if it desired, retain a "legislative veto" on the actual putting into effect of such programs. This device of advance enactment of stabilizing measures shades into the area of built-in, automatic stabilizers.

V. MONETARY POLICY

Monetary policy includes policies dealing with banking and credit—the availability of loans to firms and households, and interest rates—, the public debt and its management, and the monetary standard.

A. Banking Policy

Banking policy has for generations been held responsible for easing financial "panics." After the first World War the rather vague mandates of the Federal Reserve Act—"maintenance of sound credit conditions" and "accommodation of commerce, industry and agriculture"—came to be construed into a general concern with economic stability. During the "New Era" of the 1920's, there was a widespread impression that the policies of the Federal Reserve System were in fact achieving prosperity with steady prices. The breakdown of the "New Era" prosperity, the recurrence of a financial "panic" in 1933, and the incomplete business recovery after 1933 despite expansionist Federal Reserve policy, have raised doubts of the effectiveness of monetary policy as an instrument for maintaining economic stability. Few economists today would rely so heavily on monetary policy as was typical twenty years ago, but few would regard it as unimportant. Experience has shown that appropriate monetary policies can be helpful and that inappropriate policies can be harmful. Most economists agree on the following: (1) Tight money is a deterrent to price inflation accompanying a general excess of demand over supply; (2) Tight money can greatly accentuate a downswing of activity and may convert a mild depression into a deep one; and (3) Easy money by itself is an inadequate remedy for deep depressions, but it is helpful. Some economists think that easy money may be an adequate remedy for mild depressions, and that appropriate monetary policy may prevent mild depressions from becoming deep.

Looking ahead, there are two main lines of bank-credit policy on which to rely—qualitative controls regulating particular types of credit, and quantitative controls to produce a general tightening or easing of credit. Quantitative controls must be the main reliance, but the possibilities and limitations of qualitative controls need to be considered.

Qualitative Controls. Qualitative controls are measures designed to stimulate, restrict or stabilize loans for particular, specific purposes. Examples of stimulating controls are Federal Housing Authority insurance of mortgages and revision of bank examination standards designed to facilitate credit expansion through consumer loans and "term loans" to business. Such stimulative measures can scarcely be turned on and off on short notice, but may have their uses in case of persistent depression. The use of qualitative controls to reduce the fluctuation in bank credit is illustrated by the amendments of bank-examination standards in the late 1930's, aimed to encourage banks to judge loans and bond investments by their long-run prospects, and thus to make credit standards less cycle-sensitive. Restrictive qualitative controls are illustrated by the control of stock-exchange margins and of installment credit during and since the war.

Some opinion seems to favor primary reliance on qualitative controls in circumstances where inflationary pressures need to be checked by tight credit. Most economists are skeptical on this point, for several reasons. There seems to be no possibility of designing workable controls over loans to finance inventories, a type of loan which contributed to inflation in 1946–48, and probably in 1919–20. In general, when one type of bank credit is restricted, the activities it is hoped to restrict can usually be financed under some other label, thus evading the restriction. Further, qualitative controls necessarily affect only selected lines of activity and many economists think it undesirable that measures designed to control the general level of activity should favor or repress particular lines of activity.

Quantitative Controls. Control of the quantity of bank credit is operated through instruments affecting the reserves of the banks, since the ability of banks to make loans and investments depends on the amount of their reserves in relation to legal requirements. The reserves of the banks are their deposits in the Federal Reserve Banks. A bank cannot expand its loans or investments unless it is prepared to face a loss of reserves as borrowers, or sellers of securities, use the newly acquired funds. To expand credit, therefore, a bank must either have reserves in excess of the required minimum percentage of its deposits, or have ways to get additional reserve funds. A bank which runs short of reserves has to choose between borrowing from the Federal Reserve Bank or reversing the process of credit expansion and cutting down its outstanding loans and investments.

Policy actions by the Federal Reserve System or the United States Treasury can put the banks in an easy reserve position encouraging credit expansion, or a tight reserve position pushing them into credit contraction. The Board of Governors of the Federal Reserve System can, within limits fixed by statute, change the minimum ratio of reserves to deposits that each member bank in the System is legally required to hold. The Board can also change the "rediscount rate"—the cost to commercial banks of borrowing from the Federal Reserve Banks—though this instrument has been of little importance in recent years. The reserve position of the banks can also be altered by shifting the location of Treasury funds from commercial banks to Federal Reserve Banks, or vice versa. A shift of these funds into Federal Reserve Banks reduces deposits and reserves of commercial banks by equal amounts, thus lowering the percentage ratio of their reserves to their deposits.

The most powerful tool of monetary policy is "open market operations"—that is, the sale and purchase of government securities by the Federal Reserve or by the Treasury. A sale of securities by Federal Reserve Banks or by the Treasury results in a flow of checks from buyers to the Federal Reserve Banks. These are subtracted from the reserve accounts of commercial banks (*i.e.,* their deposits with the Reserve Banks), with the result that their reserves are lowered by the amount paid for the securities. In the other direction, a purchase of securities by a Federal Reserve Bank leads to issue of a check which, when collected by a bank from the Reserve Bank, adds directly to the reserve of that bank. The Federal Reserve buys and sells large amounts of securities every week, on its own account and as fiscal agent of the Treasury. If the net effect of these operations is an excess of sales over purchases, bank reserves are reduced. If the net effect is an excess of purchases over sales, bank reserves are expanded.

In the years 1946–48, the open-market power was used to support the prices of government securities. This limited its use to check credit expansion, since banks wishing to get more reserves could do so at will by selling such securities.

Experience suggests that quantitative monetary control is more effective in checking undesired credit expansion than in bringing about desired credit expansion. There is always a point at which shortage of reserves will curtail the growth of bank loans and investments. In the other direction, while expanding the reserves of commercial banks *permits* credit expansion, it cannot guarantee it—that depends also on the attitude of borrowers. In recession, the most that monetary policy can do may be to avoid adding credit deflation to the list of forces aiding the downswing. But if a prosperity period takes on an inflationary tinge, monetary policy has a clear responsibility to arrest credit expansion.

The destabilizing tendencies of banking could be reduced by setting higher reserve requirements. A 20 per cent reserve system, which is roughly what we have today, cannot inflate itself nearly as far on a given volume of excess reserves, or deflate itself as far in paying off a given amount of bank debt to the Federal Reserve, as the 10 per cent reserve system which we had in the 1920's.

Some economists favor going all the way to a 100 per cent reserve banking system to minimize this source of instability. In this extreme form, the proposal would involve the complete separation of the depository and check-clearance functions of existing banks from their lending functions. The existing lending functions would be taken over by new institutions, many of which, it is expected, would be formed from loan departments of existing banks and all of which would obtain their funds from the flotation of securities rather than from deposits subject to recall on demand. Proponents of this scheme maintain that it would cure the destabilizing influences now built into our banking structure, facilitate control over the quantity of money by either automatic means or discretionary authorities, and avoid excessive government regulation of the lending market. Many economists doubt that this measure would make a significant contribution to economic stability, and feel that the transitional difficulties of such a drastic change would be great and that less drastic measures can put the banking system on a satisfactory footing.

B. *Public Debt Policy*

The national debt held outside government agencies and Federal Reserve Banks now amounts to approximately $200 billion or about 90 per cent of a year's national income. (This compares with a national debt calculated on the same basis of about 50 per cent of national income in 1939.) Of the $200 billion, commercial banks hold about $65 billion and other credit institutions about $35 billion, leaving about $100 billion in the hands of individuals, corporations, and local governments. About $60 billion of the debt, including Savings Bonds, is redeemable on demand. Another $40 billion is composed of short-term Treasury securities. Interest charges on $200 billion of the debt in the hands of the public are about $4½ billion a year.

During and shortly after the war there was a standing offer by the Federal Reserve to buy government securities at stated prices. This policy made it impossible to check price inflation by tightening the bank reserve position significantly.

The standing offer of the Federal Reserve to buy government securities at stated prices rendered the large bank holdings of these securities the practical equivalent of excess legal reserves. Any bank that wanted to increase loans, or to buy investments could get reserves by selling part of its government securities to the Federal Reserve. Thus, public debt policy largely transformed the open market operations of the Federal Reserve System from a means of controlling bank credit to a means of supporting the prices of government securities and holding down interest rates.

The Federal Reserve authorities later substituted a somewhat more flexible policy of maintaining "orderly conditions" in the government security market in place of the wartime and early postwar policy of supporting government securities at stated prices. Although this new formula creates the possibility of using monetary controls as a contracyclical stabilizer, there is serious danger that excessive emphasis will be given to stabilization of government security prices.

Many economists advocate that the Federal Reserve abandon the price of government securities as a primary criterion of policy, and decide on the volume of government securities to purchase or sell on the basis of the desired tightness or ease in the money market.

Many other economists see serious drawbacks to this policy: (1) The budgetary cost might be large; (2) If such a policy resulted in disorderly conditions in the market for government securities, there might be serious repercussions on the solvency of our financial institutions—banks, insurance companies, etc.; (3) Moreover, a tightening of the structure of interest rates may take many years to reverse, so that unless the authorities can forecast with confidence that inflation will last a long time, these economists think that such a policy might do more harm than good.

Security-Reserve Possibilities. One method proposed for bringing the reserve position under control while protecting the market for government securities held by banks is to require banks to keep a reserve of government securities against deposits, in addition to present cash reserves. To be effective in controlling credit, such a requirement would have to tie down the bulk of the reserve-eligible government securities. Interest rates on other government securities would then be allowed to vary. Proposals of the Federal Reserve authorities for requirements stopping a good deal short of absorbing bank holdings might well leave banks such a wide margin of cashable securities as to be ineffective.

The security-reserve proposal was advocated during the active inflation of 1946–48 by the Board of Governors of the Federal Reserve System and by some private economists, as an emergency measure to check the inflation and as a contribution to permanent economic stabilization. In all essential respects, raising required reserve ratios by adding a security-reserve requirement is identical with a straight increase of cash reserve requirements, combined with an equivalent purchase of government securities by the Reserve Banks. The only significant difference is that the security-reserve proposal provides the member banks with the equivalent of a subsidy (in the form of interest on the bonds) to compensate for the loss of earnings on additional assets tied up as reserves. Like a straight increase in cash reserve requirements, it would reduce the possible ratio of credit expansion to excess reserves.

C. *The Monetary Standard*

The problem of monetary standards is ordinarily discussed in terms of gold. This is likely to be misleading. Gold has an importance in relation to international problems, but in relation to our domestic problems it is not very important. Our gold reserves are so enormous that maintaining the gold standard—that is, keeping gold at a price of $35 per ounce—can be no guarantee against inflation. Nor can the gold standard be any guarantee against deflation and unemployment, as may be seen from our experiences of the 1930's and earlier depressions. Moreover, attempts to manage the domestic economy by changing the gold price would be ineffective domestically and ruinous to our international relations.

Gold is a connecting link between domestic monetary policy and international problems. Currently the chief meaning of our standing offer to buy gold at $35 per ounce is that it creates a market for something produced in friendly countries we are trying to help, particularly sterling-area countries, and that it gives a value in American goods to the monetary reserves of our friends. However, political considerations aside, it is more straightforward and economical to make funds avail able to nations we seek to help in the form of open gifts than to buy gold we do not need and which they must use some of their resources to produce.

In a long-run view, most economists think is wasteful to produce gold destined only to be buried in our monetary hoards. Some urge the return to a situation in which gold plays an essential rôle in the monetary system, others, the complete elimination of the monetary rôle of gold. Many feel, however, that present international difficulties make this an inappropriate time to make a fundamental change in the rôle of gold.

One proposal for a reform of the monetary standard to promote economic stability is the commodity-reserve-currency plan ("Graham Plan"). This is a scheme for giving a stable real value to the dollar by having the government issue a standing offer to buy or sell, at a fixed price, a *composite commodity-bundle* of standardized and storable raw materials. The offer would be backed up on the buying side by the government's power to issue paper money, and by available storage facilities, and on the selling side by a reserve of commodities in storage.

The chief merit claimed for the commodity-reserve scheme is that it could be a powerful automatic stabilizer. In a recession, purchases for the commodity reserve would increase the quantity of money and check the decline in the incomes of raw-material producers and thus help also to maintain markets for goods used by these producers. In an inflationary boom, sale of commodities from the reserve would reduce the quantity of money, absorb excess spending power and add to available supplies of raw materials. This plan needs further exploration and appraisal before its practical potentialities will be clear, particularly with respect to the make-up of the "composite commodity" and its relation to farm and food policy, to international commodity agreements, and to monetary policies of other countries.

D. The Relation between Fiscal and Monetary Policy

To simplify exposition, fiscal and monetary policy have been treated separately, though they are in fact closely related and decisions about one will inevitably affect the other. Perhaps the point of most direct contact between monetary and fiscal policy is the financing of deficits and the use of surpluses.

We have seen that a stabilizing fiscal policy may call for a deficit at a time of large unemployment and for a surplus at a time of strong inflation. We have also seen that stabilizing monetary policy calls for relatively easy money at a time of large unemployment and for relatively tight money at a time of strong inflation. The two principles together require that a deficit designed to offset depressing influences be financed in a way that would contribute to monetary ease—for example, by the sale of securities to the Federal Reserve System or by the printing of currency. Similarly, the two principles require that a surplus designed to offset expansive influences be used in a way that would contribute to tight money—for example, by retiring securities owned by the Federal Reserve Banks or by destroying currency.

These simple principles have by no means always been followed. The most recent example is the policy of supporting government security prices in 1946–48, which meant that some of the restrictive effect of post–World-War II surpluses was dissipated. The combined effect of monetary and fiscal policy was in consequence to favor capital formation at the expense of consumption.

Coordination between fiscal and monetary policy is also required on a broader level: the two policies must work together and not at cross purposes. This raises broad issues, largely outside the scope of this report, about the appropriate administrative and political arrangements for the control of monetary and fiscal policies and about the standards employed to guide these policies.

In the past, fiscal policy has been directly governed by legislative action; whereas monetary policy has been largely at the discretion of the Federal Reserve System and the Treasury, though a considerable number of other agencies—the Federal Deposit Insurance Corporation, Reconstruction Finance Corporation, Federal Housing Authority, and so on—have exercised some monetary influence. Perhaps most economists feel that control over monetary policy is at present dispersed too widely to permit effective coordination. Some economists would favor concentrating control over monetary policy and adding discretionary control of fiscal policy. Others would favor reducing or eliminating the amount of discretion at present lodged in the monetary authorities—thereby placing major emphasis in both fiscal and monetary policy on essentially automatic reactions.

In the past, also, the standards for monetary action have been very vague and broad. Some economists would favor equally broad standards for governing fiscal policy. Others would favor the acceptance of a single set of more specific standards—such as stability of an index of prices or employment—to govern whatever discretionary action is authorized in both monetary and fiscal policy.

VI. SOME INTERNATIONAL FACTORS

For many countries, the problem of domestic economic stability is greatly complicated by high dependence upon external trade. A country that exports a large fraction of its own production and relies heavily upon imports to meet its internal needs will necessarily be quite sensitive to external disturbances influencing its foreign trade. This sensitiveness to outside influences will be further enhanced if its reserves of gold and foreign exchange are small and its ability to obtain aid or credit abroad is limited. A decline in external demand for its export products, owing to depressed conditions in the chief markets to which it sells, imposes upon it the necessity of quickly bringing its external payments into line with its reduced receipts. This must usually be achieved in the main through curtailment of imports, and this by itself may interfere with domestic stability. At times something may be accomplished by improving the competitive position of exports. In this situation it is possible to avert serious internal deflation by resorting to currency depreciation, imposing direct restriction on imports, or subsidizing exports; but under some circumstances such measures may have other disadvantages, so that some internal deflation may be accepted as a consequence of the falling off in external demand for its goods. For such countries the task of adjusting the external balance at least complicates, and may conflict with, the achievement of domestic economic stability.

The United States is not in that position. Indeed, among economically advanced countries the United States is in an almost uniquely fortunate position. Our problem of domestic economic stability is not significantly affected by complicating external factors. This is not due solely to our huge gold reserves. Even more important are the facts that (1) our foreign trade is a relatively small part of our total activity, and (2) at the present time, other countries have such small reserves of gold and foreign exchange and are controlling their imports from the United States so closely through direct measures that any change in our purchases from them is likely to be reflected very rapidly and fully in a corresponding change in our exports. This means that in the event of a depression in the United States, we could not get any substantial over-all domestic stimulus by raising our barriers to imports. Hence, tarriffs and import restrictions cannot be an effective anti-depression measure for the United States.

Though our foreign trade is a relatively small fraction of our activity, our imports bulk large in the activity of a considerable number of other countries. This means that foreign countries have a large stake in stable prosperity in the United States and in a broadening of our market for imports. Our record of economic instability, combined with our traditional policy of tariff protection obviously makes them reluctant to link their economies too closely to ours. In the event of a serious depression here, other countries eager to avoid a repetition of the experience of the 'thirties, would probably unite in imposing specific restrictions against imports of American goods. The result would be a partial quarantining and isolation of the United States. The general objectives of our foreign policy make it essential that we encourage other democratic countries to adopt commercial policies which emphasize interdependence with, rather than insulation from, the United States. Our success on this score will depend, first and foremost, on our actual performance in achieving stable prosperity, and second, on our willingness to have low import duties, and to refrain from such other obstacles to imports as quotas and cumbersome customs procedure. Under present world conditions, the international political importance of our success, or failure, in achieving domestic economic stability can scarcely be overestimated.

Although our domestic economy is unlikely to experience serious disturbance from unpredictable and independent fluctuations in the foreign demand for American goods, our economy is subject to other important forces from abroad. The size of our programs of foreign economic and military aid and of government-fostered private investment abroad must be based mainly on our assessment of world conditions and the requirements of foreign policy, without much reference to considerations of domestic stability. It is the task of domestic stabilization policy to compensate for unstabilizing variations in the size of those programs, as well as in our military expenditures. A worsening of the international situation, resulting in very heavy expenditures for these purposes, might confront us with as difficult a problem of controlling inflation as in wartime. Improvement in the international situation might, on the other hand, permit a sharp curtailment of military expenditures at home and military aid to others. In this event, tax reductions could go far to forestall any deflationary effect.

Although the present U.S. position permits us a wide range of freedom in choosing domestic policies, even this freedom is not complete. And in any case, we must realize when we choose between alternative stabilization programs that they have definite international implications.

VII. MARKET POLICY[1]

Wise use of the instruments of fiscal and monetary control is essential to economic stability, but there is no assurance that, under all cir-

[1] Milton Friedman makes the following comment on this section:

"I disagree with the general tenor of this section and one of its major specific conclusions.

"(1) Market policy seems to me to stand in an entirely different relation to economic stability than monetary and fiscal policy. Monetary and fiscal measures are general measures adapted to the problem of countering general changes in employment, output, and prices

cumstances, economic stability will be achieved through such controls alone. In a free-enterprise economy private policies of business and labor with respect to prices, wages and profits have a bearing upon stability, and the same is true of government policies affecting prices and incomes in particular industries, such as agriculture, transportation and public utilities.

This raises two fundamental questions. First, how should prices, wages and profits behave? Second, what steps should be taken so that prices, wages and profits will behave as they should? Since economists have not yet made much progress in analysing the effects on business fluctuations of price, wage and profit behavior, no comprehensive and precise answer can be given to the first question. And as one might guess, there are widely divergent views on both questions.

The power of organized labor today suggests that we may be faced with the danger of chronic inflation resulting from general wage increases which recurrently outrun the growth in productivity of the econ-

---

and are the appropriate techniques to use for that purpose. Changes in particular prices and particular wages are appropriate for achieving a proper allocation of resources and products among different uses; they are entirely inappropriate for countering general changes in employment, output, and prices.

"The chief reason for considering market policy at all in a report on economic instability is that inappropriate market policy—a market policy that enables special groups, whether trade unions, industrial producers, or farmers, to exercise direct control over prices or wages—may render monetary and fiscal policy largely ineffective in attaining its twin objectives of full employment and stable prices, a point that this section quite appropriately makes. The solution is to be sought in the elimination of these direct controls, not in their extension or in the substitution of governmental controls. The problem is not what behavior ought to be imposed on particular prices or wage rates but rather, what the appropriate institutional arrangements are for the determination of prices, wage rates, etc.—the problem considered in the three paragraphs that precede the final paragraph of this section.

"(2) One of the chief specific conclusions of this section is that prices of products and wages of labor require different treatment for the promotion of economic stability; that it is desirable for the general level of product prices to fluctuate over the business cycle but undesirable for the general level of wage rates to do so (paragraphs 8, 9, and 11 of this section). This seems to me false. Prices of products and wages of labor are on the same footing. Our basic objective is to minimize the fluctuations in both. Insofar as the conclusion of this section goes beyond this statement, it necessarily implies substituting rigidity for stability. When a decline in total money demand presses prices and wages down, the wage level can be kept stable only by preventing particular wage rates from falling.

"If fiscal and monetary policy prevent total money demand from falling or rising sharply, they will thereby prevent any general decline or rise in wages and prices from developing into a spiral and becoming cumulative. Declines or rises in particular prices and wage rates can then serve the useful and indispensable function of facilitating adjustments among different sections of the economy. 'The growing strength of organized labor' is, from this point of view, as harmful in periods of business contraction as in periods of business expansion (see paragraph 8 of this section). The alternative solution of a rigid wage level proposed in this section is equivalent to saying that the appropriate way to reduce temperature fluctuations in a room is to break the thermometer which controls the thermostat so it always registers the same temperature."

omy as a whole. Man-hour productivity for the economy as a whole has increased in the past at an average rate of about 2 per cent per year. A gradual upward trend in average hourly wage rates corresponding approximately to this general growth in productivity—*i.e.,* an increase of about 2 per cent a year, if past trends continue—need not result in an upward trend in the average level of prices. But general increases in wage rates exceeding the average growth of productivity raise costs and will ordinarily result in higher prices.

Chronic wage-induced price inflation would pose a dilemma for fiscal and monetary policy. Suppose wages rise at a rate of 10 per cent per year and prices by 7 or 8 per cent. Should we then adopt tight money and a budget surplus to meet this situation? If we do, the result will be not so much control of prices as a reduction of output and employment: business costs and prices will still be high but total money demand will be deficient so that men and machines will have to become unemployed. If we do not, we face the danger that the wage and price increases will continue at a rate that becomes intolerable. Thus, inflation induced by rising costs rather than excess demand offers a very grave dilemma for fiscal and monetary policy.

Opinions of economists differ regarding the likelihood that these problems will be serious. And suggestions for a solution tend to be impractical or rather general and vague. Direct governmental control of wages is incompatible with a free-enterprise economy. Even proposals for compulsory arbitration of wage disputes are opposed by both unions and employers, and there are as yet no agreed principles of income distribution policy that might establish a basis for arbitration. Limited statutory restraints upon the right to srike are unlikely to curtail seriously the bargaining strength of labor organizations. Adoption by labor leaders of a more responsible attitude on wage increases, taking account of the full effects on the economy as a whole, may be impossible unless inter-union competition becomes weaker and economic understanding of the rank and file, as well as the leaders, becomes greater. For the present, reconciling full employment with price level stability within a free-enterprise framework must be regarded as a major unsolved problem.

It should be emphasized that the relationship, noted above, between growth of productivity and increase in wage rates does not hold for a particular firm or industry. Productivity does not grow uniformly or evenly among industries and firms; the differences in rates of productivity increase are often great. If wage rates in each particular industry or firm were adjusted to the productivity change in that firm or industry, untenable disparities would develop in the wages paid by different industries for the same kind of labor. Instead, wage rates for a particular grade of labor should be approximately uniform throughout all sectors of the economy, except for regional differentials reflecting basic differences. Divergent rates of growth in productivity in particular industries should, in general, be reflected in shifts in the relative prices of their products, involving price reductions in those fields experiencing above-average progress and price increases in those fields where growth in productivity is lagging.

An average increase of about 2 per cent per year in the level of money wage rates does not, however, imply just this rate of increase for each worker or each grade of labor. Existing anomalies in the wage structure are continually being corrected. Also, progress in equalizing educational and training opportunities and in removing discriminatory barriers to entry into the more agreeable and highly paid occupations should result in narrowing somewhat the wage differentials between menial, unskilled jobs and skilled jobs through increases in rates at the lower end of the wage structure. Again, the faster-growing firms and industries may need to raise wages a little faster in order to attract labor. These factors will at times justify increases in particular wage rates of more than 2 per cent per year.

A downward spiral of wages and prices is at least as harmful to economic stability as an upward spiral. General wage cuts are likely to be unstabilizing; they may help to convert a moderate business recession into a severe depression. If such cuts are not accompanied by equivalent reductions in consumer prices, they depress business by reducing the buying power of workers. If, on the other hand, prices are promptly adjusted, the decline in wages and prices together, coming in a period of business contraction, is likely to give rise to expectations of further reductions, producing general postponement of buying, efforts to liquidate inventories, losses, pressure on borrowers to repay, and serious financial difficulties and deflation. The growing strength of organized labor, while it has increased the likelihood that an inflationary wage-price spiral will develop in periods of business expansion, has much reduced the danger that future periods of business contraction will be intensified by deflationary wage-price spirals, such as occurred in the early 'thirties.

Stability of the wage level does not imply that the level of prices must remain rigid; profit margins can and should vary through the cycle.

In a dynamic economy stable prosperity calls for a continuous re-adaptation and redirection of productive effort in response to the development of new products, new techniques of production and changing wants. In a free-enterprise economy this kind of dynamic adjustment requires willingness to adjust prices, and sometimes capacity, promptly to changed conditions of demand or supply. Marked stickiness or rigidity of particular prices may be an important factor impeding dynamic adjustment and contributing to over-all economic instability. Attempts to achieve monopoly profits by limiting output and keeping prices high tend to reduce the buying power of consumers. Some economists think that monopolistic action may prevent new investment.

General conclusions are that cumulative wage-price spirals destroy economic stability, and that the task of maintaining stable prosperity will be greatly assisted if a way can be found to combine a steady and gradual upward trend in money wage rates, corresponding to the average over-all growth in productivity, with a considerable degree of flexibility in the prices of particular goods. It is all too evident that the actual behavior of wages and prices does not correspond to this ideal. The tendency of union wages to rise excessively during periods of business expansion, and the tendency of many prices to remain fixed, or decline only sluggishly, in periods of business contraction are obstacles to economic stability. They may put an impracticable burden upon fiscal and monetary policies. There is disagreement among economists, however, on both the magnitude of these problems and the measures which should be taken to meet them.

According to one view, the government should adopt a positive, sweeping program to remove barriers to competition, so that no business corporation and no labor union would have the power to exert any significant influence over the prices of whatever it sells or buys. Prices, wages and profits would then be determined by the automatic operation of competitive markets. In those industries where economies of mass production or other factors limit the firms to such a small number that competition is not effective, government ownership or regulation would replace free, private enterprise. This approach calls for a destruction of private power over wages and prices, but with no extension of government power except where effective competition is unattainable.

According to another view, the government, instead of relying primarily on measures to enforce competition, would establish selective price and wage controls and rationing and allocation procedures in key sectors of the economy, thus securing a substantial measure of influence over the behavior of prices, wages and profits. This approach calls for a curtailment of private power, and an extension of governmental power, over both prices and wages.

According to a third view, powerful private groups, such as large corporations and labor unions, must be accepted as an inherent feature of our kind of society. Instead of undertaking extensive government controls over wages and prices, however, an attempt should be made to formulate rules of responsible private behavior for organized groups, and to secure the voluntary acceptance by these groups of such rules. This approach emphasizes not the curtailment of private power, but its responsible exercise in conformity with accepted rules. It raises the fundamental question whether private groups can satisfactorily discharge public functions. This view does not, of course, rule out attempts to make competition as effective as possible everywhere, or substitution of public ownership and operation in highly monopolistic industries.

This diversity of views and programs is significant in indicating that the problem of prices, wages and profits is as yet largely unsolved. Difficulties in this field should not, however, prevent us from using fiscal and monetary controls to do the best we can in limiting fluctuations in total income, expenditure, production, and employment.

28

The American Economic Association Committee Report on Economic Instability[*]

By *ARTHUR SMITHIES*[†]

I

I am very grateful for the opportunity to welcome this report and to congratulate the authors on their dispassionate and lucid exegesis. I also welcome the opportunity to appear as a critic rather than as an author of a full employment report. But I do not make my comments in any spirit of rivalry: the present report may contain merits that the United Nations Report does not possess, and some of the major criticisms I shall make apply equally to that report.

As the authors point out, much of the report does not deal with the conditions of today or the foreseeable future. However, the major questions to which they point as unsettled are just as relevant to present conditions as to a state of affairs that I hope we can describe as more normal; and it is on those that I want to focus most of my attention. Parenthetically, I regret the compulsive need to affirm that what I am going to say has any contemporary relevance. The traditional pessimism of economists and our chronic tendency to project present conditions, especially when they are bad, into the future have had profound effects on human history. What a different and perhaps more agreeable place the world would have been had Ricardo, Malthus, and Marx been endowed with more than human foresight.

II

If the report does represent a consensus of American economists, it means that our thinking has now reached a state of Keynesian con-

* *American Economic Review,* May 1951. Reprinted by courtesy of the American Economic Association and the author.

† Harvard University.

servatism. So far as it depends on economic doctrine, it could have been written soon after the publication of the *General Theory;* and it could not have been written before. Let those who say there has been no Keynesian revolution ponder over the validity of that assertion. According to the report, the motivating force for economic activity is the effective demand that results from the decisions of consumers, investors, the government, and foreigners. Consumers' expenditures are held to depend on the size of their incomes, and their monetary assets. Or to be more accurate, the authors mention nothing but income—not even past income—and monetary assets as determinants of consumers' expenditures.

While I have always stressed these influences on consumption myself, I now feel bound to protest if economists are being invited to accept an income-monetary theory of consumption in the same spirit as John Stuart Mill accepted the Ricardian theory of value. Is it possible to refute a theory that maintains that fluctuations in consumption as well as long-run trends stem largely from the decisions of producers of consumers' goods to produce new products, to incur selling expenses of all kinds, and to change relative prices? During and after the war we had strong evidence that changes in the production of durable consumers' goods did affect the relation of consumption to income. Is it out of the question that in more normal times decisions from the supply side may induce fluctuations in the propensity to consume?

Even if an adequate explanation of consumption must take producers' decisions into account, it may still be possible to achieve substantial stability through fiscal and monetary measures. But other possibilities for stabilization are opened up—possibilities which we may reject today but be quite ready to accept ten years from now.

It is likely that the long period of military preparation on which we are now embarking will bring permanent changes in the relation of government to business, and control measures that are inconsistent with private enterprise today may be permanent and compatible features of the economy of tomorrow. I cannot exclude the possibility that the programing of private production may become the central core of stabilization policies of the future and that fiscal and monetary policies may be reduced to a position of ancillary importance.

Beyond this general comment, I have nothing but commendation for the Committee's fiscal and monetary policy suggestions, so far as they go. I note that the authors have not found a satisfactory rule of thumb to guide budgetary policy; and that difficult and complex questions of timing discretionary policies still remain unanswered. But I have nothing useful to suggest at the present time. Let me now turn to the major questions that the report leaves unanswered.

III

Whenever one encounters a proposal for stabilization through fiscal and monetary methods, whether it be by Keynes, Beveridge, Hansen, the U. N. Report, one can be quite sure that the inflationary dilemma will be recognized but left unresolved. The present report is no exception. The consensus evaporates when it comes to questions how full employment and price stability are to be achieved at the same time. Full employment is still haunted by the prospect of a wage-price spiral.

The report sets out four possible policies: First, the extreme radical view that the government should remove all possible barriers to competition in commodity and labor markets; and that those industries where it is impossible to restore competition should be nationalized. Second, that the government should use selective price, wage, rationing, and allocation controls to stabilize key sectors of the economy. Third, that organized private groups such as large corporations and labor unions—the report does not mention organized agriculture—should voluntarily accept rules for private behavior that will achieve stability of the price level. Fourth—the minority suggestion of Milton Friedman—that the government should use fiscal and monetary measures to stabilize money income and leave it at that. In modern conditions, the proposal involves fluctuations in prices, wages, employment, and production, but cumulative movements would be avoided.

In my view, all these suggestions have elements of usefulness, but none of them affords a complete answer in itself. Some attempt must be made to achieve a synthesis.

The perfect competition proposal would resolve the dilemma if it were practicable. It would in fact create the conditions presupposed by Keynes in the *General Theory.* There he assumes perfect competition in every industry, and does not get into inflationary trouble until full employment is reached. Before that point competition holds prices down. After it, increases in effective demand produce general inflation; autonomous wage increases do occur and they result in corresponding price increases. There is no inflationary dilemma if government action holds effective demand slightly below the full employment level.

I doubt whether anyone seriously believes that it would be possible to achieve conditions of perfect competition over an area wide enough to resolve the inflationary dilemma. Any government able and willing to follow the policy proposed would probably find that nationalization would be the rule and the achievement of competition the exception.

Economic controversies can be more readily understood and economic knowledge furthered if we decide at the outset whether the author of a proposal is attempting to construct an ideal type of economic system or whether he is formulating a program for adoption in the world as it is. Both types of activity are important and useful. Unless we are completely cynical about the usefulness of economics as an independent discipline, we must favor the construction of ideal systems as anchors for our practical proposals. Without such anchors economics would become the servant of politics and economic policy would depend exclusively on the currents of political expediency. On the other hand, if ideal systems are themselves put forward in the guise of practical proposals, economists can legitimately be charged with tilting at windmills.

I regard the perfect competition proposal as an ideal system and in that sense useful. It is important to know that stability can most easily be achieved in a competitive system and that measures to increase competition should form part of a stabilization program. But to regard perfect competition as a necessary condition for stabilization seems to me to give rise to the same difficulties as to regard Prohibition as a necessary prerequisite for a good society.

The view that the inflationary dilemma can be avoided through resort to compulsory controls over prices and wages when carried too far overlooks the nature of government, particularly in a democratic state. Inflationary trouble arises either because fiscal expansion is carried too far or because organized groups within the economy contend with each other to increase their relative shares of the national product. Can we assume that groups that refuse to exercise the self-restraint needed to make a fiscal program effective will submit to a system of controls imposed by the government they themselves help to select? We are too ready, as economists, to regard the economy as a marionette theater and to make the facile assumption that those who pull the strings have no relation to the puppets they control. This is not true even in a dictatorship; it is far from true in a democratic state.

In view of these elementary political facts, I believe there is a limit to the extent to which controls can be effectively used on a permanent basis. Some economists have advanced the suggestion that the simplest, and perhaps the only, way to stability is for the government to generate a permanent state of excess demand through fiscal policy and to suppress the resulting inflation through the permanent use of direct controls. Apart from the objections to such a course in terms of economic mechanics, it should be rejected as a political monstrosity.

However, it is equally naïve to go to the opposite extreme and to argue that all exercise of direct controls by governments means that we are on the road to serfdom. I draw a sharp distinction between the occasional and selective use of controls on the one hand and the permanent incorporation of a complete control system into the economic structure on the other. Europe has provided instructive case studies on these matters in recent years. I have been impressed with the growing realization of the need for decontrol. But I have also been impressed with the fact that those countries that still make extensive use of controls seem to be no further along the road to serfdom than those that have abandoned them. However, in the United States at the present time economists will do well to emphasize the dangers of direct controls rather than to argue for their uses.

The notion that an effective stabilization policy requires co-operation of organized sectors of the economy with each other and with the government is one that I have come to accept with considerable reluctance. Fiscal and monetary measures in themselves can be regarded as steps that implement the traditional operation of a market economy, but co-operation among groups implies negation of the idea that once aggregate demand is stabilized, market forces can be relied on to determine the allocation of productive resources and the distribution of incomes. But has not the time come to recognize that the policies of organized groups form an integral part of the operation of the economy?

Whether it was true before, it is certainly true now that large corporations determine their price policy with one eye on their public relations. Since the last war we have had numerous illustrations of the fact that, in times of shortage, corporations are unwilling to charge what the traffic will bear, both because of the general public reaction and because of the effect of such a policy on their wage negotiations. And wage negotiations themselves have tended since the war to involve discussion of the relation of wages to profits as well as the more traditional relation of money wages to the cost of living.

In view of the fact that organized groups will continue to exist and probably to grow in strength, it seems eminently desirable that all possible efforts be made to harmonize their policies with the requirements of economic stabilization. Yet it would be unrealistic and undesirable to rely exclusively on their co-operation to avoid the inflationary dilemma. But we cannot contemplate with equanimity the cohesive group organization that would be required to make co-operation fully effective—because of its possible consequences on the effectiveness of competition and economic growth. Nor is such cohesiveness likely. There is still much more competition in the American economy than many are prepared to recognize. Group co-operation, in my view, must relate to the formulation of general policies and attitudes rather than to specific action.

With the Friedman dissent, we return to the realm of ideal systems. If prices and wages were sufficiently flexible, there would be much to be said for stabilizing total money income and allowing prices and wages in individual industries to find their own levels. But with modern rigidities and modern group behavior, is it realistic to suppose that this can be done? With stable money incomes, a new round of wage increases would mean unemployment that would only be cured with a general wage decrease. Attractive though such a program may be from the point of view of economic aesthetics, I cannot conceive that any government that depends heavily on labor support—as all governments do—would have the strength of purpose or even the desire to allow it to be carried out. Although the Friedman program should be brought continually to the attention of policy makers, I cannot conceive that it can be regarded as the main basis for a practical policy.

Through no desire to please everyone, I conclude that all the measures that the Committee poses as alternatives—removal of obstacles to competition, selective and occasional, and direct controls and co-operation—must be used in combination to support monetary and fiscal policy if stability of the price level is to be associated with stability of employment. And I agree with the implication of Friedman's comment that if the government attempts, by fiscal and monetary measures, to maintain full employment at all times, it is unlikely to achieve a stable price level even under the most favorable conditions. There is no simple formula or magical trick that will produce the desired result. Stability will not be achieved without a general understanding by all sectors of the economy that more is to be gained from stability than from the pursuit of immediate sectional advantage. And this general understanding must be translated into more farseeing political attitudes than those to which we are accustomed.

IV

But all that is not enough. I seriously doubt whether the struggle for redistribution can be held in check except in the context of a growing economy; and this is especially true at a time when military needs are placing increasing demands on the national product.

Labor in particular will insist on a steady increase in its material well-being, and, unless total national output is increasing, the full force of this insistence will be felt in pressure for redistribution of incomes. And although redistribution will remain an end in itself as well as a means to higher mass living standards, a sufficiently rapid increase in total product may permit it to be held within feasible bounds. With increasing total output not only can real wages increase but money wages can rise without disturbing stability of the price level. Increasing productivity has saved the country from inflation in the past and may do so in the future.

While economic growth will make the task of stabilization easier, the stabilization policies that are adopted may hinder or promote economic growth. Full employment itself should promote growth since it assures the mass markets on which capitalistic success depends. On the other hand, certain fiscal policies—notably those that involve redistributive taxation—that will produce full employment in the short run may impair entrepreneurial incentives in a way that will slow down the rates of growth. It may then be still further slowed down through the consequent increased pressure for redistribution.

The report recognizes that economic growth is an important objective of policy and that stability may not always be consistent with it. But it does not assess various stabilization alternatives in terms of their effects on growth and does not recognize that growth may be a necessary prerequisite for stability. The Committee seems to have turned a deaf ear to the theme song of the Council of Economic Advisers—that in the ability of the economy to grow lies our promise of social security and stability as well as national security.

I must regretfully conclude that, judging by the report, we as academic economists are not confronting the issues of the present and the future with the imaginative vigor displayed in the past by our predecessors.

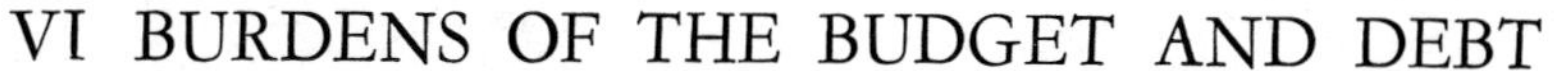

VI BURDENS OF THE BUDGET AND DEBT

29

The Burden of a Domestic Debt[*]

By B. U. RATCHFORD[†]

I

Since the beginning of modern public debts there have been serious differences of opinion as to whether they are a blessing, a curse, or a matter of indifference. During the past ten years the discussions of deficit financing have revived this issue but apparently have done little to settle it. Those who, following the Keynesian analysis, have favored deficit financing have concentrated their attention upon the income-generating potentialities of debt creation and have dismissed the question of the burden of the debt in later years with the general statement that an internally-held debt imposes no economic burden. On the other hand, those who have made special studies of the latter question have frequently arrived at a different conclusion.[1]

Since the federal debt will increase greatly during the present war, it is a matter of considerable importance to know whether that debt will be an economic burden in the post-war years. It might influence our attitude toward borrowing during the war; it would certainly affect our attitude toward deficit financing after the war.

In the discussion which follows it is assumed that the large post-war debt will be held internally, that a considerable proportion will be held by commercial banks, and that the debt will never be reduced substantially, but that interest will be paid regularly. It is also assumed that Congress will continue to frame tax laws as in the past, giving more heed to political than to economic considerations, but that the level of taxation will be much higher than in the past, with considerable re-

---

* *American Economic Review,* Sept. 1942. Reprinted by the courtesy of the American Economic Association and the author.

† Duke University.

[1] See, for example: Ursula K. Hicks, *The Finance of British Government, 1920–1936* (London, 1938), pp. 341, 348; Dan Throop Smith, "Economic Consequences of Deficit Financing: A Review," *Am. Econ. Rev.*, Supplement, Feb. 1941, XXXI, 95; David McC. Wright, *The Creation of Purchasing Power* (Cambridge, 1942), pp. 148–49.

liance upon a progressive personal income tax and a heavy corporate income tax.

It should be emphasized that the point under consideration is the burden, if any, of an internally-held public debt after it has been incurred, irrespective of the effects caused by its incurrence. Too frequently these two considerations have been confused, but as Hansen aptly states, "Once the debt has been incurred, its subsequent impact upon employment and the distribution of income will be the same regardless of the purpose for which it was incurred."[2]

II

There are two methods of analysis which may be used in attacking this problem: the "real" or barter analysis and the monetary analysis. These two methods may, in certain circumstances, lead to quite different conclusions. Much of the prevailing confusion undoubtedly arises from the unconscious switching from one method of analysis to the other.

The real or barter analysis is characteristic of classical and neoclassical theory; it has been, as Wright states, "almost the hall-mark of a trained economist."[3] Under this analysis goods exchange for goods, effective competition prevails, prices are flexible, and unemployment cannot be a serious problem. This procedure does not recognize money or monetary institutions as important elements in any problem; only the factors of production can enter into the analysis. This position is succinctly summarized in John Stuart Mill's famous statement,

> There cannot, in short, be intrinsically a more insignificant thing in the economy of society, than money; except in the character of a contrivance for sparing time and labour. It is a machine for doing quickly and commodiously, what would be done, though less quickly and commodiously, without it; and like many other kinds of machinery, it only exerts a distinct and independent influence of its own when it gets out of order.[4]

In practice the last qualification was almost invariably forgotten or disregarded.

In other words, classical theory assumed that monetary institutions merely provided a colorless or neutral medium through which the real factors of production operated. If that medium became defective and thus interfered with the free functioning of the factors of production,

---

[2] Alvin H. Hansen, *Fiscal Policy and Business Cycles* (New York, 1941), pp. 152–53. See also B. F. Haley, "The Federal Budget: Economic Consequences of Deficit Financing," *Am. Econ. Rev.*, Supplement, Feb. 1941, XXXI, 7.

[3] Wright, *op. cit.*, p. 4. See this reference for a further, and excellent, discussion of this point.

[4] *Principles of Political Economy* (Ashley ed.; London, 1921), p. 488.

that did not call for any modification of theory, but merely for a removal of the defect.

According to the monetary analysis, economic activity is dominated by the possibility of money profits. No matter how abundant the factors of production may be, they will not be used nor will exchange take place unless there is the prospect of monetary gain. Say's Law no longer reigns supreme. Expectations, the propensity to consume, and especially liquidity preference must all enter the analysis, though none of them is a factor of production. In short, this analysis recognizes that monetary institutions and arrangements may cause a shortage or a surplus of purchasing power which, in turn, may affect incomes and the level of economic activity.

Under conditions of relatively full employment these two methods of analysis may yield approximately the same results, but under other conditions the results may vary widely.

Deficit financing is usually justified by the use of the monetary analysis, which indicates that in certain circumstances monetary conditions may constitute an obstacle to the free and full use of economic resources. The remedy indicated by such analysis is to remove the obstacle by certain financial measures—the creation of purchasing power by borrowing. When this diagnosis and its corresponding prescription have been accepted and acted upon, however, its exponents are likely to switch, unconsciously, to the barter analysis to prove that the results of those financial measures (debts) cannot constitute an obstacle or burden in the future. Of course, in a barter economy they would be right. But it is submitted that greater consistency in method would provide a more valid and a more convincing analysis. It is the purpose here, with only minor exceptions, to stick to the monetary analysis.

III

A public debt will not constitute a net economic burden unless its disadvantages outweigh its advantages. Are there any advantages in the mere existence of a public debt? Hansen mentions several possible advantages. First, the English debt in the nineteenth century encouraged the growth of certain financial institutions such as banks, the stock market, and life insurance companies. Also, by offering capitalists maximum safety for a part of their funds, it encouraged them to take risks with the remainder and thus promoted the growth of new industries. Second, that same debt, together with a regressive tax system, curtailed consumption, increased savings, and thus facilitated the growth of capital and, ultimately, a rise in the standard of living. Third, because of a reversal of the above conditions, the English debt after World War I may have stimulated consumption.[5] Hansen only "suggests" this last point and does not attempt to prove it. It is not convincing to the present writer.[6]

In addition to those mentioned by Hansen, other advantages have been suggested. Some have claimed that the existence of safe public securities stimulates thrift and savings by those of low incomes and leads to financial security and self-respect. Again, the public debt is a convenient legal investment for trust and other fiduciary funds. Finally, the public debt is the most feasible vehicle for central bank open-market operations.

Concerning all of these except Hansen's last point, which is of doubtful validity, it may be said either that they are no longer of economic significance or that the conditions may be met with only a moderate debt. The big problem of the future will not be the stimulation of savings but rather the finding of suitable uses for those savings. We have the machinery, the techniques, and the institutions for assembling savings and issuing high-grade private securities; our greatest lack, in times of peace, is adequate demand for investment funds. Also, there can be no doubt that the present volume of public bonds is sufficient to provide the convenience mentioned in the last two points. The conclusion which logically follows is that there would be no economic advantage in the existence of any additional public debt.

IV

Perhaps the most popular explanation for the widely-accepted doctrine that an internally-held public debt imposes no economic burden is the "one big family" analogy; one segment of our population owes another segment, and for the group as a whole the assets and liabilities cancel out. A few years ago Professor King used a similar analogy in attempting to explain the unemployment problem, dreaming up a situation which might have arisen on George Washington's plantation. He concluded that "the illustration does not depart widely from the situation as it exists today. The United States is little more than an enlargement of Washington's plantation."[7] In reply Professor Colm pointed out that "he neglects the difference which exists between an economic order based on private enterprise and an economy in which a leader

[5] Hansen, *op. cit.,* pp. 154–57.

[6] See Hicks, *op. cit.,* pp. 356–57.

[7] Wilford I. King, "Are We Suffering from Economic Maturity?" *Jour. Pol. Econ.,* Oct. 1939, XLVII, 611–13.

tells his slaves what work they must do."[8] Those who use the family analogy do not specify whether the different members of the family maintain separate accounting systems and separate bank accounts. If they do, and if they deal with each other at arm's length, heavy debts owing from some members to others could play havoc with the family economy. If they do not, then the family is a communal unit and any analogy between it and our national economy is invalid, as Colm has indicated.

Another and more technical explanation is that a public debt is no economic burden because debt charges are "transfer" rather than "exhaustive" payments; that is, they do not tie up man power or economic resources. With certain exceptions to be noted below, this is correct as a "real"analysis. But when the economic system is operating far below capacity, as it has chronically done in recent years, available man power and economic resources do not constitute the effective limit on production. Rather, the limit is the will or desire to use those factors. In other words, the possibility of profits is the critical factor and the monetary analysis is called for. Most of the analysis which follows is an attempt to determine whether the "transfer" payments necessary to service a debt may constitute an economic burden.

V

The strongest case for the proposition that a domestic debt is not an economic burden would be one in which the bonds are held by taxpayers in the same proportion as they pay taxes. It is usually argued that in such a case taxpayers are merely transferring money from one pocket to another and that the transfer can have no economic significance. Actually we have little data on the bond holdings of individuals and business units. Even if we had such data it is doubtful whether we could distribute the tax burden in the same pattern and even more doubtful whether we should do so. For example, millions of people are unable or unwilling, for various reasons, to buy bonds during this war. Can we, twenty years from now, so shape our tax system as to exempt them from that part of the tax burden represented by debt service? Should we do it if we could? Finally, even if we solve this problem at a given time it would not remain solved, for the ownership of bonds and the factors which determine tax liability are constantly changing.[9]

---

[8] Gerhard Colm, "Comments on W. I. King: 'Are We Suffering from Economic Maturity?' " *Ibid.,* Feb. 1940, XLVIII, 115.

[9] See A. C. Pigou, *The Political Economy of War* (new and rev. ed.; New York, 1941), p. 77.

But even if the tax load could be distributed according to the ownership of bonds a public debt might, for several reasons, constitute a net economic burden. The first is the subjective reason. As Miss Ruggles has well stated:

It is very doubtful whether or not individuals would realize that part of their taxes was being returned to them in the form of interest on their bonds. Even if they realized that this was true, it is doubtful whether or not they would find their taxes less burdensome for that reason, since most individuals, who give any consideration at all to the matter when they buy government bonds, expect that the interest they will receive from their bonds will exceed the taxes they must pay for debt service.[10]

In brief, the bondholder takes his interest income for granted. He reasons, quite correctly, that he might have put his funds into other securities and therefore he should not be penalized for having bought government bonds. Even though the taxes he pays come back to him in interest he will try just as hard to escape them, he will regard them with as much distaste, and they will influence his economic decisions and actions just as much as though they went to pay interest to someone else.

More tangible—and more "real"—than the subjective factors are the various frictions involved in levying and collecting the taxes necessary to service a debt. Some writers seem to imply that when additional revenues are needed Congress merely changes a few figures in the tax laws, taxpayers make corresponding changes in their computations, and that ends the matter. They would have us believe that the taxpayer is the meekest of lambs whose only joy is to be shorn. Actually, the levy and collection of new taxes is a long, bitter, and costly fight from beginning to end. The mere mechanics of passing the laws, interpreting them, settling disputes, collecting the revenues, and paying out funds require the services of thousands of men.[11] Let us note some recent developments.

During the past ten years federal taxes have been increased sharply. A new revenue act has been passed every year—two were enacted in 1940—in contrast with the usual biennial act in the twenties. Several of the acts were marked by particularly bitter fights. From 1936 to

[10] Catherine G. Ruggles, "Social and Economic Implications of the National Debt," *Annals Am. Acad. Pol. and Soc. Sci.*, Mar. 1941, CCXIV, 200–201. Cf., "no one would buy bonds if his entire income from them were going to be taxed away." Wright, *op. cit.*, p. 143. Cf. also Haley, *op. cit.*, p. 79; and Dan T. Smith, *op. cit.*, pp. 95–96.

[11] "Moreover, the necessity of passing an increasing proportion of the national income through the public treasury is attended by growing difficulties and costs of levy, collection, and transfer." Lawrence H. Seltzer, "Direct Versus Fiscal and Institutional Factors," *Am. Econ. Rev.*, Supplement, Feb. 1941, XXXI, 105.

1938, the undistributed profits tax not only caused Congress much trouble but also was a very disturbing element in the business and financial worlds. In 1940, the start of our defense program was delayed for weeks while business men held out for tax concessions. The Revenue act of 1941 was under consideration from April to September while Congressional committees held hearings and drafted compromises. Hundreds of men spent thousands of days and more thousands of dollars preparing briefs and pleading their cases. Even the President was constrained to intervene before the fight was over. Certainly the costs of such legislation must be measured in the millions of dollars.

Tax litigation has increased greatly in recent years. The Supreme Court of the United States decides from fifty to sixty tax cases per session—more than in any other field. All large business units must have their expensive tax specialists and subscribe to elaborate tax services.[12] More accountants and lawyers are specializing in tax work.

These developments are not surprising and are perhaps unavoidable. Additional revenues mean new taxes and higher rates on old taxes, which require larger tax payments by business units and individuals with large incomes. The larger payments make it worth while for those affected to contest the constitutionality of new taxes and to try to find loopholes in old laws, all of which means more litigation. Also, in the search for new sources of revenue, Congress must resort to new and untried taxes, the constitutionality of which may be questionable. Nor can we hope for relief after we have permanently attained a higher level of taxation. The economic situation is constantly changing, requiring changes in taxes. But even if it were stable, pressure groups would be constantly at work to shift tax burdens.[13] So long as rates are high, the premium for escaping taxes will be great, and the ingenuity of man will always be at work.[14]

The total costs of these mechanical frictions, aside from their dis-

---

[12] "In recent years several factors have combined to increase greatly the business man's cost of compliance with tax laws; perhaps the most important of these factors are, first, the rapid development of various new and complicated forms of federal and state taxation applying to business. . . ." (Robert Murray Haig, "The Cost to Business Concerns of Compliance with Tax Laws." *Manag. Rev.,* 1935, XXIV, 324). He found that with the federal income tax the typical corporation had a compliance cost equal to 4.7 per cent of the tax (*ibid.,* p. 327). New York City stores found that the cost of complying with the sales tax was equal to from five to ten per cent of the tax (Carl Shoup, "The Experience of Retailers under New York City's Sales Tax," *Bull. Nat. Tax Assoc.,* 1936, XXX, 110).

[13] See "Economic Power and Political Pressures," TNEC Monograph No. 26, pp. 34–35, 117–21.

[14] Cf. Hicks, *op. cit.,* p. 261: "Chancellors have been fighting a losing battle against the ingenuity of taxpayers who believe themselves to be hardly treated—and the ingenuity of their legal advisers."

turbing influence upon the conduct of business, amounts to many millions of dollars per year. They represent a dead loss, a drag on economic production, even if the tax load is distributed in proportion to debt holdings. The uncertainties and disturbances which they arouse each year probably constitute a greater burden. So, even under the most favorable assumption of conditions which in practice are unattainable, a public debt is a burden.

VI

The most important factor determining the burden of a public debt is the effect the debt will have upon the creation of income in the future. In the past the existence of a public debt may have facilitated capital formation and the increase of real income. Taxes were regressive and the debt was held by the wealthy. This promoted savings, which were the limiting factor in the expansion of capital. Today conditions are different; investment, not savings, is the factor which limits the expansion of capital and income. It is therefore pertinent to consider how investment will be affected by the heavier taxes which will be necessary to service a large debt.[15]

It should require no extended analysis to demonstrate that heavy taxes are a deterrent to investment. We now rely, and presumably will continue to rely, heavily upon income and profits taxes. If business men are rational they will, when estimating the profitability of new investment, deduct from a third to a half of the anticipated net profits as taxes. That can mean only one thing: a drastic reduction in the range of profitable new enterprises. According to Hansen:

> Even an ideal tax structure will restrain more or less the inducement to invest, and a regressive tax structure will unduly restrict consumption. Diversion of a large part of the income stream into interest payments on government bonds would tend to raise the propensity to save, thus intensifying the savings-investment problem.[16]

Angell goes into the problem more fully and lists heavy taxation as the most important factor which has reduced the demand for invest-

[15] There would, of course, be taxes even if there were no debt. In this respect, then, the taxes for debt service may be considered as marginal taxes. If we come out of the war with a debt requiring interest payments of 5 or 6 billion dollars—an amount equal to the total of federal revenues for any year before 1940—the taxes to raise that sum may mean the difference between total taxes of 30 per cent and 35 per cent of the national income; or between 35 per cent and 40 per cent.

[16] Hansen, *op. cit.*, p. 175. Cf. "But with every increase in tax rates there is the danger that the marginal efficiency of capital and the propensity to consume will be adversely affected, and that consequently the increase in the national income may be checked" (Haley, *op. cit.*, p. 84). See also Hicks, *op. cit.*, pp. 249–50.

ment funds in recent years. He contends that both progressive income taxes and capital-gains taxes "hit especially hard those investors in the higher brackets who would otherwise take the risks of getting new enterprises started. . . ."[17] He concludes that

> There is hence no major line of escape from the conclusion . . . that in all important cases, actual or even expected increases in those taxes of which the burden varies even roughly with individual or business income from assets must necessarily reduce the volume of subsequent new private investment below what it would otherwise have been.[18]

Slichter is equally emphatic in his belief that taxes have been a major factor in restricting investment. He states that

> a deficit may cause the investment function to shift to the left, especially if it arouses the expectation of higher taxes and if the government has manifested a strong propensity to tax profits.

He then proceeds to show that the above possibility has been realized in this country.[19]

In addition to the quantitative effect upon expected profits, a large debt may deter investment in another way. Keynes and others who use his approach have emphasized the strategic part played by "expectations" or anticipations" in determining the rate of new investment. Keynes pictures quite vividly the great uncertainty out of which these expectations arise and finally concludes that we usually rely upon a convention, *i.e.,* the assumption "that the existing state of affairs will continue indefinitely except in so far as we have specific reasons to expect a change."[20] Into this state of great uncertainty a large debt injects a powerful factor on the pessimistic side—the certainty of heavy taxes. Further, if the debt is increasing or if national income is decreasing the business man has a strong reason for believing that "the existing state of affairs" will not continue indefinitely but will get worse. In fact, there may be a "multiplier" at work to increase pessimism here. If revenues for debt service must be quadrupled, a given investor may fear that his share of the taxes may be increased to an even greater extent because of discriminatory taxes or because the tax structure may be made more progressive. So long as expectations retain their

---

17 James W. Angell, *Investment and Business Cycles* (New York, 1941), p. 273 n. See also Dan T. Smith, *Am. Econ. Rev.,* Supplement, Feb. 1941, XXXI, 95–96, and Imre de Vegh, "Savings, Investment, and Consumption," *ibid.,* pp. 244–45.

18 Angell, *op. cit.,* p. 278.

19 Sumner H. Slichter, "The Conditions of Expansion," *Am. Econ. Rev.,* Mar. 1942, XXXII, 5–7.

20 J. M. Keynes, *The General Theory* (London, 1936), pp. 149–52.

present importance and so long as we use progressive taxes a large debt will be a deterrent to private investment.

Thus we have the answer to the problem of why a domestic debt, although it merely takes money from one group and gives it to another, nevertheless constitutes a net burden. It is a burden because it discourages the creation of income. A progressive tax structure which bears heavily upon capital gains and income from property—and most large incomes are from property—takes funds away from strategic or income-generating points in the income stream and restores them to the stream at less strategic points.[21] The result is a reduction in the demand for investment funds and consequently in the expansion of capital and income. Further, this analysis provides an answer to the argument, frequently advanced, that a national debt cannot be a seriously disturbing factor so long as interest payments amount to only a small part of national income. The spark plugs represent only an infinitesimal part of an automobile's weight, but the car cannot function without them. Interest payments may represent only a small part of national income but they may be equal to a very large part of business profits; a part large enough, if taxed away from the owners of business, to stop all new investment.[22]

There is a wider and more general principle involved here. Our economic system is still basically one of private property and free enterprise; a system in which we depend upon the profit motive, especially as it works out through private investment, to provide the driving power for economic activity. We still assume that the income received by the various factors of production measures roughly the value of the contributions made by those factors to economic production. There is no other rational basis for our present system. But as larger and larger parts of our national income are run through the tax mech-

---

[21] Kuznets refers to it as "a transfer of income from areas in which its power to stimulate production is great to others in which such power is less." Simon Kuznets, "National Income and Taxable Capacity," *Am. Econ. Rev.*, Supplement, Mar. 1942, XXXII, 59. See also Angell, *op. cit.*, p. 9, and de Vegh, *Am. Econ. Rev.*, Supplement, Feb. 1941, XXXI, 245.

[22] In a recent article Hansen faced this question and concluded, "Here is a question that has *got* to be solved" [italics supplied]. Alvin H. Hansen and Guy Greer, "The Federal Debt and the Future," *Harper's*, Apr. 1942, p. 498. He did not say nor indicate that it *can* be solved, yet he favors an indefinite increase in the federal debt. Here the words of J. M. Clark would seem to be appropriate; he said we should not commit "ourselves to a policy which would be disastrous if the measures should disappoint optimistic expectations. We must act daringly, but we can probably be daring without gambling our national safety on a single throw of dice. An experimental policy implies keeping open the possibility of withdrawal." *The Structure of the American Economy* (Washington, 1940), II, 26.

anism and distributed to holders of the public debt, the connection between contribution to economic production and the ultimate income enjoyed is weakened.[23] For example, if interest payments were equal to 25 per cent of the national income, producers would have to surrender 25 per cent of their economic rewards while bondholders would be able to claim that 25 per cent without making any contribution to production. Clearly that is not a good way to encourage economic production or to promote social harmony.[24]

It may be objected that the same argument would apply to interest on private debts. There are, however, two important differences. First, the parties who pay interest on private debts have received a special benefit and in most cases their earning power has been increased by the loan. With public debts it is difficult, if not impossible, to establish such a connection. Second, the creditor of a private debtor must assume, in some degree, direction and control over his funds and decide where and how they shall be used; to this limited extent he must function as an entrepreneur. This is not true with public debts.

Perhaps Adam Smith had in mind some considerations like the above when he wrote

> a creditor of the public, considered merely as such, has no interest in the good condition of any particular portion of land, or in the good management of any particular portion of capital stock. As a creditor of the public he has no knowledge of any such particular portion. He has no inspection of it. He can have no care about it. Its ruin may in some cases be unknown to him, and cannot directly affect him.[25]

The above section raises the question whether there is any real difference between private and public investment. Many have argued that when the funds are used for productive purposes in both cases there is no essential difference.[26] Both private and public investment put to use funds which have been saved (or create new funds) and thus stimulate business activity for the time being. Also, both may create utilities. But there are two important differences. First, govern-

[23] There is no escape from this conclusion unless we assume that all necessary revenues could be collected from "surplus" incomes without in any way affecting economic activity. When the needed revenue is large this is obviously a false assumption.

[24] This is especially true of a war debt. It is very difficult for anyone to explain logically why ex-soldiers and those who were hard hit by inflation during a war should, in later years, help to pay interest to those who bought bonds during a war, perhaps out of exorbitant war profits.

[25] *The Wealth of Nations* (Everyman's ed.), II, 410.

[26] See, for example, Richard V. Gilbert and others, *An Economic Program for American Democracy* (New York, 1938), pp. 63–67.

ment enterprises do not have to pass "the test of the market." Government credit is such that the promoter of a project does not have to convince those who are to provide the funds that the project will be profitable.[27] Thus an important check against the wasteful use of economic resources is avoided. It is true that this check has often worked unsatisfactorily but it may still be better than no check. As Wright aptly notes, "To assume *prima facie* that government projects which are free are not worth their cost is doubtless erroneous, but it is equally erroneous to assume that they are."[28] Further, government investment is, by tradition, restricted to low-yield fields, for the fields which promise high yields have already been exploited by private investment. Also, management is likely, in general, to be more efficient in the private field because the private business man, in order to get to the top, is subject to a more severe and rigid selection than is the politician.[29]

Second, the services rendered by public investments are paid for, not by those who use them and in proportion to that use, but by taxpayers. In other words, private activity must not only bear the costs of the utilities it creates but also pay for the utilities created by public investment.[30] We have seen that heavy taxation discourages investment and that investment funds have a strategic value. In the future the government may, in order to keep incomes up and to put savings to work, be forced to make additional investments, requiring still heavier taxes. In this way a vicious spiral may be set up, the government taking over a larger and larger portion of the economic sphere to find outlets for its investments and imposing heavier and heavier taxes upon the dwindling sphere of private economy.[31] Some contend that the increased income generated by public investment will make higher tax rates unnecessary. It has not proved so since 1933. In fact, the opposite may happen, for "The public debt may eventually be-

---

[27] On the contrary, he may have to prove that it would *not* be profitable or self-liquidating in the near future, lest it permits too rapid disinvestment or competition with private business. Cf. Paul A. Samuelson, "The Theory of Pump-Priming Reëxamined," *Am. Econ. Rev.*, Sept. 1940, XXX, 497–98.

[28] Wright, *op. cit.*, p. 145.

[29] *Cf.* Kuznets, *Am. Econ. Rev.*, Supplement, Mar. 1942, XXXII, 40–41.

[30] *Cf.* Slichter, *Am. Econ. Rev.*, Mar. 1942, XXXII, 19.

[31] One writer asks: "Is it not conceivable that a market economy, if it relies solely on the possibility of expanding planned production whenever production for market contracts, may be obliged to transform itself into its opposite in order to stave off unemployment?" John H. G. Pierson, *Full Employment* (New Haven, 1941), p. 114. Kuznets asks, "If we are to retain the system of free enterprise and individual initiative . . . how far is it possible to yield to the pressure of secular factors making for expansion of governmental activity and at the same time assure an adequate rise of the national product?" *Am. Econ. Rev.*, Supplement, Mar. 1942, XXXII, 61.

come so large that a further increase in tax rates may decrease tax revenues by decreasing the national income."[32] Furthermore, the fear of higher taxes, whether justified or not, may deter private investment as much as the reality.[33]

VII

A large domestic debt may be burdensome for other reasons. The creation of a large debt means the creation of a large *rentier* class of individuals and institutions. These normally have considerable political influence which, in the post-war period, will be exerted in favor of deflation and drastic retrenchment. At the same time taxpayers will be demanding a "return to normalcy" and sweeping tax reductions. That demand will have to be met in considerable part, for a free people will not, in time of peace, submit to the same rigorous scale of taxation which they will willingly bear in time of war.[34] The outcome of these two forces may well be a drastic reduction in the government's social expenditures during the critical reconstruction period and perhaps a failure to provide sufficient funds for national defense.

Opposing the *rentier* class—perhaps stimulated and augmented by *rentier* policies—will be certain inflationary groups such as farmers, manufacturers, debtors, and others. They may, in fact, have the first inning in the immediate post-war period, as in France after 1918. Political control may pass from one of these classes to the other, producing confusion and uncertainty in the economic world, or it may degenerate into a deadlock with the government trying to give each class a larger share of a steadily dwindling national income. The latter is essentially what happened in France after 1933; as one writer has expressed it, "they were simultaneously pursuing the policy of deflation and inflation too!"[35] There can be no doubt that the huge French debt was a major cause of the political confusion and the industrial lethargy which hung like a pall over France for the five or six years

---

[32] Haley, *Am. Econ. Rev.*, Supplement, Feb. 1941, XXXI, 84. Cf. "Business psychology being what it is at present, the accumulation of deficits seems to have reached a point at which it now deters as much private investment as Government can make, or more. This would be still more strongly true of further deficits on a basis of policy pointing to indefinite future increases, and not limited to a temporary emergency." Clark, *op. cit.*, p. 25.

[33] See Clark, *op. cit.*, p. 20.

[34] As Miss Ruggles well states, "Identical taxes involve a greater subjective burden after an emergency than during an emergency. During an emergency everyone may make sacrifices readily. But one cannot arouse enthusiasm to a very high pitch for paying taxes on account of a debt incurred during a past emergency." *Annals Am. Acad. Pol. and Soc. Sci.*, CCXIV, 200.

[35] George Peel, *The Economic Policy of France* (London, 1937), p. 210.

before 1939. In England it was found during the same period that "the hazards of a large accumulation of deadweight debt are even greater than had commonly been supposed" and that "The deflationary effect of the debt could not be side-stepped, yet it turned out to have inflationary effects just where they were not wanted."[36] In both countries the large debts were major causes of the financial, industrial, and military unpreparedness which prevailed when war came in 1939.

In brief, the point is this: In "a system of individual initiative and private enterprise . . . there must be some limit to the share of current income payments that can be withdrawn in the form of taxes."[37] If interest on the public debt consumes a larger part of that maximum, smaller amounts are left for social expenditures and for national defense. The pinch is most likely to be felt in times of depression, when a reduction of social expenditures may cause political conflicts and social unrest. Periods of depression are also periods in which wars are generated, thus the neglect of national defense may be disastrous.

Along a related line, Hansen raises the question "whether a public debt imposes any such serious rigidity upon the economy as is the case with private debt."[38] He does not think so because he does not think that the government is so likely to become insolvent. But a debt may impose rigidities and seriously curtail freedom of action without causing insolvency. In one respect, at least, public debt is like private debt; it curtails the debtor's freedom of action by prescribing in advance how a part of his income shall be allocated. The greater the debt, the greater the curtailment. In an emergency or under changed conditions, the debtor is unable to use all of his income as prevailing conditions may dictate; he must allocate a part of it in a way determined by previous commitments. In the final analysis this is probably the most important economic disadvantage of the whole institution of debt and would seem to be more significant than the purely legal fact of bankruptcy.[39]

---

[36] Hicks, *op. cit.,* pp. 358–59.

[37] Kuznets, *Am. Econ. Rev.,* Supplement, Mar. 1942, XXXII, 54. In time of peace the limit is substantially lower than in time of war. See also Ruggles, *Annals Am. Acad. Pol. and Soc. Sci.,* CCXIV, 204–5.

[38] Hansen, *op. cit.,* p. 159.

[39] Hansen contends that "An internal loan resembles ordinary borrowing [evidently he means private borrowing] only in a purely formal way, and it is obvious that *every* analogy to private borrowing must be *completely* false" [italics supplied]. *Ibid.,* p. 142. The above analysis indicates one way in which they are alike. In public borrowing there is more leeway before the limit is felt but when it is reached the consequences are all the more serious.

VIII

In one other important respect an internal debt may be a burden, at least under conditions such as those now prevailing in the United States. It may complicate and interfere with the proper control of the monetary and banking system. At the end of this war the United States will owe the largest debt ever known in history. The average rate of interest paid on the bonds will be very low. It is at least possible that the prevailing rate of interest may rise in the next ten years. If it does rise, the price of government bonds, in the absence of strong support, will drop in proportion. Since 1937 the Federal Reserve System has followed the policy of supporting the government bond market in periods of emergency. On December 8, 1941, the Board of Governors issued a statement which read in part,

> The System is prepared to use its powers to assure that an ample supply of funds is available at all times for financing the war effort and to exert its influence toward maintaining conditions in the United States Government security market that are satisfactory from the standpoint of the government's requirements.
>
> Continuing the policy which was announced following the outbreak of war in Europe, Federal Reserve Banks stand ready to advance funds on United States Government securities at par to all banks.[40]

The System is practically forced to support the market since the commercial banks of the country are holding such a large amount of government bonds—over 22 billion dollars' worth—that any substantial price decline would threaten the solvency of the whole banking system. When the Reserve Banks buy bonds to support the market, however, they are not only coining the bonds into current purchasing power but they are also creating bank reserves which may be used as the basis for credit expansion.

Many of the sales of war savings bonds now being made are accomplished under the pressure of patriotic appeal. When the war is over and patriotic fervor subsides, it is probable that many small holders will redeem their bonds in order to purchase durable consumer goods. Business units may sell bonds in order to rehabilitate and to expand their plants in order to produce those goods. Other bondholders will sell if more attractive yields are available elsewhere. The rush to purchase goods may well touch off a boom such as followed the First World War. If, in order to support the market, the Reserve Banks

[40] *Federal Reserve Bulletin,* Jan. 1942, p. 2.

are forced to buy several billion dollars of bonds they will only be adding fuel to the flames. Even if the bank reserves thus created could be sterilized or immobilized, there would still be the billions of dollars of purchasing power which would be created.

The basic fact is that it is now necessary for some agency to manipulate the price of government bonds. The only agency with sufficient resources to do that job is the central bank. But that task is, under certain conditions, inconsistent with the bank's major duty of controlling credit. It is quite evident that a situation may arise wherein it would be impossible for the Reserve Banks, with their present powers, to accomplish both of these objectives. Nor is it easy to prescribe the powers that would have to be given to the banks to enable them to deal successfully with the two problems. The only answer may be the retention by the government of its control over prices and production and an extension of direct governmental control over banking policies. In any case, the public debt will be a factor to be reckoned with; a factor which will solve no problems but which will complicate and intensify many.[41]

IX

We may briefly summarize our analysis. An internally-held public debt is an economic burden even when taxes are paid to service the debt in the same ratio as the bonds are held. This is true because of the friction of levying and collecting the taxes and because of the difference in the subjective effects of paying taxes and receiving interest. Most important, however, is the fact that such a debt is a burden because, when joined with a progressive tax system, it substantially restricts investment and thus lowers national income. Other elements of burden are the facts that a debt limits a government's freedom of action, tends to restrict social expenditures, and may preclude effective control of the monetary and banking system.

The whole analysis to this point indicates that one of the major difficulties is the progressive tax system which we are using and which we assumed at the beginning. Here we should recognize that a steeply progressive tax system and a free flow of investment funds may be incompatible. As Slichter expresses it, "There may be a clash . . . between the interest of the community in full employment and its preference concerning the distribution of wealth."[42]

[41] For a penetrating and comprehensive discussion of how the debt has complicated the problem of monetary control in England, see Hicks, *op. cit.,* Pt. 3.

[42] Slichter, *Am. Econ. Rev.,* Mar. 1942, XXXII, 17.

It has been suggested that almost the whole burden of a domestic debt may be eliminated by a "proper" tax policy. For example, Wright states that the burden is "primarily a matter of tax friction. Careful tax policy could reduce it almost to the vanishing point."[43] Similar suggestions have been made elsewhere. But in what direction should we make the change? Toward a more progressive system, or toward a regressive system? Or in some other direction? None of those making the suggestion has indicated, even in a general way, how any feasible tax plan might be developed, so we are by no means sure that it *can* be done. Present conditions would seem to indicate that it *cannot* be done within the framework of our present economic system and we must work on that assumption until there is reasonable proof to the contrary. Even if an acceptable and promising plan could be devised by the theorist, there would probably be less than an even chance that it could be enacted and administered so as to attain the desired result. Finally, it should be noted that, when the debt is large and the tax load heavy, Congress cannot exercise fine discrimination in choosing the taxes it will impose; it will levy any and all taxes that promise to bring in sufficient revenue. "When the wisest government has exhausted all the proper subjects of taxation, it must, in cases of urgent necessity, have recourse to improper ones."[44]

In brief, it is highly doubtful whether the debt burden can be dissolved by manipulating the tax structure. While the doubt remains it is dangerous to keep on piling up the debt and thus increasing the burden for, as Clark says, we should keep open the possibility of withdrawal.

Public debt is, as Hansen suggests, an instrument of public policy, but it is one which should be used with care. It is not magic; it entails a cost which has to be paid in the future. How great that cost may be will depend partly on how well we manage our finances and partly on future conditions. When we choose to remove a monetary obstacle to present production or to finance a war by creating a debt, we are able to do so because we have freedom of action. But by that act we give hostages to the future; we restrict our freedom of action to deal with new problems which may arise and at the same time create an obstacle which, according to the best of our knowledge at present, will be a chronic economic problem.

---

[43] Wright, *op. cit.,* p. 148.

[44] Adam Smith, *op. cit.,* II, 411.

30

*Functional Finance and the Federal Debt**

By ABBA P. LERNER†

Apart from the necessity of winning the war, there is no task facing society today so important as the elimination of economic insecurity. If we fail in this after the war the present threat to democratic civilization will arise again. It is therefore essential that we grapple with this problem even if it involves a little careful thinking and even if the thought proves somewhat contrary to our preconceptions.

In recent years the principles by which appropriate government action can maintain prosperity have been adequately developed, but the proponents of the new principles have either not seen their full logical implications or shown an over-solicitousness which caused them to try to save the public from the necessary mental exercise. This has worked like a boomerang. Many of our publicly minded men who have come to see that deficit spending actually works still oppose the permanent maintenance of prosperity because in their failure to see *how* it all works they are easily frightened by fairy tales of terrible consequences.

I

As formulated by Alvin Hansen and others who have developed and popularized it, the new fiscal theory (which was first put forward in substantially complete form by J. M. Keynes in England) sounds a little less novel and absurd to our preconditioned ears than it does when presented in its simplest and most logical form, with all the unorthodox implications expressly formulated. In some cases the less shocking formulation may be intentional, as a tactical device to gain serious attention. In other cases it is due not to a desire to sugar the pill but

* *Social Research,* Feb. 1943. Reprinted by the courtesy of *Social Research* and the author.

† Roosevelt College; formerly the New School of Social Research.

to the fact that the writers themselves have not seen all the unorthodox implications—perhaps subconsciously compromising with their own orthodox education. But now it is these compromises that are under fire. Now more than ever it is necessary to pose the theorems in the purest form. Only thus will it be possible to clear the air of objections which really are concerned with awkwardnesses that appear only when the new theory is forced into the old theoretical framework.

Fundamentally the new theory, like almost every important discovery, is extremely simple. Indeed it is this simplicity which makes the public suspect it as too slick. Even learned professors who find it hard to abandon ingrained habits of thought have complained that it is "merely logical" when they could find no flaw in it. What progress the theory has made so far has been achieved not by simplifying it but by dressing it up to make it more complicated and accompanying the presentation with impressive but irrelevant statistics.

The central idea is that government fiscal policy, its spending and taxing, its borrowing and repayment of loans, its issue of new money and its withdrawal of money, shall all be undertaken with an eye only to the *results* of these actions on the economy and not to any established traditional doctrine about what is sound or unsound. This principle of judging only by *effects* has been applied in many other fields of human activity, where it is known as the method of science as opposed to scholasticism. The principle of judging fiscal measures by the way they work or function in the economy we may call *Functional Finance.*

The first financial responsibility of the government (since nobody else can undertake that responsibility) is to keep the total rate of spending in the country on goods and services neither greater nor less than that rate which at the current prices would buy all the goods that it is possible to produce. If total spending is allowed to go above this there will be inflation, and if it is allowed to go below this there will be unemployment. The government can increase total spending by spending more itself or by reducing taxes so that the taxpayers have more money left to spend. It can reduce total spending by spending less itself or by raising taxes so that taxpayers have less money left to spend. By these means total spending can be kept at the required level, where it will be enough to buy the goods that can be produced by all who want to work, and yet not enough to bring inflation by demanding (at current prices) *more* than can be produced.

In applying this first law of Functional Finance, the government may find itself collecting more in taxes than it is spending, or spending more than it collects in taxes. In the former case it can keep the difference in its coffers or use it to repay some of the national debt, and in the latter case it would have to provide the difference by borrowing or printing money. In neither case should the government feel that there is anything especially good or bad about this result; it should merely concentrate on keeping the total rate of spending neither too small nor too great, in this way preventing both unemployment and inflation.

An interesting, and to many a shocking, corollary is that taxing is *never* to be undertaken merely because the government needs to make money payments. According to the principles of Functional Finance, taxation must be judged only by its effects. Its main effects are two: the taxpayer has less money left to spend and the government has more money. The second effect can be brought about so much more easily by printing the money that only the first effect is significant. Taxation should therefore be imposed only when it is desirable that the taxpayers shall have less money to spend, for example, when they would otherwise spend enough to bring about inflation.

The second law of Functional Finance is that the government should borrow money only if it is desirable that the public should have less money and more government bonds, for these are the *effects* of government borrowing. This might be desirable if otherwise the rate of interest would be reduced too low (by attempts on the part of the holders of the cash to lend it out) and induce too much investment, thus bringing about inflation. Conversely, the government should lend money (or repay some of its debt) only if it is desirable to increase the money or to reduce the quantity of government bonds in the hands of the public. When taxing, spending, borrowing and lending (or repaying loans) are governed by the principles of Functional Finance, any excess of money outlays over money revenues, if it cannot be met out of money hoards, must be met by printing new money, and any excess of revenues over outlays can be destroyed or used to replenish hoards.

The almost instinctive revulsion that we have to the idea of printing money, and the tendency to identify it with inflation, can be overcome if we calm ourselves and take note that this printing does not affect the amount of money *spent*. That is regulated by the first law of Functional Finance, which refers especially to inflation and unemployment. The printing of money takes place only when it is needed to implement Functional Finance in spending or lending (or repayment of government debt).[1]

---

[1] Borrowing money from the banks, on conditions which permit the banks to issue new credit money based on their additional holdings of government securities, must be

In brief, Functional Finance rejects completely the traditional doctrines of "sound finance" and the principle of trying to balance the budget over a solar year or any other arbitrary period. In their place it prescribes: first, the adjustment of total spending (by everybody in the economy, including the government) in order to eliminate both unemployment and inflation, using government spending when total spending is too low and taxation when total spending is too high; second, the adjustment of public holdings of money and of government bonds, by government borrowing or debt repayment, in order to achieve the rate of interest which results in the most desirable level of investment; and, third, the printing, hoarding or destruction of money as needed for carrying out the first two parts of the program.

II

In judging the formulations of economists on this subject it is difficult to distinguish between tact in smoothing over the more staggering statements of Functional Finance and insufficient clarity on the part of those who do not fully realize the extremes that are implied in their relatively orthodox formulations. First there were the pump-primers, whose argument was that the government merely had to get things going and then the economy could go on by itself. There are very few pump-primers left now. A formula similar in some ways to pump-priming was developed by Scandinavian economists in terms of a series of cyclical, capital and other special budgets which had to be balanced not annually but over longer periods. Like the pump-priming formula it fails because there is no reason for supposing that the spending and taxation policy which maintains full employment and prevents inflation must necessarily balance the budget over a decade any more than during a year or at the end of each fortnight.

As soon as this was seen—the lack of any guarantee that the maintenance of prosperity would permit the budget to be balanced even over longer periods—it had to be recognized that the result might be a continually increasing national debt (if the additional spending were provided by the government's borrowing of the money and not by printing the excess of its spending over its tax revenues). At this point two things should have been made clear: first, that this possibility presented no danger to society, no matter what unimagined heights the national debt might reach, so long as Functional Finance maintained the proper level of total demand for current output; and second

considered for our purpose as printing money. In effect the banks are acting as agents for the government in issuing credit or bank money.

(though this is much less important), that there is an automatic tendency for the budget to be balanced in the long run as a *result* of the application of Functional Finance, even if there is no place for the *principle* of balancing the budget. No matter how much interest has to be paid on the debt, taxation must not be applied unless it is necessary to keep spending down to prevent inflation. The interest can be paid by borrowing still more.

As long as the public is willing to keep on lending to the government there is no difficulty, no matter how many zeros are added to the national debt. If the public becomes reluctant to keep on lending, it must either hoard the money or spend it. If the public hoards, the government can print the money to meet its interest and other obligations, and the only effect is that the public holds government currency instead of government bonds and the government is saved the trouble of making interest payments. If the public spends, this will increase the rate of total spending so that it will not be necessary for the government to borrow for this purpose; and if the rate of spending becomes too great, *then* is the time to tax to prevent inflation. The proceeds can then be used to pay interest and repay government debt. In every case Functional Finance provides a simple, quasi-automatic response.

But either this was not seen clearly or it was considered too shocking or too logical to be told to the public. Instead it was argued, for example by Alvin Hansen, that as long as there is a reasonable ratio between national income and debt, the interest payment on the national debt can easily come from taxes paid out of the increased national income created by the deficit financing.

This unnecessary "appeasement" opened the way to an extremely effective opposition to Functional Finance. Even men who have a clear understanding of the mechanism whereby government spending in times of depression can increase the national income by several times the amount laid out by the government, and who understand perfectly well that the national debt, when it is not owed to other nations, is not a burden on the nation in the same way as an individual's debt to other individuals is a burden on the individual, have come out strongly against "deficit spending."[2] It has been argued that "it would be impossible to devise a program better adapted to the systematic undermining of the private-enterprise system and the hastening of the final catastrophe than 'deficit spending.' "[3]

[2] An excellent example of this is the persuasive article by John T. Flynn in *Harper's Magazine* for July 1942.

[3] Flynn, *ibid.*

These objections are based on the recognition that although every dollar spent by the government may create several dollars of income in the course of the next year or two, the effects then disappear. From this it follows that if the national income is to be maintained at a high level the government has to keep up its contribution to spending for as long as private spending is insufficient by itself to provide full employment. This might mean an indefinite continuation of government support to spending (though not necessarily at an increasing rate); and if, as the "appeasement" formulation suggests, all this spending comes out of borrowing, the debt will keep on growing until it is no longer in a "reasonable" ratio to income.

This leads to the crux of the argument. If the interest on the debt must be raised out of taxes (again an assumption that is unchallenged by the "appeasement" formulation) it will in time constitute an important fraction of the national income. The very high income tax necessary to collect this amount of money and pay it to the holders of government bonds will discourage risky private investment, by so reducing the net return on it that the investor is not compensated for the risk of losing his capital. This will make it necessary for the government to undertake still more deficit financing to keep up the level of income and employment. Still heavier taxation will then be necessary to pay the interest on the growing debt—until the burden of taxation is so crushing that private investment becomes unprofitable, and the private enterprise economy collapses. Private firms and corporations will all be bankrupted by the taxes, and the government will have to take over all industry.

This argument is not new. The identical calamities, although they are now receiving much more attention than usual, were promised when the first income tax law of one penny in the pound was proposed. All this only makes it more important to evaluate the significance of the argument.

III

There are four major errors in the argument against deficit spending, four reasons why its apparent conclusiveness is only illusory.

In the first place, the same high income tax that reduces the return on the investment is deductible for the loss that is incurred if the investment turns out a failure. As a result of this the *net* return on the risk of loss is unaffected by the income tax rate, no matter how high that may be. Consider an investor in the $50,000-a-year income class who has accumulated $10,000 to invest. At 6 per cent this would yield

$600, but after paying income tax on this addition to his income at 60 cents in the dollar he would have only $240 left. It is argued, therefore, that he would not invest because this is insufficient compensation for the risk of losing $10,000. This argument forgets that if the $10,000 is all lost, the net loss to the investor, after he has deducted his income tax allowance, will be only $4,000, and the rate of return on the amount he actually risks is still exactly 6 per cent; $240 is 6 per cent of $4,000. The effect of the income tax is to make the rich man act as a kind of agent working for society on commission. He receives only a part of the return on the investment, but he loses only a part of the money that is invested. Any investment that was worth undertaking in the absence of the income tax is still worth undertaking.

Of course, this correction of the argument is strictly true only where 100 per cent of the loss is deductible from taxable income, where relief from taxation occurs at the same rate as the tax on returns. There is a good case against certain limitations on permissible deduction from the income tax base for losses incurred, but that is another story. Something of the argument remains, too, if the loss would put the taxpayer into a lower income tax bracket, where the rebate (and the tax) is at a lower rate. There would then be some reduction in the net return as compared with the potential net loss. But this would apply only to such investments as are large enough to threaten to impoverish the investor if they fail. It was for the express purpose of dealing with this problem that the corporation was devised, making it possible for many individuals to combine and undertake risky enterprises without any one person having to risk all his fortune on one venture. But quite apart from corporate investment, this problem would be met almost entirely if the maximum rate of income tax were reached at a relatively low level, say at $25,000 a year (low, that is, from the point of view of the rich men who are the supposed source of risk capital). Even if all income in excess of $25,000 were taxed at 90 per cent there would be no discouragement in the investment of any part of income over this level. True, the net return, after payment of tax, would be only one-tenth of the nominal interest payments, but the amount risked by the investors would also be only ten per cent of the actual capital invested, and therefore the net return on the capital actually risked by the investor would be unaffected.

In the second place, this argument against deficit spending in time of depression would be indefensible even if the harm done by debt were as great as has been suggested. It must be remembered that spending by the government increases the *real* national income of goods and services by several times the amount spent by the government, and that the burden is measured not by the amount of the interest payments but only by the inconveniences involved in the process of transferring the money from the taxpayers to the bondholders. Therefore objecting to deficit spending is like arguing that if you are offered a job when out of work on the condition that you promise to pay your wife interest on a part of the money earned (or that your wife pay it to you) it would be wiser to continue to be unemployed, because in time you will be owing your wife a great deal of money (or she will be owing it to you), and this might cause matrimonial difficulties in the future. Even if the interest payments were really lost to society, instead of being merely transferred within the society, they would come to much less than the loss through permitting unemployment to continue. That loss would be several times as great as the *capital* on which these interest payments have to be made.

In the third place, there is no good reason for supposing that the government would have to raise all the interest on the national debt by current taxes. We have seen that Functional Finance permits taxation only when the *direct* effect of the tax is in the social interest, as when it prevents excessive spending or excessive investment which would bring about inflation. If taxes imposed to prevent inflation do not result in sufficient proceeds, the interest on the debt can be met by borrowing or printing the money. There is no risk of inflation from this, because if there were such a risk a greater amount would have to be collected in taxes.

This means that the absolute size of the national debt does not matter at all, and that however large the interest payments that have to be made, these do not constitute any burden upon society as a whole. A completely fantastic exaggeration may illustrate the point. Suppose the national debt reaches the stupendous total of ten thousand billion dollars (that is, ten trillion, $10,000,000,000,000), so that the interest on it is 300 billion a year. Suppose the real national income of goods and services which can be produced by the economy when fully employed is 150 billion. The interest alone, therefore, comes to twice the real national income. There is no doubt that a debt of this size would be called "unreasonable." But even in this fantastic case the payment of the interest constitutes no burden on society. Although the real income is only 150 billion dollars the money income is 450 billion—150 billion in income from the production of goods and services and 300 billion in income from ownership of the government bonds which constitute the national debt. Of this money income of 450 billion, 300 billion has to be collected in taxes by the government for interest payments (if 10 trillion is the legal debt limit), but after payment of these taxes there remains 150 billion dollars in the hands of the taxpayers, and this is enough to pay for all the goods and services that the economy can produce. Indeed it would do the public no good to have any more money left after tax payments, because if it spent more than 150 billion dollars it would merely be raising the prices of the goods bought. It would not be able to obtain more goods to consume than the country is able to produce.

Of course this illustration must not be taken to imply that a debt of this size is at all likely to come about as a result of the application of Functional Finance. As will be shown below, there is a natural tendency for the national debt to stop growing long before it comes anywhere near the astronomical figures that we have been playing with.

The unfounded assumption that current interest on the debt must be collected in taxes springs from the idea that the debt must be kept in a "reasonable" or "manageable" ratio to income (whatever that may be). If this restriction is accepted, *borrowing* to pay the interest is eliminated as soon as the limit of "reasonableness" is reached, and if we further rule out, as an indecent thought, the possibility of *printing* the money, there remains only the possibility of raising the interest payments by taxes. Fortunately there is no need to assume these limitations so long as Functional Finance is on guard against inflation, for it is the fear of inflation which is the only rational basis for suspicion of the printing of money.

Finally, there is no reason for assuming that, as a result of the continued application of Functional Finance to maintain full employment, the government must always be borrowing more money and increasing the national debt. There are a number of reasons for this.

First, full employment *can* be maintained by printing the money needed for it, and this does not increase the debt at all. It is probably advisable, however, to allow debt and money to increase together in a certain balance, as long as one or the other has to increase.

Second, since one of the greatest deterrents to private investment is the fear that the depression will come before the investment has paid for itself, the guarantee of permanent full employment will make private investment much more attractive, once investors have got over their suspicions of the new procedure. The greater private investment will diminish the need for deficit spending.

Third, as the national debt increases, and with it the sum of private wealth, there will be an increasing yield from taxes on higher incomes and inheritances, even if the tax rates are unchanged. These higher tax payments do not represent reductions of spending by the taxpayers. Therefore the government does not have to use these proceeds to maintain the requisite rate of spending, and it can devote them to paying the interest on the national debt.

Fourth, as the national debt increases it acts as a self-equilibrating force, gradually diminishing the further need for its growth and finally reaching an equilibrium level where its tendency to grow comes completely to an end. The greater the national debt the greater is the quantity of private wealth. The reason for this is simply that for every dollar of debt owed by the government there is a private creditor who owns the government obligations (possibly through a corporation in which he has shares), and who regards these obligations as part of his private fortune. The greater the private fortunes the less is the incentive to add to them by saving out of current income. As current saving is thus discouraged by the great accumulation of past savings, spending out of current income increases (since spending is the only alternative to saving income). This increase in private spending makes it less necessary for the government to undertake deficit financing to keep total spending at the level which provides full employment. When the government debt has become so great that private spending is enough to provide the total spending needed for full employment, there is no need for any deficit financing by the government, the budget is balanced and the national debt automatically stops growing. The size of this equilibrium level of debt depends on many things. It can only be guessed at, and in the very roughest manner. My guess is that it is between 100 and 300 billion dollars. Since the level is a result and not a principle of Functional Finance the latitude of such a guess does not matter; it is not needed for the application of the laws of Functional Finance.

Fifth, if for any reason the government does not wish to see private property grow too much (whether in the form of government bonds or otherwise) it can check this by taxing the rich instead of borrowing from them, in its program of financing government spending to maintain full employment. The rich will not reduce their spending significantly, and thus the effects on the economy, apart from the smaller debt, will be the same as if the money had been borrowed from them. By this means the debt can be reduced to any desired level and kept there.

The answers to the argument against deficit spending may thus be summarized as follows:

The national debt does not have to keep on increasing;

Even if the national debt does grow, the interest on it does not have to be raised out of current taxes;

Even if the interest on the debt is raised out of current taxes, these taxes constitute only the interest on only a fraction of the benefit enjoyed from the government spending, and are not lost to the nation but are merely transferred from taxpayers to bondholders;

High income taxes need not discourage investment, because appropriate deductions for losses can diminish the capital actually risked by the investor in the same proportion as his net income from the investment is reduced.

IV

If the propositions of Functional Finance were put forward without fear of appearing too logical, criticisms like those discussed above would not be as popular as they now are, and it would not be necessary to defend Functional Finance from its friends. An especially embarrassing task arises from the claim that Functional Finance (or deficit financing, as it is frequently but unsatisfactorily called) is primarily a defense of private enterprise. In the attempt to gain popularity for Functional Finance, it has been given other names and declared to be essentially directed toward saving private enterprise. I myself have sinned similarly in previous writings in identifying it with democracy,[4] thus joining the army of salesmen who wrap up their wares in the flag and tie anything they have to sell to victory or morale.

Functional Finance is not especially related to democracy or to private enterprise. It is applicable to a communist society just as well as to a fascist society or a democratic society. It is applicable to any society in which money is used as an important element in the economic mechanism. It consists of the simple principle of giving up our preconceptions of what is proper or sound or traditional, of what "is done," and instead considering the *functions* performed in the economy by government taxing and spending and borrowing and lending. It means using these instruments simply as instruments, and not as magic charms that will cause mysterious hurt if they are manipulated by the wrong people or without due reverence for tradition. Like any other mechanism, Functional Finance will work no matter who pulls the levers. Its relationship to democracy and free enterprise consists simply in the fact that if the people who believe in these things will not use Functional Finance, they will stand no chance in the long run against others who will.

[4] In "Total Democracy and Full Employment," *Social Change* (May 1941).

31

The "Burden of the Debt" and the National Income[*1]

By EVSEY D. DOMAR[†]

I

"Full employment after the war" has now become the subject most frequently discussed by economists. When the war is over, the level of employment and income will be determined to a great extent by the speed and character of the reconversion process. After that, hopes of maintaining full employment are based, for good or for ill, on the various backlogs developed during the war. But when both periods are over, the old and so painfully familiar problem of the disposal of intended savings will again appear.

It is possible that private investment will be able to absorb all savings year in and year out, or that private investment will at least fluctuate around a sufficiently high average so that deficits which may be incurred by the government in some years will be offset by surpluses made in others. Whether or not this will actually happen is a matter of opinion; it is a problem not discussed here. Instead I propose to examine the less optimistic case, when private investment is insufficient to absorb intended savings over a relatively long period of time.

Public investment financed by borrowing, though perhaps the most direct and evident, is by no means the only method of dealing with the situation. The income-generating properties of various kinds of taxation still remain to be explored;[2] the possibilities of encouraging

* *American Economic Review,* December, 1944, Vol. XXXIV, No. 4, and *Essays in the Theory of Economic Growth* to be published by Oxford University Press. Reprinted by the courtesy of the American Economic Association, Oxford University Press, and the author.

[1] Thanks are due to Miss Mary Painter for her assistance in the preparation of this paper.

† The Johns Hopkins University; formerly with the Board of Governors of the Federal Reserve System.

[2] See, however, P. A. Samuelson, "Full Employment After the War" in *Postwar Economic Problems* (ed. S. E. Harris) (New York, McGraw-Hill, 1943), p. 44; A. H. Hansen and H. S. Perloff, *State and Local Finance in the National Economy* (New York,

private investment by means of various tax devices have not been sufficiently worked out either; the same can be said about plans designed to reduce the propensity to save. It will be assumed here, however, either that all these measures cannot be tried, or that they have not proved sufficiently effective and therefore a continuous policy of deficit financing must still be pursued.[3]

The theory of the multiplier and our actual experience during this war have demonstrated, I believe, that money income can be raised to any desired level if the total volume of public expenditures is sufficiently high. This view will probably be accepted also by the opponents of deficit financing. Their objections to such a policy are based on several grounds, the most important being the belief that continuous government borrowing results in an ever-rising public debt, the servicing of which will require higher and higher taxes, and that the latter will eventually destroy our economy, or cause an outright repudiation of the debt.

That continuous borrowing will result in an ever-growing public debt is evident; that, with a non-falling interest rate, the interest charges will grow, is likewise true; and finally, assuming—as we shall in this paper—that all funds for payment of interest charges are to be raised by taxation,[4] there is no question that the absolute amount of taxes to be collected for that purpose will increase at the same rate. But all these *absolute* amounts do not mean much.

Whatever effects the existence and growth of the debt may have, what matters is its relation to other economic variables, such as national income, resources of the banking system, volume of private securities outstanding, and so on, the particular relation to be studied depending on the character of the problem at hand. The phrase "burden of the debt," if it has any meaning, evidently refers to the tax rate (or rates) which must be imposed to finance the service charges, and that the *tax rate* will rise is far from evident.

The belief that government borrowing must necessarily result in rising tax rates is so widespread both in technical and popular writings

Norton, 1944), pp. 245–46; L. A. Metzler, "Effects of Income Redistribution," *Rev. Econ. Stat.*, Feb. 1943, XXV, 49–57; B. Ruml, *National Fiscal Policy and the Two Super Budgets*, an address delivered before the Institute of Public Affairs, University of Virginia, June 27, 1941.

[3] At this stage, "public investment financed by borrowing" and "deficit financing" are used synonymously. The essential fact is that government absorbs the savings and spends them. The nature of these expenditures will be discussed in Section IV.

[4] This assumption is made both to simplify the argument and to protect the reader from shock. To many, government investment financed by borrowing sounds so bad that the thought of borrowing to pay interest charges as well is simply unbearable.

that no quantitative analysis of it has, to my knowledge, ever been made. It has been pointed out, however, particularly by Professor Hansen, that the debt problem should be studied in its relation to national income, and that with a growing national income the "debt burden" is likely to be confined within manageable limits.[5] The proponents of deficit financing have also argued that the burden of a domestically-held debt depends to a great extent on the distribution of the debt ownership;[6] that however large the debt may be, interest charges can still be collected because interest income constitutes a part of taxable income;[7] and finally, that a tax rate, however high, will not deter investment if losses can be offset against other incomes.[8]

No evaluation of these last three arguments will be made here. But the issues of the debt problem will appear clearer if we adopt the attitude of the opponents of deficit financing and treat this tax rate as a burden, as a price for the privilege of having a higher level of income (and employment) than would prevail without deficit financing. We shall therefore explore the behavior of the tax rate over time under several sets of assumption. In addition, it will be interesting to examine what the community gets for this payment, *i.e.,* the net income of non-bondholders after the transfer of interest charges to bondholders has taken place.

It is true that the existence and growth of the debt raise a number of other problems besides the behavior of the tax rate and of the net income of the non-bondholders. I hope it will be recognized, however, that these two variables are the most important ones, and that an analysis of their behavior will be of considerable help in the understanding of the whole problem of the debt.

The paper is based on several dynamic models which are developed mathematically. All mathematics, however, is concentrated in the Mathematical Appendix and only the final results are given in the text. As in most investigations of this character, certain simplifying

[5] A. H. Hansen and Guy Greer, "The Federal Debt and the Future," *Harper's Magazine,* Apr. 1942, pp. 489–500; A. H. Hansen, *Fiscal Policy and Business Cycles* (New York, Norton, 1941), pp. 135–85; "Moulton's *The New Philosophy of Public Debt*" in Hansen and Perloff, *op. cit.,* pp. 285–98; and his other writings.

[6] A. H. Hansen: sources given in footnote 5; A. P. Lerner, "Functional Finance and the Federal Debt," *Social Research,* Feb. 1943, X, 38–51; Stuart Chase, *Where's the Money Coming From?* (New York, Twentieth Century Fund, 1943), pp. 97–110.

[7] Lerner, *op. cit.;* S. E. Harris, "Postwar Public Debt" in *Postwar Economic Problems* (ed. Harris), pp. 169–86. Unfortunately both Lerner and Harris assumed arbitrary magnitudes of the debt and income without any analysis of their interrelationship.

[8] Lerner, *op. cit.* For a more elaborate analysis of the effects of loss offset, see E. D. Domar and R. A. Musgrave, "Proportional Income Taxation and Risk Taking," *Quart. Jour. Econ.,* May 1944, LVIII, 388–422.

assumptions will have to be made, but ways of modifying them will become apparent as the argument proceeds.

II

The burden of the debt, or the average tax rate covering the interest charges, equals, roughly speaking, the ratio of the interest charges to income; or the ratio of the debt to income multiplied by the interest rate paid on bonds.[9] *It will be assumed that this interest rate is a given constant* (i). If we now want to find the effects of deficit financing on the tax rate, we should examine its effects on the magnitude of the debt and of the national income.

The effect of borrowing on the debt is somewhat complex and will be taken up in Section III. At this stage we can only record the obvious fact that continuous borrowing will of course result in an ever-increasing debt. Indeed, this point has never been overlooked in the numerous writings on the subject.

The other relevant fact—that deficit financing may have some effect on income—has received a different treatment. Opponents of deficit financing often disregard it completely, or imply, without any proof, that income will not rise as fast as the debt. On the other hand, we sometimes get the incorrect impression that it is sufficient for the government to spend, say $100, and the national income will *rise* by $300 or $400, depending on the magnitude of the multiplier. If this were really so, there would be no debt problem at all: it would certainly pay us to *raise* the national income by $300 at the expense of some $2.00 increase in interest charges.[10]

A clear distinction should be made between *levels* of investment expenditures and income and *increments* in investment expenditures and income. With a given average propensity to save, the level of national income will be a multiple of the level of investment expenditures (public or private). Similarly, with a given marginal propensity to save, an increment in national income will be a multiple of an increment in investment expenditures. But neither of these two statements tells anything about the relation between the *level* of investment expenditures and an *increment* in income.

It should be emphasized that the stimulating effects of a given increment in expenditures tend to disappear quite soon, unless, of course, one believes in pump-priming, which does not at present find many proponents. Pump-priming aside, an increase in national income

[9] Though not quite correct, this statement will do for the time being.

[10] That is, 2 per cent of the $100 borrowed.

of, say, \$300 produced by an increase in investment expenditures of, say, \$100 will presently disappear and income will fall back to its former level. But the public debt (if investment expenditures are financed by government borrowing) has permanently increased (by \$100), and so have interest charges (by \$2.00). This is the source of the debt problem. If the national income is to be maintained at the new level, new amounts must be spent.[11]

In order to simplify the problem, *it will be assumed that the community's average and marginal propensities to save are equal and constant.*[12] Under this assumption, national income will be simply a multiple of investment expenditures, and the two series will behave in exactly the same manner.[13] To maintain a *constant* level of income it is sufficient to have a *constant* stream of investment expenditures, public and private, but to achieve a *rising* income, total investment expenditures must also be *rising.* Thus, if it is desired that income should rise at a constant absolute rate, total investment expenditures must also rise at a constant absolute rate; or if income is to rise at a constant percentage rate, investment expenditures must also rise at a constant percentage rate; and so on. In other words, by regulating the total investment expenditures, national income can be made to behave in any desired manner.

All this refers to *money* income. Nothing has been said so far about *real* income. Whether or not real income will follow the movements of money income depends on a number of circumstances which will be discussed briefly in Section IV. But it will greatly simplify our analysis if *we now assume that the price level remains constant* (whatever that means over long periods of time), *so that changes in money income and in real income are the same.*[14]

---

[11] That this is so can be easily demonstrated by means of algebra, a numerical table or a chart. For a good example, see Hansen, *Fiscal Policy and Business Cycles,* Chart 16, p. 272. It was from this chart that the present paper originated.

[12] This would be a bad assumption to make in any problem of cyclical character. It may be quite reasonable, however, in an analysis of a secular problem such as ours. More about it will be said in Section IV.

[13] This of course follows from the definition of the propensity to save. Using I for investment, Y for income and λ for propensity to save, we have $Y = I \cdot \frac{1}{\lambda}$ so that if $I = f(t)$ where t is time, $Y = f(t) \cdot \frac{1}{\lambda}$.

[14] It is well to recognize that the assumption of a constant price level considerably reduces the quality of the analysis. As a matter of fact, in three out of the four cases to be analyzed (1, 2 and 4), a constant price level is unlikely to be maintained. But the purpose of this paper is to study the debt problem in its bearing on deficit financing. It, therefore, appears worth while to sacrifice some theoretical completeness in order to bring out clearly the essence of the problem. I do not think that the validity of the final conclusions is thereby impaired.

Before proceeding to the actual analysis of our problem, two other questions have to be settled. The first refers to the distinction between national income and taxable income. Without getting into current controversies, it will be sufficient to define *national income* as the sum of all wages, salaries, dividends, etc., paid out plus undistributed corporate profits, but excluding interest paid on the public debt. *Taxable income* will be defined as the national income *plus* interest receipts on the public debt, since interest receipts are also subject to taxation. It will be assumed that service charges are raised by means of a proportional income tax imposed on the total taxable income (without any exemptions), so that the tax rate will equal the ratio of interest charges to taxable income, it being understood that taxes levied for other purposes than to service the debt have already been subtracted in arriving at this definition of national income.[15]

Since no mathematical derivations are given in the text, it will be necessary to construct numerical tables to demonstrate the argument. It must be made perfectly clear that these tables are given as an illustration only and do not represent any attempt to forecast. They cover a period of 300 years not because I expect deficit financing, in the accepted sense of the terms, to last that long, but simply to convey the notion of a long period of time.

To construct the tables, the parameters used must be given numerical values. An effort to take reasonable magnitudes could as well be made.

Let the debt at the beginning of the "experiment" = $300 billion, the national income at the beginning of the "experiment" = $130 billion, the interest rate on the debt, i, = 2 per cent.

In addition, a decision must be made with regard to the magnitude of government borrowing. To do this, we must have some idea about the community's propensity to save. An examination of Professor Kuznet's estimates shows that over the period 1879–1928 net capital formation constituted about 13 per cent of national income (in 1929 prices). This percentage appears to have been remarkably stable, with a slight downward trend; in the decade 1919–28 it was about 10.6 per cent.[16] There may be serious objections against this kind of ap-

[15] Disposable income after taxes will equal taxable income minus tax collections, *i.e.*, national income, since interest charges equal tax collections. It appears reasonable to apply the propensity to save to *disposable income*, and the fact that it equals national income considerably simplifies the mathematics of the problem.

[16] It may be well argued that non-deflated series should be used. Numerically, the difference is very small, and there is no need to elaborate this point any further here. Source: Simon Kuznets, an unpublished revision of Table 2 in *Uses of National Income in Peace and War,* Occasional Paper 6, March 1942 (New York, National Bureau of Economic Research, 1942), p. 31.

proach to an estimate of a future secular propensity to save under conditions of full employment, but it is a question which cannot be discussed here. I shall assume that the propensity to save will be 12 per cent. How this 12 per cent will be divided between private and public investment is again a matter of guesswork. It can just as well be assumed that they share in it equally. In other words, the fraction of national income borrowed by the government, to be indicated by α, will be assumed to equal 6 per cent.[17]

III

All preliminaries having been disposed of, a direct attack on the problem can now be made, which is to find out what the tax rate and other variables will be when national income is made to behave in a given manner.[18] Theoretically, there is an infinite number of patterns which the national income may be assumed to follow, but only the simplest ones will be considered here. It is clear that, in a problem of this type, it is more meaningful to express the growth of income in relative rather than absolute terms, and a function with a constant relative rate of growth will occupy the center of the discussion (Case 3).[19] But it may be also interesting to examine the situations when income is held constant (Case 1), or is increasing at a constant absolute rate (Case 2). Finally, a variable percentage of income borrowed by the government is analyzed in the so-called "War Model" (Case 4).

Case 1. When National Income Remains Constant

Since the government keeps borrowing an α fraction of national income, it is evident that the debt will increase at a constant absolute rate. The ratio of the debt to national income will therefore grow without limit and the tax rate will approach asymptotically 100 per cent.[20]

---

[17] Some remarks about a rising propensity to save and a rising α will be made in Section IV. In addition, a variable percentage of national income borrowed by the government is discussed in Case 4 (The War Model).

By referring to the Mathematical Appendix, the reader can easily construct other tables based on different numerical magnitudes of the parameters.

[18] National income is made to behave in a given manner by regulating the volume of investment expenditures. Investment expenditures are the independent variable. This must be borne in mind, because the discussion in this section might give the misleading impression that national income is the independent variable.

[19] From a realistic point of view, a function with a slowly declining relative rate of growth would probably be more significant. This paper being but a first step in an analysis of this type, I thought it better to make no use of the more complex functions. A declining relative rate of growth is, however, discussed in Section IV.

[20] It may appear strange that the tax rate does not go beyond 100 per cent, in view of the fact that the ratio of the debt to income increases without limit. But the tax rate is the ratio of the interest charges to the *taxable* income, and as the debt and therefore the interest charges grow, taxable income increases as well. It is on this fact that Harris and Lerner based their defense of a large public debt, as already mentioned in footnote 7.

The net income after taxes of non-bondholders will approach zero. The picture is rather dismal.

Actually, it takes quite a long time before conditions become really bad, depending of course on the magnitude of the parameters. As shown in Table I, after 50 years the tax rate is only about 10 per cent, and it takes almost 250 years to bring it to 25 per cent. But there is

TABLE I

THE TAX RATE AND THE RATIO OF THE DEBT TO NATIONAL INCOME WHEN NATIONAL INCOME REMAINS CONSTANT

Original debt = \$300 billion $\alpha = 6$ per cent
Original income = \$130 billion $i = 2$ per cent

Years	Tax Rate Per Cent	Ratio of Debt to National Income
0	4.41	2.31
1	4.52	2.37
2	4.63	2.43
3	4.74	2.49
4	4.85	2.55
5	4.96	2.61
10	5.50	2.91
15	6.03	3.21
20	6.56	3.51
25	7.08	3.81
30	7.60	4.11
40	8.61	4.71
50	9.60	5.31
75	11.98	6.81
100	14.25	8.31
125	16.40	9.81
150	18.44	11.31
175	20.40	12.81
200	22.25	14.31
225	24.02	15.81
250	25.71	17.31
275	27.33	18.81
300	28.88	20.31
At the limit	100.00	Infinitely large

something inherently odd about an economy with a continuous stream of investment expenditures and a stationary national income. There may exist at least two explanations:

(1) Investment expenditures do not result in a higher per manhour productivity, and there is no increase in the number of manhours worked. It is doubtful whether these expenditures should be called *investment* in the first place. But such a situation is not incompatible with full employment, if the level at which national income is kept is sufficiently high.

(2) As a result of investment expenditures, productivity per manhour rises, but there is a continuously falling number of manhours worked. It may mean an ever shortening work-week. Under present institutional conditions, it is more likely to mean ever increasing unemployment. Together with the ever rising tax rate, it would combine the bleakest prophesies of both Karl Marx and the *Wall Street Journal.*[21]

To repeat, continuous government borrowing not accompanied by a rising national income results in an ever, though slowly, rising debt burden in addition to other possible economic dislocations already mentioned. How long such a policy can be pursued is a matter of conjecture. It will be shown in Cases 2 and 3, however, that the difficulty lies not in deficit financing as such, but in its failure to raise the national income. To have a rising income, investment expenditures (public and private) must not remain constant, but must increase.

Case 2. When National Income Increases at a Constant Absolute Rate

As the fraction of income borrowed (α) is constant, by assumption, and the income grows at a constant absolute rate, the annual deficits become larger and larger, so that the debt itself grows at an accelerated absolute rate.[22] Therefore the ratio of the debt to national income will rise without limit, and the tax rate will again approach 100 per cent.

It is of course evident that in the present case the absolute magnitude of the income is larger than it was in Case 1. It is equally evident that a more rapidly growing income will, with our assumptions, result in a larger debt. We might therefore expect that the tax rate (and the ratio of the debt to income) will be the greater the more rapidly income rises. Actually, exactly the opposite holds true.

Table II compares the tax rates resulting from a constant income (as in Case 1) and from income rising at 5 and 10 billion dollars per year, respectively. After 50 years, the tax rate equals 9.6 per cent when income is constant, 5.3 per cent when it rises at 5 billions per year, and only 4.4 per cent when the rate of growth equals 10 billions. It

---

[21] There is, of course, a third possibility, namely, that of a falling price level, so that the real income would be actually rising. Such a case would exclude neither increasing productivity nor full employment. It is worth further study. What really matters is the fact that an ever increasing share of the national income goes to the bondholders. This raises grave doubts as to the advisability of fiscal and price policies resulting in a constant money and a rising real national income.

[22] Mathematically speaking, this means that while national income is linear, the debt, being a function of the integral of income, is a quadratic. See Mathematical Appendix.

takes about 280 years to raise the tax rate to 15 per cent when income increases at 10 billions per year, and only 110 years when it remains constant. And in general, it can be easily shown[23] that *the faster income rises the lower will be the tax rate,* even though a more rapidly rising income results in a larger absolute magnitude of the debt. This point will be taken up again in Case 3 and in Section IV.

TABLE II

A COMPARISON OF TAX RATES WHEN NATIONAL INCOME REMAINS CONSTANT AND INCREASES AT $5 BILLION AND $10 BILLION PER YEAR (IN PERCENTAGES)

Original debt = $300 billion — $\alpha = 6$ per cent
Original income = $130 billion — $i = 2$ per cent

Years	Constant Income	Income Increasing at $5 Billion per Year	Income Increasing at $10 Billion per Year
0	4.41	4.41	4.41
1	4.52	4.36	4.22
2	4.63	4.32	4.06
3	4.74	4.29	3.92
4	4.85	4.26	3.80
5	4.96	4.24	3.71
10	5.50	4.18	3.43
15	6.03	4.22	3.35
20	6.56	4.29	3.37
25	7.08	4.42	3.47
30	7.60	4.56	3.61
40	8.61	4.91	3.96
50	9.60	5.31	4.37
75	11.98	6.41	5.52
100	14.25	7.57	6.74
125	16.40	8.75	7.95
150	18.44	9.92	9.16
175	20.40	11.08	10.35
200	22.25	12.21	11.54
225	24.02	13.33	12.33
250	25.71	14.42	13.77
275	27.33	15.49	14.86
300	28.88	16.53	15.92
At the limit	100.00	100.00	100.00

It is still true, however, that we are confronted with an ever rising tax rate. It could therefore be expected that the net income after taxes of non-bondholders would gradually approach zero as it did in Case 1. But this growth of the tax rate is more than offset by the ever rising national income, so that the net income of non-bondholders after taxes approaches a very high asymptote.[24] It therefore follows that non-bond-

[23] See Mathematical Appendix.

[24] This asymptote is given by the expression $\frac{2b}{\alpha i}$ where b is the absolute rate of increase of the national income, and i is the interest rate paid on the debt.

holders will be much better off than they were at the beginning of the experiment, in spite of the rising tax rate.

But it is doubtful, nevertheless, whether an economy with an ever rising tax rate levied for the sole purpose of paying interest on the debt will be able to escape serious economic and social difficulties which may possibly lead to a repudiation of the debt.

What is the nature of the economy described in this model? We see that larger and larger absolute amounts are invested (publicly and privately), but in spite of this, national income rises only by the *same* amount. The explanation of this phenomenon is practically the same as in Case 1:

(1) Investment fails to raise productivity per manhour sufficiently to allow the national income to grow faster; neither is there a sufficient rise in the number of manhours worked. In other words, the result is a diminishing productivity of investment which may be due to the wasteful character of investment expenditures, or to a lack of new technological improvements.[25]

(2) Productivity per manhour rises sufficiently, but there is a continuous decline in the number of manhours worked. This may mean more voluntary leisure or more unemployment.

If it is unemployment that prevents national income from rising faster (*e.g.*, at a constant relative rate), the remedy is simple (at least in theory): investment expenditures should proceed at a faster rate. But if productivity per manhour fails to advance sufficiently, the situation is more serious. This question will be taken up in Section IV.

Case 3. When National Income Increases at a Constant Relative Rate

Since Case 3 is the most important model, the major part of the subsequent discussion refers to it. Use will be made here of three symbols, two of which have already been introduced:

α—fraction of national income borrowed,

i—interest rate paid on bonds,

and

r—relative annual rate of growth of income.

To understand the relationship between the debt and income in this case, it is necessary to make use of the following two propositions *on which the whole analysis rests:*

[25] Productivity of investment as used in this paper refers to an increment in *national income* due to a given investment, and not to return over cost received or expected by an investor, which forms the essence of Keynes's marginal efficiency of capital and allied concepts.

1. If a variable Q is the sum of $q_1, q_2, q_3, q_4, \ldots$ and so on, each of which is larger than the preceding one by r, than the addition of more and more q's makes Q itself increase at a rate approaching r.

2. If any two variables increase at the same relative rate, the ratio between them remains constant.

Mathematically, both propositions can be proved very simply.[26] The non-mathematical reader can construct numerical tables and plot the results on semi-logarithmic paper. He will find that as time goes on, his sum, whose components grow at a constant relative rate, will look more and more like a straight line, *i.e.*, its rate of growth will approach a constant. If he plots two functions growing at the same constant rate, they will be represented by two *parallel* straight lines.

Now, according to our assumption national income grows at a constant relative rate r. Since every year a constant (α) fraction of that income is being borrowed, it is clear that the deficits also grow at the rate of r per year. The total debt is simply the sum of all deficits. Therefore, according to the first proposition, the rate of growth of the debt itself will also approach r, and according to the second proposition, *the ratio between the debt and the national income will approach a constant.* This conclusion presents a striking contrast with the results ob-

---

[26] *The first proposition:*

A proof not involving the use of calculus: as stated in the text, let

$$Q = a + a(1 + r) + a(1 + r)^2 + \ldots\ldots\ldots a(1 + r)^t$$

where a is the original value of Q, r is the relative rate of increase, and t indicates the number of years. We have here a geometric progression in which $(1 + r)$ is the common ratio. Its sum is

$$Q = \frac{a[(1 + r)^{t+1} - 1]}{r}$$

As t increases, Q approaches the expression

$$\frac{a}{r}(1 + r)^{t+1}$$

which increases at the rate of r per year.

The reader familiar with calculus can use a continuous function. If

$$\frac{dQ}{dt} = ae^{rt}$$

over the interval from 0 to t, then

$$Q = a\int_0^t e^{rt}dt = \frac{a}{r}(e^{rt} - 1),$$

which increases at a rate approaching r as t becomes large.

The second proposition:

Any two variables increasing at the same rate r can be expressed as $a_1\,(1 + r)^t$ and $a_2\,(1 + r)^t$ (or a_1e^{rt} and a_2e^{rt}),

where a_1 and a_2 are constants. Their ratio equals $\frac{a_1}{a_2}$ which is also constant.

Gustav Cassel applied these principles to the relationship between capital and income. See his *On Quantitative Thinking in Economics* (Oxford, Clarendon Press, 1935), p. 24.

tained in Cases 1 and 2 where the ratio of the debt to income increased without limit.

It is shown in the Mathematical Appendix that the constant which the ratio of the debt to income approaches equals the simple expression

$$\frac{\alpha}{r}. \tag{1}$$

Similarly, the average tax rate approaches the limit expressed by

$$\frac{i}{\frac{r}{\alpha} + i}. \tag{2}$$

To obtain some idea of the magnitudes of these two expressions, numerical values must be given to r. We shall experiment with $r = 2$ per cent and $r = 3$ per cent.[27]

The ratio of the debt to national income will approach 3 when $r = 2$ per cent, and 2 when $r = 3$ per cent. The tax rate will approach 5.7 per cent and 3.9 per cent with $r = 2$ and 3 per cent respectively. These figures and the examination of expressions (1) and (2) again show that *the greater is the rate of growth of income, the lower will be the tax rate, even though a more rapidly rising income results in a larger absolute magnitude of the debt.*

The net income of non-bondholders after taxes will also grow at a rate approaching r.

We thus see that, in spite of continuous government borrowing, the tax rate does not rise indefinitely but approaches a fairly reasonable limit. Even if private (net) investment disappears altogether, and the government has to borrow all the 12 per cent of income that the community desires to save, the tax rate will approach only 10.7 per cent and 7.4 per cent with r equal to 2 per cent and 3 per cent respectively.

Table III shows the behavior of the tax rate over time with $r = 2$ and 3 per cent. It is interesting to note that when $r = 2$ per cent, the tax rate approaches its asymptote from below up; while with $r = 3$ per cent, the corresponding asymptote is reached by a downward movement.[28] This latter situation takes place because the ratio of the debt to income $300/130 = 2.3$ assumed here to exist at the beginning of the experiment is larger than the final ratio which equals 2; some doubt is, therefore, thrown on the soundness of the assump-

---

[27] A brief discussion of what r was in the past and may be expected to be in the future is presented in Section IV.

[28] In general, the movement will be up or down depending on whether the original magnitude of the debt is smaller or larger than $Y \cdot \frac{\alpha}{r}$.

TABLE III

THE BEHAVIOR OF THE TAX RATE WHEN NATIONAL INCOME INCREASES AT A CONSTANT RELATIVE RATE (IN PERCENTAGES)

Original debt = \$300 billion $\alpha = 6$ per cent
Original income = \$130 billion $i = 2$ per cent

Years	r = 2 per cent	r = 3 per cent
0	4.41	4.41
1	4.44	4.40
2	4.46	4.38
3	4.49	4.36
4	4.51	4.35
5	4.53	4.33
10	4.64	4.27
15	4.74	4.21
20	4.82	4.16
25	4.91	4.11
30	4.98	4.08
40	5.10	4.02
50	5.21	3.97
75	5.39	3.91
100	5.49	3.87
125	5.56	3.86
150	5.60	3.85
175	5.62	3.85
200	5.64	3.85
225	5.65	3.85
250	5.65	3.85
275	5.66	3.85
300	5.66	3.85
At the limit	5.71	3.85

tion that α will equal only 6 per cent. Evidently, greater fractions of national income were borrowed in the past, especially in periods of war.[29] It is of course hoped that the future will be free of wars. Still, it may be interesting to inquire what will happen to the variables if wars or other similar emergencies occur. This brings us to Case 4.[30]

[29] Strictly speaking this means that the ratio of the debt to income $\frac{300}{130}$ is inconsistent with the assumed magnitude of $\frac{\alpha}{r} = \frac{6 \text{ per cent}}{3 \text{ per cent}} = 2$. If we retain the $\frac{300}{130}$ ratio, we should change α, r or both. As will be shown in Section IV, 3 per cent is a reasonable estimate of the rate of growth of the (real) national income in the past. Therefor the magnitude of α should be raised.

[30] Case 4—The War Model—is omitted here due to lack of space. Its main conclusions are as follows:

(1) α—the fraction of national income borrowed—can be interpreted not only as a constant, but also as a weighted average of variable fractions actually borrowed.

(2) Under the assumed conditions (constant relative rate of growth of income) the ratio of debt to income declines in peace time in spite of the fact that the government does not stop borrowing and the debt itself continues to rise.

IV

In Cases 3 and 4 of the preceding section, we have established that when national income grows at a relative rate of r per year, the result at the limit is

$$\text{Ratio of debt to income} = \frac{\alpha}{r}, \tag{3}$$

and

$$\text{Tax rate} = \frac{i}{\frac{r}{\alpha} + i}, \tag{4}$$

where α can be interpreted either as a constant fraction of national income borrowed, or as a weighted average of variable fractions actually borrowed. As expression (4) for the tax rate looks rather complicated, it will be convenient—for purposes of exposition—to use an approximation to it, according to which

$$\text{Tax rate} = \frac{\alpha}{r} i.\text{[31]} \tag{5}$$

The reader is reminded that a constant price level is assumed as before, so that movements of money income and real income are identical.

Expression (5) clearly shows that the burden of the debt is directly proportional to α and i and inversely to r. If the burden is to be light (with given α and i), there must be a rapidly rising income. *The problem of the debt burden is a problem of an expanding national income.*

How can a rapidly rising income be achieved?

If this question were asked in the pre-Keynesian era, the answer would be given in terms of manhours worked, productivity, and other *real* factors. Since the appearance of the *General Theory,* analysis has run in terms of investment expenditures, the multiplier, and other *monetary* considerations. Actually, there is no conflict in these two approaches: they simply state two sides of the same problem.

The real productive powers of economy establish the ceiling beyond which real national income, at any given time, cannot go, but whether or not it will reach this ceiling depends on the volume of expenditures actually made. If a rising income is desired, there must be both rising expenditures and rising productive capacity.

[31] This expression is derived from (4) by omitting i from the denominator, since i is apt to be quite small relative to $\frac{r}{\alpha}$. By this simplification, we are in fact assuming that interest on the debt is exempt from taxation. But numerically speaking, the mistake thus made is quite small and will be more than compensated for by convenience in exposition.

As explained in Section II, national income will grow at a constant relative rate if and only if investment expenditures grow at the same rate (provided, of course, that the propensity to save remains constant). Since a stated fraction of these expenditures is assumed to be made by the government out of borrowed funds, it follows that deficits must also grow at the same relative rate. In absolute terms, the deficits must grow at an accelerated rate. It is horrifying to many to watch the public debt grow at an accelerated rate;[32] such a growth, however, is the only one which (with constant α and i) will *not* result in a rising burden of the debt.

From now on the heroic assumption is made that the stream of monetary expenditures will always be sufficient to maintain the national income at the maximum level established by the productive forces of the country. The growth of income will then be determined by the growth of these productive forces. The behavior of the latter in the past and their expected rate of growth in the future represent an important and interesting subject which can be but briefly touched upon here. As a matter of fact, available past estimates refer to actually realized real income, and it can hardly be asserted that productive resources were always fully utilized even before the collapse of 1929.

Appendix B presents rates of growth of real national income for several countries, but the data are so fragmentary that not much reliance can be placed on them.[33] For the United States, there are, fortunately, Professor Kuznets' estimates going back to 1879, which are presented in Table IV. Over the whole period 1879–1928, total and per capita income grew at 3.3 and 1.5 per cent per year, respectively.[34] It is hard to form a definite opinion about their secular trend, because up to 1919 the estimates are presented only by (overlapping) decades, and the comparison between 1919 and 1929 is not very meaningful in view of the difficulty of measuring real output in a year like 1919. The general impression one gets from these figures is that there may have been some slackening of the rate of growth of total income, and

---

[32] "Government spending tends to be like a drug, in that it takes larger and larger doses to get results, and all the time debt and taxes get higher and higher." National City Bank, *Economic Conditions* (Jan. 1944), p. 11.

[33] Appendix B is omitted due to lack of space.

[34] In regard to *money* income over the period 1879–1928, Kuznets' estimates place the rates of growth of total and per capita income at 5.0 and 3.2 per cent, respectively. A comparison of these rates with the 3.3 and 1.5 per cent at which total and per capital *real* income was growing indicates that the price level rose at an average rate of 1.7 per cent.

Since the burden of the debt depends on the rate of growth of money income, a secular rise in prices will lighten the burden. In this paper it was agreed, however, to maintain a constant price level.

possibly also of per capita income, though the performance of both rates in the twenties appears to have been extremely encouraging. Not much can be said about the period after 1929, because real output during the thirties had certainly little to do with productive powers. Also, there has been so much controversy about the measurement of real income during the present war years that it is better to postpone judgment. Estimates obtained from the U.S. Commerce Department show that, in the thirteen years 1929–42, total and per capita real income increased at an average rate of 3.4 and 2.6 per cent, respectively. Finally, there are estimates by the National Industrial Conference Board going back to 1799.

TABLE IV

PERCENTAGE RATES OF GROWTH OF REAL NATIONAL INCOME IN THE UNITED STATES, 1879–1929 (1929 PRICES)[a]

Period	Total	Per Capita
Annual averages by decades[b]		
1884–1894	2.8	0.7
1894–1909	4.2	2.4
1909–1914	3.1	1.5
1884–1914	3.6	1.7
1914–1919	1.8	0.4
1919–1924	2.9	1.5
1914–1924	2.4	0.9
1884–1924	3.3	1.5
Annual estimates		
1919–1923	5.4	3.7
1923–1929	3.5	2.1
1919–1929	4.2	2.7

Source: Simon Kuznets, an unpublished revision of Table 2 in *Uses of National Income in Peace and War*, Occasional Paper 6, March 1942 (New York, National Bureau of Economic Research, 1942), p. 31; and *National Income and Its Composition, 1919–1938*, Vol. I (New York, National Bureau of Economic Research, 1941), p. 147.

[a] All rates were computed exponentially by comparing the corresponding magnitudes at the beginning and end of each period.

[b] Each year represents the mid-point of a decade. For instance, 1884 indicates the average magnitude for the decade 1879–1888; 1924, the period 1919–1928; and so on.

The rate at which real output can be expected to grow in the future is a question about which a present-day economist has amazingly little to say. The problem of making full use of available productive capacity (except for the last few years when the war offered a solution) has been so challenging that not much attention has been devoted to the problem of long-run expansion. Indeed, one hesitates to talk about the expansion of productive powers when unemployment still looms as the most pressing post-war problem.

In general it appears very unlikely that national income, or any economic series for that matter, can grow indefinitely at some constant relative rate.[35] The rate of growth achieved in the United States in the period 1879–1928 was due to technological improvements, growth of the labor force, and the discovery of new resources. Whether much reliance can be placed on resources still to be discovered is hard to say. It is true, however, that improved technological methods find new applications for known resources and thus may have the same effect as an actual discovery of new ones. The rate of growth of the population has been slackening ever since about 1850, and the various estimates of future population growth predict a practically stationary if not declining population by 1980. Under these conditions, a 3 per cent rate of growth of real income may be too much to hope for, but a 2 per cent rate for the next 50 or even 100 years can probably be well defended.

We have to recognize that the main, and later on the only, propelling force in the economy will be technological improvements which should result in an ever-rising productivity per manhour. Only technological improvements can offset the diminishing productivity of investment which would be caused by the insufficient growth of the labor force and of natural resources. Whether new inventions will be forthcoming in sufficient numbers and whether they will be applied fast enough is hard to tell; one often gets the impression that the scientific age is just beginning, and that, once monetary problems are solved, technological advance will proceed at a tremendous rate. On the other hand, one also cannot escape the impression that certain institutional developments, particularly the growth of huge corporations and monopolies, are not conducive to rapid technological change, and that the mere assurance of an adequate effective demand will not solve the whole problem. A thorough reform of the whole process of industrial research and particularly of the application of inventions may be needed as well.

It thus follows that, if it is desired to have national income grow at a given rate, two conditions must be satisfied:

1. The total volume of monetary expenditures, public and private, must grow at the same rate;

[35] For instance, one cent invested at 2 per cent 1944 years ago would amount now to something like 768,000 billion dollars.

2. Of the total volume of these expenditures, a sufficient amount should be directed toward increasing the efficiency of production, in order to allow the required volume of monetary expenditures to take place without a rise in prices.

Since government is absorbing a part of savings, it is of course desirable that its expenditures be productive. This productivity has nothing to do, however, with such questions as whether or not the assets constructed make a direct contribution to the federal treasury or are self-liquidating. As a matter of fact, the term "investment expenditures" may be misleading, because it is too closely associated with steel and concrete.[36] If healthier people are more productive, expenditures on public health satisfy these requirements. The same holds true for expenditures on education, research, flood control, resource development and so on. Finally, if institutional forces prevent the government from spending money on anything but leaf-raking, it should still absorb the savings unused by private enterprise and spend them on leaf-raking, relying on private investment to raise the efficiency of production, rather than do nothing at all and thus create a shortage of monetary expenditures and unemployment.[37] Of course, national income would be able to advance at a higher rate if governmental expenditures were productive in our sense. In 1940 total private and public expenditures on industrial and scientific research in the United States were less than 500 million dollars. What would be the result if this amount were doubled, tripled or multiplied ten times? Indeed, large-scale governmental participation in industrial and scientific research could become one of the major propelling forces in the economy.[38]

It is possible, or even likely, that, in spite of all these efforts, national

---

[36] A substantial part of efficiency-raising expenditures is usually treated as current costs, and does not appear under the heading of capital formation or investment.

[37] It is an interesting question whether private investment would be able to take place at all in an economy characterized by a chronic shortage of monetary expenditures.

[38] Expenditures on industrial research made by private business in 1940 amounted to about 300 million dollars. To this should be added some 50 millions spent by universities; the latter figure includes their expenditures on research in social sciences as well. The figures for federal expenditures on scientific and industrial research in 1940 are not available; in 1938, they amounted to some 52 millions, the largest share going to the Department of Agriculture. See U.S. National Resources Committee, *Research—A National Resource, Vol. I—Relation of the Federal Government to Research* (Washington, 1938); U.S. National Resources Planning Board, *Research—A National Resource, Vol. II—Industrial Research* (Washington, 1941).

Since the beginning of the war, federal expenditures on research, particularly in the fields connected with the war effort, have shown a marked increase. A bill recently introduced by Senator Kilgore would authorize an annual appropriation of 250 millions on subsidies to various research organizations and on direct research by the federal government. The amount is rather small, but may prove to be a good beginning.

income will grow at a *decreasing* relative rate. Several possibilities should now be examined:

(a) The fall in the rate of growth is accompanied, or rather caused, by a declining propensity to save. The public prefers to consume a greater share of its income today; therefore, a smaller fraction is invested, and income cannot grow as fast as it otherwise would. If the decline in the propensity to save and therefore in α is proportional to that in r, the burden of the debt $\frac{\alpha}{r} i$ remains unchanged. If, however, r suffers a greater proportional decline than α, we have the next case (b).

(b) r declines while the propensity to save and α remain constant, or at least do not decline as fast (proportionally) as r. The result is a genuine diminishing productivity of investment: further investments of the same fraction of national income result in smaller and smaller relative increases in income. Under these conditions, whether the investment be made by private enterprise or by the government, it is impossible to pay a constant percentage return on the investment without increasing indefinitely the relative share of the national income going to property owners. If such a course is regarded as impossible or undesirable, the rate of return on the amounts invested must go down as well. This would mean in the case under discussion here that the interest rate on bonds must be continuously reduced.[39]

All of this discussion, with the exception of the case (a) just considered, was based on the assumption that over a period of time α remained constant. It will be worth while to examine the not improbable case when α increases, *i.e.*, when the government borrows an increasing fraction of national income. There are again several possibilities:

(c) α remains a constant fraction of the propensity to save, but the propensity to save itself rises. In other words, a larger fraction of national income is invested. If so, the rate of growth may also increase and thus leave the burden of the debt, $\frac{\alpha}{r} i$, unchanged. If, on the other hand, r does not rise—or at least does not rise as fast (proportionally) as α—the result is diminishing productivity of investment already discussed under (b).

(d) The propensity to save remains constant, but α increases. In other words, a larger fraction of total savings is absorbed by the government and a smaller one by private business. As the propensity to

[39] It is very amusing that those who appear most worried about the burden of the debt are usually least willing to advocate a lower interest rate on the debt!

save remains constant, there is no reason to expect an increase in r. Therefore, the ratio $\frac{\alpha}{r}i$ and, hence, the burden of the debt will increase.

On the face of it, such a development appears quite unfavorable, since it was agreed to regard the debt burden as an evil which should be minimized. It is presumably an evil because a part of the national income has to be taken from the public and given to the bondholders. But if interest charges on the public debt are treated in this manner, a question arises why other forms of property income should be treated differently. After all, in peacetime society has a choice (at least in theory) of having its investment undertaken by the government or by private business. In the first case, a fixed return is given to the bondholders, and presumably neither the interest nor the principal is subject to default. In the second case, society promises the investors nothing, but allows them, subject to certain rules, to get whatever they can. Which method will result in a more rapidly rising national income is a question on which many opinions have been expressed but few, if any, studies ever undertaken. Nor has any serious attempt been made (at least to my knowledge) to analyze the possible changes in the magnitude of property income produced by a replacement of private investment by government investment. Too often has it been implicitly assumed that interest on government bonds is necessarily a net *addition* to other property income, rather than a *substitution* for other forms of property income; or, in other words, that investment by government, rather than by private business, must increase the magnitude of income going to property owners. Since this may or may not be true, there is no ground as yet for asserting that government investment raises the "burden" of the total, public and private, debt, that it increases the concentration of wealth and income, that it accelerates the growth of the *rentier* class, or that it raises the community's propensity to save—thus creating new difficulties all of which would be absent if the investment were done solely by private business.

There is also the question whether the transfer of income to property owners by means of taxation is more or less "painful" to the public or disturbing to the economy than a transfer of an equal amount by means of higher prices or lower wages.

The whole problem needs further study.

It is hoped that this paper has shown that the problem of the debt burden is essentially a problem of achieving a growing national income. A rising income is of course desired on general grounds, but in addition to its many other advantages it also solves the most important aspects of the problem of the debt. The faster income grows, the lighter will be the burden of the debt.

In order to have a growing income there must be, first of all, a rising volume of monetary expenditures. Secondly, there must be an actual growth in productive powers in order to allow the increasing stream of expenditures to take place without a rise in prices.

When post-war fiscal policy is discussed, the public debt and its burden loom in the eyes of many economists and laymen as the greatest obstacle to all good things on earth. The remedy suggested is always the reduction of the absolute size of the debt or at least the prevention of its further growth. If all the people and organizations who work and study, write articles and make speeches, worry and spend sleepless nights—all because of fear of the debt—could forget about it for a while and spend even half their efforts trying to find ways of achieving a growing national income, their contribution to the benefit and welfare of humanity—and to the solution of the debt problem—would be far greater.

MATHEMATICAL APPENDIX

$Y =$ national income; $D =$ public debt; $U = Di =$ interest charges on the debt; $T = Y + U =$ taxable income; $\frac{U}{T} =$ tax rate; $Y' = Y\left(1 - \frac{U}{T}\right) =$ net income of the non-bondholders after the payment of taxes; $a =$ national income at the beginning of the "experiment"; $\alpha =$ fraction of national income borrowed by the government; $i =$ interest rate paid on the debt; $b =$ absolute annual rate of growth of national income (in Case 2); $r =$ relative annual rate of growth of national income (in Cases 3 and 4); $t =$ time (in years).

Case 1.

$$Y = a;$$
$$D = D_0 + \alpha a t;$$

(1) $$\frac{D}{Y} = \frac{D_0}{a} + \alpha t;$$

(2) $$\lim_{t \to \infty} \frac{D}{Y} = \infty;$$

$$\frac{U}{T} = \frac{Di}{Y + Di} = \frac{1}{\frac{Y}{Di} + 1};$$

(3) $$\lim_{t \to \infty} \frac{U}{T} = 1 = 100 \text{ per cent};$$

(4) $$\lim_{t\to\infty} Y' = Y\left(1 - \lim_{t\infty}\frac{U}{T}\right) = 0.$$

Case 2.

$$Y = a + bt;$$

$$D = D_0 + \alpha\int_0^t (a + bt)dt$$

$$= D_0 + \alpha t\left(a + \frac{b}{2}t\right);$$

(5) $$\frac{D}{Y} = \frac{D_0 + \alpha t\left(a + \frac{b}{2}t\right)}{a + bt};$$

(6) $$\lim_{t\to\infty}\frac{D}{Y} = \infty;$$

(7) $$\lim_{t\to\infty}\frac{U}{T} = 1 = 100 \text{ per cent};$$

$$Y' = Y\left(1 - \frac{U}{T}\right) = \frac{Y^2}{Y + U};$$

$$\lim_{t\to\infty} Y' = \frac{2b}{\alpha i}.$$

It can be readily shown from (5) that $\frac{D_1}{Y_1} < \frac{D_2}{Y_2}$ if $b_1 > b_2$, other parameters remaining the same. This also holds true for $\frac{U}{T}$.

Case 3.

$$Y = ae^{\overline{rt}}$$

$$D = D_0 + \alpha a\int_0^t e^{rt}dt = D_0 + \frac{\alpha a}{r}(e^{rt} - 1);$$

(9) $$\frac{D}{Y} = \frac{D_0}{ae^{rt}} + \frac{\alpha}{r}(1 - e^{-rt});$$

(10) $$\lim_{t\to\infty}\frac{D}{Y} = \frac{\alpha}{r};$$

(11) $$\lim_{t\to\infty}\frac{U}{T} = \frac{i}{\frac{r}{\alpha} + i}.$$

32

*Taxation, Incentives, and Financial Capacity**

By J. KEITH BUTTERS†

During considerable portions of the last decade, several of us at the Harvard Business School have been engaged in an intensive series of studies on the effects of taxes on business and investor incentives and decisions. The objective of this paper is to take a broad look at these studies and at related research in which we have been engaged, and to try to summarize the over-all findings and generalizations which characterize these studies as a whole.[1] At a broad level of generalization, then, what can be said about the findings of these studies? I shall first simply enumerate these findings in order to give direction and focus to the later discussion. The evidence underlying them will be developed in more detail in the body of the paper.

I

Over-all Effect of Taxes. The first, and most significant, finding is that the empirical evidence of these investigations substantiates none of

* *American Economic Review,* Supplement, May 1954. Reprinted by the courtesy of the American Economic Association and the author.

† Graduate School of Business Administration, Harvard University.

[1] Specifically, this paper is based mainly on the volumes in which I participated as author in the series of studies conducted through the Harvard Business School under a grant from the Merrill Foundation for Advancement of Financial Knowledge and on the data obtained in the study of the *Effects of Federal Taxes on Growing Enterprises,* by John Lintner and me. I wish to acknowledge my indebtedness to my co-authors in these studies, especially Professors Lintner and Lawrence E. Thompson, with whom I have worked most closely. I have also attempted to take full account of the findings of the other four volumes in the Merrill Foundation series, and in addition I have benefited from discussions with Professor Lintner concerning the research which he is currently doing on the subject of profits under a grant from the Rockefeller Foundation. Professors Lintner and Thompson have read this article in manuscript and have made helpful suggestions for its improvement. They are in general agreement with the findings expressed in it. My other colleagues who participated in the Merrill Foundation series have not read the manuscript and should not be regarded as being in any way committed by the views here expressed.

the extreme charges that are frequently made concerning the harmful effects of taxation on the economy. It is often alleged, for example, that the heavy tax burdens which have been imposed on the American economy for the last ten to fifteen years have destroyed or seriously impaired the basic incentives of individuals to work and their willingness and capacity to save and invest. It is also claimed that taxes have prevented new enterprises from being formed on an adequate scale; that they have made impossible the expansion of existing enterprises; and that they have caused such large numbers of independent businesses to be sold out or merged with larger companies as to affect significantly the degree of industrial concentration in the country.

While there is some factual foundation to all these charges, the weight of the evidence uncovered in this series of researches tends to minimize rather than to stress their importance. If a general statement has to be made in flat unqualified terms, the striking fact is that, by and large, the tax structure appears to have had only a relatively limited and specialized impact both on the basic incentives which motivate the private economy and on the structure of this economy. The effects of the tax structure on the aggregate levels of employment and real income realized over the last ten to fifteen years have been even more limited, as is obvious from the record levels achieved in both employment and income during this period.

Restrictions on Financial Capacity Greater Than on Incentives. To the extent that the tax structure has impaired the performance of the economy, our data point consistently to the conclusion that it has done so much more by restricting the financial capacity of key groups in the economy than by impairing the incentives of these groups. This conclusion holds especially for the effects of taxes on the rate of expansion of business enterprises, particularly of small companies with promising growth prospects. It also applies, though perhaps not to such a pronounced degree, to the effects of taxes on the flow of venture capital from private individuals to business enterprises. Moreover, in other areas where the disincentive effects of taxes have been alleged to be powerful—such as work incentives, the formation of new enterprises, and the sale, merger, or liquidation of established companies—our findings have tended to minimize rather than to stress the over-all impact of taxes.

It should be noted in passing that this emphasis on financial capacity, as contrasted with incentive effects based on income and profit expectancies, has important implications for wide ranges of economic theory. With the exception of aggregative analysis, the traditional theoretical approach has been to emphasize the latter type of effects to the near exclusion of the former. I believe that the failure to allow adequately for cash and liquidity considerations has greatly limited the relevance of much theoretical inquiry.

Explanations for Moderate Over-all Impact of Taxes. Several main factors can be cited as explanations of this moderate and comparatively optimistic conclusion concerning the effects of taxation—as compared with the popular generalizations about the highly destructive effects of the existing tax structure. The explanations, in themselves, can properly be regarded as generalized findings of our studies.

Importance of Nontax Considerations. By far the most important explanation for the relatively limited effect of taxes, even on individuals and businesses subject to very high marginal tax rates, is that nontax considerations frequently are of much greater significance than tax considerations in determining the basic decisions both of individuals in their personal capacities and of the managements of business enterprises. I believe it can be stated as a general proposition that the more basic and fundamental the decision and the greater its significance for the effective functioning of the economy, the more likely are nontax considerations to be dominant. So far as incentive effects are concerned, taxes are more likely to determine how a thing is done than they are to determine what or whether an action is taken. The more specific and technical the decision at hand, the more likely are taxes to be controlling.

A good illustration of the above propositions is the effect of taxes on executive activity. On the critical question of how hard executives work—of the intensity of executive effort and activity—the evidence indicates that taxes have had very little effect. In contrast, on the more restricted and less basic question of how executives are compensated, tax considerations have been highly influential.

To cite another example, we have found little evidence to indicate that taxes have greatly affected the desire or willingness of individuals (in the aggregate) to organize new enterprises. Once the decision is made to start such an enterprise, however, the legal form of the enterprise and the nature of its capital structure are likely to be dominated by tax considerations.[2]

As a final example, the conditions under which taxes are likely to be the main motivation for the sale or merger of one company with an-

[2] For a discussion of the effects of taxes on the legal form and financial structure of closely-held companies see Dan Throop Smith, *Effects of Taxation on Corporate Financial Policy* (Harvard Business School, Division of Research, 1952), especially Ch. 6 and 7.

other are highly specialized and do not apply to the large majority of merger transactions. Once the basic decision to sell or merge is made, however, taxes typically play an important part in the negotiations on the legal form in which the transaction is to be consummated.

Opportunities for Avoiding Full Impact of High Income Tax Rates. Another main reason why the tax structure of recent years has had only a moderate impact on incentives—and a much smaller effect on financial capacity than is usually believed—is that the impact of the existing tax structure is frequently less severe than it appears to be at first glance. Popular discussions of the harmful effects of taxes on incentives, and to some extent, also, theoretical economic analyses based on simplified models, often take for granted that all income is subject to the full impact of the personal and corporate income and excess profits taxes. While this assumption is valid in wide ranges of circumstances, there are also numerous opportunities—some of them of strategic importance—for avoiding the full impact of the ordinary income tax rates. The most important of these opportunities, but by no means the only one, is that of accumulating new investable funds and accretions to personal wealth in the form of capital gains rather than of ordinary income.

As is developed in greater detail later in this paper, the continued capacity of individuals in the upper income brackets, as a class, to accumulate large amounts of new investable funds is attributable in considerable part to the fact that many of these individuals are able to make their accumulations in ways that are not subject to the full impact of the top-bracket individual income tax rates. These same opportunities introduce a positive incentive for those top-bracket individuals who by personal disposition are inclined to be venturesome to channel substantial amounts of funds into capital gains situations such as promising young enterprises. The fact that in many cases these incentives are socially desirable in an economic sense but that at the same time they introduce serious discriminations and inequalities into the tax structure poses a major dilemma of tax policy.[3]

High Tax Rates Imposed under Conditions of Rising Incomes. A final explanation for the moderate impact of the severe tax burdens of the last ten to fifteen years is that the increased tax burdens have been imposed on an expansionary economy. For many groups in the economy and during most of this period for the economy as a whole, both real

[3] This point has been developed in more detail than is possible in this paper in J. Keith Butters, Lawrence E. Thompson, and Lynn L. Bollinger, *Effects of Taxation on Investments by Individuals* (Harvard Business School, Division of Research, 1953), pp. 62–68.

and monetary income and profits levels have been rising. As a consequence, for large portions of the economy the heavy tax burdens of recent years have not cut into existing levels of income and profits; their effect has rather been merely to absorb part of the rise in income levels which was occurring along with the tax increases.[4] For the most part, also, the tax increases have been enacted at times when business expectations were buoyant and investor attitudes optimistic.

Full weight must be given to these highly important environmental conditions in appraising the significance of our empirical findings. It would be rash, for example, to generalize from the empirical evidence of the recent past that no concern need be felt about the effect on incentives and economic activity of an indefinite continuance of the current tax structure regardless of shifts in the underling economic conditions (Butters, Thompson, and Bollinger, *op. cit.,* pages 52–75).

II

So much for a systematic statement of our major findings or generalizations. I turn now to a more detailed and specific statement of the evidence underlying these findings. Even this "detailed" discussion, however, covers such a broad range of material that it is necessarily at a summary level.

It has seemed best to organize the discussion so as to present a systematic statement of the evidence underlying my first conclusion to the effect that the over-all impact of taxes has not seriously impaired the performance of the economy during the past ten to fifteen years. In terms of the major decisions now confronting the nation in the areas of tax and expenditure policies, this is by all odds the most significant of the above findings. Illustrative material supporting the other main findings, however, will be introduced as seems appropriate at various points in the discussion.

The critical tax effects to be considered in appraising the over-all impact of taxes would seem to be (1) those affecting the basic motivations of individuals as workers and investors and (2) those affecting the crucial phases of business development (namely, the formation of new companies, the rate of expansion of existing companies, and the continued existence as separate competitive entities of existing companies). I shall discuss briefly the evidence bearing on each of these key areas.

---

[4] See, for example, the stimulating discussion of this point by Gerhard Colm and Haskell P. Wald, "Some Comments on Tax Burden Comparisons," *Nat. Tax Jour.,* Mar. 1952, pp. 1–14, and Albert C. Neisser, "The Dynamics of Tax Burden Comparisons," *Nat. Tax Jour.,* Dec. 1952, pp. 351–64.

Work Incentives. With reference to work incentives, our evidence is limited principally to tax effects on executive activity.[5] These effects, however, are of strategic importance both because business executives play a key role in a free enterprise economy and because they are subject to high marginal tax rates on their incomes and hence are in a position where tax effects on work incentives would be likely to be maximized.

In his investigation of the topic, Professor T. H. Sanders, on the basis of numerous interviews with executives and their associates in a wide range of areas and industries, arrived at the following conclusion: "The evidence . . . tends to show that the extent to which business executives have reduced their work and effort, as a result of taxes, has frequently been much exaggerated. The economy has not—as a tax consequence—lost a serious amount of such services. . . ." (Sanders, *op. cit.*, page 12.)

The gist of Professor Sanders' findings is that nonfinancial incentives typically outweigh purely financial incentives in such a basic decision as how a man spends his working life. Among the major nonfinancial incentives which Professor Sanders cites are the sheer urge to do a good job; the power, prestige, and other satisfactions associated with a responsible position regardless of the level of its financial remuneration; a sense of loyalty to an organization and an objective; and the organizational disciplines imposed on anyone working in a group activity.

Substantially similar findings were reported by Professor Challis A. Hall in his study of *Executive Compensation and Retirement Plans* and by Professor Dan Throop Smith in his summary statement on "Taxation and Executives." Professor Smith states: "As regards the direct effects of high individual taxation on executives, I fully concur with the conclusions of Professor Sanders in his recent book that their day-to-day efforts and activities are in general not lessened by taxation."[6]

These findings by no means imply that taxes have no effect at all on executive behavior. Quite the contrary. The evidence is clear that taxes have exerted a pronounced effect on methods of executive compensa-

[5] The evidence for this section of our paper is derived mainly from Thomas H. Sanders, *Effects of Taxation on Executives* (Harvard Business School, Division of Research, 1951), and Challis A. Hall, Jr., *Effects of Taxation on Executive Compensation and Retirement Plans* (Harvard Business School, 1951).

[6] Dan Throop Smith, "Taxation and Executives," *Proceedings of the National Tax Association, 1951* (Sacramento, California, 1952), p. 235. While our researches have been limited to the effects of taxes on executives, such other information as is available on the effects of taxes on work incentives in other groups of the American economy points in general to the same conclusion. See, for example, the excellent discussion of this topic by Professor Break in the December, 1953, issue of the *National Tax Journal.*

tion, tending to stimulate the use of various deferred compensation plans, especially pension plans, and also the use of such devices as stock options and stock purchase plans. Similarly, the wide range of non-taxable fringe benefits and perquisites provided to executives and claimed as business expenses, especially by the owner-managers of closely-held companies, undoubtedly is stimulated in substantial measure by tax considerations.

While developments such as these may be specialized in their impact and more concerned with the technique than the substance of what is being accomplished, they may have unintended incidental effects of substantial importance. Nonvesting deferred compensation plans, for example, tend to hold or freeze employees in their existing jobs, and hence to impair the improved allocation of resources that would be brought about by greater executive mobility. It is also suggested, though less definitely established, that deferred compensation plans often tend to develop a "play-it-safe" rather than a venturesome and enterprising management philosophy. Both these effects, through their qualitative influence on executive activity, could conceivably be of considerable importance to the long-run development of the economy, and they constitute an area which deserves examination in any fundamental revision of our tax structure. It should be noted, however, that some of the problems in this area arise not from the basic rate structure of the income tax but rather from technical features of the tax law. It could be argued with considerable merit, for example, that the tax benefits accorded qualified pension plans should be denied to plans with severely restricted vesting rights.

The matters just discussed, however, can properly be regarded as footnote qualifications to the main finding on work incentives stated above. Certainly this is true insofar as the major decisions of tax policy now confronting the country are concerned. If continued high taxes are required to finance an adequate level of defense expenditures, I know of no evidence pertaining to the United States which indicates that the harmful effect of taxes on work incentives is currently so great as to require immediate tax reductions despite these needs.

Incentives and Capacity of Upper Bracket Individuals to Save and Invest. The evidence on the question of the incentives and capacity of individuals with large incomes to save and invest falls far short of validating the claim that these individuals as a class no longer can (or do) save large amounts and that they are no longer willing to take substantial investment risks.[7]

[7] This section is summarized from Butters, Thompson, and Bollinger, *op. cit.*

This finding holds despite the indisputable evidence that the tax increases of recent years have cut severely into the incomes of upper bracket individuals and undoubtedly also into their capacity to accumulate new investable funds, provided and to the extent that their incomes bear the full brunt of the individual income tax. The data also show, however, that as a group individuals in the upper income percentiles are still accumulating large amounts of new investable funds despite existing tax rates.[8]

Two reasons appear to explain the continued large accumulations of funds by individuals in the upper income groups. First, the habit of saving appears to be so deeply ingrained in most individuals with moderate to large incomes that it has survived the impact of the severe tax burdens of the past decade. All the evidence indicates that the overwhelming majority of the individuals in the top 1 per cent of the population—ranked by size of income—are still accumulating positive savings, and that the savings of at least half these individuals amount to a fairly sizable fraction of their incomes before taxes—say, a fifth or more.

Within the group of persons receiving very large incomes, it is quite possible that those whose living standards were geared to high levels before the period of very high income taxes and whose disposable incomes have been sharply reduced by the imposition of such taxes, may have ceased to save significantly or may even be living off their capital in many instances. This group, however, appears to be more than offset by individuals whose incomes (both before and after taxes) have risen along with or after the imposition of very high tax rates. The evidence appears to indicate that as the income of such persons (say, young executive or professional persons) rises, the advance in their living standards is keyed to their disposable income rather than to their income before taxes and that, by and large, they continue to save despite the high income taxes which they must pay. In many instances, however, they obviously can do so only by accepting less luxurious living standards than their predecessors in equivalent positions were able to maintain in the era of low tax rates.

A second major explanation of the continued capacity of upper bracket individuals to accumulate substantial amounts of new investable

[8] Specific estimates of the percentage of total accumulations of new investable funds made by individuals in the top income percentiles are presented in Butters, Thompson, and Bollinger, *op. cit.*, Ch. 5. It is there estimated that the top 1 per cent of all spending units with incomes of about $15,000 and over accounted for about 30 to 35 per cent of the annual accumulations of investable funds made by all spending units in 1948, and presumably also in other postwar years. The corresponding estimates for the top 3 per cent of all spending units are 45 to 50 per cent, and for the top 5 per cent of all spending units 60 to 65 per cent.

funds is that there are numerous ways in which many groups of upper bracket individuals can accumulate new investable funds without having them subjected to the full impact of the individual income tax. In other words, for many groups in the economy the tax structure is much less severe than it appears to be on superficial examination. Since we have cited this fact as one of the major explanations for the moderate impact of the existing tax structure on incentives, it will perhaps be useful to list at this point some of the more important ways by which the full impact of the high upper bracket rates of the individual income tax can be avoided by sizable groups of individuals with large incomes.

1. There are a wide variety of circumstances under which the income received by individuals is partly or completely tax exempt. Among the more notable of these are interest on bonds issued by state and local government; interest on savings invested by individuals through insurance companies; and income offset by depletion charges in excess of the cost of the properties being depleted. Such opportunities for tax avoidance account for large amounts of tax-exempt income received by individuals with large incomes.

2. Certain categories of individuals with large incomes—notably owners of family businesses—are able to charge off substantial amounts of personal consumption expenditures as business expenses and hence to exclude them in computing their "adjusted gross income" for tax purposes. In addition, substantial components of the personal deductions—such as real estate taxes and interest payments on mortgages on owner-occupied homes—represent consumption expenditures which are, in effect, excluded from taxable income. Deductible contributions might even be so regarded if they are assumed to constitute a source of personal satisfaction to the contributors. One of the principal problems in maintaining the integrity of the individual income tax is that of resisting the constant political pressure for the enlargement of items of personal expenditures which are allowable as deductible expenses.

3. The income of family units can often be split, by the use of trusts, gifts, and family partnerships, into several entities each of which is taxed separately. By this means the income of a family unit can be concentrated to a greater degree in the lower ranges of the personal income tax brackets than would be possible if it were all lumped together for tax purposes.

4. The corporate form of business organization can sometimes be availed of to avoid the individual income tax. Owners of closely-held corporations, in particular, can cause their corporations to accumulate

undistributed profits which can frequently (though not always) be realized at the discretion of the owners at some later date. A variety of techniques exist by which such realizations may be qualified as capital gains or sometimes even be made partly or wholly tax free. Whether such accumulations of undistributed profits in closely-held corporations should be regarded as representing actual (though not taxable) income in the hands of their owners is partly a question of semantics and of personal value judgments as to the appropriate definition of income for tax purposes, but there is no doubt that they often (though not always) represent an increase in the real wealth of the owners more or less in the amount of the retained earnings.

5. The preferential treatment given to capital gains in general constitutes another major way—probably the single most important way—in which the full impact of the individual income tax rates is avoided. Once again, it is to some extent a matter of semantics whether capital gains are considered to be income, but there can be no doubt that they often constitute a source of new investable funds and of additional wealth in the hands of individuals. In this connection the increasingly large range of circumstances in which receipts formerly taxable as ordinary income now qualify as capital gains is accentuating the importance of this consideration.

6. There is a certain amount of deliberate or unintentional tax evasion which allows otherwise taxable income to escape taxation. The intensive auditing of tax returns filed by individuals with large incomes, however, severely limits such understatements of the income tax liabilities of upper bracket individuals.

While the data for appraising the extent to which advantage is taken of the opportunities of avoiding the full impact of the individual income tax are not very satisfactory, it can be safely concluded that the use made of them contributes substantially to the surprisingly large accumulations of savings still being made by individuals with large incomes.

Besides curtailing the investment capacity of individuals, taxes could restrict the supply of funds which individual investors are able and willing to invest in business equities by reducing the incentives for individuals to risk their funds in such investments. The evidence on this point indicates that, on balance, taxes have had some such effects but that these effects have not been as pronounced or as pervasive as is usually believed.

Once again, a large part of the explanation is that, so far as investment decisions by individuals are concerned, the existing tax structure is in many respects a two-edged sword. For conservative investors—those whose primary investment objective is to preserve their capital intact or to obtain a moderate income yield without incurring an undue risk of capital loss—the high upper bracket income tax rates greatly reduce the incentive for persons with large incomes to take investment risks. To such individuals, the net return after taxes often appears too small to justify the danger of capital loss present in almost any equity-type investment. The balance, however, is often reversed for venturesome investors who place a strong emphasis on capital appreciation as an investment objective. The relatively low maximum tax rates on capital gains, as compared with the much higher rates on ordinary income, often increase the willingness of essentially venturesome persons to invest in risky outlets offering the potentiality of large capital gains.

In addition, certain highly risky forms of investment—especially those in mineral and petroleum resources—receive in effect a partial tax exemption in the form of percentage depletion deductions and the current deductibility of intangible drilling costs. In a very real sense, the higher the tax rates which are assessed against other forms of income, the greater is the incentive to invest in these areas—risky though such investments may be.

On balance, our findings indicate that during the postwar years the net effect of the tax structure has been to reduce somewhat the willingness of upper bracket individuals in the aggregate to make venturesome investments, but not by a wide margin. In other words, for equity-type investments considered as a whole, the investors who were induced by taxes to shift to less risky investment positions appear to have overbalanced the opposite reaction of appreciation-minded investors. The latter group, however, may have been so stimulated by the tax structure to seek out investments offering unusually large capital gains potentialities as actually to increase the flow of capital to such situations. However this may be, it is clear that the combined impact of these effects on individual investors has fallen far short of drying up the supply of equity capital which such investors have been willing and able to make available to business enterprises in postwar years.

Business Incentives and Capital Expansion. Thus far I have been discussing the effects of taxes on work incentives and on the willingness and capacity of individual investors to save and invest. It remains to consider the effects of the tax structure on the decisions made by individuals acting as owners and managers of business enterprises. How have the heavy taxes imposed on business enterprises since 1940 affected the willingness and the capacity of the business sector of the economy to undertake the capital expansion and investments needed to maintain full employment and a vigorous rate of growth in the economy? How have taxes affected the structure of the industrial sector of the economy?

The answers to these questions, as best we have been able to ascertain them, parallel in many ways those sketched above for persons acting in their individual capacity as workers and investors. Just as there is little evidence that individuals in the aggregate have gone on an investment strike or have significantly reduced the intensity of their effort and activity because of taxes, so there is little evidence that taxes have curtailed corporate and business investment to undesirably low levels in postwar years.

No intensive or specialized inquiry is needed to justify this statement. With the exception of a slight breathing spell in late 1948 and early 1949, the economy has operated under conditions of full employment continuously since the postwar conversion period of 1945 and early 1946. The period as a whole has been characterized by upward price pressures, particularly in the industrial sectors of the economy. Private capital expansion has proceeded at an unprecedented pace. The evidence clearly indicates that the major bottleneck to the rate of new capital formation has been limitations of manpower and of technical capacity rather than the lack of adequate incentives or funds to finance this expansion.

In these aggregate terms, then, it can hardly be contended that the severe tax structure of postwar years, even with the excess profits tax, has acted as a serious brake on the economy as a whole. On the contrary, the taxes which have been imposed, along with other anti-inflationary measures, have been barely adequate to maintain a reasonable degree of financial stability in an economy characterized by extraordinarily powerful inflationary pressures.

Once again, however, it does not follow from the fact that the level of employment has been consistently high and the rate of capital formation rapid that no concern need be felt over the effect of taxes on the industrial sector of the economy. It would be quite possible for the tax structure to exert a deadening and restrictive influence on the long-run growth and vitality of the economy without necessarily bringing about conditions of unemployment and depression. These effects could be brought about if taxes should greatly restrict: (1) the rate of formation of new enterprises, particularly of new enterprises with a large growth potential; (2) the rate of expansion of such enterprises relative to their large, established competitors; and (3) the continued existence of the "centers of initiative" represented by the independently-owned and -managed small and medium-sized companies in the economy.

Our findings on the impact of taxes on the structure of the economy in these three respects can perhaps be summarized as follows.

Formation of New Enterprises. Taxes appear to have had only a limited effect on the formation of new enterprises.[9] This is particularly true insofar as the effect of taxes on the desire or incentive of individuals to undertake new enterprises is concerned; the limited restrictions which taxes place on the formation of new companies operate more through their effect on the supply of capital available for this purpose than through the incentive route.

There are perhaps two main reasons which account for the limited effect of taxes on the desire of individuals to start new enterprises—especially those new enterprises which are believed by the promoter or entrepreneur to have a large growth potential. The first is that at the time a new business is organized only the crudest estimates of its profit potentialities can be made. The impossibility of estimating profits prospects with any degree of precision at this stage of a corporation's development tends to preclude a careful evaluation of the effect of taxes on these indefinite profits prospects—unless tax rates approach confiscatory levels and are expected to remain there. The force of this point, however, becomes weaker as a business develops to the stage at which more definite estimates can be made of its profits potentialities and the impact of taxes on these potentialities can be computed with more precision.

A second reason tending to diminish the importance of the incentive effects of taxes in the formative stages of a new business is that the kind of individuals who are interested in organizing new businesses are often motivated to a marked degree by nonpecuniary considerations. They tend to be aggressive, confident in their ability to succeed, anxious to be their own boss, and desirous of developing a new "idea" in which they are intensely interested. If the organizer's primary interest is in the satisfaction of creating something new and in the power and independence that goes with a successful business development, as it often is, tax considerations tend to be viewed as of only secondary importance.

In considering the effect of taxes on the availability of funds for the inauguration of new enterprises, the appropriate starting point is to

[9] This section is based on J. Keith Butters and John Lintner, *Effect of Federal Taxes on Growing Enterprises* (Harvard Business School, Division of Research, 1945) and on our later observations, particularly the data for Butters, Thompson, and Bollinger, *op. cit.*

identify the sources from which such capital is potentially available. Our observations indicate that this type of ownership capital ordinarily must be supplied from the personal resources of the individuals directly interested in the business or by their immediate friends and relatives. Outside investors typically have very little interest in a new venture until it has advanced to a point where convincing evidence of its potential profitability can be cited. Generally speaking, until this stage of development is reached the preceding discussion of the effects of taxes on the willingness and capacity of outside personal investors to make venturesome investments is largely irrelevant to the problem of forming a new enterprise. As the enterprise progresses and is able to demonstrate more clearly its potential profitability, however, these considerations become increasingly relevant.

So far as the actual formation and the embryonic development of new enterprises are concerned, the supply of capital available for this purpose appears to be significantly affected by taxes in only one way. This is through the impact of the personal income tax on the capacity of the individuals immediately concerned to accumulate the needed funds for the development. Unless these individuals and their immediate associates can accumulate a minimum amount of capital with which to start the enterprise, the high probability is that it will never be organized. Since, however, there is no reason to believe that individuals with the desire and talents required to inaugurate a new enterprise successfully are heavily concentrated in the upper income brackets, it would hardly seem appropriate to put too much stress on this point. It is not clear, for example, that any feasible alternative tax structure would greatly alter the intensity of this tax effect for all potential new enterprises considered as a whole.

Expansion of Existing Enterprises. Inasmuch as Professor Lintner is considering this topic in detail in his paper, I shall merely state our major conclusions on this topic in order to fit them into the perspective of the present discussion. For present purposes the pertinent findings can be summarized in the following four statements: (1) The impact of taxes on the investment outlays and the rate of growth of existing enterprises appear to be much greater and more significant than most of the other tax effects considered in this paper. (2) The intensity of these effects on the growth of promising small companies is much greater than that on the growth of their large, well-established competitors. (3) Both incentive and cash (financial capacity) considerations contribute to these tax effects, but the latter are usually the more powerful. (4) The corporate income tax and the excess profits tax (if one is in effect) have a much greater impact on corporate expansion and investment outlays than does the personal income tax.[10]

Sales and Mergers of Business Enterprises. A third major way in which taxes could affect the basic structure of the economy is by stimulating the owners and managements of existing companies—mainly closely-held companies—to sell out or merge with other companies. The tax system does exert powerful pressures on the owners of many such companies to sell out or merge.

In the first place, such sales may be made to lessen the impact of the estate tax. The sales in this instance may be stimulated by the liquidity problems encountered in meeting estate tax liabilities if the business is still in the estate at death; they may also be caused by uncertainties regarding the valuation of the business for tax purposes.

In the second place, sales or mergers of closely-held businesses may be prompted by a desire to minimize the impact of the personal income tax and of the Section 102 penalty tax on unreasonable accumulations of corporate surpluses. In the most general terms, these sales are made to enable the owners to withdraw profits from the firm by the capital gains route. This is obviously an attractive alternative to having the profits distributed as dividends which would be subjected to the upper bracket rates of the individual income tax or to leaving the profits in the company and having them possibly subject to penalty taxes under Section 102.

These tax effects have undoubtedly provided a major part of the motivation for the merger or sale of many independent enterprises, and in this way tended to increase the degree of industrial concentration and to reduce the number of "centers of initiative" in the economy. But it would be incorrect to stress the importance of this fact too strongly. For the conditions under which these tax effects exert their full force are highly specialized and apply to only a small proportion of all small and medium-sized companies. Moreover, even when the tax incentives are important, they are not necessarily controlling.

The problem of whether or not to sell out a closely-held business is very complex and embraces the whole range of human motivations and interests. Frequently such matters as the desire to retire, to avoid the ever increasing red tape involved in managing an independent enterprise, to provide for management succession, to become associated

[10] Points one and three are discussed in Lintner's paper, "Effect of Corporate Taxation on Real Investment," *American Economic Review* Proceedings, May, 1954; the evidence in support of points two and four is developed in Butters and Lintner, *op. cit.* The subsequent evidence from the later study of *Investments by Individuals,* cited above, also points to the same conclusion.

sometimes as an officer or director with a nationally known company, to achieve competitive advantages, to consolidate a risky investment position, and a host of other similar reasons may far overshadow tax considerations—even when the conditions needed to make tax considerations important are met. Conversely, in other situations an owner's desire to maintain the control and management of his enterprise may be so intense that he will resist or ignore strong tax pressures to sell out or merge. In still other instances action short of a sale or a merger, such as a public sale of part of the ownership interest in the company, may be taken to alleviate the tax pressures.

All in all, it would seem misleading to place great stress on the extent to which tax-stimulated mergers have altered the basic industrial structure of the economy, or are likely to do so, in appraising the need for immediate revisions in the tax structure. As with most of the other specific problems discussed earlier in this paper, a careful investigation of the facts does not reveal a situation so acute as to justify tax reductions which would sacrifice significant amounts of tax revenues needed to maintain fiscal stability or to finance public expenditures of a high order of priority. Tax-created pressures to sell out or merge do, however, constitute one more instance in which the existing tax system exerts a stratifying and rigidifying effect on the basic competitive structure of the economy, and as such they constitute one among many considerations which demand attention in any long-run revision of the tax structure.

III

This discussion of the effects of taxes on the sale and merger of independent enterprises completes our examination of the key areas in which taxes seem most likely to impair the incentives and the financial capacity which are vital to the successful functioning and growth of the economy. Time will not permit a systematic discussion of the implications of these findings for national policy. There is, however, one point which deserves reiteration.

Insofar as the major policy issues now confronting the nation in the areas of public expenditures and taxation are concerned, the evidence clearly supports the conclusion already stated; namely, that the high taxes of the last fifteen years have not produced a crisis situation which calls for drastic and immediate action on the tax front. If the demands of national defense and fiscal stability require a continuation of the current level of tax rates for another several years, our studies have produced no evidence to indicate that the economy will suffer serious long-run damage thereby. The claim frequently voiced in Congressional quarters and elsewhere that expenditures must be greatly reduced at an early date in order to preserve economic strength at home, almost regardless of the international consequences of these reductions, is not, I believe, substantiated by the facts.

As a long-run proposition, there is substance to Secretary Humphrey's position that "our way of life is threatened, not from one, but from two sources at the same time. It can be lost just as completely by economic deterioration from within as by aggression from without." (Address by Secretary of the Treasury George M. Humphrey, April 20, 1953.) In the short run, or even in the intermediate run, extending over a considerable period of years, however, I believe that it would be a rash public policy which would evaluate the danger of economic deterioration from within, caused by the present tax structure, as being of the same order of magnitude as that of aggression from abroad. In terms of the major policy decisions now confronting the nation, this, in my judgment, is by all odds the most important policy implication of the data and analysis summarized in this paper. (Space does not permit a more extended development of the policy implications of our discussion in this paper. Some aspects of the matter are developed in more detail in Butters, Thompson, and Bollinger, *op. cit.,* pages 62–68, and in Professor Lintner's paper, *op. cit.*)

VII. FISCAL POLICY AND ECONOMIC GROWTH

33

*Economic Possibilities in the United States**

By J. A. SCHUMPETER

1. When discussing the English case, we have noticed that under modern conditions—to an extent undreamed of by nineteenth-century socialists—it is possible to extract from the bourgeois stratum, by taxation and wage policies, the bulk of what in Marxist terminology is called Surplus Value.[1] The same observation applies to the United States. To an extent which is not generally appreciated, the New Deal was able to expropriate the upper income brackets even before the war. One indication will have to suffice, one that shows no more than the effects of the increase in the (personal) Income and Surtax and these only *up to 1936:* in 1929, when Total Income Paid Out was estimated at 80.6 billion dollars, the brackets above $50,000 (taxable income) retained 5.2 billions after income and surtax; in 1936, when the total of income paid out was estimated at 64.2 billion dollars, not quite 1.2 billions.[2] Taxable income above $100,000 was *even then*

* Chapter 28, Part II, of *Capitalism, Socialism and Democracy* (New York: Harper & Bros., 1947; London: George Allen & Unwin, Ltd.). Reprinted by the courtesy of Harper & Brothers.

[1] The reader will, of course, observe that the proposition asserts nothing about the effects of such a policy upon the size—and long-run rate of increase—of the national income. In particular, it does not exclude the possibility that labor might receive less real income, in total amount and in the long run, if incomes were completely equalized than it would receive if the whole of the Marxist surplus value accrued to the "capitalist" stratum.

[2] See the highly instructive article by I. de Vegh on "Savings, Investment, and Consumption," *Am. Econ. Rev., Proceedings,* Feb. 1941, pp. 237 *et seq.* As there explained, the data from which the sums retained were calculated exclude income from wholly tax-

wholly absorbed if account be taken of estate taxes. From the standpoint of naïve radicalism, the only trouble with these and subsequent measures of confiscation is that they did not go far enough. But this does not alter the fact with which we are concerned for the moment, viz., that irrespective of the war, a tremendous transfer of wealth has actually been effected, a transfer that quantitatively is comparable with that effected by Lenin. The present distribution of disposable incomes compares well with the one actually prevailing in Russia, particularly in view of the further fact that owing to the greater importance in the upper-bracket budgets of personal services and of commodities that contain relatively much labor, the purchasing power of the upper-bracket dollar has in the United States fallen much more than has that of the lower-bracket dollar.[3] Moreover, we may also repeat another observation made earlier concerning England. The pressure on the upper brackets is, of course, not confined to "$50,000 and above." To a diminishing degree it extends down to the incomes of $5,000.

---

exempt government securities and include capital gains. Moreover, these sums are, of course, not strictly comparable with the figures of total income paid out (Commerce estimates), which may, however, be considered as indices of the comparable figures. The reason why I have not simply taken the latter (from *Statistics of Income*) is obvious, but the choice of the years of comparison needs explanation: 1929 was the year for which incomes above $50,000 after income and surtax were at an absolute maximum; 1936 has been chosen because it was the last year that was, first, unaffected by the recession of 1937–1938 and, second, completely free from war influences that asserted themselves from 1939 on.

[3] Comparison between different countries is of course difficult and perhaps never quite convincing. But the Russian act of April 4, 1940, concerning the income tax, reveals that incomes as low as 1,812 rubles per year were subject to it. It also reveals the existence of incomes of over 300,000 rubles which were then taxed at the rate of 50 per cent. Now, let us neglect the tax on the lowest incomes entirely and put the modal income in the 1,812–2,400 ruble group at 2,000 rubles; further, let us put the modal *retained* income in the highest group at no higher than 150,000 rubles (though those 300,000 rubles before tax were a lower limit). Then we discover that the higher of these modes was 75 times the lower one. Even if we put, for 1940, the American equivalent (not of course in purchasing power, but in the sense of equivalent position in the income scale) of the lower mode at as low as $1,000, we shall evidently not find much in the United States income distribution of *retained* incomes (even apart from the reductions specifically motivated by the requirements of war finance) to support, in the light of the Russian paradigma, the current phrases about atrocious inequalities, "concentration of power" as measured by concentration of income, and the like. The evidence presented in the well-known book by Bienstock, Schwarz, and Yugov on *Industrial Management* in Russia tends to support this view. Many other details point in the same direction, for instance, the fact that those ranges of the professions who could formerly but cannot now afford domestic servants in the United States, do enjoy this privilege—worth a ton of electrical household gadgets—in Russia. All this still fails to take account of advantages that do not pass through income accounts. The power and social position—which is one of the main reasons for valuing a high income—of the industrial manager, especially if leader of the local unit of the Bolshevik party, is far and away above that of an American industrialist.

Interesting phenomenon—this Lag of Ideas! Many well-meaning people in this country *now* profess horror or indignation at social inequalities which did exist fifty years ago, but no longer do. Things change, slogans remain.

And there cannot be any doubt, especially in the case of doctors in the middle ranges of professional success, that this sometimes results in loss of much-needed efficiency.

So far, then, the effect upon the social structure of the war plus the labor troubles that were its natural consequence would seem to be much the same as in England. The fact that in the United States there is no well-organized national labor party might set us speculating about the possibility of a development on the lines of guild socialism instead of one toward centralist socialism. Otherwise this fact only strengthens the case for the prognosis that has been elaborated in this book, for pressure groups are just as powerful as parties and much less responsible, hence more effective battering rams.

2. But there is another fact about the social situation in the United States that has no analogue anywhere else in the world and may conceivably affect our diagnosis concerning the chances of the private-enterprise system, at least for a short run of fifty years or so, namely, the colossal industrial success we are witnessing. Some observers seem to think that this success which has won the war and, in addition, has protected American labor from privation, will dominate the postwar situation also, to an extent that may annihilate the whole case for socialism so far as it is of a purely economic nature. Let us put this argument into its most optimistic form.

Neglecting for the moment the complex of transitional problems and fixing upon 1950 as the first "normal" year—a practice quite common with forecasters—we will put the Gross National Product—value of all goods and services produced before allowance for depreciation and depletion—evaluated by means of the B. L. S. price-level index for 1928, hypothetically at two hundred billions. This is, of course, not a prediction of the actual volume of production to be expected in that year. It is not even an estimate of what potential production at high if not "full" employment will be. It is an estimate of what this potential production might be provided certain conditions are fulfilled which will be stated presently. As such, it is high but neither unusual—higher figures have been mentioned—nor unreasonable. It conforms to past experience of the long-run average performance of the system: if we apply our "normal rate of growth of 3.7 per cent per year" (see above Chapter V) to the 1928 gross national product figure, which was about ninety billions, we get a little under two hundred billions for 1950. No undue importance should be attached to this. But I will nevertheless repeat that an objection to the effect that this extrapolation is meaningless *because* output failed to increase at that rate in the thirties would miss the point and only prove the objector's inability to grasp it. However, so far as potential production is concerned, the indications afforded by the system's actual performance during the war are certainly more convincing: if war statistics are anything to go by, the gross national product, reduced to the 1928 price level, was in 1943 pretty much what it should have been in order to reach the two hundred billion goal by 1950.

Now *suppose* that this possibility be actually realized.[4] And let us, for replacement and new "investment" (including houses), make the ample deduction of forty billions (20 per cent, equal to Professor Kuznets' average by decades, for 1879–1929).[5] The significance of the remaining one hundred and sixty billions for our subject rests upon two facts. First, short of atrocious mismanagement, the huge mass of available commodities and services that this figure (which still does not include new houses) represents, promises a level of satisfaction of economic needs even of the poorest members of society including the aged, unemployed and sick, that would (with a forty hour week) eliminate anything that could possibly be described as suffering or want. It has been emphasized in this book that the case for socialism is by no means wholly economic and also that increasing real income has so far entirely failed to conciliate either the masses or their intellectual allies. But in this instance, the promise is not only spectacular but immediate: not much more is involved in its fulfillment than that

[4] It is assumed that realization of this possibility involves a forty-hour week plus overtime at bottlenecks. But full employment is not assumed. Definitions of full employment and estimates of the amount of employment that satisfies any given definition vary widely and involve not only statistical but also some rather delicate theoretical issues. I must rest content to state that, in the conditions of the United States labor market and assuming that the total labor force will be something like sixty one millions in 1950 (counting in two or three millions in the armed forces), I do not see that the number of *statistically* unemployed women and men can possibly be, in that year, below five to six millions, a figure which includes, besides genuinely involuntary unemployment (i.e., involuntary unemployment that would be involuntary unemployment according to *any* definition), a large allowance for semi-involuntary unemployment and merely statistical unemployment. The figure does not include "hidden" unemployment. I believe it to be compatible with the two hundred billion goal for that year. It has little to do with vices specific to the capitalist system, but much with the freedom capitalist society grants to labor. Even in Sir William Beveridge's book on full employment there are chastely veiled hints at direction and compulsion. It should be added, however, that I visualize 1950 as a year of cyclical prosperity. If it is not, then our discussion should be understood to refer to the prosperous year next to it. On an average of good and bad years (statistical) unemployment should be higher than five to six millions—seven to eight perhaps. This is nothing to be horrified about because, as will be explained, adequate provision can be made for the unemployed. But the cyclical fluctuations of capitalist economy are mainly responsible for any excess above "normal" unemployment.

[5] A depreciation allowance of about 10 to 12 per cent is not unduly high for a system running at as high a level of production. Eight to ten per cent for "new" investment is certainly ample and, according to most forecasters, too much. See below, *sub* 5.

the abilities and resources that have proved their power during the war turn from production for war purposes, including the exports of consumers' goods to Allied countries, to production for the purposes of domestic consumption; after 1950 the argument would apply *a fortiori.* Second—again short of atrocious mismanagement—all this can be accomplished without violating the organic conditions of a capitalist economy, including high premia on industrial success and all the other inequalities of income that may be required in order to make the capitalist engine work according to design. *In the United States alone there need not lurk, behind modern programs of social betterment, that fundamental dilemma that everywhere else paralyzes the will of every responsible man, the dilemma between economic progress and immediate increase of the real income of the masses.*

Moreover, with gross national product at 200 billions, there is no difficulty in collecting public revenue in the amount of 40 billions without injury to the economic engine. A sum of 30 billions is sufficient, at 1928 prices, to finance all the functions actually fulfilled by the federal, state and local governments in 1939 plus a greatly enlarged military establishment plus the service of the debt and other permanent obligations that have been incurred since.[6] This will leave roughly 10 billions—at 1928 prices or a correspondingly higher amount at any higher price level that may prevail[7]—in 1950 and much more than this in another decade, for the financing of new social services or of improvements in the existing ones.

3. But it is here, namely, in the sphere of public finance and administration, that the meaning of our proviso—"short of atrocious mismanagement"—is most vividly brought home to us. For in this sphere we actually have mismanagement of national resources that is truly atrocious. With present principles and present practice, it is *not* true that 40 billions can be collected, at a 200-billion level of gross national product, without injury to the economic engine. And it is *not* true that the 30 billions—or whatever may correspond to them at price levels other than that of 1928—meet the requirements mentioned. This is only true if the whole of the public administration be rational-

[6] For the purpose in hand, it is not necessary to distinguish between public expenditure on goods and services and "transfers." But it is assumed that, roughly, the thirty billions would divide up into twenty-five billions for the former and five billions of the latter. It should be observed that this takes no account (for 1950) of veterans' pensions and other benefits, a problem that should be treated apart.

[7] Revenue cannot, in general, be assumed to change in proportion to price level. For our purpose, however, which is merely to gain a rough idea, we may adopt this simplifying hypothesis.

ized with a view to eliminating double and triple-track activities—such as we have in the case of the income taxes, to mention but one example —overlapping both of federal agencies and of federal and state and local agencies—lack of effective co-ordination and well-defined individual responsibility—which, in the federal case, is mainly due to the nonexistence of well-knit "ministries" and to the existence of a large number of semi-independent "authorities" or "boards"—and many other things that are sources of waste and obstacles to efficiency, but above all, that spirit of waste that delights in spending a billion where 100 million would do. The present state of things portends nothing but evil for public management of finance and industry and, in fact, is in itself good and sufficient reason to oppose it for many who are anything but "economic royalists."

Nor is this all. *Economy*—how unpopular this word has become!—may in a sense be less necessary in a wealthy country than it is in a poor one, namely in the sense that waste threatens want in the latter and not in the former. But in another sense, economy—that is, real economy and not the sham economy of the bureaucracy and of Congress who are ready enough to save pennies while squandering billions —is just as necessary in a rich country in order to make efficient use of its wealth as it is in a poor country in order to secure bare subsistence.[8] And this applies not only to the cost of public administration but also to the use of funds that are to be paid out in various benefits. The classic example is, of course, provision for unemployment so far as it consists in payments to individuals. Unless the behavior of workmen, in employment and out of it, be as strictly under public control as it is in Russia, economical use of the funds available for the support of the unemployed inevitably means that the benefit must be substantially below the wages the unemployed can hope to earn. As United States statistics of labor turnover suggest, there is normally in the country a large fringe of half voluntary and half involuntary unemployment, the burden of which is bound to be increased, by loose administration of unemployment benefits or by rates that are high relatively to wages, so as to destroy the possibility of attaining the two hundred billion goal.

There is still another condition that would have to be fulfilled in order to justify this possibility: "Politics" and bureaucracy must not prevent our reaching it. Nothing should be more obvious than that the business organism cannot function according to design when its

---

[8] The theory that holds the exact opposite of this will be discussed below, *sub* 5.

most important "parameters of action"—wages, prices, interest—are transferred to the political sphere and there dealt with according to the requirements of the political game or, which sometimes is more serious still, according to the ideas of some planners. Three examples must suffice to illustrate this. First, the actual labor situation, if it persist, is in itself sufficient to obstruct progress toward that goal of a two hundred billion gross national product and, still more, progress beyond it. The resulting wage rates are only one reason for this; dislocation of entrepreneurial planning and disorganization of workers even when employed are equally important. Besides preventing an otherwise possible expansion of output, these conditions also reduce employment below its otherwise possible level by putting an abnormal premium on everybody's employing as little labor as possible—they induce a sort of "flight from labor."[9]

Second, whatever the reader may believe to be its virtues, price control as practiced hitherto is another obstacle to the expansion of output. I have heard that the Stalinist régime encourages criticism of its bureaucracy. Evidently, this is not so with us. I will defer to prevailing etiquette by granting outright that many able men have done excellent service in the O. P. A.; that many others, not so able, have still done their best; and I will suppress any doubts that may exist in my mind concerning its achievements up to the present moment, especially because its most conspicuous failures link up with circumstances over which it had no control. But it should really be admitted, at least for the present and future, that the policy of encouraging in-

---

[9] It will be observed that increase in output and increase in employment are not treated as synonymous. It is, in fact, possible, within certain limits, to decrease employment without decreasing output or to increase the latter without increasing the former. The reason why in current literature output and employment are often made to vary proportionately is to be found in one of the fundamental features of the Keynesian system. This system is restricted to dealing with quite short-run chains of causation by the assumption that quantity and quality of industrial equipment remain constant so that the combination of factors of production cannot change significantly. If this were so (and in the shortest run it is approximately so), then of course they vary together though, in general, not proportionately.

It will also be observed that our argument implies that changes in money wage rates may cause changes in employment of opposite sign. I believe, in fact, that the high level of American money wage rates has always, but especially in the thirties, been a major cause of American unemployment, and that similar consequences are to be expected in the future if high-wage policies be continued. This proposition contradicts the teaching of Keynesian orthodoxy as well as that of some other economists and cannot be established here. It is therefore fortunate that, for our present purpose, and so far as 1950 is concerned and not any later development, a weaker proposition will do which would have commanded the assent of the late Lord Keynes: under the conditions that are likely to prevail in this country during the next four years, and unless compensated by additional increases in prices, higher wage rates will adversely affect both output and employment and the latter more than the former.

creases in wage rates combined with price control, unless *intended* to enforce surrender of private enterprise, is irrational and inimical to prompt expansion of output; that the disturbance of the system of relative prices resulting from the fact that the regulating agency can "keep the lid on" some prices—the prices of producers with little political pull—very much more effectively than on others—the prices of producers with plenty of political pull—reduces the degree of economic efficiency of the system; that price fixing *per se* does not define the whole extent of the damage done: equally important is the premium that the practice of "subsidizing" high-cost and "squeezing" low-cost producers puts upon inefficiency.[10]

The bureaucracy's persistent hostility, strongly supported as it is by public opinion, to industrial self-government—self-organization, self-regulation, co-operation—is a third obstacle to orderly progress and, incidentally, to a development that might solve many problems of business-cycle policy and eventually also the problem of transition to a socialist régime. Spokesmen of the bureaucracy invariably deny that there is any foundation for this view because joint action of businessmen becomes illegal and open to prosecution only if it implies "collusive restraint." But, even if this legalistic interpretation of prevailing practice could be accepted—and if the official theories of what constitutes collusive restraint or, in general, anti-social practice could also be accepted[11]—it would still remain true (a) that the concept of

[10] I do not pretend to know what will eventually come of the muddle occasioned by the presidential veto of the first Price Control Act and the passage of one a month later providing for rapid decontrol. Since, however, I am prepared to argue that the O. P. A., as it actually functioned, was bound to bar the way toward an efficient peace economy and since the possible consequences of that muddle are sure to be represented as proof positive of the necessity of retaining price control, I must ask the reader to consider two things. First, an argument for the repeal of price control is not an argument for letting it lapse, without preparation or transitional substitute, when nobody expected it or seems to have been prepared for it. Second, if in response to its defeat, the Administration hits out vindictively at targets chosen for their unpopularity rather than for any defensible reason, consequences may ensue that are entirely unconnected with the lapse of price control *per se*. As to the problem of inflation, see below *sub* 4.

[11] As a matter of fact, however, these theories cannot be accepted. They cover indeed a range of practices which everyone will agree must be outlawed by any legal system. But beyond these there is another range of practices with regard to which the legal mind simply adopts the attitude dictated by popular prejudices. An important source of examples is discrimination. Even the most competent economist will experience considerable difficulties in analyzing *all* the long-run effects of a given case. If justice is administered on nothing but general legal or popular slogans and by demonstration "drives," the element of sound sense contained in the anti-discrimination attitude may completely disappear. And the well-meant method of selective prosecution which is intended to allow for cases where formally illegal discrimination benefits *all* parties concerned—everyone who ever had an elementary course in economics knows, or should know, such cases—may then only avail to add a most irritating arbitrariness. It is only in a passing remark that we can indicate methods of remedying this state of things.

"restraint" includes the bulk of attempts at industrial co-operation with regard to price and output policy even where such co-operation does fill a much-needed function; (b) that borderline cases and cases in which the element of restraint enters without constituting the main point of an agreement are not sure to be considered with impartiality by a personnel that contains many men inadequately familiar with the nature of business problems and some who are violently opposed to the system they are to regulate or at least to the "big-business" sector of it; and (c) that the ever-present threat of prosecution for offenses which it is not always easy to distinguish from unoffending business practice may have effects on the conduct of business nobody intends it to have.

The last point illustrates an aspect of labor troubles, O. P. A. troubles, and "antitrust" troubles that never receives the attention it merits, namely, the consequent drain on entrepreneurial and managerial energy. The businessman who is incessantly thrown out of his stride not only by having to face ever new institutional data but also by having to be "up before" this or that board, has no steam left for dealing with his technological and commercial problems. It is highly revelatory of the mechanistic attitude of economists and of their remoteness from "real life" that not one in ten will recognize this particular "human element" of what is after all a human organism—though no sensible man can possibly fail, for example, to link up the relatively poor showing made by the physical-volume index of industrial production in 1945 with this element as *one* of its many causes. Nor is this all. Success in conducting a business enterprise depends under present conditions much more on the ability to deal with labor leaders, politicians and public officials than it does on business ability in the proper sense of the term. Hence, except in the biggest concerns that can afford to employ specialists of all kinds, leading positions tend to be filled by "fixers" and "trouble shooters" rather than by "production men."

It may seem to the reader that policy on the lines indicated by all this is out of the question—that it is bound to break down in a storm of righteous indignation or founder on the rocks of sabotage and other forms of resistance and that, therefore, the two hundred billion goal itself is little better than a daydream. But this does not quite follow. On the one hand, the economic engine of this country is strong enough to stand *some* waste and irrationality—including, as we know, some avoidable unemployment, the price of individual freedom. On the other hand, politicians and the public have of late displayed some signs of "coming around." And we must not forget that malleability of human nature which has been so much emphasized in this book (see especially Chapter XVIII, section II). The experiment of the New Deal and war periods may be inconclusive because the industrial bourgeoisie never expected those conditions to last. But some "education" has probably been effected. Thus relatively small adjustments of existing taxation may be all that is required, if not for maximum efficiency, yet for an adequate degree of it.[12] In another direction, a relatively small increment of legal protection—to be granted, perhaps, by means of a proper codification of industrial law—might take the sting or threat of arbitrary vexation out of the businessman's working day and increasing experience of the regulating bodies and better training

---

[12] For instance—this is not intended to be more than an example from a set of possible methods—the following measures might be substantially sufficient. (a) Elimination of the double taxation of that part of the returns to corporate industry which is paid out in dividends; in view of the British practice, this would hardly justify a "storm of righteous indignation": our practice is the German one and the purely formal argument for it is due to the German economist, Adolf Wagner (1835–1917). (b) Permission to deduct from taxable income that part of individual income which is invested. Personally, I agree with Irving Fisher's opinion that the part *saved* should be deducted (particularly in view of the danger of inflation). But in order to spare Keynesian susceptibilities I limit myself to the part invested. Technical difficulties are not serious, at least not insuperable. (c) Adoption of one of several methods that are available in order to allow full deduction of losses over time. (d) Nationalization, systematization, and development of sales or turnover taxes. This should appeal to admirers of Russia instead of sending them into paroxysms of rage. As a matter of fact, at rates like the Russian ones (e.g., thirty-one cents per pound on the best quality of wheat flour [in Moscow and for 1940] or, since translation of ruble amounts into dollar amounts is a doubtful matter, sixty-two per cent of the retail price of potatoes, seventy-three per cent of that of sugar, eighty per cent of that of salt; see P. Haensel, "Soviet Finances," *Openbare Financiën,* 1946, No. 1), and in a population so desperately poor as the Russian one, the sales tax may indeed be a terrible scourge; but at moderate rates and in a country as rich as the United States it is an excellent and perfectly harmless tool of public finance, especially useful in financing purposes that benefit exclusively the low-income groups. Five or six billions could be raised by it without anyone's feeling the burden. But since state and local governments would have to be compensated for the loss of revenue incident to the nationalization of the tax—it is not strictly correct, of course, to speak of "introduction"—and since, moreover, certain adjustments of existing excises would be necessary, the net gain to the Federal Treasury cannot be estimated at more than about two to three billion dollars, so that sales tax plus specific excises might yield something like nine to ten billions in all. (e) Nationalization and drastic downward revision, in favor of wives and children, of the estate taxes, the reason for this being that existing legislation eliminates, by confiscation above very moderate figures, one of the essential elements of the capitalist scheme of things. Whoever approves of this confiscation for extra-economic reasons is, from his standpoint, quite right in advocating a constitutional amendment to that effect; whoever approves of this confiscation on the economic argument to be found on p. 373 of Keynes's *General Theory of Employment, Interest and Money*—or a derivative of this—is quite wrong.

We are not concerned with the question what would satisfy the interests affected *politically.* As a matter of fact, however, most proposals of tax reform that have so far come from businessmen's organizations are distinctly modest which, if not otherwise relevant for our argument, seems to show how effectively the business class has been "educated."

of their staffs might do the rest.[13] Moreover, the country has given proof, not long ago, of its willingness to accept legislation like the N. R. A. And as regards the labor situation, some comfort may perhaps be derived from the fact that policy on the lines contemplated not only need not renounce a single item of what most people will consider the main achievements in social reform of the New Deal but also would provide the economic basis for further advance. It should be noticed in particular that the Annual Wage is a threat to the chance of attaining our goal only if it be introduced, administered, and financed in such ways as to do the maximum of harm. In itself, it is a perfectly possible proposition.[14]

Even so, it takes a lot of optimism to expect that these necessary adjustments will be effected—or even that the conditions of the country's politics can produce the will to undertake such serious and self-denying work, unglorified by slogans, bristling with difficulties of detail, and eminently thankless. The mass of the people would like the America that might emerge from the job but they would hate the man who takes it in hand.

4. We have not yet mentioned Transitional Problems. They are in fact not relevant to our subject except in this respect: transitional difficulties may produce situations and induce measures that are likely to impede the expansion of output quasi-permanently and to invalidate our "estimate of possibilities" completely. The most obvious as well as most serious instance is the danger of inflation. The wholesale price index for 1920 was about 2.3 times the one of 1914. This happened in consequence of a war effort that was not only much smaller and

---

[13] I am adverting here to a point that is important for many more topics than the one in hand. A good bureaucracy is a slow growth and cannot be created at will. The bureaucratic organs of the United States display the ailments of rapid growth to an extent which makes a temporary policy of taking in sails a matter not only of the public interest but of their own. Among other things, the Washington bureaucracy has not yet discovered its place. It happens again and again that individual members of it pursue programs of their own, feel themselves to be reformers and negotiate with Congressmen, Senators, and members of other agencies over the heads of their chiefs. Some idea may suddenly acquire compelling force of which nobody knows the orgin. That way lies chaos and failure.

[14] To illustrate this point, let us recall a bit of recent history. New Dealers in the early thirties adopted the practice of sneering at the slogan Reform vs. Recovery. The sneer proves that they were perfectly aware of the element of truth in it. In fact, as political slogans go, this one was perfectly fair. But it should be understood to refer to the bungling and irresponsible manner in which "reform" was carried out, not to any of its professed aims. We are in a similar position now and the misfortune is that injury to the economic process of capitalism is for some people precisely the feature of reform they like best. Reform without such injury would be all but unattractive to them. And reform paralleled by a policy that insures capitalist success would be the worst that could befall them.

shorter than the recent one in terms of goods and services but also more responsibly financed per unit of goods and services. There was nothing like the present backlog of demand. And tax privileges had provided an adequate motive for investors to keep large blocks of war bonds for good. As it is, Total Deposits Adjusted (time and demand, other than interbank and United States Government deposits, less items in process of collection) and Currency Outside of Banks amounted, in April of the current year to 174 billions (55.17 in June 1929, and 60.9 in June 1939), and there is no saying what part of the public's holdings of government bonds will be turned into cash *for purposes other than repayment of debt.* Any sensible person should be able to form an opinion about what this means under the given circumstances, especially in view of the government's encouragement of, or connivance at, the reckless but universal demand for higher money wage rates—for inflation comes through the payroll.[15] The same sensible person should not find it difficult to make up his mind regarding writers who preach that there is "no" danger of inflation[16] as well as regarding writers who see wild inflation round the corner. In order to make the one point that is relevant to our argument and in the face of the impossibility of treating the problem satisfactorily here, let me proffer my personal opinion merely for the sake of definiteness: It seems to me to be possible—*possible*—to aim, for 1950, at a price level about 50 per cent above the 1928 figure (with bursts beyond that in the interval); it seems to me to be *rational* to use, to this extent, price-level movements as an instrument of adaptation; and it seems to me that the terrors of such an increase in general prices as well as the terrors of a descent from it in later years are greatly exaggerated. But in order to keep the inevitable increase in prices within that limit, a number of measures are necessary, all of which are highly unpopular, all of which require, in order to produce their result, experience and ability that I do not see, and some of which will, to some extent, reduce the speed of the expansion of output; nobody can counteract threatening inflation without also interfering with production. Now, if, instead, nothing is done except setting up another O. P. A. and tax-

[15] The reader will please observe that this particular statement is good Keynesianism and should therefore command assent from Washington economists.

[16] Among these we must include some of those forecasters of postwar demand who predicted that, immediately upon the cessation of a great part of the government's war demand, a slump and widespread unemployment, calling for further deficit spending, was sure to follow. On these (short-run) predictions, see E. Schiff's article in a forthcoming number of the *Review of Economic Statistics.* Corresponding long-run predictions will be discussed below, *sub* 5.

ing heavily precisely those incomes from which—even according to the doctrine held by our radicals—inflation does *not* threaten and if in addition wage rates are being pushed up regardless of consequences, a situation may well arise in which, in desperation, Washington may resort to clumsy and brutal measures such as devaluation, "freezing" deposits, assuming "direct control," punishing "profiteers" and "monopolists," or some other scapegoats, keeping carefully clear of the farmers. And this may upset apple carts to such an extent as to bring us into the immediate vicinity not of the two hundred billion goal but of some half-baked socialism. *May.* There are, of course, other possibilities.

5. It remains to notice what to many economists is *the* postwar problem *par excellence:* how to secure adequate consumption. So far we have indeed seen many reasons for doubting whether the goal envisaged—a gross national product of two hundred billions in 1928 dollars—will actually be reached by 1950. But all of them were founded upon the possibility or likelihood that obstacles *external* to the business process might bar the way. The power of the business process itself to produce that result has, however, been called in question by many economists most, but not all, of whom are identified with certain articles of political as well as scientific faith. We will refer to them by a term that has gained some currency, Stagnationists.[17]

The relevant type of stagnationist theory has been developed by the late Lord Keynes. With its application to the case in hand the reader can best familiarize himself by studying one or more of those estimates of postwar demand that have been produced during the last few years.[18] Their authors agree with us in estimating *potential* production for 1950 at figures that are of the same order of magnitude as is our own so that we may, for the sake of simplicity, continue to speak of a gross national product of two hundred billions. They are even more optimistic than we in that they do not insist on the necessity of environmental conditions favorable to capitalist achievement,[19] but reason on the tacit assumption that present political, administrative, and labor practices persist. Moreover, I shall waive any objection I may have against their estimates of the inevitable minimum of unemployment, or the validity of their statistical methods, and I

[17] On some general aspects of the stagnationist thesis, see above, Chapter X.

[18] The most important of them have been critically analyzed by A. G. Hart, "Model Building and Fiscal Policy," *Am. Econ. Rev.,* Sept. 1945. Further references are therefore unnecessary.

[19] I confess that I have wondered occasionally whether they are aware of the tremendous compliment to private enterprise which this implies.

shall also accept the various hypotheses by means of which they arrive at the figures of Net National Income and of Disposable Income (the sum total of individual incomes after tax and compulsory nontax payments). For definiteness, let us suppose that this disposable income figures out at about 150 billions and that corporate undivided profits are about 6 billions.[20]

Postwar demand, that is to say, the sum total which it is expected private households will spend on consumers' goods (except new homes), is then derived by calculating, from the data for the period preceding the war, say, 1923–1940, the average relation between per capita expenditure on these consumers' goods and per capita disposable income, both deflated by the cost-of-living index, and by applying this relation to a disposable income of 150 billions.[21] If this procedure yields, for example, the sum of 130 billions, we are left with a residual in the amount of 20 billions for savings or, if we add the corporate undivided profits, with 26 billions. The argument usually goes on to survey the available outlets for this sum, the investment opportunities (new housing, additions to inventories, plant and equipment, foreign investment) and to conclude or to suggest that these cannot possibly absorb anything like as much as people will want to save at the 1950 full-employment level of national income, at least not without the help of government. Hence, the necessity of government expenditure at home or government action forcing "foreign investment." Of late, however, another recommendation has come into favor. Since, under present conditions, anyone who advocates government deficit financing is in obvious danger of making himself ridiculous, Washington economists have veered round to recommend balanced budgets, but budgets balanced at a very high level of taxation, the taxes to be highly progressive so as to eliminate the high incomes from which the menace of saving primarily proceeds. This accords with the slogan that (owing

[20] These figures approximate those of one of the postwar-demand estimators. They are not mine. Nor are they compatible with the experimental figures on which we reasoned in section II. For the procedure as applied to past periods—where hypotheses are of course replaced by facts—see, e.g., *Fed. Res. Bull.,* Apr. 1946, p. 436. It should, however, be observed, first, that these figures are in current dollars and, second, that the huge amount of "net savings of individuals" proves nothing for the saving percentages of "normal" times and that even the figures for 1937, 1938, 1939 and 1940 should not be accepted uncritically and especially not without reference to the definition of saving adopted by the Department of Commerce.

[21] Actually, the procedure is somewhat more complicated than that. The regression equations used also contain a trend factor that is to take account of possible changes of the relation over time. Moreover, some account is also taken of the effects of deferred demand and of the accumulation of liquid means. But, in order to concentrate on the salient point, we do not go into all this.

to the saving done by the receivers of high incomes) "in modern societies, the ultimate cause of unemployment is the inequality of incomes."

Thus the high level of national income to which we have looked for the solution of a good many economic and social problems is itself made out to be the most serious problem of all. Since high income means high savings and since these savings will not be entirely offset by investment expenditure, it will not be possible for the economy to keep on that high level of income and employment—unless fiscal policy keeps it there—if indeed this high level can be reached at all. It should be observed that, at least in part, this theory commands the support of public opinion and in particular of business opinions. Nothing is more common than the view that everything will be all right if only we can induce people "to use their incomes fully" or if only we can "get enough consumers' demand." It is a question of some interest why intelligent men who certainly have no stake in any political program involving government expenditure or equalization of income, should nevertheless feel concern on this score. The salesman mentality of the country coupled with the experience of the twenty years preceding the war is all the explanation I can offer for the astounding fact that the theory in question is not simply laughed out of court.

Those opponents of this theory miss the point who try to argue that gross national product, hence income, will be smaller and that investment opportunities will turn out to be greater than estimators assume who are so optimistic when it comes to estimating the former and so pessimistic when it comes to estimating the latter. There may be much truth in arguments on these and similar lines. In particular, it may be emphasized that in 1830 nobody foresaw or could have foreseen the capital requirements of the railroad age or, fifty years later, the capital requirements of the age of electricity. But the decisive argument is much simpler than all that. The theory rests upon the postulate that individuals save, according to a stable psychological law,[22] ir-

[22] This psychological law says that a *community's* expenditure upon consumption, C (hence also the amount it desires to save, S) depends upon national income, Y, in such a manner that, when Y increases by ΔY, C increases by $\Delta C < \Delta Y$ or $\frac{\Delta C}{\Delta Y} < 1$. This is the genuine Keynesian hypothesis about what is known as the Consumption Function. But Keynes himself used occasionally, and his followers use often, the stronger assumption that, as income increases, the saving *percentage* increases. We are concerned only with the genuine hypothesis. It should, however, be observed that it is a misuse of terms to call it a psychological law. Psychological laws in economics are doubtful customers at best. But the proposition in question has not even so much title to being dignified by this term as has, e.g., the proposition that our wish for one more slice of bread decreases in intensity as we go on eating more and more slices.

respective of the presence or absence of investment opportunity. Evidently this is not the normal case. Normally people save with a view to some return, in money or in services of some "investment good." It is not only that the bulk of individual savings—and, of course, practically all business savings which, in turn, constitute the greater part of total saving—is done with a specific investment purpose in view. The decision to invest precedes as a rule, and the act of investing precedes, very often, the decision to save. Even in those cases in which a man saves without specific investment purpose, any delay in coming to an investment decision is punished by the loss of return for the interval. It seems to follow, first, that unless people see investment opportunities, they will not normally save and that a situation of vanishing investment opportunity is likely to be also one of vanishing saving; and, second, that whenever we observe that people display "liquidity preference," that is to say, a desire to save unaccompanied by a desire to invest—a desire to hoard—this must be explained by special reasons and not by appeal to any psychological law postulated *ad hoc.*

Such reasons do exist, however, and there is one among them that is of considerable importance in the depth of cyclical depressions—on a broad average, in one year out of ten. When things look black and people expect nothing but losses from any commitment they might contemplate, then of course they will refuse to invest their current savings (and even to reinvest sums that currently return to them owing to the termination of previous commitments), or they will defer investment in order to profit by further reductions in prices. At the same time, savings will be not only not reduced but increased by all those who expect impending losses of income, in their business or through unemployment. This is an important element in the mechanism of depressions and public deficit spending is indeed one of the most obvious means for breaking such "vicious spirals." However, no defense of any "oversaving" theory can be based upon it because it occurs only as a consequence of a depression that hence cannot itself be explained by it. But it yields a psychological explanation of the Keynesian psychological law. The great depression of 1929–1932 and the slow recovery from it are still in everybody's mind. And the psychological law and the theory of hoarding that is based upon it are simply generalizations from that experience.[23]

Depression-hoarding is therefore not a genuine exception to our

[23] Adaptation of the above argument together with certain wartime factors will, it is hoped, explain wartime accumulations of liquid means without recourse to the hypothesis of an insatiable hunger for hoards inherent in human nature.

general proposition, viz., that decisions to save depend upon and presuppose decisions to invest, though the converse is not true, because it is obviously possible to finance an investment by a bank loan in which case there is no point whatever in speaking of anyone's saving.[24] There are genuine exceptions, besides apparent ones. But neither are of any importance. Instances of genuine exceptions are hoarding with the intention of accumulating a treasure which as everybody knows has been done extensively in India, China, and Egypt; and, temporarily, saving from a habit which once formed may outlive its rationale as may any other habit.[25] Instances of apparent exceptions, similar to our case of depression-hoarding, are accumulations for the purpose of financing a very heavy piece of investment, a possible but evidently unimportant case; or "saving" that is undertaken for the purpose of providing for contingencies, old age and so on and would be undertaken even if there were no opportunities for acquiring any "return" other than a feeling of security.[26]

---

[24] Our proposition is, however, not so simple as it may seem to readers unfamiliar with the discussion that has been carried on ever since the publication of Keynes's *General Theory* (1936). It resembles rather than repeats an old theorem of the "classical theory" (Turgot, A. Smith, J. S. Mill) and cannot be sustained by the reasoning that satisfied the classics. A long and tedious argument would be necessary in order to establish it fully, an argument which it is so discouraging to have to work out because it yields but few new and interesting results and beyond this merely destroys what has been built up with so much trouble during the thirties. Lack of space prevents us, however, from going into it. But one point must be mentioned in order to avoid a misunderstanding that would be as regrettable as it would be natural. Though our proposition shows that the stagnation thesis cannot be based upon the element of saving and though this may be expressed by saying that there is no problem of saving *in this sense,* it does not amount to saying that there are no problems of saving *in other senses.* There are. Most of them center around the case in which individual savings, by way of purchase of securities, are applied to the repayment of bank debts incurred by firms in the course of expanding their plant and equipment. But this is another matter.

[25] The persistence of saving habits that are deeply rooted in the bourgeois scheme of life, especially in the puritan variant of it, may not seem to be unimportant. But the vanishing of investment opportunities that would render those habits irrational would, in the absence of external factors, be a slow process during which adaptation could and would have time to do its work. Washington economists who wish to assert, nevertheless, that the persistence of saving habits that have become irrational is a factor in the economic situation are therefore faced by an unenviable alternative: they would have to admit *either* that the situation of the thirties was one of depression hoarding—which spells surrender of the secular-stagnation thesis—*or* that attractiveness of investment was with comparative suddenness reduced by an external factor which could be no other than the policies they themselves supported. If they adopt the latter view, it is certainly not for me to object.

[26] The unimportance of this follows mainly from two facts: first, that these accumulations are currently depleted (though, with changing national income and age distribution of the population increments and decrements will not, in general, exactly balance); and, second, that so long as there is any saving at all that is motivated by monetary returns, the presence in the total "supply" of an element that is not so motivated does not prove any tendency toward excess saving. This case needs no strengthening. But actually it may be reinforced by observing that under modern conditions insurance greatly reduces the

Thus, if the sorrows of stagnationists were the only ones to trouble us, we should entertain no misgivings about reaching the two hundred billion gross national product. And if twenty billions proved more than can be newly invested, at a rate of return satisfactory to the marginal saver, why, people would be only too happy to consume the excess. We should worry neither about measures to make them "fully use their incomes" nor about outlets for corporate and individual savings. In particular, we should not think it necessary to force foreign investment, advocacy of which under present conditions is nothing but an attempt to make palatable to the country what really amounts to imposing a war indemnity upon it.[27]

On the other hand, we should agree with the advocates of government deficit spending so far as this: Whenever there is danger, either from causes inherent to the business-cycle mechanism or from any other, of a "downward cumulative process," that is to say, whenever a situation threatens to emerge in which A's restriction of production induces B to restrict and so on throughout the economy, in which prices fall because they have fallen, in which unemployment feeds upon itself, government deficit spending will stop this "vicious spiral" and therefore, if we choose to neglect all other considerations, may be justly called an efficient remedy.[28] The true objection is not against income-generating government expenditure in emergencies once they have arisen but to policies that create the emergencies in which such expenditure imposes itself.

---

amounts necessary to attain the objects of contingency saving: of old, provision e.g. for old age and for the needs of wives and children, normally meant the accumulation of a "fortune" (though of course this was not left uninvested); now such provision is effected by "withholdings from consumption" to the amount of insurance premia. The increase in insurance during the last twenty-five years, therefore, indicates the exact opposite of what it is made to indicate in stagnationist writings.

[27] Far be it for me to say or to imply that, on moral or political grounds, a case cannot be made for large sacrifices on the part of the American people. But the case ought to be put frankly upon the moral and political grounds and not upon a denial of the reality of these sacrifices, based on questionable economics. The suggestion that part of the excessive savings might usefully be directed into channels where evidently there is no hope for repayment, let alone returns, is the more insidious because the class whose task it might be to oppose such a policy will accept it with alacrity: for under a system of government guarantees the individual businessman risks little or nothing. And he attaches little if any weight to the national loss—especially if told that this loss, owing to the employment it secures, is really a national gain.

[28] This is why the Murray bill in its original form (not only in the form in which it has been enacted) was unexceptionable *so far as purely economic considerations are concerned.* The wholesale condemnation of income-generating government expenditure under *any* circumstances is understandable and may be justifiable in people who think that, once the use of this tool be granted, the door will be wide open for all kinds of legislative and administrative irresponsibilities. But it cannot be upheld on purely economic grounds.

6. Unfortunately, however, if it were a question of predicting what will actually happen, our result would not differ so much from that of the stagnationists as the reader might expect. Though there is nothing to fear from people's propensity to save, there is plenty to fear from other factors. Labor unrest, price regulation, vexatious administration and irrational taxation are quite adequate to produce results for income and employment that will look exactly like a verification of the stagnationist theory and may indeed produce situations in which public deficit spending imposes itself. We may even witness what will look like oversaving, namely, conditions in which people will be reluctant to carry out their investment decisions. We have been discussing a possibility. We have found that there are no causes inherent in the business process itself to prevent it from being realized. We have also seen that there are causes external to the business process that may do so. Beyond this I do not pretend to know what the actual outcome will be. Whatever it is, it will be a dominant factor in the social situation not only in the United States but also in the world. But only for the next half century or so. The long-run diagnosis elaborated in this book will not be affected.

34

The Stagnation Thesis

By ALVIN H. HANSEN†

I. INVESTMENT OPPORTUNITIES

THE ROLE OF TECHNOLOGY[1]

According to the technological and innovational thesis, the electrification and motorization of the American economy dominated the period from the late nineties to 1929. From this standpoint this epoch may be compared with the period of rapid expansion in railroadization from the middle forties to the decade of the seventies. Both of these innovations caused a profound structural change in economic life and institutions. Both relate mainly to speed of communication and transportation. Both opened up enormous opportunities for real investment, not only directly in the railroads, in automobile factories, and in roads, but also in a vast network of underlying and supplementary industries, including for the last period, glass, rubber, steel, cement, electrical appliances, petroleum, and the like. These epochs are clear illustrations of the profound impact of the rise of quite new techniques giving birth to a range of new industries and expanding and developing old ones into new lines. Both epochs represent a period of rapid growth and expansion. But all new developments finally reach the stage of maturity. Thus, new railroad mileage experienced a rapidly rising trend from the middle forties to the decade of the seventies, and thereafter flattened out with, however, a major spurt in the middle eighties, and eventually in the nineties sharply declined. Similarly, the production of automobiles and the construction of roads experienced a rapid growth into the decade of the twenties. But this rate of growth could obviously not be continued indefinitely. Automobile production gradually reached an asymptotic level after 1923, and the curve of the construction of roads similarly flattened out toward the end of the twenties and thereafter declined.

---

† Harvard University.

[1] From *Fiscal Policy and Business Cycles* (New York: W. W. Norton, 1941; London: George Allen & Unwin Ltd.), pp. 38–46. Reprinted by the courtesy of W. W. Norton and the author.

In the long sweep of technological and innovational developments the decade of the thirties is, therefore, in many respects not unlike the fourth quarter of the nineteenth century,[2] with its deep depressions of the seventies and the nineties. Thus, against the background of earlier experience the decade of the thirties is more understandable.

The early expansion of the railroad served to promote vigorous booms and to cut short temporary lapses into depression. But progressively the railroad reached maturity and eventually ceased to grow. The mere slowing down in the *rate* of growth caused an absolute decline in the volume of new investment required in the plant and equipment of subsidiary industries, such as iron and steel, which manufactured the materials that went into railroad construction. Those who point to the high level of new railroad construction which continued on into the eighties miss the point. It is not enough that new railroad construction should continue at the high level reached. New construction must *continue to rise at a constant rate* if new investment in the underlying, subsidiary industries is to be maintained at the pace set. Thus, the mere slowing down in the *rate of increase* in new railroad construction was already beginning to have a damping effect on the economy long before there was an actual decline in the volume of new construction. This is the important lesson which we learn from the acceleration principle. The sharp decline in railroad construction in the decade of the nineties was a significant factor in that depressed decade.

But now a new era of buoyancy superseded the railroad era—the era of electricity and motorcars. The three decades 1900–29 witnessed

---

[2] It was in this period, when the railroadization of the country was increasingly reaching a saturation point, that Carroll D. Wright, Commissioner of Labor, made his famous declaration with respect to the exhaustion of real investment opportunities. Up to that time the central barometer of prosperity and economic activity, of which everyone was more or less consciously aware, was activity in the railroad industry. The declining role of the railroad was, indeed, the most significant single fact for this period and offers the most convincing explanation for the chronic hard times, particularly of the decade of the nineties. Wright's analysis has attracted, particularly in recent years, widespread attention and received much comment. Some, in view of the tremendous expansion ushered in by the electrification and motorization innovation beginning at the end of the century, have been disposed to criticize his analysis as shortsighted. But others regard his observation as the most penetrating and valid analysis of the economic difficulties of his time which anyone of his generation made. The investment saturation to which he called attention is evidenced by the continued difficulties which confronted not only the United States, but also the countries of western Europe for more than a decade following his lucid exposition of the deep, underlying, real factors in the situation. While others were stressing superficial aspects, Wright placed his finger upon the really significant cause of the world-wide stagnation.

See U.S. Commissioner of Labor, First *Annual Report* (Washington, D.C., Government Printing Office, 1886), dealing with industrial depressions.

the rise of four new giant industries.[3] Street cars led the way in the nineties and reached its investment peak ($2.5 billion) in the decade 1900–09. Capital outlays on telephones increased rapidly after 1900 and doubled in each of the two succeeding decades, rising to $2.5 billions in the twenties. Electric power investment first assumed large proportions in the decade 1900–09 ($1.7 billions), increased 50 per cent in the following decade, and leaped forward with a capital expenditure of $8.1 billions in the twenties. Automobile production, from only 4,000 units in 1900, rose to 187,000 units in 1910, 1,000,000 in 1915, 2,200,000 in 1920, 4,400,000 in 1925, and 5,600,000 in 1929. Garages, repair shops, and service stations multiplied throughout the country. Thus, the automobile industry not only fostered gigantic production plants, largely concentrated in a single industrial area, but also opened opportunities for thousands of small business units located in all sections of the country roughly in proportion to the consuming population. Major subsidiary industries were created or expanded on the tide of the vast purchasing power of the automobile industry, including such giants as Petroleum, Rubber, Glass Plate, and Steel. Finally, outlays on public roads, largely induced by the rise of the automobile, reached the figure of $9.9 billions in the decade 1920–29.[4]

Thus, an era of buoyant prosperity was generated by the growth of four great industries: streetrailways, telephone, electric power, and automobile industries (including Petroleum, Rubber, and Glass Plate, largely accessory to the Automobile). Also important, but nevertheless dwarfed by the four giants, were the movie, chemical, and electrical equipment industries.

Just as the railroad expansion came to an end, so also the buoyant era of 1900–29. Street railway development was largely completed in the first decade, telephone and automobile expansion in the third decade. Electric power alone remains with large prospects for further growth. The great era of expansion was over by 1930. Thus, the decade of the thirties resembles the conditions in the nineties. Technological developments making for expansion had temporarily spent their force. This does not mean, however, that eras of buoyant expansion are permanently a thing of the past. The progress of technology, we can be reasonably certain, will sooner or later open outlets for enlarged streams of investment in great new industries.

---

[3] I am indebted to John Wilson, formerly instructor in economics at Harvard University and now economist in the Department of Commerce, for the use of data in his unpublished manuscript.

[4] From TNEC, Hearings, Part 1, p. 232.

STRUCTURAL CHANGES IN AMERICAN ECONOMY

Thus far we have seen that the decade of the thirties is largely understandable in terms of past experience. But our analysis would remain incomplete if we neglected to consider one important structural change in our economy for which we have no precedent in the past. Always, in the past century, expansion has rested not merely on *intensive* investment arising from technological progress, but also on extensive growth—the occupation of new territory and the growth of population. The nineteenth century was a unique era of *extensive* growth.

Approximately in the period of 1915–30, the rate of extensive growth rapidly slowed down. The decennial increment of population growth in northern and western Europe, including the three great powers, the United Kingdom, Germany, France, and the smaller northern and western countries—Scandinavia, Finland, Belgium, Holland, Switzerland, and the Irish Free State—continued to rise, or at any rate did not decline materially until the first World War. The following table (calculated from Kuczynski's *The Balance of Births and Deaths,* p. 9) gives the approximate increases for the *eleven* countries of northern and western Europe referred to above. The period 1913 to 1926 is omitted, since the war abnormally reduced the rate of population growth. The decade 1926–36 may be regarded as representative of postwar normal rate of growth.

TABLE I

Decade	*Increase*
1883–93	10,290,000
1893–03	14,950,000
1903–13	14,510,000
1926–36	9,468,000

In the United States the decline came later, as shown in the table which follows:

TABLE II

Decade	*Increase*
1900–10	16,138,000
1910–20	14,923,000
1920–30	15,901,000
1930–40	9,218,000

In northern and western Europe the turning point came with the first World War. In the United States it came in 1924.

The expansion of Europe into new territory (in terms of both migration and foreign investments) came to an abrupt halt in the first

World War and, while resumed in the twenties, did not again attain its former level. In the United States the expansion into the great West was followed by several decades of urbanization; and then we turned (via capital export) on a large scale to less developed countries. This movement ended in the Great Depression. Doubtless, under more favorable political conditions, there is still room for considerable foreign investment in the less industrialized parts of the world, and it may be expected again sooner or later to be resumed on a fairly large scale. But no one is likely to challenge the statement that the era of development and settlement of new territory is largely over. The role of territorial expansion is likely to be much less in the next half century than was the case in the nineteenth century relative to national income.[5]

The rapid decline in population growth and the exhaustion of the world frontier may well have a causal interconnection. Certainly it is true that, so long as there were great new territories to be opened and developed, rapid population growth was a healthy economic development. With an increasing exhaustion of opportunities for settlement and exploitation of new territory, the continuation of the nineteenth-century rate of population growth would rapidly have given rise to insoluble economic problems.

It is true that the sudden and drastic decline in the rate of population growth so far has affected mainly western Europe, and highly developed industrial countries, such as the United States. It is also true that there are still areas which have a long way to go in the process of industrialization. But just as the rate of population growth in the highly industrialized countries has rapidly declined and in some is approaching zero, so also the possibilities of large outlets for foreign investment by these countries appear meager, in terms of national income and wealth, in comparison with those of the nineteenth century. While it is not possible statistically to measure the rate of decline in investment opportunities with the precision that is possible with respect to population growth, in general the two movements appear to exhibit a somewhat parallel development.

In this connection, it is well to emphasize that the economic frontier of any country must always be conceived of not in terms of its own boundaries, but in terms of the possibility of capital investment throughout the entire world. Thus, Great Britain, despite the fact that her own territory was, of course, from the beginning of the modern

[6] See Isaiah Bowman, *Limits of Land Settlement* (New York, Council of Foreign Relations, 1937).

capitalist period fully occupied, enjoyed equally with the United States a great economic frontier throughout the nineteenth century. From this standpoint, it is clearly a mistake to speak of the passing of the American frontier as the end of extensive expansion, for after this phase was over, investment abroad played an important role in the general world expansion, and this in turn reacted upon the speed of our own internal development. Moreover, of course, as far as general economic expansion is concerned, it must always be remembered that throughout the era of modern industrialization there are three strands to the process—technological innovations, the development of new territory, and the growth of population. Each has reinforced the other, but at times, when one or the other has slackened, another factor has taken an exceptional spurt. This was notably true in the United States in the period of electrification and motorization of her economy.

Population growth and territorial expansion opened vast outlets for *extensive* investment of capital. But, it is argued, may not equally favorable opportunities for *intensive* investment take their place? The answer appears to be that in the past we have enjoyed opportunities for *both* extensive and intensive investment. Now *extensive expansion* is largely over, and there remains only the possibility of intensive developments. But intensive investment is not something new. Intensive and extensive developments have proceeded together, each reinforcing the other. New technological developments underlie the nineteenth century of expansion. But population growth and the penetration into new territory, in turn, played an important role in the widening of the market and the development of mass production techniques. Extensive expansion minimized the risks of technological innovations and encouraged bold experimentation. Thus extensive expansion stimulated intensive expansion. On the other side, the pressure to find investment opportunities, in view of the slowing down of extensive growth, will be greater in the future. Industrial research is now far more systematic and more generously financed than ever before.

The era of buoyant prosperity (1844–73), based largely on the railroad, was intimately linked up with extensive growth and expansion. The next buoyant era (1900–29), based on electricity and the automobile, had less to do with mere extensive growth and expansion into new territory, and involved a much more radical transformation in consumption habits and ways of living. This sort of transformation, involving vast investment of capital, can take place without extensive growth, and under the progress of technology we shall doubtless experience again far-reaching revolutionary innovations of this sort. There is, perhaps, inherent in the process of innovation a cumulative tendency which may be described in terms of a geometric progression. That this was true, even of the past century, is at least in part supported by the fact that the percentage rate of increase in per capita real income was approximately a constant. It is, of course, always possible that the rate of technological development may in the future exceed the geometric rate of the past, but here obviously one enters a field of speculation which can be settled only by the actual course of future historical events. It is, at any rate, a question whether intensive investment can attain the buoyancy and tempo of earlier periods when technological developments were stimulated by population growth and territorial expansion.

The decline in the rate of extensive expansion may partly account for the structural change which we are witnessing in economic institutions. The economic order is undergoing progressively changes in its internal organization which affect its functioning and operation—defense mechanisms, they may be, which seek more or less blindly and experimentally to adjust the economy to an era of less rapid extensive growth.

RECENT POPULATION TRENDS[6]

In the Great Depression of the thirties there occurred for the first time in American history a drastic decline in the absolute rate of population growth. Every previous depression had been buoyed up by the capital requirements associated with an ever larger increment of population. The decade of the nineteen-thirties enjoyed no such stimulus.

In the decade of the nineteen-forties, however, there was a strong resurgence of population growth, and this in part accounts for the high level of capital requirements in the years following the Second World War. The accumulated backlog of capital needs which confronted the economy after 1945 was in some measure greater by reason of the large growth in population in the decade of the forties. By the same token the decade of the thirties suffered from a dearth of investment opportunities, partly by reason of the drastic decline in the rate of growth.

Here again, as in the case of the growth of railroad mileage, discussed above, the full impact can be understood only in terms of the acceleration principle. If the capital capacity of the heavy industries has been built up to a point adequate to take care of railroad replace-

[6] From *Business Cycles and National Income* (W. W. Norton, 1951), pp. 75–76. Reprinted by the courtesy of W. W. Norton and the author.

ment *plus* new mileage, excess capacity in these basic industries will appear whenever the *rate of growth* of mileage declines. The same holds true if the basic industries have developed a capacity adequate to take care of a given rate of population growth. Any decline in that rate will tend to have a depressional effect upon the volume of investment. After the economy has become adjusted to a rate of growth of around 16 or 17 million per decade, a decline in the rate of growth to less than 9 million could not fail to chill the outlook for investment. On the other hand, as we have just noted, the remarkable and unexpected spurt of population in the decade of the forties has raised expectations with respect to profitable investment outlets. Whether this postwar increase in population is based on fundamental factors which have altered the specific fertility rates, or whether it is merely a reflection of temporary factors stemming from the war, is not yet clear.

A large growth in population is favorable to investment and therefore to income generation and employment. This is the Keynesian view of population growth. But a population may become so large in relation to natural resources and food supply that real wages tend to fall, or at least to fall below the optimum level. This is the Malthusian view of population growth.[7]

THE NEW FRONTIER[8]

In conclusion I may briefly state my own position. It seems to me evident that the automatic factors inducing private investment outlets are not so strong as in the great days of expansion prior to World War I. We now need to develop a new frontier, so to speak, in our own back yard and thereby open new outlets for private investment. There is plenty to be done. Look at the condition of all our great metropolitan

---

[7] The following table gives the decennial increase in population in the United States during the last five decades. There was a moderate decline in the second decade, 1910–19, but any unfavorable investment effects of this decline were swallowed up in the advancing tide of wartime prosperity. Thus the decade of the thirties was the first peacetime decade to suffer a significant absolute decline in the rate of population growth.

Decade	*Increase*
1900–09	16,000,000
1910–19	13,700,000
1920–29	17,000,000
1930–39	8,900,000
1940–49	19,000,000

For a fuller discussion of the problems of extensive and intensive investment, see Alvin H. Hansen, *Fiscal Policy and Business Cycles* (W. W. Norton & Co., 1941), Ch. 1 and 17; and also the reply to George Terborgh's *The Bogey of Economic Maturity* in Hansen, *Economic Policy and Full Employment* (McGraw-Hill Book Co., 1947), Appendix B.

[8] From *Economic Policy and Full Employment* (McGraw-Hill Book Co., 1947), p. 306.

communities—rotting at the centers with ever-spreading blight. Here is a rich field for development and investment, public and private, but there are few, if any, of those familiar with the problem who believe that it can be done without the government's playing a vigorous role. We need in our day peculiarly to be ingenious about finding new outlets for investment and expansion. In the old days, with vast, rich resources untapped, it was a simple matter. For us we need ingenuity, courage, teamwork, and cooperation between government and industry.

As I have worked in recent years on regional resource development, urban redevelopment, education, public health facilities, and the like, I am impressed with the futility of much of the current discussion. When a compensatory and development program is advanced, the argument is not infrequently made that "this is all good and well, but there are no useful outlets for government outlays." On the other side, the practical people, painfully aware, in their everyday contacts, of the urgent needs, are always wondering where the money is coming from. I am convinced that economists have been grossly negligent as a profession in failing to examine the grave deficiencies in our society. Many of these cannot be overcome except by public investment in our material and human resources.

II. GROWTH OR STAGNATION IN THE AMERICAN ECONOMY[9]

A fresh look at the stagnation thesis can usefully be examined in connection with Mr. J. Steindl's book, *Maturity and Stagnation in American Capitalism*[10] which was completed in the summer of 1949, prior to Korea. At that moment the United States was experiencing a recession and all the free world was worried lest it might develop into a serious depression. The outlook seemed to point toward the continuation of rather moderate military expenditures, and it was perhaps even possible to hope for a gradual approach to a more peaceful world. Since then we have had the shock of the Korean War and the enormous increase in military outlays[11] with the prospect of continued high levels of expenditure, not indeed at the peak levels, but at levels far beyond anything envisaged in 1949.

---

[9] From *Rev. Econ. and Stat.,* Nov. 1954.

[10] J. Steindl, *Maturity and Stagnation in American Capitalism* (Oxford, Basil Blackwell, 1952).

[11] Occasionally one still encounters the argument that the increased expenditures following Korea were not expansionist because they were offset by an equivalent amount of taxes. This despite the fact that this matter has been conclusively explored by many distinguished economists including Haberler, Haavelmo, Samuelson, and many others. And as far as I know, no one who has given the matter serious thought has raised a dissenting voice.

In the kind of world now in prospect, the problem of stagnation assumes a quite different aspect from that of 1949. Indeed even in 1949, with a federal budget of about $40 billion, half of which was for national security, the situation was obviously not at all like the peacetime conditions prevailing in the thirties before the Second World War. It is amazing how many economists have been able to close their eyes and blandly announce that events since 1940 have *disproved* the stagnation thesis![12]

Perhaps Mr. Steindl might concede that under current foreseeable conditions (despite some considerable decline in military expenditures) it makes no sense to talk about stagnation except in terms of past history. But I suspect that he might disagree. And, indeed, unless fairly drastic action is taken, there is a serious danger that we may move sidewise in the United States or even slip down gradually over the next few years. Measured against the attainable growth of GNP of which we are capable, such an experience would indeed be a form of stagnation. The mere maintenance of the GNP at the level of the "second best year" would give us ten to twelve million unemployed four years hence. It is therefore perhaps not altogether a useless exercise to re-examine, as Mr. Steindl does, the stagnation thesis.

To begin with, it may be well to attempt a short classification of stagnation hypotheses, in order to give perspective to Mr. Steindl's thesis, as follows:

1. A theory based primarily on *exogenous* factors including technology, population growth and the opening up and development of new territory. This point of view is represented by my own analysis and perhaps also that of Harrod.

2. A theory based primarily on fundamental changes in social institutions, such as increasing state intervention in the form of the welfare state and related developments including the growth of the labor movement. This development, it is argued, has afflicted a formerly vigorous capitalism with a bad case of "arterial sclerosis." This point of view is represented by Schumpeter in his *Capitalism, Socialism and Democracy.*

3. A theory based on endogenous factors inherent in the development of capitalism—primarily the development of imperfect competition, monopoly and oligopoly. This point of view is represented by Steindl in the book here under review.

In his endogenous theory of stagnation, Mr. Steindl argues that already as early as the eighteen-nineties, the American economy had un-

[12] See my "Stability and Expansion" chapter in *Financing American Prosperity* (1945), p. 214. My own "full-employment" postwar federal budget, corrected for price changes, was only $37.2 billion while the actual federal budget for 1948–50 was $41.3 billion. Thus my strongly expansionist full employment budget was actually exceeded as events turned out. Hence the American economy of 1948–50 could scarcely be cited as one operating on it own steam without government support.

dergone a transition to the oligopolistic pattern. Stagnation did not come overnight. There had been going on a long process of secular change. "Hardly anybody during the 'New Era' was aware of the fact that the annual rate of growth of business capital then was only half of what it had been thirty years earlier!" (p. 166).

Stagnation is defined by reference to capital accumulation. Fundamental changes, the author asserts, began toward the end of the century in the trend of capital accumulation. Stagnation developed from long-term structural changes.

The trend toward oligopoly raised profit margins. This development tended to produce excess capacity. Excess capacity—a decline in the rate of utilization of the capital stock—led to a falling off in the rate of growth of capital. This is the essence of stagnation as Steindl sees it.

In competitive industries, excess capacity tends to be eliminated through price cutting and the consequent elimination of submarginal firms and obsolete or quasi-obsolete equipment. Thus any tendency toward excess capacity is rectified by relentless competition, and a normal level of utilization is thereby re-established.

Not so with monopoly or oligopoly. In such industries the process of throwing out surplus capital by price cutting cannot occur. The only way oligopolistic industry can respond to excess capacity is to slow up the process of expansion. Surplus capital (excess capacity) weakens the inducement to invest. Here Mr. Steindl finds the ultimate explanation for the alleged brake on the growth of capital which leads to stagnation.

In the early stages of capitalism, there was a tendency toward a cumulative process of expansion. "In fact, we may be led to wonder how this early development of capitalism ever avoided plunging into headlong inflation" (p. 136). In the early stages of capitalism the expansionist tendency was strong due to over-employment of capacity, the great need for more capital, and the low profit margins which kept capital scarce. Profit margins were low owing to low rates of increase in productivity. Thus while capital formation proceeded slowly, it grew and grew as rapidly as increases in productivity permitted. High utilization tended to promote investment to a point pressing hard on available resources.

But in later stages, large increases in productivity, combined with monopoly and oligopoly, led to high profit margins. The rate of expansion of large firms depends on the rate of internal accumulation and this depends upon profit margins. Increased profit margins will thus lead to an increase in output capacity. But monopolistic industries have great fear and apprehension of excess capacity.

This process has been going on, says Steindl, since the 1890's in the United States.[13] But compensatory factors covered up for a time the stagnation process. One important offsetting factor was the growing tendency of corporate financing by means of the issue of shares in a highly developed stock market in which a larger and larger public participated. This development had the effect of reducing the effective yield to stockholders. The trend toward lower yields had the same stimulating effect on investment as a fall in the rate of interest. In short, the process of capital growth could for awhile be carried farther than might otherwise have been possible had the cost of financing (yield on stock issues) not tended downward.

Apart from Steindl's analysis, are there any general observable changes over the last 150 years which are relative to the problem in hand? I suggest that there are, and I shall attempt here a brief summary statement.

Modern capitalism has evolved over the last 150 years from a primitive handicraft society using simple tools to a highly mechanized society using a vast amount of capital per worker. And this technological development has taken place alongside of and within the pattern of a rapidly growing population, a considerable fraction of which was moving into a vast new continent while the rest was extending, by various devices such as trade, its subsistence base. This society constitutes today the nations which possess the bulk of the economic and military power of the free world.

This society has evolved during the last 150 years from a capital poor society to a capital rich society. At the beginning of this period, starting virtually from scratch, almost the whole of gross investment was *net* investment. There was practically no replacement capital and practically no depreciation funds available for investment. At the end of the period, however, only a fraction of gross investment was *net* investment, the bulk being replacement investment financed from depreciation funds.[14] Now the use of depreciation funds for modernization of worn out equipment permits in practice a large growth in productive capacity even though there be no *net* investment whatever. John Stuart

---

[13] See, however, Stanley Lebergott, "Has Monopoly Increased?" *Rev. Econ. and Stat.*, Nov. 1953; also, M. A. Adelman, "The Measurement of Industrial Concentration," *Rev. Econ. and Stat.*, Nov. 1951; G. W. Nutter, *The Extent of Enterprise Monopoly in the United States, 1899–1939* (Chicago, 1951).

[14] See my *Fiscal Policy and Business Cycles*, pp. 309–12.

Mill, a hundred years ago, already understood the significance of this fact; he understood that there could be growth in output per capita even though there was no net saving. In the early nineteenth century nearly all gross investment had to be financed out of current *net* saving. On the one side the capital stock was scarce and the marginal efficiency of capital was high. On the other side the main source of capital was current *net* saving. Under these circumstances the rate of growth of capital accumulation was limited, not by demand, but by the amount of net current saving that could be pumped out of the community. Such a society tended to draft to the full all its productive resources. Such a society was able to "generate its own steam." There was no problem of inadequate aggregate demand.

Eventually, however, the society acquired a vast accumulated stock of capital. The society was no longer capital poor. The marginal efficiency of capital tended to decline. The bulk of gross investment was fed from depreciation funds.[15] Net savings were no longer the primary source of investment funds. Net savings thus found investment outlets less readily available than in the early periods when net savings were practically the sole source of investment funds.

On the demand side, the marginal efficiency of capital was high in a century confronted with a rich and unoccupied new territory of vast extent. The opportunities to exploit this new territory stimulated population growth. I do not believe that anyone will deny that the total population of the European stock would have been considerably smaller by 1900 had there been no great new unoccupied continent to conquer. In turn this growth of population stimulated a high level of investment.

In recent years, following the postwar increase in population growth (a spurt closely related to the Great War), I have noticed that almost everybody now places strong emphasis on population growth as a stimulating factor. This is quite in contrast with the attitude taken by many economists in the thirties. But even this recent increase in population

---

[15] See Robert Eisner, "Depreciation Allowances, Replacement Requirements and Growth," *Am. Econ. Rev.*, Dec. 1952; and Evsey Domar, "Depreciation, Replacement, and Growth," *Econ. Jour.*, Mar. 1953.

With stable prices, straight line depreciation, and constant rates of growth, depreciation charges must exceed replacement requirements by a considerable margin, since in a growing society, the age distribution of capital assets is disproportionately new. Indeed it would take a very considerable inflation to wipe out the excess of depreciation charges over replacement requirements.

See, however, Eric Schiff ("A Note on Depreciation, Replacement, and Growth," *Rev. Econ. and Stat.*, Feb. 1954), who argues that these assumptions exaggerate the excess of depreciation charges owing to the need in practice of "replacing" a durable asset in considerable part before the asset is retired from service.

growth is in fact relatively small compared with the rate of increase in the nineteenth century. A commensurate rate of population growth today would mean an increase of fifty million per decade compared with the twenty million or so which we now have. Imagine the stimulus to investment which a fifty million growth in population per decade would give us today in a situation permitting expansion into a richly endowed unoccupied continent several times the size of the North American continent. It is magnitudes such as these which one must think of if one is to weigh realistically the strength of the expansionist forces at work in the nineteenth century.

How inventive, productive, and dynamic the American private enterprise economy can be, when operating under the pull of adequate aggregate demand, has been demonstrated in a remarkable laboratory experiment during the last fifteen years. But there are sound reasons, I believe, for the proposition that the economy cannot on its own generate enough steam to provide our full potential of growth. Unaided by the massive fiscal powers of the federal government, we may not be able to achieve, in the words of the Employment Act of 1946, "maximum production, employment and purchasing power."

Growth requires that "tomorrow's" expenditures shall exceed "today's" income. This means that "tomorrow's" private investment plus government outlays must exceed "today's" current saving and taxes. Expansion requires the growth of public and private credit. Modern methods of corporate financing call for relatively little increase in bank credit. In the nineteenth century, when capital was scarce, when current net savings were the main source of funds, commercial loans played a much larger role in total financing than today. Nowadays expansion must lean more heavily on the growth in public credit. We are not likely to double our *real* GNP by 1975, as we can and should, unless we permit a more or less commensurate growth in the public debt.

Once we get our military expenditures down to a substantially smaller figure than the present level, we may discover that we cannot maintain full employment without a reduction in taxes substantially in excess of the cut in military expenditures. Under war or quasi-war conditions, the expenditures are set by the inexorable requirements of national defense. Tax rates in such periods have to be set at the levels necessary to prevent inflation, and this may well require a balanced or even overbalanced budget. Under an approach to peacetime conditions, the level of total government expenditures is subject to voluntary control. Tax rates should then be set at levels which will permit growth with stability. This requires a responsible balancing of tax financing and loan financing.

Thus the dogma of the balanced budget may well become a serious obstacle to "maximum production, employment and purchasing power" in the United States. Yet it is by now generally agreed that the present public debt, considering the manner in which it is held (combined with the current relatively favorable distribution of the tax burden) is an important element of strength in the community.

A good many economists, in conformity with either the Schumpeterian or the Steindl hypothesis respecting unfavorable structural changes, tend to the view that the incapacity of the economy adequately to "generate its own steam" stems from malfunctioning of the price system. The remedy must therefore be sought in reducing the interferences imposed upon a free price system by trade unionism, labor reformism, and state interventionism (Schumpeter) or by the elimination or amelioration of monopolistic and oligopolistic distortion (Steindl) of free, competitive price relationships. Wage and price policy (supported by *pure* monetary policy) are the remedies to be applied, not fiscal policy.

There are other economists who, skeptical or at least agnostic with respect to any stagnation *hypothesis* whatever, are none the less prepared not to rely upon automatic processes to give us full employment.[16] While stressing the importance of a well functioning price system, they are none the less not satisfied that price and wage policy will do the job. They are prepared, therefore, to agree that full employment in the United States is not likely to be maintained, either in the cyclical short run or in the long run, unless the massive fiscal powers of the federal government are employed to ensure adequate aggregate demand. This does not mean that they rely upon fiscal policy alone. These economists are dubious of all hypotheses with respect to stagnation, but they are prepared to be realistic and to support a strong fiscal policy program (supplemented by monetary policy) if and when it is needed. From the standpoint of policy it is of course not necessary to hold any views with respect to *why* the machine appears to be stalled. It is only necessary to recognize that this is in fact the case. Those who believe that adjustments in the price mechanism will suffice fall in one

---

[16] I am indebted to Carl Kaysen, Harvard University, for valuable suggestions in the section which follows. Also my attention has been called to an interesting doctor's thesis by Hyman Minsky, Brown University, which relates to the impact of the market structure upon the problem here under discussion.

school; those who believe that such adjustments (while important) will not suffice, will support the fiscal policy route to full employment not merely as an anticyclical device, but also as a necessary means to achieve our long-run growth potential.

There is, however, I suppose all will agree, still another important group which falls somewhere in between. I refer to those economists who wish to see the government take strong fiscal measures to prevent any serious depression, but are not prepared to accept the responsibility of government for sustained growth and expansion. They believe, however, that a serious depression has disastrous effects on the spirit of enterprise and breeds a psychology of stagnation. It was, they believe, the psychological effect of the Great Depression of the thirties which made it impossible to achieve full recovery. In the stagnant atmosphere of deep depression gloom, the spirit of enterprise, innovational activity, investment, expansion and growth were not possible. If, however, the government would act swiftly and adequately to prevent a serious collapse, the spirit of enterprise, buoyancy, and bold investment planning could be relied upon, in a well functioning price system sustained by active monetary policy, to generate full recovery, growth, and rising living standards. From this point of view the all important thing is not to permit any serious slump such as that of the nineteen-thirties.

It could perhaps be said that this position, as a minimum, is by now accepted by nearly all or at least by the great majority of economists. The assumption by government of responsibility for the prevention of a slump is indeed a great forward step in public policy. The British White Paper on Employment Policy in 1944 was the first firm governmental pronouncement along these lines. Until recently such a declaration by government was regarded as dangerous and illusory, and fears were often expressed that it could only give rise to hopes that might not be fulfilled.

The U.S. Employment Act of 1946 goes further than the British White Paper. The Employment Act does not even refer to the prevention of a slump. It is not cast in those terms. "The Congress declares that it is the continuing policy and responsibility of the Federal government to use all practical means . . . to promote maximum employment, production and purchasing power."

Here also, perhaps, one encounters some divergence of economic thinking. A little less ambitious with respect to goals than is indicated by the Employment Act, some economists nevertheless wish to go farther than merely to prevent serious slumps. From this point of view the all important thing is not to allow the economy to fall below the threshold of *minimum* growth; i.e., to prevent the economy from lapsing very far from the full employment trend, and yet to permit a certain range for the free play of automatic forces without more than this limited intervention of any positive governmental action other than what is provided by the continuing sustaining effect of institutional arrangements, such as a tax structure designed to promote a favorable distribution of income, social security, collective bargaining, governmental lending and insuring agencies, and adequate monetary liquidity.

Reverting again to Mr. Steindl, it may well be that his hypothesis might be a useful point of departure for further research into the 1929–33 depression. The 1929 boom seems to have been characterized by an abnormally inflated capital investment boom. What caused the feverish optimism which led to this extravagant and unmaintainable burst of investment outlays? Oligopoly, without the "countervailing power" (Galbraith) of labor or reformist government, was perhaps a factor contributing to the extraordinary stock market craze which in turn fed the capital market with incredibly cheap investment funds. The 1928–33 episode points to the danger of stimulating the economy unduly in the areas of investment and profits; it is much safer to buoy up consumption, and in particular to promote a balanced income distribution with as high wages as productivity can justify, and profits at a moderate level yet adequate for *maintainable* growth and expansion. No doubt the depression of 1929–33 was made unduly severe by the unbalanced character of the preceding boom, to which a relatively unrestrained oligopolistic economy may have contributed. Yet without the extravagant features of this particular boom, we might have experienced quasi-stagnation, given the quite inadequate institutional arrangements then in effect with respect to the money and capital markets, social security, collective bargaining, minimum wage legislation, farm prices, etc. With the exogenous factors (so powerful in the 19th century) on the wane, with the growth of oligopolistic industry, unmatched as yet by adequate "countervailing power," with 19th century social institutions still dominant and utterly inadequate for the balanced growth and expansion of the modern giant economy, the great depression (and its intractable character, unresponsive to minor stimuli) begins to be understandable. We need much more study of the interwar period.

NOTE: Professor Smithies suggested that I might comment, if I wished, on Professor Schumpeter's contribution which precedes. Adequate comments would require a long discussion. Instead I limit myself to a few brief statements.

1. I fully accept Schumpeter's definition of stagnationists (p. 392 in *Capitalism, Socialism, and Democracy* [1949 ed.]), as follows: "The power of the business process itself to produce that result [i.e., full employment] has, however, been called in question by many economists most, but not all of whom are identified with certain articles of political as well as scientific faith. We will refer to them by a term that has gained some currency, Stagnationists."

I like this definition because it stresses in a precise way the essential issue which is as follows: Can the economy *automatically* produce full employment? Can *automatic* factors alone, under modern conditions, be relied upon to the degree that was possible in the expansionist nineteenth century?

2. I agree fully that "a situation of vanishing investment opportunity is likely to be also one of vanishing saving" (p. 395, *Capitalism, Socialism, and Democracy*), but Schumpeter's conclusion is not valid.

This statement, in itself quite correct, means that at low levels of investment, income will fall, and *as a result,* saving will also decline until at the new equilibrium position investment and saving are equal at a low level.

But this unfortunately is not really what Schumpeter means. In his view, the economy always (apart from temporary lapses) tends toward full employment, even though investment has fallen, and so excess saving keeps piling up until an increase in real assets causes a rise in consumption. This is Say's law all over again.

Now this is not what actually happens at all. This section, and many other statements scattered about in Schumpeter's writings, disclose quite clearly that he was never prepared to face up with the problem in terms of the consumption function analysis. Other illustrations of this can be found in his reference (p. 396) in this contribution to "the persistence [in depression] of savings habits that have become irrational," and in his statement "that the situation of the thirties was one of depression hoarding." Arguments such as these completely ignore the analysis upon which the case of his opponents rests, and thus evade or sidestep the issues involved.

Classified Bibliography of Articles on Fiscal Policy

WILBUR A. STEGER

The compilation of a lengthy bibliography is both a rewarding and frustrating experience. Insight into a specialized subject is gained, but it must be translated arbitrarily into classes and subclasses. Since there are many articles that fall into more than one category, the reader must be warned that the classification is not mutually exclusive. Another difficulty in classification arises from the several functions of bibliographies: what is suitable for the instructor preparing a reading list may be less useful for the research student interested in a special branch of the subject. No cross referencing is included in this bibliography, but in most cases the subject headings should provide sufficient leads to the researcher.

The classification headings used in this bibliography are shown in the accompanying table of contents. Only a few points require special comment. The delimitation of fiscal policy from other specialized fields in economics is itself highly arbitrary. While this bibliography encompasses subjects not covered in the articles included in the text of this book, no great departure from the general field is intended. While some of the headings such as "Taxation and Investment" and "Budgeting Theory and Policy" are on the borderline of the larger subjects of public finance and public administration, others such as "Public Debt Policy and Economic Stability" border on the province of monetary theory and policy. Overlapping with previous bibliographies in this series, while necessary for adequate coverage, has been reduced to the minimum. For this reason, the subsection on "Monetary Policy versus Fiscal Policy," for example, has been limited to a few of the most basic articles on this subject.

Coverage has been attempted only in English language journals, and is more complete for journals dealing mainly with economics than for journals dealing with the social sciences generally, such as the *Annals of the American Academy of Social Sciences.* Time limitations have prevented coverage of foreign language periodicals in this bibliography: this is a severe limitation, but it is believed to be less serious than it would be in many other branches of economics. Articles originally appearing in periodicals and reprinted in a book are included, as are articles published in multi-author books. The relative youth of the subject has made the coverage in terms of years fairly comprehensive.

Articles within each heading are arranged chronologically by years; articles published in the same year are alphabetized. This arrangement was chosen to indicate the timeliness of the writing on fiscal policy and the tendency of the literature to parallel the stage of the economic cycle at the time of the writing.

I should like to express my appreciation to Mrs. J. R. Lindsay, who made available the extensive files she had maintained in compiling bibliographies for the Fiscal Policy Seminar in the Graduate School of Public Administration at Harvard University.

Classified Bibliography of Articles

I. INTRODUCTION

A. Over-all Discussion, General

GORDON, R. A., Fiscal policy as a factor in stability, *Annals of the American Academy of Political and Social Science,* CCVI (1939), 106–13.

HARDY, C. O., Fiscal policy and the national income: a review, *American Economic Review,* XXXII (1942), 103–10.

COLM, G., Fiscal policy, *The New Economics* (ed. S. E. HARRIS), pp. 450–67. New York: Alfred A. Knopf, 1947.

HANSEN, A. H., Keynes on economic policy, *The New Economics* (ed. S. E. HARRIS), pp. 197–207. New York: Alfred A. Knopf, 1947.

HARRIS, S.E., Keynes' influence on public policy, *The New Economics* (ed. S. E. HARRIS), pp. 12–25. New York: Alfred A. Knopf, 1947.

SCHUMACHER, E. F., Public finance—its relation to full employment, *Economics of Full Employment,* pp. 85–125. Oxford Institute of Statistics, Oxford: Basil Blackwell, 1949.

BUEHLER, A. G., Taxation and the economy, *National Tax Journal,* III (1950), 121–33.

HAYES, H. G., Keynesism and public policy, *Twentieth Century Economic Thought* (ed. G. HOOVER), *pp.* 211–44. New York: Philosophical Library, 1950.

SCAMMEL, W. M., The changing aims of fiscal policy, *Westminster Bank Review,* May, 1950, pp. 1–8.

POOLE, K. E., Background and scope of American fiscal policies, *Fiscal Policies and the American Economy* (ed. K. E. POOLE), pp. 1–54. New York, Prentice-Hall, 1951.

VANDERMEULEN, A. J., Criteria of "adequate" governmental expenditure and their implications, *Journal of Finance,* VI (1951), 19–32.

STRAYER, P. G., An appraisal of current fiscal policy, *American Economic Review,* XLII (1952, Supplement), 138–46.

SHOUP, C. S., Taxation and fiscal policy, *Income Stabilization for a Developing Democracy* (ed. M. MILLIKAN), pp. 261–302. New Haven: Yale University Press, 1953.

B. Integration of Fiscal Policy with Other Counter-Cylical Techniques

ECCLES, M. S., Controlling booms and depressions, *The Lessons of Monetary Experience* (ed. A. D. GAYER), pp. 3–22. New York: Farrar & Rinehart, 1937.

OHLIN, B., Can world prosperity be maintained?, *Svenska Handelsbanken's Index,* Oct. 1937, Supplement.

BRATT, E. C., What can we do about depressions?, *Harvard Business Review,* XVI (1938), 273–80.

KROUT, J. A. (ed.), Essentials for sustained recovery, *Proceedings of the Academy of Political Science,* XVIII (1938), 1–122.

SPRAGUE, O. M. W., The recovery problem in the United States, *American Economic Review,* XXVIII (1938), 1–7.

HALASI, A., The problem of full employment, *International Post-war Problems,* I (1943), 41–85.

SIMONS, H., Economic stability and antitrust policy, *Economic Policy for a Free Society* (ed. H. SIMONS), pp. 107–20. Chicago: University of Chicago Press, 1948. Originally in *University of Chicago Law Review,* XI (1944), 338–48.

CLARK, J. M., Financing high level employment, *Financing American Prosperity* (ed. P. T. HOMAN and F. MACHLUP), pp. 71–126. New York: Twentieth Century Fund, 1945.

GOLDENWEISER, E. A., Post-war problems and policies, *Federal Reserve Bulletin,* XXXI (1945), 112–21.

SLICHTER, S., How to stimulate postwar employment, *Annals of the American Academy of Political and Social Science,* CCXXXVIII (1945), 158–66.

BEVERIDGE, W., Life, liberty and the pursuit of happiness (1950 model), *Review of Economic Statistics,* XXVIII (1946), 53–59.

GRAHAM, F. D., Full employment without public debt, without taxation, without public works, and without inflation, *Planning and Paying for Full Employment* (ed. A. P. LERNER and F. D. GRAHAM), pp. 40–66. Princeton, N.J.: Princeton University Press, 1946.

HALASI, A., Toward a full employment program: a survey, *ibid.*, Ch. 1, pp. 1–33.

BARAN, P. A., National economic planning, *Survey of Contemporary Economics* (ed. B. F. HALEY), Vol. II, pp. 355–403. New York: Irwin Press, 1952.

BREMS, H., Business cycles and economic policy, *Journal of Political Economy,* LXII (1954), 246–54.

II. FISCAL POLICY AND MONETARY POLICY

A. PUBLIC DEBT POLICY AND ECONOMIC STABILITY

EBERSOLE, J. F., The money management powers of the treasury and federal reserve banks, *Harvard Business Review,* XV (1936), 1–9.

HUBBARD, J. B., Absorption of the United States debt, *Review of Economic Statistics,* XVIII (1936), 126–33.

ROBEY, R. W., Fiscal policy and credit control, *Academy of Political Science,* XVII (1936, Proceedings), 10–17.

LELAND, S. E., Debt retirement and the national budget, *American Economic Review,* XXVII (1937, Supplement), 75–85.

JOHNSON, G. G., JR., The significance of the government trust funds for monetary policy, *Public Policy,* Vol. I, pp. 212–46. Cambridge, Mass.: Graduate School of Public Administration, 1940.

SELTZER, L. H., Direct versus fiscal and institutional factors, *American Economic Review,* XXX, No. 5 (1941), 99–107.

WILLIAMS, J. H., The implications of fiscal policy for monetary policy and the banking system, *American Economic Review,* XXXII (1942, Supplement), 234–49. Reprinted in J. H. WILLIAMS, *Postwar Monetary Problems* (Oxford: Basil Blackwell, 1949).

MITNITZKY, M., Some monetary aspects of government borrowing, *American Economic Review,* XXXIII (1943), 21–37.

SPERO, H. and LEAVITT, J. A., Inflation as a post-war problem, *Journal of Political Economy,* LI (1943), 356–60.

HANSEN, A. H., How shall we deal with the public debt?, *Postwar Goals and Economic Reconstruction* (ed. A. J. ZURCHEN and R. PAGE), pp. 133–56. New York: Institute on Postwar Reconstruction, New York University, 1944.

———, Inflationary potentialities of the public debt, *Curbing Inflation through Taxation,* pp. 39–50. Tax Institute Symposium, 1944.

POINDEXTER, J. C., Fallacies of interest-free deficit financing, *Quarterly Journal of Economics,* LVIII (1944), 438–59.
Reply by D. M. WRIGHT, *ibid.,* 637–46.
Rejoinder by POINDEXTER, *ibid.,* LX (1945), 154–65.

SIMONS, H., On debt policy, *Journal of Political Economy,* LII (1944), 356–61. Reprinted in H. SIMONS, *Economic Policy for a Free Society* (Chicago: University of Chicago Press, 1948), pp. 220–30.

ABBOTT, C. C., Management of the federal debt, *Harvard Business Review,* XXIV (1945), 96–108.

ROBINSON, R. I., Monetary aspects of national debt policy, *Public Finance and Full Employment,* pp. 69–83. Postwar Economic Studies, No. 3. New York: Board of Governors of the Federal Reserve System, 1945.

SAMUELSON, P. A., The effect of interest rate increases on the banking system, *American Economic Review,* XXXV (1945), 16–27.

SELTZER, L., Is a rise in interest rates desirable or inevitable?, *American Economic Review,* XXXV (1945), 831–50.

CARR, H. C., The problem of bank-held government debt, *American Economic Review,* XXXVI (1946), 833–42.

POINDEXTER, J. C., A critique of functional finance through quasi-free bank credit, *American Economic Review,* XXXVI (1946), 311–23.

SELTZER, L. H., The changed environment of monetary-banking policy, *American Economic Review,* XXXVI (1946, Supplement), 65–79.

SIMONS, H., Debt policy and banking policy, *Review of Economic Statistics,* XXVIII (1946), 85–89. Reprinted in H. Simons (ed.), *Economic Policy for a Free Society* (Chicago: University of Chicago Press, 1948), pp. 231–39.

WALLICH, H. C., Debt management as an instrument of economic policy, *American Economic Review,* XXXVI (1946), 292–310.

BACH, G. L., Monetary-fiscal policy, debt management and the price level, *American Economic Review,* XXXVII (1947, Supplement), 228–42.

BURKHEAD, J. V., Full employment and interest-free borrowing, *Southern Economic Journal,* XIV (1947), 1–13.

THOMAS, W., The heritage of war finance, *American Economic Review,* XXXVII (1947, Supplement), 205–15.

WICKENS, A. J., The public debt and national income, *American Economic Review,* XXXVII (1947, Supplement), 184–91.

WOODWARD, D. B., Public debt and institutions, *American Economic Review,* XXXVII (1947, Supplement), 157–83.

HARDY, C. O., Fiscal operations as instruments of economic stabilization, *American Economic Review,* XXXVIII (1948, Supplement), 395–403.

MUSGRAVE, R., Credit controls, interest rates, and management of public debt, *Income, Employment and Public Policy,* pp. 221–54. New York: W. W. Norton & Co., 1948.

WIGGINS, A. L. M., Fiscal policy and debt management, *Academy of Political Science,* XXIII (1948, Proceedings), 69–80.

BECKHART, B. H., A debt policy for a prosperous America, *Annals of the American Academy of Political and Social Science,* CCLXVI (1949), 186–95.

CHANDLER, L. V., Federal reserve policy and the federal debt, *American Economic Review,* XXXIX (1949), 405–29.

HARRIS, S. E.; SELTZER, L. H.; ABBOTT, C. C.; MUSGRAVE, R. A.; and HANSEN, A. H., How to manage the national debt, *Review of Economics and Statistics,* XXXI (1949), 15–32.

RATCHFORD, B. U., The monetary effects of public debts, *Public Finance,* IV (1949), 5–18.

WHITTLESEY, C. R., Memorandum on the stability of demand deposits, *American Economic Review,* XXXIX (1949), 1192–203.

MCCRACKEN, P. W., The present status of monetary and fiscal policy, *Journal of Finance,* V (1950), 24–48.

MILLER, D. C., Reconciling monetary management and debt management policies, *Journal of Finance,* V (1950), 368–86.

COHEN, J., On the theory and measurement of treasury interest saving, *Southern Economic Journal,* XVII (1951), 257–69.

FORD, J. S., The monetary controversy in the U.S.A., *Oxford Economic Papers* (NS), III (1951), 221–39.

GUTHMANN, H. G., Financial institutions as a factor in fiscal policy, *Fiscal Policies and the American Economy* (ed. K. E. POOLE), pp. 252–309. New York: Prentice-Hall, 1951.

HARRIS, S. E.; CHANDLER, L. V.; FRIEDMAN, M.; HANSEN, A. H.; LERNER, A. P.; and TOBIN, J., The controversy over monetary policy, *Review of Economics and Statistics,* XXXIII (1951), 179–200.

MCCRACKEN, P. W., The public debt and economic stability, *Yale Review,* XL, (1951), 669–80.

MURPHY, H. C., Debt management, *Fiscal Policies and the American Economy* (ed. K. E. POOLE), pp. 158–200. New York: Prentice-Hall, 1951.

ROBINSON, R. I., Monetary aspects of fiscal policy, *ibid.,* pp. 55–98.

ROSA, R. V., Interest rates and the central bank, *Money, Trade and Economic Growth,* pp. 270–95. New York: Macmillan & Co., 1951.

SPROUL, A., Changing concepts of central banking, *ibid.,* pp. 296–325.

THOMAS, W., Lessons of war finance, *American Economic Review,* XLI (1951), 618–31.

WALLACE, R. F., Some reflections on current war financing, *Journal of Finance,* VI (1951), 300–10.

WHITE, M. I. and MILLER, M., Note on an income effect of changing interest rates, *Public Finance,* VI (1951), 139–44.

ALHADEFF, D. A., Monetary policy and the treasury bill market, *American Economic Re-*view, XLII (1952), 326–46.

MUELLER, F. W., JR., The treasury-federal reserve accord, *Journal of Finance,* VII (1952), 580–99.

ROOSA, R. V., Integrating debt management and open market operations, *American Economic Review,* XLII, Supplement (1952), 214–35.

The new flexible open market policy, *Institute of International Finance,* Bull. 179, School of Business of New York University, 1952.

DAANE, J. D., Interest rate movements since 1945, *Southern Economic Journal,* XX (1953), 23–34.

HART, A. G., Monetary policy for income stabilization, *Income Stabilization for a Developing Democracy* (ed. M. MILLIKAN), pp. 303–46. New Haven: Yale University Press, 1953.

Realistic credit and debt management policies, *Institute of International Finance,* Bull. 184, School of Business of New York University, 1953.

Refunding the public debt, *ibid.,* Bull. 181, 1953.

TOBIN, J., Monetary policy and the management of the public debt: the Patman inquiry, *Review of Economics and Statistics,* XXXV (1953), 118–27.

DONOVAN, C. H., Debt management and federal reserve credit policy since 1945, *Southern Economic Journal,* XX (1954), 231–42.

WALKER, C. E., Federal reserve policy and the structure of interest rates on government securities, *Quarterly Journal of Economics,* LXVIII (1954), 19–42.

B. MONETARY POLICY VERSUS FISCAL POLICY

ANGELL, J. W., Monetary prerequisites for employment stabilization, *Stabilization of Employment* (ed. C. F. ROSS), pp. 206–26. Bloomington, Indiana: Principia Press, 1933.

CURRIE, L., The failure of monetary policy to prevent the depression of 1929–32, *Journal of Political Economy,* XLII (1934), 145–77.

HICKS, J. R., Mr. Keynes and the "classics"; a suggested interpretation, *Econometrica,* V (1937), 147–59. Reprinted in *Readings in the Theory of Income Distribution,* 1946.

HYTTEN, T. F., The limits of monetary policy, *Economic Record,* XV (1939, April Supplement), 76–93.

WARBURTON, C., The monetary theory of deficit spending, *Review of Economic Statistics,* XXVII (1945), 74–84.
Comment by H. W. ARNDT, *ibid.,* XXVIII (1946), 90–92.
Reply by WARBURTON, *ibid.,* 92–94.

TOBIN, J., Liquidity preference and monetary policy, *Review of Economics and Statistics,* XXIX (1947), 124–31.

VICKREY, W., Limitations of Keynesian economics, *Social Research,* XV (1948), 403–16.

ELLIS, H. S., The rediscovery of money, *Money, Trade, and Economic Growth,* pp. 253–69. New York: Macmillan, 1951.

III. RELATIONSHIP BETWEEN FISCAL POLICY AND NATIONAL INCOME AND EMPLOYMENT

A. IMPACT OF PUBLIC EXPENDITURE AND TAXATION ON NATIONAL INCOME AND EMPLOYMENT

BERNSTEIN, E. M., Public expenditure, prices and national income, *Southern Economic Journal*, II (1936), 34–46.

COLM, G., Public revenue and public expenditure in national income, *Studies in Income and Wealth,* Vol. I, Pt. V, pp. 175–228. New York: National Bureau of Economic Research, 1937.
Discussions by J. M. CLARK, S. KUZNETS, M. NEWCOMER, G. COLM, *ibid.*, pp. 228–48.

KALECKI, M., A theory of commodity, income, and capital taxation, *Economic Journal,* XLVII (1937), 444–50.

TINBERGEN, J., On the theory of business cycle control, *Econometrica,* VI (1938), 22–39.

HICKS, J. R., and HICKS, U. K., Public finance in the national income, *Review of Economic Studies,* VI (1939), 147–55.

GILBERT, D. W., Taxation and economic stability, *Quarterly Journal of Economics,* LVI (1942), 406–29.

SAMUELSON, P. A., Fiscal policy and income determination, *Quarterly Journal of Economics,* LVI (1942), 575–605.

SOMERS, H. M., Impact of fiscal policy on national income, *Canadian Journal of Economics and Political Science,* VIII (1942), 364–85.

STERN, E. H., Public expenditure in the national income, *Economica* (NS), X (1943), 166–75.

WARBURTON, C., Relation of government financing to gross income flow, *Survey of Current Business, XXIII* (Apr. 1943), 17–22.

NEISSER, H., Government net contribution and foreign balance as offset to savings, *Review of Economic Statistics,* XXVI (1944), 216–20.

WALLICH, H. C., Income-generating effects of a balanced budget, *Quarterly Journal of Economics,* LIX (1944), 78–91.

HAAVELMO, T., Multiplier effects of a balanced budget, *Econometrica,* XIII (1945), 311–18.
Analysis by G. HABERLER, *ibid.,* XIV (1946), 148–49.
Analysis by R. M. GOODWIN, *ibid.,* 150–51.
Further analysis by E. E. HAGEN, *ibid.,* 152–55.
Reply by HAAVELMO, *ibid.,* 156–58.

SHACKLE, G. L. S., The deflative or inflative tendency of government receipts and disbursements, *Oxford Economic Papers,* No. 8 (1947), 46–64.

SAMUELSON, P. A., The simple mathematics of income determination, *Income, Employment, and Public Policy,* pp. 133–55. New York: W. W. Norton & Co., 1948.

SMITHIES, A., The multiplier, *American Economic Review,* XXXVIII (1948, Supplement), 299–305.

SOMERS, H. M., An economic analysis of the capital gains tax, *National Tax Journal,* I (1948), 220–26.

TEW, B., A note on the multiplier, *Economic Record,* XXIV (1948), 109–11.

ARNDT, H. W., Public finance and the national income, *ibid.,* 243–45.

DUE, J. F., A general sales tax and the level of employment: a reconsideration, *National Tax Journal,* II (1949), 122–30.

GEHRELS, F., Inflationary effects of a balanced budget under full employment, *American Economic Review,* XXXIX (1949), 1276–78.

MCKEAN, R. N., The Keynesian framework and money income, *American Economic Review,* XL (1950), 620–22.

BROWN, E. C., Analysis of consumption taxes in terms of the theory of income determination, *American Economic Review,* XL (1950), 74–89.

SOLOWAY, A., Purchase tax and fiscal policy, *National Tax Journal,* IV (1951), 304–14.

WHITE, W. H., Measuring the inflationary significance of a government budget, *Staff Papers,* International Monetary Fund, I (1951), 355–78.

TURVEY, R., Some notes on multiplier theory, *American Economic Review,* XXLIII (1953), 275–95.

PESTON, M. H., A note on the balanced budget multiplier, *American Economic Review,* XLIV (1954), 129–30.

B. THE EFFICACY OF BUILT-IN FLEXIBILITY

BRETHERTON, R. F., The sensitivity of taxes to fluctuations of trade, *Econometrica,* V (1937), 171–83.

EDELBERG, V., Flexibility of the yield of taxation—some econometric investigations, *Journal of Royal Statistical Society,* CIII (1940), 153–79.

SLITOR, R. E., The flexibility of income-tax yield under averaging, *Journal of Political Economy,* LIV (1946), 266–68.

SUMBERG, T. A., Leakage problems in flexible taxation, *Journal of Political Economy,* LV (1947), 572–75.

MUSGRAVE, R. A., and MILLER, M., Built-in flexibility, *American Economic Review,* XXXVIII (1948), 122–28.

SLITOR, R. E., The measurement of progressivity and built-in flexibility, *Quarterly Journal of Economics,* LXII (1948), 309–13.

VICKREY, W., Some limits to income elasticity of income tax yields, *Review of Economics and Statistics,* XXXI (1949), 140–46.

WALTERS, J. E., Tax sensitivity, *Southern Economic Journal,* XVII (1951), 422–37.

LUSHER, D. W., The stabilizing effectiveness of budget flexibility, *Conference on Policies to Combat Depressions,* pp. 1–18. National Bureau of Economic Research, 1954. Comments by S. COHN, B. CAPLAN, G. COLM, A. G. HART, M. I. WHITE, C. H. KAHN and D. M. HOLLAND, *ibid.,* 19–49.

PECHMAN, J. A., Effect of built-in flexibility and rate and exemption changes on the yield of the federal individual income tax during a recession," *ibid.,* Ch. 4, pp. 1–38. Reprinted in *National Tax Journal,* VII (1954), 1–16.
Comment by P. G. STRAYER, *ibid.,* pp. 39–42.

C. TAXATION AND INVESTMENT

COLM, G., Tax policy and capital formation, *Capital Formation and Its Elements,* pp. 73–85. New York, National Industrial Conference Board, 1930.

BUTTERS, J. K., Discriminatory effects of the annual computation of the corporation income tax, *Quarterly Journal of Economics,* LIV (1939), 51–72.

SHACKLE, G. L. S., A means of promoting investment, *Economic Journal* LI (1941), 249–60.

BERGSON, A., The incidence of an income tax on savings, *Quarterly Journal of Economics,* LVI (1942), 337–40.

DOMAR, E. D., and MUSGRAVE, R. A., Proportional income taxation and risk-taking, *Quarterly Journal of Economics,* LVIII (1944), 389–422.

BALOGH, T., Taxation, risk-bearing and investment, *Bulletin,* Oxford Institute of Statistics, VII (1945), 181–92.

BUTTERS, J. K., Taxation and new product development, *Harvard Business Review,* XXIII (1945), 451–59.

MAGILL, R., Business expansion and the tax structure, *Academy of Political Science,* XXI (1945, Proceedings), 28–34.

MUSGRAVE, R. A., Federal tax reform, Postwar Economic Studies, No. 3, Board of Governors of the Federal Reserve System, 1945.

WALLICH, H. C., Effect of taxation on investment, *Harvard Business Review,* XXIII (1945), 442–50.

BROWN, E. C., Business income taxation and investment incentive, *Income, Employment and Public Policy,* pp. 300–316. New York: W. W. Norton & Co., 1948.

MUSGRAVE, R. A. and PAINTER, M. S., The impact of alternative tax structures on personal consumption and saving, *Quarterly Journal of Economics,* LXII (1948), 475–99.

KEITH, E. G., Tax policy and investment, *Annals of the American Academy of Political and Social Science,* CCLXVI (1949), 77–84.

———, Repercussions of the tax system on business, *Fiscal Policies and the American Economy* (ed. K. E. POOLE), Ch. 7, pp. 310–58. New York: Prentice-Hall, 1951.

SCHRAM, E., Taxation and venture capital, *Annals of the American Academy of Political and Social Science,* CCLXVI (1949), 85–93.

OHLIN, G., and SHELTON, J. P., A Swedish tax provision for stabilizing business investment, *American Economic Review,* XLII (1952), 375–80.

SLITOR, R. E., The corporate income tax: a re-evaluation, *National Tax Journal,* V (1952), 289–309.

BROWN, R. S., JR., Techniques for influencing private investment, *Income Stabilization for a Developing Democracy* (ed. M. MILLIKAN), Ch. 9, pp. 397–496. New Haven: Yale University Press, 1953.

DOMAR, E. D., The case for accelerated depreciation, *Quarterly Journal of Economics,* LXVII (1953), 493–519.

STREETEN, P., The effect of taxation on risk-taking, *Oxford Economic Papers,* N.S., V (1953), 271–87.

THOMPSON, L. E., and BUTTERS, J. K., Effects of taxation on the investment policies and capacities of individuals, *Journal of Finance,* VIII (1953), 137–51.

IV. THE ROLE OF FISCAL POLICY IN SHORT AND LONG-TERM ECONOMIC FLUCTUATIONS

A. FISCAL POLICY AND THE CONTROL OF DEPRESSION

1. Role in Preventing Depressions and Stimulating Recovery

LEISERSON, W. M., The problem of unemployment today, *Political Science Quarterly,* XXXI (1916), 1–24.

MACGREGOR, D. H., Public authorities and unemployment, *Economica,* III (1923), 10–18.

HAWTREY, R. G., Public expenditure and the demand for labour, *Economica,* V (1925), 38–48.

CLARK, J. M., Effects of public spending on capital formation, *Capital Formation and Its Elements,* pp. 54–72. New York: National Industrial Conference Board, 1930.

KAHN, R. F., The relation of home investment to unemployment, *Economic Journal,* XLI (1931), 173–98.

KEYNES, J. M. An economic analysis of unemployment, *Unemployment as a World Problem* (ed. Q. WRIGHT), pp. 1–42. Chicago: University of Chicago Press, 1931.

PRIBRAM, K., World unemployment and its problems, *ibid.,* 43–150.

FAIRCHILD, F. R., Government saves us from depression, *Yale Review,* XXI (1932), 661–83.

HAWTREY, R. G., Public expenditure and trade depression, *Journal of Royal Statistical Society,* XCVI (1933), 438–58.
Discussion, *ibid.,* 459–77.

KEYNES, J. M., Open letter to the president, *New York Times,* December, 1933.

UNIVERSITY OF CHICAGO ROUNDTABLE, Balancing the budget: federal fiscal policy during depression, Public Policy Pamphlet, No. 1, 1933.

BULLOCK, C. J., Inflation by public expenditure, *Review of Economic Statistics,* XVI (1934), 213–16.

GROVES, H. M., Recovery through taxation, *Current History,* XXXIX (1934), 661–67.

HANSEN, A. H., Capital goods and the restoration of purchasing power, *Academy of Political Science,* XVI (1934, Proceedings), 11–19.

CANNING, J. B. and NELSON, E. G., The relation of budget balancing to economic stabilization; a suggested federal treasury policy, *American Economic Review,* XXIV (1934), 26–37.

ROBEY, R. W., Fiscal problems of recovery, *Annals of the American Academy of Political and Social Science,* CLXXII (1934), 22–25.

DOUGLAS, L. W., Sound recovery through a balanced budget, *Atlantic Monthly,* CLVI (1935), 676–80.

MARTIN, P. W., Expansionist technique in the United States, *Index, Svenska Handelsbanken,* X (1935), 56–65.

COLM, G., and LEHMANN, F., Public spending and recovery in the United States, *Social Research,* III (1936), 129–66.

ECCLES, M. S., How are we to put idle men, money and machines to work?, Address before the Harvard Business School Alumni, June 1936. Reprinted in *Economic Balance and a Balanced Budget* (ed. R. L. WEISSMAN), pp. 254–71. New York: Harper & Bros., 1940.

HAIG, R. M., Facing the deficit, *Yale Review,* XXV (1936), 685–701.

KALDOR, N., Wage subsidies as a remedy for unemployment, *Journal of Political Economy,* XLIV (1936), 721–42.

NEISSER, H., Secondary employment: some comments on R. F. Kahn's formula, *Review of Economic Statistics,* XVIII (1936), 24–30.

HENDERSON, H. D., The trade cycle and the budget outlook, *Lloyd's Bank Limited Monthly Review,* N.S., VIII (1937), 290–98.

ROBBINS, L., How to mitigate the next slump, *ibid.,* 234–44.

BRESCIANI TURRONI, C., The multiplier in practice: some results of recent German experience, *Review of Economic Statistics,* XX (1938), 76–88.

HAIG, R. M., Fiscal policies, *American Economic Review,* XXVIII (1938, Supplement), 132–35.

GAYER, A. D., Fiscal policies, *ibid.,* 90–112.

HANSEN, A. H., Pump priming, new and old, *Barron's,* April 11, 1938. Reprinted in *Full Recovery or Stagnation?,* pp. 290–312. New York: W. W. Norton & Co., 1938.

———, The consequences of reducing expenditures, *Academy of Political Science,* XVII (1938, Proceedings), 466–78. Reprinted in *Full Recovery or Stagnation?,* pp. 275–89. New York: W. W. Norton & Co., 1938.

HUMPHREY, D., The relation of surpluses to income and employment during depression, *American Economic Review,* XXVIII (1938), 223–34.

KÄHLER, A., Business stabilization in theory and practice, *Social Research,* V (1938), 1–18.

LUTZ, H., Federal depression financing and its consequences, *Harvard Business Review,* XVI (1938), 129–41.

MORGENTHAU, H., Jr., Federal spending and the federal budget, *Academy of political Science,* XVII (1938, Proceedings), 534–42.

SLICHTER, S., The downturn of 1937, *Review of Economic Statistics,* XX (1938), 97–110.

SMITH, D. T., An analysis of changes in federal finances, July, 1930—June, 1938, *ibid.,* 149–60.

CLARK, J. M., An appraisal of the workability of compensatory devices, *American Economic Review,* XXIX (1939, Supplement), 194–208.

GALBRAITH, J. K., Fiscal policy and the employment-investment controversy, *Harvard Business Review,* XVIII (1939), 24–34.

HARDY, C. O., An appraisal of the factors which stopped short the recovery development in the United States, *American Economic Review,* XXIX (1939, Supplement), 170–82.

LEWIS, B. W., The government as competitor: the effect on private investment, *American Economic Review,* XXIX (1939), 286–98.

POOLE, K. E., Tax remission as a means of influencing cyclical fluctuations, *Quarterly Journal of Economics,* LIII (1939), 261–74.

SALANT, W. S., A note on the effects of a changing deficit, *Quarterly Journal of Economics,* LIII (1939), 298–304.

SMITH, D. T., Is deficit spending practical?, *Harvard Business Review,* XVIII (1939), 35–43.

COLM, G., Full employment through tax policy?, *Social Research,* VII (1940), 447–67.

SAMUELSON, P. A., The theory of pump-priming reexamined, *American Economic Review,* XXX (1940), 492–506.

TIRUMALACHAR, B., Deficit financing, *Indian Journal of Economics,* XX (1940), 567–86.

HALEY, B. F., The federal budget: economic consequences of deficit financing, *American Economic Review,* Vol. XXX, No. 5 (1941), pp. 67–87.

HIGGINS, B., and MUSGRAVE, R. A., Deficit finance—the case examined, *Public Policy,* Vol. II, pp. 136–207. Cambridge, Mass.: Graduate School of Public Administration, 1941.

WEBBINK, P., Unemployment in the United States, 1930–40, *American Economic Review,* Vol. XXX, No. 5 (1941, Proceedings), 248–72.

WILLIAMS, J. H., Deficit spending, *ibid.,* 52–66.

HANSEN, A. H., and GREER, G., Toward full use of our resources, *Fortune,* XXVI (1942), 130–33.

BENOIT-SMULLYAN, E., Net investment, consumption and full employment, *American Economic Review,* XXXIV (1944), 871–74.
Reply by A. R. SWEEZY, *ibid.,* 875–78.
Rejoinder by BENOIT-SMULLYAN, *ibid.,* 878–79.

COPELAND, M. A., How to achieve full and stable employment, *American Economic Review,* XXXIV (1944, Supplement), 134–47.

GARLAND, J. M., Some aspects of full employment, *Economic Record,* XX (1944), 152–69, and XXI (1945), 23–36.

HUBBARD, J. C., Income creation by means of income taxation, *Quarterly Journal of Economics,* LVIII (1944), 265–89.

LUTZ, H., Debt, taxation and functional finance, *Tax Review,* V (1944). Reprinted in *Guideposts to Free Economy,* pp. 114–28. New York: McGraw-Hill, 1945.

HAHN, L. A., Compensatory reactions to compensatory spending, *American Economic Review,* XXXV (1945), 28–39.

HANSEN, A. H., Three methods of expansion through fiscal policy, *American Economic Review,* XXXV (1945), 382–87.

KALECKI, M., Full employment by stimulating private investment?, *Oxford Economic Papers,* No. 7 (1945), pp. 83–92.

MCLEOD, A. N., The financing of employment-maintaining expenditures, *American Economic Review,* XXXV (1945), 640–45.

LUTZ, H. L., Post-war budgets and taxes, *Tax Review,* VI (1945), 5–9.

HOWENSTINE, E. J., Jr., Some principles of compensatory action, *Quarterly Journal of Economics,* LXI (1946), 165–68.

MEYERS, A. L., Some implications of full employment policy, *Journal of Political Economy,* LIV (1946), 258–65.

SMITHIES, A., The American economy in the thirties, *American Economic Review,* XXXVI (1946, Supplement), 11–27.

WILLIAMS, K. B., Employment and wage policies, *Prices, Wages, and Employment,* Post-war Economic Studies, No. 4, Board of Governors of the Federal Reserve System, 1946, pp. 28–66.

BISHOP, R. L., Alternative expansionist fiscal policies: a diagrammatic analysis, *Income, Employment and Public Policy,* pp. 317–40. New York: W. W. Norton & Co., 1948.

HUBBARD, J. C., The proportional personal income tax as an instrument of income creation, *Economic Journal,* LIX (1949), 56–67.

WHITE, M. I., Personal income tax reduction in a hypothetical contraction, *Review of Economics and Statistics,* XXXI (1949), 63–68.

VILLARD, H. H., The Council of Economic Advisers and depression policy, *American Economic Review,* XL (1950), 600–604.

BROCKIE, M. D., Economic fluctuations and governmental policy, *Southern Economic Journal,* XVIII (1951), 46–60.

ROOSE, K. D., The role of net government contribution to income in the recession and revival of 1937–38, *Journal of Finance,* VI (1951), 1–18.

GURLEY, J. G., Fiscal policies for full employment: a diagrammatic analysis, *Journal of Political Economy,* LX (1952), 525–33.

PHILBROOK, C., The re-examining of Keynesian economics and employment experience, *Southern Economic Journal,* XIX (1952), 21–27.

CREAMER, D., Importance of government offsets to cyclical losses in personal income, *Conference on Policies to Combat Depressions,* Ch. 3, pp. 1–26. National Bureau of Economic Research, 1954.

GOODE, R., Corporate income tax in a depression, *ibid.,* Ch. 5, pp. 1–33.
Comments by R. A. MUSGRAVE, *ibid.,* pp. 34–38.

2. Utilization in Specific Expenditure Programs

MALLERY, O. T., A national policy—public works to stabilize employment, *Annals of the American Academy of Political and Social Science,* LXXXI (1919), 56–61.

———, Long-range planning of public works, *Business Cycles and Unemployment,* pp. 231–61. New York: McGraw-Hill, 1923.

———, Set up a reserve of public works to stabilize employment, *American Labor Legislation Review,* XIV (1924), 157–59.

DICKINSON, F. G., Public construction and cyclical unemployment, *Annals of the American Academy of Political and Social Science,* CXXXIX (1928, Supplement), 175–209.

BIELSCHOWSKY, G., Business fluctuations and public works, *Quarterly Journal of Economics,* XLIV (1930), 286–319.

KAHN, R. F., The financing of public works—a note, *Economic Journal,* XLII (1932), 492–95.

RORTY, M. C., How may business revival be forced?, *Harvard Business Review,* X (1932, Supplement), 385–97.

HARRINGTON, J. L., Self liquidating public works as a factor in equalizing employment in times of depression, *Stabilization of Employment* (ed. F. ROOS), pp. 108–16. Bloomington, Indiana: Principia Press, 1933.

KAHN, R. F., Public works and inflation, *Journal of American Statistical Association,* XXVIII (1933, Supplement), 168–73.

LOUCKS, W. N., Municipal public works as a stabilizer of employment, *Stabilization of Employment* (ed. F. ROOS), pp. 98–107. Bloomington, Indiana: Principia Press, 1933.

SLICHTER, S., Making booms bear the burden of relief—some implications of unemployment reserves, *Harvard Business Review,* XI (1933), 327–35.

WOLMAN, L., Employment stabilization through public works, *Stabilization of Employment* (ed. F. ROOS), pp. 85–97. Bloomington, Indiana: Principia Press, 1933.

MITNITZKY, M., The effects of a public works policy on business activity and employment, *International Labor Review,* XXX (1934), 435–56.

SLICHTER, S., The economics of public works, *American Economic Review,* XXIV (1934, Supplement), 174–85.

CLARK, J. M., Cumulative effects of changes in aggregate spending as illustrated by public works, *American Economic Review,* XXV (1935), 14–20.

WALKER, E. R., Public works as a recovery measure, *Economic Record,* XI (1935), 187–201.

COYLE, D. C., Financing of public works—an expansionist point of view, *Annals of the American Academy of Political and Social Science,* CLXXXIII (1936), 207–11.

KAZAKÉVICH, V. D., Public works in two depressions, *Science and Society,* II (1938), 471–88.

Public works as a factor in economic stabilization, *International Labor Review,* XXXVIII (1938), 727–57.

RICHTER-ALTSCHAEFFER, H., A note on the "Economics of public investment," *Journal of Political Economy,* XLVI (1938), 414–16.

ANDERSON, C. J., The development of pump-priming theory, *Journal of Political Economy,* LII (1944), 144–59.

TAIT, D. C., Social aspects of a public investment policy, *International Labor Review,* XLIX (1944), 1–18.

ANDERSON, C. J., The compensatory theory of public works expenditure, *Journal of Political Economy,* LIII (1945), 258–74.

HEIMANN, E., Developmental schemes, planning and full employment, *Planning and Paying for Full Employment* (ed. A. P. LERNER and F. D. GRAHAM), pp. 99–115. Princeton, N.J.: Princeton University Press, 1946.

STETTNER, W. F., Public works and services in the postwar economy, *Housing, Social Security, and Public Works,* pp. 63–95. Postwar Economic Studies, No. 6, Board of Governors of the Federal Reserve System, 1946.

TAIT, D. C., Development works and full employment, *International Labor Review,* LIV (1946), 309–20.

WANTRUP, S. V., Resource conservation and economic stability, *Quarterly Journal of Economics,* LX (1946), 412–52.

HIGGINS, B., Keynesian economics and public investment policy, *The New Economics* (ed. S. E. HARRIS), pp. 468–81. New York: Alfred A. Knopf, 1947.

BENOIT-SMULLYAN, E., Public works in the depression, *American Economic Review,* XXXVIII (1948), 133–39.

HOWENSTINE, E. J., Jr., An inventory of public construction needs, *American Economic Review,* XXXVIII (1948), 353–66.

LUTIN, D. L., Government control of residential construction as an anti-cyclical device, Graduate Economics Seminar of Syracuse University, No. 5, 1951.

GREBLER, L., Draft memorandum on housing policies to combat recession, *Conference on Policies to Combat Depressions,* Ch. 6, pp. 1–20. National Bureau of Economic Research, 1954.
Comment by D. BLANK, *ibid.,* pp. 21–23.

OWEN, W., Self-liquidating public works to combat depression, *Conference on Policies to Combat Depressions,* Ch. 7, pp. 1–54. National Bureau of Economic Research, 1954.
Comments by S. G. TICKTON and W. LINDOW, *ibid.,* pp. 54–60.

B. FISCAL POLICY AND THE CONTROL OF INFLATION

SPRAGUE, O. M. W., Loans and taxes in war finance, *American Economic Review,* VII (1917, Supplement), 198–213.

HOLLANDER, J. H., Do government loans cause inflation?, *Annals of the American Academy of Political and Social Science,* LXXV (1918), 105–12.

MILLER, A. C., War finance and inflation, *ibid.,* 113–34.

NOYES, A. D., The argument against inflation from government loans, *ibid.,* 135–39.

SNYDER, C., War loans, inflation, and the high cost of living, *ibid.,* 139–46.

SCHUMPETER, E. B., English prices and public finance, 1660–1822, *Review of Economic Statistics,* XX (1938), 21–37.

KEYNES, J. M., The income and fiscal potential of Great Britain, *Economic Journal,* XLIX (1939), 626–39.

PIGOU, A. C., War finance and inflation, *Economic Journal,* L (1940), 461–68.

RICHES, E. J., Deferred pay: the Keynes plan, *International Labor Review,* XLI (1940), 557–81.

ANGELL, J. W., Defense financing and inflation: some comments on Professor Hansen's article, *Review of Economic Statistics,* XXIII (1941), 78–82.

GALBRAITH, J. K., The selection and timing of inflation controls, *ibid.,* 82–85.

HANSEN, A. H., Defense financing and inflation potentialities, *ibid.,* 1–7.

HART, A. G., Safeguards against inflation, *ibid.,* 85–87.

SHOUP, C. S., Choice of tax measures to avert inflation, *ibid.,* 88–90.

HICKS, U. K., Lags in tax collection—a neglected problem in war finance, *Review of Economic Studies,* VIII (1941), 89–99.

LUTZ, H., Financing the defense program, *Bulletin of the National Tax Association,* XXVI (1941), 132–41.

———, Loans vs. taxes in defense financing, *Annals of the American Academy of Political and Social Science,* CCXIV (1941), 207–15.

MADGE, C., Public opinion and paying for the war, *Economic Journal,* LI (1941), 36–46.

PIGOU, A. C., Types of war inflation, *Economic Journal,* LI (1941), 439–48.

PLUMPTRE, A. F. W., An approach to war finance, *Canadian Journal of Economics and Political Science,* VII (1941), 1–12.

POLAK, J. J., Rationing of purchasing power to restrict consumption, *Economica,* VIII (1941), 223–38.

ROSA, R. V., A multiplier analysis of armament expenditure, *American Economic Review,* XXXI (1941), 249–65.

SMITH, D. T., Economic consequences of deficit financing: a review, *American Economic Review,* Vol. XXX, No. 5 (1941), pp. 88–98.

WEINTRAUB, S., Compulsory savings in Great Britain, *Harvard Business Review,* XX (1941), 53–64.

BRONFENBRENNER, M., Diminishing returns in federal taxation?, *Journal of Political Economy,* L (1942), 699–717.

BUEHLER, A. G., Compulsory loans in war financing, *Harvard Business Review,* XXI (1942), 115–23.

FELLNER, W., War finance and inflation, *American Economic Review,* XXXII (1942), 235–54.

HART, A. G., Use of flexible taxes to combat inflation, *ibid.,* 87–102.

LELAND, S. E., Income versus sales taxation as anti-inflationary control, *Financing the War,* pp. 105–32. New York: Tax Institute, 1942.

LUTZ, H., A tax on gross income payments to individuals, *ibid.,* 133–35.

SALANT, W. S., The inflationary gap, *American Economic Review,* XXXII (1942), 308–14.

BLAKEY, R., and BLAKEY, G. C., Federal sales tax or spendings tax, *Taxes—The Tax Magazine,* XXI (1943), 148–53, 183–84.

FRIEDMAN, M., The spendings tax as a wartime fiscal measure, *American Economic Review,* XXXIII (1943), 50–62.

HARRIS, S. E., Subsidies and inflation, *American Economic Review,* XXXIII (1943), 557–72.

HARRISS, C. L., Revenue implications of a progressive-rate tax on expenditures, *Review of Economic Statistics,* XXV (1943), 175–91.

POOLE, K. E., Problems of administration and equity under a spendings tax, *ibid.,* 63–73.

SHOUP, C. S., Problems in war finance, *ibid.,* 74–97.

SWANSON, E. W., Some aspects of value and capital in a war economy, *ibid.,* 852–67.

WEILER, E. T., Wartime savings and postwar inflation, *Survey of Current Business,* XXIII (July 1943), 13–18.

ECCLES, M. S., Possibilities of postwar inflation and suggested tax action, *Curbing Inflation through Taxation,* pp. 225–38. Tax Institute, 1944.

FARIOLETTI, M., A federal sales tax as a fiscal device for curbing inflation in wartime, *Curbing Inflation through Taxation,* Pt. 3, pp. 63–82. Tax Institute, 1944.

NELSON, G., The retail sales tax, *ibid.,* pp. 83–91.

BUEHLER, A. G., The spendings tax and excises, *ibid.,* pp. 91–111.

BLOUGH, R., The individual income tax as a method of inflation control, *ibid.,* pp. 112–24.

SHOUP, C. S., Forced loans, *ibid.,* pp. 126–36.

HARRIS, S. E., Social security taxes and inflation, *ibid.,* 137–50.

WOYTINSKY, W. S., Prospects of permanent full employment, *International Post-war Problems,* I (1944), 498–515.

HANSEN, A. H., Inflation, *Yale Review,* XXXV (1946), 692–711.

FELLNER, W., Postscript on war inflation; a lesson from World War II, *American Economic Review,* XXXVII (1947), 76–91.

GALBRAITH, J. K., The disequilibrium system, *ibid.,* 287–302.

VINER, J., Can we check inflation?, *Yale Review,* XXXVII (1947), 193–211.

HARRIS, S. E.; SLICHTER, S.; MILLS, F. C.; DAVIS, J. S.; HABERLER, G.; BOULDING, K. E.; MACHLUP, F.; KALECKI, M.; LERNER, A. P.; and HEFLEBOWER, R. B., Ten economists on the inflation, *Review of Economics and Statistics,* XXX (1948), 1–29.

SHERE, L., Taxation and inflation control, *American Economic Review,* XXXVIII (1948), 843–56.

FETTER, F. W., The Economic Reports of the President and the problem of inflation, *Quarterly Journal of Economics,* LXIII (1949), 273–81.

LERNER, A. P., The inflationary process: 1. some theoretical aspects, *Review of Economics and Statistics,* XXXI (1949) 193–200; HARRIS, S. E., The inflationary process: 2. In theory and recent history, *ibid.,* 200–210.
Comments by F. MACHLUP, H. M. SOMERS, and H. H. VILLARD, *ibid.,* 210–16.

MARTIN, J. W., American taxation and World War II, *Public Finance,* IV (1949), 112–20.

TOBIN, J., Taxes, saving and inflation, *American Economic Review,* XXXIX (1949), 1223–32.

BERNSTEIN, E. M., Latent inflation: problems and policies, *Staff Papers,* Vol. I, pp. 1–16. International Monetary Fund, 1950.

BUEHLER, A. G., The spendings tax, *Public Finance,* V (1950), 8–22.

HAGEN, E. E., Direct vs. fiscal-monetary controls: a critique, *Journal of Finance,* V (1950), 49–62.

HORSEFIELD, J. K., The measurement of inflation, *Staff Papers,* Vol. I, pp. 17–48. International Monetary Fund, 1950.

An economists' statement on anti-inflationary measures, *American Economic Review,* XLI (1951), 82–84.

RITTER, L. S., Alternative anti-inflationary fiscal policies, *Review of Economic Studies,* XVIII (1950–51), 129–39.

DUE, J. F., The sales tax as an anti-inflationary measure, *Public Finance,* VI (1951), 385–94.

HAGEN, E. E., The control of inflation, *Current Economic Comment,* XIII (1951), 3–15.

HELLER, W. W., Compulsory lending: the World War II experience, *National Tax Journal,* IV (1951), 116–28.

GOODE, R., Anti-inflationary implications of alternative forms of taxation, *American Economic Review,* XLII (1952, Supplement), 147–60.

THOMAS, W., Recent experience with monetary-fiscal measures to combat inflation, *ibid.,* 273–88.

PEACOCK, A. T., Social security and inflation: a study of the economic effects of an adjustable pensions scheme, *Review of Economic Studies,* XX (1953), 169–73.

C. Fiscal Policy during Mobilization and Demobilization

Rosenson, A., Proposals for cushioning the transition to a peacetime economy, *American Economic Review,* XXXII (1942), 117–22.

Colm, G., Fiscal policy in economic reconstruction, *Postwar Reconstruction* (ed. S. E. Harris), pp. 253–74. New York: McGraw-Hill, 1945.

Hart, A. G., Postwar effects to be expected from wartime liquid accumulations, *American Economic Review,* XXXV (1945, Supplement), 341–51.

Machlup, F., Summary and analysis, *Financing American Prosperity* (ed. P. T. Homan), pp. 394–496. New York: Twentieth Century Fund, 1945.

Slichter, S., Public policies and postwar employment, *ibid.,* 266–336.

Sweezy, A. R., Fiscal and monetary policy, *American Economic Review,* XXXVI (1946, Proceedings), 291–303.

Wald, H. P., Fiscal policy, military preparedness, and postwar inflation, *National Tax Journal,* II (1949), 51–62.

Smithies, A., Fiscal aspects of preparedness for war, *American Economic Review,* XXXIX (1949, Supplement), 356–65.

Blough, R., Fiscal policy in a defense economy, *National Tax Journal,* III (1950), 273–82.

Haley, B. F., Are price control and rationing necessary?, *American Economic Review,* XL (1950, Supplement), 199–208.

Musgrave, R., Fiscal and monetary problems in a high-level defense economy: a study in taxable capacity, *ibid.,* 209–21.

Butters, J. K., et al., Tax program for a sustained mobilization, *Harvard Business Review,* XXIX (1951), 119–24.

Chandler, L. V., The nature of war finance problems, *Economic Mobilization and Stabilization* (ed. L. V. Chandler and D. H. Wallace), Pt. 3, pp. 181–90. New York: Henry Holt, 1951.

Shoup, C. S., Problems in war finance, *ibid.,* 190–213.

Graham, F. D., A plea for adequate war taxation, *ibid.,* 213–23.

Blough, R., The individual income tax as a method of inflation control, *ibid.,* 223–34.

Graham, F. D., and Farioletti, M., Federal sales taxes and wartime inflation control, *ibid.,* 234–51.

Shoup, C. S., Forced loans in war finance, *ibid.,* 262–72.

Galbraith, J. K. The strategy of direct control in economic mobilization, *Review of Economics and Statistics,* XXXIII (1951), 12–17.

Hart, A. G., General strategy of economic policy for less-than-total war, *American Economic Review,* XLI (1951), 51–59.

Shaw, E. S., and Tarshis, L., A program for economic mobilization, *ibid.,* 30–50.

Director, A. (ed.), The role of fiscal policy, *Defense, Controls and Inflation,* pp. 68–121. Chicago: University of Chicago Press, 1952.

Fagan, E. D., A fiscal program for high-level mobilization, *National Tax Journal,* V (1952), 120–29.

Hildebrand, G. H., Defense expenditures and the problem of deflation, *American Economic Review,* XLIV (1954, Supplement), 410–22.

D. Fiscal Policy Program for Economic Stability

1. Proposed and Analyzed by Individuals

Newman, W. H., The building industry and building cycles, *Studies in Business Administration,* Vol. V, No. 4 (1935). School of Business, University of Chicago.

Kaldor, N., Stability and full employment, *Economic Journal,* XLVIII (1938), 642–57.

Lindblom, C. E., Long-run considerations in employment stabilization and unemployment compensation, *Quarterly Journal of Economics,* LVI (1941), 145–51.

PRIBRAM, K., Employment stabilization through pay roll taxation, *Quarterly Journal of Economics,* LVII (1942), 142–52.

LINDBLOM, C. E., Pay roll taxation and employment stabilization, *ibid.,* 657–58.

GREBLER, L., Housing policy and the business cycle, *Review of Economic Statistics,* XXIV (1942), 66–74.

HANSEN, A. H., and PERLOFF, H. S., Regional resource development, Planning Pamphlets, No. 16, National Planning Association, 1942.

SIMONS, H., Hansen on fiscal policy, *Journal of Political Economy,* L (1942), 161–96. Reprinted in *Economic Policy for a Free Society,* pp. 184–219. Chicago: University of Chicago Press, 1948.

BISSELL, R., Postwar private spending and public spending, *Postwar Economic Problems* (ed. S. E. HARRIS), pp. 83–110. New York: McGraw-Hill, 1943.

HANSEN, A. H., The postwar economy, *ibid.,* pp. 9–26.

RUML, B., and SONNE, H. C., Fiscal and monetary policy, Planning Pamphlets, No. 35, National Planning Association, 1944.

YNTEMA, T. O., Full employment in a private enterprise system, *American Economic Review,* XXXIV (1944, Supplement), 107–17.

COLEAN, M. L., Stabilizing the construction industry, Planning Pamphlets, No. 41, National Planning Association, 1945.

HANSEN, A. H., Stability and expansion, *Financing American Prosperity* (ed. P. T. HOMAN), pp. 199–265. New York: Twentieth Century Fund, 1945.

HART, A. G., Model building and fiscal policy, *American Economic Review,* XXXV (1945), 530–58.

KALECKI, M., The maintenance of full employment after the transition period. A comparison of the problem in the United States and the United Kingdom, *International Labor Review,* LII (1945), 449–64.
Notes by W. S. WOYTINSKY, *American Economic Review,* XXXVI (1946), 641–45.
Rejoinder by A. G. HART, *ibid.,* 632–36.

MUSGRAVE, R., Alternative budget policies for full employment, *American Economic Review,* XXX (1945), 387–400.

———, Fiscal policy, stability and full employment, Postwar Economic Studies, No. 3, pp. 1–21. Board of Governors of the Federal Reserve System, 1945.

SCHMIDT, E. P., Mitigating depressions, *Post-war Readjustments,* Bull. No. 15, Chamber of Commerce of the United States of America, 1945.

UPGREN, A. R., Objectives and guides to policy, *American Economic Review,* XXXV (1945, Supplement), 67–84.

WILLIAMS, J. H., Free enterprise and full employment, *Financing American Prosperity* (ed. P. T. HOMAN), pp. 337–93. New York: Twentieth Century Fund, 1945.

HANSEN, A. H., Federal fiscal policy for full employment, New York University, Institute on Postwar Reconstruction, 1946.

KALECKI, M., Three ways to full employment, *Economics of Full Employment,* pp. 39–58. Oxford Institute of Statistics. Oxford: Basil Blackwell, 1946.

LERNER, A. P., An integrated full employment policy, *Planning and Paying for Full Employment,* pp. 163–220. Princeton, N.J.: Princeton University Press, 1946.

MELVILLE, L. G., Some post-war problems, *Economic Record,* XXII (1946), 4–22.

MINTS, L. W.; HANSEN, A. H.; ELLIS, H. S.; LERNER, A. P.; and KALECKI, M., A symposium on fiscal and monetary policy, *Review of Economic Statistics,* XXVIII (1946), 60–84.

MOSAK, J. L., National budgets and full employment policy, *American Economic Review,* XXXVI (1946), 20–43.
Rejoinder by KALECKI, *ibid.,* XXXVII (1947), 391–97.
Reply by MOSAK, *ibid.,* 637–41.

NEISSER, H., Realism and speculation in employment programs, *Planning and Paying for Full Employment* (ed. A. P. LERNER and F. D. GRAHAM), pp. 84–98. Princeton, N.J.: Princeton University Press, 1946.

STONE, R., and JACKSON, E. F., Economic models with special reference to Mr. Kaldor's system, *Economic Journal,* LVI (1946), 554–67.

BRONFENBRENNER, M., Sales taxation and the Mints plan, *Review of Economic Statistics,* XXIX (1947), 39–42.

COLM, G., The nation's economic budget—a tool of full employment policy, *Studies in Income and Wealth,* X (1947), 85–93. New York: National Bureau of Economic Research.

COPLAND, D. B., Public policy—the doctrine of full employment, *The New Economics* (ed. S. E. HARRIS), pp. 208–18. New York: A. A. Knopf, 1947.

DOBRETSBERGER, J., A critical review of the discussions on full employment, *Kyklos,* I (1947), 19–25.

FISHER, A. G. B., Less stabilization: more stability, *ibid.,* 1–18.

BENOIT-SMULLYAN, E., On the meaning of full employment, *Review of Economics and Statistics,* XXX (1948), 127–34.

COLM, G., On the road to economic stabilization, *Social Research,* XV (1948), 265–76.

———, The government's budget and the nation's economic budget, *Public Finance,* III (1948), 5–14.

DOWNING, R. I., Housing and public policy, *Economic Record,* XXIV (1948), 72–86.

Federal taxation and economic stability (Note), *Yale Law Journal,* LVII (1948), 1227–55.

FRIEDMAN, M., A monetary and fiscal framework for economic stability, *American Economic Review,* XXXVIII (1948), 245–64.

NEFF, P., Professor Friedman's proposal: a comment, *American Economic Review,* XXXIX (1949), 946–49.
Rejoinder by M. FRIEDMAN, *ibid.,* 949–55.
Final comment by NEFF, *ibid.,* 955–56.

MUSGRAVE, R., Fiscal policy in prosperity and depression, *American Economic Review,* XXXVIII (1948, Supplement), 383–94.

PERLOFF, H. S., Dynamic elements in a full employment program, *Income, Employment and Public Policy,* pp. 199–217. New York: W. W. Norton & Co., 1948.

WARBURTON, C., Hansen and Fellner on full employment policies, *American Economic Review,* XXXVIII (1948), 128–34.

GREBLER, L., Stabilizing residential construction—a review of the postwar test, *American Economic Review,* XXXIX (1949), 898–910.

BACH, G. L., Economic requisites for achieving economic stability, *American Economic Review,* XL (1950, Supplement), 155–64.

BROWNLEE, O. H., The theory of employment and stabilization policy, *Journal of Political Economy,* LVIII (1950), 412–35.

DESPRES, E.; HART, A. G.; FRIEDMAN, M.; SAMUELSON, P. A.; and WALLACE, D. N., The problem of economic instability, *American Economic Review,* XL (1950), 505–38.

STRAYER, P. G., Stabilization of personal incomes—a limited fiscal policy, *American Economic Review,* XL (1950), 827–44.

OLIVER, H. M., Fiscal policy, employment and the price level, *Fiscal Policies and the American Economy* (ed. K. E. POOLE), Ch. 3, pp. 99–157. New York: Prentice-Hall, 1951.

OSER, J., Agricultural policy and the business cycle, *Social Research,* XVIII (1951), 32–54.

COLM, G., The American economy in 1960. Planning Pamphlets, No. 81, National Planning Association, 1952.

SIMMONS, E. C., The uses and limitations of monetary-fiscal policy in economic stabilization, *Southern Economic Journal,* XVIII (1952), 510–15.

WILSON, T., Professor Robertson on effective demand and the trade cycle, *Economic Journal,* LXIII (1953), 553–78.

GORDON, R. A., Types of depressions and programs to combat them, *Conference on Policies to Combat Depressions,* Ch. 1, pp. 1–39. National Bureau of Economic Research, 1954.

HART, A. G., Government measures designed to promote regularization of business investment, *Regularization of Business Investment,* pp. 451–457. National Bureau for Economic Research, 1954.

2. Proposed and Analyzed by Organized Groups

BENOIT-SMULLYAN, E., Seventeen postwar plans—the Pabst post-war employment awards, *American Economic Review,* XXXV (1945), 120–127.

NATIONAL PLANNING ASSOCIATION, National budgets for full employment, Planning Pamphlets, No. 43 and 44. Washington, D.C., 1945.

COMMITTEE FOR ECONOMIC DEVELOPMENT, *Taxes and the Budget: a Program for Prosperity in a Free Economy.* New York, 1947.

HAGEN, E. E., Some implications of the C.E.D.'s stabilizing budget policy, pp. 481–91. National Tax Association, Proceedings, 1948.

STEIN, H., The C.E.D. on budget policy, *ibid.,* 474–80.

COMMITTEE FOR ECONOMIC DEVELOPMENT, *Monetary and Fiscal Policy for Greater Economic Stability.* New York, 1949.

CLARK, J. M.; KALDOR, N.; SMITHIES, A., ET AL., *National and International Measures for Full Employment.* New York: United Nations, 1949.

NATIONAL PLANNING ASSOCIATION, Federal expenditure and revenue policy for economic stability, *American Economic Review,* XXXIX (1949), 1663–67.

University economists' statements on fiscal policy, Princeton, Sept. 16–18, 1949. Reproduced in *A Collection of Statements submitted to the Subcommittee on Monetary, Credit and Fiscal Policies of the Joint Committee by Government Officials, Bankers, Economists and Others,* 81st Congress, 1st Session, Nov. 7, 1949, p. 437.

COMMITTEE FOR ECONOMIC DEVELOPMENT, *Tax and Expenditure Policy for 1950.* New York, 1950.

———, *The Stabilizing Budget Policy: What It Is and How It Works: A Review of a Proposal for Stabilizing Federal Taxing and Spending.* New York, 1950.

WALLICH, H. C., United Nations report on full employment, *American Economic Review,* XL (1950), 876–83.

VINER, J., Full employment at whatever cost, *Quarterly Journal of Economics,* LXIV (1950), 385–407.

COMMITTEE FOR ECONOMIC DEVELOPMENT, *Defense against Recession: Policy for Greater Economic Stability.* New York, 1954.

———, *Taxes, National Security and Economic Growth.* New York, 1954.

3. Analysis of the British and United States Full Employment Acts.

GRAGG, C. I., and TEELE, S. F., The proposed full employment act, *Harvard Business Review,* XXIII (1945), 323–37.

HANSEN, A. H., A new goal of national policy: full employment, *Review of Economic Statistics,* XXVII (1945), 102–3.

HARRIS, S. E.; HABERLER, G.; SLICHTER, S.; and MCNAIR, M. P., Comments on the Murray Bill, *ibid.,* 104–16.

KALDOR, N., The quantitative aspects of the full employment problem in Britain, *Full Employment in a Free Society* (ed. W. H. BEVERIDGE), Appendix C. New York: W. W. Norton & Co., 1945.

MCNAIR, M. P., The full employment problem, *Harvard Business Review,* XXIV (1945), 1–22.

ROBINSON, E. A. G., Sir William Beveridge on full employment, *Economic Journal,* LV (1945), 70–76.

SMITHIES, A., Full employment in a free society, *American Economic Review,* XXXV (1945), 355–67.

SCHMIDT, E. P., Can government guarantee full employment?, Postwar Readjustments, Bull. No. 13. Chamber of Commerce of the United States of America, 1945.

SIMONS, H., The Beveridge program: an unsympathetic interpretation, *Journal of Political Economy,* LIII (1945), 212–33.

ANDERSON, R. V., Full employment in a free society, *Canadian Journal of Economics and Political Science,* XII (1946), 192–203.

JEWKES, J., Second thoughts on the British White Paper on employment policy, The Manchester School of Economics and Social Studies, Vol. XIV, No. 2 (1946), pp. 65–84.

HANSEN, A. H., The first reports under the Employment Act of 1946, *Review of Economic Statistics,* XXIX (1947), 69–74.

VINER, J., The Employment Act of 1946 in operation, *ibid.,* 74–79.

NATIONAL INDUSTRIAL CONFERENCE BOARD, An appraisal of official economic reports, Studies in Business Economics, No. 16, 1948.

HARRIS, S. E., The January, 1949, Economic Report of the President—introduction, *Review of Economics and Statistics,* XXXI (1949), 165–66.
Appraisals by T. WILSON, F. W. PAISH, H. S. ELLIS, G. TERBORGH, and E. E. HAGEN, *ibid.,* 166–81.

WILLIAMS, J. H., The Employment Act of 1946, *Postwar Monetary Plans and Other Essays,* pp. 205–15. Oxford: Basil Blackwell, 1949.

E. FISCAL POLICY AND GROWTH

1. *Fiscal Policy and Long-term Economic Trends*

KEYNES, J. M., Some consequences of declining population growth, *Eugenic Review,* XXIX (April 1937), 13–17.

FLEMING, J. M., Secular unemployment, *Quarterly Journal of Economics,* LIV (1939), 103–30.

HANSEN, A. H., Economic progress and declining population growth, *American Economic Review,* XXIX (1939), 1–15.

HARROD, R. F., An essay in dynamic theory, *Economic Journal,* XLIX (1939), 14–33.

FRANZSEN, D. G., The secular stagnation thesis and the problem of economic growth, *South African Journal of Economics,* X (1942), 282–94.

KUZNETS, S., Review of Hansen's *Fiscal Policy and Business Cycles, Review of Economic Statistics,* XXIV (1942), 31–36.

SLICHTER, S., The conditions of expansion, *American Economic Review,* XXXII (1942), 1–21.

HARROD, R. F., Full employment and security of livelihood, *Economic Journal,* LIII (1943), 321–42.

WRIGHT, D. M., The great guessing game: Terborgh vs. Hansen, *Review of Economic Statistics,* XXVIII (1946), 18–22.

———, Income redistribution reconsidered, *Income, Employment and Public Policy,* pp. 159–76. New York: W. W. Norton & Co., 1948.

———, Inflation and equality, *American Economic Review,* XXXVIII (1948), 892–97.
Comment by G. ACKLEY, *ibid.,* XXIX (1949), 960–64.
Rejoinder by WRIGHT, *ibid.,* 965–66.

SLICHTER, S., Long-term economic trends, *American Economic Review,* XL (1950, Supplement), 457–69.

SPENGLER, J. J., Prospective population and income growth and fiscal policy, *National Tax Journal,* III (1950), 36–63.

ROLPH, E. R., Equity versus efficiency in federal tax policy, *American Economic Review,* XL (1950, Supplement), 391–404.

DUE, J. F., Government expenditures and their significance for the economy, *Fiscal Policies and the American Economy* (ed. K. E. POOLE), Ch. 5, pp. 201–51. New York: Prentice-Hall, 1951.

ADLER, J. H., Fiscal and monetary implementation of development programs, *American Economic Review,* XLII (1952, Supplement), 584–600.

BERNSTEIN, E. M., and PATEL, I. G., Inflation in relation to economic development, *Staff Papers,* International Monetary Fund, II (1952), 363–98.

RAO, V. K. R. V., Full employment and economic development, *Indian Economic Review,* I (August 1952), 43–57.

FITCH, L. C., Trends in federal, state, and local government expenditures since 1890, *American Economic Review,* XLIII (1953, Supplement), 216–33.

GOODE, R., Taxation and economic development, *National Tax Association* XLVI (1953, Proceedings), 225–36.

GURLEY, J. G., Fiscal policy in a growing economy, *Journal of Political Economy,* LXI (1953), 523–35.

MUSGRAVE, R., and CULBERTSON, J. M., The growth of public expenditures in the United States, 1890–1948, *National Tax Journal,* VI (1953), 97–115.

SAMUELSON, P. A., Full employment versus progress and other economic goals, *Income Stabilization for a Developing Democracy* (ed. M. MILLIKAN), Ch. 12, pp. 547–80. New Haven: Yale University Press, 1953.

WEINBERG, R. S., "Full employment" 1955–60—A feasibility test, *American Economic Review,* XLIII (1953), 860–83.

RAO, V. K. R. V., Deficit financing, capital formation, and price behavior in an underdeveloped economy, *Indian Economic Review,* I (Feb. 1953), 55–91.

WANG, N. T., A note on Dr. Rao's dynamic model, *Indian Economic Review,* I (Aug. 1953), 94–104.

FELLNER, W., Full use or underutilization: appraisal of long-run factors other than defense, *American Economic Review,* XLIV (1954, Supplement), 423–33.

2. Effect of Redistribution of Income on Stability and Growth

PETTENGILL, R. B., Division of the tax burden among income groups in the United States in 1936, *American Economic Review,* XXX (1940), 60–71.

STAUFFACHER, C., The effects of governmental expenditures and tax withdrawals upon income distribution, 1930–1939, *Public Policy,* Vol. II (1941), pp. 232–61. Cambridge, Mass.: Graduate School of Public Administration.

TARASOV, H., Who does pay the taxes?, *Social Research,* IX (1942, Supplement).

BAER, W., Equality and prosperity, *Social Research,* X (1943), 118–22.

METZLER, L. A., Effects of income distribution, *Review of Economic Statistics,* XXV (1943), 49–57.

WILLIAMS, R. S., Fiscal policy and the propensity to consume, *Economic Journal,* LV (1945), 390–97.

NORRIS, H., Fiscal policy and the propensity to consume, *Economic Journal,* LVI (1946), 316–18.

FISHER, A. G. B., Full employment and income inequality, *Economic Journal,* LVI (1946), 18–26.

KLEIN, L. R., Theories of effective demand and employment, *Journal of Political Economy,* LV (1947), 108–31.

LUBELL, H., The effects of redistribution of income on consumers' expenditures, *American Economic Review,* XXXVII (1947), 157–70, and correction, *ibid.,* 930.

PIERSON, J. H. G., The underwriting approach to full employment: an explanation, *Review of Economics and Statistics,* XXXI (1949), 182–92.

ADLER, J. H., The fiscal system, the distribution of income, and public welfare, *Fiscal Policies and the American Economy* (ed. K. E. POOLE), Ch. 8, pp. 359–421. New York: Prentice-Hall, 1951.

MUSGRAVE, R.; CARROLL, J. J.; COOK, L. D.; and FRANE, L., Distribution of tax payments by income groups: a case study for 1948, *National Tax Journal,* IV (1951), 1–53.
TUCKER, R. S., Distribution of tax burden in 1948, *ibid.,* 269–85.
Comments by G. COLM and H. P. WALD, *National Tax Journal,* V (1952), 1–14.
Rejoinder to Tucker by MUSGRAVE and FRANE, *ibid.,* 15–35.
Rebuttal by TUCKER, *ibid.,* 36–38.
Concluding note by MUSGRAVE and FRANE, *ibid.,* 39.

JOHNSON, H. G., The effects of income-redistribution on aggregate consumption with interdependence of consumers' preferences, *Economica,* N.S. XIX (1952), 131–47.

JAMES, S. F., and BECKERMAN, W., Interdependence of consumer preferences in the theory of income redistribution, *Economic Journal,* LXIII (1953), 70–83.
Comment by H. G. JOHNSON, *ibid.,* 83.

TUCKER, R. S., The distribution of government burdens and benefits, *American Economic Review,* XLIII (1953, Supplement), 518–34.
Comments by H. M. GROVES, E. R. ROLPH, and R. B. GOODE, *ibid.,* 535–43.

CONRAD, A. H., Redistribution through government budgets in the United States, 1950, *Income Redistribution and Social Policy* (ed. A. T. PEACOCK), pp. 178–267. London: Jonathan Cape, 1954.

JOHNSON, H. G., The macro-economics of income redistribution, *ibid.,* 19–40.

V. BURDEN OF THE PUBLIC DEBT

STUDENSKI, P., The limits to possible debt burdens—federal, state and local, *American Economic Review,* XXVII (1937, Supplement), 58–74.

WRIGHT, D. M., The economic limit and economic burden of an internally held national debt, *Quarterly Journal of Economics,* LV (1940), 116–29.

COLEMAN, R., Government bonds and the balanced budget, *Harvard Business Review,* XX (1941), 75–80.

RUGGLES, C. O., Social and economic implications of the national debt, *Annals of the American Academy of Political and Social Science,* CCXIV (1941), 199–206.

KUZNETS, S., National income and taxable capacity, *American Economic Review,* XXXII (1942, Supplement), 37–75.

RATCHFORD, B. U., The burden of a domestic debt, *American Economic Review,* XXXII (1942), 451–67.
Comment by D. M. WRIGHT, *ibid.,* XXXIII (1943), 115–19.

BROWN, H. G., The danger in the mounting national debt, *American Journal of Economics and Sociology,* III (1943), 1–14.

HARRIS, S. E., Postwar public debt, *Postwar Economic Problems* (ed. S. E. Harris), pp. 169–85. New York: McGraw-Hill, 1943.

KALECKI, M., The burden of the national debt, Bulletin V, pp. 76–80. Oxford Institute of Statistics. Oxford, 1943.

LERNER, A. P., Functional finance and the public debt, *Social Research,* V (1943), 38–51.

DOMAR, E. D., The burden of the debt and the national income, *American Economic Review,* XXXIV (1944), 798–827.
Comment by B. U. RATCHFORD, *ibid.,* XXXV (1945), 411–14.
Rejoinder by DOMAR, *ibid.,* 414–18.

SHIRRAS, G., Methods of estimating the burden of taxation, *Journal of the Royal Statistical Society,* CVI (1943), 214–36.

BALOGH, T., The burden of the national debt, *Economic Journal,* LV (1945), 461–63.

CHAMBERLAIN, N. W., Professor Hansen's fiscal policy and the debt, *American Economic Review,* XXXV (1945), 400–407.

CLARK, C., Public finance and changes in the value of money, *Economic Journal,* LV (1945), 371–89.

DOMAR, E. D., Public debt and the national income, *Public Finance and Full Employment,* pp. 53–68. Postwar Economic Studies, No. 3, Board of Governors of the Federal Reserve System, 1945.

WALLICH, H. C., Public debt and income flow, *ibid.*, 84–100.

LANSTON, A. G., The crucial problem of the federal debt, *Harvard Business Review*, XXIV (1946), 133–50.

LERNER, A. P., The burden of the national debt, *Income, Employment and Public Policy*, pp. 255–75. New York: W. W. Norton & Co., 1948.

RATCHFORD, B. U., The economics of public debts, *Public Finance*, III (1948), 299–310.

STETTNER, W. F., Carl Dietzel, public expenditures and the public debt, *Income, Employment and Public Policy*, pp. 276–99. New York: W. W. Norton & Co., 1948.

CLARK, C., The danger point in taxes, *Harper's Magazine*, 1950, 67–69.

PREST, A. R., Government revenue and the national income, *Public Finance*, VI (1951), 238–52.

GOODE, R., An economic limit on taxes: some recent discussions, *National Tax Journal*, V (1952), 227–33.

HELLER, W. W., Limitations of the federal individual income tax, *Journal of Finance*, VII (1952), 185–202.

———, The limits of taxation, *Proceedings of the National Tax Association*, XLV (1952), 243–45.

PECHMAN, J. A., and Mayer, T., Mr. Colin Clark on the limits of taxation, *Review of Economics and Statistics*, XXXIV (1952), 232–42.

RATCHFORD, B. U., Practical limitations to the net income tax—general, *Journal of Finance*, VII (1952), 203–13.

SMITH, D. T., Note on inflationary consequences of high taxation, *Review of Economics and Statistics*, XXXIV (1952), 243–47.

HIGGINS, B., A note on taxation and inflation, *Canadian Journal of Economics and Political Science*, XIX (1953), 392–402.

BROWNLEE, O. H., Taxation and the price level in the short run, *Journal of Political Economy*, LXII (1954), 26–33.

VI. FISCAL POLICY AND SECULAR INFLATION

BOOKER, H. S., Have we a full employment policy?, *Economic Journal*, LVII (1947), 37–47.

DUNLOP, J. T., Wage-price relations at high level employment, *American Economic Review*, XXXVII (1947, Supplement), 243–53.

FELLNER, W., Hansen on full employment policies, *Journal of Political Economy*, LV (1947), 254–56.

HAHN, L. A., Wage flexibility upwards, *Social Research*, XIV (1947), 148–67.

HANSEN, A. H., Cost functions and full employment, *American Economic Review*, XXXVII (1947), 552–65.

SINGER, H. W., Wage policy in full employment, *Economic Journal*, LVII (1947), 438–55.
Comment by J. H. RICHARDSON, *ibid.*, LVIII (1948), 421–24. Rejoinder by SINGER, *ibid.*, 424–25.

BRONFENBRENNER, M., Postwar political economy: the President's Reports, *Journal of Political Economy*, LVI (1948), 373–91.

PHELPS, O. W., Collective bargaining, Keynesian model, *American Economic Review*, XXXVIII (1948), 581–97.

REDER, M. W., The theoretical problems of a national wage-price policy, *Canadian Journal of Economics and Political Science*, XIV (1948), 46–61.
Comment by B. HIGGINS, *ibid.*, XV (1949), 203–6.
Further comment by REDER, *ibid.*, 206–10.

HIGGINS, B., The optimum wage rate, *Review of Economics and Statistics*, XXXI (1949), 130–39.

WORSWICK, G. D. N., The stability and flexibility of full employment, *Economics of Full Employment,* pp. 59–84. Oxford Institute of Statistics. Oxford: Basil Blackwell, 1949.

BOULDING, K. E., Collective bargaining and fiscal policy, *American Economic Review,* XL (1950, Supplement), 306–20.

DUNLOP, J. T., Review of E. C. Lindblom's *Unions and Capitalism, American Economic Review,* XL (1950), 463–68.

MORTON, W. A., Trade unionism, full employment and inflation, *American Economic Review,* XL (1950), 13–39.

CLARK, J. M., Criteria of sound wage adjustment, with emphasis on the question of inflationary effects, *The Impact of the Union* (ed. D. M. WRIGHT), pp. 1–33. New York: Harcourt Brace & Co., 1951.

FRIEDMAN, M., Some comments on the significance of labor unions for economic policy, *ibid.,* 204–34.

HABERLER, G., Wage policy, employment and economic stability, *ibid.,* 34–62.

Selections from the discussion of the Clark and Haberler papers, *ibid.,* Ch. 3, 63–79.

MORTON, W. A. Keynesianism and inflation, *Journal of Political Economy,* LIX (1951), 258–65.

JACK, D. T., Full employment in retrospect, *Economic Journal,* LXII (1952), 731–49.

MEIDNER, R., The dilemma of wage policy under full employment, *Wage Policy under Full Employment* (ed. R. TURVEY), pp. 16–29. London: William Hodge & Co., 1952.

REHN, G., The problem of stability: an analysis and some policy proposals, *ibid.,* pp. 30–54.
Critique by E. LUNDBERG, *ibid.,* pp. 55–71.
Reply by REHN, *ibid.,* pp. 72–79.

BROEHL, W. G., Trade unions and full employment, *Southern Economic Journal,* XX (1953), 61–73.

LINDBLOM, C. E., Labor policy, full employment and inflation, *Income Stabilization for a Developing Democracy* (ed. M. MILLIKAN), Ch. 11, pp. 515–46. New Haven: Yale University Press, 1953.

PEACOCK, A. T., and RYAN, W. J. L., Wage claims and the pace of inflation, *Economic Journal,* LXIII (1953), 385–92.

REES, A., Wage levels under conditions of long run full employment, *American Economic Review,* XLIII (1953), 451–57.

SULTAN, P. E., Full employment on trial, *Canadian Journal of Economics and Political Science,* XIX (1953), 210–21.

SLICHTER, S., Do the wage-fixing arrangements in the American labor market have an inflationary bias?, *American Economic Review,* XLIV (1954, Supplement), 322–46.

VII. FISCAL POLICY AND THE INTERACTION OF GOVERNMENTAL UNITS

A. FISCAL POLICY AND FEDERAL, STATE, AND LOCAL GOVERNMENTS

LOUCKS, W. N., Public works planning and economic control: federal, state, and municipal, *Annals of the American Academy of Political and Social Science,* CLXII (1932), 114–20.

GILBERT, D. W., Cycles in municipal finance, *Review of Economic Statistics,* XXII (1940), 190–202.

PERLOFF, H. S., Fiscal policy at the state and local levels, *Postwar Economic Problems* (ed. S. E. Harris), pp. 221–38. New York: McGraw-Hill, 1943.

BLAKEY, R., Postwar fiscal policies—state and local, *Taxes,* XXII (1944), 63–68.

COUNCIL OF STATE GOVERNMENT, TAX COMMITTEE, Wartime fiscal policies for state and local government, *Materials on Budgeting: An Instrument of Planning and Management, Unit III,* pp. 32–37. American University, 1944.

SULLIVAN, J. L., Intergovernmental fiscal relations in wartime: coordination of fiscal policies of various levels of government necessary, *ibid.,* 27–31.

BIRD, F. C., Municipal fiscal policy and the business cycle, *National Tax Association Proceedings,* XXXVIII (1945), 208–13.

HOWENSTINE, E. J., Jr., Methods of federal financing of postwar public works, Bulletin of the National Tax Association, XXX (1945), 130–38.

MITCHELL, G. W.; LITTERER, O. F.; and DOMAR, E. D.; State and local finance, *Public Finance and Full Employment,* Postwar Economic Studies, No. 3, pp. 101–30. Board of Governors of the Federal Reserve System, 1945.

SHERE, L., Tax reserves for state and local governments, *National Tax Association Proceedings,* XXXVIII (1945), 187–99.
Discussion by E. D. DOMAR, *ibid.,* 200–201.

LOGSDON, C. S., Some comments upon the effectiveness of state and local area development programs, *Southern Economic Journal,* XV (1949), 303–10.

SOMERS, H. M., The multiplier in a tri-fiscal economy, *Quarterly Journal of Economics,* LXIII (1949), 258–72.

GROVES, H. M., and KAHN, C. H., The stability of state and local tax yields, *American Economic Review,* XLII (1952), 87–102.

NYGAARD, K. O., State and local government receipt and expenditure programs, *Survey of Current Business,* XXXIII (Jan. 1953), 11–16.

NEWCOMER, M., State and local financing in relation to economic fluctuations, *National Tax Journal,* VII (1954), 97–109.

WHITE, M. and WHITE, A., The impact of economic fluctuations on municipal finance, *ibid.,* 17–39.

B. FISCAL POLICY AND THE INTERNATIONAL ECONOMY

WARMING, J., International difficulties arising out of the financing of public works during depression, *Economic Journal,* XLII (1932), 211–24.

WOYTINSKY, W. S., International measures to create employment: a remedy for the depression, *International Labor Review,* XXV (1932), 1–22.

MEADE, J. E., *Public Works in Their International Aspect.* London: New Fabian Research Bureau, 1933.

WILLIAMS, J. H., The world's monetary dilemma—internal vs. external stability, *Proceedings of the Academy of Political Science,* XVI (April 1934), 62–68. Reprinted in J. H. WILLIAMS, *Postwar Monetary Plans.* Oxford: Basil Blackwell, 1949.

SALANT, W. A., Foreign trade policy in the business cycle, *Public Policy,* Vol. II, pp. 208–31. Cambridge, Mass.: Graduate School of Public Administration, 1941.

METZLER, L. A., The transfer problem reconsidered, *Journal of Political Economy,* L (1942), 397–414. Reprinted in *Readings in the Theory of International Trade.* Philadelphia: Blakiston, 1949.

MARSH, D. B., Fiscal policy and tariffs in post-war international trade, *Canadian Journal of Economics and Political Science,* IX (1943), 507–31.

BARNA, T., Domestic economic policy and international trade, *Britain and Her Export Trade* (ed. M. ABRAMS), pp. 51–76. Pilot Press, 1946.

BENHAM, F., Full employment and international trade, *Economica,* N.S., XIII (1946), 159–69.

BUCHANAN, N. S., American national income and foreign investment, *Planning and Paying for Full Employment* (ed. A. P. LERNER and F. D. GRAHAM), pp. 154–62. Princeton, N.J.: Princeton University Press, 1946.

GILBERT, J. C., Professor Polanyi's full employment and free trade, *The Manchester School of Economics and Social Studies,* Vol. XIV, No. 2 (1946), pp. 85–97.

KALECKI, M., Multilateralism and full employment, *Canadian Journal of Economics and Political Science,* XII (1946), 322–27.

TRIFFIN, R., National central banking and the international economy, *International Monetary Policies,* Postwar Economic Studies, No. 7, pp. 46–81. Board of Governors of the Federal Reserve System, 1946.

KAHN, A. E., The British balance of payments and problems of domestic policy, *Quarterly Journal of Economics*, LXI (1947), 368–96.

KURIHARA, K. K., Foreign investment and full employment, *Journal of Political Economy*, LV (1947), 459–64.

NURSKE, R., Domestic and international equilibrium, *The New Economics* (ed. S. E. Harris), pp. 264–92. New York: Alfred A. Knopf, 1947.

POOLE, K. E., National economic policies and international monetary cooperation, *American Economic Review*, XXXVII (1947), 369–75.

SMITHIES, A., Multilateral trade and employment, *American Economic Review*, XXXVII (1947, Supplement), 560–68.

HIRSCHMAN, A. O., Disinflation, discrimination and the dollar shortage, *American Economic Review*, XXXVIII (1948), 886–92.

MEADE, J. E., Financial policy and the balance of payments, *Economica*, XV (1948), 101–15.

BALOGH, T., The international aspects of full employment, *Economics of Full Employment*, pp. 126–80. Oxford Institute of Statistics. Oxford: Basil Blackwell, 1949.

BROWN, A. J., International equilibrium and national sovereignty under full employment, *International Affairs*, XXV (1949), 434–42.

HIRSCHMAN, A. O., International aspects of a recession, *American Economic Review*, XXXIX (1949), 1245–53.

HAWTREY, R. G., Multiplier analysis and the balance of payments, *Economic Journal*, LX (1950), 1–8.

KALDOR, N., Employment policies and the problem of international balance, *Review of Economic Studies*, XIX(1) (1950–51), 42–49.

ROSTOW, W. W., The United Nations' Report on full employment, *Economic Journal*, LX (1950), 323–50.

STOLPER, W. F., A note on multiplier, flexible exchanges—the dollar shortage, *Economia Internazionale*, III (1950), 765–83.
Comment by T. BALOGH, *ibid.*, IV (1951), 435–40.

———, The multiplier, flexible exchanges and international equilibrium, *Quarterly Journal of Economics*, LXIV (1950), 559–82.

FETTER, F. W., International aspects of fiscal policy, *Fiscal Policies and the American Economy* (ed. K. E. POOLE), Ch. 9, pp. 422–56. New York: Prentice-Hall, 1951.

WILSON, T., Some international aspects of employment policy, *Oxford Economic Papers*, N.S., III (1951), 30–38.

SMITHIES, A., Modern international trade theory and international policy, *American Economic Review*, XLII (1952, Supplement), 168–76.

VIII. POLITICAL AND ADMINISTRATIVE ASPECTS OF FISCAL POLICY

A. BUDGETING THEORY AND POLICY

BASTABLE, C. F., The new budget and the principles of financial policy, *Economic Journal*, IX (1899), 204–11.

DALTON, H., Unbalanced budgets, *Unbalanced Budgets* (ed. H. DALTON and others), Ch. 2, pp. 11–16. London: George Reutledge and Sons, 1934.

SUNDELSON, J. W., The emergency budget of the federal government, *American Economic Review*, XXIV (1934), 53–68.

FAIRCHILD, F. R., An analysis of the government's financial reports, with special reference to the deficit, *American Economic Review*, XXV (1935), 31–43.

SUNDELSON, J. W., Fiscal aspects of planned public works, *Economics of Planning Public Works* (ed. J. M. CLARK), pp. 169–94. Washington, 1935.

HEINIG, K., The state budget and public works, *International Labor Review*, XXXIV (1936), 153–76.

COYLE, D. C., Balance what budget?, *Harper's Magazine,* CLXXV (1937), 449–59.

COLM, G., Comment on extraordinary budgets, *Social Research,* V (1938), 168–81.

COPELAND, M. A., Public investment in the United States, *American Economic Review,* XXIX (1939, Supplement), 33–41.

MUSGRAVE, R., The nature of budgetary balance and the case for the capital budget, *American Economic Review,* XXIX (1939), 260–71.

MYRDAL, G., Fiscal policy in the business cycle, *American Economic Review,* XXIX (1939, Supplement), 183–93.

KEY, V. O., The lack of a budgetary theory, *American Political Science Review,* XXXIV (1940), 1137–44.

PERLOFF, H. S., Budgetary symbolism and fiscal planning, *Public Policy,* Vol. II, Ch. 2, pp. 36–62. Cambridge, Mass.: Graduate School of Public Administration, 1941.

SIMKIN, C. G. F., Budgetary reform, *Economic Record,* XVII (1941), 192–209.

THOMPSON, S., The investment budget, *Public Policy,* Vol. II, Ch. 2, pp. 63–77. Cambridge, Mass.: Graduate School of Public Administration, 1941.

COPELAND, M. A., The capital budget and the war effort, *American Economic Review,* XXXIII (1943), 38–49.

MAXWELL, J. A., The capital budget, *Quarterly Journal of Economics,* LVII (1943), 450–65.

SMITH, H. D., Fiscal policy and budget operations in war and peace, *Materials on Budgeting: An Instrument of Planning and Management,* Unit II (ed. C. SECKLER-HUDSON), pp. 23–30. Washington, D.C.: American University Press, 1944.

———, The budget as an instrument of legislative control and executive management, *Public Administration Review,* IV (1944), 181–88.

BURKHEAD, J. V., Budget classification and fiscal planning, *Public Administration Review,* VII (1947), 228–35.

MARCHAL, J., The state and its budget, *Public Finance,* III (1948), 23–34.

SMITHIES, A., Federal budgeting and fiscal policy, *Survey of Contemporary Economics,* pp. 179–209. Philadelphia: Blakiston, 1948.

BANFIELD, E. C., Congress and the budget: a planner's criticism, *American Political Science Review,* XLIII (1949), 1217–28.

BURKHEAD, J. V., The outlook for federal budget making, *National Tax Journal,* II (1949), 289–99.

TINBERGEN, J., Government budget and central economic plan, *Public Finance,* IV (1949), 195–99.

BARRÉRE, A., The problem connected with budgetary equilibrium—summary, *Public Finance,* V (1950), 180–82.

LEPPO, M., The double-budget system in the Scandinavian countries, *Public Finance,* V (1950), 137–46.

BAKKER, O., The budget cycle in public finance in the United States of America, *Public Finance,* VI (1951), 273–305.

FIELDER, C., Reform of the legislative budget, *National Tax Journal,* IV (1951), 65–76.

LOEFFLER, H. C., Alice in budget-land, *National Tax Journal,* IV (1951), 54–64. Comment by M. S. MARCH, *ibid.,* V (1952), 155–73.

PHILLIPS, J., The hadacol of the budget makers, *National Tax Journal,* IV (1951), 255–68.

SECKLER-HUDSON, C., Current trends in public budgeting in the United States, *Public Finance,* VI (1951), 319–29.

SINGH, B., A concept of optimum budget, *Public Finance,* VI (1951), 376–82.

SECKLER-HUDSON, C., Performance budgeting in the government of the United States, *Public Finance,* VII (1952), 327–45.

COLM, G., Fiscal policy and the federal budget, *Income Stabilization for a Developing*

Democracy (ed. M. MILLIKAN), Ch. 5, pp. 213–59. New Haven: Yale University Press, 1953.

BURKHEAD, J. V., The balanced budget, *Quarterly Journal of Economics,* LXVIII (1954), 191–216.

DIRKS, F. C., Recent progress in the federal budget, *National Tax Journal,* VII (1954), 141–54.

B. ADMINISTRATION OF FISCAL POLICY

MUND, V. A., Prosperity reserves of public works, *Annals of the American Academy of Political and Social Science,* Pt. II, CXLIX (1930), 1–49.

COMPTON, K. T., Long-range budgeting of public capital expenditures, *Annals of the American Academy of Political and Social Science,* CLXII (1932), 127–32.

SAWYER, D. H., Federal planning of public works, *American Labor Legislation Review,* XXII (1932), 83–88.

ICKES, H., Public works in the United States of America, *International Labor Review,* XXXV (1937), 775–802.

BRATT, E. C., Timing pump-priming expenditures, *American Economic Review,* XXXI (1941), 97–98.

HIGGINS, B., Problems of planning public works, *Postwar Economic Problems* (ed. S. E. HARRIS), pp. 187–205. New York: McGraw-Hill, 1943.

HOWENSTINE, E. J., Jr., Public works program after World War I, *Journal of Political Economy,* LI (1943), 523–37.

LEONTIEF, W., Economic statistics and postwar policies, *Postwar Economic Problems* (ed. S. E. HARRIS), pp. 159–65. New York: McGraw-Hill, 1943.

ABBOTT, C. C., Administration of fiscal policy, *Harvard Business Review,* XXIII (1944), 46–64.

HIGGINS, B., The United States public works reserve—an experiment in the co-ordination of public investment planning, *International Labor Review,* L (1944), 581–602.

———, Public work and our postwar economy, *Postwar Goals and Economic Reconstruction* (ed. A. J. Zurcher and R. Page), pp. 73–92. New York University Institute on Postwar Reconstruction. New York, 1944.

SMITH, H. D., Public works and national welfare, *Materials in Budgeting: an Instrument of Planning and Management,* Unit IV (ed. C. SECKLER-HUDSON), pp. 120–29. Washington, D.C.: American University, 1945.

WALLACE, H. A., The use of statistics in the formulation of a national full employment policy, *Journal of American Statistical Association,* XL (1945), 11–19.

HART, A. G., Facts, issues and policies, *American Economic Review,* XXXVI (1946, Proceedings), 280–90.

HOWENSTINE, E. J., Jr., Dovetailing rural public works into employment policy, *Review of Economic Statistics,* XXVIII (1946), 165–69.

———, Public works policy in the twenties, *Social Research,* XIII (1946), 478–500.

KLEIN, L. R., A post-mortem on transition predictions, *Journal of Political Economy,* LIV (1946), 289–308.

LOVEDAY, A., The informational requirements for full employment policies, *Commercial and Financial Chronicle,* CLXIII (1946), 3201, 3230–31.

FLANDERS, R. E., Administering the employment act—the first year, *Public Administration Review,* VII (1947), 221–27.

HAGEN, E. E., The reconversion period: reflections of a forecaster, *Review of Economic Statistics,* XXIX (1947), 95–101.

WOYTINSKY, W. S., What was wrong in forecasts of postwar depression?, *Journal of Political Economy,* LV (1947), 142–51.

BRATT, E. C., Business-cycle forecasting, *Journal of Business of the University of Chicago,* XXI (1948), 1–11.

———, Data needed to forecast the business cycle, *ibid.*, 168–79.

HAGEN, E. E., The problem of timing fiscal policy, *American Economic Review,* XXXVIII (1948, Supplement), 417–29.

HART, A. G., Timing and administering fiscal policy: how to give relevant counsel, *American Economic Review,* XXXVIII (1948, Supplement), 430–42.

ENSLEY, G. W., Suggested lines of economic research needed to carry out objectives of the Employment Act, *American Economic Review,* XXXIX (1949, Supplement), 453–63.

MAISEL, S. J., Timing and flexibility of a public works program, *Review of Economics and Statistics,* XXXI (1949), 147–52.

MARGOLIS, J., Public works and economic stability, *Journal of Political Economy,* LVII (1949), 293–303.

SAPIR, M., Review of economic forecasts for the transition period, *Studies in Income and Wealth,* Vol. XI, pp. 275–351. New York: National Bureau of Economic Research, 1949.

Comments by L. R. KLEIN, E. E. HAGEN, C. GEHMAN, M. A. COPELAND, R. S. TUCKER, *ibid.,* 352–67.

STRAYER, P., Public expenditure policy, *American Economic Review,* XXXIX (1949), 383–404.

COLM, G., Experiences in the use of social accounting in public policy in the United States, *Income and Wealth,* Series I, pp. 75–111. International Association for Research in Income and Wealth, 1951.

HOWENSTINE, E. J., Jr., The alleged inflexibility of compensatory public works policy, *Journal of Political Economy,* LIX (1951), 233–41.

SAMUELSON, P. A., Principles and rules in modern fiscal policy: a neo-classical reformulation, *Money, Trade and Economic Growth,* pp. 157–76. New York: Macmillan, 1951.

DAHL, R. E., and LINDBLOM, C. E., Variation in public expenditure, *Income Stabilization for a Developing Democracy* (ed. M. MILLIKAN), Ch. 8, pp. 347–96. New Haven: Yale University Press, 1953.

EMERSON, T. I., Administration of stabilization policy, *ibid.,* Ch. 15, pp. 659–702.

HAGEN, E. E., The role of economic forecasting in income stabilization, *ibid.,* Ch. 4, pp. 169–212.

TINBERGEN, J., The analysis of unemployment figures and the alleged correspondence between causes and cures, *Metro-economica,* V (1953), 43–49.

C. POLITICS OF FISCAL POLICY

TAYLOR, O. H., Economics versus politics, *Economics of the Recovery Program* (ed. D. V. BROWN and others), pp. 160–88. New York: Whittlesey House, 1934.

ROBERTSON, D. H., The state and economic fluctuations, *Authority and the Individual,* pp. 37–47. Cambridge, Mass.: Harvard University Press, 1936. Reprinted as "The snake and the worm," *Essays in Monetary Theory,* pp. 104–13. London: King, 1940.

ROEPKE, W., Socialism, planning and the business cycle, *Journal of Political Economy,* XLIV (1936), 318–38.

HERRING, E. P., The politics of fiscal policy, *Yale Law Journal,* XLVII (1938), 724–49.

HOOVER, C. B., Economic planning and the problem of full employment, *American Economic Review,* XXX (1940, Supplement), 263–71.

BLOCH, H. S., Fiscal policy and social reform as it may affect the potentialities of the personal income tax, *American Philosophical Society Proceedings,* LXXXVIII (1944), 36–42.

HAHN, L. A., Deficit spending and private enterprise, *Postwar Readjustments,* Bull. No. 8. Chamber of Commerce of the United States of America, 1944.

SCHMIDT, E. P., Full employment—its politics and economics, *Postwar Readjustments,* Bull. No. 9. Chamber of Commerce of the United States of America, 1944.

WALSH, J. R., America's rendezvous with destiny, *International Post-war Problems,* I (1944), 236–44.

WRIGHT, D. M., Hopes and fears—the shape of things to come, *Review of Economic Statistics,* XXVI (1944), 206–15.

GRATTAN, C. H., Full employment through the wringer, *Harper's Magazine,* CXC (1945), 577–84.

GRIFFITH, E. C., Deficit financing and the future of capitalism, *Southern Economic Journal,* XII (1945), 130–40.

WRIGHT, D. M., The future of Keynesian economics, *American Economic Review,* XXXV (1945), 284–307.

LANDAUER, C., Prosperity, democracy and planning, *Planning and Paying for Full Employment* (eds. A. P. LERNER and F. D. GRAHAM), pp. 67–83. Princeton, N.J.: Princeton University Press, 1946.

LYDALL, H. F., Unemployment in an unplanned economy, *Economic Journal,* LVI (1946), 366–82.

SUITER, W. O., Divergent theories of national debt, *Southern Economic Journal,* XIII (1946), 53–64.

BAUER, P. T., Lord Beveridge on full employment, *Kyklos,* I (1947), 166–76.

NOURSE, E. G., Economics in the public service, *American Economic Review,* XXXVII (1947, Supplement), 21–30.

———, Public administration and economic stabilization, *Public Administration Review,* VII (1947), 85–92.

ALEXANDER, S. S., Opposition to deficit spending for the prevention of unemployment, *Income, Employment and Public Policy,* pp. 177–98. New York: W. W. Norton & Co., 1948.

COOPER, W. W., Some implications of a program for full employment and economic stability, *Political Science Quarterly,* LXIII (1948), 230–56.

MARX, F. M. (ed.); APPLEBY, P. H.; NOURSE, E. G.; DAVEY, H. W.; CANNON, C.; FAINSOD, M.; and LONG, N. E., Formulating the federal government's economic program: a symposium, *American Political Science Review,* XLII (1948), 272–336.

BACH, G. L., Monetary-fiscal policy reconsidered, *Journal of Political Economy,* LVII (1949), 383–94.

BLUM, W., Tax policy in a democratic society, *National Tax Journal,* II (1949), 97–109.

CROOME, H., Liberty, equality and full employment, *Lloyd's Bank Review,* N.S., No. 13 (July 1949), 14–32.

NATIONAL PLANNING ASSOCIATION, The position of business on fiscal and wage policy in depression, Memorandum to members of the National Planning Association, Special Report No. 25, 1949.

BLOUGH, R., Political and administrative requisites for achieving economic stability, *American Economic Review,* XL (1950, Supplement), 165–78.

———, The argument phase of taxpayer politics, *University of Chicago Law Review,* XVII (1950), 604–15.

CLARK, J. M., Employment policy in a divided world, *Social Research,* XVII (1950), 157–67.

NOURSE, E. G., Economic analysis and political synthesis, *American Philosophical Society Proceedings,* XCIV (1950), 311–16.

STRAYER, P. G., The Council of Economic Advisers: political economy on trial, *American Economic Review,* XL (1950, Supplement), 144–54.

CIKINS, W., The Council of Economic Advisers: political economy at the crossroads, *Public Policy* (eds. C. J. FRIEDRICH and J. K. GALBRAITH), Vol. IV (1953), pp. 94–115.

COKER, F. W., Income stabilization and the American political tradition, *Income Stabilization for a Developing Democracy* (ed. M. MILLIKAN), Ch. II, pp. 77–110. New Haven: Yale University Press, 1953.

JONES, V., The political framework of stabilization policy, *ibid.,* Ch. 13, pp. 583–624.

LASSWELL, H. D., Stabilization technique and patterns of expectation, *ibid.,* Ch. 14, 625–58.

OXENFELDT, A. R., and HAAG, E. V., Unemployment in planned and capitalist economies, *Quarterly Journal of Economics,* LXVIII (1954), 43–60.

IX. EXPERIENCE WITH FISCAL POLICY IN COUNTRIES OTHER THAN THE UNITED STATES

FISHER, A. G. B., Crisis and readjustment in Australia, *Journal of Political Economy,* XLII (1934), 753–82.

HUGHES, T. J., Public works and their finance, *Unbalanced Budgets* (ed. H. DALTON and others), pp. 234–50. London: George Reutledge and Sons, 1934.

REEDMAN, J. N., The stabilization of the budget and the franc, *ibid.,* 273–78.

THOMAS, B., Public works policy, *ibid.,* 138–60.

BRIGDEN, J. B., and others, Recovery measures in Australia and New Zealand, *Economic Record,* XI (March 1935, Supplement).

GREBLER, L., Work creation policy in Germany, 1932–1935, *International Labor Review,* XXXV (1937), 329–51, 505–27.

BELLMAN, H., Business recovery and the housing program in Great Britain, *Journal of Land and Public Utility Economics,* XIV (1938), 111–19.

MÖLLER, G., The unemployment policy, *Annals of the American Academy of Political and Social Science,* CXCVII (1938), 47–71.

WIGFORSS, E., The financial policy during depression and boom, *ibid.,* 25–39.

HOLT, L. W., Public finance and control of investment in New Zealand, *Economic Record,* XV (1939, Supplement), 58–68.

JÁSZI, G., The budgetary experience of Great Britain in the great depression, *Public Policy,* Vol. I, pp. 176–211. Cambridge, Mass.: Graduate School of Public Administration, 1940.

PARKINSON, J. F., Some problems of war finance in Canada, *Canadian Journal of Economics and Political Science,* VI (1940), 403–23.

THOMAS, B., How Britain is avoiding inflation, *Financing the War,* pp. 269–83. New York: Tax Institute, 1942.

BEATTIE, J. R., Some aspects of the problem of full employment, *Canadian Journal of Economics and Political Science,* X (1944), 328–42.

BEVERIDGE, W., The government's employment policy, *Economic Journal,* LIV (1944), 161–76.

Post-war planning in Sweden—employment investment and monetary policy, *International Labor Review,* L (1944), 750–57.

ARNOLD, A. Z., Controlling inflation in the USSR, *Curbing Inflation through Taxation,* Pt. IV, pp. 153–62. New York: Tax Institute, 1944.

TESORO, G. A., Italy's experience in curbing inflation through fiscal devices, *ibid.,* 163–87.

EATON, A. K., Canadian experience in curbing inflation through fiscal devices, *ibid.,* 188–200.

MURPHY, M. E., England's experience in curbing inflation through fiscal devices, *ibid.,* 201–222.

DOWNING, R. I., The planning of public investment in Australia, *International Labor Review,* LII (1945), 352–79.

MERRY, D. H. and BRUNS, G. R., Full employment, the British, Canadian, and Australian White Papers, *Economic Record,* XXI (1945), 223–35.

URQUHART, M. C., Public investment in Canada, *Canadian Journal of Economics and Political Science,* XI (1945), 535–53.

MANDELBAUM, K., An experiment in full-employment controls in the German economy, 1933–1938, *Economics of Full Employment,* pp. 181–203. Oxford Institute of Statistics, Oxford: Basil Blackwell, 1946.

SADIE, J. L., Public finance and the business cycle in South Africa, 1910–40, *South African Journal of Economics,* XIV (1946), 132–60.

WILSON, J. S. G., Prospects of full employment in Australia, *Economic Record,* XXII (1946), 99–116.

HOUGHTON, D. H., Changing emphasis in public finance, *South African Journal of Economics,* XV (1947), 60–67.

DACEY, W. M., The budget, overseas borrowing and domestic investment, *Lloyd's Bank Review,* July 1948, 34–51.

HIRSCHMAN, A. O., Inflation and deflation in Italy, *American Economic Review,* XXXVIII (1948), 598–606.

KLOPSTOCK, F. H., Western Europe's attack on inflation, *Harvard Business Review,* XXVI (1948), 597–612.

SCHUMANN, C. G. W., Aspects of the problem of full employment in South Africa, *South African Journal of Economics,* XVI (1948), 115–32.

SNIDER, D. A., French monetary and fiscal policies since the liberation, *American Economic Review,* XXXVIII (1948), 309–27.

CARTER, C. F., British public finance and the progress of inflation, *Public Finance,* IV (1949), 28–48.

PAISH, F. W., and TRESS, R. C., The budget and economic policy, *Bulletin, London and Cambridge Economic Service,* XXVII (1949), 42–48.

ROSA, R. V., The problem of French recovery, *Economic Journal,* LIX (1949), 154–70.

CARTER, C. F., Rearmament and public finance in Britain, *Public Finance,* V (1950), 199–222.

HELLER, W. W., The role of fiscal-monetary policy in German economic recovery, *American Economic Review,* XL (1950, Supplement), 531–47.

TRESS, R. C., How much disinflation?, *Westminister Bank Review,* Feb. 1950, 1–7.

MARCUS, E., The effectiveness of Canadian fiscal policy, *Journal of Finance,* VII (1952), 559–79.

ROBERTSON, W., Unemployment in Belgium and full employment policy, *Economica,* N.S., XIX (1952), 176–92.

HIGGINS, B., Government measures to regularize private investment in other countries than the United States, *Regularization of Business Investment,* pp. 459–81. National Bureau Committee for Economic Research. Princeton, N.J.: Princeton University Press, 1954.

Index to Bibliography

This book has been set on the Linotype in 12 and 10 point Garamond No. 3, leaded 1 point. Chapter numbers and titles are in 24 point Garamont. The size of the type page is 27 by 46½ picas.